Systems of Psychotherapy
A Transtheoretical Analysis
Fourth Edition

James O. Prochaska
University of Rhode Island

John C. Norcross
University of Scranton

Brooks/Cole Publishing Company

I(T)P® An International Thomson Publishing Company

Pacific Grove • Albany • Belmont • Bonn • Boston • Cincinnati • Detroit
Johannesburg • London • Madrid • Melbourne • Mexico City • New York
Paris • Singapore • Tokyo • Toronto • Washington

Sponsoring Editor: *Eileen Murphy*
Marketing Team: *Steve Catalano, Jean Thompson*
Editorial Assistant: *Julie Martinez*
Production Coordinator: *Keith Faivre*
Production Service: *Professional Book Center*
Manuscript Editor: *Kelly Winters*

Permissions Editor: *Fiorella Ljunggren*
Interior Design: *Lee Ballentine*
Cover Design: *Laurie Albrecht*
Photo Research: *Terry Powell*
Typesetting: *Professional Book Center*
Printing and Binding: *R.R. Donnelly & Sons, Crawfordsville*

Photo Credits: 25, Sigmund Freud, Courtesy, National Library of Medicine; 69, Alfred Adler, Courtesy, Alfred Adler Institute of Chicago; 95, Rollo May, Courtesy, Rollo May; 133, Carl Rogers, Land Marks, Doug Land; 163, Fritz Perls, Courtesy, National Library of Medicine; 199, Eric Berne, Photo submitted by Cole Weston; 235, Thomas G. Stampl, Courtesy, Dr. Thomas Stampfl; 271, Joseph Wolpe, Courtesy, Pepperdine University; 321, Albert Ellis, Courtesy, Albert Ellis; 357, Virginia Satir, Avanta, The Virginia Satir Network; 399, Corbis; 437, Insoo Kim Berg, Courtesy, Insoo Kim Berg; 457, Arnold Lazarous, Courtesy, Arnold Lazarous; 487, Illustration by Laurie Albrecht.

For more information, contact:

BROOKS/COLE PUBLISHING COMPANY
511 Forest Lodge Road
Pacific Grove, CA 93950
USA

International Thomson Editores
Seneca 53
Col. Polanco
11560 México, D.F., México

International Thomson Publishing Europe
Berkshire House 168–173
High Holborn
London WC1V 7AA
England

International Thomson Publishing GmbH
Königswinterer Strasse 418
53227 Bonn
Germany

Thomas Nelson Australia
102 Dodds Street
South Melbourne, 3205
Victoria, Australia

International Thomson Publishing Asia
60 Albert Street
#15-01 Albert Complex
Singapore 189969

Nelson Canada
1120 Birchmount Road
Scarborough, Ontario
Canada M1K 5G4

International Thomson Publishing Japan
Hirakawacho Kyowa Building, 3F
2-2-1 Hirakawacho
Chiyoda-ku, Tokyo 102
Japan

Printed in the United States of America.

10 9 8 7 6 5 4 3 2 1

Library of Congress Cataloging-in-Publication Data

Prochaska, James D. [date]
   Systems of psychotherapy : a transtheoretical analysis / James O.
Prochaska, John C. Norcross. — 4th ed.
     p. cm.
   Includes bibliographical references and index.
   ISBN 0-534-35704-0
   1. Psychotherapy.   I. Norcross, John C. [date].   II. Title.
RC480.P73 1998   98-28468
616.89'14—dc21   CIP

To Jan and Nancy

About the Authors

JAMES O. PROCHASKA earned his baccalaureate, master's, and doctorate in clinical psychology from Wayne State University and fulfilled his internship at the Lafayette Clinic in Detroit. At present, he is professor of psychology and director of the Cancer Prevention Research Consortium at the University of Rhode Island and a clinical psychologist in part-time private practice. Dr. Prochaska has over 30 years of psychotherapy experience in a variety of settings and has been a consultant to a host of clinical organizations, including the University of Texas and the Veterans Administration. He has been the principal investigator on grants from the National Institutes of Health totaling over $40 million and has been recognized by the American Psychological Society as one of the five most-cited authors in psychology. His 30 book chapters and over 100 scholarly articles focus on self-change and psychotherapy from a transtheoretical perspective, the subject of both his 1984 professional book, *The Transtheoretical Approach* (with Carlo DiClemente), and his 1994 popular book, *Changing for Good* (with John Norcross and Carlo DiClemente). An accomplished speaker, he has offered workshops and keynote addresses throughout the world and served on various task forces for the National Cancer Institute, National Institute of Mental Health, National Institute of Drug Abuse, and the American Cancer Society. Jim makes his home in southern Rhode Island with his wife, two children, and Samoyed.

JOHN C. NORCROSS received his baccalaureate *summa cum laude* from Rutgers University, his master's and doctorate in clinical psychology from the University of Rhode Island, and completed his internship at the Brown University School of Medicine. He is professor and former chair of psychology at the University of Scranton and a clinical psychologist in part-time independent practice. Author of more than 125 scholarly articles, Dr. Norcross has written or edited 10 books, the most recent being *Psychologists' Desk Reference* (with Gerry Koocher and Sam Hill), *Insider's Guide to Graduate Programs in Clinical and Counseling Psychology* (with Tracy Mayne and Michael Sayette), and *Handbook of Psychotherapy Integration* (with Marvin Goldfried). He is codeveloper of the APA Psychotherapy Videotape  Series and has served on the editorial board of a dozen journals. Dr. Norcross has also served as a clinical and research consultant to a number of organizations, including the National Institute of Mental Health, and has given workshops and lectures in 15 countries. He has received numerous awards for his teaching and research, such as fellowship status in professional associations, the Krasner Memorial Award from the American Psychological Association's Psychotherapy Division, and the Pennsylvania Professor of the Year Award from the Carnegie Foundation. John lives, works, and plays in the northern Pocono Mountains with his wife, two children, and their two deranged cats.

Contents

Preface

THIS BOOK PROVIDES a systematic, comprehensive, and balanced survey of the leading theories of psychotherapy. It is designed, however, to be more than just a survey, since we strive toward a synthesis both within each psychotherapy system and across the various systems. Within a particular system of therapy, this book follows the integrative steps that flow from the system's theory of personality to its theory of psychopathology and culminates in its therapeutic process and therapeutic relationship. Across the various systems of therapy, this book offers an integrative framework that highlights the many similarities of therapy systems without blurring their essential differences. The emerging comparative and transtheoretical analysis clearly demonstrates how much psychotherapy systems agree on the processes producing change while disagreeing on the content that needs to be changed.

Systems of Psychotherapy: A Transtheoretical Analysis is intended, primarily, for advanced undergraduate and graduate students enrolled in introductory courses in psychotherapy and counseling. This course is commonly titled Systems of Psychotherapy, Theories of Counseling, Foundations of Psychotherapy, or Introduction to Counseling and is offered to psychology, counseling, social work, psychiatry, nursing, human relations, and other students. Our volume is intended, secondarily, for psychotherapists of all professions and persuasions seeking a comparative overview of the burgeoning field of psychotherapy. We have been immensely gratified by the letters and comments from readers who have used this text in preparing for comprehensive exams, licensure tests, and board certification as well as from those who have found it instrumental in acquiring a more integrative perspective on clinical work.

Our Objectives

The content and goals of this fourth edition embody our personal objectives as psychotherapy practitioners, teachers, researchers, and theorists.

As integrative practitioners, we appreciate the vitality and meaning that different clinical approaches can have for different clients and therapists. We attempt to communicate the excitement and depth of understanding emanating from these conceptual scaffolds constructed to guide us through the inner and outer worlds of our patients. Accordingly, we avoid simple descriptions of each system as detached observers in favor of immersing ourselves in each system as advocates.

As practitioners we are also convinced that any treatise on such a vital field as psychotherapy must come alive to do the subject matter justice. To this end, we have included a wealth of case illustrations drawn from our combined 45 years of clinical practice. Further, we demonstrate how the same complicated psychotherapy case—Mrs. C.—is formulated and treated by each system of psychotherapy. This and all of the other case material counterbalances the theoretical considerations and illustrates technical concepts; in this way, theories become pragmatic and consequential—relevant to what transpires in the psychotherapeutic hour. The details of individual clients have been altered, of course, to preserve their anonymity.

As psychotherapy teachers, we recognize the complexity and diversity of concepts underlying these leading theories of psychotherapy. This volume endeavors to present the essential concepts clearly and concisely but without resorting to oversimplification. Our students occasionally complain that theorists seem to have a knack for making things more complicated than they really are. We hope that as readers move through these pages they gain a deeper appreciation for the complexity of the human condition or, at least, the complexity of the minds of those attempting to articulate the human condition.

Our decades of teaching and supervising psychotherapy have also taught us that students desire an overarching structure to guide the acquisition, analysis, and comparison of information. Unlike edited psychotherapy texts with varying writing styles and chapter content, we use a consistent structure and voice throughout the book. Instead of illustrating one approach with Mrs. Apple and another approach with Mr. Orange, we systematically present a detailed treatment of Mrs. C. for each and every approach.

As psychotherapy researchers, the empirical literature has taught us that psychotherapy has enormous potential for impacting patients in a positive (and occasionally a negative) manner. In this view, therapy is more analogous to penicillin than to aspirin. With interventions expected to produce strong rather than weak effects, we should be able to demonstrate the effectiveness of therapeutic systems even in the face of error caused by measurement and control problems. This book includes, therefore, a summary of controlled outcome studies and meta-analytic reviews that have evaluated the efficacy of each of the therapy systems.

Research and practice have further taught us that each psychotherapy system has its respective limitations and contraindications. For this reason, we offer cogent criticisms of each approach from the vantage points of behavioral, psychoanalytic, humanistic, contextual (systems and culture-sensitive), and integrative perspectives. The net effect is a balanced coverage combining sympathetic presentation and critical analysis.

As psychotherapy theorists, we do not endorse the endless proliferation of psychotherapy systems, each purportedly unique and superior despite the absence of empirical evidence. What our amorphous discipline *does* need is a continuing effort to pull together the essential variables operating in effective therapies and to discard those variables unrelated to effective practice. From our comparative analysis of the major systems of therapy, we hope to move toward a higher level of integration that will yield a transtheoretical approach to psychotherapy. And from comparative analysis and research, we hope to contribute to an empirically supported psychotherapy in which particular treatment methods and therapeutic relationships—derived from these major systems of therapy—will be tailored to the needs of the individual client. In this way, we believe, the efficacy, efficiency, and applicability of psychotherapy can be permanently enhanced.

Changes in the Fourth Edition

Innovations appear and vanish with bewildering rapidity on the diffuse psychotherapeutic scene. One year's treatment fad—say, Neurolinguistic Programming—fades into oblivion in just a few years. The volatile nature of the psychotherapy discipline requires continuing education and regular revisions in order for practitioners and students to stay abreast of contemporary developments.

The evolution of this book closely reflects the changing landscape of psychotherapy. The first edition in 1979 was relatively brief and only hinted at the possibility of sophisticated psychotherapy integration. The second edition added sections on object relations, cognitive, and systems therapies and on advances that had been made in building a transtheoretical model of psychotherapy. The third edition brought new chapters on gender-sensitive/culture-sensitive therapies and integrative/eclectic therapies, new sections on interpersonal therapies and short-term psychodynamic therapies, the introduction of an *Instructor's Resource Manual*, and the addition of a coauthor (John Norcross).

This fourth edition, in turn, brings a host of revisions and additions that reflect recent trends in the field. Among these are:

- An entirely new chapter (13) on solution-focused and constructive therapies
- New sections on brief forms of therapy within existing chapters
- A reorganized and retitled chapter (8) on exposure and flooding therapies, including additional information on exposure methods and new information on eye movement desensitization and reprocessing (EMDR)
- The addition of material on reality therapy (in chapter 4), motivational interviewing (in chapter 5), and psychotherapy for men (in chapter 12)
- An Alternative Table of Contents as an Appendix for those who wish to focus on the change processes cutting across theories, rather than the psychotherapy theories themselves
- Increased reliance on quantitative reviews of controlled outcome studies and meta-analytic studies on each psychotherapy system (in place of reviewing individual outcome studies)
- New section on The Future of Psychotherapy (in chapter 15)

- Tightening the presentation of the personality theory of each psychotherapy system by deleting the "rules for living" material

- Expansion of the *Instructor's Resource Manual,* including a computerized test item package, now coauthored by two exceptional psychotherapy teachers, Dr. Linda Campbell (University of Georgia) and Dr. Anthony Giuliano (University of Hartford)

- And, reflecting our entry onto the information superhighway, an Internet website for the book: http://www.brookscole.com

Of course, we have also updated and altered content throughout the entire book.

With these additions, the text now surveys 35 leading systems of psychotherapy and provides a more thorough analysis of 16 of these, thus affording a broader scope than is available in most textbooks. Guiding all these modifications, however, has been the unwavering goal of our book: to provide a comprehensive, rigorous, and balanced survey of the major theories of psychotherapy. Expansion of the breadth of *Systems of Psychotherapy* has been accomplished only within the context of a comparative analysis that seeks to explicate both the fundamental similarities and the useful differences among the therapy schools.

Acknowledgments

Our endeavors in completing previous editions and in preparing this edition have been aided immeasurably by colleagues and family members. Anyone who has ever struggled with the mass and complexity of such a project as this would freely admit, in the words of John Donne, that no man is an island, entire of himself, or in the more modern lyrics of the Beatles, that it was accomplished with (more than) a little help from our friends.

In particular, special appreciation is extended to our good friends and close collaborators, Dr. Carlo DiClemente and Dr. Wayne Velicer, for their continuing development of the transtheoretical approach. We thank seven anonymous colleagues for their detailed and constructive reviews of the previous edition and are grateful to the following reviewers of the fourth edition: Linda F. Campbell, University of Georgia; Melvin T. Henderson, Metropolitan State University; Lynda Kayser, Eastern Illinois University; Daniel Sonkin, Sonoma State University. Dr. Klaus Grawe and Dr. Michael Reicherts in Switzerland helped to access and translate a considerable body of outcome literature conducted in Europe. We are also indebted to Marie Kobayashi, Betty Nebesky, and Elaine Taylor for their tireless efforts in word-processing the manuscript.

Three groups of individuals deserve specific mention for their support over the years. First, we are grateful to the National Institutes of Health, the University of Rhode Island, and the University of Scranton for their generous financial support of our research. Second, we are indebted to our clients, who continue to be our ultimate teachers of psychotherapy. And third, we are appreciative of the good people at Brooks/Cole for seeing this new edition of *Systems of Psychotherapy: A Transtheoretical Analysis* to fruition, especially Eileen Murphy, sponsoring editor.

Finally, we express our deepest appreciation to our wives (Jan; Nancy) and to our children (Jason and Jodi; Rebecca and Jonathon), who were willing to sacrifice for the sake of our scholarship and who were available for support when we emerged from solitude. Their caring has freed us to contribute to the education of those who might one day use the powers of psychotherapy to make this a better world.

James O. Prochaska
Kingston, Rhode Island

John C. Norcross
Mt. Cobb, Pennsylvania

Defining and Comparing the Psychotherapies: An Integrative Framework

THE FIELD OF PSYCHOTHERAPY has been fragmented by future shock and staggered by over-choice. We have witnessed the hyperinflation of brand-name therapies during the past three decades. In 1959, Harper identified 36 distinct systems of psychotherapy; in 1976, Parloff discovered more than 130 therapies in the therapeutic marketplace or, perhaps more appropriately, the "jungle place." In 1979, *Time* magazine was reporting more than 200 therapies. Recent estimates put the number at over 400 and growing. The proliferation of therapies has been accompanied by an avalanche of rival claims: each system is proposed as differentially effective and uniquely applicable. Developers of new systems usually claim 80% to 100% success, despite the absence of controlled outcome research. A healthy diversity has deteriorated into an unhealthy chaos. Students, practitioners, and patients are confronted with confusion, fragmentation, and discontent. With so many therapy systems claiming success, which theories should be studied, taught, or bought?

A book by a proponent of a particular therapy system can be quite persuasive. We may even find ourselves using the new ideas and methods in practice while reading the book. But when we turn to an advocate of a radically different approach, the confusion returns. Listening to proponents compare therapies does little for our confusion, except to confirm the rule that those who cannot agree on basic assumptions are often reduced to calling each other names. We believe that fragmentation and confusion in psychotherapy can best be reduced by a comparative analysis of psychotherapy systems that highlights the many similarities across systems without blurring essential differences.

A comparative analysis requires an adequate understanding of each of the individual systems of therapy to be compared. In discussing each system, we first present a brief clinical example and introduce the developer of the system. We then trace the system's theory of personality as it leads to its theory of psychopathology and culminates in its therapeutic processes, therapeutic content, and therapeutic relationship. Following a summary of controlled research on the effectiveness of that system, we review central criticisms of that psychotherapy from diverse perspectives. Each chapter concludes with an analysis of the same patient (Mrs. C.), a review of future directions, and suggestions for further reading on that particular approach. In outline form, our examination and comparative analysis of each psychotherapy system follows this format:

- A clinical example
- A sketch of the founder
- Theory of personality
- Theory of psychopathology
- Theory of therapeutic processes
- Therapeutic content
- Therapeutic relationship
- Practicalities of the therapy
- Effectiveness of the therapy
- Criticisms of the therapy
- Analysis of Mrs. C.
- Future directions
- Suggestions for further reading

In comparing systems, we will use an integrative model to demonstrate their similarities and differences. An integrative model was selected in part because of its spirit of *rapprochement,* seeking what is useful and worthwhile in each therapy system rather than looking primarily for what is most easily criticized. Integration also represents the mainstream of contemporary psychotherapy: research consistently demonstrates that integration/eclecticism is the most popular orientation of mental health professionals (for reviews, see Jensen, Bergin, & Greaves, 1990; Norcross & Newman, 1992).

Lacking in most integrative endeavors is an adequate, comprehensive model that provides an intellectual framework for thinking and working across systems. Later in this chapter, an integrative model is presented that is complex enough to do justice to the complexities of psychotherapy yet simple enough to reduce confusion in the field. Rather than having to work with 400-plus theories, the model assumes that there are ten basic processes of change that underlie contemporary systems of psychotherapy. The model further demonstrates how the content of therapy can be reduced to four different levels of personal functioning.

Psychotherapy systems are compared on the particular process, or combination of processes, used to produce change and on the level of personal functioning to be changed. The systems are also compared on how they conceptualize the most common problems that occur at each level of personal functioning, such as low self-esteem, lack of intimacy, and impulse dyscontrol. Since clinicians are concerned primarily with the real problems of real people, we do not limit our comparative analysis merely to concepts and data. Our analysis also includes a comparison of how each major system conceptualizes and treats the same complex client.

We have limited our comparative analysis to 15 major systems of therapy. Systems have been omitted because they seem to be dying a natural death and are best left undisturbed, because they are so poorly developed that they have no identifiable theories of personality or psychopathology, or because they are primarily variations on themes already considered in the book. The final criterion for exclusion is empirical: no system was excluded if at least 1% of American mental health professionals endorsed it as their primary theoretical orientation. Table 1.1 summarizes the self-identified theories of over 1,000 psychologists, psychiatrists, counselors, and social workers from several representative studies, including two of our own.

Defining Psychotherapy

An appropriate opening move in a psychotherapy text would be to define psychotherapy—the subject matter itself. However, no single definition of psychotherapy has won universal acceptance. Depending on one's theoretical orientation, psychotherapy can be conceptualized as interpersonal persuasion, psychosocial education, professionally coached self-change, behavioral technology, a form of reparenting, the purchase of friendship, a contemporary variant of shamanism, health care, and many others. As Perry London (1986) once quipped, it is easier to practice psychotherapy than to explain or define it.

From our integrative perspective, an acceptable definition of psychotherapy possesses several necessary features (Norcross, 1987b). First, the definition should operationalize the clinical phenomena in a relatively concrete manner. Second, it will be theoretically and, insofar as possible, semantically neutral. Third, it will eventually be consensual, subject to agreement and verification by psychotherapists of diverse persuasions. And fourth, our generic definition should be, for want of a better word, respectfully evenhanded. That is, it should treat theories equitably without sacrificing the integrity of any particular approach.

Our working definition is as follows (from Norcross, 1990, p. 218):

> Psychotherapy is the informed and intentional application of clinical methods and interpersonal stances derived from established psychological principles for the purpose of assisting people to modify their behaviors, cognitions, emotions, and/or other personal characteristics in directions that the participants deem desirable.

This admittedly broad definition is nonetheless a reasonably balanced one and a relatively neutral one in terms of theory, method, and format. We have, for example, not specified the number or composition of the participants, since different

Table 1.1 Primary Theoretical Orientations of American Psychotherapists

Orientation	Clinical Psychologists	Counseling Psychologists	Psychiatrists	Social Workers	Counselors
Adlerian	1%	2%	1%	1%	2%
Behavioral	13%	8%	1%	4%	6%
Cognitive	24%	11%	1%	4%	10%
Eclectic/ Integrative	27%	40%	53%	34%	37%
Existential/ Humanistic	3%	6%	1%	3%	13%
Gestalt	1%	2%	1%	1%	2%
Interpersonal	5%	2%	3%	1%	1%
Psychoanalytic/ Psychodynamic	18%	12%	35%	33%	11%
Rogerian/Person-Centered	1%	8%	0%	2%	8%
Systems	4%	5%	1%	13%	7%
Other	3%	4%	3%	4%	3%

Sources: Norcross, Karg, & Prochaska (1997a); Norcross, Strausser, & Missar (1988); Watkins, Lopez, Campbell, & Himmell (1986).

theoretical orientations and client needs call for different formats. Similarly, the precise training and qualifications of the psychotherapist have not been delineated. We recognize multiple processes of change and the multidimensional nature of change; no attempt is made here to delimit the methods or content of therapeutic change. The requirement that the methods be "derived from established psychological principles" is sufficiently broad to permit clinical and/or research validation.

The definition also explicitly includes both "clinical methods and interpersonal stances." In some therapy systems, the active change mechanism has been construed as a technique; in other systems, the therapeutic relationship has been regarded as the primary focus and source of change. Here, the interpersonal stances and experiences of the therapist are placed on an equal footing with methods and interventions. Finally, we firmly believe that any activity defined as psychotherapy should be conducted only for the "purpose of assisting people" toward mutually agreed-upon goals. Otherwise—though it may be labeled psychotherapy—it becomes a subtle form of coercion or punishment.

The Role of Theory

The term *theory* has multiple meanings. In popular usage, theory is contrasted with practice, empiricism, or certainty. In scientific circles, theory is generally defined as a set of statements used to explain the data in a given area (Marx & Goodson, 1976). In psychotherapy, a theory (or system) is a consistent perspective on human behavior, psychopathology, and the mechanisms of therapeutic change (Norcross, 1985b). These appear to be the necessary, but perhaps not sufficient, features of a psychotherapy theory. Explanations of personality and human development are frequently included, but, as we shall see in the behavioral and integrative models, are not characteristic of all theories.

When colleagues learn that we are revising a text on psychotherapy theories, they occasionally question the usefulness of theories. Why not, they ask, simply produce a text on the actual practice or accumulated facts of psychotherapy?

Our response takes many forms, depending on our mood at the time, but goes something like this. One fruitful way to learn about psychotherapy is to learn what the best minds have had to say about it and to compare what they say. Further, "absolute truth" will probably never be attained in psychotherapy, despite impressive advances in our knowledge and despite a growing body of research. Instead, theory will always be with us to provide tentative approximations of "the truth."

Without a guiding theory or system of psychotherapy, clinicians would be vulnerable, directionless creatures bombarded with literally hundreds of impressions and pieces of information in a single session. Is it more important to ask about color preferences, early memories, parent relationships, life's meaning, disturbing emotions, environmental reinforcers, thought processes, sexual conflicts, or something else in the first interview? At any given time, should we empathize, confront, teach, model, support, question, restructure, interpret, or remain silent in a therapy session? A psychotherapy theory describes the clinical phenomena, delimits the amount of relevant information, organizes that information, and integrates it all into a coherent body of knowledge that prioritizes our conceptualization and directs our treatment.

The model of humanity embedded within a psychotherapy theory orientation is not merely a philosophical issue for purists. It affects which human capacities will be studied and cultivated, and which will be ignored and underdeveloped. Treatment interventions inevitably follow from the clinician's underlying conception of pathology, health, reality, and the therapeutic process (Kazdin, 1984). Systems of therapy embody different visions of life, which imply different possibilities of human existence (Messer & Winokur, 1980).

In this regard, we want to dispute the misconception that any psychotherapist possessing an identifiable theoretical orientation is dogmatic and antiquated. This pervasive misconception suggests that psychotherapists aligning themselves with a particular theory are unwilling to adapt their practices toward the demands of the situation and the patient. The confusion on this issue revolves around the process of selecting and identifying a theoretical orientation. A voluntary decision to label oneself an adherent of a specific theory does not constitute a lifetime commitment of strict adherence or reverence (Norcross, 1985b). Good clinicians are flexible, and good theories are widely applicable. Thus, we see theories being adapted for use in a variety of contexts and clinicians borrowing heavily from divergent theories. As Goldfried (1980) has documented, a preference for one orientation does not preclude the use of strategies or interventions from another. Put another way, the primary problem is not with narrow-gauge therapists, but with therapists who impose that narrowness at the expense of their patients (Stricker, 1988).

Therapeutic Commonalities

Despite theoretical differences, there is a central and recognizable core of psychotherapy. This core distinguishes it from other activities, such as banking, farming, or physical therapy, and glues together variations of psychotherapy. This core is composed of *common factors* or nonspecific variables common to all forms of psychotherapy and not specific to any one. More often than not, these therapeutic commonalities are not specified by theories as being of central importance, but the research suggests exactly the opposite (see Lambert, 1992, for a review).

Mental health professionals have long observed that disparate forms of psychotherapy share common elements or core features (Arkowitz, 1992a; Goldfried & Newman, 1986; Thompson, 1987). As early as 1936, Rosenzweig, noting that all forms of psychotherapy have cures to their credit, invoked the famous Dodo Bird verdict from *Alice in Wonderland*, "Everybody has won and all must have prizes," to characterize psychotherapy outcomes. He then proposed as a possible explanation for roughly equivalent outcomes a number of therapeutic common factors, including psychological interpretation, catharsis, and the therapist's personality. In 1940, Watson reported the results of a meeting held to ascertain areas of agreement among psychotherapy systems (Sollod, 1981). The participants, including such diverse figures as Rosenzweig, Adler, and Rogers, concurred that support, interpretation, insight, behavior change, a good therapeutic relationship, and certain therapist characteristics were common features of successful psychotherapy approaches (Watson, 1940).

If indeed the multitude of different psychotherapy systems can all legitimately claim some success, then perhaps they are not as diverse as they appear on the surface. They probably share certain core features that may be the "curative" elements—those responsible for therapeutic success. To the extent that clinicians of different theories are able to arrive at a common set of strategies, it is likely that what emerges will consist of robust phenomena, as they have managed to survive the distortions imposed by the different theoretical biases (Goldfried, 1980).

But, as one might expect, the common factors posited to date have been numerous and varied in both composition and characterization (Karasu, 1986; Patterson, 1989). Different authors focus on different domains or levels of psychosocial treatment; as a result, diverse conceptualizations of these commonalities have emerged.

Our consideration of common factors will be guided by the results of a study (Grencavage & Norcross, 1990) that reviewed 50 publications to discern convergence among proposed therapeutic commonalities. A total of 89 commonalities were proposed in all. The analysis revealed that the most consensual commonalities were clients' positive expectations and a facilitative therapeutic relationship, each of which will be discussed in turn.

Positive Expectations

Expectation is one of the most widely debated and heavily investigated of the nonspecific variables. Torrey (1972) described this commonality as the "edifice complex"—the patient's faith in the institution itself, the door at the end of the pilgrimage, the confidence in the therapist and the treatment. Our computer search of the literature yielded at least 150 studies that have been conducted to determine the amount of therapy outcome accounted for by the particular expectations patients have toward therapy. The hypothesis of most of these studies is that the treatment is enhanced by the extent to which clients expect the treatment to be effective. Some critics hold that psychotherapy is nothing but a process in which we induce an expectation in our clients that our treatment will cure them, and that any resulting improvement is a function of the client's expecting to improve. Surely many therapists wish on difficult days that the process were so simple!

The available evidence suggests no such simple solution. The studies are divided as to whether expectations induced in clients even affect improvement, let alone determine outcome (DuPont, 1975; Garfield, 1986; Wilkins, 1971, 1977, 1979). Of the studies reporting expectation effects, virtually all demonstrate that a high, positive expectation adds to the effectiveness of such treatments as systematic desensitization. Up to half of successful psychotherapy outcomes may be attributable to the fact that both the healer and the patient believe strongly in the effectiveness of the treatment (Roberts, Kewman, Mercier, & Hovell, 1993).

But psychotherapy can by no means be reduced to expectation effects alone. A sophisticated analysis of multiple outcome studies found that psychotherapy was more effective than well-designed, nonspecific factors conditions, which in turn were more effective than no treatment at all (Barker, Funk, & Houston, 1988). The ranking for therapeutic success is psychotherapy, placebo, and control (do-nothing or wait). In fact, psychotherapy is nearly twice as effective as "nonspecific" or "placebo" treatments, which seek to induce positive expectations in clients (Grissom, 1996).

On the basis of the research, then, we will assume that expectation is an active ingredient in all systems of therapy. Rather than being the central process of change, however, a positive expectation is conceptualized as a critical precondition for therapy to continue. Most clients would not participate in a process that costs them dearly in time, money, and energy if they did not expect the process to help them. In order for clients to cooperate in being desensitized, hypnotized, or analyzed, it seems reasonable that most of them would need to expect at least some return on their investment. It is also our working assumption that therapists consciously strive to cultivate hope and enhance positive expectancies.

Psychotherapy research need not demonstrate that treatment operates free from such nonspecific or common factors. Rather, the task is to demonstrate that specific treatment techniques considered to carry the burden of client change go beyond the results that can be obtained by credibility alone (Kazdin, 1979). Research will also need to operationally define the general term *expectancy*: in some instances, it designates a client's expectation with regard to positive outcome with a particular therapist; in other instances, it refers to a client's expectation about procedures in psychotherapy, the length of treatment, the role of the therapist, and the like (Garfield, 1986; Tinsley, Bowman, & Ray, 1988).

Therapeutic Relationship

Psychotherapy is at root an interpersonal relationship. The single greatest area of convergence among psychotherapists in their nominations of common factors (Grencavage & Norcross, 1990) and in their treatment recommendations (Norcross, Saltzman, & Guinta, 1990) is the development of a strong therapeutic alliance.

This most robust of common strategies has consistently emerged as one of the major determinants of psychotherapy success. Across various types of psychotherapy, at least 10% of psychotherapy outcome—why patients improve in psychotherapy—is due to the therapeutic relationship (Horvath & Luborsky, 1993). To summarize the conclusions of an exhaustive review of the psychotherapy outcome literature (Bergin & Lambert, 1978): The largest variation in therapy outcome is accounted for by preexisting client factors, such as expectations for change and severity of the disorder. The therapeutic relationship accounted for the second largest proportion of change, with technique variables coming in a distant third.

Still, the desirable type and relative importance of the therapeutic relationship are areas of theoretical controversy. At one end of the continuum, some psychotherapy systems, such as the radical behavior therapies, view the relationship between client[1] and therapist as being of little importance; the processes and content that must occur in therapy could just as readily occur with only a programmed computer, without the therapist's presence. For these systems, a therapist is included for practical reasons only, because our technology in programming therapeutic processes and content is not developed fully enough to allow the therapist to be absent.

Toward the middle of the continuum, some therapy schools, such as cognitive therapies, view the relationship between clinician and client as one of the preconditions necessary for therapy to proceed. From this point of view, the client must trust and collaborate with the therapist before being able to participate in the process of change.

At the other end of the continuum, Rogers' client-centered therapy sees the relationship as *the* essential process that produces change. Since Carl Rogers (1957) has been most articulate in describing what he believes are the necessary conditions for a therapeutic relationship, let us briefly outline his criteria so that we can use these for comparing systems on the nature of the therapeutic relationship.

---

1. We will employ the terms *client* and *patient* interchangeably throughout the text because neither satisfactorily describes the therapeutic relationship and because we wish to remain theoretically neutral on this quarrelsome point.

1. Of the two people in the relationship, the therapist must be more congruent or emotionally healthy than the client.

2. The therapist must relate in a genuine manner.

3. The therapist must relate with unconditional positive regard.

4. The therapist must relate with accurate empathy.

These—and only these—conditions are necessary and sufficient for positive outcome, according to Rogers.

Then there are those psychotherapy systems, such as psychoanalysis, that see the relationship between therapist and patient primarily as the source of content to be examined in therapy. In this view, the relationship is important because it brings the content of therapy (the patient's interpersonal behavior) right into the consulting room. The content that needs to be changed is thus able to occur during therapy, rather than the person's having to focus on content issues that occur outside of the consulting room.

In light of these various emphases on the role of the therapeutic relationship in the conduct of psychotherapy, it will be necessary to determine for each therapeutic system whether the relationship is conceived as (1) a precondition for change, (2) a process of change, and/or (3) a content to be changed. Moreover, in each chapter that follows, we will consider the relative contribution of the therapeutic relationship to eventual success, as well as the therapist behaviors designed to facilitate that relationship.

Hawthorne Effect

Psychologists have known for years that many people can improve in such behaviors as work output solely as a result of having special attention paid to them. In the classic Hawthorne studies (Roethilsberger & Dickson, 1939) on the effects of improved lighting on productivity in a factory, it was discovered that participants increased their output as a result of simply being in a study and having special attention paid to them. Usually such improvement is assumed to be due to the increase in morale and esteem that people experience from having others attend to them.

One commonality among all psychosocial treatments is that the therapist gives special attention to the client. Consequently, attention has been assumed to be one of the nonspecific or common factors that impact the results of therapy. Anyone who has been in therapy can appreciate the gratification that comes from having a competent professional give undivided attention for an hour. This special attention may indeed affect the course of therapy—including those occasional cases in which patients do not improve because they do not want to surrender such special attention.

Researchers have frequently found that attention does indeed lead to improvement, regardless of whether the attention is followed by any other therapeutic processes. Paul (1967), for example, found that 50% of public-speaking phobics demonstrated marked improvement in their symptoms following treatment with an attention placebo that was intended to control for such nonspecific variables as attention. Equally striking was his finding that a group receiving similar attention plus insight-oriented therapy demonstrated no greater improvement than the group receiving attention placebo alone, while a group receiving attention plus desensitization showed much greater improvement. Although there were problems with the fairness of Paul's test of insight therapy, his study does suggest that attention can be a powerful common factor in therapy.

To be able to conclude that any particular therapy is more than an attention placebo, it is necessary that research include controls for attention effects. It is not enough to demonstrate that a particular therapy is better than no treatment, because the improvement from that particular therapy may be due entirely to the attention given the patients.

Several research designs are available to measure or control for the effects of attention in psychotherapy. The most popular design is to use attention placebo groups, as in Paul's study, where control subjects were given as much attention as clients in therapy but did not participate in processes designed to produce change. An alternative design is to examine studies that compare the effectiveness of one school with that of another, such as psychoanalytic therapy with person-centered therapy and cognitive therapy. If one therapeutic approach does better than the other, we can conclude that the differential improvement is due to more than just attention, because the less-effective treatment included—and therefore controlled for—the effects of attention. However, we do not know whether the less-effective therapy is anything other than a placebo effect, even if it leads to greater improvement than no treatment. Finally, in such comparative studies, if both therapies lead to significant improvement, but neither therapy does better than the other, we cannot conclude that the therapies are anything more than Hawthorne effects, unless an attention placebo control has also been included in the study. To be considered an adequately controlled evaluation of a psychotherapy's efficacy, studies must include controls for the Hawthorne effect and related factors.

Other Commonalities

In his classic *Persuasion and Healing*, Jerome Frank (1961; Frank & Frank, 1991) posits that all psychotherapeutic methods are elaborations and variations of age-old procedures of psychological healing. The features that distinguish psychotherapies from each other, however, receive special emphasis in the pluralistic, competitive American society. Because the prestige and financial security of psychotherapists hinge on their being able to show that their particular approach is more successful than that of their rivals, little glory has traditionally been accorded to the identification of shared or common components.

Frank argues that therapeutic change is predominantly a function of factors common to all therapeutic approaches. These factors include an emotionally charged, confiding relationship; a healing setting; a rationale or conceptual scheme; and a therapeutic ritual. Other consensual commonalities include a warm, inspiring, and socially sanctioned therapist; opportunity for catharsis; acquisition and practice of new behaviors; exploration of the "inner world" of the patient; suggestion; and interpersonal learning (Grencavage & Norcross, 1990). Many observers now conclude that features shared by all therapies account for an appreciable amount of observed improvement in clients.

So powerful are these therapeutic commonalities for some clinicians that explicitly "common factors" therapies have been proposed. Garfield (1980, 1992), to take one prominent example, finds the mechanisms of change in virtually all approaches to be rooted in the therapeutic relationship, emotional release, explanation and interpretation, reinforcement, desensitization, confronting a problem, and skill training. Other common-factors clinicians structure the powerful determinants slightly differently, but all are impressed with the commonalities of psychotherapy (see, for example, Arkowitz, 1992a, 1992b; Beitman, 1986, 1992; Orlinsky & Howard, 1987; Palmer, 1980).

Specific Factors

At the same time, common factors theorists recognize the value of unique—or specific—factors in disparate psychotherapies. Psychotherapy research has demonstrated differential effectiveness of a few therapies with specific disorders, such as behavior therapy for specific symptoms, cognitive therapy for depression, and systemic therapy for marital conflict (Lambert & Bergin, 1992).

We now turn to the processes of change—the relatively specific or unique contributions of a therapy system.

Processes of Change

There is, as we said in the introduction to this chapter, an expanding morass of psychotherapy theories and a seemingly endless proliferation of specific techniques. Consider the relatively simple case of smoking cessation: In one of our early studies, we identified more than 50 formal treatments employed by health professionals and 130 different techniques used by successful self-changers to stop smoking. Is there no smaller and more intelligible framework within which to examine and compare the psychotherapies?

The *transtheoretical*—across theories—model reduces the number of therapeutic techniques to ten basic processes of change. We will probably never reach common ground in the theoretical or philosophical realm, and a search for commonalities across approaches in the realm of specific techniques will probably not reveal much more than minor points of similarity. By contrast, the *processes of change* represent a middle level of abstraction between global theories (such as psychoanalysis, behaviorism, and systems) and specific techniques (such as dream analysis, progressive muscle relaxation, and family sculpting), in which meaningful points of both convergence and contention may be found among psychotherapy systems. Table 1.2 (adapted from Goldfried & Safran, 1986) illustrates this intermediate level of abstraction represented by the processes of change.

Table 1.2 Levels of Abstraction

Level	Abstraction	Examples
High	Theoretical frameworks	Psychodynamic, Gestalt, behavioral
Medium	Change processes	Consciousness raising, self-liberation, counterconditioning
Low	Clinical techniques	Interpretation, two-chair technique, self-monitoring

Source: Adapted from Goldfried & Sefran (1986).

Processes of change are the covert and overt activities that people engage in to alter affect, thinking, behavior, or relationships related to a particular problem or more general patterns of living. The change processes are used within psychotherapy, without psychotherapy, and between therapy sessions. These processes were derived theoretically from a comparative analysis of the leading systems of psychotherapy (Prochaska, 1979).

Consciousness Raising

Traditionally, increasing an individual's consciousness has been one of the prime processes of change in psychotherapy. Consciousness-raising programs sound so contemporary, yet therapists from a variety of persuasions have been working for decades to increase the consciousness of clients. Beginning with Freud's basic objective "to make the unconscious conscious," all so-called "verbal psychotherapies" begin by working to raise the individual's level of awareness. It is fitting that the verbal or awareness therapies work with consciousness, which has frequently been assumed to be a human characteristic that emerged with the evolution of language.

Although much about expanding awareness remains to be discovered, some aspects of consciousness raising are directly relevant to systems of psychotherapy. With language and consciousness, we do not respond reflexively to the energy in a stimulus. Thus, for example, the mechanical energy from a hand hitting against our back does not cause us to react with movement. Instead, we respond to the information contained in the stimulus, such as whether the hand touching us is that of a friend patting us on the back, a robber grabbing us, or a spouse hitting us. In order to respond effectively, we must process adequate information to guide us in making a response appropriate to the stimulus. Therapies that involve increasing consciousness are assumed to increase the information available to individuals so that they can make the most effective responses to the stimuli impinging on them.

For each of the processes of change, the psychotherapist's focus can be on producing change either at the level of the individual's experience or at the level of the individual's environment. When the information given clients is contained in the stimulation generated by the individual's own actions and experiences, we call that *feedback.* An example of the feedback process occurred in the case of a stern and proper middle-aged woman who was unaware of just how angry she appeared to be. She could not connect her children's avoidance of her or her recent rash of automobile accidents with anger, because she kept insisting that she was not at all angry. After viewing videotapes of herself interacting with members of a psychotherapy group, however, she was stunned. All she could say was, "My God, how angry I seem to be!"[2]

When the information given in therapy is contained in stimulation generated by environmental events, we call this *education*. An example of therapeutic movement due to education occurred in the case of an aging man who was distressed over the fact that his time to attain erections and reach orgasms had increased noticeably over the past few years. He was very relieved when he learned that such a delay was what Masters and Johnson (1966) found to be normal in older men.

One of the most important areas for education and feedback in psychotherapy is information regarding the cognitive structures that individuals use to ward off threatening information about themselves. These defensive structures are like blinders or the "rose-colored glasses" that some people use to selectively attend only to positive information about themselves and the world and ignore negative input. Cognitive blinders prevent individuals from being able to increase their consciousness without feedback or education from an outside party. For example, my (JOP's) wife, who is also a psychotherapist, confronted me with the following information that made me aware of one set of blinders I was wearing. We were trying to see if we could anticipate who would be on our partner's list of sexually attractive individuals. I was absolutely sure that my first three guesses would be high on my wife's list. When I said a friend's name, my wife laughed and said that she knew I always thought that, but she wasn't attracted to him. She also said that she was now sure that his wife was on my list. My next two guesses were also wrong, but my wife was quickly able to guess that I found their wives attractive. I was amazed to realize how much I had been projecting over the years and how my projection kept me from being aware of the qualities in men that my wife found appealing.

Because our conceptualization of consciousness raising focuses on information processing, using the more current label of *cognitive approaches* to therapy might seem preferable to using the label *consciousness-enhancing approaches*. The concept of changes in consciousness is used, however, partly because it has a much longer history in psychotherapy. Even more important, the term *cognitive processes* might be misleading if it implied that the information processed in therapy produced only a cognitive response in clients. Obviously, the information in therapy is usually very personal and likely to produce as strong an affective reaction as a cognitive response.

This occurred during a session with a family that had entered therapy in part because the stepfather had beaten his 16-year-old stepson when he found him

---

2. In the case of this woman, as with so many clients, we cannot demonstrate that the way we conceptualize the person's problems is, in fact, the way things really are. We cannot, for example, demonstrate in an empirical manner that this woman's problems were due to angry feelings that were outside of her awareness. Nevertheless, it can still be useful in therapy to make assumptions about the origins of a client's problems. As future case illustrations are presented, they will be described in the manner that we found most helpful for the purposes of treatment, without assuming some ultimate validity of the clinical interpretations.

smoking marijuana. For several years the stepfather had lectured the boy about the dangers of drinking and drugging, but the boy could not understand why his stepfather got so livid over the issue. Finally, the stepfather revealed that he had been an alcoholic for ten years and had spent a year in a hospital struggling to overcome his disorder. The stepfather said he had withheld this information because of the effect it might have on his stepson's feelings and actions toward him. We assume that information such as this, central to personal conflicts, always carries the potential for producing emotional and behavioral changes as well as cognitive change.

How can our awareness of such information lead to a change in our actions or experiences? Without definitive answers from research, we must at times rely on analogies to further our understanding. If we think of our consciousness as a beam of light, then the information unavailable to us is like a darkness in which we can be lost, held back, or directed without knowing the source of the influence. In the darkness, we are like blind individuals, knowing that a wide array of stimuli may be influencing us, but not having enough light on the stimuli to guide us effectively in our lives. For example, without being aware of how aging normally affects a man's sexual response, the aging man would not know whether the best direction for himself was to admit he was over the hill and give up on sex, to eat two raw eggs a day as an aphrodisiac, or to enjoy his present ability to respond without trying to live up to some stereotype of male sexuality.

As we will see, many psychotherapy systems agree that people can change as a function of increasing consciousness. A translation of traditional terms will also demonstrate that these systems are involved in the process of making available experiential or environmental information that was previously unavailable to the individual. The disagreement among some of these consciousness raising systems is on the concrete techniques that are most effective in helping people process information that can profoundly affect them.

Catharsis

Catharsis has one of the longest traditions as a process of therapeutic change. It is well established that the ancient Greeks believed that evoking emotions was one of the best means of providing personal relief and behavioral improvement.

Historically, catharsis has been based on a hydraulic model of emotions, in which unacceptable affects, such as anger, guilt, or anxiety, are blocked from direct expression. The damming off of such emotions results in pressure from affects seeking some form of release, however indirect, as when anger is expressed somatically through headaches. If emotions can be released more directly in therapy, then their reservoir of energy is discharged, and the person is freed from a source of symptoms.

In a different analogy, the patient with blocked emotions is seen as emotionally constipated. What these patients need to release the stress on their psyches is a good emotional bowel movement. In this analogy, psychotherapy serves as a psychological enema that allows patients to purge their emotions and be free from fighting such feelings. The therapeutic process is aimed at helping patients break through their emotional blocks. By expressing the dark side of themselves in the presence of another, the individuals are presumably more able to accept such emotions as natural phenomena that need not be so severely controlled in the future.

Most often, this therapeutic process has been at the level of individual experience, in which the stimuli that elicit cathartic reactions come from within the individual. We shall call this form of catharsis *corrective emotional experiences*.

A fellow clinician related a cathartic experience several years ago when he was trying to fight off a bout of depression. He had not been able to get in touch with the source of his depression, so he took off a mental health day from work. Alone at home, he put on some music and started to express some of his feelings in a free form of dance that he could perform only when no one else was present. After some very releasing movements, he began to experience some childhood rage toward his father for always being on his back. He soon let himself express his intense anger by tearing to shreds the shirt on his back. By the time his wife arrived home, he felt quite relieved, although she thought he had flipped when she saw his shirt.

The belief that cathartic reactions can be evoked by observing emotional scenes in the environment dates back at least to Aristotle's writings on theater and music. In honor of this tradition, we will call this source of catharsis *dramatic relief*. A patient suffering from headaches, insomnia, and other expressions of depression found himself weeping heavily during Ingmar Bergman's *Scenes from a Marriage*. He began to experience how disappointed he was in himself for having traded the possibility of a satisfying marriage for security. He felt his depression beginning to lift because of the inspiration he felt from Bergman to leave his hopelessly devitalized marriage.

Choosing

The role of choice in producing individual change has been in the background of many psychotherapy systems. The concept of choosing has lacked respectability in the highly deterministic world view of most scientists. Many clinicians have not wanted to provide ammunition for their critics' accusations of tender-mindedness by openly discussing freedom and choice. Consequently, we will see that many therapy systems seem to assume that clients will choose to change as a result of psychological treatment but do not articulate the means by which clients come to use the process of choosing.

Because there has been so little open consideration of choosing as a fundamental change process (with the exception of the existentialists), it is predictably difficult to suggest what choice is a function of. Some theorists suggest that choice is irreducible, because to reduce choice to other events is to advance the paradox that such events determine our choices. Human action is seen as freely chosen, and to say that anything else determines our choice is to show bad faith in ourselves as free beings. Few therapists, however, accept such a radical view of freedom for their clients; they usually believe that many conditions limit choice.

From a behavioral perspective, choice would be a partial function of the number of alternative responses available to an individual. If only one response is available, there is no choice. From a humanistic perspective, the number of responses available can radically increase if we become more conscious of alternatives that we have not previously considered. Thus, for a variety of therapy systems, an increase in choice is thought to result from an increase in consciousness.

The freedom to choose has traditionally been construed as a uniquely human response made possible by the acquisition of consciousness that accompanies the development of language. Responsibility is the burden that accompanies the awareness that we are the ones able to respond, to speak for ourselves. If choice and responsibility are made possible by the emergence of language and consciousness, it seems only natural that the therapeutic process of becoming freer to choose is a verbal or awareness process.

The easiest choices in psychotherapy follow from accurate information processing that entails an awareness of the consequences of particular alternatives. If a woman were informed, for example, that birth control pills eventually caused cancer in all women, then her best alternative would be to follow the information she has just processed. With the pill, however, as with so many life decisions, we are not aware of all the consequences of choice, and the consequences are rarely absolute. In these situations, there are no clear external guidelines of which to become aware, and we are confronted with the possibility of choosing an alternative that might be a terrible mistake. Then our ability to choose is more clearly a function of our ability to accept the anxiety inherent in taking responsibility for our future.

An example of so-called existential anxiety was seen in a student in one of my classes who came to see me about the panic attacks she was having since she informed her parents of her pregnancy. They insisted that she get an abortion, but she and her husband wanted to have the baby. They were both students, and entirely dependent on her wealthy parents for financial support. Her parents had informed her that the consequence of having a baby at this time would be disinheritance, because they believed she would not finish college once she had a baby. In 21 years she had never openly differed with her parents, and although she was controlled by them, she had always felt protected by them as well. Now after just a few sessions, she became more aware that her panic attacks reflected her need to choose. Her basic choice was not whether she was going to sacrifice her fetus to her family's fortune, but whether she was going to continue to sacrifice herself.

At an experiential level, then, an increase in choosing involves the individual's becoming aware of new alternatives, including the conscious creation of new alternatives for living. This process also involves the individual's experiencing the anxiety inherent in being responsible for which alternative is followed. We will call this experiential level of increased choosing a move toward *self-liberation*. When changes in the environment make more alternatives available to individuals, such as more jobs open to gay people, we will call this a move toward *social liberation*. Therapists working for such social changes are usually called advocates.

Conditional Stimuli

At the opposite extreme from changing through choosing is changing by making modifications in the conditional stimuli that control our responses. Alterations in conditional stimuli are necessitated either when the individual's behavior is elicited by classically conditioned stimuli (CS) or when stimuli are discriminable (S^D) occasions for individuals to emit responses that are operantly conditioned. When troublesome responses are conditioned to such stimuli, then being conscious of the stimuli will not produce change, nor can conditioning be overcome just by choosing to change.

Again, either we can modify the way we behave to particular stimuli, or we can modify the environment to minimize the probability of the stimuli occurring. Changing our responses to the stimuli is referred to in our model as *counterconditioning*, whereas changing the environment involves *stimulus control*.

Counterconditioning was used in the treatment of a new bride with a penetration phobia who responded to intercourse with involuntary muscle spasms. This condition, known as vaginismus, prevented penetration. She did not want to modify her environment, but rather to change her response to her husband. As in most counterconditioning cases, the procedure involved a gradual approach to the CS of intercourse while experiencing a response, such as relaxation or sexual arousal, that is incompatible with the undesired response of anxiety and muscle spasms that had previously been elicited by intercourse.

Stimulus control procedures involve restructuring the environment so that the probability that a particular conditional stimulus will occur is significantly reduced. A high-strung college student had a host of anxiety symptoms, including considerable distress when driving his car. Whenever the car began to shake in the slightest, the student would also begin to shake. He attributed this particular problem to a frightening episode he had experienced earlier in the year, when the universal joint on his car broke with a startling noise. Not once but three times it broke before a mechanic discovered that the real cause was a bent drive shaft. Because the problem appeared to be a function of conditioning, a counterconditioning approach was the treatment of choice. Before the treatment was under way, however, the student traded in his car for a van. Because his anxiety response did not generalize to his van, he solved his problem through his own stimulus control procedure.

Contingency Control

Almost axiomatic for many behavior therapists is that behavior is under the control of the consequences to which it leads. As most of us have learned, if a reinforcement is made contingent on a particular response, then the probability is increased that we will make that response. If, on the other hand, a punishment is made contingent on a particular response, then we are less likely to emit that response. By changing the contingencies that govern our behavior, it is widely assumed that we change our behavior, including psychopathology. The extent to which particular consequences control behavior is a function of many variables, including the immediacy, saliency, and schedule of the consequences. From humanistic and cognitive-behavioral points of view, the individual's valuing of particular consequences is also an important variable affecting contingency control.

If changes in an individual are made by modifying the contingencies in the environment, we call this *contingency management*. For example, a graduate student with a bashful bladder wanted to increase his ability to use public rest rooms; he also wanted more money to improve his style of living. Therefore, he made a contingency contract with me (JOP) that earned him two dollars for each time during the week he urinated in a public rest room. I am pleased to say that I lost money on that case.

Very seldom have behavior therapists considered the alternative, but there are important means by which individuals can modify their experience or response to anticipated consequences without changing the consequences themselves. Modifying responses to consequences without changing contingencies will be called *re-evaluation*.

A very shy man continued to desire a relationship with a woman but avoided asking anyone out because of his anticipation that he would be rejected. After several intensive discussions, he began to accept that when a woman turns down a date, it is a statement about her and not about him. We do not know whether she is waiting for someone else to ask her out, whether she doesn't like mustaches, whether she is afraid of men, or whether she doesn't know him well enough—we simply don't know what her saying no says about him. After reevaluating how he would interpret being turned down for a date, the fellow began asking out women, even though he was rejected on his first request for a date.

Initial Integration of Processes of Change

An overview of the basic processes of change is presented in Table 1.3. The processes of consciousness raising, catharsis, and choosing represent the heart of the traditional verbal or awareness psychotherapies, including both the psychoanalytic and the humanistic traditions. These schools focus primarily on the subjective aspects of the individual—the processes occurring within the skin of the organism. This perspective on the individual sees greater potential for inner-directed changes that can counteract some of the external pressures from the environment.

The processes of conditional stimuli and contingency control represent the core of action or behavioral psychotherapies, including those in the behavioral and systemic traditions. These schools focus primarily on the external and environmental forces that set limits on the individual's potential for inner-directed change. These are what the existentialists would call the more objective level of the organism.

Our integrative, transtheoretical model suggests that to focus only on the awareness processes of consciousness, catharsis, and choice is to act as if inner-directedness is the whole picture and to ignore the genuine limits the environment can place on individual change. On the other hand, the action emphasis on the more objective, environmental processes selectively ignores the potential for inner, subjective change that individuals possess. An integrative model posits that a synthesis of both awareness and action processes provides a more balanced view that moves along the continuous dimensions of inner to outer control, subjective to objective functioning, and self-initiated to environmentally induced changes. These continuous dimensions afford a more complete picture of individuals by accepting their potential for inner change while recognizing the limits that environments and contingencies can place on such change.

Table 1.3 Change Processes at Experiential and Environmental Levels

	Change Process	Experiential Level	Environmental Level
Awareness Therapies	Consciousness raising	Feedback	Education
	Catharsis	Corrective emotional experience	Dramatic relief
	Choosing	Self-liberation	Social liberation
Action Therapies	Conditional stimuli	Counterconditioning	Stimulus control
	Contingency control	Reevaluation	Contingency management

Therapeutic Content

The processes of change are the distinctive contributions of a system of psychotherapy. The content to be changed in any particular therapy is largely a carry-over from that system's theory of personality and psychopathology. Many books purportedly focusing on psychotherapy frequently confuse content and process and wind up examining the content of therapy, with little explanation about the processes. As a consequence, they are really books on theories of personality rather than theories of psychotherapy.

The distinction between process and content in psychotherapy is a fundamental one (Held, 1991). As we shall see, psychotherapy systems without theories of personality are primarily process theories and have few predetermined concepts about the content of therapy. Behavioral, eclectic, systemic, and solution-focused theories attempt to capitalize on the unique aspects of each case by restricting the imposition of formal content (Held, 1991). Other systems, such as Adlerian, existential, and culture-sensitive therapies, which adopt change processes from other therapy systems, will have things to say primarily about the content of therapy. Many systems of therapy differ primarily in their content, while agreeing on the change processes. Put differently, theories of personality and psychopathology tell us *what* needs to be changed; theories of process tell us *how* change occurs (Arkowitz, 1989).

Because psychotherapy systems have many more differences regarding the content of therapy, it is much more difficult to bring order and integration to this fragmented field. A refreshing guide is Maddi's (1972, 1996) comparative model for personality theories. We have adapted parts of Maddi's model in synthesizing and prioritizing the vast array of content in psychotherapy.

In Maddi's (1972, 1996) terms, most systems of therapy assume a conflict view of personality and psychopathology. Conflict-oriented theories differ in the level of personality functioning on which they focus. Some see personal problems as a result of conflicts within the individual. Maddi calls these intrapsychic conflicts, but we shall use the term *intrapersonal conflicts,* indicating that the conflicts are among forces within the person, such as a conflict between desires to be independent and fears of leaving home. Other theories focus on the *interpersonal conflicts* in personality, such as chronic disagreements between a woman who likes to save money and her husband who likes to spend money. Another group of theories focuses primarily on the conflicts that occur between an individual and society. We shall call these *individuo-social conflicts;* an example is the tension of an individual who wants to live an openly gay life but who is afraid of the ostracism that may result from society's mistrust of homosexuality. Finally, an increasing number of therapies are concerned with helping individuals go beyond conflict to fulfillment.

In our integrative model, we assume that different groups of clients have dysfunctions emanating from conflicts at different levels of personality functioning. Some patients express intrapersonal conflicts, others evidence interpersonal conflicts, and still others are in conflict with society. Some clients have resolved their principal conflicts and turn to psychotherapy with questions as to how they can best create a more fulfilling existence.

Because different patients are troubled at different levels of functioning, we will compare the psychotherapy systems and determine how each would conceptualize and treat the problems that most commonly occur at each level of conflict and growth. At the intrapersonal level, we will examine the approach of each therapy to conflicts over anxiety and defenses, self-esteem, and personal responsibility. At the interpersonal level, we will consider problems with intimacy and sexuality, communication, hostility, and interpersonal control. At the individuo-social level, we will compare their perspectives on adjustment versus transcendence and impulse control. At the level of transcending conflicts to fulfillment, we will examine therapeutic approaches to the fundamental questions of meaning in life and the ideal person that would emerge from successful therapy. Table 1.4 summarizes the most common therapeutic content that occurs at different levels of personality.

Honest differences abound over whether particular problems, such as addictive, sexual, and family disorders, are most profitably conceptualized as intra- or interpersonal conflicts, and we expect disagreement over our assignment of problems to a particular level of personality functioning. We also recognize that any viable theory of personality can reduce all problems to a single level of functioning that the theory assumes to be critical to personality. For example, an intrapersonal theory of personality can present a convincing case that sexual disorders are primarily due to conflicts within the individuals, such as conflicts between sexual desires and performance anxieties. By contrast, an individuo-social theory could summon a coherent argument that sexual disorders are primarily due to the inevitable tensions between an individual's sexual desires and society's sexual prohibitions. Our integrative assumption is that a comparative analysis of therapies will demonstrate that particular systems have been especially effective in conceptualizing and treating problems related to their level of personality theory.

In comparing psychotherapy systems, we will also discover that a theory's level of personality will largely dictate the number of people in the consulting room and the focus of the therapeutic transaction. If a theory focuses on the intrapersonal level of functioning, then the therapy is much more likely to work solely with the individual, because the basic problem is assumed to lie within the individual. If a theory concentrates on the interpersonal level, on the other hand, it is more likely to involve two or more persons in conflict, such as a husband and wife or family

Table 1.4 Therapeutic Content at Different Levels of Personality

1. Intrapersonal conflicts
   a. Anxieties and defenses
   b. Self-esteem problems
   c. Personal responsibility

2. Interpersonal conflicts
   a. Intimacy and sexuality
   b. Communication'
   c. Hostility
   d. Control of others

3. Individuo-social conflicts
   a. Adjustment versus transcendence
   b. Impulse control

4. Beyond conflict to fulfillment
   a. Meaning in life
   b. The ideal person

members. Therapies that focus on individuo-social conflicts will work to change the individual, if the therapist's values are on the side of society. For example, in working with a pedophiliac who has no inner conflict over having sexual relations with children, a therapist will work to change the individual, assuming that the therapist's values converge with society's values that this sexual behavior is unacceptable. However, if the therapist's values are on the side of the individual in a particular conflict, such as a gay person wanting to be free to be openly homosexual, the therapist is more likely to work with or support movements that are working to change society. In comparing therapies, then, we will examine which level of personality functioning they emphasize and whether such an emphasis leads to working primarily with individuals alone, with two or more individuals together, or with groups seeking to change society.

⎯ THE CASE OF MRS. C ⎯

Therapy systems are not merely a static combination of change processes, theoretical contents, and research studies. The systems are, first and foremost, concerned with the serious disorders of real people. In comparing systems, it is essential to present a picture of how the psychotherapies conceptualize and treat the presenting problems of a real client. The client we have selected for comparative purposes is Mrs. C.

Mrs. C. is a 47-year-old mother of six children: Arlene, 17; Barry, 15; Charles, 13; Debra, 11; Ellen, 9; and Frederick, 7. Without reading further, an astute observer might be able to discern Mrs. C.'s personality configuration.

The orderliness of children named alphabetically and of childbirths every two years are consistent with other features of an Obsessive-Compulsive Disorder (OCD). For the past ten years, Mrs. C. has been plagued by compulsive washing. Her baseline charts, in which she recorded her behavior each day before treatment began, indicated that she washed her hands 25 to 30 times a day, 5 to 10 minutes at a time. Her daily morning shower lasted about two hours with rituals involving each part of her body, beginning with her rectum. If she lost track of where she was in her ritual, then she would have to start all over. A couple of times this had resulted in her husband, George, going off to work with his wife in the shower only to return eight hours later with her still involved in the lengthy ritual. To avoid lengthy showers, George had begun helping his wife keep track of her ritual, so that at times she would yell out, "Which arm, George?" and he would yell back, "Left arm, Martha." His participation in the shower ritual required George to rise at 5:00 A.M. in order to have his wife out of the shower before he left for work at 7:00 A.M. After two years of this schedule, George was ready to explode.

George was, understandably, becoming increasingly impatient with many of his wife's related symptoms. She would not let anyone wear a pair of underwear more than one day and often wouldn't even let these underwear be washed. There were piles of dirty underwear in each corner of the house. When we had her husband gather up the underwear for the laundry, we asked him to count them, but he quit counting after the thousandth pair. He was depressed to realize that he had more than $1,000 invested in once-worn underwear.

Other objects were scattered around the house, because a fork or a can of food dropped on the floor could not be retrieved in Mrs. C.'s presence. Mrs. C. had been doing no housework—no cooking, cleaning, or washing—for two years. One of her children described the house as a "state dump," and my visit to the home confirmed this impression.

Mrs. C. did work part-time. What would be a likely job for her? Something to do with washing, of course. In fact, she was a dental assistant, which involved washing all of the dentist's equipment.

As if these were not sufficient concerns, Mrs. C. had become very unappealing in appearance. She had not purchased a dress in seven years, and her clothes were becoming ragged. Never in her life had she been to a beautician and now she seldom combed her own hair. Her incessant washing of her body and hair led to a presentation somewhere between a prune and a boiled lobster with the frizzies.

Mrs. C.'s washing ritual also entailed walking around the house nude from the waist up as she went from her bedroom bath to the downstairs bath to complete her washing. This was especially upsetting to Mr. C. because of the embarrassment it was producing in their teenage sons. The children were also upset by Mrs. C.'s frequently nagging them to wash their hands and change their underwear, and she would not let them entertain friends in the house.

Consistent with OCD features, Mrs. C. was a hoarder; she had two closets filled with hundreds of towels and sheets, dozens of unused earrings, and her entire wardrobe from the past 20 years. She did not consider this hoarding a problem because it was a family characteristic, which she believed she inherited from her mother and from her mother's mother.

Mrs. C. also suffered from a sexual arousal disorder or, in common parlance, she was "frigid." She said she had never been sexually excited in her life, but at least for the first 13 years she was willing to engage in sexual relations to satisfy her husband. However, in the past two years she had had intercourse just twice, because sex had become increasingly unpleasant for her.

To complete the list, Mrs. C. was currently clinically depressed. She had made a suicide gesture by swallowing a bottle of aspirin because she had an inkling that her psychotherapist was giving up on her and her husband was probably going to send her to a mental hospital.

Mrs. C.'s compulsive rituals revolved around an obsession with pinworms. Her oldest daughter had come home with pinworms ten years earlier during a severe flu epidemic. Mrs. C. had to care for a sick family while pregnant, sick with the flu herself, and caring for a demanding 1-year-old child. Her physician told her that to avoid having the pinworms spread throughout the family, Mrs. C. would have to be extremely careful about the children's underwear, clothes, and sheets and that she should boil all of these articles to kill any pinworm eggs. Mr. C. confirmed that they were both rather anxious about a pinworm epidemic in the home and were both preoccupied with cleanliness during this time. However, Mrs. C.'s preoccupation with cleanliness and pinworms continued even after it had been confirmed that her daughter's pinworms were gone.

The C. couple acknowledged a relatively good marriage before the pinworm episode. They had both wanted a sizable family, and Mr. C.'s income as a business executive had allowed them to afford a large family and comfortable home without financial strain. During the first 13 years of their marriage, Mrs. C. had demonstrated some of her obsessive-compulsive traits, but never to such a degree that Mr. C. considered them a problem. Mr. C. and the older children recalled many happy times they had had with Mrs. C., and they seemed to have been able to keep alive the warmth and love that they had once shared with this now preoccupied person.

Mrs. C. hailed from a strict, authoritarian, and sexually repressed Catholic family. She was the middle of three girls, all of whom were dominated by a father who was 6 feet, 4 inches tall and weighed 250 pounds. When Mrs. C. was a teenager, her father would wait up for her after dates to question her about what she had done; he once went so far as to follow her on a date. He tolerated absolutely no expression of anger, especially toward himself, and when she would try to explain her point of view politely, he would often tell her to shut up. Mrs. C.'s mother was a frigid, compulsive woman who repeatedly regaled her daughters about her disgust with sex. She also frequently warned her daughters about diseases and the importance of cleanliness.

In developing a psychotherapy plan for Mrs. C., one of the critical differential diagnostic questions was whether Mrs. C. was plagued with a severe obsessive-compulsive disorder or whether her symptoms were masking a latent schizophrenic process. A full battery of psychological testing was completed, and the projective test results were consistent with those from previous tests that had found no evidence of a thought disorder or other signs of psychotic processes.

Mrs. C. had previously undergone a total of six years of mental health treatment, and throughout this time the clinicians had always considered her problems to be severely neurotic in nature. The only time schizophrenia was offered as a diagnosis was after some extensive individual psychotherapy that failed to lead to any improvement. The consensus in our clinic was that Mrs. C. was demonstrating a severe obsessive-compulsive neurosis that was going to be extremely difficult to treat.

At the end of each of the following chapters, we will see how each of the psychotherapy systems might explain Mrs. C.'s problems and how their treatment might help her to overcome these devastating preoccupations.

Suggestions for Further Reading

Beutler, L. E., & Crago, M. (Eds.). (1991). *Psychotherapy research*: *An international review of programmatic studies*. Washington, DC: American Psychological Association.

Frank, J. D., & Frank, J. (1991). *Persuasion and healing* (3rd ed.). Baltimore: Johns Hopkins University Press.

Freedheim, D. K. (Ed.). (1992). *History of psychotherapy*: *A century of change*. Washington, DC: American Psychological Association.

Gabbard, G. O. (Ed.). (1995). *Treatments of psychiatric disorders* (2nd ed.). Washington, DC: American Psychiatric Press.

Garfield, S. L., & Bergin, A. E. (Eds.). (1994). *Handbook of psychotherapy and behavior change* (4th ed.). New York: Wiley.

Lipsey, M. W., & Wilson, D. B. (1993). The efficacy of psychological, educational, and behavioral treatment: Confirmation from meta-analysis. *American Psychologist, 48,* 1181–1209.

Maddi, S. R. (1996). *Personality theories*: *A comparative analysis* (6th ed.). Pacific Grove, CA: Brooks/Cole.

Saltzman, N., & Norcross, J. C. (Eds.). (1990). *Therapy wars: Contention and convergence in differing clinical approaches*. San Francisco: Jossey-Bass.

Zeig, J. K., & Munion, W. M. (Eds.). (1990). *What is psychotherapy? Contemporary perspectives*. San Francisco: Jossey-Bass.

Journals: *American Journal of Psychiatry; American Journal of Psychotherapy; Archives of General Psychiatry; British Journal of Psychotherapy; Clinical Psychology and Psychotherapy; In Session: Psychotherapy in Practice; International Journal for the Advancement of Counseling; International Journal of Psychotherapy; International Journal of Short-Term Psychotherapy; Journal of Child and Adolescent Psychotherapy; Journal of College Student Psychotherapy; Journal of Consulting and Clinical Psychology; Journal of Contemporary Psychotherapy; Journal of Counseling and Development; Journal of Counseling Psychology; Journal of Mental Health Counseling; Journal of Psychosocial Nursing and Mental Health Services; Journal of Psychotherapy Practice and Research; Psychiatric Quarterly; Psychiatry; Psychotherapy; Psychotherapy and Psychosomatics; Psychotherapy in Private Practice; Psychotherapy Patient; Psychotherapy Research; Social Casework; Voices: The Art and Science of Psychotherapy.*

2

Psychoanalytic Therapies

Sigmund Freud

KAREN WAS TO BE TERMINATED from her nursing program if her problems were not resolved. She had always been a competent student who seemed to get along well with peers and patients. Now, since beginning her rotation on 3 South, a surgical ward, she was plagued by headaches and dizzy spells. Of more serious consequence were the two medical errors she had made when dispensing medications to patients. She realized that these errors could prove fatal and was as concerned as her nursing faculty that she understand why such problems had begun in this final year of her education. Karen knew she had many negative feelings toward the head nurse on 3 South, but she did not believe these feelings could account for her current dilemma.

After a few weeks of psychotherapy, we realized that one of Karen's important conflicts revolved around the death of her father when she was 12 years old. Karen had just gone to live with her father after being with her mother for seven years. She remembered how upset she was when her father had a heart attack and had to be rushed to the hospital. For a while it looked as though her father was going to pull through, and Karen began enjoying her daily visits to see him. During one of these visits, her father clutched his chest in obvious pain and told Karen to get a nurse. She was unclear as to why, but she remembered how helpless she felt when she could not find a nurse. Her search seemed endless, and when she finally found a nurse, her father was dead.

I don't know why, but I asked Karen the name of the ward on which her father had died. She paused and thought, and then to our surprise, she blurted out, "3 South." She cried heavily as she expressed how confused she was and how angry she felt toward the nurses on that ward for not being more available, although she thought they had been involved with another emergency. After weeping and shaking and expressing her resentment, Karen felt calm and relaxed for the first time in months. My psychoanalytic supervisor said her symptoms would disappear, and sure enough they did. He knew we would have to go much deeper into what earlier conflicts this adolescent experience represented, but for now, Karen's problems in the nursing program were relieved.

A Sketch of Sigmund Freud

Early in his career, Sigmund Freud (1856–1939) was quite impressed by the way some of his patients seemed to recover following cathartic recollections of an early trauma. But he soon discovered that more profound, lasting changes required changes in his own approach. Over time, he switched from hypnosis to catharsis to a dynamic analysis that radically increased not only the consciousness of his clients but also the consciousness of his culture.

Freud's genius has been admired by many, but he complained throughout his life about not having been given a bigger brain (Jones, 1955). Freud himself believed that his outstanding attribute was his courage. Certainly it took tremendous daring and inquisitiveness to descend into the uncharted depths of humanity and then to declare to such a strict Victorian culture what he had discovered.

Freud once observed that scientific inquisitiveness is a derivative of the child's sexual curiosity, the sublimation of anxiety-laden questions of "Where do I come from?" and "What did my parents do to produce me?" These questions exercised a particular fascination for Freud and later assumed a central position in his theory of personality because of his own intricate family constellation. His mother was half his father's age, his two half-brothers were as old as his mother, and he had a nephew older than he (Gay, 1990). He was the prized "golden child" born into a lower-class Jewish family.

For years he struggled for success. Beginning in 1873, with his entry into the University of Vienna at age 17, to his work as a research scholar in an institute of physiology, to earning his MD in 1891 and his residency in neurology, he expected that his hard work and commitment would result in recognition and financial success. He had never intended to practice medicine, but he found the rewards of research to be quite restricted and the opportunities for academic advancement for a Jew to be limited. Finally, after marrying at age 30, he began to develop a rewarding private practice. Yet Freud was willing to risk his hard-earned financial success in order to communicate to his colleagues what his work with patients had convinced him of: the basis of neurosis was sexual conflict—or, more specifically, the conflict between the id's instinctive desires and society's retribution for direct expression of those desires.

Freud's profound insights were met with professional insults, and his private practice rapidly declined. For months he received no new referrals. For years he had to rely on his inner courage to continue his lonely intellectual pursuits without a colleague to share his insights. During this same period of the 1890s, he began his lonely and painful self-analysis, in part to overcome some neurotic symptoms and in part to serve as his own subject in his studies of the unconscious. Surprisingly, Freud was not basically alienated by his professional isolation. He was able to interpret the opposition he met as part of the natural resistance to taboo ideas.

Finally, in the early 1900s, Freud's risky work began to be recognized by scholars, such as the dying William James, as the system that would shape 20th-century psychology. Shape it he did, along with the incredibly brilliant group of colleagues who joined the Vienna Psychoanalytic Society. Most of these colleagues contributed to the development of psychoanalysis, but Freud insisted that as the founder he alone had the right to decide what should be called psychoanalysis. This led some of the best minds, including Adler and Jung, to leave the Psychoanalytic Society to develop their own systems. Freud's insistence may also have set a precedent for a dogmatism that relied more on authority than on evidence in revising psychotherapy theories. Freud himself, however, continued throughout his lifetime to be critical of his own theories and would painfully discard selected ideas if experience contradicted them.

Success did not diminish Freud's commitment to his scholarly work or to his patients. He worked an 18-hour day that began with seeing patients from 8:00 A.M. until 1:00 P.M., a break for lunch and a walk with his family, patients again from 3:00 P.M. until 9:00 or 10:00 P.M., dinner and a walk with his wife, followed by writing letters and books until 1:00 or 2:00 A.M. His dedication to his work was remarkable, although it is also striking that this man, dedicated to understanding sex and its vicissitudes, left little time or energy for his own sexuality. Nevertheless, his commitment to work right up until his death from bone cancer at age 85 resulted in the most comprehensive theory of personality, psychopathology, and psychotherapy ever developed.

Theory of Personality

Freud's theory of personality was as complex as he was. He viewed personality from six different perspectives: the topographic, which involves conscious versus unconscious modes of functioning; the dynamic, which entails the interaction of psychic forces; the genetic, which is concerned with the origin and development of psychic phenomena through the oral, anal, phallic, latency, and genital stages; the economic, which involves the distribution, transformation, and expenditure of energy; the structural, which revolves around the persistent functional units of the id, ego, and superego; and the adaptive view, implied by Freud and developed by Hartmann (1958), which involves the inborn preparedness of the individual to interact with an evolving series of normal and predictable environments. We will focus primarily on his dynamic, genetic, and structural perspectives, because these are most directly related to his theories of psychopathology and psychotherapy.

Freud believed that the basic dynamic forces motivating personality were Eros (life and sex) and Thanatos (death and aggression). These complementary forces are instincts that possess a somatic basis but are expressed in fantasies, desires, feelings, thoughts, and most directly, actions. The individual constantly desires immediate gratification of sexual and aggressive impulses. The demand for immediate gratification leads to inevitable conflicts with social rules that insist on some control over sex and aggression if social institutions, including families, are to remain stable and orderly. The individual is forced to develop *defense mechanisms* or inner controls that restrain sexual and aggressive impulses from being expressed in uncontrollable outbursts. Without these defenses, civilization would be reduced to a jungle of raping, ravaging beasts.

The development of defense mechanisms keeps individuals from becoming conscious of basic inner desires to rape and ravage. The assumption here is that if individuals are unaware of such desires, they cannot act on them, at least not directly. The defenses serve to keep the individual out of danger of punishment for breaking social rules. Defenses also keep the individual from experiencing the anxiety and guilt that would be elicited by desires to break parental and social rules. For defenses to work adequately, the person must remain unconscious of the very mechanisms being used to keep sexual and aggressive impulses from coming into awareness. Otherwise, the individual is faced with a dilemma akin to keeping a secret from a 3-year-old child who knows you have a secret—the constant badgering to know what is being hidden can be overwhelming.

The core of the Freudian personality is the unconscious conflict among the individual's sexual and aggressive impulses, society's rules aimed at controlling those impulses, and the individual's defense mechanisms controlling the impulses in such a way as to keep guilt and anxiety to a minimum while allowing some safe, indirect gratification of the impulses (Maddi, 1972, 1996). The difference between a normal personality and a neurotic one, of course, is a matter of degree. It is when the unconscious conflicts become too intense, too painful, and the resultant defense mechanisms too restrictive, that neurotic symptoms begin to emerge.

While all personalities revolve around unconscious conflicts, people differ in the particular impulses, rules, anxieties, and defenses that are in conflict. The differences depend on the particular stage of life at which an individual's conflicts occur. For Freud, the stages of life are determined primarily by the unfolding of sexuality in the oral, anal, phallic, and genital stages. Differences in experiences during each of these stages are critical in determining the variety of traits and personalities that ensue.

Oral Stage

During the first 18 months of life, the infant's sexual desires are centered in the oral region. The child's greatest pleasure is to suck on a satisfying object, such as a breast. The instinctual urges are to passively receive oral gratification during the oral-incorporative phase and to more actively take in oral pleasure during the oral-aggressive phase. Sucking on breasts or bottles, putting toys, fingers, or toes in the mouth, and even babbling are some of the actions a child takes to receive oral gratification. As adults, we can appreciate oral sexuality through kissing, deep kissing, fellatio, cunnilingus, or oral caressing of breasts and other parts of the body.

The infant's oral sexual needs are intense and urgent, but the child is dependent on parental figures to provide the breasts or bottles necessary for adequate oral gratification. How the parents respond to such urgent needs can have a marked influence on the child's personality. Parents who are either too depriving or overindulgent can make it difficult for a child to mature from the oral stage to later stages of personality development. With deprivation, the child can remain fixated at the oral stage: energies are directed primarily toward finding the oral gratification that was in short supply during childhood. With overindulgence, the child can also become fixated at the oral stage, but energies are directed toward trying to repeat and maintain the gratifying conditions. Fixation due to either deprivation or overgratification leads to the development of an oral personality that includes the following bipolar traits (Abraham, 1927; Glover, 1925): optimism/pessimism, gullibility/suspiciousness, cockiness/self-belittlement, manipulativeness/passivity, and admiration/envy.

Although it is by no means a rule, it is easiest to think of overindulgence leading to preverbal images of the world and oneself that result in traits on the left side of each pair. Optimism would come from an image that things have always been great, so there is no reason to expect that they will not continue to be so. Gullibility would derive from the experience of finding early in life that whatever one received from people was good, so why not swallow whatever people say now. Cockiness would ensue from feelings of having been something super for parents to dote on.

Manipulativeness would relate to the mental set that comes from being able to get parents to do whatever one wants. Finally, admiration would be due to feelings that other people are as good as oneself and one's parents.

Deprivation, on the other hand, is more likely to lead to pessimism; the mental set from the start is that one's needs will not be met. Suspiciousness comes from a feeling that if parents cannot be trusted, there are few whom one can trust. Self-belittlement derives from an image of having been awful, if one's folks could not care enough. Passivity follows from the repeated conclusion that no matter how hard one kicks or cries, parents will not care. Envy is an inner craving to have the traits that would make one lovable enough for people to provide special care.

Besides these traits, fixation at the oral stage brings a tendency to rely on more primitive defenses when threatened or frustrated. *Denial* derives from having to finally close one's eyes and go to sleep as a way of shutting out the unmet oral needs. On a cognitive level, this defense involves closing off one's attention to threatening aspects of the world or self. *Projection* has a bodily basis in the infant's spitting up anything bad that is taken in and making the bad things part of the environment. Cognitively, projection involves perceiving in the environment those aspects of oneself that are bad or threatening. *Incorporation* on a bodily level includes taking in food and liquids and making these objects an actual part of oneself. Cognitively, this defense involves making images of others part of one's own image.

In the oral stage, children are inherently dependent on others to meet their needs. Individuals fixated at this stage, therefore, are especially concerned with defending against separation anxiety. Oral personalities are anxious that if their loved ones knew how selfish, demanding, and dependent they really are, their loved ones might leave or withdraw their love. With experience, they learn that they had better control their intense desire to be cuddled, cared for, fed, and suckled, lest they be left alone. So they learn to deny or project such stingy, narcissistic wishes, although deep down they continually crave to passively receive without giving or to aggressively take without deserving.

The well-defended oral personality is not to be considered pathological but rather an immature person, like all of the pregenital personalities we shall discuss. There certainly are many people who are overly optimistic, gullible, and cocky, who deny faults in themselves or others, without considering themselves or being considered by others as pathological. Likewise, there are many people who believe it is wise to be suspicious, expect too little from this world, and perceive selfishness and manipulativeness in others. These people are also rarely judged to be pathological.

Anal Stage

In a society that assigned functions of the anus to the outhouse, that gagged at the sight or smell of the products of the anus, it must have been ghastly to think that a physician like Freud believed that this dirty area could be the most intense source of pleasure for children between the ages of 18 months and 3 years. Even in our ultra-clean society, many people still find it difficult to imagine that their anuses can be a source of sensuous satisfaction. In the privacy of their own bathrooms, however, many people admit to themselves that the releasing of the anus can be the real "pause that refreshes." As one of my constipated patients said, it is his most pleasurable time of the month.

Children in the anal stage are apt to learn that intense urges to play with the anus or its products bring them into conflict with society's rules of cleanliness. Even the pleasure of letting go of the anus must come under the parental rules for bowel control. Before toilet training, the child was free to release the sphincter muscles immediately as soon as tension built up in the anus. But now society, as represented by the parents, demands that the child control the inherent desire for immediate tension reduction. In Erikson's (1950) terms, the child must now learn to hold on and then to let go. Not only that, but the child must also learn the proper timing of holding on and letting go. If the child lets go when it is time to hold on—trouble; and if the child holds on when it is time to let go—more trouble!

The child is most likely to become conflicted and fixated at the anal stage if the caretakers again are either too demanding or overindulgent. The bipolar traits that develop from anal fixation have been clearly articulated by Freud (1925) and Fenichel (1945): stinginess/overgenerosity, constrictedness/expansiveness, stubbornness/acquiescence, orderliness/messiness, meticulousness/dirtiness, punctuality/tardiness, precision/vagueness.

Much of Freud's concern was with the overdemanding or overcontrolling parents who forced toilet training too quickly or too harshly. The individual receiving this caretaking style was seen as more likely to develop an anal personality dominated by holding-on tendencies. The child's unarticulated experience appears to have been a sense of having been forced to let go when the child didn't want to let go. Then when the child did let go, what did the parents do with the present to them? Just flushed it down the toilet. Now such individuals react as if they will be damned before they again let go against their will. So these personalities hold tightly to money (stinginess), their feelings (constrictedness), and their own way (stubbornness). In the process of harsh toilet training, however, people also learn that they are punished if they are not really clean or meticulous, if they are not punctual and orderly about where they go, and if they do not handle their matters precisely.

Overindulgent parents who are lackadaisical about toilet training are more likely to encourage a child to just let go whenever any pressure is felt. This route to an anal personality results in people who are more likely to easily let go of money (wasteful), let go of feelings (explosiveness), and let go of their wills (acquiescent). Lack of concern with such a basic social rule as proper toilet training is assumed to encourage a child to be generally messy, dirty, tardy, and unconcerned with details (vagueness).

Conflicts during the anal stage are also assumed to lead to the development of particular defenses. *Reaction formation,* or experiencing the opposite of what one really desires, develops first as a reaction to being very clean and neat, as the parents demand, rather than expressing anal desires to be messy. *Undoing,* or atoning for unacceptable desires or actions, occurs when the child learns that it is safer to say, "I'm sorry I let go in my pants," rather than saying, "I like the warm feeling the poo in my pants gives me." *Isolation,* or not experiencing the feelings that would go with the thoughts, emerges in part when the child has to think about an anal function as if it is a mechanical act rather than an instinctual experience. *Intellectualization,* or the process of neutralizing affect-laden experiences by talking in intellectual or logical terms, is partly related to such experiences as talking about the regularity of bowel movement as being soothing to one's gastrointestinal system.

Anal characters use these and other defenses to control anal desires to soil wherever and whenever they want and to control their anal erotic desire to pleasure their anus by touching it, caressing it, or putting things into it. Even individuals from overindulgent families discover that they really cannot exercise their anuses whenever they want without receiving punishment from their peers or from parental figures like teachers. Both types of anal characters also use these defenses to remain unaware of the immense hostility and aggression that is related to conflicts over toilet training and other areas of life in which the culture insists on controlling the individual's instincts. Again, a well-defended anal character is considered immature, not pathological. Anal people are very likely to take pride in their neatness and punctuality and even to be admired by others for these traits.

Phallic Stage

The name of this stage, which refers specifically to male genitalia, suggests a problem that Freud had with theorizing too much about men and then generalizing to women. For both, the sexual desires during the phallic stage are thought to be focused on the genitalia. From ages 3 to 6, both sexes are presumed to be very interested in their own genitalia and to increase their frequency of masturbation. They are also very interested in the opposite sex and engage in games of doctor and patient in which they examine each other to satisfy their sexual curiosity.

The conflict for youngsters is not with their genital desires, since theoretically other kids could satisfy these desires. The conflict is over the object of their sexual desires, which in this stage is the parent of the opposite sex. The boy's desire for his mother is explained as a natural outgrowth of the mother's serving as the major source of gratification for his previous needs, especially the need for sucking. Therefore, it seems logical to assume that the son will direct his genital sexual desires initially toward his mother and would expect her to gratify him. The *oedipal conflict,* of course, is that the father already has the rights and privileges of enjoying the mother. The son's fear is that the father might punish his rival by removing the source of the problem—the son's penis. This *castration anxiety* eventually causes the son to repress his desire for his mother, repress his hostile rivalry toward his father, and identify with his father's rules, in the hope that if he acts as his father would have him act, he can avoid castration.

Why a girl ends up desiring her father rather than her mother is more difficult to explain, since the mother is presumed to be the main source of instinctual gratification for daughters as well as sons. Freud asserted that girls become hostile toward their mothers when they discover that their mothers cheated them by not giving them a penis. Why Freud assumed that females would conclude that there was something wrong with them because they lacked a penis, rather than vice versa, has always been something of a mystery. For example, a non-Freudian colleague tells the story of his 5-year-old daughter's discovery of her 3-year-old brother's penis. Rather than envying his penis, she went yelling, "Mama, Mama, Andy's 'gina fell out."

Nevertheless, and in spite of understandable protest by enlightened women, many classical analysts still assume that girls initially envy penises, that they become enraged toward the mother, and that they turn their desires to the father in part to be able to at least share his phallus.

Again, a critical issue is how the parents respond to the genital desires of their children. Both overindulgence and overrejection can produce fixations at the phallic stage that result in formation of the following bipolar traits: vanity/self-hatred, pride/humility, stylishness/plainness, flirtatiousness/shyness, gregariousness/isolation, brashness/bashfulness.

Overrejection, in which parents give their opposite-sex children little affection, few hugs or kisses, and no appreciation of their attractiveness, is likely to lead to the following self-image: "I must be hateful if my parent wouldn't even hug or kiss me. Why flirt, dress stylishly, be outgoing or brash, or take pride in myself if the opposite sex is sure to find me undesirable?" On the other hand, a person who has had an overindulgent parent, whether seductive or actually incestuous, can more readily develop feelings of vanity. They feel they must be really something if Daddy preferred them over Mommy, or vice versa. The flirting, stylishness, pride, and brashness would all be based on maintaining an image of being the most desirable person in the world.

Conflicts over sexual desires toward one's parent are not solely due to how the parent reacts, however. The child also has to defend against castration anxieties, including the female's supposed anxiety that her rivalrous mother might damage her further. The child must also defend against society's basic incest taboo. These conflicts lead to repression as the major defense against incestuous desires. By becoming unaware even of fantasies about one's opposite-sex parent, the youngster feels safe from incest and the consequent castration or taboos that would accompany it. However, as with all conflicted desires, the impulse is omnipresent and can be kept at bay only by unconscious defenses.

Latency Stage

In classical psychoanalytic theory, this stage involved no new unfolding of sexuality, but rather was a stage in which the pregenital desires were largely repressed. Freud associated no new personality development with this stage, believing that all pregenital personality formulation had been completed by age 6. Latency was seen primarily as a lull between the conflicted, pregenital time and the storm that was to reemerge with adolescence—the beginning of the genital stage.

Genital Stage

In Freudian theory, an individual does not progress to the genital stage without at least some conflict between instinctual desires and social restraints. Some individuals will be fixated at the oral, anal, or phallic stage and will demonstrate the related personality type. Others will experience conflicts at each of the stages and will demonstrate a mixed personality that is a combination of traits and defenses of each stage. But no one becomes a fully mature, genital character without undergoing a successful analysis. Because such a personality is the ideal goal of analysis, we will delay discussion of it until the section on this theory's ideal individual.

Theory of Psychopathology

Because all personalities are at least partially immature due to inevitable conflicts and fixations at pregenital stages, all of us are vulnerable to regressing into psychopathology. We are more vulnerable if our conflicts and fixations occurred earlier in life, because we would be dependent on more immature defenses for dealing with anxiety. In addition, the more intense our pregenital conflicts are, the more vulnerable we are, since more of our energy is bound up in defending against pregenital impulses, and less energy is available for coping with adult stresses and conflicts. As indicated earlier, however, well-defended oral, anal, phallic, or mixed personalities may never break down unless placed in environmental circumstances that precipitate stress and lead to an exacerbation of defensive mechanisms and symptom formation.

Precipitating events, such as the death of a loved one, an offer of an affair, or an illness, stimulate the impulse that individuals have been controlling all their lives. They react on an unconscious level to this current event as if it were a repetition of a childhood experience, such as rejection by a parent or a desire for taboo sex. Their infantile reactions make them panicky that their impulses may now get out of control and that the punishment they have dreaded all their lives, such as separation or castration, will occur. These individuals are also panicky because they feel their very personality is threatened with disintegration. Their personality configuration has always been a delicate balance of traits and defenses that kept impulses and anxieties at a safe level. Like children, they are terrified that their adult personality will break down and that they will become entirely dominated by infantile instincts and fears. These individuals are reexperiencing at an unconscious level the same infantile conflicts that were once the cause of their personality development and now threaten to be the cause of their personality disintegration.

In the face of such threats, the person is highly motivated to spend whatever energy is necessary to keep impulses from coming into consciousness. This may translate into an exacerbation of previous defenses to the point where they become pathological. For example, a married woman who has been offered an affair and has an intense desire for taboo sex may rely more heavily on repressing such desires. Soon she is entirely fatigued and may show other symptoms of neurasthenia, but at least she does not have the energy to act on an affair even if she wanted to. While she constantly complains about her fatigue, for her it is better to be tired than to be in terror of acting out her infantile desires. A woman who did not have such intense fixations and conflicts over taboo sex might simply decline the offer or might accept if she thought it was worth the risks.

When a person overreacts to life's events to such an extent that symptoms develop, it is clear to the Freudians that the symptoms are defending against unacceptable impulses and childish anxieties. In many cases, the symptoms also serve as indirect expressions of the person's unacceptable wish. An example: Karen's symptoms of headaches, dizziness, and medical errors diverted her attention from emerging rage toward the nurses on 3 South and the accompanying anxiety. Her medical errors also provided some expression of her hostile wishes without her being at all aware that she was even angry, to say nothing of being threatened by internal rage. When symptoms serve both as defenses against unacceptable impulses and as indirect expressions of these wishes, then the symptoms are doubly resistant to change. Other benefits from symptoms, such as special attention from loved ones or doctors, are secondary gains and make symptoms even more resistant to change.

But why does a person like Karen overreact in the first place to an event like being assigned to 3 South? Why did she respond to the current 3 South as if she were a 12-year-old again? Why didn't she just make the logical discrimination between an old 3 South and the current 3 South? Obviously, Karen was not aware of responding to 3 South as if she were a 12-year-old. If her response to 3 South was primarily on a conscious level, then she could indeed have made such logical distinctions based on her conscious, secondary thought process. But unconscious responses like Karen's follow *primary-process* thinking, which is *alogical*. Logical thinking includes reasoning from the subjects of sentences, as in: (1) All men are mortals; (2) Socrates was a man; therefore, (3) Socrates was mortal. In primary-process thinking, reasoning frequently follows the *predicates* of statements, so that we think: (1) The Virgin Mary was a virgin; (2) I am a virgin; therefore, (3) I am the Virgin Mary. Or in Karen's case: (1) The ward where they let my father die was 3 South; (2) the ward where I am now is 3 South; therefore, (3) this 3 South is where they let my father die.

When people like Karen respond on an unconscious level, they do not systematically proceed through any reasoning process; rather, their primary-process reaction is automatically alogical. Primary-process responding is also *atemporal,* with no differentiation among past, present, and future. Therefore, on an unconscious level, Karen's response makes no distinction between the 3 South of ten years ago and the 3 South of now. On an unconscious level, all is now, and so the same impulses and anxieties are elicited that were present ten years ago. Primary-process experiencing is also *condensed,* so that the energies that are connected to a complex set of ideas and events are focused on one idea. Thus, for Karen, 3 South elicited all of the energies that were originally attached to the sequence of father dying, running for help, no nurses available, father dead.

Another characteristic of primary-process thinking is *displacement,* which involves placing the energies from highly charged ideas onto more neutral ideas. In this case, Karen displaced the intense anger she felt toward her father for leaving onto her image of the more neutral people responsible for 3 South. Primary-process thinking is also *symbolic,* which means *pars pro toto,* that any part of an event represents the total event; thus, the name 3 South became a symbol for the many feelings stirred up over the death of Karen's father. Finally, primary-process experiencing includes both *manifest* and *latent content*: the content that is conscious, or manifest, is only a minor portion of the hidden, or latent, meaning of events. Karen was thus originally aware of only the manifest event of becoming upset on her new ward; she was not even aware of the latent significance of the name 3 South until it was uncovered in psychotherapy.

With this understanding of primary-process responding, we can more fully appreciate why Karen's unconscious response to being placed on the present 3 South appeared to be irrational, or alogical. We can also appreciate why she was reacting in a manner more appropriate to an angry child and why her response involved much more energy and meaning than could be understood from a relatively neutral stimulus like the name fo the ward, 3 South.

If we went even deeper into the latent meaning of this event for Karen, we would probably find that her experience at age 12 represented her original loss of her father when she was 5. The rage that threatened to break out toward the nurses on 3 South may have been in part displaced from her original rage toward her mother, who Karen imagined caused her father to leave at an age when she so desired him. Being on 3 South may also have threatened to bring to awareness feelings of sexual desire for her father mixed with hostility for his leaving when she needed him so. Even the fantasy that she might wish his death could damage Karen's image of herself as the caring daughter who would have saved her father if she had been a nurse ten years before. To protect her image of herself, to protect herself from acting out or experiencing dangerous impulses, and to protect herself from all the anxiety and guilt such impulses would elicit could be the reasons for her symptoms as defenses of last resort.

If the essence of psychopathology lies at an unconscious level and if the person has no awareness of the psychological significance of precipitating events, the impulses that are being elicited, the anxieties that threaten panic, and the defensive yet gratifying nature of symptoms, then how can individuals be helped to overcome their disorders?

Theory of Therapeutic Processes

For Freud, only one process could succeed in making the unconscious conscious. Before we can respond to environmental events in a more realistic manner, we must first be conscious of how our pathological responses to the environment derive from the unconscious, primary-process meaning we attribute to environmental events. To remove symptoms, we must become conscious of our resistance to letting go of the symptoms because they both defend against and give partial release to unacceptable impulses. We must gradually recognize that our impulses are not as dangerous as we thought as children and that we can use more constructive defenses to keep our impulses in control, in part by allowing more mature expressions of our instincts. Finally, to prevent future relapses, we must use our conscious processes to release our pregenital fixations so that we can continue to develop to mature, genital levels of functioning. Such radical increases in consciousness require considerable work on the part of both patient and analyst.

Consciousness Raising

The Patient's Work. The work of *free association* sounds very simple—to freely say whatever comes to mind, no matter how trivial the thought or association may seem. If patients could let their minds go and associate without defending, then their associations would have to be dominated by instincts. Because the instincts are the source of all energy and therefore the strongest forces in the individual, and because the instincts are always pressing to emerge into consciousness, then patients would immediately associate to thoughts, feelings, fantasies, and wishes that express instincts. But the person's earliest lessons in life were that such direct, uncontrolled expressions of instincts are most dangerous. The person also learned at the time symptoms developed that a loosening of defenses can be terrifying and can lead to pathology. Now, just because the analyst has ordered the patient to lie on the couch and say everything that comes to mind, does not mean that the patient can do so without considerable resistance or defensiveness.

To help the patient continue to work in the face of potential terror and resulting defensiveness, the analyst must form a working alliance with the part of the person's ego that wants relief from suffering and is rational enough to believe that the analyst's directions can bring such relief. Through this alliance, patients also become willing to recall in detail dreams and childhood memories, even though such material brings them even closer to threatening impulses.

The Therapist's Work. The therapist's work begins with evaluating the patient to determine whether he or she is indeed a suitable candidate for psychoanalysis. As Greenson (1967) succinctly puts it, "People who do not dare regress from reality and those who cannot return readily to reality are poor risks for psychoanalysis" (p. 34). This generally means that patients diagnosed as schizophrenic, manic-depressive, schizoid, or borderline personalities are considered poor risks for classic psychoanalysis.

If analysis does proceed, the therapist uses four procedures—*confrontation, clarification, interpretation,* and *working through*—in analyzing the patient's resistance to free associating and the transference that emerges as the patient regresses and expresses instinctual desires toward the analyst (Bibring, 1954; Greenson, 1967).

Confrontation and Clarification. The first two are fundamentally feedback procedures. In analytic confrontation, the therapist makes sure patients are aware of the particular actions or experiences that are being analyzed. For example, in confronting a particular transference phenomenon, the analyst might give the patient the following feedback: "You seem to be feeling angry toward me," or "You seem to have sexual feelings toward me." Clarification, which frequently blends with confrontation, is sharper and more detailed feedback regarding the particular phenomenon that the patient is experiencing. Greenson (1967, p. 304) gives an example of how, after confronting a patient with his hatred for the analyst, he helped the patient clarify the exact details of his hatred:

He would like to beat me to a pulp, literally grind me up and mash me into a jelly-like mass of bloody, slimy goo. Then he'd eat me up in one big "slurp" like the god damned oatmeal his mother made him eat as a kid. Then he'd shit me out as a foul-smelling poisonous shit. And when I asked him, "And what would you do with this foul-smelling shit?" he replied, "I'd grind you into the dirt so you could join my dear dead mother!"

Interpretation. Confronting and clarifying a patient's experience are preparatory steps for the most important analytic procedure: interpretation. Greenson (1967, p. 39) defines interpretation in such a way as to make it almost synonymous with analysis itself:

> To interpret means to make an unconscious phenomenon conscious. More precisely, it means to make conscious the unconscious meaning, source, history, mode, or course of a given psychic event. The analyst uses his own unconscious, his empathy and intuition as well as his theoretical knowledge for arriving at an interpretation. By interpreting we go beyond what is readily observable and we assign meaning and causality to a psychological phenomenon.

Because interpretation goes beyond the experience of the patient, it is more than just feedback to the patient. The meaning and causality assigned to psychological phenomena are determined, at least in part, by psychoanalytic theory. Therefore, the information patients are given regarding the meaning and causality of their responses is in part an education on how psychoanalysis makes sense of people and their problems. This is not to say that interpretations are given in theoretical terms. They certainly are personalized for the individual, and in that respect are feedback. Nevertheless, through interpretations patients are taught to view their conscious experiences as caused by unconscious processes, their adult behavior as determined by childhood experiences, their analysts as if they were parents or other significant figures from the past, and so on.

Therapists committed to psychoanalytic theory assume that patients accept such teachings because the psychoanalytic interpretations hold true for the patient. After all, it is the patient's response that verifies an interpretation. If patients gain insight—that is, if they have a cognitive and affective awakening about aspects of themselves that were previously hidden—then analysts have some evidence for the validity of their interpretations. The most critical response for verifying interpretations is whether the interpretations eventually lead to a change for the better in the client.

The problem with improvement as the criterion for the verification of interpretations is that improvement in analysis is expected to be a slow, gradual process. First, the analyst and the patient must interpret the repeated resistance the client throws up against becoming conscious of threatening forces from within. The client misses appointments, comes late, recovers dramatically and wants to leave therapy, wants to leave because of not recovering, represses dreams, and does a million other things to shore up defenses. Then, as blind resistance is gradually reduced through insightful interpretations, the client begins to release hidden instincts toward the therapist. The patient wants to satisfy impulses by displacing frustrated sexual and aggressive impulses onto the therapist, and gradually a neurotic transference develops in which the patient relives all of the significant human relationships from childhood. For weeks or months, the therapist is experienced as the nongiving, miserly mother who does not care about the patient; then the analyst is the lecherous father who wants to seduce the patient; or the wonderful, wise parent who can do no wrong; or the stupid fool who is always wrong. Transference reactions serve as intense resistances: why mature further when you feel so good beating on your therapist or feel so safe with such a wise, caring parent? Painfully, through repeated interpretations, the patient must realize that these intense feelings and impulses come from within and represent the patient's pregenital conflicts, not realistic feelings elicited by the relatively blank-screen analyst.

Working Through. The slow, gradual process of working again and again with the insights that have come from interpretations of resistance and transference is called working through. In this last and longest step of psychotherapy, patients are acutely conscious of their many defensive maneuvers, including symptoms. They are undeniably aware of the impulses they have tried to defend against and the many ways in which they are still expressed, such as in symptoms. They realize that they need not fear their impulses to the degree they once did as children, because in transference relationships they expressed impulses in intense words and were not castrated, rejected, or overwhelmed. Gradually the person becomes aware that there are indeed new and more mature ways of controlling instincts that allow some gratification without guilt or anxiety. Gradually the patient channels impulses through these new controls and gives up immature defenses and symptoms. The use of new defenses and the radical increase in consciousness are seen by Freudians as actual structural changes in personality, in which energies that were bound up in pregenital conflicts are now available to the more mature ego of the individual.

Other Processes

Most analysts accept that corrective emotional experiences can lead to temporary relief of symptoms, especially for traumatic neuroses. Catharsis, however, even if used by an analyst, is not considered part of the analytic process. There is only one fundamental change process in analysis, and that is to increase consciousness; all the steps in analysis are part of that process.

Therapeutic Content

Intrapersonal Conflicts

Psychoanalysis obviously focuses on intrapersonal conflicts in therapy, with the individual's inner conflicts among impulses, anxiety, and defenses being of central concern. Problems may be acted out at an interpersonal level, but the origin and resolution of such problems can be derived only through an analysis of each individual's intrapsychic conflicts.

Anxieties and Defenses. We have already discussed anxiety due to threats of separation and castration. The Freudians also postulate primal anxiety, which is due to the assumed birth trauma of being overwhelmed with stimulation. Primal anxiety is the bodily basis for panic, which is the adult threat of being overwhelmed with instinctual stimulation. Moral anxiety, or guilt, is the threat that comes with breaking the rules that have been internalized.

In psychotherapy, anxiety is a motivator that may drive a person to seek relief because of its aversive properties. Once in therapy, however, an analyst must be careful not to uncover impulses too quickly lest the person panic and either flee therapy or have a psychotic experience of being overwhelmed. Anxiety is one of the central reasons therapy moves slowly—partly because anxiety signals the person to shore up resistance when dangerous associations are being approached, and partly because analysts feel that immature egos cannot hold up under high levels of anxiety.

Defenses or *resistance,* as defenses are called when they occur in therapy, are half of the content of psychoanalysis. Almost any behavior in therapy can serve defensive functions—talking too fast or too slowly, too much or too little, feeling good toward the therapist or feeling hostile, focusing on details or avoiding details. So the analyst is never without material to process. It is just a matter of which defenses are most likely to be accepted by the client as resistance, such as missing appointments or not being able to recall dreams. The analytic goal is not to remove defenses, but rather to replace immature and distorting defenses with more mature, realistic, and gratifying defenses.

Self-Esteem. Self-esteem has not been a major content area for psychoanalysis. It seems to be taken for granted that patients will have conflicts over self-esteem. Some will have unrealistically low self-esteem—deprived oral characters who engage in continual self-belittlement or rejected phallic characters who feel ugly and undesirable, to name but two. Others will have unrealistically high self-esteem, such as overindulged oral characters who are cocky or overindulged phallic characters who are vain and brash. Pregenital personalities cannot feel fundamentally good about themselves as long as they are dominated by infantile desires to be selfishly taken care of, hostilely controlling, or seductively narcissistic. Lack of genuine self-esteem, however, is the result of personality problems, not the cause of such problems, and analysts do not treat esteem problems directly. Acceptance of infantile characteristics may bring temporary relief, but what the pregenital personality really needs is a personality transplant. The best that can be done is to help patients consciously restructure their personalities into a more genital level of functioning, and only then can individuals experience a stable sense of self-esteem.

Responsibility. In a deterministic system like psychoanalysis, how can we talk about individual responsibility? In practice, the analyst expects the patient to be responsible for the bill, to keep appointments three to six times a week, and to free-associate as well as possible. But theoretically, there is no freedom and no choice in psychoanalysis and, therefore, no responsibility. How can we hold a person responsible for any action, whether it be murder, rape, or just not paying a bill, if all pathological and immature behavior is determined by unconscious conflicts and pregenital fixations? This difficulty in holding an individual responsible for his or her actions is one of the reasons why Mowrer (1961) said that Freud freed us from a generation of neurotics and gave us a generation of psychopaths.

Freud was a determinist, yet his theory is a psychology of freedom (Gay, 1990). His *psychic determinism* held that just as there is no event in the physical universe without its cause, so there is no mental event or mental state without its cause. Nothing is chance in the psychological world. Yet psychoanalysis is ultimately designed to make us more aware of our repressed conflicts and mental defenses, and thereby free us from the tyranny of the unconscious.

Interpersonal Conflicts

Intimacy and Sexuality. Intimacy, the revealing and sharing between two people as they really are, is fundamentally impossible for an immature personality. The problem of intimacy is basically a transference problem. The pregenital personality cannot relate to another person as the other person really is, but distorts the other according to childhood images of what people are like. In Piagetian terms, the person's earliest interpersonal experiences with parents result in internalized schemas that are primitive concepts of what people are like. Any new experience of a person is assimilated into this schema through selective attention to that person's actions.

While Piaget (1952) suggests that children's schemas of people change to accommodate new experiences, the Freudian concept of *fixation* suggests that pregenital personalities do not continue to develop their schemas of people. Rather, immature individuals distort their experiences of people to fit internalized images. For example, if individuals develop a concept of people as untrustworthy and rejecting, then they would attend to the slightest reason for mistrust and the slightest sign of rejection as evidence that a new, potential intimate is the same as all the rejecting people they have known from the time they were born.

A thorough psychoanalysis is the only way such people can mature to a level where they can perceive individuals with the freshness and uniqueness that each deserves. It is only by being fully aware of how we have distorted our relationships in the past that we can avoid destructive distortion in the present.

Sexual relationships for immature people are also primarily transference relationships. Two immature people can only engage in object relationships in which the other is seen as perhaps finally being the one who will satisfy ungratified pregenital instincts. So the oral character may relate sexually with a clingy and demanding manner that smothers a spouse. The anal personality may relate sexually in a very routinized manner, such as each night when the 11:00 news is over rather than when sex is spontaneously desired. The phallic character may relate as the teasing, seductive person who promises so much in bed but has so little to give. The ability to relate to another as a mature, heterosexual partner results only after a satisfying working through of one's pregenital fixations. Otherwise we are reduced to two objects bumping in the night.

Communication. Most interpersonal communication between two immature people is interlocking monologue, not a genuine dialogue. Immature personalities are locked into their egocentric worlds, in which others are only objects for their gratification. They do not respond to what the other says, but rather to their own desires that they want satisfied by the other. They do not talk to each other, but rather speak to their internal images of what the other is supposed to be. The messages they send have a manifest content that is also directed at hiding what the person really wants to say. If it takes an analyst years of "listening with the third ear" (Reik, 1948) to interpret what the person really means, how can a spouse with two blocked ears be expected to hear? From a classical Freudian view-point, attempts at marital therapy between two immature personalities will only produce absurd dialogue that is best left to modern playwrights.

Hostility. The violence in our urban era is seen by Freudians as a reflection of the hostility inherent in humans. Just as the work of ethologists such as Tinbergen (1951) and Lorenz (1963) suggested that animals have instincts to release aggression, the work of Freud suggested that the human animal has aggressive instincts to strike out and destroy. But humans also desire to live in civilized societies, and the stability of social organizations—marriage, the family, and communities, to name a few—is continually threatened by the hostile outbursts of poorly defended personalities. With paranoid personalities barely controlling their rage, defenses must be strengthened through supportive therapy or medication rather than uncovered by analysis. With overcontrolled neurotics, the best we can expect is to rechannel hostility into more socially acceptable outlets such as competition, assertiveness, or hunting. Otherwise, we will all be hunters and the hunted.

Control. Struggles over interpersonal control are frequently struggles over whose defenses will dominate the relationship. The more rigid the defenses, the more likely it is that individuals will insist on others' conforming to their view of the world and their ways of acting. For example, the person who repeatedly projects hostility onto the world is likely to put considerable pressure on others to see the world as a hostile place. Conversely, if a person defends with repressive, rose-colored glasses, then interactions will be focused on only the cheery aspects of the world. If two people with incompatible defenses try to interact, there will be conflict. An insignificant issue like deciding what movie to see can turn into a heated conflict for control when it involves a spouse with rose-colored glasses who wants to see a light comedy and a hostility-projecting spouse who wants to see a war flick.

Individuals also expect to control relationships when they experience the other person as nothing more than an object that exists to gratify their infantile desires. Each pregenital type of personality has its unique style of controlling others: oral characters control by clinging, anal characters control through sheer stubbornness, and phallic characters control through seductiveness. The most intensely controlling people seem to be anal personalities who have come from overcontrolling families. These individuals feel they were once forced to give in on the toilet and thereby lost control over their bodies. Now they act as if they are determined never to give in again.

An anal-restrictive woman was raised by a governess who seemed to enjoy giving her cold-water enemas to force her to let go when she was 2 years old. She married a man who was toilet trained at 10 months of age. He was complaining that his wife could never let go and really enjoy their sexual relationship. She went along with his demands for sex but seemed unable to let go to have an orgasm. The trauma that brought them into psychotherapy followed the wife's decision to solve her problem. She read Masters and Johnson and reserved a room in New York so they could have a sexual holiday. Once in New York, she became very aroused as she approached her husband, but he was now unable to get an erection. He was so determined to control their sexual relationship that he shut off his penis to spite his wife.

In treatment, the analyst must be keenly aware of how a patient is trying to control. The analyst will recognize when controlling behavior is serving defensive purposes of resistance or gratifying purposes of transference. The analyst must confront and clarify the patient's attempts to control and then interpret the meaning and causality of controlling maneuvers. The analyst's most effective method of countercontrol is silence: no matter what response the patient insists on, the analyst can respond with silence. It is like trying to fight with a spouse who clams up—it can be terribly frustrating, since the quiet one is in control.

Individuo-Social Conflicts

Adjustment Versus Transcendence. Freud (1930) believed there was a fundamental and unresolvable conflict between an organized society's need for rules and an individual's basic desires for immediate gratification without consideration for the needs of others. This represents, in a nutshell, the superego versus the id, the reality principle versus the pleasure principle. Freud certainly believed that cultures did not have to be as oppressive about childhood sexuality as was his Victorian age. Without doubt, he more than any other individual was responsible for our modern sexual revolution. Nevertheless, the idea that culture must be repressive to some degree was accepted by Freud. Being the civilized individual that he was, he threw his weight behind civilization and was willing to treat its discontents.

Some radical Freudians, such as Norman Brown (1959), believe that individuals need not be repressed. All of the destructive expressions of the death instinct, such as violence and tearing nature down through scientific analysis and commercial construction, are the result of repeated frustration of the life instinct. If we adopt more childlike, spontaneous lifestyles, in which we give free expression to playing in bed and in fields, then we need not be frustrated and so aggressive. Those who assume a radical Freudian view usually accept sexuality as an instinct but see aggression as due to the frustration that comes from repression of our desires for spontaneous sexuality. Radical Freudians generally believe that individuals should be encouraged to transcend their particular culture and find fulfillment by following their own unique paths in the face of possible social ostracism. But Freud himself, as radical as he was in numerous ways, was convinced that even the most conscious individuals must make considerable compromises with the culture in which they live and leave fantasies of transcendence to the angels.

Impulse Control. It is obvious that Freud believed that human sexual and aggressive impulses must be controlled. We are animals covered with a thin veneer of civilization. For psychotherapists to encourage the removal of that veneer is ultimately to encourage raping and rioting in the streets. Some believe that Freud himself contributed to removing this thin veneer. They see sexuality and aggression as out of control in our post-Freudian society. Dependency on drugs, alcohol, and food is rampant; violence seems to dominate the streets. Deviances such as homosexuality and bisexuality are accepted as healthy, and gonorrhea and other venereal diseases are epidemic. Freud, however, was one of the earliest to recognize that it is much easier for therapists to loosen the controls of neurotics than to produce controls for impulse-ridden personalities. He did not preach removal of the thin veneer of controls, but rather believed that the best hope for individuals and society was to replace the rigid but shaky infantile veneer with a more mature and realistic set of controls.

Beyond Conflict to Fulfillment

Meaning in Life. Although Freud believed we could not go beyond conflict, he did suggest that we could find meaning in life in the midst of conflict. Meaning is found in love and work (*lieben und arbeiten*). Work is one of society's best channels for sublimating our instincts; Freud himself could sublimate his sexual curiosity into his work of analyzing his patients' sexual desires. *Sublimation* is a mature ego defense that allows us to channel the id's energy into more acceptable substitute activities: oral sucking can become cigar smoking, anal expression can become abstract art, and so on.

Freud's total acceptance of the meaning of work came mainly from his total involvement in his own work. His voluminous productivity could come only from a person with a passion for work. A clearer source of meaning is love—the atmosphere that allows two people to come together, the most civilized expression of sexuality, and therefore the safest and most satisfying. Obsessive ruminating about meaning in life can come only from someone too immature to love and to work.

Ideal Individual. The ideal individual for Freud, and the ultimate goal of psychoanalysis, is a person who has analyzed pregenital fixations and conflicts sufficiently to attain, and maintain, a genital level of functioning. The *genital personality* is the ideal. The genital personality loves heterosexuality without the urgent dependency of the oral character, is fully potent in work without the compulsivity of the anal character, and is satisfied with self without the vanity of the phallic character. This ideal individual is altruistic and generous without the saintliness of the anal character, and is fully socialized and adjusted without immeasurable suffering from civilization (Maddi, 1972).

Therapeutic Relationship

There are two parts of the patient-analyst relationship, and they serve two different functions for therapy. The *working alliance* is based on the relatively non-neurotic, rational, realistic attitudes of the patient toward the analyst. This alliance is a precondition for successful analysis, because the rational attitudes allow the patient to trust and cooperate with the analyst even in the face of negative transference reactions.

Transference is one of the most important sources of content for analysis. In transference reactions, the patient experiences feelings toward the analyst that do not befit the analyst but actually apply to significant people from the patient's past. Through displacement, impulses, feelings, and defenses pertaining to people in the past are shifted to the analyst. These transference reactions represent the conflicts between impulses and defenses that are the core of the person's pregenital personality. Repeating these impulses and defenses in relation to the analyst provides the actual content of psychopathology for analysis. The person does not just talk about past conflicts, but actually relives these conflicts in the current relationship with the analyst. Experiencing transference reactions is not a curative process per se, because the essence of the transference is unconscious. Patients know they are having intense reactions toward the analyst but are unaware of the true meaning of their reactions. It is the analysis, or making conscious the unconscious content of the transference reactions, that is the therapeutic process.

The analyst's own reaction to the patient must be a delicate balance between being warm and human enough to allow a working alliance to develop, yet depriving and blank enough to stimulate the patient's transference reactions. The stereotype has emerged that an analyst is just a blank screen and therefore cool and aloof. Even such an orthodox analyst as Fenichel (1941), however, has written that above all the analyst should be human. Fenichel was appalled at how many of his patients were surprised by his own naturalness in therapy. In order for the patient to trust the analyst and believe the analyst cares, the analyst must communicate some warmth and genuine concern.

Analysts, of course, would disagree with Rogers's (1957) assumption that it is therapeutic to be genuine throughout therapy. If analysts become too real, they will interfere with the analysand's need to transfer reactions onto them from people in his or her past. Patients can transform a blank screen into almost any object they desire, but it would take a psychotic transference to distort a three-dimensional therapist into an object from the past.

While analysts agree with Rogers's general assumption that it is best to adopt a nonjudgmental attitude toward a patient's productions in order to allow for a freer flow of associations, they do not respond with unconditional positive regard. Frequently, neutral responses such as silence are more likely to stimulate transference reactions, and thus an analyst's reactions to the patient's productions are best described as unconditional neutral regard.

Analysts would agree with Rogers that accurate empathy is an important part of therapy. Empathy is a prime source of useful interpretations, after all. Psychoanalysts also agree that an analyst must be healthier or, in Rogers's terms, more congruent than patients.

Analysts must be aware of their own unconscious processes, as another source of accurate interpretations and as a guard against reacting toward their patients on the basis of *countertransference*—feelings that represent the analysts' desires to make clients objects of gratification of their own infantile impulses. For example, the analyst must be able to analyze hostile withholding of warmth or support because a patient reminds the analyst of a sibling. Likewise, an analyst must be able to recognize that giving too much of oneself to a client may represent encouragement to the patient to act out sexual desires with the analyst. Basically the analyst must be healthy enough to discriminate what is coming from the patient and what the analyst is encouraging, because a patient in the midst of transference reactions cannot be expected to make such important discriminations.

Practicalities of Psychoanalysis

In order for analysts to be considered competent to analyze their own countertransference reactions, they must have been psychoanalyzed by a training analyst and must have graduated from a psychoanalytic institute—a process that takes four to six years, depending on how much time is spent per week at the institute. Early on, most analysts in the United States were psychiatrists, because it was very difficult for nonphysicians to be admitted to analytic institutes—even though Freud (1959) supported the practice of lay analysis, which is analysis by a nonphysician. In the past two decades, however, nonmedical mental health professionals have been routinely accepted into formal psychoanalytic training.

"But where and how is the poor wretch to acquire the ideal qualifications which he will need in this profession? The answer is in an analysis of himself, with which his preparation for his future activity begins." So asked and answered Freud (1937/1964, p. 246) in enjoining psychoanalysts to complete personal analysis themselves. Research has indeed found that 99% of psychoanalysts and 88% of psychoanalytic psychotherapists have undergone personal therapy themselves and that their therapy experiences are typically lengthier than psychotherapists of other persuasions, averaging 400 to 500 hours (Norcross, Strausser, & Missar, 1988).

Although classical analysts prefer seeing patients four or five times per week, treatment can still be considered psychoanalysis if it occurs at least three times a week. Psychoanalysis currently costs between $80 and $150 per 45- to 50-minute session, with the cost varying according to the city and the reputation of the analyst. Theoretically, analysis has been considered interminable, in that there is always more in the unconscious that could be made conscious, but the actual work with an analyst is completed in an average of four to six years.

In orthodox analysis, patients agree, if possible, not to make any major changes—such as marriage or relocation—while in analysis. Above all, they should make no important decisions without thoroughly analyzing them. At times, patients are asked to give up psychotropic medications and chemicals such as alcohol or tobacco.

The psychoanalysis itself involves the patient (or analysand) and the analyst interacting alone in a private office. The patient lies on a couch with the analyst sitting in a chair at the head of the couch. The patient does most of the talking; the analyst is frequently silent for long periods of time when the patient is working well alone. Patients are subtly encouraged to associate primarily to their past, their dreams, or their feelings toward the analyst. The analyst keeps self-disclosures to a minimum and never socializes with patients. Needless to say, the analyst becomes a central figure in the patient's life, and during the neurotic transference, the analyst is the central figure. Following termination, the analyst remains one of the most significant persons in the patient's memory.

Major Alternatives: Ego Psychology, Object Relations, and Psychoanalytic Psychotherapy

Although we have focused on classical psychoanalysis so far in this chapter, it should be emphasized that in practice most contemporary followers of Freud lean more heavily upon ego psychology, object relations, and psychoanalytic psychotherapy than upon classical psychoanalysis. A case in point: When hundreds of psychologists conducting psychotherapy were recently asked to declare their theoretical orientation, 12% embraced psychoanalytic theory, but a larger proportion (21%) identified themselves as psychodynamic/neo-Freudian (Norcross, Prochaska, & Farber, 1993). Furthermore, many psychotherapists consider themselves neo-Freudians although they have been trained in settings other than psychoanalytic institutes—including social work, clinical psychology, and counseling training programs.

These neo-Freudian or psychodynamic approaches attempt to extend and complete Freud's original ideas. In general, the psychoanalytic emphasis on the id and intrapsychic conflicts is transformed in psychodynamicism into an emphasis on the ego and interpersonal conflicts. Freud's original emphasis on biological forces and defense mechanisms is also shifted to social forces and coping or mastery experiences. To appreciate the evolving orientation of these psychoanalytic revisionists, we will now turn to a discussion of three major alternatives to classical psychoanalysis—ego psychology, object relations, and psychoanalytic psychotherapy—and then to brief psychoanalytic psychotherapy, widely known as short-term dynamic therapy.

Ego Psychology

Classical psychoanalysis has been based primarily on an id psychology, in which the instincts and conflicts over such instincts are seen as the prime movers of personality, psychopathology, and psychotherapy. While id psychology remains the theory of choice of some analysts, others have followed the lead of Hartmann, Kris, and Loewenstein (1947), Erikson (1950), and Rapaport (1958), who have helped establish an influential *ego psychology*.

Whereas id psychology assumes that the ego derives all of its energies from the id, ego psychology assumes that there are ego processes, such as memory, perception, and motor coordination, that are also inborn (Rapaport, 1958) and that possess energy separate from the id. Whereas id psychology assumes that the ego serves only a defensive function in trying to find a safe and satisfying balance in the ongoing conflicts between instincts and the rules of society, ego psychology assumes that there are conflict-free spheres of the ego (Hartmann et al., 1947) that involve the individual's adaptation to reality and mastery of the environment (Hendricks, 1943). The ego's striving to adapt to and master an objective reality is a primary motivation in the development of the personality. Ego analysts certainly do not deny that conflicts over impulses striving for immediate gratification are important influences on development. They just assume that the separate striving of the ego for adaptation and mastery is an equally important influence.

Although development of impulse control is regarded as one of the early ego tasks (Loevinger, 1976), it is by no means the only task. Individuals are also striving to be effective and competent in relating to reality (White, 1959, 1960). The emergence of effectiveness and competence requires the development of ego processes other than defense mechanisms. Learning visual motor coordination, discrimination of colors, and language skills, for example, are some of the tasks that individuals can be motivated to master, independent of longings for sexual or aggressive gratification. With its own energies, then, the ego becomes a major force in the development of an adaptive and competent personality. Failure to adequately develop such ego processes as judgment and moral reasoning can lead to the development of psychopathology just as readily as can early sexual or aggressive fixations. The person with inadequate ego development is, by definition, poorly prepared to adapt to reality.

Once the ego is assumed to have its own energies and developmental thrust, it becomes clear that more is involved in the stages of maturation than only the resolution of conflicts over sex and aggression. The psychosexual stages of Freud are no longer adequate to account for all of personality and psychopathology. Development of the conflict-free spheres of the ego during the first three stages of life is just as important as defending against the inevitable conflicts over oral, anal, and phallic impulses. Furthermore, the strivings of the ego for adaptability, competency, and mastery continue well beyond the first five years of life. As a result, later stages of life are as critical in the development of personality and psychopathology as are the early ones.

The latency stage, for example, is seen by Erikson (1950) as critical in the development of a sense of industry, which involves learning to master many of the skills used in work. Freud, on the other hand, saw the latency stage as a quiet timeout during which no new personality traits developed. From Erikson's point of view, some individuals fail to develop a sense of industry not because of unconscious conflicts but because their culture discriminates against people of particular races or religions and fails to educate them adequately in the tools of that culture's trade. Failure to develop a sense of industry leads to a sense of inadequacy and inferiority. A sense of inferiority can lead to such symptoms as depression, anxiety, or avoidance of achievement. Thus, individuals can develop problems later in life even if they have developed a basically healthy personality during the first three stages of life. Of course, serious conflicts from early stages can make it more difficult for later stages to progress smoothly. A person with serious dependency conflicts from the oral stage, for example, will probably have more problems developing a sense of industry than would a person free from such conflicts.

The important point for psychotherapy here is that ego analysts will be as concerned with later developmental stages as they are with early developmental stages. By no means are all problems reduced to repetitions of unconscious conflicts from childhood. The adolescent stage, in particular, brings very real issues of developing ego identity versus ego diffusion (Erikson, 1950). Young adults must use their maturing ego processes if they are to move toward intimacy rather than lapse into isolation. Mid-adulthood involves the ego energies in creating a lifestyle that brings a sense of generativity, creating something of worth with one's life lest a sense of stagnation take over. And aging adults must look back over their lives to see if they can maintain ego integrity in the face of death, if they can look back and affirm their entire life cycle as worth living. If not, they are drained by despair.

Issues of identity, intimacy, and ego integrity are critical concerns of ego analysts. Much of therapy is focused on such contemporary issues of clients. Treatment goes back into history only as far as necessary to analyze the unresolved childhood conflicts that might be interfering with the person's present adaptation to life.

Clearly, the content of ego analysis will differ from the content of classical analysis. The process of ego analysis may, however, be very similar to the classical process, with long-term intensive therapy and use of free association, transference, and interpretation being the rules of some ego analysts. On the other hand, many ego analysts tend to follow the more flexible format of psychoanalytic psychotherapy.

Object Relations Theory

Psychoanalysis is a continually evolving system. One of the ways that psychoanalysis evolves is through new theorists emphasizing different aspects of personal development as the core organizing principles for personality and psychopathology. Freud emphasized conflicts over gratification and control of id processes as the central organizing principle of people's lives. Anal characters, for example, organize their lives around patterns of both controlling and gratifying anal impulses. Ego analysts emphasize the ego as the central organizing principle; the resolution of ego issues, such as basic trust, autonomy, and initiative, determine the individual's way of life. Object relations theorists, such as Fairbairn (1952), Kernberg (1975, 1976), and Kohut (1971, 1977), emphasize relationships between the self and objects as the major organizing principle in people's lives.

Object relations are intrapsychic structures, not interpersonal events (Horner, 1979). Object relations are very much affected by early interpersonal relationships and, in turn, profoundly affect later interpersonal relationships. Object relations are the mental representations of self and others (the objects). *Object* is the term Freud (1923) used for others, because in id psychology others serve primarily as objects for instinctual gratification rather than as authentic individuals with needs and wants of their own.

Object relations theorists differ on the importance of id forces in the relationship between child and parent. Kernberg (1976), for one, views object relations as partly energized by basic instincts, especially aggression. Fairbairn (1952) and Kohut (1971), on the other hand, deemphasize id impulses in early relationships. Kohut (1971) assumes that children have inherent needs to be mirrored and to idealize. These needs obviously require others who can serve as objects that reflect the developing self and as objects that the self can idealize as models for future development.

The self develops through stages that are different from the classic oral, anal, phallic, and genital stages that have been emphasized in the development of id and ego processes (Mahler, 1968). The first stage of self development is normal autism, which comes in the first few months of life. In this primary, undifferentiated state, there is neither self nor object. Fixation at this stage results in the severe pathology of primary infantile autism, which is characterized by a failure of attachment to objects and a failure of mental organization due to a lack of self-image (Horner, 1979).

Through the process of *attachment,* described by Bowlby (1969, 1973), the child enters the stage of normal symbiosis. In this stage, there is confusion in the child's mind as to what is self and what is object, because neither is perceived as independent of the other. This stage normally lasts two to seven months.

The child then enters the differentiation period, during which the child practices separating and individuating from significant others (Mahler, 1968). Crawling away from parents and then crawling back, walking away from parents and then running back, and even playing peek-a-boo, where the parent disappears for a moment and then reappears, are patterns of physical play that allow children to mentally differentiate themselves as separate from the parents to whom they are attached. A failure to differentiate can result in symbiotic psychosis, reflecting a fixation at the symbiotic stage.

Under normal conditions, the stages of differentiation shift at about 2 years of age into an integration stage. Through integrating processes, the self and object representations, which have become independently perceived, are now fit into relationships with each other. Parent and self are perceived as both separate and related. When all goes well, children at this stage can learn to relate without having overwhelming fears of losing their autonomy, their individuality, or their sense of self.

During the integration stage, the child also begins to integrate the good and the bad self-images into a single, ambivalently experienced self. Similarly, the child needs to integrate the good and the bad object images into a single, ambivalently experienced object. Experiences that originate from within the person that were not integrated into the early self-representation, such as the image of oneself as capable of anger, continue to be split off from the sense of self. If these experiences are evoked later in life, they can produce a state of disintegration, with the person's sense of self falling apart.

According to Kernberg (1976), the task of development is not only differentiation and integration, but also the emergence of a sense of identity. In the earliest stage, children vacillate between different ways of thinking and acting, expressing first one part of themselves and then another. This instability is due to *splitting*, a defensive attempt to deal with being overwhelmed by more powerful parents (Kernberg, 1976). If the child splits off bad self-images, such as the angry self, then there is less to fear from punitive parents. Similarly, if children can split off bad object images, such as the angry mother, then the object becomes less threatening. The next step in identity development involves *introjection*, which is the literal incorporation of objects into the mind. This tends to occur during symbiosis: mother can be experienced as less threatening if mother and child are one. A more mature identity, however, requires the process of identification, in which objects have influence but need not be "swallowed whole." With a more mature sense of identity, individuals can value both autonomy and community; they are open to influence from others without the fear of being overwhelmed by others.

According to Kohut (1971), the ideal type of identity is an autonomous self, characterized by self-esteem and self-confidence. Secure in this identity, the person is not excessively dependent on others and is also not merely a replica of the parents. Developmentally, the ideal situation is for children to have both their need to be *mirrored* and their need to idealize met through interaction with the parents. Who the parents are is more important than how the parents intend to interact. If the parents have accepted their own needs to shine and succeed, then their children's exhibitionism will be accepted and mirrored. If the parents have adequate self-esteem, then they can be comfortable with their children's needs to idealize them.

If, during the stages of self development, the parents are not able to meet the child's needs to be mirrored and to idealize, the child will develop a troubled identity. Kohut (1971) focuses on different types of narcissistic personalities that develop from insufficient mirroring or idealizing. Mirror-hungry personalities, for example, are famished for admiration and appreciation. They incessantly need to be the center of attention. These people tend to shift from relationship to relationship, performance to performance, in an insatiable attempt to gain attention. Ideal-hungry personalities are forever in search of others whom they can admire for their prestige or power. They feel worthwhile only as long as they can look up to someone.

From Kohut's (1977) perspective, narcissistic personalities cannot be treated by traditional psychoanalysis, in which the analyst alternates between being a blank screen and raising consciousness through verbal interpretations. Psychoanalysis is successful when patients are able to project emotions toward others onto the therapist by means of transference experiences. Persons with self disorders, however, cannot project emotions and images consistently, because they are too personally preoccupied. These clients must be mirrored (appreciated and respected) and must be permitted to idealize the therapist. In order to be idealized, therapists must be willing to let themselves be known rather than remain shadows for the clients' projections. By combining Rogers's emphasis on empathy and unconditional positive regard (mirroring) and the existential emphasis on being authentic (idealizing), the therapist can fill the void that clients experienced in childhood. By meeting some of the clients' unmet narcissistic needs, they enable clients to begin to develop either a mirroring transference or an idealizing transference. After such transferences are developed, the analyst can use the traditional consciousness-raising technique of interpretations to help patients become aware of how they try to organize their lives around narcissistic relationships. Clients can then begin to participate in the development of a more autonomous self.

Kernberg (1979) would agree that traditional psychoanalysis can be effective with neurotic patients who can develop neurotic transference relationships. But patients with severe self disorders, such as the borderline patients with whom Kernberg specializes, cannot be effectively treated merely with interpretations of transference and resistance. Borderline patients have the potential for developing psychotic transference and can thus experience the therapist as the split-off "bad parent." Profound fears of being overwhelmed, uninhibited, rejected, or abandoned can cause such patients to leave therapy or can prevent the development of a working alliance.

Kernberg (1975) emphasizes the importance of setting limits with borderline patients. Setting limits on telephone calls, on acting out aggression toward the therapist, and on how often the therapist can be seen are critical with borderline patients. Setting limits on acting-out will provoke anxiety that helps to clarify the underlying meaning of the acting out. Only by setting clear limits with such clients will the therapist maintain the opportunity for interpretations to be effective. In a therapeutic relationship that combines emotional support with clear limit setting, clients can gradually become conscious of the parts of themselves that have been split off. Without clear limits, the split-off parts of self and objects can threaten to produce disintegration within the individual or within the therapeutic relationship.

Psychoanalytic Psychotherapy

Variations in the standard operating procedures of analysis have occurred throughout the history of psychoanalysis. At times, innovations in therapy have resulted in rejection of the unorthodox analyst by more classical colleagues, and the innovator has gone on to establish a new system of psychotherapy. At other times, variations in orthodox analysis have been seen as a practical necessity, because particular patients lacked the ego or financial resources to undergo the stress of long-term, intensive analysis. Establishing more flexible forms of psychoanalytic therapy as truly acceptable alternatives within psychoanalysis has usually been credited to Franz Alexander (1891–1963) and his colleagues at the Chicago Institute of Psychoanalysis.

Alexander and French (1946) argued that orthodox analysis had been developed by Freud to serve as a scientific means of gathering knowledge about neuroses, as well as a means for treating neuroses. Once the fundamental explanations for the development of personality and psychopathology had been established, however, there was no justification to proceed with all patients as if each analyst were rediscovering the oedipal complex. With a thorough understanding of the psychoanalytic principles of psychopathology, therapists could begin to design a form of psychoanalytic therapy that fit the particular patient's needs, rather than trying to fit the patient to standard analysis.

There are patients who do indeed require classical analysis—namely, those with chronic neuroses and character disorders. These patients are in the minority, however. Much more common are the milder chronic cases and the acute neurotic reactions resulting from a breakdown in ego defenses due to situational stresses. Clients with milder or more acute disorders can be successfully treated in a much more economical manner than previously thought. Alexander and French (1946) reported 600 such patients who were treated with psychoanalytic therapy that lasted anywhere from 1 to 65 sessions. The therapeutic improvements they reported with their abbreviated therapy were previously believed to be achievable only through long-term, standard psychoanalysis.

Following the principle of flexibility, psychoanalytic therapy becomes highly individualized. The couch may be used, or therapy may proceed face-to-face. Direct conversations may be substituted for free association. A transference neurosis may be allowed to develop, or it may be avoided. Drugs and environmental manipulations will be included when appropriate. Therapeutic advice and suggestions will be included along with dynamic interpretations.

Because daily sessions tend to encourage excessive dependency, psychotherapy sessions are usually spaced over time. Daily sessions can also lead to a sense of routine in which the client fails to work as intensely as possible because tomorrow's session is always available. As a rule, sessions are usually more frequent at the beginning of therapy to allow an intense emotional relationship to develop between client and therapist, and then sessions are spaced out according to what seems optimal for the individual client. After therapy has progressed, it is usually desirable for the therapist to interrupt treatment to give clients a chance to test their new gains and to see how well they can function without therapy. These interruptions also pave the way for more successful termination.

Transference is an inevitable part of any psychoanalytic therapy, although the nature of the transference relationships can be controlled. A full-blown transference neurosis is usually what accounts for the length of standard analysis, so brief therapy will frequently discourage a transference neurosis from developing. A negative transference can also complicate and extend therapy, and may be discouraged with particular clients. When the transference relationship is controlled and directed, and when the therapist relies on a positive transference to help influence clients, then therapy can usually proceed more rapidly. A client with a positive father transference toward the therapist, for example, is much more likely to accept the therapist's suggestions to leave a destructive marriage or change to a more constructive job than would a client involved in a negative transference.

The nature of the transference can be controlled through the proper use of interpretations. If it has been decided that a transference neurosis is unnecessary or perhaps even damaging, the interpretations will be restricted to the present situation, because interpretation of the infantile neurotic conflicts encourages regression and dependency. Regression to early stages of functioning can also be interpreted as a means of avoiding dealing with present conflicts. Attention to disturbing events in the past would be used only to illuminate the motives for irrational reactions in the present.

The psychotherapist can also control the transference by being less of a blank screen and more the type of person that clients would expect to find when they go to someone for help with personal issues. When the therapist is more real, neurotic transference reactions will be more clearly seen as inappropriate to the present situation and will be less likely to develop. Countertransference reactions in the therapist can also help foster a more therapeutic relationship. Such reactions in the therapist need not be analyzed away; rather, the therapist must consciously decide which reactions will be helpful to therapy and must express those reactions. If a client had a very rejecting father, for example, then remaining a blank screen may engender a negative transference, while expressing more accepting attitudes could foster a more therapeutic relationship.

The development of a safe and trusting therapeutic relationship determines whether or not clients can express the troubling emotions and feelings that have been blocked off because of early conflicts with parents. The expression of previously defended emotions and feelings, such as anger, erotic desires, and dependency, is what leads to therapeutic success. Corrective emotional experiencing, then, is a more critical process than the consciousness raising stressed in orthodox analysis. Of course, a flexible attitude toward therapy does not see the process as an either/or issue. Therapy at its best should involve corrective emotional experiences integrated into conscious ego functioning through intellectual insights into the history of troubled emotions.

Brief Dynamic Psychotherapy

The past two decades have witnessed a proliferation of brief psychodynamic therapies that are principally derived from psychoanalytic psychotherapy. Leading theorists and practitioners in this vein include Habib Davanloo (1978, 1980), Lester Luborsky (1984; Luborsky & Crits-Cristoph, 1990), David Malan (1976a, 1976b), James Mann (1973; Mann & Goldman, 1982), Peter Sifneos (1973, 1992), and Hans Strupp (Levenson, 1995; Strupp & Binder, 1984). Despite their differences, these psychodynamic treatments are united by several characteristics:

- Setting a time limitation on treatment, typically 12 to 40 sessions
- Targeting a focal interpersonal problem within the first few sessions
- Adopting a more active or less neutral therapeutic stance
- Establishing a rapid and strong working alliance
- Employing interpretation and transference interpretation relatively quickly

As direct descendants of psychoanalysis, all short-term psychodynamic therapists incorporate the cardinal psychoanalytic principles, including the presence of resistance, the value of interpretation, and the importance of a strong working alliance. But all have also responded to the emerging empirical literature that strongly questions the value of lengthy over briefer analytic psychotherapy and to the escalating socioeconomic constraints on the number of psychotherapy sessions permitted by insurance carriers.

Briefer therapy requires thorough case formulation and planning. Calling upon all that is known about a particular client and all that is known about the dynamics of psychopathology, the psychodynamic therapist plans a more precise treatment that fits the needs of a particular client. Modest and achievable goals are set, such as an improved interpersonal pattern, greater attunement to feelings, or a resolution of a specific conflict (Messer & Warren, 1995). Where standard analysis might let the treatment take its own course, the short-term dynamic therapist decides whether it should be oriented primarily toward supporting the ego, uncovering the id impulses, or changing the external conditions of the client's life. Obviously not all the details of treatment can be planned, and the therapist will rely on conscious use of various techniques in a flexible manner, shifting tactics to fit the particular needs of the moment.

The brief dynamic therapist is obviously more active and directive in procedure and more interactive in the relationship than orthodox psychoanalysts. In traditional analytic treatment, the therapist allows the transference to emerge slowly over time, with gradual and frugal interpretations. In short-term dynamic treatment, the therapist actively engages the patient early in the process, focuses on a core interpersonal theme, and offers frequent transference interpretations regarding links among the patient's behavior toward the therapist, current life figures, and significant past figures.

For example, the transference interpretation might concern Vera's frequent stomach cramps for which no medical reason could be identified and for which she presented to psychotherapy. These cramps are experienced only in the presence of her mother in the past, in the presence of her boyfriend in the present, and now in the presence of the therapist in the consulting room. One interpretation is that the cramps are her habitual way of dealing with her difficulty in expressing aggression; instead of expressing her anger directly, she swallows it and turns it against herself (Messer & Warren, 1995).

Short-term dynamic therapy embodies the paradigm shift in psychoanalysis from drive reduction to the relational paradigm. The *relational model* posits that the therapist is unavoidably embedded in the relational field of the treatment; the pulls and feelings of the therapist are regarded as related to the patient's dynamics and as providing potentially useful information (Mitchell, 1988, 1993). Instead of assiduously avoiding countertransference, interpersonal psychoanalysts accept it as an invaluable source of information about the patient's character and difficulties in living. Mitchell (1988, p. 293) captures this idea in a passage from his book, *Relational Concepts in Psychoanalysis*:

> Unless the analyst affectively enters the patient's relational matrix or, rather, discovers himself within it—unless the analyst is in some sense charmed by the patient's entreaties, shaped by the patient's projections, antagonized and frustrated by the patient's defenses—the patient is never fully engaged and a certain depth within the analytic experience is lost.

The locus of change for Freud was inside the patient's head; for relational psychoanalysts, the locus is between people. The analyst's role is thus transformed from lofty, cerebral detachment to concerned, active involvement. The analyst creates a different emotional presence in order to get the patient to hear and experience him or her in a different way. In this manner, the patient undergoes a corrective emotional experience and learns new skills within the context of an empathic relationship.

Effectiveness of Psychoanalytic Therapies

While psychoanalysis has been concerned with the distortions emanating from transference and countertransference, this system has not been nearly as careful in controlling for the possible distortions involved in analyzing the effectiveness of psychoanalysis. For nearly 50 years, the effectiveness of psychoanalysis has been supported almost entirely by selected case studies reported by enthusiastic analysts. Such case studies are the empirical starting point for all therapy systems, even though such studies are too open to bias to establish the efficacy of any system (Meltzoff & Kornreich, 1970). Following the typical history of outcome research, psychoanalysts switched first to survey studies with subjective criteria and then to survey studies with more objective criteria.

Probably the best known of the psychoanalytic survey studies is that of Knight (1941), who surveyed dispositions of patients who stayed in psychoanalysis for at least six months. The data involved the analysts' judgments of whether patients were "apparently cured," much improved, improved, unchanged, or worse when analysis was terminated. This survey study had the advantage of being cross-cultural, in that it included data on patients seen at psychoanalytic institutes in Berlin, London, Topeka, and Chicago. Dividing patients by diagnostic category, Knight reported the results shown in Table 2.1. Across patient diagnoses, approximately half of the patients completing classical psychoanalysis were apparently cured or much improved. Subsequent surveys on the outcomes of psychoanalysis show similarly positive results (e.g., Bachrach, Galatzer-Levy, Skolnikoff, & Waldron, 1991; Fonagy & Target, 1996); however, virtually all of this research entails retrospective, uncontrolled studies with outcome measures of untested validity. Survey research is subject to considerable bias, such as therapists' judging the outcome of their own patients, but it is a starting point for controlled experiments.

Unfortunately, there are no controlled studies on the outcomes of classical psychoanalysis with either adults (Grawe et al., 1998) or children (Weisz et al., 1995). Merton Gill (1994, p. 157), himself a passionate analyst, lamented before his death that psychoanalysis is "the only significant branch of human knowledge and therapy that refuses to conform to the demand of Western civilization for some kind of systematic demonstration of its contentions." Thus, the efficacy of classical psychoanalysis has not been adequately tested. One can probably state with reasonable confidence that psychoanalysis is superior to no treatment at all, but one cannot safely conclude that psychoanalysis has proved itself more effective than a credible placebo therapy.

Table 2.1 Early Survey Results on the Effectiveness of Psychoanalysis by
Patient Diagnosis

Diagnostic Category	Number of Patients	Cured or Much Improved	No Change or Worse
Neuroses	534	63%	37%
Sexual disorders	47	49%	51%
Character disorders	111	57%	43%
Organ neurosis and organic conditions (e.g., colitis, ulcers)	55	78%	22%
Psychoses	151	25%	75%
Special symptoms (e.g., migraine, epilepsy, alcoholism, stammering)	54	30%	70%

Data from Knight (1941).

The available controlled research is on psychoanalytic psychotherapy or time-limited psychodynamic therapy. Let us review the findings of three important outcome studies on these psychotherapies and then consider quantitative reviews.

The Menninger Foundation's Psychotherapy Research Project began in 1959 and lasted nearly 20 years. The study included 42 adult outpatients and inpatients who were seen in psychoanalysis or psychoanalytic psychotherapy. Psychoanalysis lasted an average of 835 hours; psychotherapy lasted an average of 289 hours. In Kernberg's (1973) summary of the project results, the majority of patients improved on the Health—Sickness Rating Scale, but there was no difference in improvement between those in psychoanalysis and those in psychoanalytic psychotherapy. Direct comparisons between the two treatments are difficult to make, however, because patients were not randomly assigned but differed systematically between the two groups. Further limiting the conclusions on the efficacy of the two therapies was the absence of both a placebo therapy group and a no-treatment group.

In his 1986 book *Forty-Two Lives in Treatment,* Wallerstein extensively chronicles, over a 30-year span, the treatment careers and subsequent life changes of the 42 patients seen in the Menninger project. Paralleling the earlier report by Kernberg (1973), Wallerstein drew the following overaraching conclusions from this extensive study: The traditional distinction between "structural change" and "behavioral change" is highly suspect; intrapsychic conflict resolution is not always a necessary condition for change; the supportive psychoanalytic therapy produced greater-than-expected success; and classical psychoanalysis produced less-than-expected success. The treatment results tended to converge rather than diverge in outcome.

In a rigorous study conducted at Temple University, Sloane, Staples, Cristol, Yorkston, and Whipple (1975) compared the effectiveness of short-term psychoanalytic psychotherapy with that of short-term behavior therapy. There were 30 patients randomly assigned to each of the therapy conditions, and 34 assigned to a waiting-list control group. The patients were treated at the Temple University Hospital Outpatient Clinic. Two-thirds of the patients were diagnosed as neurotics and one-third as exhibiting personality disorders. The therapists were matched for experience. Each patient was assessed initially by one of three experienced psychiatrists who were not connected with the study. Together the patient and assessor identified three major target symptoms on a five-point scale.

Treatment lasted for four months, with an average of 14 sessions. The behavior therapists were free to use whatever techniques they believed would be most helpful. The senior therapist relied almost exclusively on counterconditioning techniques, the second therapist emphasized cognitive restructuring, and the junior therapist seemed to show no preference. The psychoanalytic therapists emphasized the importance of the therapeutic relationship, followed by the exploration and expression of feelings and insight. Free association, dream analysis, and uncovering of defenses were also apparent in their approaches.

The most striking findings of the study were that, at the end of four months of therapy, both treatment groups were significantly more improved than the no-treatment group, and neither form of psychological treatment was more effective than the other. On symptom ratings, 80% of the patients in each therapy group were considered either improved or recovered, compared to 48% in the control group. On ratings of overall adjustment, 93% of the patients in behavior therapy were considered improved, compared with 77% of the psychoanalytic psychotherapy group and 47% of the waiting list. Only two patients, one in psychotherapy and one on the waiting list, were rated as worse. The extremely high percentage of waiting-list subjects rated improved may be due to the fact that this rating could be given if patients were seen as "a little better." Of course, the same holds true for the therapy patients. A one-year follow-up after the start of therapy indicated that initial gains were maintained across groups.

In the Vanderbilt Project, Strupp and his colleagues (see Henry & Strupp, 1991, for a summary) contrasted the treatment experiences of a group of neurotic patients treated by college professors specifically selected for their understanding and warmth with those of a comparable group of patients treated by experienced, psychodynamically oriented psychotherapists. More than a test of the efficacy of psychodynamic psychotherapy, this study sought to separate the effects of nonspecific (or common) factors, represented in the warmth and understanding of college professors, and specific factors, represented in the specific techniques provided by the professional therapists. All patients were 17- to 24-year-old men with a 2–7–0 (depression-psychosthenia-social introversion) profile on the Minnesota Multiphasic Personality Inventory (MMPI). Both treated groups had outcomes superior to the untreated controls. However, the original group analyses did not demonstrate statistical superiority in outcomes for the professional therapists, and subsequent analyses indicated only a trend for professional therapists to be more effective with the healthier patients. Neither group of therapists was notably effective in treating patients with more characterological problems.

The efficacy of psychoanalytic psychotherapy and psychodynamic therapies has been addressed in recent years through *meta-analysis,* a statistical technique that quantitatively combines the results of many different studies. A benchmark meta-analysis was undertaken by Smith, Glass, and Miller (1980; Smith & Glass, 1977) to examine the benefits of psychotherapy using a total of 475 studies. Approximately 29 studies were found at that time on psychodynamic treatments and 28 on psychodynamic-eclectic treatments, producing average effect sizes of .69 and .89, respectively. An effect size (ES), as shown in Table 2.2, is an index of the magnitude and direction of therapy effects. Each ES can be thought of as reflecting a corresponding percentile value; that is, the percentile standing of the average treated patient after psychotherapy relative to untreated patients. Patients treated with psychodynamic therapy (ES = .69) were, on average, more improved than 76% of the untreated patients According to consensual rules of effect-size interpretation (Cohen, 1977), these are large effects (.20 is small, .50 is moderate, and .80 is a large effect). When compared with effect sizes for other forms of therapy, the psychodynamic therapies were judged to be comparably effective to slightly less effective, depending on one's interpretation of the data.

In an attempt to replicate Smith and Glass's study with an improved design, Shapiro and Shapiro (1982) only considered studies that had at least two treatment groups and one control group. The majority of these 143 studies examined behavioral therapies. Shapiro and Shapiro concluded that their more rigorous study largely reproduced the earlier meta-analysis by Smith and Glass, with an average effect size of approximately 1.0. There were few differences in average outcome as a result of different treatments, but there was a modest but undeniable superiority of behavioral and cognitive methods and a corresponding relative inferiority of dynamic therapies. This was a small difference; more treatment outcome could be accounted for by the type of problem being treated than by the type of treatment.

In a comprehensive review of 897 controlled outcome studies on various psychotherapies with adult patients published in the United States and Europe, Grawe and colleagues (1998) found the outcomes of psychoanalytic and psychodynamic therapies (grouped together) to be inferior to those of cognitive and behavioral treatments. Similarly, Weisz and colleagues (1995) found the effects of "insight-oriented" psychotherapy with children in nine studies to be less than that of various behavioral and cognitive therapies. The average effect size of the insight-oriented treatment was .30, statistically below the .54 for behavioral therapy and the .57 for cognitive-behavioral treatments.

Three meta-analyses have been conducted specifically on the efficacy of brief psychodynamic psychotherapy with adults. In the first, Crits-Christoph (1992) examined 11 well-controlled studies that compared brief dynamic therapy to a control group, nonpsychiatric treatment, or alternative psychotherapy. When the effect sizes (.81, .82, and 1.10 for three different categories of outcome measures) were translated into percentages, the average brief dynamic therapy patient was better off than 79% to 86% of waitlist patients. Large effects, then, were found relative to waitlist controls. In the nine direct comparisons to alternative forms of therapy, brief dynamic therapy showed a slight inferiority. In a meta-analysis of 19 overlapping studies, Svartberg and Stiles (1991) also found that short-term psychodynamic psychotherapy was superior to no treatment but was inferior to alternative psychotherapies at posttreatment, and even more so at one-year follow-up.

Table 2.2 The Interpretation of Effect Size (ES) Statistics

Effect Size	Percentile	Type of Effect	Cohen's Standard
1.00	84	Beneficial	
.90	82	Beneficial	
.80	79	Beneficial	Large
.70	76	Beneficial	
.60	73	Beneficial	
.50	69	Beneficial	Medium
.40	66	Beneficial	
.30	62	Beneficial	
.20	58	Beneficial	Small
.10	54	No effect	
.00	50	No effect	
−.10	46	No effect	
−.20	42	Detrimental	
−.30	38	Detrimental	

Adapted from Weisz, Donenberg, Han, & Weiss (1995).

More recently, Anderson and Lambert (1995) performed a meta-analysis on 26 studies to determine the effectiveness of short-term dynamic therapy. Short-term dynamic therapy obtained effect sizes of .71 and .34, relative to waitlist and minimal treatment groups, respectively. The authors found no evidence that it was superior or inferior to other forms of psychotherapy, in contrast to the earlier two meta-analyses.

All in all, the controlled outcome research consistently finds that the measurable outcomes of psychoanalytic psychotherapy and short-term psychodynamic psychotherapy are superior to no-treatment and slightly to considerably inferior to alternative psychotherapies. The question of "How effective is short-term psychodynamic therapy?" has been answered with certainty in one respect—it is definitely superior to no treatment at all—and with doubt in another respect—perhaps a little worse or perhaps just as good as alternative psychotherapies.

Much debate continues over the meaning of these differences uncovered by meta-analyses. Differences in effect sizes between psychotherapies can be due to a variety of factors, including the theoretical orientation of the researchers, the type of problems treated, the reactivity of the measures used, and the type of patients studied. Because the majority of comparative studies have been conducted by cognitive and behavior therapists, these therapists may consciously or unconsciously design studies that involve variables and measures that favor their preferred therapy. Relatively minor statistical advantages in such controlled studies do not necessarily mean that cognitive and behavior therapies invariably possess clinical superiority in real-world settings.

Criticisms of Psychoanalysis

From a Behavioral Perspective

Behavioral criticisms of psychoanalysis have been frequent and intense. One set of criticisms revolves around the view that as a theory, psychoanalysis is much too subjective and unscientific. The psychoanalytic notions of unconscious processes, ego, and defenses are almost entirely mentalistic, and incapable of being linked to observable behavior in a way that can be objectively measured and validated. All too frequently, Freudians have reified rather than verified their concepts, such as the ego and the id. Freud's ideas about superego formation, female sexuality, dream interpretation, and other fanciful notions simply do not stand up under scientific scrutiny (Fisher & Greenberg, 1996).

The notion that "insight" itself is frequently therapeutic is another mentalistic fiction. As B. F. Skinner (1971, p. 183) wrote,

> Theories of psychotherapy which emphasize awareness assign a role to autonomous man which is properly, and much more effectively, reserved for contingencies of reinforcement. Awareness may help if the problem is in part a lack of awareness, and "insight" into one's condition may help if one then takes remedial action, but awareness or insight alone is not always enough, and it may be too much. One need not be aware of one's behavior or the conditions controlling it in order to behave effectively—or ineffectively. On the contrary, as the toad's inquiry of the centipede demonstrates, constant self-observation may be a handicap.

But there is a more devastating behavioral reaction. Behaviorists do not argue with psychoanalytic theory; they ignore it. Why bother learning how psychoanalysis is supposed to work when there are no data to demonstrate that it does work? The absence of any controlled experiments designed to evaluate the effectiveness of psychoanalysis after 100 years of practice is a scientific disgrace! Even a few experiments every decade would be slower than the average analysis. Freud himself can be excused as a genius too committed to theory construction to gather controlled data, but surely not all of his followers can hide behind that excuse. Unless psychoanalytic institutes demonstrate empirically that their form of treatment is more than just a placebo therapy, we will continue to ignore this once-dominant system as if it were a therapeutic dinosaur, too slow to survive.

From an Existential Perspective

In contrast to the behavioral view, psychoanalysis is much *too* objective for existentialists—not empirically, but theoretically and practically. Just look at the psychoanalytic concept of object relationships. Psychoanalysis conceives of human beings as objects, mere bundles of instinctual and defensive energy. This psychoanalytic conception of human beings has filtered into the very core of our self-concepts, becoming one of the dominant forces in the dehumanization of modern human beings. Where are freedom, choice, and responsibility, the subjective experiences that allow humans the option of being different from all the objects of the universe? How can a system that has placed so much emphasis on consciousness as the process of freeing people from psychopathology not take freedom and choice seriously? A conscious object sounds paradoxical and absurd.

From a Contextual Perspective

Freud was indeed the grandfather of psychotherapy, and as is unfortunately true of many patriarchs, he legitimized dysfunctional intrapsychic and androcentric (male-centered) biases adopted by generations of subsequent psychotherapists. Virulent attacks have been leveled over the years against psychoanalysis from a contextual perspective, which emphasizes the impact of systemic, gender, and cultural forces on individuals.

For starters, the broader social context is practically ignored in psychoanalytic treatment. The exclusive focus on the intrapsychic makeup of the individual neglects the self as a subsystem of the family. Disorders and fixations are attributed to internal conflicts rather than family dysfunction or social problems. An exemplar: Early on, Freud courageously attributed many of his female patients' disorders to the childhood sexual abuse they had encountered, but later he retracted this position and characterized these allegations as fantasies. As a result, generations of therapists treated childhood sexual abuse as an intrapsychic fantasy rather than an actual assault.

When psychoanalysts do venture from their internal psychopathological orientations to consider relationships, it is largely to engage in mother-bashing. One study (Caplan, 1989) analyzed a decade of psychological research to determine the nature and extent of mother blaming. Of four categories—things that mothers do, things that mothers fail to do, things that fathers do, and things that fathers fail to do—only one regularly turned out to be viewed as problematic: things that mothers do. Mothers have been blamed for causing more than 70 different disorders in their children, including bedwetting, schizophrenia, and learning disabilities. The father's role is assumed to be peripheral. Psychoanalysts define "good enough mothering"; what about "good enough fathering" (Okun, 1992)? The impact of the father, the family, and the culture on the child are minimized, at least when development goes awry. Mothers must be to blame.

Freud's infamous declaration that "biology is destiny" represents an attempt to restrict women's power and status. A classic illustration of the sexist nature of classic psychoanalysis is penis envy. A girl, we are told, concludes that something is wrong with her because she does not have a penis and cathects with her father to share his phallus. This convoluted and unsubstantiated reasoning, however, does not apply to boys. Why is there no vagina envy? Freud focused too much on sexual fantasy and not enough on sexist ideology.

Psychoanalytic theory is so clearly patriarchal and Eurocentric in form and structure that much more could be criticized about it—the upper-class male values, the paucity of female psychoanalysts in Freud's inner circle, its historical orientation, its lengthy and inefficient process, its focus on personality restructuring at the expense of behavior change, to name a few. All in all, to borrow Harriet Lerner's (1986) words, contextualists cast a mote in Freud's eye.

From an Integrative Perspective

It is the essence of integration to seek what is of value in any therapy system, especially one as rich and complex as psychoanalysis. Some integrative therapists use a dynamic approach in their work, especially in their formulation of the problems with which they are working. Psychoanalysis is one of the few theories with enough personality and psychopathology content to be the core of a diagnostic manual or the content of a Rorschach evaluation. Most integrationists will also use the concepts of defenses and transference in their thinking about the content of therapy.

As an overall system of therapy, however, classical psychoanalysis has become much too dogmatic for integrative tastes. As in most systems, the disciples of a genius like Freud are usually less creative and, therefore, less flexible. With Freud, theory and therapy continued to evolve, but to many of the present practitioners of psychoanalysis, it seems more important to be orthodox than to be innovative and face possible ostracism for acting out their countertransference.

We are much more at home with the flexibility of psychoanalytic psychotherapy and time-limited psychodynamic therapies. However, we are not comfortable with the fact that psychoanalytic psychotherapy, like psychoanalysis, has not been demonstrated to be more effective than any other form of therapy. One certainly cannot justify recommending classical psychoanalysis to clients when it is the lengthiest and most expensive alternative. Psychoanalysis may provide a rich source of therapy content, but it has not yet established any real advantage in therapy outcome.

⟶ A PSYCHOANALYTIC ANALYSIS OF MRS. C. ⟵

During the early years of her marriage, Mrs. C. apparently made an adequate though immature adjustment. As an obsessive or anal personality, she expressed such traits as excessive orderliness in the alphabetical ordering of her children's names, meticulousness in her concern with cleanliness, stinginess in holding onto unused clothes while buying no new ones, and constrictedness in never letting go of her sexual feelings and becoming excited. These were probably the result of Mrs. C.'s interactions in the anal stage with overcontrolling and overdemanding parents. We know Mrs. C.'s mother was a compulsive person who was overly concerned with cleanliness and disease. Her father overcontrolled Mrs. C.'s expression of aggression and her interest in men. We can imagine that such parents could be quite harsh in their demands on such issues as toilet training and could produce many conflicts in their daughter over holding on and letting go of her bowels and other impulses. From psychoanalytic theory, we could hypothesize that Mrs. C.'s anal characteristics developed, in part at least, as defenses against anal pleasures such as being dirty and messy and against impulses to express anger.

Why did the experiences surrounding her daughter's case of pinworms precipitate a breakdown in Mrs. C.'s previously adaptive traits and defenses and lead to the emergence of a full-blown neurosis? Illness and fatigue from the Asian flu and from caring for so many sick children would place stress on Mrs. C.'s defenses. But the precipitating event was also of such a nature as to elicit the very impulses that Mrs. C. had come to defend against since early childhood. First of all, how would anyone feel when a daughter brings home pinworms when the family is already down with the Asian flu and the mother is burdened with pregnancy and a toddler in diapers? Relatively unrepressed parents would be upset, even though they might not express their anger directly because the child did not intend to get pinworms. But Mrs. C. was not free to express anger as a child and would probably have to defend against it as a parent.

A case of pinworms is also characterized by anal itching, with the pinworms locating in the anus. In fact, to confirm that the problem was pinworms, Mrs. C.'s physician directed her to examine her daughter's anus with a flashlight while her daughter was sleeping. So while on one level the pinworms were painful, on another level the possibility of contracting pinworms could be a temptation to exercise that secret pleasure that can come from scratching an itchy anus. With defenses weakened by illness and fatigue, and with threatening impulses of aggression and anal sexuality stimulated by her daughter's contracting pinworms, the conditions were set for the emergence of neurotic symptoms that both defend against as well as give indirect expression to Mrs. C.'s unacceptable impulses.

Look at how her neurotic symptoms provided further defense against her threatening impulses. The compulsive showers and hand washing are an intensification of her long-standing preoccupation with cleanliness. If danger lies in being dirty, then wash! These compulsive symptoms are in part an intensification of her reaction formation of keeping clean in order to control desires to play with dirt and other symbols of feces. If desires to damage her daughter were also breaking through, then her washing could serve both as a means of removing Mrs. C. from interactions with her daughter in the morning and as a means of undoing any guilt over aggression by washing her hands clean of such bloody thoughts. The underwear piled in each corner literally served to isolate Mrs. C. and her family from more direct contact with anal-related objects.

How did Mrs. C.'s neurotic symptoms allow some gratification of her desires? The shower ritual is most obvious, since each time she lost her place in her ritual, she had to go back to giving herself anal stimulation. In the process of isolating dirty materials like the underwear and things that dropped to the floor, Mrs. C. was also able to make a mess of her house. It does not take much of an interpretation to appreciate how Mrs. C. was expressing her aggression toward her husband by making him get up at 5:00 A.M. and toward her children by not cooking or adequately caring for them.

Why was Mrs. C. unable to express some of her feelings and desires directly and thereby prevent the need for a neurotic resolution of her conflicts? First of all, such direct expression would be entirely contrary to her core personality concerned with controlling such impulses. Second, the regression induced by her defenses' weakening would cause Mrs. C. to react to her current situation more on a primary-process level than on a rational, secondary-process level. At the unconscious primary level, Mrs. C. would be terrified that loosening controls would result in her going totally out of control and being overwhelmed by her impulses. Being overwhelmed by instinctual stimulation produces its own panic, but Mrs. C. would also be panicky about facing the wrath of her overcontrolling parents for being a bad girl who soiled her pants or expressed the slightest anger. At an atemporal, unconscious level, Mrs. C. would not experience herself as the adult parent who is safe to express some anger, but as the controlled little girl who had better not express her resentment.

In considering psychoanalysis for Mrs. C., an analyst would have to be quite confident that Mrs. C.'s problem was indeed obsessive-compulsive neurosis and not pseudoneurotic schizophrenia, in which the neurotic symptoms are masking a psychotic process. Given how much she has already regressed and how much her life is dominated by defensive symptoms, there could be a real risk in encouraging her to regress further in psychoanalysis. If the analyst felt that further evaluation confirmed previous reports that Mrs. C. did not show evidence of a psychotic process, then psychoanalysis might proceed.

When directed to lie on the couch and say whatever comes to mind, Mrs. C. would become quite anxious about having to give up some of her controls to the analyst. Obviously, she has to trust enough to believe that her analyst knows what to do and will not let her get out of control entirely. Resistance to letting her thoughts go would begin immediately. It might take the form of returning immediately to her obsession with pinworms whenever she became anxious. The analyst would have to confront and clarify her pattern of talking about pinworms whenever she became anxious and then interpret this pattern in a way that would allow Mrs. C. to become aware that she uses her obsession to defend against experiencing associations that are even more threatening than pinworms. The analyst would also have to deal with Mrs. C.'s well-established defense of isolating her affect. The analyst would slowly confront her pattern of saying only what she thinks about events and not what she feels about them. The analyst would also be very sensitive to occasions when Mrs. C. is being excessively warm and affectionate, because such expressions would likely be reactions to her true feelings of hatred and loathing for the nongiving, controlling therapist.

As Mrs. C. very gradually became aware of the defensive nature of her symptoms and her other patterns of behavior in analysis, she would be more able to experience intensely the feelings that would be emerging toward the analyst. As she regressed, she might become aware of fears that her analyst was trying to control her sex life, just as her father seemed to want to control it when he followed her on a date during her teens. Even more threatening would be her desires to have her fatherlike analyst control her sexuality and thereby satisfy his and her desires together. As she regressed further, she might become aware of desires to have her fatherlike analyst satisfy her by having anal intercourse or to have her motherlike analyst pleasure her by wiping her rear.

Mrs. C.'s transference reactions would include considerable hostile feelings that would be displaced from both of her parents onto her analyst, so she would be frequently enraged that the analyst was demanding and controlling while being ungiving, as were both her mother and her father. But she could not become conscious of hostile and sexual impulses without also becoming conscious of fears that her parent/analyst was going to destroy her or reject her by sending her to a state hospital. She would then become acutely aware of how frequently she would try to control both her anxiety and her impulses by expressing the opposite of what she felt, by apologizing, or in other ways undoing her reactions, or by isolating her impulses into more neutral thoughts.

As Mrs. C. worked through the neurotic transference with her analyst, she would gradually gain insight into the meaning and causes of her neurosis. She would eventually become conscious of ways in which she could channel her dangerous impulses into more mature outlets that provide both controls and gratification for her desires, such as expressing her anger in words. Over many years, Mrs. C. might be able to consciously restructure her personality enough to give her ego some flexibility in expressing hostile and sexual impulses without having to panic when situations threatened to stimulate them.

Future Directions

Many a psychotherapist in the past century has sounded the death knell for psychoanalysis. They are convinced that psychoanalysis will disappear as a body of knowledge and as a form of treatment. Allusions to psychoanalysis as a "dinosaur" and as a "gas-guzzler in an era of compacts" reflect this sentiment. However, we and many others agree with Silverman's (1976) assessment of psychoanalytic theory—borrowed from Mark Twain's famous quip when confronted with news reports of his own demise—that "the reports of my death are greatly exaggerated."

Bewildering changes in practice confront the new generation of psychoanalysts. These include a diminishing number of patients for analysis proper; an increasing number of nonpsychoanalytically-based psychotherapies; a systematic retreat from adequate insurance coverage for long-term psychotherapeutic care; a growing preoccupation with cost-effectiveness and cost containment; and the increased use of peer review and quality assurance systems, with their inevitable infringements on the confidentiality of the therapeutic relationship (Wallerstein & Weinshel, 1989).

For all these reasons, the future of psychoanalysis probably lies in time-limited psychodynamic therapy. Both the empirical evidence suggesting few outcome differences between long-term psychoanalytic therapy and short-term psychodynamic therapy and the financial constraints favoring use of the latter drive this conclusion. Surveys of practitioners' theoretical orientations, reviewed in Chapter 1, already demonstrate a decisive shift from psychoanalysis to psychodynamicism.

In addressing the future of psychodynamic psychotherapy, Strupp (1992) offers a number of forecasts. First, increasing attention is being paid to disturbances in infancy and early childhood. The Oedipus complex, once regarded as the watershed of psychic difficulties, is now no longer considered a universal phenomenon and has given way to the treatment of residues of pathogenic parent—child relationships. John Bowlby's (1969, 1973) seminal writings on child-parent *attachment style,* in particular, are serving as useful clinical guidelines for psychoanalytically-inspired psychotherapists. Second, and concomitantly, the treatment focus has shifted from the classical neurotic conditions of anxiety hysteria, phobias, and obsessive-compulsive disorders to more serious and characterological disorders, such as borderline and narcissistic personality disorders. The psychoanalytic treatment of these conditions, along the lines established by James Masterson (1976, 1981), Otto Kernberg (1975, 1984; Kernberg, Selzer, Koenigsberg, Carr, & Applebaum, 1989), and Heinz Kohut (1971, 1977), is now considered to be one of the "treatments of choice." Third, treatment manuals for psychoanalytic and psychodynamic therapies are likely to proliferate. Analogous to a flight plan or a road map, *treatment manuals* contain directions concerning appropriate therapist stances and techniques. They have provided much-needed specificity in research, training, and practice.

Two additional directions we foresee for psychoanalysis can be summed up by the terms *interpersonal* and *integration.* Although there is honest disagreement as to the permanence of the resurgence of interest in psychoanalysis, almost all observers concur that this is attributable to its interpersonal and relational emphasis. New attention is being paid to the dyadic character of the therapeutic relationship. Both patient and therapist continually and reciprocally contribute to the therapeutic situation, which always contains real and transference elements. The notion of "pure" transference (and countertransference) has proven an illusion. Contributing to the renewed vitality and the interpersonal evolution of psychoanalysis is the tremendous interest in incorporating advances in neuroscience, feminism, and more directive psychotherapies.

In practice, few therapists are "purists." Integration dominates the contemporary scene (see Chapter 15), and the modern psychodynamic therapist demonstrates greater openness to tailoring treatment to the needs of the patient and adapting to changing circumstances. While the intellectual descendents of Sigmund Freud maintain an underlying psychodynamic appreciation and formulation of the case, behavioral, cognitive, humanistic, and systemic methods are being routinely added to their therapeutic armamentaria.

Suggestions for Further Reading

Crits-Christoph, P., & Barber, J. P. (Eds.). (1991). *Handbook of short-term dynamic psychotherapy.* New York: Basic.

Fisher, S., & Greenberg, R. P. (1996). *Freud scientifically reappraised: Testing the theories and therapy.* New York: Wiley.

Freud, S. (1900/1953). *The interpretation of dreams.* First German edition, 1900; in *Standard edition* (Vols. 4 & 5), Hogarth Press, 1953.

Freud, S. (1933/1964). *New introductory lectures on psychoanalysis.* First German edition, 1933; in *Standard edition* (Vol. 22), Hogarth Press, 1964.

Greenson, R. R. (1967). *The technique and practice of psychoanalysis* (Vol. 1). New York: International Universities Press.

Holt, R. R. (1989). *Freud reappraised*. New York: Guilford.

Kernberg, O. (1976). *Object-relations theory and clinical psychoanalysis*. New York: Jason Aronson.

Kohut, H. (1977). *The restoration of the self*. New York: International Universities Press.

Luborsky, L. (1984). *Principles of psychoanalytic psychotherapy*. New York: Basic.

Neressian, E., & Kopff, R. G. (Eds.). (1996). *Textbook of psychoanalysis*. Washington, DC: American Psychiatric Press.

Journals: *American Journal of Psychoanalysis; Bulletin of the Menninger Clinic; Contemporary Psychoanalysis; Dynamic Psychotherapy; International Review of Psycho-Analysis; Issues in Ego Psychology; Journal of Analytic Social Work; Journal of Clinical Psychoanalysis; Journal of the American Psychoanalytic Association; Modern Psychoanalysis; Psychoanalysis and Contemporary Thought; Psychoanalysis and Psychotherapy; Psychoanalytic Dialogues; Psychoanalytic Inquiry; Psychoanalytic Psychology; Psychoanalytic Quarterly; Psychoanalytic Review.*

3

Adlerian Therapy

Alfred Adler

MAX WAS PREOCCUPIED with trying to get into Harvard Medical School. He was convinced that acceptance at such a superior school was his only chance of being able to demonstrate to others that he was not a clod. His own deep-seated feelings of inferiority were attributed to the fact that his younger brother had been favored at home and was superior at school. Max himself had always been a good student but never outstanding. He believed that his college performance was handicapped by his concern that other students were spreading rumors about his being homosexual. Max was afraid that he might one day reach out and grab the penis of one of his fellow students in his all-male Catholic college.

In spite of what others might think, Max was certain that he was not homosexual. He said he had never desired sex with a man and had experienced two fairly satisfying relationships with women. Max believed that his obsession to reach out and grab his fellow students was a hostile desire to strike back at those who were bothering him. His goal in therapy was to extinguish his obsession with penises and with what fellow students thought, so that he could succeed with his quest for Harvard.

One of Max's previous therapists, himself a Harvard MD, had assured Max that he was Harvard material. In spite of a glowing letter from the therapist, Max had failed to get into Harvard or any other medical school, for that matter.

When I suggested to Max that his goals might be unreasonable and unnecessarily high, he didn't want to hear it. He was zealously doing postgraduate work to improve his scores on the premed test, and there was no holding him back. As our relationship developed, I expressed my admiration for his ambition but felt he was overly preoccupied with himself. He agreed, but countered that if he received his M.D. from Harvard, then he could really do something for others. Taking a lead from Adler, I challenged Max to prove that he really cared about others. I challenged him to find a way to make at least one person a little happier each day for the next week.

That particular week the staff at a state hospital happened to be on strike. Max met my challenge by volunteering each day to help care for some of the most troubled patients. Then he went even further. He became quite upset over the way the patients were treated in the hospital and began organizing the other volunteers and some of the patients to form a citizens group for patients' rights. When he learned that such an organization already existed, he combined forces and was elected to the citizens advisory board.

As his concern for others increased, Max's preoccupation with penises and his peers' opinions faded. He began an intense relationship with a woman volunteer who was a strong advocate for patients' rights. His goal to get into Harvard, however, became even stronger, as he decided to eventually go into psychiatry in order to make a real impact on the state hospital system.

A Sketch of Alfred Adler

Alfred Adler (1870–1937) was the first person to formulate how feelings of inferiority could simulate a striving for superiority, as evidenced by Max. Adler himself had striven to be an outstanding physician, in part to compensate for the frailty he had experienced as a youngster with rickets. As the second son in a family of six, he was also spurred to stand out by his rivalry with his older brother and his somewhat unhappy relationship with his mother. His strongest support, both emotionally and financially, came from his grain-merchant father, who encouraged him to complete his MD at Vienna University.

In 1895 Adler began to practice as an ophthalmologist and then switched to a general practice, which he maintained long after he became known as a psychiatrist. As a psychiatrist in Vienna, he could not help but consider the theories of Freud, which were creating such a stir and generating so much criticism. Adler was quick to appreciate the importance of Freud's ideas, and he had the courage to defend the controversial system. Freud responded by inviting Adler to join his select Wednesday evening discussion circle.

Frequently cited as a student of Freud, Adler was actually a strong-minded colleague who was in harmony with Freud on some issues and in conflict on others. Adler's book *Study of Organ Inferiority* (1917) was highly praised by Freud. On the other hand, when Adler introduced the concept of the *aggression instinct* in 1908, Freud disapproved. It was not until long after Adler had rejected his own aggression-instinct theory that Freud incorporated it into psychoanalysis in 1923.

By 1911, the differences between Adler and Freud were becoming irreconcilable. Adler criticized Freud for an overemphasis on sexuality, while Freud condemned Adler's emphasis on conscious processes. At a series of tense meetings, Adler discussed his criticisms of Freud and faced heckling and jeering from the most ardent of Freud's followers. Following the third meeting, Adler resigned as president of the Vienna Psychoanalytic Society and soon resigned as editor of the society's journal. Later that year, Freud indicated that no one could support Adlerian concepts and remain in good standing as a psychoanalyst. Freud thus pressured other members to leave the society, while at the same time setting an unfortunate precedent of stifling serious dissent.

Adler quickly established himself as the leader of an important emerging approach to therapy. He called his system *individual psychology* to underscore the importance of studying the total individual in therapy. His theoretical productivity was interrupted by service as a physician in the Austrian army during World War I. Following the war, he expressed his interest in children by establishing the first of 30 child-guidance clinics in the Viennese school system. Adler expressed his social interest by speaking out strongly for school reforms, improvements in child-rearing practices, and the rejection of archaic prejudices that persistently led to interpersonal conflict.

Adler's interest in common people was expressed in part by his commitment to avoid technical jargon and to present his work in a language readily understood by nonprofessionals. Unlike many intellectuals, he was eager to speak and write for the public, and his influence among the public probably spread further than his professional influence. As an indefatigable writer and speaker, he traveled extensively to bring his message to the public. His influence seemed to peak just prior to the advent of Hitler, when 39 separate Adlerian societies were established.

There has been a resurgence of interest in Adler's ideas, especially in the United States (Hoffman, 1994). Adler himself had seen the United States as a place of great potential for his ideas. In 1925, at a relatively late age, he was struggling to learn English so he could speak to American professionals and to the public in their own language. He became a professor of psychiatry at the Long Island School of Medicine and settled in New York in 1935. Two years later, at the age of 67, he ignored the urging of his friends to slow down and died from a heart attack while on a speaking tour in Scotland.

Adler's influence on others was as much personal as intellectual. Besides his serious compassion for those suffering from social ills, Adler also had a light side and loved good food, music, and the company of others. He entertained both his guests and his audiences with his excellent humor. In spite of his own fame, he abhorred pomposity. He was committed both professionally and personally to expressing his commonality with his fellow human beings.

Theory of Personality

Striving for superiority is the core motive of the human personality. To be superior is to rise above what we currently are. To be superior does not necessarily mean to attain social distinction, dominance, or leadership in society. Striving for superiority means striving to live a more perfect and complete life. It is the superordinate dynamic principle of life; striving for completion and improvement encompasses and gives power to other human drives.

Striving for superiority can be expressed in many ways. Ideals of the perfect life vary from "peace and happiness throughout the land" to "honesty is the best policy" to "Deutschland über Alles." Perfection is an ideal created in the minds of humans, who then live as if they can make their ideals real. Individuals create their own fictional goals for living and act as if their personal goals are the final purpose for life. This *fictional finalism* reflects the fact that psychological events are determined not so much by historical circumstances as by present expectations of how one's future life can be completed. If a person believes that a perfect life is found in heaven as the reward for being virtuous, then that person's life will be greatly influenced by striving for that goal, independent of whether heaven exists or not. Such fictional goals represent the subjective cause of psychological events. Humanity is not merely a historically determined accident, an objective consequence of past external conditions. Human beings evolve as self-determined subjects who influence their futures by striving for internally created ideals. Each of us creates an *ideal self* that represents the type of perfect person we might strive to become.

What are the sources of this striving for superior ideals? Striving to be superior is the natural reaction to inescapable feelings of inferiority, an inevitable and virtually innate experience of all humans. Subjective feelings of inferiority may be based on such objective facts as *organ inferiorities*—physical weaknesses of the body that predispose us toward such ailments as heart, kidney, stomach, bladder, and lung problems. An organ inferiority is a stimulus to compensate by striving to be superior. The classic case is that of Demosthenes, who compensated for his early stuttering by becoming one of the world's great orators.

Feelings of inferiority—or, more broadly, an *inferiority complex*—can arise from subjectively felt psychological or social weaknesses as well as from actual bodily impairments. Young children, for example, are aware of being less intelligent and less adept than older siblings, and they strive toward a higher level of development. To feel inferior is not abnormal. To feel inferior is to be aware that we are finite beings who are never wise enough, fast enough, or able enough to handle all the contingencies of life. Feelings of inferiority have been the stimulus for every improvement that has been made in humanity's ability to deal more effectively with the world.

Feeling inferior and consequently striving for superiority applies to gender as well. Adler's notion of *masculine protest* refers chiefly to a woman protesting against her feminine role. Unlike Freud's proposal that a woman wishes to be a man and desires his anatomical structure, Adler recognized that a woman wishes to have a man's freedom and desires his privileged position in society. Status, not genitalia, is the real goal. A man, too, can suffer from masculine protest when he believes his masculinity is in some fashion inferior and consequently compensates by adopting hypermasculine behaviors. Preoccupation with big trucks, large guns, body building, and other symbols of male power may reflect such compensation.

The particular feeling of inferiority a person experiences can influence the *style of life* that person chooses for becoming superior. A person who felt intellectually inadequate as a child, for example, may choose to become a superior intellectual. An intellectual style of life then becomes the integrating principle of the person's life. An intellectual arranges a daily routine, develops a set of reading and thinking habits, and relates to family and friends in accordance with the goal of intellectual superiority. An intellectual style of life is a more solitary and sedentary existence than is the active life of a politician, for example.

A lifestyle is not the same as the behavioral patterns of a person's existence. All of a person's behavior springs from that individual's unique style of life. A lifestyle is a cognitive construction, an ideal representation of what a person is in the process of becoming.

People construct their lifestyles partly on the basis of early childhood experiences. The child's position in the family constellation—the *birth order* or *ordinal position*—is an especially important influence on his or her lifestyle. A second or middle child, for example, is more likely to choose an ambitious style of life, striving to surpass the older sibling. The oldest child faces the inevitable experience of being dethroned by a new center of attention. Having to give up the position of undisputed attention and affection produces feelings of resentment and hatred that are part of sibling rivalry. The oldest child enjoys looking to the past when there was no rival and is likely to develop a more conservative style of life. The youngest child has older siblings who serve as pacemakers to goad development. Youngest children never have the experience of losing attention to a successor and are more likely to expect to live the life of a prince or princess.

Although such objective facts as organ inferiorities and birth order will influence the lifestyle a person constructs, they do not ultimately determine how a person lives. The prime mover of the lifestyle is the *creative self*. As such, the creative self is not easily defined. It is a subjective power that gives humans the unique ability to transform objective facts into personally meaningful events. The creative self keeps a person from becoming just a product of biological and social circumstances by acting upon these circumstances to give them personal meaning. The creative self is an active process that interprets the genetic and environmental facts of a person's life and integrates them into a unified personality that is dynamic, subjective, and unique. From all the forces impinging on a person, the creative self produces a personal goal for living that moves that person toward a more personal and perfect future.

Although each style of life is a unique creation, each must take into account the society that is the background from which the figure of the person emerges. Every style of life must come to grips with the fact that humans are social beings born into a system of interpersonal relationships. A healthy style of life reflects the *social interest* that is an inherent potential for all human beings. A healthy personality is aware that a complete life is possible only within the context of a more perfect society. A healthy personality identifies with the inferiorities that are common to us all. The areas of ignorance that we all share, such as how to have peace in the world or how to be free from dreaded diseases, spur the healthy personality to help humanity transcend these weaknesses. As Adler (1964, p. 31) wrote, "Social interest is the true and inevitable compensation for all the natural weaknesses of individual human beings."

Although social interest is an inherent potential that can capture the commitment of any person, it will not develop on its own. Social interest must be nourished and encouraged within a healthy family atmosphere that fosters cooperation, mutual respect, trust, support, and understanding. The values, attitudes, and action patterns of family members, especially the parents, make up a family atmosphere that can, if healthy, encourage children to reject purely selfish interests in favor of the greater social interests of all humanity. Healthy personalities are those that are encouraged by the prospect of living a more complete life by contributing to the construction of a more perfect world.

Theory of Psychopathology

Pathological personalities are those that have become discouraged from being able to attain superiority in a socially constructive style. Pathological personalities tend to emerge from family atmospheres of competition and distrust, neglect, domination, abuse, or pampering, all of which discourage social interests. Children from such families are more likely to strive for a more complete life at the expense of others. Children discouraged from social interests tend to choose from one of four selfish goals for attaining superiority: attention seeking, power seeking, revenge taking, and declaring deficiency or defeat (Dreikurs, 1947, 1948). Although Dreikurs saw these selfish goals as the immediate strivings of children who misbehave, they can also become the final traits that lead to pathological lifestyles (Maddi, 1972).

A pampered lifestyle is encouraged when parents dote on their children, doing tasks for them that are well within the children's abilities to do themselves (Adler,

1936). The message the children receive is that they are not capable of doing things for themselves. If children conclude that they are inadequate, they develop an inferiority complex that is more than just inferiority feelings; they acquire a total self-concept of inadequacy. Inferiority complexes lead pampered personalities to avoid tackling the basic life tasks of learning to work, relating to the opposite sex effectively, and being a constructive part of society. Lacking adequate social interest, they attempt to compensate through constant attention seeking. The world view of people with pampered lifestyles suggests that the world should continue to take care of them and attend to them even when they are noncontributing adults.

In striving to be the center of attention, the pampered person can become a nuisance who disrupts satisfying social interactions. The more passive, pampered lifestyle results in laziness, in which the clear message is a dependent desire to be taken care of. Lazy adolescents or adults actually receive considerable negative attention from family and friends trying to goad them into a more constructive style of life. If being a nuisance or being lazy fails to bring sufficient attention or nurturance, the pampered person is likely to withdraw further from society into angry pouting.

Children reared under parental domination will also tend to develop an inferiority complex, based on a profound sense of being powerless to direct their own lives. Feeling powerless as children, they will shun life's basic tasks in favor of a more destructive goal. The consuming goal of those who have been constantly dominated is to attain power so that they never again will have to experience the acute inferiority that comes from being dominated. The active power seeker may become a rebel who opposes the authority of society in order to justify seeking personal power over others. Rebels may hide behind a variety of social slogans, but their final goal is to seize enough power to never again be dominated by another person. The more passive power seeker may strive for control over others by being stubborn and unwilling to compromise with even the smallest wishes of others.

One of the most common neurotic styles to emerge from parental domination is the *compulsive lifestyle* (Adler, 1931). The constant nagging, scolding, deriding, and faultfinding of dominating parents can lead to an inferiority complex in which the compulsive person feels powerless to solve life's problems. Afraid of ultimate failure in life's tasks, compulsives move into the future in a hesitating manner. When feeling powerless to handle their futures, they will hesitate, using indecision and doubt to try to hold back time. They may also resort to rituals to keep dreaded time from moving ahead. Besides giving a sense of timelessness by repeating the same act over and over, rituals serve as a safeguard against further loss of self-esteem. The compulsive can always say, "If it weren't for my compulsiveness, look how much I could have done with my life."

Compulsions are even more important as a compensatory means by which compulsives can develop an almost godlike sense of power. The compulsive ritual is experienced as the arena for a tremendous struggle between the good and evil forces of the universe that only the compulsive has the power to control. Compulsives act as if they have the power to save the world from hostile forces, from death or dreaded diseases, if they only carry out their rituals. So they check and recheck to see if the gas is off; they put knives on the table at just the proper angle; or they drive back around the block to make sure that no one has been hurt. To fail to re-peat their compulsions is to risk evil consequences for the world. If compulsives feel they cannot succeed on the stage of life, they can at least create their own sec-ondary theater of operations, their own dramatic rituals, that are under their power and control. The compulsive can ultimately declare a superior triumph: "See, I have succeeded in controlling my own urges."

Children who have been abused, beaten, and battered are more likely to want to take revenge on society than to help it. As adolescents and adults, these individu-als often develop a vicious style of life that actively seeks superiority by aggressing against a society that seems so cold and cruel. More passive revenge can be taken by those who adopt a passive-aggressive style of life and hurt others through con-stant inconsideration.

People raised with neglect and indifference are apt to declare defeat. They can-not expect to succeed in a society that does not care. They wish to demonstrate their personal superiority over society by withdrawal and isolation. The message in their withdrawal is that they are above needing others. To shore up their shaky sense of superiority, such isolates may actively denigrate others and convince them-selves that they really have not lost anything of value. The more passive isolates de-spair and declare that, because of such overwhelming personal deficiencies, there is no way they can be of interest or service to others.

The destructive goals of pathological personalities are typically under-standable, given the family atmospheres that encourage such goals. Though under-standable, these goals are mistakes, nonetheless. Pathological personalities con-struct maladaptive goals by making such *basic mistakes* as generalizing about the nature of all of society on the basis of the very small sample they have experienced. Particular parents or siblings may be cruel or indifferent and encourage revenge or withdrawal. If it weren't for distorted perceptions, however, such troubled persons could find evidence of kindness and caring from more constructive relationships. Pathological personalities also make the basic mistake of forming conclusions about themselves based on distorted feedback from just a few people. Neglected children, for example, may erroneously conclude that they are unlovable because one or both of their parents were unable to truly care for them.

The final fictions that troubled persons strive to make real will also be seen, at least by others, as basic mistakes. Over the course of their lives, it will become ap-parent that the pathological styles of life that have been constructed to fulfill a de-structive goal do not lead to a more perfect life. The neurotic nuisance, for exam-ple, may ultimately realize that rather than becoming a perfect person, he or she has become a perfect nuisance. The vicious revengers may discover that in the end they traded superiority for criminality. And the passive drinkers who have with-drawn into being high above it all through alcohol may find complete happiness only through complete drunkenness.

Theory of Therapeutic Processes

With their lifestyles having been created at a young age, most patients are too pre-occupied with trying to follow the details of their cognitive maps to be fully aware of the overall pattern of their lifestyles and the goals toward which they are directed. Many clients do not even want to think about the fact that their troubled lives are the result of their self-created styles of life. They prefer to experience themselves as the unfortunate victims of external circumstances. As a result, therapy must involve an analysis of the cognitive lifestyles of patients in order to help them become more fully conscious of how they are directing their own lives toward destructive goals.

Consciousness Raising

The Client's Work. Because the lifestyle is expressed in all that an individual does, clients really cannot help but reveal the general nature of their styles of life. Their styles of behaving, speaking, sitting, writing, responding, asking questions, and paying bills all have the personalized stamp of a unique style of life. If the cognitive lifestyles are to be brought into bold relief and clear consciousness, however, clients must be willing to reveal special phenomena in therapy, including their dreams, earliest memories, and family constellation. Besides revealing important information, clients are encouraged to participate actively in the analysis of their lifestyles and the goals toward which those styles are directed.

Becoming more aware of one's lifestyle and disorder can be accelerated by reading books written by others, a process known as *bibliotherapy,* Adler and his followers were amongst the first psychotherapists to pen self-help books for the lay public, and clients are frequently asked to read these and related works. The Adlerian goals for bibliotherapy are embodied in six "E's" (Riordan, Mullis, & Nuchow, 1996):

Educate by filling in psychological knowledge and gaps

Encourage by reading inspirational materials

Empower by reviewing goal formation and attainment

Enlighten by increasing self- and other-awareness

Engage with the social world through modeling and social mentoring

Enhance by reinforcing specific points and lifestyle changes addressed in psychotherapy

The Therapist's Work. In raising consciousness, Adlerian therapists rely a great deal on interpreting the important information that clients present. Adlerian interpretations are not concerned with making causal connections between past events and present problems. The past is connected to the present only to demonstrate the continuity of a patient's style of life. Interpretations are concerned mainly with connecting the past and the present to the future. Interpretations help clients become aware of the purposive nature of their lives, of how their past and present experiences are directed toward fulfilling future goals or purposes. Clients become aware of how all their behaviors, including their pathological behaviors, serve the goal of making real the fictional finalisms that were created early in life.

To become aware of the overall pattern and purpose of a patient's life, the therapist must conduct a fairly complete analysis of the lifestyle. A *lifestyle analysis* includes a summary of the client's family constellation. The order of birth, the gender of siblings, the absence of a parent, and the feelings of which child was favored are all important factors in a family constellation that can be interpreted as influencing the lifestyle a client decided to follow. An interpretation of the client's earliest recollections *(anamnesis)* will give a picture of whether the client felt encouraged or discouraged to compensate for inferiority feelings in a socially constructive style.

A lifestyle analysis will also include an interpretation of the *basic mistakes* the client made in constructing a view about the nature of the world. The most common cognitive mistakes include (1) overgeneralizations, such as "nobody cares"; (2) distortions of life's demands, such as "you can't win at life"; (3) minimization of one's worth, such as "I'm really inadequate" or "I'm only a housewife"; (4) unrealistic goals to be secure, such as "I must please everyone"; and (5) faulty values, such as "get ahead, no matter whose it is" (Mosak & Dreikurs, 1973).

Unlike many therapists, Adlerians do not stop at analyzing the problems of clients. They are just as concerned with giving clients feedback about their personal assets. Thus, a summary of a client's strengths is included as part of a lifestyle analysis. After completing an analysis of the patient's lifestyle as part of the early assessment phase of therapy, Adlerians present a summary of the lifestyle to the client in a teacher-to-student fashion. The lifestyle summary is offered as if the therapist is presenting at a case conference, but here the client has a chance to cooperate in the analysis. Clients can indicate whether they agree or disagree with the therapist's summary. Therapists can make necessary changes in their view of the client's lifestyle, or they can interpret the client's response as resistance to a more complete view of the lifestyle if clients are indeed resisting seeing themselves more completely.

The interpretations and the presentation of a lifestyle summary include both feedback and education. Individual clients are given personal feedback about their unique family constellation, their personal feelings of inferiority, and their particular assets and basic mistakes. At the same time, clients are educated in a theory of lifestyle construction that emphasizes such concepts as the creative self, social interest, and the striving for superiority. In interpreting life goals and demonstrating the basic mistakes in living for selfish values instead of social interests, Adlerians teach clients a new philosophy of life. In fact, Adlerians believe that a therapy is incomplete if it does not include an adequate philosophy of life (Mosak & Dreikurs, 1973).

Whether or not clients are changing their basic styles of completing life's tasks is best determined by an analysis of dreams. Dreams are a means of solving future problems, and that person's manner of dreaming will indicate how that person is currently attempting to resolve the problems of everyday life. Dreams are a rehearsal of possible alternatives for future action. Thus, if clients wish to postpone action, they will tend to forget dreams. If they wish to convince themselves to avoid particular actions, they will frighten themselves with nightmares. Clients who are making little movement in therapy may have brief dreams with little action. Clients who are ready to tackle their problems head on will throw themselves into creative analysis of their dreams. By helping clients interpret their own dreams, therapists are helping them become aware of new and creative alternatives for completing life's tasks.

Contingency Control

The Client's Work. As a cognitive approach to change, Adlerian therapy is directed at weakening the effects of present contingencies by having clients reevaluate their future goals. By reevaluating their goals pertaining to power, revenge, and attention, clients decrease the reinforcing effects of such consequences as being the center of attention or controlling others. In the process of reevaluating selfish goals, patients may experiment with behaviors directed toward a social interest in order to experience the consequences that result from striving for social interest. After experiencing the good feelings that come from helping another person, clients are in a better position to realistically compare and reevaluate the consequences that they had been receiving from a self-centered life.

The Therapist's Work. One of the techniques that therapists use to help a client reevaluate the consequences of selfish goals is to create images that capture the essence of the client's goals. Clients who are constantly striving to be the center of attention may be asked to imagine themselves as Bozo the Clown, who becomes the center of attention by having people throw things at him, such as insults or sarcastic remarks. When clients find themselves playing the buffoon, they can imagine that they are like Bozo the Clown sitting on a stool over a pool of water just egging people on to knock him down. These and related images encourage clients to laugh at their styles rather than to condemn themselves. Once clients can laugh about playing Bozo the Clown or Caesar the Conqueror, they can devalue the desire for attention or control.

Adlerians also assign tasks to clients designed to help them experiment with expressing a social interest. A therapist might, for example, assign a patient the task of doing something each day that gives pleasure to another person. In the process of completing such tasks, clients are able to experience for themselves the valuable consequences that come from doing something for someone other than themselves.

As values are changing, therapists may still have to provide techniques that help patients avoid slipping back into old habits of responding to selfish goals. *Catching oneself* is a technique that encourages clients to think about catching themselves with their hands in the cookie jar. They should try to actually catch themselves in the process of acting out a destructive behavior—for instance, overeating or overdrinking. With practice, including the internal practice of anticipating putting a hand in a cookie jar, clients can learn to anticipate a situation and to turn their attention to more constructive consequences rather than automatically responding to destructive goals.

Choosing

The Client's Work. Just as patients originally chose particular lifestyles as children, so too are they capable of choosing to radically change their lifestyles at a later age. Once they are more fully conscious of the fictional finalisms that they are trying to make real, and once they have evaluated selfish goals in comparison with social goals, clients are freer to choose to stay with their old styles or to create a new life. Some goals, such as having power over others or being the center of attention, are highly valued by many people, and there is no assurance that clients will choose to give up such goals in the name of social interest. Beyond the consensual value of some goals, clients may choose to stay with the security of an unsatisfying style of life because it is at least a known quantity. To consider choosing a radically new lifestyle can threaten a loss of security, and clients may opt to reaffirm their longstanding lifestyles.

The Therapist's Work. Rather than have clients face a sudden and dramatic decision to throw themselves into the darkness of a new and unknown style of life, therapists can use techniques that encourage clients to experiment with new alternatives for living. One such technique is the *as if*. For example, a 35-year-old widow had decided that now, after having known the security of six years of relying only on herself, she valued the idea of developing an intimate relationship with a man. She had met a man to whom she was attracted at her Parents Without Partners group, but he had not asked her out. Because she had not been making any progress in pursuing her goal for more intimacy, I suggested that she ask him if he would like to go for coffee after the meeting. She said she really found that alternative exciting, but insisted that she was not the kind of person who could do such a thing. Using an Adlerian technique, I suggested that she only act "as if" she were a liberated woman, rather than worrying about becoming such a person. With considerable courage, she was able to act as if she were more liberated and was able to get closer to the man. At the same time, she discovered that if she acted as if she were more liberated, she could soon transform such fiction into reality.

For clients who insist that they would change if only they could control overpowering emotions, a *push-button technique* is used to demonstrate that they can indeed choose to control their emotions. Using fantasy, clients are instructed to close their eyes and imagine very happy incidents in their pasts. They are to become aware of the feelings that accompany the scenes. Then clients are instructed to imagine a humiliating, frustrating, or hurtful incident and note the accompanying feelings. Following this, the pleasant scenes are imagined again. By pushing the button on particular thoughts, clients are taught that they can indeed create whatever feelings they wish by deciding what they will think about. After practicing cognitive control of emotions, clients are impressed with their enhanced ability to determine emotions. With an increased ability to choose whether to be angry or not, or depressed or not, clients are in the process of liberating their lifestyles from emotions that once seemed overwhelming.

Therapeutic Content

Intrapersonal Conflicts

Psychological problems are primarily intrapersonal in origin, reflecting the destructive lifestyle that was constructed by the individual at an early age. With its focus on the lifestyle of the individual, Adlerian therapy was traditionally carried out in an individual format. Nevertheless, Dreikurs (1959), a prominent student of Adler, is credited with being the first to use group therapy in private practice. Since destructive lifestyles are acted out interpersonally, a group setting yields firsthand information on how patients create problems in relating to others.

Anxiety and Defenses. However self-defeating or destructive a lifestyle may be, it at least provides a sense of security. When a therapist questions or threatens lifestyle convictions, anxiety is aroused and the client is ready to resist further treatment. Anxiety can be used to frighten the therapist from pushing ahead, as when the patient threatens to go into a panic if the therapist continues to probe. Anxiety serves a primary purpose, then, of keeping the client from having to take action and move ahead into the future. Anxiety can also serve as a secondary theater of operations, allowing clients to turn their attention from solving life's tasks to trying to solve the considerable anxiety they are creating by their constant self-preoccupation. Therapists need not worry about treating anxiety directly. However, they must be aware of tendencies to avoid being direct in analyzing a self-aborted lifestyle out of their fear of the tremendous amount of anxiety clients can create as an excuse for holding onto a secure but unsuccessful style of life.

The most common and important defense mechanism is *compensation*. Compensation serves not as a defense against anxiety per se but rather as a defense against the aversive feelings of inferiority. Compensation itself does not produce problems. It is the goal toward which a person strives in order to be superior that determines whether or not compensation leads to problems. A person with intense feelings of organ inferiority might compensate and strive for superiority by becoming the community's most plagued hypochondriac. Or the same person could have been encouraged to compensate by becoming the community's most revered physician. The issue in psychotherapy is not to remove feelings of inferiority or to replace compensation with more effective coping mechanisms. Therapy is intended to help clients redirect their compensatory strivings from selfish, self-absorbing goals toward socially useful, self-enhancing values.

Self-Esteem. Enough has been said about feelings of inferiority to indicate that problems with self-esteem are central in Adlerian therapy. The secret to solving problems of esteem is not to reassure maladjusted people that they are indeed well. Nor is self-esteem particularly enhanced through encouraging self-absorption by having clients analyze all the intricate details of their early years. The paradox of self-esteem is that it vanishes as a problem when people are encouraged to forget themselves and begin living for others. A solid sense of self-esteem can be created only by creating a style of life that is of value to the world. Live a life that affirms the value of fellow human beings, and the unintended consequence will be the creation of a self that is worthy of the highest esteem.

Responsibility. Those who would be free from pathology must have the strength to carry the double burden of both personal and social responsibility. In becoming aware that one's own creative self is ultimately responsible for transforming the objective facts of life into personally meaningful events, a person is confronted with the ultimate responsibility of choosing in the present the goals that will allow the most perfect future to unfold. Once individuals accept responsibility for shaping their own lives, they must also accept their responsibility for the impact that their lifestyles have on society. Will they, for instance, attempt to live a more complete life by helping to create a more perfect personality while at the same time producing a more polluted place to live? The person who can hope to attain a condition of wholeness is one who can respond to the hopes of humanity.

Interpersonal Conflicts

Intimacy and Sexuality. People who are committed to selfish interests should not be surprised that their self-centeredness prevents them from experiencing intimacy. Intimacy includes being able to place concern for a valued other above one's own immediate interests. Intimacy also requires the ability to truly cooperate with others in pursuing commonly shared goals. The selfishness that is inherent in psychopathology preempts such intimate cooperation. Yet so many people are surprised that they cannot have life both ways—that they cannot dedicate themselves to a life of selfish competitiveness, for example, without that competitiveness eventually tearing apart their marriages or their families. People would like to pretend that a lifestyle can be fragmented into convenient parts, with competition, domination, and ruthlessness at work and cooperation, equality, and caring at home. This pretense may work for a while, but eventually the goals of selfish success will take their toll on intimate relationships.

Although Adler rejected sexuality as being the prime mover of life, it was accepted as one of the important tasks of life. The biological fact of life is that we exist in two sexes. A task of life is to learn how to relate to that fact in a manner that allows both sexes to find mutual pleasure and significance in sexual relating. Defining our sex roles in part on the basis of cultural definitions and stereotypes, we must strive to relate to the other sex, not the opposite sex (Mosak & Dreikurs, 1973). Other people of either sex need not be transformed into the enemy. Thinking in terms of the *other* sex as the *opposite* sex tends to encourage competition and conflict rather than the cooperation that comes from being fellow human beings. Without such cooperation, partners cannot expect to teach each other what is needed for sex to be a mutually rewarding experience.

Communication. The inherent preparedness for language acquisition indicates that humans are born to be social beings. Language alone, however, does not guarantee effective communication. Problems with communication are fundamentally problems with cooperation. Effective communication is, by its very nature, a cooperative endeavor. If one person is holding back information out of self-interest, or if another is sending misleading messages to gain a competitive advantage, then communication is bound to be conflicted. Couples with conflicts over competition, such as sex role competition, will frequently complain of problems in communicating with each other, even though each is able to communicate effectively with a friend of the same sex. The task in therapy is not to correct communication patterns, but rather to help the couples reorient their values toward common goals so that their communications can be for shared rather than selfish interests.

Hostility. Adler originally considered the aggressive instinct to be the most important human drive. He later elaborated his position to include hostility as one expression of the basic will to power. Now we understand hostility as perhaps the worst of many mistaken paths of striving for superiority. For those discouraged from being able to attain perfection through social contributions, violence seems to provide a sense of superiority. To beat up someone, to hold another person at gunpoint, to threaten someone's very life can transform the most inferior-feeling individual into a giant who is almost godlike in the ability to destroy another existence. To resort to hostility is, of course, to deny the value of another human being. Hostility is the worst expression of the belief that self-interest is of higher value than social interest. The tragic rise in violence in modern society may well be testimony to the prevalence of the belief that only the self and never the society is really sacred.

Control. All people have a need to be able to control, to master certain situations and exercise restraint over others. Pathological personalities, however, are frequently preoccupied with dominating others. The most blatant controller is the person who was once dominated by parents and has made a commitment to seek power over others in order to never again feel the intense inferiority that comes from being under another person's domination. The pampered personality is a more subtle despot, using neurotic symptoms such as anxiety, depression, and hypochondriasis to get others to satisfy every whim. Pampered people are trained to use the services of others for solutions to problems rather than to become self-reliant. As adults, pampered people rely on symptoms to control others, including therapists, in order to get others to care for them.

Control over others brings a sense of security, a position of superiority, and an exaggerated conviction of self-value. With these gains from control, many clients can be expected to rely on subtle and not-so-subtle maneuvers to control therapy. Effective therapists will be aware of patients' efforts to control, and they can respond with countercontrol techniques. Clients who try to control therapy, for example, by insisting on how bad off they are and how unable they are to progress, may cry out in exaggerated self-worth, "I bet you've never had such a tough case as me before." The therapist may refuse to be impressed by responding, "No, not since last hour." The therapist is not attempting to win some control game, but rather to communicate to the client that the therapist is unwilling to cooperate with the client's maneuvers.

Individuo-Social Conflicts

Adjustment Versus Transcendence. The issue of adjustment versus transcendence should not pit the individual against society. Striving for transcendence is synonymous with striving for superiority; both entail finding fulfillment by continuing to transcend a present level of personal adjustment by attaining a higher and more complete level of life. Healthy people will resist notions that fulfillment requires placing oneself against the system. Healthy people do not place self-esteem over social esteem in an attempt to rise above the society to which they are integrally related. Social transcendence is for snobs and elitists who can feel superior only at the expense of the commoners that surround them. Healthy people are committed to helping the entire society transcend its present level of functioning in order to become a more perfect social system.

Impulse Control. The civilizing role of parents and clinicians is not to inhibit bad impulses but to strengthen social interest. Children are not primarily biological beasts that must have controls imposed on destructive drives. Children are social beings who are prepared to cooperate if encouraged by parents and teachers. Accordingly, impulses must be directed toward prosocial goals as part of the total lifestyle. Drives do not have inherent direction, such as to destroy or to dominate. Drives are simply expressions of the primary thrust toward completion. Thus, impulses such as sex and aggression can be brought to completion for higher social interests, as in providing a pleasure bond between spouses or aiding in the defense of a society against aggressors. Impulses become a problem for society only when the overall direction of a lifestyle is antisocial rather than prosocial in nature. Impulses threaten to break out of control not because of an excess of civilization but because some individuals lack a full appreciation of and dedication to civilization.

Beyond Conflict to Fulfillment

Meaning. We create meaning out of our lives by the lives we create. We are not born with intrinsic meaning in our existence, but we are born with a creative self that can fashion intrinsic meaning from our existence. From the raw materials of our genetic endowment and our childhood experiences, we shape and mold the goals and the means to the goals that will give significance to our existence. If our vision is good enough and our goals are noble enough, then the lifestyles we construct may be truly valued works of art that are dedicated to the best in humanity. If, out of discouragement and distortion, we dedicate our lives to banal goals, then our lifestyle may reflect more basic mistakes than basic meaning. A basic mistake that has resulted in the alienation of many is that existence can have meaning if it is dedicated to becoming a shrine to the self. The creative self seeks completion not by turning inward and drawing away from the world, but by reaching out to become connected to the greatest needs and the highest aspirations of humanity.

Ideal Person. Inspired by goals that transcend any immediate wants or worries, the superior person is drawn to life with excitement and anticipation. Esteem is granted in knowing that the world really needs people who care. Energies are not wasted on evasive defenses or on neurotic patterns that provide ready-made excuses for failing to add to the world.

The healthy person is at home in the world. The ideal person embraces *Gemeinschaftsgefühl*, the social interest that allows us to contribute to the common welfare of humanity. Social interest is not just an idealistic value that provides inspiration for life, it is also a pragmatic goal that produces mental health in life. The interests of the self and the interests of others are not experienced as being in basic conflict by those who care enough to find completion through cooperation. The ubiquitous social values of security and success are rejected in favor of the even higher social value of the common good. Healthy people do not place themselves against, above, or below others. They are egalitarians who experience profound relatedness with others by identifying with the imperfections that we all share and with the aspirations of those who truly care.

Therapeutic Relationship

The therapeutic relationship is a central part of the process of helping clients overcome their longstanding discouragement so that they can be freer to reorient themselves toward a healthy social interest. Therapists help draw clients toward a genuine social interest by showing the personal interest they have for the well-being of their clients. In many ways, the therapeutic relationship is a prototype of social interest. The classical values of love, faith, and hope for the human condition are essential to both social interest and an effective therapeutic relationship.

The therapist's positive regard for the client reflects the love and caring of an individual dedicated to the well-being of human beings. The therapist's willingness to relate as a genuine equal communicates a faith in the client's ability to actively contribute to finding solutions to serious problems. The therapist is not the doctor who acts upon the client, no matter how helpless pampered clients may act in order to persuade the doctor-therapist to take over their lives. The therapist is more like a teacher who has faith in the unused potential of the student-client to create a fulfilling style of life. The teacher-therapist is willing to recommend readings (bibliotherapy), assign homework experiments, and offer personal encouragement. The genuineness of the therapist reveals a willingness to make mistakes, to be perfectly human, which communicates a faith that imperfect human beings have the power to enhance life. Patients who are well aware of being imperfect need not look to a perfect healer for help, but can share the faith of the therapist that the imperfect client is capable of striving for a more complete life.

The faith and love that the patient experiences through the therapeutic relationship give him or her hope that counteracts the discouragement that prevents meeting life head on. Experiencing genuine love, faith, and hope from an empathic therapist is an undeniable event that makes clients profoundly aware of the intrinsic value that social interest from one human being can have for another. With renewed hope and a vital awareness of the value of social interest, clients are provided fresh opportunities to break out of a self-centered existence and begin caring and living for others.

Practicalities of Adlerian Therapy

Adlerians are comparatively flexible and innovative in the formal aspects of psychotherapy. Formats vary from a traditional individual style, to conjoint family sessions, to a multiple-therapist approach (two or more therapists working together with one patient), to group approaches with multiple therapists as well as clients. The multiple-therapist approach was originated by Dreikurs (1950) as a means of preventing serious transference or countertransference problems from interfering with therapeutic progress. The presence of two therapists also allows clients to become aware of how two individuals can really differ and still cooperate.

As part of the educational orientation toward solving or preventing mental health problems, Adlerian workshops have become a popular format for teaching parents how to raise children to cooperate, to care, and to strive as individuals while living in the context of a warm, supportive social group that still insists on clear limits through democratic rules. Similar workshops are available for marital couples, who can attend the educational sessions and either just sit back and learn from others or come to center stage and discuss issues in their marriage, with the audience giving considerable support and positive suggestions for solving problems. Adlerians have also established social clubs to help foster social interest both within and outside of mental hospitals. Within the social clubs, the strengths of individuals are stressed, as they are encouraged to enjoy the social aspects of the clubs rather than focusing on their weaknesses through therapy.

Adlerian approaches to therapy are also flexible with regard to such matters as fees and time limits. As a reflection of their own social interests, clinicians are encouraged to provide a significant contribution to the community without charge. This *pro bono* service may be done through free Friday evening marital workshops, free workshops for parents, or some private therapy hours for clients unable to pay.

While Adlerians have traditionally worked with a full range of clients, they are especially active in working with delinquents, criminals, families, and organizations. The resurgence of Adlerian activity in these areas reflects a concern with social relationships in danger of disintegrating because of excessive self-interest. Following Adler's original example, Adlerians are heavily involved in school settings, especially with guidance counselors eager to help students clarify their values in order to find constructive goals for their energies. Of late, Adlerian priniciples and methods have been increasingly applied to workplace problems and organizational changes (Barker & Barker, 1996; Ferguson, 1996).

The Adlerian movement is now largely centered in the United States, with several training institutes that offer certificates in psychotherapy, counseling, and child guidance. Becoming an Adlerian therapist is more a matter of the individual's social values than of formal credentials—at least as compared to the countervailing priorities in other psychotherapy systems of psychotherapy. As a consequence,

Adlerian institutes have been receptive to educators, clergy, and even paraprofessionals, as well as to members of the traditional mental health professions.

Brief Adlerian Therapy

The course of psychotherapy is expected to be relatively short-term. The Adlerians were among the first to advocate time-limited treatment and to develop active methods to accelerate the therapeutic process. In fact, many of the methods embraced by brief therapists—clinican flexibility, group and family treatment, homework assignments, psychoeducational materials, lifestyle analysis, optimistic perspective, and collaborative relationship—were pioneered by the Adlerians (Sperry, 1992).

Effectiveness of Adlerian Therapy

Although many of Adler's seminal concepts—ordinal position, earliest childhood memories, social interest, to name a few—have been extensively investigated (Watkins, 1982, 1983, 1992), little empirical research has been conducted on the actual effectiveness of Adlerian therapy. The Smith, Glass, and Miller (1980) meta-analysis of 475 studies located only four that included an Adlerian type of therapy. The average effect size for Adlerian therapy in the admittedly small set of available studies was .62, not significantly different from the average effect size of .56 for placebo treatments. Similarly, recent literature reviews fail to locate any substantial body of controlled outcome research on Adlerian therapy on either adults (e.g., Grawe, Donati, & Bernaver, 1998) or on children (e.g., Weisz et al., 1987, 1995).

A handful of controlled studies, all with different foci, is inadequate to draw any firm conclusions about the efficacy of Adlerian therapy. Perhaps the most we can say at this time is that Adlerian therapy is superior to no treatment and, when compared with alternative treatments, it has been found to be as effective as client-centered therapy and psychoanalytic therapy in several studies. With the resurging interest in Adlerian therapy and with the increasing availability of scientific methodology to examine idiographic data, our hope is that more extensive outcome studies will be completed in the near future.

Criticisms of Adlerian Therapy

From a Psychoanalytic Perspective

Freud anticipated that Adler's break with psychoanalysis would lead to the development of a superficial and sterile theory (Colby, 1951). In rejecting psychoanalysis, Adler acted as if he had rejected half of the human personality. The result is a one-dimensional theory that emphasizes the ego or self at the expense of the id, consciousness at the expense of the unconscious, social strivings at the expense of biological drives, compensation at the expense of other defenses, and the perfectible at the expense of the imperfectible. Here we have a yin without a yang, half of the person presented as if it were the whole.

As a result of the holes in Adler's holism, there emerges a naive therapy that suggests that people can be truly helped with all types of cute gimmicks. Just have a frightened, submissive woman act "as if" she is liberated, and she will be liberated. Just push a button, and an embittered recluse can change his fantasies and feelings as fast as he can change the television channel. The power of positive thinking has been peddled as a lasting cure for centuries, when in fact it is nothing but a temporary pep talk. Patients are not really emotionally crippled; they are only mistaken. People are not really locked into unconscious conflicts; they are only discouraged. Just have hope, faith, and charity, and that is the way to live successfully. Adler does indeed promise a rose garden to those who are willing to share his rose-colored glasses that filter out the truly dark side of life.

From a Behavioral Perspective

Adlerians have been unable to decide whether they are social learning theorists who attribute maladaptive behavior to family constellations and other environmental conditions or mystics who attribute distorted lifestyles to an undeveloped creative self that sounds much like a soul. Why Adlerians feel the need to resort to the mythical concepts of choice and a creative self when observable behaviors of parental pampering, abusing, ignoring, and dominating would serve as explanations is unclear.

It is clear, however, that theoretical propositions concerning the effects of birth order can be defined and tested, while such concepts as striving for superiority and the creative self are vague and totally unamenable to scientific investigation. Perhaps Adlerians hold to such concepts in order to place the responsibility for change on the clients, because the therapy system has been unable to generate techniques powerful enough to produce adequate change in the behavior of clients. Whatever the reasons, the Adlerian school remains a strange combination of a theory that borders on scientific respectability and a religion that dedicates the soul to social interest.

From a Contextual Perspective

Adler is properly seen as a pioneer in moving away from the overly sexual nature of Freud's classic drive theory and toward an appreciation of the broader family and contextual forces at work. But he did not go far enough. No matter how you repackage it, Adlerian theory represents the same old sexist, intrapsychic perspective in more social terms. Problems are still attributed to individuals, not social ills. Intrapsychic forces of superiority and inferiority still rule the mental roost. The lifestyle analysis considers the impact of the family constellation, but the patient is still responsible for the illness and the cure. Change the sick patient, not the sick society.

Women fare a bit better under Adler than under Freud, but not much. Adlerian theory seems willing to accept psychotherapy as an extension of the socialization process. Be more socialized and civilized, and you will be free from psychopathology. That may be true for many men and children in need of socialization or resocialization, but what of the many women who are troubled because they are over-socialized? The ever-polite and proper client with colitis and frigidity will not be freed by striving to be more perfect. She needs to express her anger and resentment over always having to stifle herself for the sake of social harmony. The self-sacrificing spouse who experiences an existential crisis of having no sense of self because she has always lived for others doesn't need to be encouraged to just make someone else happy once a day. She needs to know how to care for herself and to assert herself for her own interests when necessary.

From an Integrative Perspective

There is much of value in Adlerian therapy to those committed to integrating the psychotherapies. Alfred Adler broadened the exclusive reliance on insight and private knowledge to include action-oriented and psychoeducational processes in therapy. The therapeutic relationship was construed and offered as more egalitarian and more real than it was in psychoanalysis. Individuality and relatedness were accorded equal consideration in psychotherapy, reversing a trend toward self-contained individualism (Guisinger & Blatt, 1994). Adler and his followers were more flexible in their formats, innovative in their practices, and eclectic in their techniques than Freud and his disciples. Not surprisingly, many contemporary eclectics, including Arnold Lazarus (see Chapter 14), have been heavily influenced by Adler's work and are enthusiastic about his general approach to psychotherapy.

On pragmatic grounds, systemization and evidence are sorely needed (Dryden & Lazarus, 1991). Although there are many interesting constructs and a prescribed lifestyle analysis, there is little systematic direction regarding which interventions should be used with which patients with which disorders. Just do the same thing for all patients—not a notion likely to be endorsed by any genuine eclectic! The empirical evidence on the effectiveness of Adlerian therapy, moreover, is far too scant for an eclectic to even consider wholly adopting its theory or its interventions.

On more theoretical grounds, it is ironic that Adler called his approach individual psychology, when in fact he ultimately valued social interests over the interests of the individual. Adler attempted to resolve the inherent conflicts between society and the individual by suggesting that the individual's best interests are really served by subjugating self-interest to the interests of society. Adlerian theory may indeed help balance therapeutic approaches that worship only the self at the expense of others. Nevertheless, it would be a mistake to conclude that a complete life can be found only in living for social interests and never for self-interest.

AN ADLERIAN ANALYSIS OF MRS. C.

Mrs. C. is a person almost entirely preoccupied with herself. Other people are mere shadows, minor characters who move in and out of her dramatic rituals. Her life has become a parody of a great epic. She is in a mortal struggle with the dreaded evil of pinworms, and only she can be powerful enough and perfect enough to prevent the pinworms from becoming the victors. She has obviously switched her striving for superiority from solving the primary tasks of life to a secondary theater of operations in which she can be the heroine, the star in her own style of life.

Mrs. C.'s dramatic dilemma is common to those with a compulsive personality. Having been raised under the constant castigation and derision of dominating parents, Mrs. C. was discouraged from believing that she was capable of facing life's tasks successfully. She had indeed failed at the task of coming to grips with her own sexuality. She was in the process of failing at the work of caring for five children with a sixth on the way. The intense inferiority complex that she had accepted early in life was in danger of proving to be all too true. What she decided as a child was becoming a self-fulfilling prophecy: she was too inferior to find completion through life's tasks. Her solution was to switch the arena to a neurotic struggle that was more of her own making and more under her control.

Quickly Mrs. C. became the perfect compulsive, the most complete washer others had ever known. What a special person she is, how unusual! She has already stumped several clinicians and a prominent mental hospital. Yet she continues to insist that she could really live, could really care for her children and husband, if it weren't for her neurosis. Her compulsive lifestyle serves, then, as a compensation for her inferiority complex of being unable to solve life's tasks, as a built-in excuse for not doing more with her life, as a means of freezing time by repeating the same rituals that seem to keep life from moving ahead, and as a dramatic struggle that proves how superior she is at holding back the evil forces of the world.

Progress in therapy would be a real threat to Mrs. C. She has judged herself as too inferior to progress in life. She has made a basic mistake of evaluating herself on the basis of early recollections of how her parents perceived her—as an inferior being, requiring constant control and domination. What distortions she may have added to these recollections may never be known. Did her parents never support her strengths or her strivings for independence? Did she encourage their domination because she found security in being protected from sex, disease, or boys? Were there not adults in her life, teachers or neighbors, who encouraged her, even if her folks were really such tyrants? Again, answers to such questions may never be known.

What must become known to Mrs. C. is that she continues in her neurotic patterns because she concluded early in life that she was ultimately unable to succeed in life. She must come to understand that she is not special or disturbed because she has intense feelings of inferiority, but that she shares these feelings with all human beings. Her disturbance is the result of striving to be special and trying to compensate for her inferiorities by investing all her energies in a completely self-centered life.

If Mrs. C. continues to withdraw from living with and for others, she is indeed at high risk of becoming psychotic. Her thinking and communication are of little social interest. They are almost entirely directed toward pinworms, toward her fears, and toward convincing others how special are her life circumstances. The social ties that connect thinking with social reality can break down if others continue to be of no interest to Mrs. C.

Given Mrs. C.'s almost total self-preoccupation, it will be difficult to engage her with another human being acting in the role of therapist. Because she has had considerable individual therapy, and because she seems only to have convinced herself of how special she is, it would be better to start her out in an Adlerian group. Although she would probably resist group therapy, on the grounds that she is too troubled and too in need of individual attention, being placed in a group would give the direct message that, in fact, she is not so special. She would have the opportunity to discover that others also have serious problems and serious feelings of inferiority, and yet some of them are moving ahead in life. Bibliotherapy would also advance this message. Finding herself unable to really care about others, Mrs. C. might insist that if she were not so preoccupied with her own problems, then she could care about the others. The therapist or group members could correct such mistaken thinking by indicating that the reverse idea is really true: if she can begin to learn to care about others in the group, she can begin to forget about herself for a while.

Mrs. C. would also be encouraged to participate in a full analysis of her life script, including such basic mistakes as judging herself inadequate because she felt dominated by her parents. Her earliest recollections would be interpreted, as would her perceptions of her position in her family constellation. The group could be especially supportive in helping Mrs. C. to become more fully conscious of her inferiority complex. Finding that others share intense feelings of inferiority can give Mrs. C. the opportunity to rediscover a genuine interest in others.

Experiencing the caring of her therapist and of special group members can begin to reorient Mrs. C. from sheer self-interest to an emerging social interest. Tasks would be assigned to encourage interest in others, such as assigning Mrs. C. to call certain group members who are in a crisis to see how they are doing each evening. Mrs. C. would be encouraged to step further out of her special drama back into the world of others by being assigned simple tasks to add pleasure to her children's lives, such as baking them a pie. Any reasons for avoiding these tasks would be interpreted as excuses. In the process of experimenting with such tasks, Mrs. C. can become aware of the healing effect that caring for others can have on self-preoccupation.

Assigning tasks can help Mrs. C. begin to reevaluate the consequences of living for others versus living to ward off pinworms. Acting as if she is free, for the moment at least, to create something of value for others, even a simple pie, can demonstrate that she indeed has some choice in how she is going to continue living. Ultimately, she will have to confront the choice of whether or not to come off the stage of her limited theater of operations to reengage the world. After so many years of living for her own drama, Mrs. C. may choose to hold onto the security and esteem of being the world's greatest container of pinworms, rather than risk creating a life that might be more useful to others, even if it is a bit more mundane.

Future Directions

Adler was clearly ahead of the learning curve in psychotherapy. His social recasting of Freudian theory predated the evolution of psychodynamic therapy; his task assignments foreshadowed the development of behavioral and other directive therapies; his specific techniques involving imagery and "as if" anticipated the cognitive therapies; and his community outreach and psychoeducational programs foreshadowed contemporary community mental health. Many of Adler's ideas have quietly permeated modern psychological thinking, often without notice. Ellenberger (1970, p. 645) concluded that "it would not be easy to find another author from which so much has been borrowed from all sides without acknowledgment than Adler."

In some cases, success of a psychotherapy system begets more success and popularity. In other cases, success begets gradual disappearance as a distinct system and incorporation by other systems and the public. The fate of Adlerian therapy definitely seems to be following the second track.

The future impact of Adlerian therapy, then, will probably be more indirect than direct. Adler's influence will be represented in the cognitive and behavioral therapies it inspired. His system will be embodied, unknowingly in most instances, in the eclectic and integrative therapies it helped to spawn. The concepts of inferiority complex, superiority strivings, social interest, ideal self, and ordinal position, among others, have been widely incorporated, often without acknowledgment of Adler, into many psychotherapy systems and, indeed, into the public lexicon. Thus incorporated and assimilated, Adlerian therapy may gradually disappear as a distinct orientation as a result of its own success.

The principal direction for Adlerians is to go "on beyond Adler." A special issue of *Individual Psychology* (December 1991, vol. 47, no. 4) with that title contains many articles dedicated to building on Adler's ideas and, concurrently, moving beyond them. Manaster (1987a, 1987b), editor of *Individual Psychology*, has pointed out that the continuing battle over who or what is (or is not) Adlerian has served to fragment Adlerian efforts, to eliminate some who wished to identify themselves as Adlerians, and to exclude and depreciate change in the original theory. What's needed are evolutionary Adlerians who will view Adler as an ancestor but who will do so critically, noting where they think he was essentially correct and where he may have missed the mark (Hartshorne, 1991). This evolution will certainly entail combining Adlerian techniques with those of other systems in a coherent and purposeful brief therapy (Kovacs, 1989; Solis & Brink, 1992) "On beyond Adler" may well become the rallying cry of those who desire to avert the premature disappearance of Alfred Adler's seminal theory as a distinct system of psychotherapy.

Suggestions for Further Reading

Adler, A. (1917). *Study of organ inferiority and its physical compensation*. New York: Nervous and Mental Diseases Publishing.

Adler, A. (1929/1964). *Social interest: A challenge to mankind*. New York: Capricorn.

Adler, A. (1929/1964). *Problems of neurosis*. New York: Harper.

Ansbacher, H. L., & Ansbacher, R. R. (Eds.). (1964). *Superiority and social interest*. New York: Viking.

Dinkmeyer, D. C., Dinkmeyer, D. C., Jr., & Sperry, L. (1990). *Adlerian counseling and psychotherapy* (2nd ed.). Englewood Cliffs, NJ: Prentice Hall.

Dreikurs, R., & Soltz, V. (1964). *Children: The challenge*. New York: Meridith.

Manaster, G. J., & Corsini, R. J. (1982). *Individual psychology*. Itasca, IL: Peacock. Mosak, H., & Shulman, B. (1988). *Life style inventory*. Muncie, IN: Accelerated Development.

Sweeney, T. J. (1998). *Adlerian counseling: A practitioner's approach* (4th ed.). Bristol, PA: Accelerated Development.

Journal: *Individual Psychology: Journal of Adlerian Theory, Research and Practice*.

4

Existential Therapies

Rollo May

MARK HAD BEEN in psychoanalytic therapy for two years, and he had become much more aware of the historical and intrapsychic reasons for his avoiding intimate relationships with women. But now his cherished psychotherapist was leaving town. And now Mark wanted to determine whether he could relate fully to a woman. An existential crisis loomed.

For 20 years since puberty, Mark had exclusively maintained homosexual relationships and had assiduously avoided physical contact with women, except for a single petting experience with a girl when he was 17. He was currently afraid that if he went out with a woman and she wanted to go to bed with him, he would have to try lest she see him as impotent. I confronted him with the fact that he was acting as if he had no choice in determining if and when he would relate sexually to a woman. Just as he respected a woman's freedom to set her limits, so too was he free to set his own limits. He would need to express his honest feelings that if a woman wanted instant sexual intimacy, he was not the person for her.

Mark liked this idea and dated a woman for the first time in 20 years. She was in a hurry. Mark, however, was able to accept this fact as a statement about her and not a put-down of himself. Later he met Leesa through a mutual friend. Leesa liked Mark and agreed with his feelings about their getting to know each other gradually rather than jumping into instant intimacy. For a few months they gradually became more comfortable with each other, including more sexually comfortable. They had not had intercourse yet when they went away to the mountains of Vermont for a New Year's weekend. Mark's supervisor from work and her husband accompanied them. Mark was convinced that both she and her husband believed he was gay. Mark said their jaws hit the floor when they saw how turned on Leesa was with Mark, nibbling at his ears and caressing his body.

When I saw Mark on the Monday after the holiday, he was all smiles and related with delight that he had made love four times with Leesa and each time it was great for both of them. From my heterocentric view, I assumed that psychotherapy was just about over, but Mark soon discovered that he was now confronted with one of the most profound choices of his life. Previously he had never really believed that he could enjoy heterosexual relationships. Now he had, but he had also discovered that for him heterosexuality was not so radically different from his previous homosexual relationships. Mark believed that he had the choice of following a homo-, hetero-, or bisexual style of life. At the same time, he felt frozen by the anxiety of knowing that his future would depend on his free choice and not on past conditioning or intrapsychic conflicts.

A Sketch of Two Early Existential Therapists

Ludwig Binswanger (1881–1966) was one of the first mental health professionals to emphasize the existential nature of the crisis that Mark was experiencing in therapy. Binswanger believed that crises in psychotherapy were usually critical choice points for the people involved. His commitment to a person's freedom to choose in therapy went as far as his acceptance of the suicide of one of his patients, Ellen West, who found death to be her most legitimate alternative (Binswanger, 1958a).

Existentialists, like Binswanger, do not run from the dark side of life. Following the example of Kierkegaard (1954a, 1954b), the Danish philosopher, existentialists are willing to face aspects of life that are awful but meaningful at the same time.

Binswanger had originally struggled to find meaning in madness by translating the experience of patients into psychoanalytic theory. After reading Heidegger's (1962) profound philosophical treatise, *Sein und Zeit* (*Being and Time*), however, Binswanger (1958b) became more existential and phenomenological in his approach to patients. The phenomenological approach enabled Binswanger to face directly the immediate experience of patients, and to understand the meaning of such phenomena in the patient's language rather than in terms of the therapist's abstract theory.

Binswanger began applying his emerging existential ideas in the Sanatarium Bellevue in Kreuglinger, Switzerland, where he succeeded his father as chief medical director in 1911. After interning under the famous psychiatrist Eugen Bleuler, from whom he learned much about the symptoms of schizophrenia, he became increasingly intrigued with understanding the actual structure of existence of the people experiencing psychopathological states. He continued in his work until his retirement in 1956 and his death in 1966 at the age of 85.

Medard Boss (1903–1991), a second early and influential existential psychotherapist, had a career remarkably similar to Binswanger's. Born in Switzerland in 1903, he also worked under Bleuler in Zurich. Like Binswanger, he knew Freud and was heavily influenced by his thinking. Heidegger was his most important influence and, like Binswanger, he was concerned with translating Heidegger's philosophical position into an effective approach to psychotherapy. Boss's particular concern was to integrate the ideas of Heidegger with the methods of Freud, as indicated in the title of his major work, *Daseinanalysis and Psychoanalysis* (1963). Boss worked for many years in the medical school as professor of psychoanalysis at the University of Zurich, which continues to be the European center of *Daseinanalysis* (being-there or existential analysis) even after his 1991 death (Craig, 1988).

Although most existential therapists draw upon the clinical formulations of Binswanger and Boss, neither dominates existentialism the way Freud dominated psychoanalysis or Rogers eclipsed person-centered therapy. One reason is that neither developed a comprehensive system or theory of psychotherapy. Boss, in fact, seems even antitheoretical in a letter to Hall and Lindzey (1970), in which he wrote:

> I can only hope that existential psychology will never develop into a theory in its modern meaning of the natural sciences. All that existential psychology can contribute to psychology is to teach the scientists to remain with the experienced and experienceable facts and phenomena, to let these phenomena tell the scientists their meaning and their references, and so do the encountered objects justice.

Existential therapy has been defined as an attitude that transcends orientation (May, Angel, & Ellenberger, 1958), a dynamic therapy that addresses life's ultimate concerns (Yalom, 1980), or practically any antideterministic psychotherapy (for example, Edwards, 1982). Not surprisingly, then, the existential movement is a diffuse school of theorists and practitioners more aligned in their philosophical emphases than in concrete techniques or practical consequences. Put another way, existential therapy is more a philosophy about psychotherapy than a system of psychotherapy.

Several American psychotherapists have been involved, however, with pulling together the many strands of existentialism into a coherent clinical approach. They combine the philosophical base of existentialism, as enunciated by Søren Kierkegaard, Martin Heidegger, Jean-Paul Sartre, and Martin Buber, among others; the clinical themes of the early existential therapists, principally Binswanger and Boss; and their own therapy experiences and contributions into a recognizable system of psychotherapy. Central among these American systematizers are Rollo May (1958a, 1958b, 1967, 1977, 1981, 1983), James Bugental (1965, 1987, 1990), Irving Yalom (1980), and Ernst Keen (1970), from whose work we will draw in this chapter.

Theory of Personality

Existentialists are uncomfortable with the term *personality* if it implies a fixed set of traits within the individual (Boss, 1983). For them existence is an emerging, a becoming, a process of being that is not fixed or characterized by particular traits. *Being* is a verb form, a participle, implying an active and dynamic process. Nor does existence occur just within the individual, but rather between individuals and their world.

Existence is best understood as *being-in-the-world*. The use of hyphens is the best we can do in English to convey the idea that a person and the environment are an active unity. Existentialists reject the Cartesian dualism that assumes a split between mind and body, experience and environment. Being and world are inseparable, because they are both essentially created by the individual. Phenomenologically, the world we relate to is our own construction that to a greater or lesser extent reflects the construction of others, depending on how conventional we are. For example, a traditional Christian's world includes a Superior Being that can be communicated with, while the atheist's existence contains no such spiritual being. In therapy, a psychoanalyst experiences dynamics in patients that a behaviorist would swear are figments of the Freudian imagination. The behaviorist might argue that eventually we will all respond to the same world once it is defined by the scientific method, but the existentialist argues that the scientific method itself is a human construction, inadequate for understanding the very being that created it. Rather than reconciling differences in world views, the existentialist accepts that to understand a particular human being is to understand the world as that person construes it.

We exist in relation to three levels of our world. In German these are called *Umwelt*, *Mitwelt*, and *Eigenwelt* (Binswanger, 1963; Boss, 1963; May, 1958b). *Umwelt* connotes ourselves in relation to the biological and physical aspects of our world, and we will translate it as being-in-nature. *Mitwelt* refers to the world of persons, the social world; we will call it being-with-others. *Eigenwelt* literally means own-world and refers to the way we reflect upon, evaluate, and experience ourselves; it will be translated as being-for-oneself.

Personalities differ in their ways of existing at each of these three levels of being. Imagine being on a beautiful, secluded beach by the ocean. One person may be afraid to set foot in the ocean because it is the home of sharks waiting to attack, whereas another person dives in eagerly seeking refreshment in the cool waters. One person experiences a desire for a lover in such a sensuous setting, while another feels all alone. One person walks along looking at the nearby land as a golden opportunity for a seaside housing development, whereas another feels sad about the encroachment of houses already under construction nearby. Still others feel at one with the ocean from which all life has come, while someone, somewhere wants to join the ocean to end life.

When *we-are-with-others,* we know that they are conscious beings who can reflect upon us, evaluate us, and judge us. This may cause us to fear others and want to run from them. We may choose to clam up or to talk only about superfluous topics like the weather lest we reveal something about ourselves that others would dislike. Frequently we anticipate what others are thinking or feeling about us, and we guide our observable behavior in order to have a favorable impact on them. This is the way, unfortunately, we typically are with others, a level of existence known as *being-for-others.* This mode of existence is similar to Reisman's (1961) characterization of the modern personality as other-directed.

Fortunately, there are precious times with special others in which we can let ourselves be, whether we are silly or sad, anxious or mad, without having to worry about what the other person is thinking about us. When we are *being-for-ourselves,* we are the ones who are reflecting upon, evaluating, or judging our own existence. Because self-reflection can be very painful at times, we may choose not to be introspective. Or we may choose to think about ourselves only after having a few drinks or a few joints to deaden the pain somewhat. Or we may become incessantly introspective and have difficulty with being at the other two levels of existence. For existentialists, however, the risk of pain or self-preoccupation is the price we may have to pay to achieve the considered, conscious life that is so important in creating a healthy existence.

In the process of trying to create a healthy existence, we are faced with the dilemma of choosing the best way to be in-nature, with-others, and for-ourselves. With the emergence of consciousness, we realize how ambiguous the world is and how open it is to different interpretations. In this book alone, we are considering over a dozen different interpretations that could serve as guides for interpreting the natural, social, and personal aspects of our world. What is the existential alternative for living? The best alternative is not necessarily to choose to maximize reinforcements and minimize punishments, as some behaviorists would suggest, or to adapt our instinctual desires to the demands of our environment, as some Freudians would suggest.

The best alternative is to be authentic. For the existentialists, *authenticity* is its own reward. An authentic existence brings with it an openness to nature, to others, and to ourselves, because we have decided to meet the world straight on without hiding it from us or us from it. Openness means that authentic individuals are much more aware, because they have chosen not to hide anything from themselves. An authentic existence also brings the freedom to be spontaneous with others, because we do not have to fear that we might reveal something about ourselves that contradicts what we have pretended to be. A healthy existence brings with it an awareness that any relationship we do have is authentic and that if anyone cares about us, it is really us they care about and not some facade constructed on their behalf. Authentic relationships allow us to truly trust others because we know they will be honest about their experience and not tell us what they think we want to hear.

An authentic existence is healthy in part because the three levels of our being are integrated, or in-joint, rather than in conflict. We experience ourselves as together: the way we are in nature is the way we present ourselves to others and also the way we know who we are. We do not get caught up in idealizing images about ourselves that prevent us from being intimate with others lest they tell us what we do not want to hear. Nor do we get so preoccupied with ourselves that we cannot get involved in the world around us. A healthy existence, then, involves a simultaneous and harmonious relationship to each level of being without emphasizing one level at the expense of others, such as sacrificing our self-evaluation for the approval of others.

With authenticity promising so much, why don't we all choose to be authentic? Why do so many of us seem to have the inner terror that if other people really knew us they wouldn't want to be with us? Why does the other-directed personality seem to be the stereotype of our time? What is the dread that comes with being more fully aware of ourselves and our world?

The theologian Paul Tillich (1952) outlined certain conditions inherent in existence that tempt us to run from too much awareness. These conditions fill us with a dread called *existential anxiety*. The first source of anxiety comes with our acute awareness that at some unknown time we must die: being implies *nonbeing*. Death may be denied by our culture, including psychology, as not being particularly relevant to life, yet the fact that our total existence will end in nothingness can make us shudder. When we are honest, we are also aware that our most significant others can die at any time, ending not only their existence but also the part of our being that was intimately connected with them.

Many summers ago my wife and I were swimming with our young son and daughter in a salt pond near the ocean. A woman came over to borrow a paper cup, and when she turned around she immediately realized that her 4-year-old son was missing. She was convinced he was in the water, so we began diving and diving and diving. The more we dove the more anxious we became, hoping we would find him, then gradually hoping that we wouldn't. Two hours later, when the fire department pulled him out of the deepest waters where no one expected him to be, all we could do was shudder and hold each other close.

Once we become conscious beings, we are aware that inherent in existence is a necessity-to-act. We must make decisions that will profoundly affect the rest of our lives, such as where we go to school, what career we choose, if and whom we choose to marry, and whether or not we have children. We must act, and yet in modern times, we are less and less certain about the basis for deciding. We cannot know beforehand with any degree of certainty how our decisions will turn out, and so we are continually under the threat of being profoundly guilty. We must make decisions in relative ignorance of their ramifications, knowing that we will hurt people regularly without intending to.

In critical choices, we alone are responsible. Inherent in our responsibility is the anxiety of knowing that we will make serious mistakes, but not knowing whether this choice is one of those mistakes. For example, when I (JOP) was originally deciding whether or not to spend a year of my life writing the first edition of this book, I was quite anxious that such a decision might be a miserable mistake and might lead me to avoid other attractive pursuits. (Some of you may now believe that I had good reason to be anxious!)

The threat of *meaninglessness* is another contingency of human existence that produces anxiety. In our orientation to life, we want to see what we do as meaningful. The particular meaning may vary from love for one person, to sex for another, to faith for still another. But when we honestly reflect on ourselves and begin to question the significance of our existence, the issue becomes whether life itself means anything. We can rarely go to the theater or a modern museum or read a current novel without being confronted with this issue. For many of us, what we once believed in—our former religions, our former politics, or our former therapies—no longer seem as significant as they once did. This suggests that our current source of meaning may also disappear. All therapists see formerly vital marriages that have become entirely devitalized, with nothing left but deadly boredom. We see people trapped in previously gratifying jobs that are now nothing more than a means of structuring time, ruts that lead nowhere. Our clients become anxious, and so do we.

Part of our anxiety comes from knowing that we are the ones who created the meaning in our lives, and we are the ones who let it die. Therefore, we must be the ones to continue to create a life worth living.

The prospect that existence has no significance whatsoever can be terrifying. The conclusion that one's existence is totally absurd can be immobilizing. This immobilization is exemplified by the main character in John Barth's (1967) *The End of the Road*. If there is no meaning in life, then there is no basis on which to make a decision, so he could not act. His therapist had the ingenious solution that because nothing mattered, he could do just as well by applying arbitrary principles when faced with the necessity to act. His principles for living included alphabeticity and sinistrality: when confronted with a choice in life, he would choose the option that began with the first letter of the alphabet or the option on the left.

Our *isolation*, our fundamental *aloneness* in the universe, is another condition of life that brings anxiety (Bugental, 1965). Regardless of how intimate I am with others, I can never be them, nor can they be me. We share experiences, but we are always under the threat of never totally understanding each other. Furthermore, we know that choosing to follow our unique direction and create our own meaning in life may lead to others' not wanting to be with us. The possibility of such rejection brings forth the anxiety of being literally alone.

These multiple sources of existential anxiety attest to the defining characteristic of the human condition: *finiteness*. Death reflects the finiteness of our time; accidents represent the limits of our power; anxiety over decisions, the inadequacy of our knowledge; the threat of meaninglessness, the finiteness of our values; isolation, the finiteness of our empathy; and rejection, the finiteness of control over another human being.

These contingencies of life have also been called the realm of *nonbeing*. These givens are matters of necessity—we must die, we must act—and hence are a negation of being, which is by definition open-ended and in the realm of possibility. Nonbeing is the ground against which the figure of being is created. Death is the ground that accents the figure of life in bold relief. Chance is the ground that determines the limits of our choice. Meaninglessness is the ground against which meaning can be seen. And isolation is the ground from which intimacy emerges. The figure of our being is conscious, chosen, and free, whereas the realm of nonbeing is without light, closed, and necessary. In daily living, we experience being as our "subjectness," in which we are the active subject or agent in directing our own lives; nonbeing is experienced as our "objectness," in which we are objects determined by forces other than our will.

Authentic being survives to the extent that it takes nonbeing into itself. It perishes to the extent that it attempts to affirm itself by avoiding nonbeing. Our self as a conscious, choosing, and open subject can *be* only through confronting and surviving the anxiety of existence. To avoid existential anxiety is to avoid nonbeing in its various forms. To avoid choice and its anxiety, for example, is to fail to be a choosing subject. An authentic personality is aware that existence is a constant flow from nonbeing into being and back into nonbeing again. This can be seen most clearly in the overall course of our existence, as we come from the darkness of having never been, live in the light of consciousness, and then return to the darkness of death. Our daily cycle is similar, as our present existence emerges from the yesterday that no longer exists into the being of the present and thrusts into the unconscious nonbeing of tomorrow. This is why authentic being is said to occur only in the present.

Theory of Psychopathology

Lying is the foundation of psychopathology. Lying is the only way we can flee from nonbeing, to not allow existential anxiety into our experience. When confronted with nonbeing, such as the drowning of the 4-year-old boy, we have two choices: to be anxious or to lie. We may choose to lie by telling ourselves that if we keep a constant eye on our family, we can prevent accidents. We hold close our children and our spouse, and when they are in sight we feel relaxed. The lie has worked. We have avoided an encounter with the existential anxiety of accidents, but nonbeing is always there, threatening to emerge into our consciousness. Lying always leads to a closing off of part of our world; in this case, we must close off any thoughts about the man who slipped right in front of his family and broke his neck. Consciousness of such events not only brings existential anxiety but also threatens to expose our lie.

Lying also leads to *neurotic anxiety*. If we become anxious, for example, just because our children are momentarily out of sight, we are experiencing neurotic anxiety. Neurotic anxiety is an inauthentic response to being, whereas existential anxiety is an honest response to nonbeing. Our children's leaving our sight is essential to many expressions of their own being; they do not exist to shore up our lies. We decide that they need to be in sight in order for us to be more comfortable; they decide to be away from us in order to exist more fully and freely. We choose our lies, however, and are stuck with the consequences. The consequence now is that unless we are aware of our family at all times, we are anxious. Like a mother I saw in therapy, we may have to have our children play in the living room at all times. We may choose to walk them to and from school, to go see them at recess and lunch time, or be anxious. We may call our spouse repeatedly on the phone pretending to have something to say but wanting only to be reassured that our spouse is well. If we try not to call, the anxiety may become extremely intense, and we tell ourselves we have no choice—we must call.

When neurotic anxiety leads to the decision that we must act on that anxiety, we develop symptoms of psychopathology, such as a compulsion to check on our family. By saying that we must check on our family, we have become an object that no longer has the choice to let our family be. Symptoms of psychopathology are in fact *objectifications* of ourselves. In the area of our pathology, we experience ourselves as objects without will. This can be terrifying, like the nightmares in which we are being chased by someone and want to run, but no matter how hard we will it, we cannot run. We are trapped as a consequence of our own lies.

Psychopathology is also characterized by an overemphasis on one level of being at the expense of other levels of being. In this case, there is an overemphasis on being-with-others—namely, our family—at the expense of being-in-nature or being-for-oneself. We must be-with-others lest we become filled with neurotic anxiety.

Lying can occur at any level of existence. There are many examples of lying-in-nature. Many people pretend that their biological drives control their lives rather than accept the responsibility for finding healthy expressions for their natural desires. These people tell themselves they must eat and eat and eat or they must drink, must smoke, must rape. There are some theories of therapy, such as psychoanalysis, that support such a biological objectification of humanity. However, we are the ones who choose to believe such a myth about ourselves.

Hypochondriacs lie about the nature of illness and healing. They fabricate a theory that diseases of nature can be avoided if only they see the doctor often enough and fast enough. Their bodies are constant sources of anxiety that send them scurrying to a doctor with every ache and twitch. "If only I run soon enough, I can outsmart nature at her games of chance," they lie. After convincing themselves they must run, trying not to run fills their being with neurotic anxiety. They have given up their will to their aches and their medicine man. "You take over, doctor," they seem to say. "This business of living is too scary for me." Lying-in-nature drastically reduces their freedom to be-with-others or to be-for-themselves, because all they can talk about or think about is their most recent attack of this or that.

Some people of a paranoid persuasion decide that nature is filled with evil forces out to destroy them. There is poison in the food, the water, or the air, so we must constantly beware. Others of a more manic temperament can make nature into an all-loving universe; they thrust themselves into space, seeking a universal orgasm. Some people fighting off depression can conclude that it is the world that is falling apart, the world that is going to the dogs. The good old days are gone forever, and it is only downhill from here.

Perhaps the most common level of lying is for others. Early in life, we learn that we can misrepresent ourselves to others with some success. As children we are smart enough to see that the option to lie can be a tremendous source of power. How to influence others by faking sad or mad or innocent, depending on their weak spot, is a lesson not missed by many. But, of course, every lie is accompanied by fear of discovery and the shame of being caught in a lie by others. Over the years, the impending shame builds and leaves us feeling that if people really knew what we are they would leave us alone. So we spend much of our time lying-for-others, seldom free to be-with-others.

Some slaves brag of their ability to lie-to-others. Selling themselves, they call it—the royal road to success. People want them to smile, they smile; people want their egos built up, they build. The other people may be the customer, the boss, or the professor—same difference. These people have the tokens, and if they buy the liar's act, everyone is happy. The liars are happy to sell themselves—a small price for success, they think. The lie up their sleeves, of course, is that someday they will be free to be themselves. They promise themselves that when they get their PhD, then they will really live their own lives—or maybe they better wait until they'd get their first job, or tenure, or that final promotion, or that new position.

But can this be pathological? we ask. It is so common, so natural. The ability to delay gratification, even the gratification of being ourselves, is a necessary part of succeeding in society. The ability to play roles is essential for making it in the academic or mental health marketplaces. Those elitist European existentialists would reserve health for only the authentic few. But what they really ask is that we not become so alienated that we equate statistically normal self-estrangement with health. If we are going to compromise ourselves away for others, then let us at least remain healthy enough to hurt about it, rather than hide behind the data that show we all do it to some extent.

Lying-for-ourselves is more complicated. First, we must consciously choose to lie; then at some point, usually beginning when we are children, we come to believe our own lies. For years I (JOP) believed that I never got angry. I became depressed all right, but never angry. When I finally got tired of getting depressed, I became aware in therapy that I could indeed get angry. To protect my idealized image of myself as a character who never lost his cool, I had to close off most of my feelings and be cold and depressed, but never angry.

The psychoanalysts would say that I was unconsciously repressing my anger. But the existentialists argue that in order to close off the "bad" parts of ourselves like anger, we have to first know that the anger is "bad." Otherwise, we have an image of an ego that is like a conscious person within a person, and the ego decides that the anger is bad and must be repressed. Sartre (1956) argues that all we need to assume is one conscious person who uses self-deception and chooses what aspects of the self to turn away from. Once we act on such *bad faith* in ourselves, we are faced with the impending guilt of knowing who we really are; as a result, our lying snowballs into symptoms, such as having to get depressed in order to never be angry.

Lying-for-oneself can occur in a wide range of pathologies. Some individuals can flee the anxieties of finitude by deceiving themselves into believing they are God. One man was so convinced that he was Christ that he persuaded his 6-year-old son that he must die during his 33rd year. So on Good Friday, his son shot him.

Many people are convinced they can attain perfection—be beyond criticism and, therefore, free from rejection—if they only work harder. So they become workaholics. Others protect their saintly self-concepts by turning their backs on their sexuality, modeling the Virgin Mary. Still others are convinced they are the perfect spouse and yet are afraid to come in for marital therapy. They send their partner. Once the doctor straightens out their spouse, their marriage can be perfect again.

In the process of lying, people construct a phenomenal world that may seem to be a house of cards but is very real to them nonetheless. Understanding their pathology involves an empathy for their world, including the basic psychological categories of time, space, and causality.

Keen (1970) cites several forms of time that occur quite frequently in pathological reactions. A *deteriorating future* is one in which a person feels that life and the world are on a downhill course. Deterioration is the eventual outcome for all objects, and the phenomenon of their own future filled with deterioration reflects how much of an object they have become. A *status-striving future* is characteristic of people who promise themselves that someday they will really live. In the process of saving their money, their time, or their being for the future, they are unable to exist in any authentic way. They act as if meaning will come from objects outside themselves, such as material possessions, degrees, or status positions, rather than from the scary but free decisions that emerge from within. A *fantastic future* involves wishing that someday things will be different: a rich spouse will come along and endow us with wealth, or a terrific therapist will reawaken us with a magic wand. This fantasy negates the continuous flow of time in which our present grows out of our past decisions and actions and our future emerges out of commitments we make right now. Keen does not mention the pathological pasts that many patients live in, but certainly the *omnipresent past* is one of the most common time zones for troubled people. Such past-tense living frequently reflects the dreaded regrets that people have over mistakes they have made. They hold onto the past as if they believe the childhood rule that "slips go over"—that they can take back a previous decision rather than accept that their errors have hurt, but need not halt, their personal development.

Spatial relations differ not only for brain-damaged patients but for all people. Some patients always keep their distance, which reflects how far away they feel from almost everyone. In some marriages, we find spouses so egocentric that they fill the vital space of their home, leaving little room for their partner's identity to emerge. Other people find that the object closest to them is the bar or the refrigerator, which is just a sigh away. Still others live in a clouded space, darkened by depression or distorted by drugs. This notion of a personal space has drifted into lay language, so that people may declare what a "bad space" they're in today or may check with their friends on where they are "at" today.

Concepts of causality also vary on a personal basis. What we believe causes our future critically affects how we act today. If we are overly objective, we may lose any basis on which to choose, and experience ourselves as being tossed and turned by the wind. Through lying, we may lose contact with the source of our personal direction, our *intentionality*. Intentionality is the creation of meaning, the basis of our identity. Sartre (1967) wrote that "man is nothing else but what he makes of himself. Such is the first principle of existentialism."

Our intentionality involves taking a stand in life. Our stance determines what we attend to—as when one person attends to the beauty of a beach while another person attends to its business potential. The posture or orientation we choose in life is the source of what our lives mean, and the source of the meaning we attribute to a beach. Lying, however, may convince us that our life is determined by a pathology that attacks us like an infectious illness—an accident over which we have no control.

Theory of Therapeutic Processes

Because lying is the source of psychopathology, honesty is the solution for dissolving symptoms. With authenticity as the goal of existential psychotherapy, increasing consciousness becomes one of the critical processes through which people become aware of the aspects of the world and of themselves that have been closed off by lying. Because lying also leads to an objectification of oneself in which the ability to choose is no longer experienced, therapy must involve processes through which individuals can again come to experience themselves as subjects or agents capable of directing their own lives through an increase in choosing.

Techniques are slighted in existential therapy because technology is an objectifying process in which the therapist as subject decides the best means by which to change the patient as object. While many patients want their therapists to fix them as a mechanic repairs a car, a technical focus can only add to the problem of patients' experiencing themselves as mechanical objects. The emphasis in existentialism is to encourage clients to enter into an authentic relationship with a therapist and thereby become increasingly aware of themselves as subjects, free to differ with the therapist even to the point of choosing at any time when treatment will end. Although technique is deemphasized, we shall see that in practice the classical existentialists, such as Binswanger, Boss, and May, draw heavily upon psychoanalytic techniques, especially in the early stages of therapy.

Consciousness Raising

The Client's Work. If the explicit direction in psychoanalysis is to say whatever comes to mind, the implicit direction in existentialism is to be whatever you want to be. Patients are allowed to present themselves as they typically would relate to the world, with little intervention from the therapist early in therapy. Existentialists share the analytic assumption that patients will repeat their previous patterns of relating and will begin to form transference relationships. While psychoanalysts assume that the transference is due to instinctual fixations, existentialists see it as a result of the patients' objectification of themselves, which keeps them from being flexible and open to new and more authentic ways of being-in-the-world-of-therapy. Patients will impose their psychological categories onto therapy, so that if, for example, their experience of space with-others is a distant space, they will keep their distance from the therapist. If a patient's time is the omnipresent past, then the patient will talk in therapy primarily about the past.

Gradually patients are encouraged to engage in a process similar to free association but perhaps more appropriately called *free experiencing*. Here patients are encouraged to express freely and honestly whatever they are experiencing in the present, although traditionally such "free" expression has in fact been limited to expression through language, not action. In trying to freely experience, patients can become increasingly conscious that they are repeating the same patterns of being, such as being-in-the-past or in the fantastic future. They can become aware that there are parts of themselves and their world that they are not open to experiencing or expressing—for instance, their angry self or the reality of the therapist.

Patients will ordinarily try to maneuver the therapist into agreeing with their reasons for closing off such experiences, but since the reasons are lies, they will run into disagreement with the authenticity of the therapist. For example, in saying "Don't you agree that it is immature to get angry?" the patient is pressuring the therapist for validation, but may instead meet with an honest response such as "No, I get angry at times, and I don't feel like a baby."

Eventually the patient is encouraged to change from a more egocentric experiencing of the process and person of the psychotherapy to a more authentic dialogue. By the time the client is able to enter into an ongoing dialogue, however, therapy is ready for termination.

The Therapist's Work. Unfortunately, classical existentialists have not made clear the methods they use to increase the consciousness of clients. As with personality, many existentialists view existentialism as the philosophy they embrace in therapy and not as a system they use. As a result, many existentialists would oppose a systematic approach to therapy as contrary to an authentic encounter between the participants.

From the writings of Binswanger (1963), Boss (1963), Keen (1970), and May (1958a), however, we do get some idea of the variety of strategies traditional existentialists use in therapy. They seem to agree that the therapist's work begins with understanding the phenomenal world of the patient. The *phenomenological method* focuses on the immediacy of experience, the perception of experience, the meaning of that experience, and observation with a minimum of a priori biases (Spiegelberg, 1972). The therapist attempts to experience the patient's unique construal of the world without imposing any theoretical or personal preconceptions onto the patient's experience. In understanding the patient's phenomenological world, most existentialists seem to use a *clarification* type of feedback through which they more fully illuminate the patient's experience, using the patient's own language rather than any theoretical language. Such illuminating feedback helps patients to become more conscious of their being, including some aspects that have been closed off.

Once the therapist has gained a phenomenal understanding of the patient, the therapist chooses what techniques to follow. As Rollo May (1909–1994), one of the fathers of American existential psychotherapy, states, therapeutic technique follows understanding, in contrast to the more common reverse order in which a clinician tries to understand a patient via the therapist's preferred theory and techniques. Existentialists vary most at this step. Some, such as Boss (1963) and Bugental (1965), rely mainly on interpretation to analyze or make conscious the patient's transference reactions or repeated patterns of being. Although Boss and Bugental use psychoanalytic explanations of the patient's reactions when they fit, they also rely heavily on existential explanations, such as pointing out how the patient repeatedly runs from experiences related to death, decisions, or other aspects of nonbeing.

Other traditional existentialists seem to prefer a type of *confrontation,* in which the information they provide the patient is generated by the therapist's genuine reaction to the patient. Existential confrontation differs from psychoanalytic confrontation in that existentialists reveal their own experience of the patient and do not just reflect the patient's experience. The existentialist is by no means concerned with remaining a blank screen, as the analyst is, because it is the honest feedback from the existentialist's experience that is seen as most able to grate up against and eventually break through the patient's closed world.

An example of such confrontation occurred when my (JOP's) wife, Jan, and I were conducting conjoint therapy with a couple in which the husband was complaining that his wife was refusing to have sex with him. At one intense point when the man insisted on dominating and degrading his wife, Jan told him, "You make me want to vomit." He was beside himself; he did not respond. He just fumed and the next morning came to see me individually, declaring that no woman had ever responded to him like that before. He couldn't imagine why, especially when the woman was a therapist. As I encouraged him to consider that maybe at times he stirred up similar feelings in his wife but she was afraid to express them because of his anger, he began to think that maybe, just maybe, he had something to do with his wife's feeling sick when he approached her sexually. His idealized image of himself had been shaken by Jan's intense confrontation, and he tried to shore up his lies by pressuring me into agreeing that a responsible therapist doesn't talk like that. When I encouraged him to face Jan's honest feedback, his lying-for-himself began to come out into the open, and he began to see himself as the not-so-perfect man who perhaps had real trouble in being-with-women and not just with his "selfish" wife.

Although therapy may begin with interpretations, in order for it to become existential, the therapist must eventually confront the patient with the therapist's own authentic being. If the therapist cannot be authentic, the patient may remain in a transference relationship, and this may be the reason psychoanalysis seems interminable. How can a patient be authentic with the therapist if the analyst remains an objectified blank screen?

By being authentic the therapist allows an encounter to develop, which is a new relationship that opens up new horizons rather than a transference relationship that repeats the past (Ellenberger, 1958). Patients may continually try to freeze the therapist into the categories of their pathological world—keeping the therapist distant or casting her as a controlling authority figure, for instance. By being authentic, the therapist refuses to be frozen. By remaining authentic in the face of the patient's demands, the therapist confronts the patient, both verbally and experientially, with the patient's attempts at freezing the therapist and thereby keeping the patient frozen as a role or a symptom. Gradually the patient becomes aware that the therapist is taking risks to be honest and sees that the therapist can remain authentic in the face of such existential anxieties as being rejected by the patient or making mistakes. The patient becomes aware of a new alternative for being and is then confronted with the choice of changing his or her existence.

Choosing

The Client's Work. Clients are confronted with the burden of choosing from the very beginning of therapy, when they must decide whether they will commit themselves to working with this particular person. Patients are also confronted with having to decide what they will talk about in therapy and how they will be in therapy. The therapist will encourage clients to consider new alternatives for being, such as new alternatives for relating to a sexually turned-off wife, but the clients are expected to carry the burden of creating new alternatives in order for them to experience themselves as subjects capable of finding new directions for living. Once conscious of new alternatives, it is the client who must experience and exist with the anxiety of being responsible for which alternative to follow. The burden of choosing, then, is clearly on the client.

This burden is perhaps most evident when clients are faced with what Ellenberger (1958) calls *kairos*, which are the critical choice points in therapy at which a client is faced with deciding whether to risk changing a fundamental aspect of existence, such as to be homosexual or heterosexual or bisexual, to be separate or married, to remain in the security of symptoms or to enter the anxiety of authenticity. The clients are the ones who must look deep into themselves to see if they can muster up the courage to leap into the unknown future, knowing there is no guarantee that they will not fall flat on their faces. As an existential friend (Atayas, 1977) puts it, once clients become conscious that at least one person can be authentic, then they no longer have the choice of being a slave who is blind to better alternatives. The patient must now choose between being a coward and becoming a free person.

The Therapist's Work. The existential therapist takes every opportunity to clarify the choices that patients continually confront in their treatment, whether the choice pertains to what they should talk about each hour, how they should structure their relationship to the therapist, or whether they will return for future sessions. With such clarification, the patient becomes acutely conscious of being a subject in spite of frequent protestations about being a patient, a helpless victim of psychopathology. The therapist also encourages patients to use their uniquely human processes of consciousness—their imagination, intellect, and judgment—to create rational alternatives to an apparently irrational way of being.

The therapist will remain with patients throughout their small choices and their kairos, empathizing with their anxiety and their turmoil but knowing that the road to being an authentic subject rather than an objective symptom is basically a lonely one on which the patient alone must take responsibility for the choices that are made. To jump in and rescue the patient, no matter how much the patient pulls on the therapist's rescue fantasies, would be to reinforce the lie that patients by definition are inadequate to direct their own lives.

Keen (1970, p. 200) provides the following excellent example of an existential therapist confronting a patient both with the responsibility she has for choosing to change and with the boring way that she is being.

PATIENT: I don't know why I keep coming here. All I do is tell you the same thing over and over. I'm not getting anywhere. (Patient complaining that therapist isn't curing her; maintenance of self-as-therapist's-object.)

DOCTOR: I'm getting tired of hearing the same thing over and over, too. (Therapist refusing to take responsibility for the progress of therapy and refusing to fulfill patient's expectations that he cure her; refusal of patient-as-therapist's-object.)

PATIENT: Maybe I'll stop coming. (Patient threatening therapist; fighting to maintain role as therapist's object.)

DOCTOR: It's certainly your choice. (Therapist refusing to be intimidated; forcing patient-as-subject.)

PATIENT: What do you think I should do? (Attempt to seduce the therapist into role of subject who objectifies patient.)

DOCTOR: What do you want to do? (Forcing again.)

PATIENT: I want to get better. (Plea for therapist to cure her.)

DOCTOR: I don't blame you. (Refusing role of subject curer and supporting desire on part of patient-as-subject.)

PATIENT: If you think I should stay, okay, I will. (Refusing role of subject-who-decides.)

DOCTOR: You want me to tell you to stay? (Confrontation with patient's evasion of the decision and calling attention to how the patient is construing the therapy.)

PATIENT: You know what's best; you're the doctor. (Patient's confirmation of her construing therapy.)

DOCTOR: Do I act like a doctor?

Keen does not mention it, but if in fact the therapist acts like a doctor or some other authority figure who will cure the patient, then the therapist is lost. The patient's construal of therapy as a doctor-object relationship would be accurate, rather than a lie that allows her to run from her necessity-to-act as a responsible subject. With the therapist being authentic, however, this is neither a game nor a form of combat. It is an honest confrontation between one person who experiences the potential of the other to choose and the other's desire to shore up the lie that she is not really capable of choosing.

Therapeutic Content

Existentialism is a relatively comprehensive theory of existence that is concerned with the individual at all four levels of personal functioning. Being-for-oneself is focused on intrapersonal functioning; being-with-others is the existential concept for interpersonal functioning; being-in-the-world includes, but is more than, the individual's relationship to society; and the search for authenticity reflects the goal of existentialists to go beyond conflict to fulfillment.

Intrapersonal Conflicts

Anxiety and Defenses. Anxiety is an ontological characteristic of every person, rooted in our very existence as a threat of nonbeing. The acceptance of freedom and the awareness of finitude will unavoidably result in anxiety, or as Kierkegaard called it, the dizziness of freedom. Anxiety is not something we have, but something we are (May, 1977).

The existential approach retains Freud's basic dynamic structure but has a radically different content. The old Freudian formula of "instinctual drive produces anxiety which produces defense mechanisms" is replaced in existential therapy by "awareness of ultimate concerns produces anxiety which produces defense mechanisms" (Yalom, 1980). Accordingly, much of the focus is on the conflicts within the individual between the existential anxieties that are inherent in being and the lies that individuals use as defenses against such anxieties. As with psychoanalysis, anxiety is a central concept in existential therapy, but anxiety is viewed as a natural consequence of becoming conscious of nonbeing. Rather than approach anxiety gradually in therapy, existentialists frequently confront it head on, especially during the periods of kairos. The only solution to existential anxiety is that suggested by Tillich (1952) in *The Courage to Be*: we must find courage within ourselves to accept existential anxiety as part of the price we pay for being uniquely human. In return, we can gain the excitement of being a unique human being.

Since existential anxiety is a consequence of consciousness, the only defense against it is conscious lying—turning our attention away from threats of nonbeing by pretending to be something we are not, such as immortal, omnipotent, omniscient, or anything other than finite humans. We can give different names to different forms of lying if we prefer. Projection would be the lie that the responsibility for particular experiences belongs outside of us. Denial would be the lie of insisting that either we or the world are not what we honestly know them to be.

Over time, these and other defenses can become an unconscious and habitual part of our objectified selves. But defenses can remain frozen only if we continue to run from the anguish of being more open and authentic. Lying-for-others can succeed, for example, only when our lies are hidden from others. Choosing to let others, such as a therapist, become aware of our pretenses removes the power inherent in lying. Likewise, for lies to work on ourselves, we must continue to pretend that we are not lying. To confront or be confronted with our lying-for-ourselves frees us from the need to be something we are not.

Self-Esteem. In spite of what many behavioral scientists might say, self-esteem is not a function of how much other people value us. That is social esteem. If we make the same mistake as many behavioral scientists and base our self-esteem on social esteem, then we are reduced to being-for-others, which usually includes lying-for-others in order to win or maintain their approval. The fact that researchers report high correlations between how we value ourselves and how others value us may just support Reisman's (1961) theory that we have indeed become an other-directed society.

An inner-directed person accepts that self-esteem occurs at the level of being-for-oneself and as a function of self-evaluation. An authentic person accepts that approval by oneself must come above approval by others. To strive to be free from what others think of us is romantic nonsense. We can be free, however, by caring more about what we think of ourselves than about what others think of us. When we are honest with ourselves, we know that we can feel genuinely good about ourselves only when we are genuine.

An existential therapist is not concerned with boosting a patient's shaky self-esteem. For example, if a patient becomes depressed over living an empty life, the therapist might say something along the lines of "It's natural that you are depressed. I would be worried about you if you could feel good about the way you've been living." The existentialist knows that all a therapist can do is boost a patient's social esteem through such measures as unconditional positive regard and positive reinforcements. In doing so, however, the therapist risks reinforcing the patient to remain a pigeon of other people—in this case, the therapist's pigeon. Self-esteem is the hard-earned natural response that patients can make only to themselves after struggling to be authentic.

Responsibility. Much has already been said about the centrality of responsibility in existential therapy. We have seen how, in the process of choosing to be authentic, individuals are confronted with the existential anxiety of being responsible for who they become. We should also point out that to choose against authenticity—to lie, to conform, to cop out—makes us responsible for missing an opportunity to be ourselves, and we are faced with existential guilt (May, 1958a). Existential guilt is a consequence of having sinned against ourselves. If our lives become essentially inauthentic—whether obviously pathological, as with the neurotic or psychotic, or normally pathological, as with the conventional conformist—we may at some time find ourselves faced with an overwhelming neurotic guilt. Neurotic guilt is a more total self-condemnation for having abdicated our responsibility to become a genuine human being and not just a ghost of a person. Such self-condemnation can be so intense that some individuals may want to destroy their lives without having really existed.

Guilt if we choose against ourselves; anxiety if we choose for ourselves; with no guarantee that we will create something of value in our one short life—no wonder Sartre has said that we are "condemned to be free." A patient comes to turn over some of the burden of lies to a therapist, and the existentialist insists that the patient be strong enough to become more responsible and hence freer and more authentic.

Interpersonal Conflicts

Intimacy and Sexuality. Being intimate with others is an integral part of being human. The existential ideal for intimacy is poetically expressed in Buber's (1958) book, *I and Thou.* Intimate relationships involve the caring and sharing of what is most central in the lives of two authentic people. Although this is the ideal, the reality is that all too many people feel safe to relate only to objectified others and are able to enter only into I–it relationships. Perhaps even more frequently, the interactions of two objectified people result in it–it relationships, which are at best two human objects relating as roles with each other. Such relationships are safe, predictable, and most efficient, but are devoid of giving or receiving anything unique to the two people involved. Any two people or even two robots could fill the roles, and it would make no essential difference to the relationship.

Sexuality is less of an issue for existentialists than is intimacy. The assumption seems to be that if individuals are free to be intimate, they will be free to be sexual if that is what they choose. Sexual conflicts are considered to the extent that it is the person's sexuality that has been disowned or idealized in the process of self-objectification. In contrast to what psychoanalysts believe, sexuality is certainly not seen as the essence of humanity. It is bad faith to say either that we must be sexual or that we cannot be sexual. We can be sexually free, which means the freedom to say yes to our own sexuality when we believe it is best to say yes, and the freedom to say no to our sexuality when it is best for us to say no. It is only in response to our highly repressive culture, which has traditionally said no to sexuality, that we have adopted a perverted notion that sexual freedom means saying only yes. Existential sexual therapy would include helping people to be free to say no in sexual relationships, whether to the demands of a spouse or to some internal calendar that says you are falling behind the national average of a couple of times a week. Existential sexual therapy would be better described as sensual therapy, with clients encouraged to experience their whole body as sensual beings who enjoy touching and being touched from head to toe and not just genital to genital.

Communication. Existentialists suggest that conflicts in communication are almost inherent in our isolation. Because we can never enter directly the experience of another, we can never know fully what the other is attempting to communicate. Our own perspective is bound to do some violence to what the other is communicating; therefore, we again experience some existential guilt over our inability to fully be-with-others. Such guilt need not lead to withdrawal from others, but can motivate us to be more sensitive so that we do the least damage possible to another's experience. Guilt can also help us to be authentically humble as we recognize that, no matter how hard we try, we can never be smart enough or sensitive enough to know just what the other is experiencing. We cannot sit back smugly as we listen and say, "I know, I know, the same thing happened to me"—because it never did.

Problems in communication are inevitable also because of the meager way in which language reflects experience. Experience is so much richer than the abstraction that words usually relay. It is no wonder that existentialists sound like poets or novelists when they attempt to communicate the most significant experiences of themselves or their clients. The meagerness of words and the isolation of persons are no excuses, however, for a therapy or a science of humans to try to omit experience from the realm of understanding. Communication through the medium of words can still present a rich enough picture of an individual's experience if the receiver drops theoretical decoders and listens with the openness of a trained phenomenologist.

Hostility. To experience hostility is to experience the threat of nonbeing, because hostility is one of the quickest and surest means to end the being of ourself or another. This hostility can elicit existential anxiety and drive us to lie and tell ourselves or others we never get angry. The repression that follows can lead to our being unwilling to enter into intense relationships with others because such relationships are always potentially frustrating and thus may lead to hostility. To close off our aggression can also lead to feelings of depression and emptiness as we close off one of our body's sources of vital assertions.

Just as we lie if we say we cannot get angry, so too we lie if we say we cannot control our hostility. Some choose to be hostile in order to deny their finitude so they can be God and decide who will live and who will die. Once they tell themselves lies, they are free to be possessed by the power of violence, the power to end an existence. The people they choose to destroy will be people who threaten to remind them of their nonbeing, such as by rejecting them. The killer says, in effect, "You cannot reject me if you no longer exist." Favorite targets for violence are people like Jesus Christ, John F. Kennedy, Martin Luther King, Jr., and Malcolm X, who are threats because they remind some individuals of how empty and inauthentic their own lives are in comparison.

For existentialists, however, violence is not always a pathological act. As Camus and Sartre learned from their most meaningful days in the French underground, one of their most authentic acts was to help in the violent destruction of the Nazis. Camus (1956) later suggested, in his beautiful book *The Rebel,* that the first question of existence is suicide: to be or not to be is what we decide each day we go on living. The second is the equally violent question of homicide: to let another be or not. The power to kill, whether it be oneself or another, tells us just how free we can be. If freedom is our first principle, then nihilism is justified, and we are free to destroy others in the faith that something better may emerge. But if we are to control our freedom to kill, then our first principle is the affirmation of life, not freedom. Camus concludes that we can be free to kill if revolution is the only means available to remove the oppression that prevents others from being free to exist.

Control. For Sartre, the attempt to control another person is psychologically the most violent thing we can do to the other. Because freedom is the essence of existence, to control other human beings is essentially to destroy them. Sartre (1955) is well aware, however, that most people have a strong desire to control others; this is one of the reasons for his saying "Hell is other people." To control another person is to objectify that person, to deny that individual the freedom to be able to leave us or hurt us or to remind us that we are not as special as we pretend to be. To seek to control others is, in part, to pretend that our basic security comes from being on top of things, rather than to accept that any genuine security, no matter how limited or fleeting, can come only from accepting oneself as a very special person.

The existential therapist teaches patients the futility of attempting to control others by remaining unwilling to be controlled. No matter whether the patient threatens to quit therapy, not pay a bill, go crazy, or commit suicide, the existentialist is enjoined to respond only out of honesty, never fulfilling a patient's desire to find false security through controlling others.

Individuo-Social Conflicts

Adjustment Versus Transcendence. The only way a life based on adjustment might be healthy is if the society a person is adjusting to is basically honest. Few observers of our age would argue that honesty is a hallmark of our society. A majority of business managers admit to having surreptitiously broken the law in order to succeed; a large percentage of college students say they will cheat if given the chance; practically all politicians routinely misrepresent their constituencies in order to get elected, to the point where we expect no less of them. How can you be sane in a society that seems unable or unwilling to discriminate between truth and delusion?

The only way to rise above the morass of lies and inauthenticity is to become conscious of how the forces of socialization and industrialization prefer to make us automatons, easily controlled and manipulated. Once we become conscious of the pressures to sacrifice ourselves for success or security, we must take responsibility for becoming our own person rather than someone else's pigeon. Consciousness and choice are the uniquely human characteristics through which we can become uniquely human. We can still be-with-others and be-in-the-world without having to be owned by others or bought out by the world.

We must not delude ourselves into thinking we can in any way transcend all that we have been thrown into. The givens of our life—our time in history, our native language, our genetic makeup—put real limits on our freedom. As Camus (1956) has suggested, transcendence begins with choosing that which is necessary. To fight against our bodies, for example, as by trying to fly to the sun, can only destroy the limited freedom we do have for rising above our society. Freedom is not just another word for nothing more to lose; it is a commitment to the core of our being that nothing our society can give us is worth the loss of our one chance at creating ourselves.

Impulse Control. Unlike psychoanalysts, existentialists do not fear that choosing one's own rules will precipitate dyscontrol over impulses because of a weakening of social controls. Some people may indeed choose a hedonistic lifestyle if that is most authentic for them. Other authentic individuals, such as Gandhi, may choose to control even such a basic impulse as hunger for 40 days in order to express a stand for freedom. To say that we must eat too much, drink too much, have sex too much, or get angry too much shows bad faith in our potential for being self-directed individuals. People with impulse-control problems lie daily: "I'll just have one beer, or one potato chip"; or "Now that I've started, I may as well eat the whole thing"; or "You made me get angry." They tell themselves assorted lies rather than honestly acknowledge that they prefer to eat or drink rather than feel bored, anxious, or depressed. Impulses are not the dominant forces in human beings, although many people let them become dominant. The processes of consciousness and choice are what direct a mature person, so that being freer does not mean becoming a beast or a Dionysian irrationalist who is authentic only when expressing every spontaneous desire.

Beyond Conflict to Fulfillment

Meaning in Life. One does not discover meaning in life; one creates meaning out of life. The question is not what is the answer to life; the answer is that life is an ongoing process to be experienced, not a problem to be solved. The meaning of our existence emerges out of what we choose to stand for. Individuals can choose to take quite different but nevertheless authentic stances in their existences, and thus we find a multitude of conflicting meanings throughout history. Jesus stands for love, Marx stands for justice, Sartre stands for freedom, Galileo stands for truth, Picasso stands for creativity, Martin Luther stands for faith, Hitler stands for power, and Martin Luther King, Jr., stands for equality.

To know what the meaning of our existence is, we must ask ourselves: What do we stand for? Do we take a stand? Is what we are to become worth the price we pay, worth all the other possibilities we give up in choosing to be this particular person? These are questions of meaning that can haunt us but also motivate us in times of kairos to break out of the safe or successful route if what we see emerging is not significant enough to spend our existence on. If we do not break out during these critical periods of life, then we may at some later date break down because of the overwhelming depression, terror, or nausea that can come with the awareness that we can no longer stand what we stand for. Many such breakdowns are the result of breakthroughs of the sense of meaninglessness; but rather than being just symptoms of an inadequate existence, they can be seen as fresh opportunities to begin a more meaningful life.

Ideal Individual. The ideal for living, and therefore for psychotherapy, is to make oneself authentic by making the choices in life that create meaning and value out of our existence. In Heidegger's terms, later borrowed by Sartre, an authentic life is one based on an accurate appraisal of the human condition and a fulfillment of one's potentialities. A person is authentic to the degree to which that person's being in the world is unqualifiedly in accord with the givenness of his or her own nature and of the world (Bugental, 1976).

Authenticity requires awareness of one's self, relationships, and the world; recognition and acceptance of choices; and acceptance of full responsibility for those choices. To make choices requires the courage to be responsible for acting in the face of limited information on how our life may turn out. An authentic person must also find the courage to exist in the face of the fact that the very meaning we intend in our life can be negated at any time by the forms of nonbeing, such as death or isolation. The only value a person *must* follow to become authentic is to be honest, even in the face of nothingness.

Once a patient finds the courage to be basically honest, then we can no longer predict what that person will be. We can only predict what a conventional person will be, a reflection of the norms and expectations of the society, or what a pathological person will be, a reflection of the frozen past. To attempt to further define authentic individuals is to attempt to freeze them within the limits of our ideal. Authentic people refuse to be frozen, even by the ideals of their therapists.

Therapeutic Relationship

The central task of the existential psychotherapist is to understand the client as a being-in-the-world. All technical and theoretical considerations are subordinate to this understanding. The therapeutic relationship is a direct relationship of two people, *I–Thou,* a sharing and experiencing together that leads to an elucidation of the patient's mode of being with an enlightened understanding of the implications for existence. The chief characteristic of the therapeutic relationship is a "being-together" of the therapist and client in the spirit of "letting be" (Hora, 1959, 1960). The concept of *letting be* means the authentic affirmation of the existence of another person.

The therapeutic relationship is both part of the process of change and the prime source of content for existential psychotherapy. In attempting to engage a patient in an authentic encounter, the psychotherapist helps the patient become aware of the ways in which he or she avoids an encounter, such as insisting on remaining a patient rather than a person. The therapeutic relationship provides one of the best opportunities for patients to choose to enter into a deep and authentic encounter, because the existential therapist is committed to responding authentically. If a patient has the courage to choose to be-authentic-with-the-therapist, then the patient has radically changed from lying-for-others or lying-for-self to being-with-another.

As a source of content, the therapeutic relationship brings into the here and now the patient's pathological styles of being and lying. For psychoanalytically inspired existentialists such as Boss (1963) and Binswanger (1963), these lies and objectifications result in a transference relationship that is the first content to be analyzed or made conscious in order for a patient to be free to enter an encounter. For other existentialists, the fact that the patient's lying-for-others or lying-for-self is occurring right in the consulting room allows patients to be confronted with their pathological ways of being. Patients cannot hide the pathological content of their existence, because it is occurring in their immediate relationship to the existential analyst. Patients, for example, will eventually be forced to become conscious of their running from the existential anxiety of responsibility by the therapist's remaining unwilling to take over for the patient.

In Rogerian terms, existentialists would agree that the therapist initially must be more congruent or authentic than the patient. Congruency on the therapist's part is necessary for the therapist to be genuine in therapy. If the patient is equally congruent and genuine, the two could have a rewarding encounter, but then there would really be no need for therapy. Existentialists also agree with Rogers's requirement of accurate empathy: the therapist strives to experience the world as the patient experiences it. Dasein—the therapist literally "being there" with the patient —means an unconditional meeting of experience and relational presence (Bolling, 1995).

Existentialists do not agree, however, that a therapist must maintain unconditional positive regard toward the patient. In order to be authentic, the therapist can respond with positive regard only toward honesty and authenticity but never toward lying and pathology. That the therapist at first allows the patient to lie and objectify without overt judgment is accepted in order for the therapist to experience the patient's phenomenal world. But an authentic therapist can hold no positive regard for a patient's lying.

Practicalities of Existential Therapy

Existential analysts seem to be too unconcerned with mundane practicalities to write about them. Therapy schedules, fees, and formats are rarely broached in the existential literature. The impression one gathers is that much of existential analysis is similar to psychoanalytic psychotherapy, except during times of kairos. That is, a regular appointment seems to last 50 minutes and is scheduled weekly. When a patient is in one of the critical crises, however, the existentialist seems to become much more flexible and may spend extended hours with the patient. Boss (1963), for example, reports spending four days at the bedside of an obsessive-compulsive patient as the patient lived through a psychotic experience brought on by his repulsion at his own existence.

To our knowledge, traditional existentialists have no formalized criteria for judging the preparedness of someone to be an existential therapist. Existential work depends heavily on getting into the subjectivity of clients and thus calls extensively on the subjectivity of therapists. Enriching a therapist-to-be's own subjectivity would entail intensive personal psychotherapy experiences, considerable life experiences in the larger world, extensive reading of both fiction and nonfiction portraying the human experience, and internships that nurture the sensitivities, skills, and innovation of the trainee (Bugental, 1987). Existentialists have been quite flexible about the formal educational backgrounds of their colleagues; medicine, psychology, education, theology, and philosophy are just some of the disciplines represented among existential analysts.

Existentialists seem to be less amenable than other psychotherapists to the use of medication as an adjunct to therapy. They prefer to have patients experience authentic though acutely painful emotions such as anxiety and guilt rather than pop a pill, thereby deadening the hurt but also risking deadening themselves by treating themselves as objects that can be free from existential anxiety.

Brief Existential Therapy

Who is to say whether existential therapy should be lengthy or brief? Why, the patient, of course. In a freely-choosing relationship, the content, goals, and length of the psychotherapy will be largely determined by the client. In the spirit of "being together" and "letting be," the client is responsible for her choices. The existential therapist will weigh in with an honest and authentic opinion, but trying to predict or control a freedom-enhancing psychotherapy would be antithetical to its purpose.

To the limited extent that one can generalize, existential analysis appears to be comparatively lengthy along the lines of psychoanalytic psychotherapy. Discussion of intentionally "brief" or "time-limited" existential therapy is absent from the burgeoning literature on brief therapies (for example, Budman & Gurman, 1988; Wells & Giannetti, 1990).

At the same time, the major alternatives to existential analysis lend themselves more readily to briefer therapy. The centrality of choice, the I–Thou relationship, the here-and-now orientation, and the imperative to act in the face of inevitable existential anxiety—all catalyze the therapeutic process. We now turn to these briefer alternatives to existential analysis.

Major Alternatives: Existential-Humanistic, Logotherapy, Reality Therapy

The focus of this chapter so far has been on traditional or classical existential psychotherapy, also known as existential analysis, Daseinanalysis, and existential-analytic therapy. The early existential analysts, as we have seen, were originally trained in psychoanalysis and then created and converted to an existential orientation to clinical work. Subsequent generations of existential therapists, however, have less frequently come from a psychoanalytic background. Instead, they are likely to hail from the humanistic and Rogerian traditions or been trained explicitly as "existentialists."

Moreover, owing to existential therapy's paucity of technical procedures and practice guidelines, therapists committed to an existential stance have been free to choose from a variety of therapeutic approaches that are compatible with the major tenets of existentialism. Although the traditional practice has been to follow the format of a modified psychoanalysis, there are those who prefer client-centered, Gestalt, bioenergetic, transactional analytic, Adlerian, or even cognitive-behavioral methods within an existential philosophy (for example, Denes-Radomisli, 1976; Dublin, 1981; Edwards, 1990; Maddi, 1978). These therapies are examined elsewhere in this volume. Here we will briefly consider existential-humanistic therapy, logotherapy, and reality therapy as three alternatives to classical existential analysis.

Existential-Humanistic Therapy

Clinical experience and published literature suggest that at least two types of existential therapy exist: existential analysis and existential-humanistic therapy. Existential analysis, or Daseinanalysis, can be viewed as an intermediate step between psychoanalysis proper and contemporary humanistic existentialism (Norcross, 1987a). Existential-humanistic therapy operates at the interface of existentialism and humanistic theory and is closely allied with the "third force" in psychology (psychoanalysis being the first force and behaviorism the second; Maslow, 1962). A related, but not identical, distinction (Yalom, 1980) is that between the "old country cousins" (existential analysts) and their "flashy American cousins" (existential-humanistic therapists). Whereas the Europeans are more likely to discuss limits, acceptance, anxiety, life meaning, apartness, and isolation, the American existential humanists focus on potential, awareness, peak experiences, self-realization, I—Thou, and encounter.

James F. T. Bugental (1915-), a prominent American example, identifies himself as an existential-humanistic psychotherapist. The kind of existential psychotherapy he practices no longer carries the adjective "analytic," although it still owes much to the insights of psychoanalysis. Instead, he prefers to speak of it as "humanistic" to emphasize a value system less concerned with finding components (analysis) than with fostering the realization of human possibilities. He has in mind as a goal of therapy the increase in the true livingness of those who engage in the process (Bugental, 1991, 1992).

A phenomenological study of the reported therapy practices of 22 self-identified existential-humanistic therapists and 11 self-identified existential-analytic therapists also supports the distinction. Not surprisingly, the existential analysts reported using significantly more classic psychoanalytic techniques—analysis of the transference and interpretations, for instance—than did their existential-humanistic colleagues. In contrast, the existential-humanistic therapists reported substantially more physical contact (touching, holding, embracing) with their patients and more Rogerian-type warmth and positive regard than did their existential-analytic counterparts (Norcross, 1987a). Limiting existentialists to two types may be a crude categorization, but these catagories seem to accurately capture variation in existential practice.

Logotherapy

Of the four forms of nonbeing, *logotherapy* is most concerned with meaninglessness (*logo* = meaning). After suffering through years in Nazi concentration camps in which his mother, father, brother, and wife perished, Viktor Frankl (1905–1997) became convinced that a *will-to-meaning* is the basic sustenance of existence (Frankl, 1969). Stripped to a bare existence, he experienced the truth of Nietzsche's dictum: "He who has a why to live for can bear with almost any how." But facing the horror of World War II and the madness of a nuclear future, more and more people find their lives becoming *existential vacuums*. Patients come in greater numbers doubting the meaning of work, of love, of death, of life. Psychotherapies may be adequate for resolving discrete psychological disorders and mental conflicts, such as those between drives and defenses. But a relevant modern therapy must also be a philosophical therapy—a therapy of meaning for those confronted with the existential frustration of being unable to find a "why to live for."

Frankl himself survived Nazi concentration camps and the death of his family by creating meaning in his helping others face the ordeal. In his classic *Man's Search for Meaning*, Frankl (1963) writes movingly of the terrifying death of his wife, parents, and brother in the concentration camps, the brutality of his own imprisonment in four of the camps, and his encroaching apathy. In the midst of this seemingly overwhelming trauma, he found meaning by helping his fellow prisoners restore their own health. For Frankl and others, the search for meaning is the cornerstone of psychological well-being and the antidote to suicide.

"Why don't you kill yourself?" can be a threatening but effective question for beginning therapy with some clients. After the initial startle, the person can begin to realize that the reasons given for not committing suicide contain the seeds of a meaning that can blossom into a profound purpose for living. By facing each form of nonbeing, clients can become aware of a meaning for living. The accidents of one's unique genetic composition and family heritage place limits on who one can become but can also help form the contours of one's unique identity. Death is seen as a negation of being that also brings a responsibility for acting, because if life were endless, decisions could be postponed indefinitely. Even in the face of fate, a person is responsible for the attitude that is assumed toward fate. The victims of concentration camps, for example, could choose to die for the sake of a fellow prisoner, collaborate with the enemy for the sake of survival, or give meaning to the future by struggling to hold on for a better day (Frankl, 1963, 1978).

The meaning of life is not an abstraction. People who are preoccupied with asking "What is the meaning of life?" should realize that it is life that asks us what meaning we give to our existence. We can respond to life only by being responsible. We accept our responsibility when we accept the categorical imperative of logotherapy: "So live as if you were living already for the second time and as if you had acted the first time as wrongly as you are about to act now" (Frankl, 1963). Facing each moment with such acute awareness and with such responsibility enables us to find the meaning of life that is unique to us at this unique moment in our life.

Logotherapy is quite similar in content to classical existential analysis, although Frankl gives meaning an even more central position in therapy. Whereas existential analysis relies on a form of therapy that is very similar to psychoanalysis, logotherapy is closer in form to some of the briefer therapies such as Adlerian. Although philosophical issues will often be discussed in a warm, accepting manner, logotherapists will also confront, instruct, reason, and work in a variety of ways to convince a client to take a more conscious and responsible look at the existential vacuum that life has become. Therapy transcripts (Frankl, 1963, 1967) indicate that therapeutic techniques include interpretations and confrontations but also rely on persuasion and reasoning to a considerable extent. Logotherapy appears to be a form of consciousness raising that relies on a combination of personal feedback and persuasive education in a philosophy of existence.

In treating traditional psychological problems, Frankl has developed two special techniques. Clients with anxiety neuroses and phobic conditions are plagued by *anticipatory anxiety*. They anticipate dreadful consequences from feared encounters and struggle to avoid such encounters. In struggling to avoid, however, they only increase their anxious anticipation of what will happen if they are forced into a feared encounter. Frankl calls their avoidance and withdrawal from dreaded areas of life "wrong passivity." To reverse this neurotic pattern, clients are encouraged to adopt an attitude of self-detachment and humor toward themselves and to intend to do the very thing they are dreading. With this *paradoxical intention*, clients find that the way they anticipated acting is not the way they in fact will act. A student who was afraid that he would vomit if he went into the student union was instructed by me to go into the union and vomit intentionally. We joked about how he could explain his vomiting, and with sufficient self-detachment he entered the union only to discover that when he intended that which he feared, he actually ended up having much more control over his anxiety than he had anticipated.

Anxious patients frequently use "wrong activity" in efforts to fight off obsessive ideas or compulsive acts. Instead of excessively attending and intending to control obsessive-compulsive behaviors, clients are instructed in *de-reflection*. In de-reflection, clients are instructed to ignore that which they are obsessed with by directing their awareness toward more positive aspects of life. By attending to a life full of potential meaning and value, clients substitute the "right activity" of actualizing personal potentials for the "wrong activity" of trying to fight off psychopathology.

Reality Therapy

Whereas logotherapy emphasizes a lack of meaning as the central concern in therapy, reality therapy emphasizes a lack of responsibility. Some readers may be surprised to find reality therapy presented as an alternative to classical existential therapy. However, the developer of reality therapy, William Glasser (1925–   ), did in fact derive many of his principles of therapy from Helmuth Kaisar, one of the first existential therapists in America. Furthermore, many of the central concerns of reality therapy parallel an existential approach toward personality and psychopathology. Glasser's (1975, 1984) approach to therapy, however, appears to be a unique blend of existential philosophy and behavioral techniques similar to the self-control procedures of behavior therapists.

Across all cultures, establishing an identity is the one basic requirement for being fully human. Identity is based on the uniquely human awareness that we are somehow separate and distinct from every other human being on the face of the earth. Our awareness of unique being brings with it a profound sense of responsibility concerning what we are going to make of our existence. We strive to give meaning to our identity by the actions we take. The fundamental meaning of identity can best be expressed as a success identity or a failure identity. Creating a success identity involves the conviction that we are succeeding in moving toward our personal goals because we have been willing to take responsibility for our actions and to respond to reality as it is, not as we wish it to be.

To attain our goals, we must have adequate control over our environment. According to Glasser's (1984) *control theory*, the human brain functions like a thermostat that seeks to regulate its own behavior in order to change the world around it. All behavior is aimed at fulfilling the four psychological needs of belonging, power, enjoyment and freedom, and the physical need for survival. Successful satisfaction of these needs results in a sense of control.

The need for belonging motivates us to learn to cooperate and function as a unit, such as in marriages, families, teams, clubs or religious organizations. Power does not imply exploitation of others but rather achievement, competence, and accomplishment. These consequences provide a sense of control—we can make things happen. The need for fun or enjoyment balances our need for achievement. Life is meant to be enjoyed, not endured. Finally, the need for freedom, independence or autonomy implies that, to function in a truly human manner, we must have the opportunity to make choices and to act on our own. A successful identity develops from experiences of having the power and the pleasure of choosing to meet our own needs.

A failure identity is likely to develop when a child has received inadequate love or been made to feel worthless. Regardless of how cruel or unusual our early childhood has been, however, that is no excuse to avoid taking responsibility for our present behavior. In fact the only way we can transcend an early failure identity is to begin taking responsibility for what we do now. Obviously the past cannot be changed. The past is closed and fixed, a part of nonbeing. The present and future are open to us, however, and can come more under our control if we will take responsibility for our present actions.

Troubled people are those who maintain a failure identity because they are unwilling to accept responsibility and face reality honestly. Mental illness is the name we give to the variety of strategies that people use to ignore or deny reality and responsibility. People with grandiose delusions, who believe they are God or Napoleon, are attempting to deny failure by creating a false identity. Other patients attempt to develop a sense of being worthwhile by becoming preoccupied with how special their symptoms are. Psychopathic patients believe they can ignore reality and succeed by breaking the rules, laws, and other realistic limits set by society. Once people begin to ignore or deny reality, they are more likely to repeat their failures. A person who has failed to gain adequate love, for example, might deny the need for love and withdraw from others, and by this very withdrawal fail to find the love that could produce a sense of being worthwhile.

Therapy begins with helping clients become aware of what they are doing in the present to make themselves disturbed. The question for a depressed patient, for example, is not "What's making you depressed?" but rather "What are you doing to make yourself depressed?" If past difficulties are focused on by patients, the question is not why the person got into such difficulties, but rather why they didn't get into even more difficulty. Such a focus helps clients to become aware that even in the process of making difficulties for themselves, they still maintained some strengths and some sense of responsibility that kept them from totally destroying their own lives or the lives of others. Clients are taught to focus on the strengths they have, not on the failures they have had. With increasing awareness of their strengths, clients can begin to realize that they have abilities that they can use to succeed without denying or ignoring reality.

Therapy is primarily present-centered. The past is important only as it relates to present actions. Obviously the present is where clients can choose to change. Blaming present problems on past abuses is one of the common cop-outs of clients that unfortunately has been reinforced all too often by traditional therapists. Reality therapists do not, however, point a cold, blaming finger at patients. Clients have already had enough coldness and condemnation. Therapy needs to be personal, with a warm, real, and caring therapist providing some of the love and confirmation that were missing in the client's early life.

The personal nature of reality therapy does not imply an all-accepting therapist. Value judgments must be made, but it is the judgment of clients that is critical. Having the therapist make the value judgments only serves to take responsibility away from clients. If clients are to succeed they must come to judge their behavior as acceptable when it is responsible, which means good for the client and for those with whom the client is meaningfully related. If what clients are doing is hurting themselves or others, then their hurtful actions are irresponsible and should be changed. Effective change comes only after there is a responsible awareness of how one's actions are destructive to self or others.

The patient decides whether present actions are irresponsible or not. Choice is really the main process of change. Therapeutic change is the result of responsible choice based on the awarenesss of the hurt that one has been creating. One of the therapist's tasks is to call clients on their cop-outs. Certainly therapists should not engage in the irresponsible activity of excusing clients' misbehavior though theoretical interpretations that blame personal problems on the past actions of parents or on the present conditions of society. Successful people know they can work within the reality of society without being swallowed up by the immorality that exists. The starting point for changing any immoral aspect of society is to accept responsibility for one's own actions.

Once a client chooses to change irresponsible behavior, the therapist is present to help the person create specific plans for changing specific behaviors. The therapist is assumed to have more of a success identity and thus to be more aware of how to succeed in society. The therapist serves as a guide for people who are failing to progress in reality. Plans are made that have a chance of succeeding from week to week. If clients are taking on more than they can realistically accomplish within their present limits, then the therapist's task is to give feedback and to help the clients design more realistic plans for the week. What clients need are experiences of success, not more experiences of failure. Reality therapists seem to encourage a behavioral form of successive approximation in which a success identity is gradually established through weekly plans that bring increasing consequences of success. Success comes, however, not through the therapist's management of contingencies, but rather through the client's self-management of behavior.

Weekly plans are put in writing, frequently in the form of a contract. Putting a plan in writing is a much clearer commitment to change. Written contracts also avoid the cop-outs of forgetting or distorting what was said. The therapist asks for details of the plan to see how realistic it is and how much chance it has for succeeding. Obviously plans, even written plans, are not absolutes. If a plan does not succeed, then it can be changed in response to feedback from reality. No excuses are accepted, however, if a plan does not work. The client takes responsibility, including the responsibility for choosing to change the plan. Most of us realize that things usually go wrong because people do not do what they said they were going to do. Blaming or deprecating does not help. The critical question is: Are you going to fulfill your commitment or not? If so, when? Or the therapist might say, "The plan didn't work. Let's change it."

Part of accepting reality is accepting limits, including the limits that life sets on our ability to succeed at our goals. Failure comes in not reaching our limits. Failure comes in not assuming the responsibility for succeeding to the very limits of our capacity and our reality.

Effectiveness of Existential Therapy

Our review of the existential literature and the psychotherapy outcome research revealed no controlled research to evaluate the effectiveness of existential therapy, traditional or otherwise. The standard meta-analytic studies, similarly, do not report on any outcome studies on existential therapy with children or with adults (Grawe et al., 1998; Weisz et al., 1987, 1995). Apparently, existential therapists do not tally conventional "success" rates, whether based on subjective or objective outcome criteria.

Of course, this resistance to standard empirical research is consistent with the existential distaste for ordinary "scientific" research. Objective research is seen as adding to the dehumanization of people by reducing their experience to test scores or aggregate data. The abstraction of people into numbers further objectifies patients, whereas existential therapy is committed to helping people experience their unique subjectiveness while giving up their escapes into self-objectification. On the basis of phenomenological principles, existentialists have been opposed to contributing to the myth that the usual experimental methods of science can do justice to the study of humanity.

Logotherapy has experienced the same paucity of published, empirical outcome research. We and others are unable to identify any controlled studies testing the effectiveness of logotherapy.

Frankl was an early proponent of paradoxical interventions, but by no means the only or most systematic. Family-systems therapists have been far more specific and prolific of late in examining the efficacy of paradoxical interventions. Meta-analyses of paradoxical interventions in general, not Frankl's paradoxical intention in particular, have shown that they are as effective as, but no more effective than, typical treatment modes. The mean effect size for paradoxical interventions compared to no-treatment controls was .99, a large effect. Thus, on average, a treated patient would be more improved than 84% of the control group (Hill, 1987). One meta-analysis also found that paradoxical interventions showed relatively greater effectiveness than other interventions with more severe cases (Shoham-Salomon & Rosenthal, 1987). These results, we should reiterate, do not directly attest to the demonstrated efficacy of logotherapy, but to a broad class of techniques that includes Frankl's single technique of paradoxical intention.

Criticisms of Existential Therapy

From a Behavioral Perspective

With no controlled outcome studies, we can see why some existentialists prefer to consider their approach a philosophy about psychotherapy and not a theory of psychotherapy. But what kind of authentic philosophy would be unwilling to fall or stand on the basis of its effectiveness in helping patients overcome their pathologies? Let the existentialists use phenomenological analyses if they prefer, but let them also demonstrate that such approaches result in greater authenticity than alternative approaches, including the placebo effect of expecting patients to be more open and honest.

As a theory, existentialism attempts to take a giant step backward with such romantic-sounding ideas as love and will (May, 1969), which held back a science of humanity for so long. Not only is such philosophizing damaging to the human sciences, it is also, as Skinner (1971) has so cogently argued, damaging to human societies. The continued emphasis on the myths of freedom and dignity can do nothing more than lead to the continued disintegration of our society. If existentialists are truly concerned with alienating phenomena such as the fragmentation of our communities, then let them use their eloquence in support of well-designed communities in which the contingencies are sane and the consequences of rule-breaking severe. To sacrifice society in the name of the elitist authentic individual is a luxury we can no longer afford.

From a Psychoanalytic Perspective

How can existential analysis borrow so much of psychoanalytic technique and yet reject so much of psychoanalytic theory? How can existentialists be authentic and still act as psychoanalysts in therapy? Doesn't that violate their own principles, and doesn't it also show that effective therapy necessitates a relationship in which transference can be developed?

As a theory, existentialism does serious injustice to patients in the midst of unconscious conflicts by insisting that they are responsible for and even choose the very pathologies from which they struggle to extricate themselves. Can the existential therapist really believe that patients with severe compulsions to wash or psychotic delusions of persecution have any choice over what they are driven to do? The logical but ludicrous consequence of the theory can be seen in Binswanger's (1958a) analysis of the phenomenological meaning of his patient's suicide rather than his attempting to prevent her from lethally directing her hostility inward.

Mowrer blamed Freud for giving us a generation of psychopaths, but existentialism is the more likely culprit. As an emerging philosophy of our modern times, existentialism's emphasis on the freedom to choose and on individual rules for living is more responsible than psychoanalysis for the breakdown of social order.

From a Humanistic Perspective

Lest anyone erroneously conclude that all humanists are sympathetic to traditional existential analysis, here is a quote from Maslow (1960, p. 57) regarding the concept of nonbeing:

> I do not think we need take too seriously the European existentialist's harping on dread, on anguish, on despair, and the like, for which their only remedy seems to be to keep a stiff upper lip. This [is] high I.Q. whimpering on a cosmic scale.

From a Contextual Perspective

Dead white European men develop another elitist individual psychotherapy that ignores the realistic context of people's lives. Sound familiar?

Existentialism has been roundly attacked by feminist, family-systemic, multicultural, and other therapists advocating a contextualist position. The dearth of influential women in existential theory and the predictable neglect of their phenomenological worlds convey a distinct impression of existentialism as a bastion of male intelligentsia. In viewing each individual client as a unique essence, existential therapists fail to see or treat the family system as a whole. The passive stance of the therapist and the abstract nature of the concepts would make family therapy difficult in any case. The lack of direction and concrete solutions make existential therapy particularly unsuitable for minority clients seeking relief. Kairos brought upon them by poverty, racism, homelessness, and crime will surely not be solved by analysis of their existential concerns, but such analysis might provoke a few more suicides in the face of the existentialist's benign neglect. The money and time would be much better spent in solving real problems in their Umwelt and Mitwelt than in interminable philosophizing about their Eigenwelt. Even if disadvantaged patients change internally, as existentialists maintain, they see little hope for—or have little choice or impact on—their external realities. Only in existentialism and the movies do people possess unlimited freedom, construct their own meanings, and execute boundless choices. Save it for the wealthy, worried well.

From an Integrative Perspective

Existentialism is rich in its appreciation of the human condition, yet meager in its theory of therapy. For example, the traditional existential analyst focuses on the existential anxiety of responsibility at the expense of the other equally important forms of nonbeing. The existential analysts provide little insight into their therapeutic procedures other than repeating much of psychoanalysis combined with a few slogans about therapist authenticity. The inadequate development of therapeutic procedures has proven May's (1958a) fear that existentialism might degenerate into an anything-goes anarchy.

The existential rejection of scientific evaluation of psychotherapy has also encouraged an irrationalism in which many therapists feel no responsibility to evaluate the effectiveness of their work. What criteria are we going to use to judge the honesty of different therapists? Are we left with a solipsism in which one person's truth is another person's lie? Existentialists would do well to recognize the truth in Bronowski's (1959) seminal book, *Science and Human Values*, that honesty is the fundamental value of science and that the scientific method is the most honest method we have. There is nothing inherent in the scientific method that says we cannot compare the phenomenological description of patients following different forms of therapy. Existentialists need to participate in the shared honesty of such comparisons, which can lead to the truth as to which approaches are most effective with which problems.

⟶   AN EXISTENTIAL ANALYSIS OF MRS. C.   ⟵

An existential analysis of Mrs. C. is restricted by the case description, which contains just the facts and little of the phenomena of her existence. From the facts, it looks as if Mrs. C.'s pre-pinworm existence was already heavily objectified. In sexual relations she was unable to be-in-nature, because she was nonorgasmic and thus unable to let herself be free to fully enjoy the natural joys of sexuality. Because her mother had lied about sex being disgusting, Mrs. C. at some point probably began to tell herself that she was not sexual in order to close off anything about herself that would be experienced as disgusting. The original existential anxiety associated with sexuality was probably expressed in isolation in the form of rejection for being disgusting. In everyday affairs Mrs. C. had also objectified herself by being so orderly, as exemplified by her cataloging her children alphabetically and scheduling them exactly two years apart. This suggests that she reduced her anxiety over the responsibility of having and naming children by placing the responsibility outside of herself onto an alphabet and a calendar. In spite of considerable objectification, Mrs. C. was seen as no more pathological than most conventional people who try to control the anxieties of life through arbitrary rather than authentic principles.

A crisis occurred when the Asian flu infected her family at a time when Mrs. C. was tired from caring for five children and a sixth on the way. When the pinworms infested her daughter, an authentic response for Mrs. C. would have been to experience the intense anxiety that no matter how hard she cleaned and cared for her children, they were still infected and were now faced with the possibility of additional infestation. Mrs. C. had never been authentic at facing such threats of nonbeing, but under the additional stress of her own illness, she chose to lie to escape the anxiety related to the prospect of further diseases. The lie was ready-made in the form of the physician's orders for her to boil clothes and wash intensely. At this point she was not particularly responsible for the orders, but she was responsible for telling herself "If I just wash enough, I can keep the nonbeing of diseases away from my children and myself." So she washed. With her washing based on this lying-about-nature, she was now faced with neurotic anxiety over not washing. Her conclusion was that she must wash, and her bad faith resulted in the objectification of herself into a human washing machine.

With full self-objectification in place, Mrs. C. experienced herself as unable to keep from washing. Causality in her life was no longer intentional, but a compulsive drive like a motor that automatically switched on in the presence of dirt or other threats of diseases. With so much of her time and energy dedicated to washing, Mrs. C. was bound to be faced with existential guilt over the many opportunities she was missing to be-for-herself and to be-intimate-with-her-family. Her washing would also serve as an attempt to cleanse herself of existential guilt. However, the longer she continued her washing compulsion, the less she was guilty over what she was doing and the more she was faced with the possibility of experiencing neurotic guilt for what she was becoming—a washing machine in human clothes, unable to care or share with her family and unable to let herself be spontaneous in the world.

After years of compulsive washing, to be confronted with the choice not to wash would also be to confront the tremendous existential anxiety over how meaningless her past decade had been. To face the choice of not washing would also be to face self-condemnation for having wasted precious years of her life and for having hurt her family by not joining the critical years of their development. Better to hold onto the lie that she must wash! At least that way she is not responsible: she has not failed in life; her physician has failed her. When her psychotherapist said he was washing his hands of her case, she made a suicide gesture to force him to remain responsible for her by arranging for someone else to cure her. We can further see Mrs. C.'s desire to run from responsibility by the way she pressured her husband into assuming responsibility not only for the family but even for her very compulsion. "You tell me, George, what to wash next because I am so mechanical I cannot remember or decide what to wash" is the essence of her communication to her husband.

The reason Mrs. C. began her washing ritual with her anus is that the anus was the locus of pinworms and was seen in her phenomenological world as a source of disease, as it is with many compulsive people. Even if Mrs. C. could not control all the sources of illness in the universe, she could keep her own anus clean and could pretend that no germs would penetrate her immaculate body.

Mrs. C. lived in the vigilant future where she kept an ever-watchful eye open for any signs of disease. Her space was surrounded by germs and worms, her symbols of nonbeing. She could be secure in such a dreaded world only if she remained clean, not only of dirt but also of any responsibility and, therefore, any guilt for having let her family down. In effect, she was attempting to literally wash her hands clean of the whole mess—a Pontius Pilate maneuver to absolve herself of responsibility and to avoid authenticity.

As with many obsessive-compulsive patients who devote their lives to making themselves into objects, it could be extremely difficult to engage Mrs. C. in an authentic encounter. But this would be one of the few ways we would have to keep her from becoming totally washed up as a human being. To help Mrs. C. experience her own subjectivity, an existentialist would look for every possibility of confronting her with choices in psychotherapy. For example, when we went to my office for our first meeting, Mrs. C. stopped at the door and waited for me to open it so that she could avoid any possible contact with germs. Right at that point, the existentialist would confront Mrs. C. with the choice of seeking help by opening a new door to therapy or returning to her secure but deadening patterns from the past.

Given the choice of what to talk about in therapy, Mrs. C. would probably ramble endlessly about her preoccupation with pinworms and the details of her washing. At some point, her obsessive preoccupations would have to be interpreted as her means of remaining a patient so that she would not have to face her therapist as a person. The therapist might also choose to confront Mrs. C. with the therapist's own feelings, for example: "I am sick and tired of hearing the endless details about pinworms and washing. I want to see if you still exist within that laundromat you call a life. I know it will be scary and hurt like hell to open yourself up, but look, my hands are not clean either."

If Mrs. C. could respond by sharing herself with the therapist, there would be *kairos* during which Mrs. C. would feel overwhelmed with guilt and anxiety. Both she and her therapist might fear that her compulsive symptoms did indeed cover a psychosis, but they would have to recognize that one cannot face a decade of waste without being overwhelmed with the existential anxiety and guilt that are the authentic responses to such absurd waste. The therapist would do Mrs. C. an injustice to try to minimize her anxiety and guilt as only *feelings* of anxiety and guilt; she would *be* anxious and guilty, and the only route to health would be to live through her confrontation of having not been authentic. The therapist can no more cleanse Mrs. C. of her guilt and anxiety than she could cleanse herself. By remaining with her through such crises, however, the therapist can communicate that new options do exist for the future and that she can choose not to waste her options, including the chance to be-authentic-with-the-therapist.

Future Directions

Existentialism has a rich and established basis in psychology, sociology, education, and the humanities; in other words, as Medard Boss put it, a potential voice in "everything with which human beings have something to do" (quoted in Craig, 1988). In psychotherapy, the historical influence of existentialism is equally established, but its future is equivocal.

In many respects, existentialism's contemporary influence on psychotherapy is far greater than the small percentage of psychotherapists (see Chapter 1 for details) endorsing it as their primary theoretical orientation. The existential orientation frequently underlies clinical practice without explicit recognition (Norcross, 1987a; Rubinstein, 1994). Core existential concepts—meaning, freedom, responsibility, individuality, authenticity, choice—have been incorporated into most contemporary systems of psychotherapy. Existentialism is a "strange yet oddly familiar" orientation to psychotherapy and life (Yalom, 1980).

What does this implicit but selective incorporation portend for the future of existential therapy? As long as there are philosophically inclined psychotherapists and angst-plagued patients, existential therapy will surely survive as a distinct orientation, but its overriding contribution to the 21st century will probably be as an indirect social force. It will serve as a vital counterbalance to the flourishing victimology in the world: when people convincingly deceive themselves into believing they are the unwitting, choiceless victims of fate, existentialists will confront them with the undeniable existence of active choice and personal responsibility. Existential therapy will promote the possibility and power of self-initiated change: when people delude themselves about the necessity of formalized professional assistance, existentialists will challenge them with the efficacy of personal change and individual autonomy. These will be social forces more than therapeutic endeavors, but powerful correctives nonetheless.

Looking specifically at existential-humanistic psychotherapy, Bugental and Bracke (1992) propose that this orientation gives promise of being particularly valuable in aiding a growing number of clients complaining of feelings of emptiness and lack of personal meaning. Economic, political, and social forces over the past decades have drastically assailed the capacity of being oneself, complicating the quest for meaning, freedom, and authenticity. Existentialism offers fulfillment in an age of emptiness; it embraces authenticity in an era of medicalization; it addresses, in the words of Frankl's (1978) book title, *The Unheard Cry for Meaning*. Existential therapy will help clients find meaning in their suffering, be it chronic pain, social ostracism, or post-traumatic stress disorder. The meaning in trauma and terror can then be used for self-transcendent giving to the world, as in the case of Viktor Frankl himself (Lantz, 1992).

Although the rise of managed health care at first glance would seem a threat to insight-seeking, life-changing therapy, the short-term and problem-centered treatment services offered by managed care may stimulate, paradoxically, a desire for more life-changing therapy in the existential-humanistic tradition. Patients' appetites for deeper self-exploration may be whetted by brief treatment, kindling a desire for more comprehensive exploration into one's inner life. While existentialists are probably overly optimistic about the paradoxical demand for long-term therapy in a short-term therapy market, the full impact of enhanced freedom from the information age and increased isolation from the technological revolution just may fuel a resurgence in the existential perspective on psychotherapy and, indeed, life.

Suggestions for Further Reading

Binswanger, L. (1963). *Being-in-the-world: Selected papers of Ludwig Binswanger.* New York: Basic.

Boss, M. (1963). *Daseinanalysis and psychoanalysis*. New York: Basic.

Buber, M. (1958). *I and thou*. New York: Charles Scribner.

Bugental, J. F. T. (1965). *The search for authenticity*. New York: Holt, Rinehart & Winston.

Bugental, J. F. T. (1987). *The art of the psychotherapist*. New York: Norton.

Frankl, V. (1963). *Man's search for meaning*. New York: Washington Square.

Frankl, V. (1967). *Psychotherapy and existentialism: Selected papers on logotherapy*. New York: Washington Square.

May, R. (1977). *The meaning of anxiety* (rev. ed.). New York: Norton.

May, R. (1983). *The discovery of being: Writings in existential psychology*. New York: Norton.

May, R., Angel, E., & Ellenberger, H. (Eds.). (1958). *Existence: A new dimension in psychology and psychiatry*. New York: Basic.

Yalom, I. D. (1980). *Existential psychotherapy*. New York: Basic.

Journals: *International Forum for Logotherapy; Journal of Humanistic Psychology; Journal of Phenomenological Psychology; Review of Existential Psychology and Psychiatry.*

5

Person-Centered Therapy

Carl Rogers

MARTY WAS WEALTHY financially but impoverished emotionally. He rotated through glamorous houses in Miami, Newport, and New York, but his life was superficial. Golf, tennis, polo matches, parties, and dining out helped pass the time. But his wife, his children, and his friends were moving away from Marty. His superficial conversations, his sarcastic jokes, his negative attitude, and his limited feelings were causing others to seek more enriching relationships elsewhere.

At first, Marty was enraged at others. He blamed his increasing isolation on other people's self-centeredness or on the fact that he was no longer so important since selling his major company. Then, Marty tried to deny that being alone even bothered him. He preferred his independence; he had always been a lone wolf. Who needed others anyhow?

It wasn't until his wife separated from him and moved to New York and left him alone in Newport that Marty's denial began to break down. He asked his wife to join him in psychotherapy, and he began to experience and express emotions. Instead of talking about his golf game or the polo match, he began to share his fantasies and his dreams. He dreamed about dolphins, and he believed they represented the type of person he wanted to become. The dolphins could jump for joy at the surface of the sea, but they could also dive to the depths of experience. They could communicate acutely with sounds and signals; they were sensitive and caring about each other's needs.

Through a caring and empathic therapeutic relationship, Marty discovered that he was not emotionally retarded, as he had originally feared. He began to discover that he had learned to close off his feelings because of his mother's teaching that men don't show emotions. He had replaced genuine feelings with silly jokes. As an awkward teenager, he had defended himself with cutting comments and a cognitive scanning for any signs of rejection. He had supplanted genuine relationships with social events.

In psychotherapy, Marty gradually reduced his defensiveness. He discovered that men could exchange emotions without threats of being sissies. He found that he could get close to his wife without being hurt by her. As all of this was occurring and as Marty was becoming more of the person he wanted to be, I asked him what about therapy was the most helpful to him. He replied immediately: "You really listen, and you really care."

Carl Rogers taught generations of psychotherapists the profound value of active listening and human caring. Later he added the importance of genuine sharing.

A Sketch of Carl Rogers

Carl Ransom Rogers (1902–1987) demonstrated a profound openness to change, beginning with his movement away from the almost fundamentalist Protestantism of his Wisconsin farm family to the liberal religion of Union Seminary in Manhattan. His strict ascetic and religious family allowed no drinking, dancing, card playing, or theater going. Foreshadowing his later research interests, he showed scientific interests early and became a serious student of agriculture at the age of 14, thus gaining an early appreciation of experimental design and empiricism (Sollod,

1978). After two years of preparation for the ministry, Rogers made a move common to a number of actual or potential clergy, toward training in psychotherapy. He received his PhD in clinical psychology in 1931 from Columbia in a highly Freudian atmosphere.

Beginning as an intern in 1927–28, Rogers spent 12 years as a psychologist at a child guidance clinic in Rochester, New York. During this time, he let his own clinical experience be the basis for his theorizing and therapy. In the midst of a very busy but fertile schedule, he found time to put together his first book, *The Clinical Treatment of the Problem Child*, published in 1939. Rogers found both inspiration and confirmation of his views in the work of Otto Rank (1936), who emphasized the importance of the humanity of therapists rather than their technical skills in remedying human problems.

In 1940, Rogers moved to Ohio State University to train students in psychotherapy. As is so often true of students, they taught Rogers several important lessons. One of these lessons was that his ideas were in fact a new view of the nature of effective therapy and not a distillation of generally accepted principles, as Rogers had originally thought. They also convinced him that if his new theory was going to be accepted by scientifically minded students, he would have to demonstrate its efficacy through controlled research. With his own strong commitment to the scientific method, Rogers began an extended series of outcome studies with his students both at Ohio State and later at the University of Chicago, where he moved in 1945.

The clarity of Rogers's clinical and theoretical writings in such books as *Counseling and Psychotherapy* (1942) and *Client-Centered Therapy* (1951) and the controls in his scientific research brought widespread recognition. For such a humanistic psychologist, Rogers was tremendously successful in the traditional academic world, and in 1957 he returned to his home state at the University of Wisconsin. Here he was willing to make the acid test of any therapy, to see if his system could be effective in producing profound change in schizophrenic clients. During the five-year study, Rogers and the other therapists found themselves becoming more actively genuine, disclosing more of their inner experiencing, which seemed to lead to greater improvement in such clients.

In 1964, Rogers moved to the Western Behavioral Sciences Institute in La Jolla, California, and began working with groups of normal individuals struggling to improve their human relations abilities. In 1968, Rogers and some of his research colleagues established their own Center for Studies of the Person in La Jolla. As a world figure in humanistic approaches to therapy, Rogers became as deeply involved in trying to inspire humanistic changes in education, business, marriage, and world relations (Rogers, 1970, 1977, 1983, 1987b) as he was in helping individuals to more fully realize their basic humanity. His long-time commitment to peacemaking led to many workshops between warring factions and culminated in the Rust Workshop on Central America in 1985 (Solomon, 1990). Enlarging the focus of his work from psychotherapy and clients to human interactions and all people was accompanied by a name change from the "client-centered" to the "person-centered" approach.

When Carl Rogers spoke, it was apparent that the audience was in the presence of a great man. The aura around him was warm and gentle, though his words were strong. He was willing to field any question and respond to even the most critical comments. When asked how he as a therapist could be both genuine and nondisclosing, he surprised us with his candor. He said that over the years of working first with psychiatric clients and then with growth-oriented groups, he had come to see that his model of a therapist as reflective and nondirective had been very comfortable for a person like him. For most of his life he had been rather shy and therefore nondisclosing. In the sunny climate of California, with its emphasis on openness in groups, he had come to recognize that too much of his former style was a convenient role that had protected him from having to reveal much of himself. Right until his death, Rogers was realizing more fully in psychotherapy, as in his life, the genuineness he had always valued but never fully actualized.

Theory of Personality

All humanity has but one basic motivational force, a tendency toward *actualization*. Rogers (1959, p. 196) defines the actualizing tendency as "the inherent tendency of the organism to develop all its capacities in ways which serve to maintain or enhance the organism." This includes not only the tendency to meet physiological needs for air, food, and water and the tendency to reduce tensions, but also the propensity to expand ourselves through growth, to enhance ourselves through relating and reproducing. It also refers to expanding our effectiveness, and hence ourselves, through the mastery of cultural tools, as well as moving from control by external forces to control from within.

We are also born with an organismic *valuing* process that allows us to value positively those experiences perceived as maintaining or enhancing our lives and to value negatively those experiences that would negate our growth. We are born, then, with actualizing forces that motivate us and with valuing processes that regulate us; what's more, we can trust that these basic organismic processes will serve us well.

In relating to the world, we respond not to some "real" or "pure" reality, but rather to reality as we experience it. Our world is our experienced or phenomenal world. If others wish to understand our particular actions, they must try to place themselves as much as possible into our internal frame of reference and become conscious of the world as it exists within our subjective awareness. Our reality is certainly shaped in part by the environment, but we also participate actively in the creation of our subjective world, our internal frame of reference.

As part of our actualizing tendency, we also begin to actively differentiate—to see the difference between experiences that are part of our own personal being and functioning and those that belong to others. The special experiences that we come to own are *self-experiences*. We are able to become conscious of self-experiences by representing these experiences symbolically in language or other symbols. This representation in awareness of being alive and functioning becomes further elaborated through interaction with significant others into a concept of self. Our concept of self includes our perceptions of what is characteristic of "I" or "me," our perceptions of our relationships to others and to the world, and the values attached to these perceptions (Rogers, 1959, p. 200).

As our self consciousness emerges, we develop a need for *positive regard* for that self. Although this need is universal in human beings, Rogers (1959) seems to agree with his student Standal (1954) that we actually learn to need love. This need for positive regard—the need to be prized, to be accepted, to be loved—is so addictive that it becomes the most potent need of the developing person. "She loves me, she loves me not" is the endless puzzle of the emerging individual who looks to the mother's face, gestures, and other ambiguous signs to see if she holds the child in positive regard. Although a mother's love has been emphasized, positive regard from all others, especially significant others, becomes compelling.

Whenever another person, such as a parent, responds to a particular behavior with positive regard, our total image of how positively we are prized by the other is strengthened. On the other hand, let a parent respond to a behavior with a frown or another expression of negative regard, and our total perception of how much we are loved by our parent is weakened. Consequently, the expression of positive regard by significant others is so powerful that it can become more compelling than the organismic valuing process. The individual becomes more attracted to the positive regard of others than to experiences that are of positive value in actualizing the organism. When the need for such love becomes dominant, individuals begin to guide their behavior not by the degree to which an experience maintains or enhances the organism, but by the likelihood of receiving love.

Soon individuals learn to regard themselves in much the same way as they experience regard from others, liking or disliking themselves as a total configuration for a particular behavior or experience. This learned self-regard leads to individuals' viewing themselves and their behavior in the same way that significant others have viewed them. As a result, some behaviors are regarded positively that are not actually experienced organismically as satisfying, such as feeling good about ourselves for getting an A after spending many dull hours memorizing tedious material. Other behaviors are regarded negatively that are not actually experienced as unsatisfying, such as feeling bad about masturbating.

When individuals begin to act in accordance with the introjected or internalized values of others, they have acquired *conditions of worth*. They cannot regard themselves positively as having worth unless they live according to these conditions. For some, this means they can feel good about themselves, feel lovable and worthy, only when achieving, no matter what the cost to their organism; others feel good about themselves only when they are nice and agreeable and never say no to anyone. Once such conditions of worth have been acquired, the person has been transformed from an individual guided by values generated from organismic experiencing to a personality controlled by the values of other people. We learn at a very early age to exchange our basic tendency for actualization for the conditional love of others and ourselves.

Theoretically, such a trade need not be made. As Rogers (1959, p. 227) states so clearly, "If an individual should experience only unconditional positive regard, then no conditions of worth would develop, self-regard would be unconditional, the needs for positive regard and self-regard would never be at variance with organismic evaluation, and the individual would continue to be psychologically adjusted and would be fully functioning." Unfortunately, such a hypothetical situation does not appear to occur in actuality, except perhaps in psychotherapy.

Theory of Psychopathology

The more conditional the love of parents, the more pathology is likely to develop. Because of the need for self-regard, individuals begin to perceive their experiences selectively, in terms of their parents' conditions of worth, which have been internalized. Experiences and behaviors consistent with conditions of worth are allowed accurate representation in awareness. Individuals whose parents insisted on achievement, for instance, should be able to perceive and accurately recall experiences in which they were indeed doing well. Experiences and behaviors that conflict with conditions of worth, however, are distorted in order to fit the conditions of worth, or may even be excluded from awareness. People who must achieve in order to feel good about themselves may, for example, distort their vacations into achievement times, as they count the number of historical sites, museums, or states they visit. Some workaholics may deny entirely that they have any desire to play or just lounge around. "Fun is for fools" is their motto.

As some experiences are distorted or denied, there is *incongruence* between what is being experienced and what is symbolized as part of a person's self-concept. An example of such incongruence was suggested earlier when I (JOP) indicated that I could not allow myself to experience anger and still feel good about myself. I perceived myself as one of those rare individuals who never gets angry. My wife has since told me that in situations where I would be expected to get angry, I would first begin to pucker my lips. If the frustration continued, I would then begin to whistle. I never allowed myself to become aware of these somatic clues of anger even though I was going around like a whistling teapot ready to explode. For Rogers, the core of psychological maladjustment is the incongruity between the organism's total experience and what is accurately symbolized as part of the self-concept.

The incongruence between self and experience is the basic estrangement in human beings. Because of conditions of worth, there are now organismic experiences that are threatening to the self. The person can no longer live as a unified whole, which is the birthright of every human being. Instead, we allow ourselves to become only part of who we really are. Our inherent tendencies toward full actualization do not die, however, and we become like a house divided against itself. Sometimes our behavior is directed by the self we like to believe we are, and at other times behavior can be driven by those aspects of our organism that we have tried to disown. Psychopathology reflects a divided personality, with the tensions, defenses, and inadequate functioning that accompany a lack of wholeness.

Psychological maladjustment is a result of this basic estrangement of human beings. For the sake of maintaining the positive regard of others, we no longer remain true to who we really are, to our own natural organismic valuing of experience. At a very early age, we begin to distort or to deny some of the values we experience and to perceive them only in terms of their value to others. This falsification of ourselves and our experience is not the result of conscious choices to lie, as the existentialists would hold; rather, it is a natural, though tragic, development in infancy (Rogers, 1959).

As individuals live in a state of estrangement, experiences that are incongruent with the self are subceived as threatening. *Subception* is the ability of the organism to discriminate stimuli at a level below what is required for conscious recognition. By subceiving particular experiences as threatening, the organism can use perceptual distortions, such as rationalizations, projections, and denial, to keep from becoming aware of experiences like anger, which would violate conditions of worth. If individuals were to become aware of unworthy experiences, their concepts of themselves would be threatened, their needs for self-regard would be frustrated, and they would be in a state of anxiety.

Defensive reactions, including symptoms, are developed in order to prevent threatening experiences from being accurately represented in awareness. People who feel unlovable for getting angry, for instance, may deny their anger and end up with headaches. The headaches may not feel good organismically, but at least most other people can love someone who is sick. Those who have self-regard only for success may develop compulsions to work. They may drive themselves into the late hours of the night with the aid of stimulants, feeling good about each success while their body experiences tremendous stress. Some people are so threatened by experiencing sexual desires that they distort their perceptions to the point where they believe that they are pure and innocent and godlike, while others are trying to make them think dirty, rotten thoughts. One patient I tested at a state hospital looked at the first Rorschach card I gave him, threw it down, and shouted, "Why the hell don't you go show these pictures to the goddamned communists? They're the ones that are perverting our kids with all of their sex education."

All human beings are threatened by some experiences incongruent with their self-concepts. To a lesser or greater degree, then, we all use some defenses or symptoms to preserve our self-regard and to prevent undue anxiety. While defenses help preserve positive self-regard, they do so only at a price. Defenses result in an inaccurate perception of reality due to distortion and selective omission of information. Early in my (JOP) career, a 45-year-old man walked into my office and said, "Oh, you're younger. You must be in favor of open marriages. I won't be able to work with you." He requested a referral to another psychotherapist without even asking about my views on open marriage. In rigidly trying to defend their views of the world and of themselves, people end up becoming rigid and inadequate in their styles of information processing. The more defensive and pathological the person, the more rigid and inadequate are the person's perceptions.

Some individuals have such a significant degree of incongruence between self and experience that particular events can prevent their rigid defenses from functioning successfully and can lead to disorganization of their personalities. If the event threatens to demonstrate the degree of incongruence between self and experience, and if the event occurs suddenly or obviously, then such individuals are flooded with anxiety because their very concepts of themselves are threatened. With their defenses not working successfully, previously disowned experiences are now symbolized accurately in awareness. For these individuals, the organized self-images are shattered by unacceptable experiences.

Panic and disorganization were experienced by a sophomore who came to see me following a bad trip with LSD. Before the experience, he had been convinced that he was a true follower of Jesus. He had seen himself as basically loving and kind and working for the well-being of others through a radical Christian movement. During the recent experience with acid, he saw himself as an egomaniac, misusing his leadership role in his Christian group to win a following of female admirers and to see his picture in the news. He said he kept running in a circle, trying to catch his picture of himself from the papers, but he had this eerie feeling that the picture was a stranger. He could not rationalize these self-perceptions as being due to acid. He was so panicky and disorganized that he thought he might jump off a bridge to destroy his life in order to save his self. Fortunately, with the aid of crisis intervention from the counseling center and the support of some friends, he decided to enter psychotherapy to begin the arduous process of reintegrating a sense of self that was more complete and less idealized.

Whether a person enters therapy because of a breakdown, because of inadequate functioning due to perceptual distortions, because defensive symptoms are hurting too much, or because of a desire for greater actualization, the goal is the same: to increase the congruence between self and experience through a process of integration. Because Rogers conceptualizes the reintegration of self and experience as emerging from the therapeutic relationship, we will break with our standard format and present Rogers's view of the therapeutic relationship before examining his theory of therapeutic processes.

Therapeutic Relationship

Rogers (1957, 1959) has stated very explicitly that the necessary and sufficient conditions for therapy are contained within the therapeutic relationship. Six conditions are necessary for a relationship to result in constructive personality change. Taken together, these conditions are sufficient to account for any therapeutic change. That is, these and only these conditions are hypothesized to produce therapeutic personality changes in all clients, in all therapies, and in all situations.

1. Relationship. Obviously, two persons must be in a relationship in which each makes some perceived difference to the other.

2. Vulnerability. The client in the relationship is in a state of incongruence and is therefore vulnerable to anxiety because of the potential for subceiving experiences that are threatening to the self, or is anxious because such subception is already occurring. The vulnerability to anxiety is what motivates a client to seek and to stay in the therapeutic relationship.

3. Genuineness. The therapist is congruent and genuine in the therapeutic relationship. *Genuineness* means that therapists are freely and deeply themselves, with the actual experiences of the therapists being accurately represented in their awareness of themselves. It is the opposite of presenting a facade. This does not mean that therapists are always genuine and congruent in all aspects of life, but it is necessary when entering a therapeutic relationship. Rogers (1957, 1959) originally believed that within this condition there was no necessity for therapists to disclose their genuine experiences to clients overtly; it seemed necessary only that therapists not deceive clients or themselves. Following client-centered work with schizophrenic clients (Rogers, Gendlin, Kiesler, & Truax, 1967) and work in human relations groups (Rogers, 1970), Rogers (1970) came to the conclusion that therapist genuineness includes self-expression.

The degree of self-disclosure by Rogers himself actually seems rather minimal when compared with the extensive spontaneous disclosure characteristic of many leaders of encounter groups. The following excerpt from a session with a schizophrenic client is an example that Rogers uses to demonstrate his increased willingness to express his own feelings of the moment.

CLIENT: I think I'm beyond help.

ROGERS: Huh? Feeling as though you're beyond help. I know. You feel completely hopeless about yourself. I can understand that. I don't feel hopeless, but I realize you do. (Meador & Rogers, 1973, p. 142)

We shall see that other client-centered therapists go considerably further in expressing their own immediate feelings.

4. Unconditional Positive Regard. The therapist must experience *unconditional positive regard* for the client. The client's incongruence is due to conditions of worth that have been internalized from others' conditional positive regard. In order for the client to be able to accept experiences that have been distorted or denied to awareness, there must be a decrease in the client's conditions of worth and an increase in the client's unconditional self-regard. If the clinician can demonstrate unconditional positive regard for the client, then the client can begin to become accurately aware of experiences that were previously distorted or denied because they threatened a loss of positive regard from significant others. When clients perceive unconditional positive regard, existing conditions of worth are weakened or dissolved and are replaced by a stronger unconditional positive self-regard. If the therapist is able to prize and consistently care about clients, no matter what the clients are experiencing or expressing, then the clients become free to accept all that they are with love and caring.

5. Accurate Empathy. The therapist experiences *accurate empathy* of the client's inner world and endeavors to communicate this understanding to the client. Through empathy we sense the client's private world as if it were our own, without our own anger, fear, or confusion getting bound up in the experience. With this clear sense of the client's world, we can communicate our understanding, including our awareness of the meanings in the client's experience of which the client is scarcely aware.

Without deep empathic understanding, clients could not trust the therapist's unconditional positive regard. Clients would feel threatened that once the therapist came to know them more fully, there would be aspects of the client that would not be accepted with positive regard. With accurate empathy and unconditional positive regard, clients come close to being fully known and fully accepted (Rogers, 1959).

6. *Perception of Genuineness.* The client perceives, at least to a minimal degree, the acceptance and understanding of the therapist. In order for the client to trust the caring and empathy of the therapist, the therapist must be seen as genuine and not as just playing a role.

Theory of Therapeutic Processes

Although Rogers has written extensively about the conditions of the client–therapist relationship that allow for positive change, he has had much less to say about the actual processes that occur in the interactions between client and therapist to produce such change. Throughout the 1950s, it seemed adequate to postulate that the facilitative conditions of therapist genuineness, positive regard, and accurate empathy were all that was necessary to release a client's inherent tendency toward actualization. During the 1960s, Rogers and his colleagues (Rogers et al., 1967) began to theorize that the curative process involved the direct and intense expression of feelings, leading to corrective emotional experiences. Later, client-centered theorists (for example, Wexler, 1974; Zimring, 1974) began to view client-centered therapy as a process of expanding consciousness or awareness through therapists' helping to bring about more effective information processing in clients. Currently, then, the processes of change in client-centered therapy are most accurately conceptualized as a combination of consciousness raising and corrective emotional experiencing that occurs within the context of a genuine empathic relationship characterized by unconditional positive regard.

Consciousness Raising

The Client's Work. Given an atmosphere of unconditional positive regard, clients are free to discuss whatever they wish in sessions. Clients, rather than therapists, direct the flow of therapy. This is the primary reason Rogers (1942) originally used the label *nondirective* to describe his therapy. Because clients come to treatment out of distress, however, they can be expected to express information related to personal experiences that are troubling them. The responsibility of clients, then, is to take the initiative to inform the therapist about their personal experiences and to be available for feedback from the therapist.

The Therapist's Work. Traditionally, the therapist's work in increasing the client's consciousness was seen as being almost entirely a function of *reflection.* As a mirror or a reflector of the client's feelings, the therapist would communicate to the client messages that said, in essence, "You really feel. . . ." The specifics might be "You really feel disappointed in your father for leaning on alcohol," or "You feel envious because your roommate has a special boyfriend and you wish you did." Through a commitment to understand the client with accurate empathy, the therapist is not dogmatically, authoritatively, or interpretively telling the client how or what to feel. The therapist is instead able to sensitively and exquisitely capture the essence of the experiences the client is expressing. The therapist can reflect so empathically and accurately in part because there is no distortion caused by having to be interpretive or self-expressive. The therapist is free to listen actively and reflect accurately the essential feelings of the client.

With such a caring and congruent mirror available, clients are able to become more fully conscious of experiences that previously were partly distorted or denied. These experiences, of course, included their feelings, or more important, their real feelings. Perhaps of even greater significance, clients begin to be more fully aware of the *You* the therapist is reflecting—the You with increasing richness; the You who produced experiences once judged to be unworthy of self-regard, but which are now prized and shared by a significant other. Gradually the You that clients become aware of through empathic feedback from the therapist is a richer and more congruent human being.

More recently, person-centered therapists have recognized that erroneously equating the specific technique of reflection with the complex attitude of empathy has resulted in severe limitations on modes of empathic response (Bohart, 1993b; Bozarth, 1984). Rogers (1987a, p. 39) wrote later in his life, "I even wince at the phrase *reflection of feeling*." He regretted that this simple intellectual skill was being (mis)taught as an accurate description of a complex type of interpersonal reaction. The evolving definition of empathy and the expanding role of the person-centered therapist emphasize the therapist's experiencing the world of the client by developing more active and idiosyncratic means of empathy predicated upon the particular client.

The contemporary view is that the therapist's work in raising consciousness involves more than just a feedback function. Anderson (1974) and Wexler (1974) posit that part of the person-centered therapist's work is to help clients reallocate their attention so that they can make greater use of the richness that exists in the information generated by their feelings. By more flexibly and fully attending to the client's feelings, the therapist helps clients break through some of their perceptual rigidities and distortions in order to attend to the personal meaning of experiences that previously have not been processed into awareness. The client-centered therapist can thereby serve as a surrogate information processor. In compensating for the client's more rigid and deficient style of information processing, the therapist first serves an attentional function whereby the client's experiences, especially threatening experiences, can be held in awareness for further processing. If the therapist did not reflect some of the client's threatening experiences, the client's selective attentional processes would cause such information to be lost in short-term memory, crowded out by other information that is receiving attention.

A case in point: In talking about her roommate's boyfriend, a shy sophomore was expressing a variety of feelings, including her close relationship to her roommate, her admiration of the boyfriend, and some vague feelings of envy. Because envy was not a feeling she could accept, this client would have focused her attention on her admiration or her sense of closeness and would have lost the opportunity to become aware of feelings of envy that might be the source of her recent arguments with her roommate.

Because there is always more information impinging on a client than the client can attend to, information from threatening experiences is most likely to be lost unless it is empathically reflected by the therapist and thereby kept available for further processing. By selecting out such threatening information to process into awareness, the person-centered therapist is, in fact, quite directive, but in a subtle and noncoercive style, and only by responding to information that is already in process in the client. In other words, person-centered therapists are relatively controlling of the process of therapy, but not its content.

As a surrogate information processor for the client, the therapist also helps the client to adopt a more optimal mode of organizing information. As clients approach feelings that threaten self-regard, they can become anxious, confused, or defensive, and may be unable to find adequate words or symbols for organizing and integrating such feelings into conscious experience. Some clients may anxiously search for words to organize their previously unacceptable feelings of anger or envy, while others will quickly give up and go on to something else. Therapists can move the work ahead by empathically organizing the information from a client's experience in a concise and accurate manner. Organized information is then more fully available to awareness.

An example of such helpful organization occurred with a 55-year-old woman who was expressing a variety of upsetting feelings toward her husband. She was angry because he wouldn't spend money to fix up the house for their daughter's wedding. She was depressed over how many years she had worked to make their restaurant a success, but now that they had money she still wasn't happy. She was trying to understand her husband's view that it would be better to remodel the house after they saved up the money rather than cash in one of their bonds. She said she felt torn and confused. When I told her, "You feel impatient with his promises that someday the two of you are really going to live," she broke into tears and said, "Yes, that's it, that's it, that's what he's always been holding out in front of me."

A more actualizing style of experiencing includes a pattern of processing that organizes information using structures, symbols, or schemas that evoke richer, more intense, and more conscious expressions of life. Therapists help clients develop evocative structures for processing information by using symbols or words that are active, vivid, potent, and poignant. All too frequently, the language and symbols of clients are conventional, repetitive, dull, and safe, reflecting the defensive ways clients process their experiences into awareness. Evocative symbols threaten to bring experiences into awareness that have previously been damaging to the client's self-regard. As clients become aware of how therapists can capture the client's own feelings in more vital and enriched language, they have the opportunity to begin to use symbols that allow them to be conscious of how vital their lives can really be.

Zimring (1974) uses the philosophy of Wittgenstein (1953, 1958) to explain that as clients become aware of more vital, enhancing, and actualizing modes of expressing themselves, their experiences in fact become more vital, more enhancing, and more actualizing. In Wittgenstein's view, expression and experience are a unity. Experiences do not exist somewhere in the organism, waiting to be expressed into awareness. Experiences are created by expression. Thus, the richer, the more potent, and the fuller the symbols that clients learn to use in expressing themselves, the richer, the more potent, and the fuller human beings they become.

Catharsis

In the process of increasing consciousness, person-centered therapists have emphasized the primacy of the client's feelings. The therapist's continual focus on "You really feel. . . ." helps clients to become more aware of feelings but also to release, express, and own their most powerful feelings. For Rogers (1959), feelings have both emotional and personal meaning components. In the previous section, we examined the expression, organization, and integration of the personal meaning, informational, or cognitive component of feelings. Now we will examine the cathartic release of the emotional component of feelings, which is equally important in the curative process. Although Rogers considers the expression of emotional and cognitive components of feelings as inseparable, we have taken the liberty of discussing them separately while recognizing their experiential unity.

The Client's Work. In the process of expressing themselves, clients usually begin by avoiding emotionally laden experiences. When feelings are talked about early in therapy, they are described as past experiences that are external to self (Rogers & Rablen, 1958). Clients will talk about emotional problems, but describe such problems as coming from outside themselves. "My roommate is driving me up a wall"; "My folks are really on my back"; and "My studies are giving me a bad time" are some examples of early communications. Gradually, in response to the therapist's accurate empathy and positive regard, clients begin to describe their feelings, but they are still primarily past emotions and thus lacking in intensity. As clients experience themselves as accepted, they can begin to describe present feelings more freely, but they are not yet fully living and expressing their emotional experiences. Part of the work of clients involves staying with emerging emotions even though anxiety is aroused and their defensive responses are mobilized to selectively disattend to such threatening emotions.

Eventually, clients begin to fully express their feelings of the moment. These feelings are owned and accepted as coming from within the person and being worthy of positive regard. At the same time, emotional experiences that were previously denied are bubbling up. Rather than continue to deny all such feelings, clients gain more confidence that emotions can be valued and valuable. They discover that experiencing feelings with immediacy and intensity is a possible guide for living. They begin to trust their feelings and base more of their valuing on what they like or dislike, what makes them happy or sad, what produces joy or anger. With the release and owning of emotional experiences, clients begin to be in touch once again with their inherent organismic basis for valuing their genuine feelings. The release and acceptance of such feelings are frequently vivid, intense, and dramatic as clients discover an internal basis for directing their own lives rather than having to be dominated, distorted, and threatened by the internalized values of others.

The Therapist's Work. Originally, the therapist's work seemed to be simply to allow clients to get in touch with their most basic feelings by demonstrating an attitude of unconditional prizing of all the feelings a client was releasing. Now it is recognized that therapists help clients get in touch with and express threatening emotional experiences by continually redirecting the client's attention to the feeling aspect of whatever is being discussed. As the therapist empathically reflects back to the client the essence of what the client is feeling implicitly, the client eventually becomes able to attend to and explicitly feel the emotion and the meaning of experiences.

More recently, many client-centered therapists have begun to follow Rogers's lead of directly expressing some of the emotion and meaning of their own feelings. Especially in group work, therapists might express such emotions as "I feel angry about the way you're attacking Tom," or "I feel deeply moved and saddened by what you've expressed," or "I really do care about you." The theoretical justification for person-centered therapists' expressing their own emotional experiences of the moment is that it allows for greater genuineness or congruence. Furthermore, if psychotherapists use nondirectiveness as an excuse to suppress their own annoyance because the poor, weak client could not take it, an attitude of fundamental disrespect for the client's powers will be communicated (Barton, 1974).

The empirical justification for therapist self-expression is the discovery (Rogers et al., 1967) that therapists who speak genuinely out of their strong feelings tend to encourage and liberate clients to release and express their own emotional experiences. In important respects, the self-expressing therapist may actually create emotional experiences in clients through such transactions, rather than releasing some feelings that are implicitly present within the client. The traditional view in client-centered therapy, however, is that threatening emotions are implicitly present in clients and are not being released because of the client's defensiveness. Through the therapist's self-expression of emotions and, most important, through the therapist's empathic communication of client feelings, clients are gradually freed from having to deny or distort their emotions and can begin to speak and live out their strongest feelings.

Therapeutic Content

Intrapersonal Conflicts

Person-centered therapy is more of a process than a content theory, but it has had important things to say about many of the common content issues in treatment. As we have seen, person-centered theory has been especially concerned with intrapersonal conflict between the client's concept of self and the total experience of the client, which includes feelings that are threatening to the person's self-concept. Even in the movement toward group therapy and institutional consultation, person-centered therapists remain centrally committed to establishing an atmosphere of unconditional positive regard to help individuals overcome incongruence in order to be more fully functioning.

Anxiety and Defenses. Anxiety is not the cause of people's problems but the troubling result of a divided life. Although anxiety is frequently what drives people into treatment, our task is not to desensitize anxiety but rather to listen sensitively to the client's expression of anxiety in order to discover more fully what organismic experiences are threatening to enter awareness.

In practice, person-centered therapists respect the potentially disorganizing effects of anxiety, and thus do not flood a client with threatening emotional experiences. Instead, they allow a more gradual corrective emotional experiencing to occur. The person-centered style of catharsis may be slower and less dramatic than the emotional flooding therapies, but it is also seen as less risky because of the belief that anxiety causes incongruent people to become disorganized.

The defense against anxiety-arousing experiences is either to deny the experiences, banishing them from awareness entirely, or to use a whole range of distorting perceptions, such as projection or rationalization, that process experiences in a manner slanted in favor of maintaining the person's self-concept. In Piaget's terms, distorting defenses involve the assimilation of new experiences into the schema of the self with no accommodation of the self-concept to those new experiences. The self is left unthreatened, but only at the loss of opportunity to grow.

Self-Esteem. Rogers places the need for self-esteem at the center of intrapersonal problems, only he called it *self-regard*. Vulnerability to low self-esteem is in direct proportion to the distance between who we think we were and who we really are. The problem is not that we have too-great concepts of ourselves that we cannot live up to; the problem is that our concepts of ourselves are too meager to let us be all that we were born to be. Striving for self-esteem is a trap that keeps us locked into trying to actualize self-concepts that were created out of the confining conditions of our parents' prying. The more restrictive the striving, the more we can feel good about ourselves only when we do not allow ourselves to feel much at all. The solution lies not in increasing self-esteem but rather in expanding our conditions of worth so that we can prize all that we can be and not only who we believe we are supposed to be.

Responsibility. Being the scientist that he was and having been educated in a time in which the sciences of humanity assumed complete determinism, Rogers did not include freedom and responsibility as core constructs in his original theory. In later years, however, he placed freedom and responsibility at the cornerstone of his work with married couples, educational systems, and international relations.

In the context of the clinical setting, the troubled person is the victim needing parental regard that was all too conditional. The therapist is responsible for providing four of the six conditions necessary for effective therapy; clients provide themselves and a willingness to relate to the therapist. Even within this seemingly deterministic system, we can see that freedom is experienced in the process of releasing a safe but restrictive self-concept in order to actualize the inherent tendencies to be all that we can be. Becoming responsible means learning again to respond to our natural organismic valuing process rather than to the internalized values of others. The responsible person is the actualizing person who moves from *heteronomy*, or control by others and the environment, to *autonomy*, or inner control.

Interpersonal Conflicts

Intimacy and Sexuality. Intimacy is therapeutic, and therapy is intimate. In defining the necessary and sufficient conditions for a therapeutic relationship, Rogers presents an excellent ideal for an intimate relationship: unconditional prizing, accurate empathy, and interpersonal genuineness. The major difference is that in an ongoing intimate relationship both partners are, or at least become, relatively equal in their levels of congruence in order for the relationship to truly progress, whereas treatment is ready for termination when such a level of intimacy is reached, often to the sadness of both therapist and client.

Because there is much similarity between therapy and intimacy, some incongruent people can make major strides toward actualization without receiving professional assistance. Unfortunately, truly intimate relationships are rare, in part because it is so difficult for us to grant to others what we withhold from ourselves: our love of our humanness, including our blemishes, our defects, our imperfections. To love and to feel intimate, most people must distort their perceptions of their partners to fit their conditions of what is worthy of love, just as they distort their perceptions of themselves. Eventually, when they discover who they are really relating to, they are likely to believe that the faults and the gaps in their relationship are due to their partner's incompleteness rather than to the narrow conditions of their own love.

Our society has traditionally placed much too narrow conditions on our sexual worth. These restrictive conditions have led too many people to disown the fullness of their sexuality so that they can hold themselves in high regard. In reacting to the plethora of prohibitions against being sexual, we may have gone to the opposite extreme of believing that to feel worthy we have to be sexually successful, to be routinely orgasmic or even multiply orgasmic, to always be aroused and maintain lubrication or erections, to never ejaculate too quickly but to always ejaculate. Much of the performance anxiety that Masters and Johnson (1970) describe so well may indeed be a reflection of restrictive conditions of worth that say we must be sexually successful rather than sexually natural in our relationships.

A more natural sexuality, one that is neither goal-consumed nor performance-oriented, is most likely to occur within an intimate relationship. In such a relationaship, we are most likely to jettison either overly restrictive or overly demanding conditions of worth regarding either our own or our partner's style of sexual relating. When things go wrong sexually, as they will at times for nearly everyone, there is little threat of rejection in an intimate relationship. The atmosphere is present for the couple to work through their own sexual difficulties. Rogers (1972) himself revealed a very intimate experience of how his wife's unconditional regard allowed her to remain available to help him work through a period of erectile dysfunction. If therapists focus only on sexual dysfunctions without cultivating more intimate relationships, they are liable to leave couples in relationships that will continue to need therapy when things go wrong.

Communication. At one time communication problems were believed to be inevitable, given the inadequacy of words to express feelings. With our enhanced awareness of accurate empathy, however, we now know that we can indeed understand the fullness of what another is communicating if we truly care to listen. The problem of communication is no longer a language problem; it is a problem in caring. The testimony of clients from many forms of effective therapy indicates how fully people feel they can communicate and be understood when someone really cares to listen. Just as we can train therapists (Truax & Carkhuff, 1967) and paraprofessionals (Carkhuff, 1969) to increase their ability to listen actively, so too have we learned how to train parents (Gordon, 1970) and teachers (Gordon, 1974) to listen actively and communicate effectively.

Hostility. From his humanistic point of view, Rogers sees the natural actualizing tendency as bringing people toward each other rather than driving them against each other. Hostility is not an inherent drive that must be controlled. It is, in part, a reaction to being overcontrolled by the restrictive conditions of parental regard. Hostility is, at times, our organismic way of rebelling against having to disown parts of our lives in order to be prized by others. It can also manifest itself when people cannot express angry feelings without feeling guilty or unworthy. There are, of course, individuals who use hostility against others with little caring, but such hostile individuals were most likely raised in dehumanizing atmospheres in which they themselves experienced all too little caring.

Control. Control becomes a problem in interpersonal relationships when individuals attempt to impose their conditions of worth on others. In subtle or not-so-subtle ways, such individuals communicate that they will continue to care only if others live up to their images of lovable human beings. Be nice, be a winner, be assertive, be deferential, be witty, be quiet, be sexy, and behave are just a few of the conditions that people place on their partners or their children. We let ourselves be controlled by others because we value maintaining their regard above what is organismically pleasing. We, in turn, act in restricted ways to control the positive regard of others. As long as our conditions of worth coincide, we tend to go on controlling each other without feeling conflict. Issues of control become acute when conditions of worth conflict, as when some people can feel worthy only when they keep others waiting. To give up being controlled and to give up controlling, people must work hard in therapy at giving up their restrictive conditions of worth.

Individuo-Social Conflicts

Adjustment Versus Transcendence. Going beyond one's internalized conditions of worth to become a whole person suggests some need to transcend one's personal enculturation process. But once a person is in the process of becoming more congruent, there is no inherent conflict between being an actualizer and being part of a society. Rogers's (1959) view of the natural actualizing tendencies includes being part of a society in order to relate, to create, and to grow through the mastery of cultural tools. Rogers is certainly in favor of humanizing social institutions, such as marriages, families, schools, universities, and businesses. Perhaps because so much of Rogers's professional life was spent in universities and growth-oriented centers, probably two of the most humane institutions of society, he seemed confident that autonomous clients can go out into society, be fully functioning, and still be at home in the world.

Impulse Control. The natural organismic valuing process provides inherent regulation over impulses. A person raised in a humanistic atmosphere will eat, drink, or relate sexually in a manner that is organismically enhancing and not organismically destructive. Attempts at bringing particular impulses under control through fancy techniques or faddish diets may produce short-term gain but little long-term maintenance, because they fail to focus on enhancing natural abilities for self-regulation. Once people feel good about who they really are and are not under constant stress to be what others want, they will not need to resort to overeating, drinking, or smoking in order to feel good for the moment or to reduce stress. Acceptance of self begets control of impulses.

Beyond Conflict to Fulfillment

Meaning. Meaning emerges from the process of actualizing our tendencies to become all that we are by nature intended to be. Those who are obsessed with the belief that there must be something more to life than natural living have probably not experienced all that there is to their lives. The haunting notion that there must be something more to life represents a subception that there is indeed a good deal more to life than what they are experiencing, but what's missing is to be found within them and not outside them. There is no need to give life meaning for those in the process of living a congruent, complete life.

The locus of evaluation, the source of evidence for meaning, is found within the individual. The person should be the center of his or her meaning, rather than having a meaning being imposed by other individuals or society as a whole. The criterion for values is the actualizing tendency: does this action or experience enhance the organism?

Ideal Individual. Rogers's (1961) ideal for the good life is found in a *fully functioning* person. This ideal type of individual would, of course, demonstrate organismic trusting. Being open to each new experience, the person would let all of the significant information in a situation flow in and through them and would trust in the course of action that emerges as the best response to the current event. The person would not have to ruminate about decisions, but would find the best decision emerging as a result of not distorting or denying any information that is relevant to current living. The openness to experiencing indicates a person who is living primarily in the present, who is neither processing information that belongs to the past nor omitting information that belongs to the present. The fully functioning person does not process experience through a rigid or structured set of categories—through a rigid concept of self, for example. Instead, in what Rogers (1961) calls *existential living,* people let the self and the personality emerge from experience: they discover a sense of structure in experience that results in a flowing, changing organization of self and personality. Self is now experienced as a process—a rich, exciting, challenging, and rewarding process—rather than a constricted structure that can process only what is consistent with internalized conditions of worth.

Organismic trusting, openness to experiencing, and existential living in the present result in an experiential freedom in which people have the power to choose and direct their lives from within, regardless of the sad fact that actions may indeed be somewhat predictable on the basis of past experiences. The greatest sense of freedom comes in being creative, in being able to produce new and effective thoughts, actions, and entities, because the person is in touch with the spring of life.

Practicalities of Person-Centered Therapy

The central focus of person-centered therapy on "self-authority" tends to militate against the use of psychometric tests and routine assessment in psychotherapy. Three conditions suggest the use of tests in person-centered counseling: the client may request testing; clinic policy may demand that tests be administered; and tests may be administered as an "objective" way for the client and clinician to consider a decision for action, as in making vocational and career choices (Bozarth, 1991).

Because the person of the psychotherapist is more important than formal training in person-centered work, therapists from a diversity of backgrounds are welcomed. Counseling psychology, counseling education, and pastoral counseling have been especially well represented in the Rogerian approach. Rogers has also had considerable influence on many programs in clinical psychology and some programs of social work, especially those in the Rankian tradition. Client-centered counselors have been among the most active in developing training approaches for paraprofessionals, such as students participating in self-help groups (Carkhuff, 1969). Through methods developed by Truax and Carkhuff (1967), students are trained through modeling, role playing, videotaping, and feedback to learn the skills involved in becoming increasingly empathic, genuine, and unconditional in their regard. Personal therapy is seen as desirable, though not essential; however, aspiring person-centered therapists are frequently encouraged to participate in growth-oriented group experiences. Any experience that enhances the sensitivity of the clinician and that fosters full functioning is regarded as valuable training.

Unfortunately, academic efforts to enhance trainees' empathy has become confused with mindless parroting or a sterile technique. In one of his last articles before his death, Rogers (1987, p. 39) deplored the teaching of empathy as a cognitive skill: "Genuine sensitive empathy, with all its intensity and personal involvement, cannot be so taught." "I even wince at the phrase *reflection of feeling*. It does not describe what I am trying to do when I work with a client." Training in empathy—or rather experiencing and witnessing empathy—will come about only in authentic, I–Thou relationships, including experiential groups and personal therapy.

Fees seem to follow the going rate for other forms of therapy in a given locale. The genuine therapeutic relationship typically translates into a face-to-face encounter, with no intervening desk.

Over the past 20 years, person-centered therapy (like most psychotherapies) has increasingly expanded into couples, group, and family therapy formats. Following Rogers's lead in moving from strictly individual work to more systems interventions, contemporary person-centered clinicians are active in group therapy (see review by Raskin, 1986a, 1986b), couples and family therapy (see August 1989 special issue of *Person-Centered Review* for an overview), and indeed entire communities and nations (see Levant & Shlien, 1984, for illustrations). Enlarging the scope of practice from the consulting room to planetary concerns, such as nuclear war and international relations, reaffirms the name change from "client-centered therapy" to "person-centered approach."

Brief Person-Centered Therapy

The terms "brief" and "person-centered therapy" are rarely used in the same sentence. Rogers' own therapy cases almost always ran into two-digit numbers of sessions and frequently went into three digits. While years of psychotherapy are unnecessary, due to the client's self-actualizing tendencies, the most common practice was to see clients individually once a week for 6 to 12 months. Thus, little clinical or research attention was paid to brief or short-term person-centered therapy (Budman, 1981; Koss & Shiang, 1994).

In the past, person-centered therapy's historical stricture against authority, teaching, and telling have made counselors hesitant to experiment with means to accelerate the therapeutic process. As Arthur Combs (1988, p. 270), a respected person-centered psychologist, humorously observed, "Anyone who has watched a group of person-centered counselors decide where to go on a picnic must surely have asked themselves whether there are not speedier ways of reaching good decisions." In the present, the time-efficiency and brevity of treatment constitute central challenges to person-centered theory and practice.

A Major Alternative: Motivational Interviewing

As some person-centered therapists have become more cognitive, relying on information processing perspectives, others have become briefer and more directive.

William Miller defines his *Motivational Interviewing* as a brief, directive client-centered approach to eliciting behavior change by helping clients explore and resolve ambivalence (Rollnick & Miller, 1995). As such, it combines elements of both person-centered style (e.g., warmth, empathy) and technique (e.g., key questions, reflective listening).

Miller (1978) began his career by applying behavioral self-control techniques to the treatment of problem drinkers. As a good empiricist, he was struck (and annoyed) by his findings that the control group showed excellent improvement, comparable in magnitude to that of clients receiving ten therapy sessions. The control group had received initial assessments, encouragement, advice, and a self-help book (Miller & Munoz, 1982).

Miller so disbelieved the results that he replicated them twice after increasing the intensity of therapy to 18 sessions (Miller & Taylor, 1980). In one of the studies, the in-therapy behavior of the counselors was observed and rated on the empathy scale developed by Truax and Carkhuff (1967). Although the treatment and control groups showed comparable outcomes, the empathy ratings of the therapists could account for outcomes at 6 months ($r = .82$), 12 months ($r = .71$), and 2 years ($r = .51$). Miller concluded that the empathy and reflective listening advocated by Rogers must be a central part of any effective brief therapy.

From a comparative analysis of effective brief therapies, six elements were identified and are summarized by the acronym FRAMES (Miller & Sanchez, 1994). Most brief therapists conducted assessments followed by *Feedback* of individual findings. Many stressed the individual's personal *Responsibility* for change, emphasizing that changing is a matter of free choice and a decision that no one else can make for the person. All of the brief therapies included an element of direct *Advice* to make healthy changes and many offered a *Menu* of different ways in which change could be accomplished. The therapist style entailed *Empathy*. Finally, effective brief interventions contained elements to strengthen the individual's *Self-efficacy* for change, reinforcing optimism and the ability to succeed.

In Motivational Interviewing the counselor carefully avoids the classic confrontation in which the therapist asserts the need for change ("You have to quit drinking!") while the client denies it. Instead of seeking to persuade directly, the counselor systematically elicits *from the client* and reinforces reasons for concern and for change. The counselor maintains a warm and empathic atmosphere that permits patients to explore ambivalent feelings about changing. Resistance is not confronted head-on but is skillfully deflected to encourage open exploration. Underlying this process is a goal of developing with the client a motivational discrepancy between present behaviors (real self) and desired goals (more ideal self). Evidence indicates that such discrepancy provides motivation that triggers behavior change (Miller & Rollnick, 1991).

In Project MATCH, the largest psychotherapy outcome study ever completed, four sessions of Motivational Enforcement Therapy (MET) were compared to 12 sessions of Cognitive Behavioral Coping Skill Training and to 12 sessions of Twelve-Step Facilitation Therapy (Project MATCH Research Group, 1993, 1997). Two parallel but independent randomized clinical trials were conducted, one with 952 alcohol-dependent clients receiving outpatient psychotherapy and one with

774 clients receiving aftercare therapy following alcohol inpatient treatment. The first two sessions of MET included motivational interviewing and personal feed-back based on intensive assessments of problems related to alcohol abuse, including physical health, brain functioning, interpersonal relationships, and occupational functioning. The last two session of MET were basically booster sessions (Miller et al., 1992). What was clear was that the briefer MET was just as effective at each follow-up as the lengthier and more established Twelve Step and Cognitive Behavioral treatments. Of special note was that, at long term follow-up, the MET was more effective than Cognitive Behavioral Coping Skills Training with patients who initially were less motivated to change as measured by being in earlier stages of readiness for change. Just as Carl Rogers predicted, clients can go a long way in a short time when provided with facilitative conditions, an accepting therapist, and considerable autonomy.

Effectiveness of Person-Centered Therapy

Rogers has consistently stood for an unusual combination of a phenomenological understanding of clients and an empirical evaluation of psychotherapy. He and his followers have demonstrated that a humanistic approach to conducting therapy and a scientific approach to evaluating therapy need not be incompatible. In one of his last articles, which addressed the future development of the person-centered approach, Rogers (1986, pp. 258–259) continued to emphasize the need for empirical research:

> There is only one way in which a person-centered approach can avoid becoming narrow, dogmatic, and restrictive. That is through studies—simultaneously hardheaded and tender minded—which open new vistas, bring new insights, challenge our hypotheses, enrich our theory, expand our knowledge, and involve us more deeply in an understanding of the phenomena of human change.

Strupp (1971, p. 44) concludes that "the impetus given research by client-centered therapy is at least equal in importance to Rogers's theoretical contributions or the effectiveness of his form of psychotherapy."

Two separate lines of research on the effectiveness of person-centered therapy have been pursued. The first concerns the veracity of Rogers's necessary and sufficient conditions hypothesis; the second line of research relates to the overall efficacy of person-centered therapy. We will consider each in turn.

Rogers's (1957) provocative identification of purportedly "necessary and sufficient conditions of therapeutic personality change" precipitated scores of published studies, at least ten reviews, and even a "review of reviews" (Patterson, 1984). The empirical research on empathy, genuineness, and prizing, which Rogers anticipated eagerly, has demonstrated that these facilitative interpersonal conditions are valuable contributors to outcome but are neither necessary nor sufficient. Dispassionate reviews conclude that "patients' positive perceptions of therapist facilitative attitudes have a modest tendency to enhance treatment gains" (Beutler, Crago, &

Arezmendi, 1986, p. 279), and that "the evidence for the therapeutic conditions hypothesis [as necessary and sufficient] is not persuasive. The associations found are modest and suggest that a more complex association exists between outcome and therapist skills than originally hypothesized" (Parloff, Waskow, & Wolfe, 1978, p. 251).

Most person-centered therapists now concede the point and have reformulated the original hypothesis. Mitchell, Bozarth, and Krauft (1977, p. 481), for instance, conclude that the evidence, "although equivocal, does seem to suggest that empathy, warmth, and genuineness are related in some way to client change but that their potency and generalizability are not as great as once thought." Raskin (1992), an influential client-centered practitioner, summarized his position on the original Rogerian qualities by saying they were not necessary, perhaps sufficient, definitely facilitative. Few researchers seriously suggest that these conditions are necessary and sufficient, even within person-centered psychotherapy (Bohart, 1993b; Norcross & Beutler, 1997).

At the same time, the accumulating research demonstrates that the interpersonal qualities of warmth, empathy, and genuineness are indeed facilitating for most people and most circumstances. This conclusion also applies to comparatively technical forms of treatment, such as cognitive-behavior therapy (Burns & Nolan-Hoeksema, 1992). In their monumental review of the relevant literature, Orlinsky and Howard (1986, p. 365) conclude, "Generally, 50 to 80 percent of the substantial number of findings in this area were significantly positive, indicating that these dimensions were very consistently related to patient outcome." Related and facilitative, yes, but neither necessary nor sufficient in person-centered or other systems of psychotherapy.

The general pattern of early findings was that person-centered therapy outperformed no-treatment and waitlist control groups in samples of college students and mildly disturbed clients. In the early 1960s, Rogers and his colleagues (1967) courageously applied person-centered therapy to a group of institutionalized schizophrenics—one of the few psychotherapies now or then to be tested with this seriously disturbed population. The overall pattern of results demonstrated little effectiveness. Satz and Baraff (1962) also failed to find client-centered group therapy effective in treating hospitalized nonchronic, paranoid schizophrenics.

Turning to the overall effectiveness of person-centered therapy with nonpsychotic clients, let us examine the conclusions of several meta-analyses on the subject. Aggregating about 60 studies, the Smith and Glass (1977; Smith, Glass, & Miller, 1980) meta-analysis found that Rogerian person-centered therapy showed an average effect size of .63. This was interpreted as a respectable and moderate effect, clearly superior to no treatment, but just barely higher than the average effect of .56 for placebo treatment. Person-centered therapy was found to be comparable in effectiveness to psychodynamic, transactional analytic, and other insight-oriented therapies, but slightly below—some would say negligibly below—that of systematic desensitization and focused behavioral treatments (Shapiro & Shapiro, 1982). The one type of outcome measure on which client-centered therapy demonstrated higher change than a number of other orientations was in self-esteem, an area particularly prized by the person-centered approach (Rice, 1988).

A reassessment of the 17 published studies on client-centered therapy contained in the Smith et al. (1980) meta-analysis indicated that the apparent effectiveness of client-centered therapy was largely based on the treatment of problems that occur in academic settings (Champney & Schulz, 1983). Caution was recommended in generalizing the effectiveness of Rogerian therapy beyond academic problems and educational counselors to medical settings and private practices.

More recent reviews of client-centered therapy similarly show that it is definitely superior to no treatment, probably superior to an active placebo treatment, but also probably inferior in its effects to cognitive-behavioral psychotherapies. In a comprehensive review of 897 adult outcome studies on various psychotherapies published in the United States and Europe, Grawe and colleagues (1998) found client-centered therapy to produce statistically significant benefits compared to waitlist or no treatment in over 90% of the studies. At the same time, in direct comparisons, client-centered therapy produced less benefits than cognitive and behavioral treatments. Likewise, Greenberg, Elliot, & Litaer (1994) found that, in studies comparing classic client-centered therapy with no treatment, client-centered therapy achieved an average effect size of .95, a large impact to be sure. However, when client-centered therapy was compared with cognitive-behavioral therapies in five direct comparisons, client-centered therapy fared slightly poorly (Reicherts, 1998).

Similar conclusions are apparent in meta-analyses of the effectiveness of client-centered psychotherapy with children and adolescents. Weisz, Weiss, Alicke, & Klotz (1987) located approximately 20 controlled studies that included client-centered therapy. The average effect size was .56, similar to the .63 reported for adults treated with person-centered therapy. However, this effect size was smaller than those obtained for various behavioral treatments (ranging from .75 to 1.19). In a subsequent meta-analysis of child and adolescent psychotherapy outcome research, Weisz and colleagues (1995) identified six new studies testing the effectiveness of client-centered therapy. The effect size was again significantly lower than that found for a variety of behavioral, cognitive, modeling, parent training, and social skills interventions.

Criticisms of Person-Centered Therapy

From a Behavioral Perspective

Rogerians should be praised for their willingness to place person-centered therapy under scientific scrutiny. They must realize, however, that they are open to criticism for the many methodological errors found in their experiments. Fatal flaws in their studies include (1) using control subjects who are not candidates for therapy; (2) omitting an untreated control group; (3) failing to control for placebo effects; (4) relying on self-report measures, which are so open to demands to please the therapist or experimenter; and (5) neglecting the actual behavior and functioning of clients in favor of ratings of their subjective experiences.

Even when sufficient controls and rigorous methods are employed, the general meta-analytic conclusion is that behavior therapy is more efficacious than person-centered therapy. Perhaps greater use of empathy and warmth by behavior therapists would be useful, but the therapist's interpersonal behavior is rarely sufficient to conquer behavioral disorders. Don't stop with "touchy, feely" therapist qualities when specific, teachable behavioral techniques have been found to be more effective.

From a theoretical perspective, client-centered therapy is also open to serious question. Beneath all the rhetoric, Rogers is advocating a treatment that is apparently based on a fuzzy form of extinction. Troubled responses are assumed to have been conditioned by the contingent love and regard of parents. The therapist is supposed to reverse the process by establishing a social-learning environment in which there are no contingencies, no conditions for positive regard. The client is allowed to talk on and on about troubled behavior without being reinforced or punished. Eventually, the absence of contingencies leads to an extinction of talking about troubles. Of course, we cannot determine from the verbal extinction paradigm alone whether the client's troubled behavior itself has changed or whether the client has just quit talking about it. But why rely upon extinction when it is necessarily lengthy and can lead to complications, such as spontaneous recovery of the extinguished responses? Furthermore, when only extinction is used, there is no way of telling which new behaviors will be learned in place of the maladaptive responses that are being extinguished.

Rogers advocates trusting in some mysterious organismic actualizing tendency. This tendency is reminiscent of the ancient belief in teleology, which assumed an acorn would grow straight and tall if we only kept our foot off it. Of course, we now know that the manner in which even an acorn develops is in part a function of how it is nourished by its ongoing environment.

From a Psychoanalytic Perspective

The Rogerian approach is an exemplar of how our perceptions can be distorted by the people we are most likely to see for psychological treatment. Person-centered therapy is an inspirational theory of humanity of enormous appeal to college students because it was based primarily on work with students. It is a theory and therapy for ambitious individuals whose typically American drive to achieve is mistaken for some inherent tendency to actualize. Where was such a driving tendency to actualize in the chronic schizophrenics that Rogers and his colleagues (1967) failed to make into fully functioning individuals?

What person-centered therapy actually provides is a transference relationship that has all the elements of an idealized maternal love. Clients are promised a rose garden in which all that they are, their worst as well as their best, will be met with unconditional love. The fact is that research (for example, Truax, 1966) has demonstrated that even Carl Rogers made his responses to clients highly conditional upon the clients expressing feelings. When clients expressed particular feelings, Rogers was much more likely to show interest or express empathy. To pretend to be unconditional in our love is to do our clients a disservice, because the real world is, in fact, conditional with love. Such pretense can encourage clients to believe that, compared to the rest of the world, only a therapist could really love them.

From a Contextual Perspective

The person-centered disregard of the larger environment beyond the therapeutic relationship often leads to naiveté and ineffectiveness. The social milieu in humanistic theories is treated simplistically as an obstacle to self-realization, rather than as an arena in which the self will be either lost or realized. Downplaying external "reality" or the "real world," concepts Rogers often placed in quotation marks, can only confirm the public image of psychotherapy as unrealistic, self-indulgent, expensive talk about one's inner feelings and potentials. "Reality" consists of much more than emotions expressed in 50-minute sessions; family relationships, social institutions, economic considerations, and political power, to name just a few, routinely exert more influence on selfhood than person-centered therapists care to admit.

Rogers's preoccupation with selfhood, individuation, and self-actualization is culture-specific. His position both reflects and reinforces the high value that Western culture places on individualism (Usher, 1989). Not all cultures share this emphasis on "self." In at least one culture, the term for "self" does not even exist (Pervin, 1993). Less radically, some ethnic groups favor an external (not internal) locus of evaluation and function quite well. Person-centered therapists may be comparatively nondirective in the content addressed in therapy, but the underlying values are anything but nondirective. The value on separateness and autonomy over interdependence and connectedness, as another example, reflects a Western (and masculine) perspective.

Unlike Rogers, feminists insist that it is not enough for a woman to alter her self-perception. "To imply that such an internal change would eliminate all cultural, economic, legal, and interpersonal obstacles to a woman's physical and psychological actualization is absurd" (Lerman, 1992, p. 15). Vigorous group advocacy, not gradual individual change, will better solve most of the contemporary problems plaguing women and minorities.

From an Integrative Perspective

Rogers can be praised for the outstanding contributions he has made in articulating what constitutes a therapeutic relationship. The problem is, however, that he seems to have gone too far and concluded that what may be necessary conditions for therapy to proceed are also sufficient conditions for therapy to succeed. His promise of facilitative therapist qualities sounds like a Hollywood melodrama in which one unconditional love relationship comes along and emancipates a fully functioning person who lives happily ever after. What power he attributes to one caring relationship that usually meets only one hour per week! We are asked to believe that one special relationship alone is powerful enough to overcome the crippling effects of the conditional relationships that characterize our past and present lives.

Rogers's overemphasis on relationship variables can also encourage the fantasy that being an effective psychotherapist is merely a matter of feeling and relating and not of knowing much. His system suggests that anyone who is congruent, whether it be a peer counselor or a paraprofessional, can do effective psychotherapy with all patients and problems, without necessarily having any knowledge about personality or psychopathology.

Knowledge in Rogers's system is of little consequence; it certainly is not a necessary condition for effective therapy. Yet one wonders if it is sheer coincidence that master therapists, such as Freud, Adler, May, and Rogers himself, have been individuals with intense intellectual commitments as well as an enormous capacity for caring.

Finally, Rogers embodied unitary formulations and singular treatments for all clinical encounters (Norcross & Beutler, 1997). All clients suffer from the same essential problem, and all require the identical treatment. For all his avowed interest in an individualistic psychology, Rogers rarely managed to individualize his therapy approach to fit the particular client! Some patients thrive on a comparatively passive and unstructured form of psychotherapy, such as person-centered therapy, but other people do not. Instead, they require directive therapy and await active advice. History taking, confronting, teaching, interpreting, directing, and advising are all essential clinical activities in treating some clients with some problems. In these situations, person-centered therapy is contraindicated at best, poor practice at worst.

— A PERSON-CENTERED ANALYSIS OF MRS. C. —

Mrs. C. was raised in an extremely rigid atmosphere in which her parents' conditions of worth centered on being clean, being free from germs, being asexual, and being meek and nonaggressive. From her present compulsive pattern of existence, we can imagine that her own internalized conditions of worth are just as rigid as those of her parents. The only experiences she lets herself possess are those in which she is obsessed with proving how clean and free from disease she is.

Apparently in her early years of marriage she had felt loved and regarded highly enough to be more flexible and better adjusted. Just what went wrong is open to speculation. Her family was struck with a severe flu, and then the possibility of a pinworm epidemic might have threatened her self-regard by confronting her with not having been clean enough and careful enough with her family. At a more central level, she may have been threatened by a subception that she could not really love her children when they were sick or dirty. Mrs. C. may well have been experiencing the rigid limits of her love in relationship to her sick children and may have been threatened by doubts about the kind of mother she was if she could not really love her children when they needed her the most. But she had internalized the lesson from her parents that love is really contingent, that love is much too scarce to waste on the dirty or the diseased.

Although we do not know the exact experiences that were threatening to emerge into awareness, we do form the impression of a person who panicked, who was confronted with intense and undeniable experiences of being unlovable. Much of her life became disorganized as she struggled to hold onto what little self-regard she could maintain by organizing her life around washing and avoiding germs. If we empathize with the communications contained in her symptoms, we may hear how desperately she cries out: "I am worthy. I am lovable. Look how clean I am. I am not diseased. Don't send me away. I will make myself more lovable, more worthy of your regard. I will work harder, be cleaner."

If she could express her genuine feelings, she might go on: "My therapist and my family can love me only if I stop washing; I can love myself only if I am clean and pure. I am in a trap where I gain their regard at the loss of my own, or hold onto what little self-worth I have by continuing to clean and risk losing the few people who have any regard left for me. Suicide seems like the only alternative in this no-win situation."

Is Mrs. C.'s view just the distorted perception of a very troubled person? Do we not cast aside the dirty and the diseased? In our society, in which every major religious group values cleanliness more than mature love (Rokeach, 1970), should we be surprised that some people, like Mrs. C., base their existence on distorted social values and sacrifice their own organismic experiencing? Mrs. C. is a tragic prototype of a culture that is so enamored with social values such as cleanliness as to be estranged from organismic values like love.

Mrs. C.'s family and therapist have indeed made their caring as rigidly conditional as she has. They say, "Don't wash and we will care about you"; she says, "Only when I wash can I care about myself." An effective psychotherapist must establish an atmosphere in which Mrs. C. is held in high regard when she washes as well as when she doesn't, when she talks about washing as well as when she doesn't. When we appreciate that we are talking with a woman who is obsessed with maintaining what little self-regard and self-love she has left, we will not feel a need to have her give up her one remaining source of esteem—her washing.

First, she needs to experience the positive regard of those who care, whether she washes or not, whether she is obsessed or not. Then, and only then, can she begin to understand that being positively regarded is not contingent on either washing or not washing. Only then can she begin to gradually become a little freer to consider that maybe she, too, can love herself whether she washes or does not wash.

Caring is the fundamental issue, not cleaning. Mrs. C. has been providing unconditional cleaning, cleaning whether it is warranted or not, when what she really wants is unconditional caring, caring whether she at this moment warrants it or not.

Future Directions

As with Adler and the existentialists, Rogers's major contributions have been gratefully incorporated by most practitioners whose preferred orientations are not Rogerian. These lasting influences include the centrality of accurate empathy, the importance of the *person* of the therapist, the primacy of the relationship over technique, and the healing power of the therapeutic relationship. As a result of this widespread assimilation, the person-centered approach to psychotherapy has recently declined in popularity and research (Lietaer, 1990). As a distinct, 50-year-old system, person-centered therapy is definitely on the wane in the United States, (although it is more popular on the European continent).

The section titles of a volume devoted to client-centered and experiential psychotherapy in the 1990s (Lietaer, Rombauts, & VanBalen, 1990) epitomize its future directions: "Dialogue with Other Orientations" and "Specific Problems and Settings." Many practitioners of person-centered therapy argue for the supplementation of its communication and process focus with specific, validated interventions from other orientations (Bohart, 1993b; Tausch, 1990). Within and outside client-centered therapy, the facilitative therapist qualities have been profitably integrated with specific technical interventions from other systems of psychotherapy. There need be no inherent conflict between relationship and technique as long as the experience of the client remains the continuous touchstone for what is introduced by the therapist.

Laura Rice (1988; Rice & Greenberg, 1984) makes a crucial distinction between the primary relationship conditions and the specialized therapist interventions that are indicated by certain client *markers*. These markers represent an expressed or inferred readiness for specific change tasks. Confrontations, for instance, would be particularly useful when a therapist picks up discrepant messages from the client. Offered in an accepting relational context, even confrontation can be an extension of advanced accurate empathy (Greenberg et al., 1994; Norcross & Beutler, 1997; Sachse, 1990). Behavioral tasks outside the therapy session might be mutually designed when a client expresses a desire to implement some specific actions outside of the therapeutic relationship. By selecting those interventions that are missing in client-centered therapy as it is usually practiced and that are internally consistent with the primary client-centered relationship conditions, therapists could have the best of both worlds—the relationship and the techniques.

Empathy as a core of psychotherapy may be making a comeback (Bohart & Greenberg, 1997). As clients tire of short-term, technical interventions delivered in a few sessions by a hurried practitioner "managed" by an insurance carrier, they may hunger for a real human relationship that is a genuine meeting of two individuals. As therapists reacquaint themselves with the relational world of their clients, they may discover an empathic perspective surprisingly similar to that of Rogers, as has been experienced recently in psychoanalysis (e.g., Kahn, 1985), cognitive therapy (e.g., Safran & Segal, 1990), and yes, even in behavior therapy (e.g., Goldfried & Davison, 1994). As researchers work through the theoretical and practical struggles of assessing empathy (Duan & Hill, 1996), they too may return to the compelling awareness that psychotherapy is most fruitfully conceived and studied as a human relationship, rather than as a technical enterprise.

Person-centered therapy will also continue to adapt to new clinical settings and challenges. Health psychology, child therapy, couple therapy, and family therapy are likely up-and-comers for this therapy system (see Lietaer et al., 1990, and Wexler & Rice, 1974, for examples). Patient-centered training for medical professionals, especially physicians and nurses, should thrive in a consumer-oriented and holistic health care system. Perhaps most important, person-centered therapy will need to maintain an openness to new theoretical ideas (Combs, 1988) and to active and eclectic interventions (Lambert, 1986) in the era of short-term treatments. This openness is exactly what Rogers's own life demonstrated and what his later writings (1986, p. 259) implored: "Open new vistas, bring new insights, challenge our hypotheses, enrich our theory, expand our knowledge, and involve us more deeply in an understanding of the phenomena of human change."

Suggestions for Further Reading

Bohart, A. C., & Greenberg, L. S. (Eds.). (1997). *Empathy reconsidered: New directions in psychotherapy.* Washington, DC: American Psychological Association.

Farber, B. A., Brink, D. C., & Raskin, P. M. (Eds.). (1996). *The psychotherapy of Carl Rogers: Cases and commentary.* New York: Guilford.

Fiftieth anniversary of the person-centered approach [Special issue]. (1990). *Person-Centered Review,* 5(4).

Levant, R. F., & Shlien, J. M. (Eds.). (1984). *Client-centered therapy and the person-centered approach.* New York: Praeger.

Lietaer, G., Rombauts, J., & VanBalen, R. (Eds.). (1990). *Client-centered and experiential psychotherapy in the nineties.* Leuven, Belgium: Leuven University Press.

Miller, W. R., & Rollnick, S. (1991). *Motivational interviewing: Preparing people for change.* New York: Guilford.

Rogers, C. R. (1951). *Client-centered therapy.* Boston: Houghton Mifflin.

Rogers, C. R. (1961). *On becoming a person.* Boston: Houghton Mifflin.

Rogers, C. R. (1980). *A way of being.* Boston: Houghton Mifflin.

Journals: *Journal of Humanistic Education and Development; Journal of Humanistic Psychology; Person-Centered Review.*

Gestalt Therapy

Fritz Perls

AS LONG AS SEX WAS going well for Howard, all was well with the world. From ages 17 to 27, he had been very active sexually, with most of his time and energy spent in erotic adventures or in fantasizing about such adventures. Sexual relating was by far the most significant and satisfying activity in his life. No wonder he was so puzzled at the onset of his impotence. Except for his first experience with a prostitute at age 17, he had never had any difficulty performing in bed. In fact, Howard loved to perform and prided himself on what a great lover he was. But now, no matter how hard he tried, he just could not succeed. Needless to say, he was quite depressed and anxious.

Fortunately, Howard had a special partner named Ginny, whom he cared for deeply. She wanted to be with him sexually in spite of his impotence, and was willing to join him in sex therapy. We began therapy with the standard, Masters and Johnson (1970) type of sensate focusing. The results were discouraging because of the amount of depression and anxiety Howard continued to experience in the nondemanding, pleasuring exercises. Since his erections remained basically inhibited when he was with Ginny, we decided to try systematic desensitization and then come back to sensate focusing. Although Howard progressed to the point of imagining intercourse without anxiety, he did not show much generalization to the actual sensate-focusing situation.

Finally, I decided to use some Gestalt work and concepts to help Howard discover the significance of the intense pressure he was having over his sexual drive. I asked Howard to imagine as vividly as he could that he was his penis and that his penis had something to say. As he got into the fantasy, I encouraged him to just let the mouth of his penis say whatever it spontaneously desired, and here is what came out: "You're asking too much of me, Howard. You've been asking me to carry the whole meaning of your life on my back, and that's just too big a load for any one penis to carry. I'm bound to bend under such weight."

A Sketch of Fritz Perls

Frederich (Fritz) Perls (1893–1970) was the developer of Gestalt therapy and the master of using Gestalt work to assist people to become more deeply aware of themselves and their bodies. Perls did not start out with such an action-oriented approach, however. Like so many procreators of psychotherapy systems, his early career was heavily influenced by his studies of psychoanalysis with Freud. After receiving his MD in Berlin, where he was born, he studied at the Berlin and the Vienna Institutes of Psychoanalysis. He was analyzed by Wilhelm Reich (considered in Chapter 8), who had a profound influence on his development. Perls (1969b) said that if it had not been for the advent of Hitler, he probably would have spent his total professional career doing psychoanalysis with a few select clients.

As an aware individual, however, he anticipated the horrors of Hitler; and in 1934, when Ernst Jones announced a psychoanalytic position in Johannesburg, South Africa, Perls accepted. Besides establishing a practice, he also began the South African Institute for Psychoanalysis. Over the next dozen years, he developed what he initially considered a revision and elaboration of psychoanalysis. In 1947 he published his first book, *Ego, Hunger and Aggression: A Revision of Freud's Theory and Method*. At that time he was still committed to an instinct theory but argued for the acceptance of hunger as an instinct as critical to the survival of the individual as the sexual instinct is to the survival of the species. In the face of the many other revisions that Perls was suggesting for psychoanalysis, it became obvious that he was really beginning a new system, and when he republished his first book in 1969 he subtitled it *The Beginning of Gestalt Therapy*.

With the death of Jan Smuts in South Africa and the rise of apartheid, Perls again chose to leave a country heading toward unacceptable oppression. He emigrated to the United States in 1946, and with his therapist wife, Laura, began the New York Institute for Gestalt Therapy. In 1951, with Ralph Hefferline and Paul Goodman, he published *Gestalt Therapy: Excitement and Growth in the Human Personality*, a book that is exciting because of its engaging presentations of Gestalt exercises.

As a person, Perls was very much like his writings, both vital and perplexing. It was probably his many workshops with clinicians more than his writings that had such an impact on the psychotherapy profession. People saw him as keenly perceptive, provocative, manipulative, evocative, hostile, and inspiring. Many professionals came away from an encounter with Perls feeling more alive and more complete. Those who went out to spread the Gestalt gospel talked affectionately and almost worshipfully of Fritz. He certainly did not discourage such a cult. Believing that modesty is for modest people, Perls (1969b) wrote in his autobiography: "I believe that I am the best therapist for any type of neurosis in the States, maybe in the world. How is this for megalomania. At the same time I have to admit that I cannot work successfully with everybody."

Such unabashed egotism was fashionable in the 1960s and many people flocked to Esalen in Big Sur, California, where Perls held court. If it was uniqueness, honesty, and spontaneity they sought in Fritz, they were not disappointed; if it was a grandfatherly unconditional positive regard they desired, they were frustrated. As a result of his personal impact and his professional writings, the Gestalt movement became a very significant force in the last decade of Perls's life. He wanted to close out his life by building a Gestalt Training Center and Community in British Columbia, so he moved there just before his death in 1970.

With Fritz's death, Gestalt therapists lost their touchstone of just what Gestalt therapy can and should be. As one would expect from such a dynamic and spontaneous force as Fritz, there were many changes in his approach over the years. Consistency was not one of his concerns. Most Gestaltists, however, point to the 1969 publication of *Gestalt Therapy Verbatim* as the best representation of Perls's latest approach to Gestalt theory and therapy, and so this book serves as the main source for our presentation of Gestalt therapy.

Theory of Personality

In spite of the centuries-old wish to disown our bodies, we humans must accept that we are basically biological organisms. Our daily goals, or *end-goals* as Perls

(1969a) prefers to call them, are based on our biological needs, which are limited to hunger, sex, survival, shelter, and breathing. The social roles we adopt are the *means-whereby* we fulfill our end-goals. Our role of psychotherapist, for instance, is a means-whereby we earn a living, which is a means-whereby we fulfill such end-goals as hunger and shelter. As healthy beings, our daily living centers around the particular end-goals that are emerging into awareness in order to be fulfilled. If we listen to our body, the most urgent end-goal emerges, and we respond to it like an emergency—that is, without any obsessive doubt that the most important action we can take at this moment is to fulfill the particular end-goal emerging into awareness. We then interact with the environment to select the substances we need to satisfy that end-goal.

End-goals are experienced as pressing needs as long as they are not completed; they are quiescent once they are given closure through an adequate exchange with the environment. If we are thirsty, for example, we experience a need to bring completeness to our thirst by responding to our need with an adequate supply of water from our environment. It is this continual process of bringing completeness to our needs, the process of forming wholes or *Gestalts*, that Perls posits as the one constant law of the world that maintains the integrity of organisms.

The really serious concerns in living, then, are with the completion of these organismic needs, as is well known by the millions of starving poor in the world. In a spoiled society such as the United States, we spend little of our time or energy in completing our natural needs. Instead we preoccupy ourselves with social games that are best seen as nothing more than social means to natural ends. Once we experience these social means as end-goals, we identify with them as essential parts of our ego, so that we act as if we must put almost all our energy into playing roles such as student, teacher, or therapist. Much of our thinking is involved with practicing how we can better act out our roles in order to more effectively manipulate our social environment and convince ourselves and others of the inherent value of our roles. As we repeatedly practice our roles, they become habits—rigid behavioral patterns that we experience as the essence of our character. Once we develop our social character and have a fixed personality, we have transformed our basic natural existence into a pseudosocial existence.

In a healthy natural existence, our daily life cycle would be an open, flowing process of organismic needs emerging into awareness. This process would be accompanied by a means-whereby we bring closure to the most pressing need of the moment, followed by the emergence of another end-goal into awareness. As long as we remain centered on what is occurring within us right now, we can trust our wisdom as organisms to select the best means-whereby we adequately complete the most pressing need of the moment.

In a healthy existence, our entire life cycle involves a natural process of maturation in which we develop from children dependent on environmental support into adults who can rely on self-support for our own existence. Our development begins as unborn children entirely dependent on our mothers for support—for food, oxygen, shelter, everything. As soon as we are born, we have to do our own breathing at least. Gradually we learn to stand on our own two feet, to crawl, to walk, to use our own muscles, our senses, our wit. Eventually we have to accept that wherever we go, whatever we do, whatever we experience, is our own responsibility and only ours. As healthy adults, we are aware that we possess the ability to respond, to have thoughts, reactions, and emotions that are uniquely ours. This mature responsibility is fundamentally the ability to be what one is. For Perls (1969a), "responsibility means simply to be willing to say 'I am I' and 'I am what I am.'"

As healthy adults, we are also aware that other maturing organisms are equally able to respond for themselves, and the maturation process includes shedding responsibility for anyone else. We give up our childish feelings of omnipotence and omniscience and accept that others know themselves better than we can ever know them and can better direct their own lives than we can direct them. We allow others to be self-supporting, and we give up our need to interfere in the lives of others. Others do not exist to live up to our expectations, nor do we exist to live up to theirs.

The healthy personality does not become preoccupied with social roles, since these roles are nothing more than a set of social expectations that we and others have for ourselves. The mature person does not adjust to society, certainly not to an insane society like ours. Healthy individuals do not repeat the same old, tired habit patterns that are so safe and so deadly. In taking responsibility for being all that they can be, such people accept Perls's attitude of living and reviewing every second afresh. They discover that there are always new and fresh means-whereby they can complete their end-goals. This freshness is what the creative cook discovers, what the joyful sex partner experiences, and what the vital therapist thrives on.

With these attractive possibilities emerging from the natural process of maturation, how is it that most people remain stuck in the immature, childish patterns of dependency? There are several childhood experiences that can interfere with the development of a healthy personality. In some families, parents withdraw needed environmental support before children have developed the capacity for inner support. The child can no longer rely on the safe, secure environmental support, nor can the child rely on self-support. The child is at an *impasse*. Perls's (1970) example of an impasse is a blue baby that has had the placenta severed and cannot rely on oxygen from the mother but is not yet prepared to breathe on its own—a very scary situation. Another example of an impasse occurs when parents demand that a child stand without support before the child's muscles and balance are adequately developed. All the child can experience is the fear of falling. Experiencing impasses can result in becoming stuck in the maturation process.

A more frequent source of interference comes from parents who are convinced that they know what is best for their children in all situations. In such families, children may fear "the stick," which is some form of punishment for trusting their independent direction when it differs from what the parents believe is best. The child develops *catastrophic expectations* for independent behavior, such as "If I take the risk on my own, I won't be loved anymore or my parents won't approve of me." Perls (1969a) suggests that catastrophic expectations are frequently projections onto the parents of the child's own fears of the consequences of independence, rather than memories of how parents actually responded to the child's display of more mature behavior.

As we become more aware, we realize that marching to a different drummer can indeed be risky. If we are different from our parents or peers, we may risk losing their love or approval. But they are not responsible if we choose to avoid the risks of being our own person. There are even more serious risks in our society if we refuse to play roles or to adjust to social expectations. We can lose jobs, friends, money, and even face crucifixion for being outside the boundaries of society. But we still cannot blame society if we refuse to take the risks of being healthy.

Fear of repercussions for being independent is a major cause of maturational delays, but it is not the most common. More people get stuck because they have been spoiled by parents who overindulged them as children. Perls believes that too many parents want to give their children everything they never had. As a result, the children prefer to remain spoiled and let their parents do everything for them. Many parents are also afraid to frustrate their children; yet it is only through frustration that we are motivated to rely on our own resources to overcome what is frustrating us. By giving too much and not frustrating enough, parents establish an environment that is so secure and satisfying that the children become stuck with a desire to maintain constant environmental support. Perls's emphasis on being stuck by being spoiled is reminiscent of Freud's emphasis on overindulgence as one source of infantile fixations.

Perls does not blame the parents, however, for the spoiled child remaining stuck. These children are still responsible for using all of their resources to manipulate the parents and others in the environment to take care of them. These children develop a whole repertoire of manipulations, such as crying, if that is what it takes to get support, or being the nice little child, if that is the role that gets others to respond. To allow immature personalities to blame their parents for their problems is to allow them to avoid responsibility for their lives, which is such a critical part of the maturation process.

Theory of Psychopathology

The pathological person is the one who has become stuck in the natural process of growth or maturation. No wonder that Perls preferred the term *growth disorders* rather than *neuroses* to refer to the most common problems in living, although he frequently relied on the more traditional term *neurosis* when talking about psychopathology.

For Perls (1970), there are five different layers or levels of psychopathology: (1) the phony, (2) the phobic, (3) the impasse, (4) the implosive, and (5) the explosive. The *phony layer* is the level of existence in which we play games and play roles. At this level, we behave *as if* we are big shots, *as if* we are ignorant, *as if* we are demure ladies, *as if* we are he-men. Our *as if* attitudes require that we live up to a concept, live up to a fantasy that we or others have created, whether it comes out as a curse or an ideal. We may think it is an ideal to act *as if* we were Christ, for example, but Perls would see it as a curse, because it is still an attempt to get away from who we really are. The result is that neurotic people have given up living in a way in which they can actualize themselves; they live in order to actualize a concept. Perls (1970) compares such pathology to an elephant that would rather be a rosebush and a rosebush that tries to be a kangaroo.

We remain stuck in childhood fantasies because we do not want to be what we are. We want to be something else because we are dissatisfied with what we are. We believe we could get more approval, more love, more environmental support if we were something else.

What we create in place of our authentic selves is a fantasy life that Perls (1969a) calls *maya*. Maya is part of the phony level of existence that we construct between our real selves and the real world, but we live as if our maya is reality. Our maya serves a defensive purpose, because it protects us from the threatening aspects of ourselves or our world, such as the possibility of rejection. Much of our mental life is involved with making us better prepared to live in maya. Thinking, for example, is seen as a rehearsal for acting, for role playing, and this is one of the reasons that Perls says he disesteems thinking. We become so preoccupied with our concepts, our ideals, and our rehearsals that soon we no longer have any sense of our real nature.

In the struggle to be something we are not, we disown those aspects of ourselves that may lead to disapproval or rejection. If our eyes cause us to sin, we cast out our eyes. If our genitals make us human, we disown our genitals. We become alienated from the properties of ourselves that we and significant others frown upon, and we create the holes, the void, the nothingness where something should exist. Where the voids are, we build up phony artifacts. If we disown our genitals, for example, then we can act as if we are by nature pious and saintly. We try to create the characteristics that are demanded by our society for approval and that are eventually demanded by the part of ourselves that Freud called the superego.

In the process, we create our phony characters—phony because they represent, at best, only half of who we are. If the character we construct is mean and demanding, for instance, then we can be sure that below the surface is the opposite polarity of wanting to be kind and yielding. Our phony characters attempt to shield us from the fact that authentic existence involves, for each individual, facing a continuing sequence of personal *polarities* (Polster & Polster, 1973). We may rigidly adhere to being pious and saintly, for example, to keep from experiencing our opposite desires to be devilish and sexual. The healthy person attempts to find wholeness in life by accepting and expressing the opposite poles of life. Pathological individuals attempt to hide unacceptable opposites by pretending that their lives are composed entirely of their phony characters.

Perls called the most famous of the Gestalt polarities *Top Dog* and *Under Dog*. We experience Top Dog as our conscience, the righteous part of us that insists on always being right. Top Dog attempts to be master by commanding, demanding, insisting, and scolding. Under Dog is the slavish part of us that appears to go along with the bullying demands of Top Dog's ideals, but in fact attempts to control through passive resistance. Under Dog is the part of us that acts stupid, lazy, or inept as a means of trying to keep from successfully completing the orders of Top Dog. As long as people avoid accepting that they are also the opposite of what they pretend to be—that they are strong as well as weak, cruel as well as kind, and master as well as slave—they are unable to complete the Gestalt of life, to experience the whole of life.

To try to face all that we really are, to try to be whole, leads us to confront the *phobic layer* of our pathology. At this layer, we are phobic about the pain that ensues from facing how dissatisfied we are with parts of ourselves. We avoid and run from emotional pain, even though such pain is a natural signal that something is wrong and needs to be changed. The phobic layer includes all of our childish catastrophic expectations—that if we confront who we really are our parents will not love us, or if we act the way we really want to act our society will ostracize us, and so forth. These phobic responses frequently help us avoid what is really hurting; thus, most people come to therapy not to be cured, but to have their neuroses improved.

Below the phobic layer is the most critical level of psychopathology, the *impasse*. The impasse is the very point at which we are stuck in our own maturation. It is what the Russians call the *sick point*. The impasse is the point at which we are convinced that we have no chance of survival because we cannot find the means within ourselves to move ahead in the face of withdrawal of environmental support. People will not move beyond this point because of terrors that they might die or fall apart because they cannot stand on their own feet. But neurotics also refuse to move beyond this point because it is still easier for them to manipulate and control their environment for support. So they continue to play helpless or stupid or crazy or enraged in order to get others to take care of them, including their therapists. It is easier to continue these control maneuvers, because so much of the developmental time and energy of the neurotic has gone into creating and refining effective manipulation rather than into developing self-reliance. No wonder the neurotic is both afraid and unwilling to move through the impasse to the implosive layer of neurosis.

To experience the *implosive layer* is to experience deadness, the deadness of parts of ourselves that we have disowned. Neurotics would experience the deadness of their ears, or of their heart, or their genitals, or their very soul, depending on what fundamental processes of living they have run from. Perls (1970) compares the implosive layer to a state of catatonia, in which the person is frozen like a corpse. The catatonia is due to the investment of energy in the development of a rigid, habitual character that seems safe and secure but oh, so dead. To go through the implosive level, the person must be willing to shed the very character that has served as a sense of identity. The person is threatened with experiencing his or her own death in order to be reborn, and that is not easy, says Perls (1969a).

To let go of one's roles, of one's habits and one's very character, is to release a tremendous amount of energy that has been invested in holding back from being a responsible and fully alive human being. The person is now confronted with the *explosive layer* of neurosis, which entails an emancipation of life's energies, the size of the explosion depending upon the amount of energy bound up in the implosive layer. In order to become fully alive, the person must be able to explode into orgasm, into anger, into grief, and into joy. With such explosions, the neurotic has moved well beyond the impasse and the implosive and has taken a giant stride into the joy and sorrow of maturity.

Theory of Therapeutic Processes

Explosively breaking out of a neurotic life sounds like an exciting cathartic experience. The powerful release of the emotions of anger, orgasm, joy, and grief promises to bring a profound sense of wholeness and humanness. No wonder so many people sought out Fritz Perls as he traveled throughout the country. But Fritz quickly let people know that cathartic explosions could be attained only after the struggle to increase their consciousness of the phony games and roles they play and of the parts of themselves they have disowned. They have to become aware of how they are stuck in childish fantasies, of how they try to be something they are not.

Consciousness Raising

Consciousness raising in Gestalt therapy is aimed at liberating people from maya, from the phony, fantasy layer of existence. Since maya is a mental world, a world of concepts, ideals, fantasies, and intellectual rehearsals, Perls says the way for us to become free from maya is to "lose our mind and come to our senses." This loss of mind is actually a radical change in consciousness from future-oriented thinking and theorizing to a present-oriented sensory awareness. At this phenomenological level of consciousness, we can experience with all of our senses the reality of ourselves and the world rather than only experiencing our theoretical or idealistic conceptions of how things are supposed to be. We can have an experience of *satori,* or waking up. Suddenly the world is there again, right in front of our eyes. We wake up from an intellectual trance as we wake up from a dream. And with our senses we are again able to be in touch with all that we are.

The Client's Work. The client's work actually sounds quite simple—to stay in the *here and now.* Awareness of the moment allows clients to work on the healthy Gestalt principle: that the most important unfinished situation will always emerge into consciousness and can be resolved. But clients soon discover that staying in the here and now is not so simple. As soon as clients enter the "hot seat," indicating that they are ready to be the focus of the Gestalt therapist, they can be expected to reenact the phony layer of their neurosis. Some clients will play the helpless role, unable to proceed without more encouragement or direction from the therapist; others will play stupid, unable to understand just what the therapist means; others will strive to be the "perfect patient" with their Top Dog insisting that they should be able to do just what is expected of them.

Patients will then be asked to participate in Gestalt exercises designed to help them become more aware of the phony roles or games they are playing. These exercises are not an end in themselves; they are employed as a method to prevent avoidance of conflictual emotions. In the Top Dog/Under Dog exercise, for example, the client sits in one chair as Top Dog shouting out the "shoulds" at Under Dog, then switches to Under Dog's chair to give all of the excuses for not being perfect. Or the patient may be asked to become more aware of and dramatically repeat a nonverbal behavior, such as a kicking leg or an anxious smile.

As clients struggle to participate in the Gestalt exercises, they can also become more deeply aware of their phobic layer, of what they run from in the here and now and the catastrophic expectations that they use as excuses to run. For example, they may feel extremely angry at the therapist for not being supportive, but refuse to express their anger for fear that the therapist may want nothing more to do with them. The clients may then be asked to *own the projection* of rejection and to role-play who is actually threatening to reject them, such as their parents or their conscience. At each step in the exercises, the clients do not talk about what is entering their awareness. Clients are asked to express their conscious experiences in action—for example, by taking the chair that represents their parents or their Top Dog and expressing exactly what that person would say. Through such active expression, they become much more profoundly aware of what is interfering with their ability to exist in the here and now.

The Therapist's Work. The therapist's work in consciousness raising is, first and foremost, to frustrate the patient. More precisely, therapists frustrate the client's desires to be protected and to be shielded from unpleasant emotions, and the client's efforts to deny responsibilities for choices. Frustration itself is a by-product of the Gestalt interaction and the therapist interventions that are designed specifically to elicit something the patient is attempting to avoid. Client attempts to manipulate the therapist into taking responsibility for the client's well-being must be blocked, producing frustration. If the therapist is committed to "helping" the client, the therapist is lost from the start. Such a helping attitude is paternalistic, and the client will be determined to make the therapist feel inadequate as compensation for needing the therapist.

Early in treatment, the Gestalt therapist instructs clients on just how responsible they are for what they do in therapy. Perls (1969a, p. 79) used the following type of instructions in beginning a workshop:

> "So if you want to go crazy, commit suicide, improve, get 'turned-on,' or get an experience that will change your life, that's up to you. I do my thing and you do your thing. Anybody who does not want to take the responsibility for this, please do not attend this seminar. You come here out of your own free will, I don't know how grown up you are, but the essence of a grown-up person is to be able to take responsibility for himself— his thoughts, feelings, and so on. Any objections? . . . OK." And he begins.

Gestalt therapists are aware, of course, that such instructions alone will not keep clients from trying to turn their lives over to mental health professionals. Ultimately, the only way therapists can keep from being manipulated is to be mature individuals who take responsibility for their own lives and give up trying to be responsible for others. Mature individuals, be it clinicians or clients, have adequate inner support so that they are not dependent on others' liking or needing them, nor are they afraid of colleagues' condemning them. Perls (1969a) was not afraid to write, for example, that if a client rattled on in a meaningless monologue, he would take a snooze if he felt sleepy, even though such a response would be frowned upon by traditional therapists and clients alike. Such an honest response, however, would be sure to frustrate a client who was trying to make Perls responsible for making therapy an exciting adventure.

Part of the Gestalt therapist's responsibility is to be in the here and now just as clients are invited to be in the present. Being present-centered means that Gestalt therapists cannot use any predetermined pattern of exercises. An exercise is selected because at that moment the Gestalt therapist believes that it can allow the client to become more aware of what is keeping the client from remaining in the here and now. If clients continue to drift back into resentment of the past by blaming their parents for their problems, for example, the Gestalt therapist may employ an *empty chair* technique. Here the client is asked to imagine that the parent is present in the empty chair and they are now free to express to the parent what they always held back from saying. Such expression in the present of unfinished resentments can begin to allow clients to bring closure to their blaming game with their parents.

Although the pattern of exercises cannot be predetermined, the Gestalt therapist does have a wealth of exercises that can be called upon at any time to increase awareness. In *Gestalt Therapy* (Perls et al., 1951), a variety of these exercises are systematically presented so that readers can experience their own blocks of awareness. Theoretically, the types of exercises are limited only by the creativity of the clinician. In practice, however, most Gestalt therapists seem to fall back on the classical exercises devised by Perls (1947, 1969a; Perls et al., 1951). Levitsky and Perls (1970) have articulated the most commonly used Gestalt exercises or games. The exercises that are most involved in consciousness raising include the following:

1. *Games of dialogue,* in which patients carry on a dialogue between polarities of their personality, such as a repressed masculine polarity confronting a dominant feminine polarity.

2. *I take responsibility,* in which clients are asked to end every statement about themselves with "and I take responsibility for it."

3. *Playing the projection,* in which clients play the role of the person involved in any of their projections, such as playing their parents when they blame their parents.

4. *Reversals,* in which patients are to act out the very opposite of the way they usually are in order to experience some hidden polarity of themselves.

5. *Rehearsals,* in which patients reveal to the group the thinking or rehearsal they most commonly do in preparation for playing social roles, including the role of patient.

6. *Marriage counseling games,* in which spouses take turns revealing their most positive and negative feelings about each other to each other.

7. *May I feed you a sentence?,* in which the therapist asks permission to repeat and try on for size a statement about the patient that the therapist feels is particularly significant for the patient.

Gestalt therapists do not interpret what clients have to say while participating in Gestalt work. Interpretation is seen as a representation of the traditional therapist's maya—the therapist's fantasy that the real meaning of a client and the client's world can be found in a favorite theory rather than in the client's present experience. It is just another form of one-upmanship. It is a way for therapists to convince clients that they should listen to the magnificent mind of the therapist rather than to their own senses. In practice, however, the use of "May I feed you a sentence?" comes awfully close to straight interpretations, although Gestaltists prefer to see this exercise as feedback in which the client is free to actively spit out the therapist's message if it doesn't fit.

Gestalt therapists increase the consciousness of their clients by allowing the clients' own eyes and ears to serve as a source of feedback that provides them with information about themselves that has not been in their awareness. Clients are already aware of the sentences they have spoken, so Gestalt therapists do not reflect their clients' words as would Rogerian therapists. Gestalt therapists are much more in touch with clients' nonverbal expressions—the quality of their voices, their posture, and their movements. Gestalt therapists feed back what they see or hear, especially what they see as bodily blocks to greater awareness. They ask clients not only to attend to their nonverbal expressions, such as their arms folded across their chest, but also to "become" their arms in order to express how they are tensing up the muscles to keep from opening up the feelings in their hearts. With the assistance of these action-oriented exercises, clients begin to experience a deeper awareness that emerges from the depths of their bodies rather than off the top of their heads.

Catharsis

As clients become increasingly aware of their phony games and social roles, as they become more aware of their bodily resistances and phobic avoidance of the here and now, they are less and less able to run from themselves. The fear of being themselves, however, can bring them to an impasse. They will want to communicate to the therapist that they are able to continue on their own, that the therapist must take over for them or they will go crazy, panic, or terminate treatment. They try to convince the therapist that their catastrophic expectations are real and not just residual childhood fantasies. By pressing ahead, therapists communicate through their actions that they believe that clients do indeed have the inner strength to continue on past the impasse into their areas of deadness. Through sensitively selected exercises, clients can begin to reown the aspects of their personality that were sacrificed in the name of roles and games. Clients can begin to release all of the emotions that others will not love or approve of them if they are truly human.

The Client's Work. Cathartic releases require that clients take responsibility for continuing in therapy when they most want to run. The therapist will not try to talk them into staying in the "hot seat" if they feel it is getting too hot; they can and often do leave before the explosive fireworks begin. If clients do stay in the hot seat, however, they must be responsible for really throwing themselves into the suggested exercises and not merely play passively at going along with therapy.

If clients are prepared to take back and own what has been dead within, then they must be willing to participate in Gestalt dream work. Dreams are used in Gestalt therapy because they are seen as the most spontaneous part of one's personality. Dreams are the time and place in which people can express all parts of themselves that have been disowned in the rat race to succeed at daily roles. For dreams to be cathartic, however, clients cannot just talk about their dreams; they must act them out. Clients are encouraged to "become" each detail of a dream, no matter how insignificant it may seem, in order to give expression to the richness of their personality. Only when we become as rich and as spontaneous as our dreams can we be healthy and whole again.

At a time when I (JOP) was preoccupied with my promotion and my tenure, I found myself unable to experience any joy, not even the joy of sex. I sought the assistance of a friend who is a Gestalt therapist, and she asked me to conjure up a daydream rather than a dream. The daydream that emerged spontaneously was of skiing. She asked me to be the mountain, and I began to experience how warm I was when I was at my base. As I got closer to the top, what looked so beautiful was also very cold and frozen. She asked me to be the snow, and I expressed how hard and icy I could be near the top. People tripped over me there and were unable to cut through me because of how hard I was. But near the bottom people ran over me easily and wore me out. When we finished, I did not feel like crying or shouting; I felt like skiing. So I went, leaving my articles and books behind. In the sparkle of the snow and the sun, I realized again what Goethe had suggested through Faust: our joy in living emerges through deeds and not through words. In my rush to succeed, I was committing one of the cardinal sins against myself, the sin of not being active.

Because catharsis in Gestalt therapy occurs primarily as a result of clients' expressing their inner experiences, such as their dreams, we can talk about the process as a form of *corrective emotional experiencing*. Gestalt therapy also entails *dramatic relief*, inasmuch as it is often conducted in groups or workshops; the corrective emotional experiences of the person on the hot seat serve as cathartic releases for the people who are actively observing what is occurring there.

The *empty chair dialogue* pioneered by Perls and systematized by his followers demonstrates the therapeutic value of dramatic relief followed by a corrective emotional experiencing. The empty chair is used when emotional memories of other people trigger the reexperiencing of unresolved emotional reactions; for example, *unfinished business* with a dead parent or unavailable ex-spouse. The client is to express feelings fully to the imagined significant other, such as an alcoholic parent, in an empty chair. This act helps remobilize the client's suppressed needs and give full expression to them, thereby empowering the client to separate emotionally from the other. The critical components of the resolution of the unfinished business appear to be the arousal of intense emotions, the declaration of a need, and a shift in the view of the other person (Greenberg et al., 1994).

The Therapist's Work. Because catharsis in Gestalt therapy can be very dramatic, we can conceive of the therapist's work as beginning with setting the stage for the event. The group waits with anticipation for someone to step forward to fill the emotionally charged hot seat. The therapist's attention is then focused on the client like a spotlight. The therapist suggests that the best scene for now is some particular exercise—let's say, dream work. The script is created mostly by the client, who decides what dream to act out. Once the client enters the scene, the therapist is like a director who is prepared to help the client live, rather than just play a part in, the dramatic exercise.

Like a good director, the Gestalt therapist will observe carefully and listen for a *process diagnosis*—the emergence of markers of particular types of affective problems with which the client is currently struggling, such as splits between two parts of the self (Greenberg, 1995). When a marker emerges, the therapist will suggest a specific in-session experiment or task to facilitate conflict resolution. Although Perls was able to do much of this automatically, contemporary Gestalt therapists have tried to delineate specific markers for specific in-session experiments. The emergence of splits, for example, is a marker for a two-chair dialogue, unfinished business is a marker for the empty-chair dialogue, and a client expression of genuine vulnerability is a marker for empathic affirmation.

Gestalt therapists must also be aware of times when clients are trying to avoid the pain and fear of taking off their masks. Therapists try to block these avoidances by providing feedback and directing the client's attention to maneuvers that are being used to avoid, such as expressing important parts of a dream in a soft voice. If feedback alone does not produce change, then the Gestalt therapist will challenge clients to put more of themselves into the exercises, like a famous director challenging actors to give their best performance. Challenging clients to be more intense is especially effective in our competitive society, where people are so geared to meet any challenge. "OK, let's try it again with a fuller voice!" the Gestaltist might yell out. Such challenges also communicate the therapist's belief that clients do indeed have the inner resources to throw themselves more fully into the work, even when they are facing frightening or embarrassing scenes.

The Gestalt therapist can use other techniques of the theater to intensify the situation. Clients may be challenged to use the *repetition or exaggeration* game (Levitsky & Perls, 1970) until the true affect is expressed. Exaggeration or repetition is exemplified in the following excerpt from Perls (1969a, p. 293):

FRITZ: Now talk to your Top Dog! Stop nagging.

JANE: (loud, pained) Leave me alone.

FRITZ: Yah, again.

JANE: Leave me alone.

FRITZ: Again.

JANE: (screaming it and crying) Leave me alone!

FRITZ: Again.

JANE: (she screams it, a real blast) Leave me alone! I don't have to do what you say! (Still crying) I don't have to be that good! I don't have to be in this chair! I don't have to. You make me. You make me come here! (screams) Aarhh! You make me pick my face (crying), that's what you do. (Screams and cries) Aarhh! I'd like to kill you.

FRITZ: Say this again.

JANE: I'd like to kill you.

FRITZ: Again.

JANE: I'd like to *kill* you.

Gestalt therapists will also direct clients to change their lines toward a more emotional and responsible direction, following the rule of using "I" language (Levitsky & Perls, 1970). Fritz Perls (1969a, p. 115) demonstrates this direction with Max.

MAX: I feel the tenseness in my stomach and in my hands.

FRITZ: *The* tenseness. Here we've got a noun. Now *the* tenseness is a noun. Now change the noun, the thing, into a verb.

MAX: I am tense. My hands are tense.

FRITZ: Your hands are tense. They have nothing to do with you.

MAX: I am tense.

FRITZ: You are tense. How are you tense? What are you doing?

MAX: I am tensing myself.

FRITZ: That's it.

An outstanding therapist like Perls is also able to use *comic relief* to reduce tension and humor to release joy. An example of comic relief occurred with a client who was plagued by an incredible inferiority complex. He felt uglier than everyone and more inadequate than anyone. After several sessions of tense therapy he said, "I hope you don't misunderstand this but I'm beginning to feel inferior to everyone but you." I spontaneously responded, "That makes me feel real good." He laughed and I laughed and after a while he said, "You don't know how good it feels to say that to someone."

The creative process in Gestalt therapy means that the clinician will be an artist, not a scientist or a technician (Zinker, 1991). Fritz was admired for his artistic spontaneity, including his humor, which emerged in his workshops. Perhaps it is in humor that it is most obvious that a Gestalt therapist cannot predetermine the steps of effective therapy. For humor to be effective, the therapist must be free to be spontaneous, to capture the moment in creative humor. Cathartic experiences appear to be the dramatic results of clients who are struggling to be spontaneous interacting with therapists who are able to be spontaneous.

Therapeutic Content

Intrapersonal Conflicts

The most important problems for Gestaltists are conflicts within the individual, such as those between Top Dog and Under Dog, or between the person's social self and natural self, or between the disowned parts of the person and the catastrophic expectations that keep the person from expressing polarities that may meet with disapproval or rejection. Although Perls conducted Gestalt therapy in groups, his therapy was not really a group treatment in which the important content is the relationship between people in the group. Perls's therapy was principally individual treatment occurring in a group setting. The important content occurs within the individual as he or she acts out Gestalt exercises that bring an enhanced awareness and a cathartic release. Other individuals in the workshop relate to the person on the hot seat vicariously rather than directly.

Anxiety and Defenses. Anxiety is the gap between the now and then, the here and there (Perls, 1969a). Whenever we leave the reality of now and become preoccupied with the future, we experience anxiety. If we are anticipating future performances, such as exams, lectures, or therapy sessions, then our anxiety is nothing more than stage fright. How will I perform on the exam? How will my lecture go over? What will I do with that difficult client? We can also experience anxious anticipation over wonderful things that will happen: I just can't wait for that vacation to come! Many people fill this gap between the now and the future with all types of planned activities, repetitive jobs, and insurance policies to make the future predictable. These people try to replace anxiety with the security of sameness, but in the process they lose the richness of future possibilities. The problem is that in a rapidly changing society the people who try to hold onto the status quo can become more and more panicky about the changing future.

For Perls, the solution to anxiety is obvious: live in the here and now, not in the gap. By learning to be fully in the present, clients can transform anxiety into excitement. Rather than ruminating anxiously about aging, for example, people can experience the excitement of making fresh contact each day with an ever-changing environment.

Most people, however, avoid direct and immediate contact with the here and now through a variety of defensive maneuvers (Perls et al., 1951; Polster & Polster, 1973). *Projectors* distort experiences of themselves and their world by attributing the disowned parts of themselves to others in the environment. They avoid the excitement of their own sexuality, for example, by perceiving others, such as therapists, as being preoccupied with sex. *Introjectors* appear to take in the world, but in a passive and nondiscriminating manner. They never really integrate and assimilate new experiences into their personal identity. They are like the gullible oral characters who swallow anything others tell them.

Retroflectors withdraw from the environment by turning back upon themselves what they would like to do to someone else, or by doing to themselves what they would like someone else to do to them. A woman who would have loved to chew out her mother, to take one example, avoided the risk of explosion by chronically grinding her teeth. An introverted man avoided reaching out for sensual strokes from others by becoming preoccupied with masturbation.

Two other common defenses against anxiety are deflection and confluence. *Deflectors* avoid direct contact by acting or reacting in a chronically off-target manner. They may go off on tangents when talking, speak in generalities to avoid more emotion-laden specifics, or in other ways fail to get to the point of an interaction. Deflectors can avoid an impact from others, including therapists, by experiencing themselves as bored, confused, or in the wrong place. *Confluence* is a means whereby individuals avoid the excitement of novelty and difference by emphasizing the superficial similarities of any new contacts. Confluence frequently involves an agreement not to disagree and ultimately leads to phony conformity because of the security that is gained by going along with the crowd rather than acting from the center of oneself.

Perls (1969a) also emphasized how often thinking is used as a means of avoiding the here and now. Perls agreed with Freud's statement that "Denken ist Probearbeit"—thinking is trial work, or as Perls prefers, thinking is rehearsing. Thinking is a means whereby we prepare ourselves for social role playing.

Perls (1969a) suggests that most people play two kinds of intellectual games as part of social role playing. The *comparing game,* or "more than" game, is a form of one-upmanship in which intellect is used to convince others that "My house is better than yours," or "I'm greater than you," or "I'm more miserable than you," or "My therapy is better than yours," or "My theory is more valid than yours." The other intellectualizing game is the *fitting game,* in which we try to fit other people or other therapies into our favorite concepts of how the world is supposed to be. Or even worse, we may struggle to fit ourselves into our favorite concept of what we are supposed to be.

Self-Esteem. Shaky self-esteem is not the source of neurosis but one of the results of remaining immature and dependent. As long as our esteem remains dependent on the approval and evaluation of others, we will remain preoccupied with what others think of us and with trying to meet their expectations. A solid sense of esteem seems to be one of the natural rewards of discovering that we indeed have the inner strength to be self-supportive. Mental health professionals who perform supportive psychotherapy, which includes trying to shore up their patients' shaky esteem, in the long run contribute to the patients' esteem problems by implicitly telling them that they do not have the inner resources to support themselves. On the other hand, the tough stance of the Gestalt therapist, who refuses to give unnecessary support even when the patient is crying for it, is implicitly telling patients that they have the inner strength to stand on their own. By tapping into that inner strength, clients will find a solid basis on which to feel good about themselves.

Responsibility. We have already seen that accepting responsibility for one's life is a critical part of being a healthy, mature human being. Developmentally, people avoid taking responsibility either because they were spoiled and find it easier to manipulate others into taking care of them or because they fear parental disapproval or rejection if they respond in a manner that is too different from what their parents expect. Unlike traditional existentialists, Perls does not see avoidance of responsibility as deriving from inherent existential anxiety. For Perls, decisions about end-goals emerge naturally when one is centered as a natural organism. Problems with decisions occur only when people are not centered.

With a source of direction that is so natural, there is little need for existential guilt in the Gestalt system. Perls (1969a) suggests that most of what people call guilt is really unexpressed resentment. Guilt over premarital sex, for example, is frequently unexpressed resentment toward one's parents or church for trying to keep one from satisfying the natural sexual end-goals that emerge when the person is truly present-centered. Express the resentment either directly or in an empty chair exercise, and the guilt will soon be gone.

Perls does not directly address the difficult aspect of responsibility that involves an obligation to live up to a commitment that one has made. He does make it clear that when he talks about responsibility he is not talking about obligations. Since a mature person does not accept responsibility for others, perhaps there are no obligations for a person who lives in the now other than to be true to oneself. For people living in the now, it may be clear that making commitments is future-oriented and foolish because we cannot predict that at some future point it will be most important to act on a commitment that was made in the past.

Interpersonal Conflicts

Intimacy and Sexuality. Luthman (1972) paints an exciting picture of intimacy from the Gestalt perspective. Contrary to convention, intimate relationships begin with a commitment to ourselves, not to another. We are committed to presenting ourselves as we are, not pretending to be something the other expects or prefers. If who we really are is not liked by another, then it is best for us to learn that early rather than waste our time on a relationship that is bound to fail no matter how much we pretend otherwise.

As we relate, we accept differences as opportunities for growth, not as reasons for conflict. Differences are bound to bring frustration, but for Gestaltists frustration is welcome as a stimulus for further maturation. As we relate, we also accept that what we like and dislike is a statement about us and not a put-down of our partner. If we don't like our partner's cooking, for example, that is a statement about our taste and not a reason for saying that our partner is a lousy cook.

As differences emerge, we have to be willing to stay with an issue until all of our feelings are out in the open. We can then make compromises up to the limits or boundaries of who we are as individuals. We cannot compromise ourselves away just to keep a relationship going, because such compromises will generate smoldering resentment that will eventually poison the relationship. Our limits should not be seen as attempts to control the other person, but rather as the contours of who we are. We may find that once all of our feelings are in the open, neither of us can compromise far enough to allow the relationship to continue. Such a discovery is not a reason to blame or to hate, but rather to accept that we simply cannot make it together. On the other hand, if we do make it together, we can love even more because we are with a person who is strong enough to be authentic first and our partner second.

Although Perls has written little about sex, others such as Rosenberg (1973) and Otto and Otto (1972) have presented a series of exercises directed at helping sex to be a more total or holistic experience. The Gestalt emphases on being in touch with our bodies, on getting back to our senses, and on breaking out of old habits and responding spontaneously with our whole organism are critical in freeing people to experience how sex can be so much more than genital orgasm. Learning more integrated breathing, more natural pelvic movements, how to make fantasies reality, how to enjoy the humor in sex, and how to explode into orgasm are part of making sex a more total experience.

Communication. Since Perls worked mainly with individuals and not with ongoing relationships, he had little to say about communication conflicts. He does seem to suggest, however, that most communication is just part of social role playing. People chatter away about how great they are, how important or miserable or meager their roles in life are. As an action-oriented therapist, Perls prefers to get away from so much talk and to let real feelings be expressed in action, such as dancing to communicate joy or weeping to express sorrow. Perls was certainly astute at helping people become aware of their nonverbal communication, of what their body was attempting to say in its various postures and movements.

When we must resort to words, conflicts can be kept to a minimum by following several rules of Gestalt therapy. First of all, we should try to communicate as much as possible in the imperative form, because the demand is the only real form of communication for Perls (1970). When we ask someone a question, for example, we are really placing a demand on that person. Instead of saying, "Would you like to go to the movies tonight?" we should be direct and say, "Let's go to the movies tonight!" When we use direct demands, the person with whom we are communicating knows exactly where we are and what we want. That person then can choose to respond directly to our demands, rather than to a question. Second of all, since what we have to say is really a statement about us and not about the other, we should own our statements by talking mainly in "I" language. Rather than say, "You really make me angry because of how rotten you treat me," we would say, "I am angry because I let you treat me so rotten. From now on, treat me with more consideration!"

Hostility. Problems with hostility are boundary problems. Those aspects of the world that we identify with and that we include within our ego boundaries are experienced as friendly, lovable, and open to our kindness. Those parts of the world that we experience as outside of our boundaries are alien, threatening, and subject to our hostility. Those white Americans who identify with white supremacy, for example, and exclude African-Americans from their ego boundaries feel free to direct hostility toward blacks and be at war with them. For other whites, who identify with the goals of African-Americans and support their efforts for wholeness in our society, racists become enemies who are outside their ego boundaries and fair game for their hostility.

In intimate relationships, we expand our boundaries to include the other within our identity and create an experience of "we-ness." But even in intimate relationships, we usually cannot accept all aspects of another because we do not own all the aspects of ourselves. What we are most likely to be hostile toward in our intimates are their qualities that remind us of what we have disowned and projected outside of our boundaries. As the old saying goes, "We despise that in others which we fear most in ourselves." If we are hostile toward the tardiness of a friend, we should look within to see if we have disowned certain desires to not have to live our lives by the clock.

If we do not express resentments toward our intimates, we will begin to close off communication with them out of fear that openness might lead to expression of our hostility. We have failed to bring closure to an issue, and the resentment is an important signal that a Gestalt is pressing for completion. *Unfinished business* is then at hand. In psychotherapy, clients are encouraged to express intensely the hostility and resentment toward the empty chair that represents intimates with whom they are having trouble communicating. After releasing their hostility, clients need to begin to forgive their intimates for not being perfect so that they can begin to forgive themselves for not being perfect.

Control. Immature people are constantly involved in battles over interpersonal control. They either play a helpless, sick role, trying to manipulate others to take care of them, or they play a perfectionist Top Dog role in which they assume the responsibility for trying to get others to see the light and be more like them. They are acting out on an interpersonal level their intrapersonal pathology in which there is a constant struggle for control between the Top Dog and Under Dog. Only with maturation and integration can people give up the constant struggle for control and live by the Gestalt creed (Perls, 1970, p. 1):

I do my own thing and you do your thing.
I am not in this world to live up to your expectations,
And you are not in this world to live up to mine.
You are you, and I am I,
And if by chance we find each other, it's beautiful.
If not, it can't be helped.

Individuo-Social Conflicts

Adjustment Versus Transcendence. Gestalt is clearly a therapy of transcendence. Adjustment to society might have been an acceptable therapy goal at some time in the past when society was more stable and healthy. But like many critics of modern society, Perls (1970, p. 23) says: "I believe we are living in an insane society and that you only have the choice either to participate in this collective psychosis or to take risks and become healthy and perhaps also crucified."

To some extent, all healthy individuals will experience themselves as outside the boundaries of society. They will experience themselves as aliens, always potential targets for the violence of society. Alienation is thus the condition of the mature person, of the fully aware person, as long as society remains insane.

To adjust to a brutalizing society means to give up more and more of yourself (Denes-Radomisli, 1976). To adjust to riding in the New York subways, for example, we are forced to give up our sense of being human, deserving of some courtesy, and must be willing to be jostled and shoved and to shove and jostle in return. In order to be relatively comfortable in such a situation, we have to cover or deny our awareness of being mistreated and of mistreating others. With successful adjustment, we will soon be unable to feel human at all and get along just fine as a role or a robot.

Unfortunately, the alternatives for most people are alienation from society, in which the healthy person is one of the strangers in a strange land, and alienation from oneself, in which the unhealthy person is self-estranged. The final resolution for Perls was to seek transcendence by creating a Gestalt community in Canada in which a limited number of healthy individuals could both be themselves and be integrated within a community of whole people.

Impulse Control. Organismic impulses need not be controlled but need to be completed. Seeking food when hungry and sex when aroused are not dangerous to the individual; rather, completing these organismic needs is what helps create an individual. These impulses are a biological source of motivation and direction that allow individuals to rise above being just a social role. These biological sources of self-direction are relatively culture-free, and individuals can trust in their bodies, rather than social conformity to an insane society, to lead them to a healthy life. If people were raised to trust the messages from within their bodies, we could have a society of free and fulfilled people who let each other be rather than a society of rapers and ravagers.

Beyond Conflict to Fulfillment

Meaning. The meaning that comes from living in the now is found in the awareness that every second in our one existence is being lived afresh. No fuller life can be imagined. No regrets occur among those who jump into the stream of the present, since regrets are the plague of those stuck in the past. There are no preoccupations about the future, since we trust that our healthiest future emerges out of a present in which we attend to and complete our most urgent Gestalts. There is only one authentic goal for the future: to actualize ourselves as responsible and whole human beings. If that is not meaningful enough, then why not try to be a kangaroo or a king?

Ideal Individual. The ideal outcome for Gestalt therapy is to have people discover that they do not and never really did need a psychotherapist. Ideal clients accept that, despite all their manipulations to the contrary, they have the inner strength to stand on their own and be themselves. Such individuals have discovered the center of their lives, the awareness of being grounded in oneself. In being centered, they take full responsibility for the direction of their lives and do not blame anything on their parents or their past. From their core they find the strength to take the risks of being spontaneous and unpredictable, including the risks of being ostracized or crucified if that is the ultimate consequence of being themselves. In return for risking, the ideal individual earns the freedom to be creative, to be truly funny, to dance with joy, to be overwhelmed with grief, to be outraged with anger, and to be totally engaged in orgasm.

Therapeutic Relationship

In Rogerian terms, Perls certainly endorsed the need for therapists to be more congruent—or, as he would prefer, more mature—than clients. If therapists are to be self-supporting enough to resist pressures to match client expectations, they must have developed adequate maturity in their own lives. It is also a rule of Gestalt therapy (Levitsky & Perls, 1970) that the relationship should be an *I–Thou* relationship, or what Rogers would call a genuine encounter. In practice, however, Perls has been criticized by his colleagues (for example, Kempler, 1973) for always playing the Top Dog, thereby forcing the client into an Under Dog or patient role. Kempler is certainly correct that in the available transcripts of Perls's work, the personal Perls, or Perls as an "I," is missing. The very format of the hot seat puts clients in an Under Dog position in which they are directed in exercises by the Top Dog therapist. If clients confronted Perls to look at his own behavior, he would counter with a psychoanalytic type of move that forced the clients to look at their own motives for making such suggestions.

Both in theory and in practice, Perls agreed with Rogers on the therapist's need to respond with accurate empathy. In Gestalt work, clinicians must be able to experience the projections that clients are placing on them or the parts of the clients' personalities that are being disowned and then accurately feed back these blind spots. Neither in theory nor in practice did Perls accept the Rogerian concept of unconditional positive regard. For Perls, such behavior on the therapist's part would encourage infantilization. Patients must learn in treatment that if they act in immature or irresponsible ways, then mature people, including psychotherapists, will react with anger, impatience, boredom, or other negative responses.

At its best, the Gestalt therapeutic relationship is part of both the process and the content of therapy. As part of the process of being in the here and now, the therapist insists on remaining present-centered regardless of the patient's attempts to flee from the now. Therapists block immature attempts to make them take over the life of a client who is playing helpless, crazy, suicidal, or seductive. Through such frustrations in the relationship, clients are forced to grow, to become more aware of the games they are playing in order to remain unaware and immature. Gestalt therapists use their own awareness to realize when patients are attempting to avoid parts of who they are and to block avoidance by introducing exercises or exhortations designed to break through the patient's blocks. The relationship between the therapist's greater awareness, greater maturity, and ability to be in the now and the client's inability to stay in the now or to accept responsibility for avoiding being natural is an important part of the Gestalt process.

As part of the content of Gestalt therapy, clients' projections of disowned parts of their personalities onto the therapist are centrally important. Patient enactments of developmental immaturities and their various defenses are also confronted and frustrated in the context of the relationship. In addition, to the extent that Gestalt therapists do indeed encourage a Top Dog–Under Dog relationship, they provide a present battleground for clients to fight out their conflicts with authority and with their conscience or internalized parent.

To the extent that Gestalt books such as Perls and associates' (1951) *Gestalt Therapy* and Rosenberg's (1973) *Total Orgasm* suggest that people can radically expand their consciousness and cathartically release their energies by participating in the prescribed exercises, they imply that a therapeutic relationship is not absolutely necessary. No one disputes that a mature relationship can enhance the effectiveness of Gestalt work, but the relationship may not be essential for healthy growth to occur through Gestalt exercises. In part, disagreement on the necessity of the therapeutic relationship in Gestalt work revolves around the definition of "relationship." Gestalt work, as we have seen, does not require that the participants maintain a relationship in ongoing therapy together, nor that they have a therapeutic relationship before working together in a workshop. The requisite relationship, in Perls's eyes, is a state of common ground or attunement between a client and a therapist living in the here and now. This relationship or attunement *is* fundamental to the therapeutic process, and exercises without this relationship will likely be hollow, superficial, and even potentially harmful to the client (S. Forfar, personal communication, 1990). Did Perls desire an empathic and genuine bond to guide the appropriate use of technique? Absolutely. Did Perls insist that an ongoing relationship was necessary for growth? No.

Perls himself became concerned late in his life that all too many protégés were attempting only to learn techniques, instead of letting their work be a natural consequence of who they were and letting their responses be a natural consequence of an authentic therapist–client relationship (Kempler, 1973). But Perls had unwittingly contributed, both in his writings and in his workshops, to the belief that the Gestalt exercises were more essential to the content and process of Gestalt therapy than an authentic relationship was.

More recent considerations of the Gestalt relationship have amplified the need for Perls's concept of authentic *contact* (see Robine, 1991; Wheeler, 1990). Contact is the appreciation of differences in direct exchanges between persons and groups of persons (Perls, 1969a). Unlike the psychoanalytic object relations theory (Chapter 2), contact does not yet designate an object or another person. Rather, the term designates a sensorimotor pattern, ways of feeling and moving, a going toward and taking from (Robine, 1991). This contact plays a huge part in the creation of the therapeutic bond—empathically sensing each other's emotions and existence, authentically responding to the other in the here and now, sensitively making a connection in the Buberian I–Thou tradition, revealing the personhood of the therapist, and respectfully acknowledging the differences between the two existences now in contact. This renewed emphasis on contact in the Gestalt relationship softens the harsh, confrontational edge that some students experience in it and reminds us that Perls was capable of immense sensitivity to pain when clients confronted it directly. Furthermore, the emphasis on relational contact brings Gestalt therapy closer, in theory and in practice, to the desired therapeutic relationship of other systems in the existential-humanistic tradition, particularly the person-centered and existential perspectives.

Practicalities of Gestalt Therapy

Perls said that to do his psychotherapy, all he needed was a chair for the hot seat, an empty chair for the client's role playing, a client willing to enter the hot seat, and an audience or group willing to participate in the work between therapist and client. Perls seldom saw clients in an office, especially in his most famous years; most of his work was done in workshops, lectures, or seminars under the sun at Esalen. Many of his clients had only one clinical encounter with Perls, and yet the number of people who believed Perls had an impact on them is amazing. Apparently just watching Perls work with another person could produce a dramatic impact.

Gestalt therapists still prefer to conduct psychotherapy in a group setting, even though their work occurs primarily between the therapist and the person in the hot seat, not among group members. Our impression of the literature, however, is that the proportion of Gestalt therapy now conducted in an individual format rivals that performed in a group format. Increasingly, too, Gestalt therapists work with couples and families (see Greenberg & Johnson, 1988; Wheeler & Backman, 1994; Zinker, 1994).

Most Gestalt therapists tend to see their clients weekly, although as a rule they prefer at least two hours with a group and frequently longer, including marathon sessions. In Perls's workshops, clients did not pay extra for the therapy they received while in the hot seat but rather just paid the entrance fee to the workshop or lecture. It was the client's responsibility to secure therapy by requesting or assertively taking the hot seat.

In terms of professional disciplines, Gestalt therapists include psychologists, social workers, psychiatrists, pastoral counselors, and educators. Although many tend to be more informal about their Gestalt training, the more respectable route includes a minimum of one year of intensive training at one of the Gestalt training institutes. As a group, Gestalt therapists are also more informal about patient screening and outcome follow-up, following Perls's precedent that it is the client's responsibility to decide to enter or terminate treatment. Length of treatment seems to vary considerably, from one workshop session, to a marathon, to weekly meetings for six months, to a year or longer.

Training in Gestalt and experiential therapy is experiential. The medium is personal therapeutic work emphasizing individual awareness, emotional growth, and attendant personality change. The idea is that the individual grows as a result of contact with others, and this boundary contact nourishes and triggers a creative process. Personal development is thus integrated with professional training. Much of the learning occurs in therapy groups in which fellow students offer themselves as real-life clients to the therapists and the others to observe. This essentially comprises *circular learning,* in which individuals learn and teach each other by doing and observing (Napoli & Wolk, 1989). Some newer work attempts to teach the skills of Gestalt therapy in a more systematic fashion through a combined didactic-experiential and skill training program (Greenberg & Goldman, 1988).

Brief Gestalt Therapy

Several inherent elements of Gestalt therapy contribute to its brief and focused nature (Harman, 1995). For one, initial development of a contract with the client helps to narrow the focus on what issues the client would most like to resolve. For another, the here-and-now focus uses the present as the point of reference, as contrasted to extended analysis of the there-and-then. For still another, the active and directive techniques, such as the empty chair dialogue to resolve "unfinished business" (Paivio & Greenberg, 1995), can bring conflicts into full awareness and move them toward resolution in just a few sessions. Brief Gestalt therapy appears to be the rule rather than the exception, just as it was originally with Perls.

A Major Alternative to Gestalt: Experiential Therapy

Experiential therapy refers generally to a broad class of psychosocial treatments in the humanistic tradition that emerged in the 1950s and 1960s, largely as a reaction and alternative to the then-predominant psychoanalytic and behavioral perspectives. Some include person-centered and Gestalt therapies in this category; however, we will restrict our usage of this term specifically to those therapies identifying themselves by the moniker "experiential." Among the prominent examples of specific experiential therapies are the process-experiential approach of Leslie Greenberg and associates (Greenberg & Goldman, 1988; Greenberg & Johnson, 1988; Greenberg, Rice, & Elliott, 1993), the symbolic-experiential family therapy of Carl Whitaker (Whitaker & Bumberry, 1988; Whitaker & Keith, 1981), the focusing method of Eugene Gendlin (1981, 1996), and the experiential therapy of Alvin Mahrer (1983, 1986, 1989b, 1996). We will briefly examine Mahrer's version of experiential therapy as an alternative to Gestalt therapy because Mahrer has written extensively about its theory of human functioning and has systematized its process of therapy.

For Mahrer (1986; 1996; Mahrer & Fairweather, 1993), the core construct of personality and the central axis of change is therapeutic *experiencing*. Personality is understood in terms of potentials for inner "ways of being" or experiencing, which is a mode of apprehension characterized by its immediate, holistic, contextual, and bodily nature (Bohart, 1993a). Accessing deeper experiencing is the precious jewel of experiential therapy, it is what the patient can become, and it is the criterion for the success of a session.

In this view, change does not occur through attaining insight, resolving transference, receiving support or warmth, altering behavioral contingencies, restructuring cognitions, or other traditional means. Rather, change occurs by means of experiencing—that is, accessing a deeper potential, undergoing a good relationship with the potential, and then becoming a new person on the basis of this potential.

Accordingly, much of the therapist activity associated with other theoretical persuasions becomes irrelevant, if not counterproductive, in experiential therapy. Completing an initial assessment, taking a clinical history, performing evaluations, making diagnoses, formulating case dynamics, and targeting problematic behaviors have no place in this system (Mahrer, 1991). The therapist's work is solely to enable therapeutic experiencing.

Each session, every session, proceeds through the same four steps of therapeutic experiencing and achieves as much personal change as the patient is ready and willing to achieve in that session (Mahrer, 1989b). As we will see, the process of Mahrer's experiential therapy represents an interesting combination of emotional expression (catharsis), commitment to a new way of being (self-liberation), and then acquisition and practice of this new way of being and behaving that is incompatible with the old way (counterconditioning).

The first step is *being in a moment of strong feeling and accessing the inner experience*. This step enables the client to identify a scene of strong feeling, to discover the precise moment of this strong feeling in the scene, and to enter into and be that strong feeling in order to access the inner experiencing. Being in the exact moment of strong feeling is the royal road toward accessing whatever inner experiencing may be present. This experiencing then serves as the template for the balance of the session.

The second step, *integrative good relationship with the inner experiencing*, enables the person to accept, welcome, appreciate, and have an integrative good relationship with the accessed inner experiencing. The methods include naming and describing the inner experiencing—for example, being tough and hard, or feeling angry—and then accepting and welcoming that anger.

Step three, in turn, is *being the inner experiencing in earlier life scenes*. This temporal change from the present to the past enables the client to disengage from the ordinary person and enter into being the new person who is the inner experiencing. However, this change is accomplished within the relative safety of previous life situations. The therapist instructs the client to identify an earlier scene in life in which she was, to follow our example, extremely angry and to *be* the inner experiencing in that earlier scene and other scenes evoking the same strong feeling of anger. The person would temporarily relive and reexperience anger in, for example, being betrayed by a childhood friend or being cheated by a salesperson or being mistreated by a lover.

Having accessed the inner experience in the present, having accepted and welcomed the inner experiencing, and having been it in earlier life contexts, the patient is instructed in step four in *being the new person in the present*. The process jumps from the present, to the past, and now into the present and the future. This final step enables the person to be and to behave like the new person in likely new scenes—to sample what it is like to be a new person in the extratherapy world. The therapist helps the client select prospective scenes from the next few days, as well as ways of behaving in those scenes. In the session, the client mentally and emotionally rehearses these new ways of behaving, and refines effective and useful behaviors. The client might imagine a future episode of being mistreated again by her lover and then responding with assertion rather than passivity; a refinement might be for her to assert herself verbally and then behaviorally by leaving the theater or restaurant. The final element in the fourth step is to obtain from the client a personal commitment to new ways of being and behaving in the extratherapy world once the session is complete.

The next session, and each subsequent session, opens once again with the client identifying scenes of strong feeling. These may well include scenes related to the new ways of behaving that the client personally committed to at the end of the previous session. The principal, if not sole, measures of therapeutic success are the effective completion of the four steps in the session and the degree of being and behaving differently between sessions. Similarly, experiential dream work proceeds through the same four steps, and its effectiveness is evaluated according to the same criteria (Mahrer, 1989a). The dream provides ready-made scenes of strong feeling, in accord with the first step of each experiential session. The client reenters the dream experience, in contrast with the traditional method in which the therapist provides a dream interpretation.

Mahrer (1989b, p. 1) writes that his experiential therapy is "appropriate for virtually any adult," provided that he or she is ready and willing to do the work, and chooses to do so. A premium is placed, as in Gestalt therapy, on the patient's active participation in the work. Once trained in the four steps, patients and others may well undertake the four steps by themselves or with helpful partners. In practice, however, the three most common patterns of psychotherapy are for a client to have between 5 and 20 sessions over several months, 50 to 70 sessions over a period of a year, or 100 to 150 sessions over a few years (Mahrer, 1989b).

Quite distinctive to experiential therapy are the physical arrangements of treatment and the therapeutic relationship. Sessions generally last 75 to 120 minutes each, in a room with plentiful sound insulation and low light illumination. The therapist and client both sit or recline in large, comfortable chairs situated alongside (not across from) each other. And both have their eyes closed throughout the entire session in order to enhance experiencing, to avoid discussing the interpersonal relationship between therapist and patient, and to minimize other distracting influences. This side-by-side, closed-eyes configuration is unique; no other experiential therapist requests or insists on such an arrangement.

In experiential therapy, the clinician operates as an instruction giver, a fellow traveler into the inner world, and as the "voice" of the patient's experiencing. Forging a therapeutic alliance and examining the relationship represent a "trap" that interferes with accessing experiencing and, as such, has no place in this system. The therapist has few private thoughts or personal agendas; instead, what the patient says comes in and through the therapist in a very active and advanced form of empathy. The experiential therapist relates in the same way with all clients in every session; the *way* of relating and the four steps are fixed and universal for all clients. At the same time, the *person* of the therapist is almost wholly tailored by the client in the unique here and now of the moment, in that the therapist deliberately tries to be the voice of whatever the client is experiencing at that moment. Put another way, the experiential relationship is rigidly fixed and invariant for each patient in terms of the therapy *process* or steps, but is simultaneously flexible and tailored to each patient in terms of the therapy *content* (Mahrer, 1993).

All told, Mahrer's form of experiential psychotherapy constitutes a vital and novel system, to be sure, but one that some mental health professionals "experience" as untested and radical. The proscriptions against problem identification, history taking, and alliance formation, as well as the prescriptions to keep eyes closed at all times, to speak with and for the client's experiencing, and to follow the same four steps for each patient in each session, are radical departures from conventional practice. Nonetheless, experiential therapy is gradually emerging as a major alternative to Gestalt therapy, but one in the same general family. A particular advantage is that the operations of a leading experiential therapy have been identified and codified in a treatment manual, which can now be systematically taught and rigorously evaluated.

Effectiveness of Gestalt Therapy

As a humanistic approach, Gestalt psychotherapy has not eagerly embraced the traditional scientific method of empirical research. As a growth-oriented approach, Gestalt therapy has been evaluated largely for its enhancement of functioning, not recovery from symptoms. Compared to cognitive and behavioral treatments, there is little systematic research on the outcomes of Gestalt and other experiential psychotherapies (Greenberg, et al., 1994), and the research that has been conducted frequently concerns growth experiences, decisional conflicts, and nondiagnosable conditions.

Quantitative reviews conducted in the 1980s on the efficacy of Gestalt therapy are partially supportive. Across 475 studies examining various types of psychotherapy, Smith, et al. (1980) found an overall effect size of .85, a large effect. Across 18 studies testing the efficacy of Gestalt therapy, the researchers found an average effect size of .64, a number closer to the moderate effect range. This effect size indicates that Gestalt therapy is consistently superior to no treatment but barely higher than placebo treatment (average effect size = .56).

A thorough review by Greenberg and colleagues (1994) on the very small amount of outcome research conducted on Gestalt therapy in the past decade demonstrates that it is superior to waitlist or no-treatment controls. No recent studies have compared it to an "active" placebo. At the same time, in five direct comparisons between Gestalt therapy and alternative psychotherapies, Gestalt therapy led to slightly lower gains four of the five times (Greenberg et al., 1994).

All in all, Gestalt therapy has not been found to be consistently superior to any other tested system of psychotherapy and, depending on one's perspective on statistical versus clinical significance (as discussed in Chapter 2), is perhaps inferior to tested cognitive and behavioral methods of therapy. Gestalt therapy has not been sufficiently researched with children and adolescents to be included in meta-analyses of that body of literature (Weisz, et al. 1987; Weisz, et al., 1995).

Turning to experiential therapy, no controlled outcome studies have been published to date on Alvin Mahrer's form of experiential therapy. Hence, its effectiveness has not been demonstrated in comparison to no treatment, placebo treatment, or other systems of psychotherapy.

Several studies have examined the effectiveness of Leslie Greenberg's *process-experiential therapy* (Greenberg, et al., 1993). This treatment combines a client-centered relationship with more active, Gestalt interventions, such as two-chair work for resolving splits and empty chair dialogues for unfinished business. The results of process-experiential therapy are consistently and impressively good compared to both no-treatment and alternative treatments (Greenberg et al., 1994), but are unfortunately based primarily on studies concerning marital distress and decisional conflict, not diagnosable "neurotics" (Reicherts, 1998).

The effectiveness of Gestalt and experiential therapies will probably be determined in the future by programmatic research aimed at identifying the specific disorders and particular people for whom it is most indicated. In a series of studies, Beutler and colleagues (see reviews by Beutler, Mohr, Grawe, Engle, & MacDonald, 1991; Beutler & Consoli, 1992) have examined the efficacy of *Focused Ex-*

pressive Psychotherapy (FEP) (Daldrup, Beutler, Engle, & Greenberg, 1988), a Gestalt-based group treatment that encourages affective arousal by intensifying awareness and facilitating unwanted emotions. FEP was compared to both cognitive therapy (CT) and a supportive/self-directed (S/SD) therapy in groups of four to eight depressed outpatients who met weekly over 20 weeks. Groups were led by experienced psychologists, and therapist compliance with the therapeutic model was closely monitored. An intensive battery of assessment measures administered throughout treatment, at termination, and after 3-, 6-, and 12-month follow-up periods indicated that all the treatments were effective in combating depression.

As expected, the three treatments did not differ in overall effectiveness. However, also as expected, differential effectiveness emerged when the three treatments were cross-matched to compatible patients. Specifically, depressed patients who cope by acting out and projecting (the externalizers) tended to fare best in CT because their personality dispositions contrasted with the introspective and awareness methods of the other treatments. By contrast, depressed patients who cope by using intrapunitive methods (the internalizers) tended to do better with FEP. As further predicted, the directive treatments (CT and FEP) were of greatest benefit to patients who had low resistance, whereas the S/SD treatment was differentially effective with highly resistant patients. In sum, Gestalt-based therapies were most effective for internalizing, low-resistant, overly socialized clients. This research conclusion perfectly describes the prototypical patients with whom Fritz Perls worked during the development of his system of psychotherapy.

Criticisms of Gestalt Therapy

From a Behavioral Perspective

We must recognize that, at a societal level, the ultimate outcome of Gestalt therapy would be anarchy. "You do your thing and I do my thing" may sound romantic to some, but it is a shallow slogan that reinforces the development of narcissistic and egocentric individuals who have little reason to be concerned with others. Perls states directly that his ideal individual would not take responsibility for anyone else. What happens, then, to the socializing responsibility of parents? Is there any evidence that human beings can live in relatively harmonious and secure societies if social expectations and approval are rejected as consequences for helping to direct human behavior? Perls seems to forget that his work at Esalen was appealing to those who had already gone through a socialization process and tended to reject violence or force as means-whereby they satisfied such organismic end-goals as sex. Let the Gestaltists test their psychotherapy with undersocialized individuals, such as psychopathic prisoners, to see what kind of community they would create.

If it is not bad enough that there is pitifully little controlled outcome research on Perls' Gestalt therapy and none at all on Mahrer's experiential therapy, then consider the sobering conclusion of a review on negative outcome in psychotherapy. A review of 46 studies on negative effects for adult, nonpsychotic persons in psychotherapy found that expressive-experiential therapies produce higher rates of deterioration than other psychotherapies (Mohr, 1995). So let us get this straight:

Few research findings attest to Gestalt therapy's effectiveness, and convergent findings suggest its higher risk for negative effects. Not our idea of an empirically supported therapy!

From a Psychoanalytic Perspective

Where ego was, let there be id! The naive Gestaltist would like to deny that there are indeed biological impulses that can overwhelm both the individual's mental well-being and the social order. How would Gestaltists treat paranoid and other patients whose ego processes are in danger of being overwhelmed by rage? Encourage more rage? So much talk about responsibility, and yet the Gestaltists encourage professional irresponsibility by suggesting to potential patients that if they want to go crazy or commit suicide, that's up to them. Such a philosophy may work fine in workshops filled with growth-seeking normals. But it is certainly dangerous as an approach to a typical caseload of patients that includes people barely able to hold onto their sanity, let alone able to be mature, self-supporting, whole human beings.

From a Contextual Perspective

The emphasis in Gestalt therapy on awareness, self-support, and responsibility magnifies the role of the individual *qua* individual, separate and distinct from other people, often with little attention to important ongoing relationships and cultural systems (see Saner, 1989; Shepherd, 1976). Isolation and occasional dalliances with others are the probable results. Who will tend to families and communities? Surely not the Gestaltists! The Gestalt prayer (Perls, 1973) reminds us that "I am I, and you are you. I'm not in this world to live up to your expectations, and you're not in this world to live up to mine. I is I, and you is you." All the "I-ness" has driven out the "We-ness." No wonder Perls predicted that the ideal person would be socially alienated; such people are merely reaping the "I-ness" they have sown. When problematic relationships are not dismissed as inconvenient or fatalistic enterprises ("It can't be helped"), they are discarded as our projections.

Social problems aren't the real culprits, Gestalt therapy tells us. They are merely handy intellectual excuses for the failure to take responsibility for our own behavior. Perhaps that's true for mildly neurotic, wealthy people luxuriating on the idyllic beaches of Big Sur, California, but for most of us, the real social forces of poverty, illness, sexism, racism, crime, and death are at least contributing culprits. Where else but in California, and when else but in the 1960s, could one seriously promise a life full of integration, expression, and freedom?

It is a major hunk of work for women to integrate all the social, political, and economic forces and to arrive at a harmonious personal sense of self in which no experience needs to be discriminated against as inadmissable or unworthy (Polster, 1974). But speaking of "disowned" parts and of getting in touch with "polarities" begins to erroneously locate the disturbance solely within a person and unrealistically suggests that emotionally expressive work will free her from these social forces. Not in most neighborhoods. The Gestalt injunction to accept individual responsibility for change quickly deteriorates into blaming the victim. Genuine liberation for the oppressed must also come from without, not only from within.

From an Integrative Perspective

Although Perls believed that he was following the existential heritage, which includes rejecting the Cartesian dualism that overvalues mind at the expense of body, what Perls in fact left us is a reverse dualism that overvalues body at the expense of mind. Perls's disesteeming of thinking encourages an irrational anti-intellectualism that could result in empty-headed organisms that are no more whole than the disembodied products of the Cartesian tradition. Gestalt therapy is obviously in need of a cognitive theory to balance its overemphasis on biology. Many observers (for example, James & Jongeward, 1971; Martin, Paivio, & Labadie, 1990; Tosi, Rudy, Lewis, & Murphy, 1992) have suggested an integration of Gestalt with cognitive therapy. Until some integration is achieved that gives equal weight to the cognitive capacities of human beings, Gestalt therapy will remain a movement that attempted to balance Descartes by speaking for the body but unfortunately ended up flipping the philosophical cart, with the body now the Top Dog.

Like most "true believers," Perls and his fellow Gestalt enthusiasts overextended the usefulness of the therapy into indiscriminate applications with promises that cannot be met. Gestalt work is most effective with overly socialized, restrained, and constricted individuals. With less-organized and more seriously disturbed individuals, Gestalt work becomes a risky proposition. And with individuals whose problems center on impulse dyscontrol—acting out, delinquency, explosive disorders—it is probably contraindicated (Shepherd, 1976). The eclectic directive is to selectively use what works, not to indiscriminately use it all the time.

— A GESTALT ANALYSIS OF MRS. C. —

Like so many people in our society, Mrs. C. was raised to disown the socially unacceptable aspects of her body. For most of her life she succeeded in disowning the sources of her sexual desires and the bodily basis for her angry feelings. Since the onset of her full-blown neurosis, Mrs. C. has been engaged in trying to disown her entire body by washing it away. Fortunately, the biological basis of her existence will not just lie down and die; her body keeps sending out messages that remind her that she is human and therefore subject to diseases, anger, and sexual desires. Mrs. C. refuses to listen to her body and instead keeps obsessing in her mind and compulsing in her actions, "Wash away body, wash away," until she is now little more than a washed-out dishrag.

Mrs. C. reports that her childhood disowning of sex and anger was due to catastrophic expectations that her parents would punish her if she did not play the role of a good, clean little girl. How much these catastrophic expectations were based on reality and how much on fantastic projections cannot be established from the record. The important point is that these fears were part of the phobic layer that motivated Mrs. C. to spend most of her existence in the phony layer of playing the model child, model mother, and now model neurotic.

At the time her symptoms began, Mrs. C. was probably becoming increasingly dissatisfied with how responsible she had to be for everyone else, with no time or energy to realize who she really was. Five kids and a pregnancy, diapers, dishes, disease, and pinworms on top of it all! Who wouldn't want to yell out in anger and in despair? But Mrs. C. never had the guts to stand up for herself, to do what she really wanted to do, so why would we expect her to do it now? Instead, she projected the responsibility for her problems onto the pinworms and then proceeded to spend her life trying to wash away the pinworms and herself. If she had confronted who she really was—a person able to get very angry, a person desiring to be free, and a person more egocentric than she ever dared to be—her childish catastrophic expectations would tell her that she would be rejected and hurt. So don't think about who you really are; think only about the pinworms and the washing!

The reason the pinworm episode represented an impasse, a sick point, was that Mrs. C. had never become a mature person, never developed the capacity to be responsible for herself. Now there were clearly too many kids, too much illness, and too many demands for Mrs. C. to move ahead on her own. With the development of dramatic symptoms, Mrs. C. could get others, including her psychotherapists, to try to take care of her. It was also apparent that Mrs. C. was using her symptoms to manipulate others, such as getting George to attend to her by keeping track of her shower ritual. Apparently Mrs. C. was finding it easier to remain sick and manipulative than to become healthier and stand on her own.

To work through her impasse, Mrs. C. would have to face the implosive layer of her neurosis. She would need to experience the deadness of her genitals, the total emptiness of her past ten years, and the loss of her very center. Because she had projected the responsibility for her miserable life onto pinworms, it is no wonder that her life now centered around pinworms. Mrs. C. had no energy left to feel alive, because her organismic energy was all tied up in the rigid, neurotic patterns that had become her life.

With almost all of her energy invested in neurosis, Mrs. C. would need to experience some tremendous explosions to be born again. She would explode into grief over the loss of a whole decade of her life. She would release all of her anger toward her daughter, her husband, her parents, and herself for letting her play the role of such a good daughter and such a good mother. Mrs. C. would also reach way back into the earliest years of her life to see if she could discover the bodily basis for her sexuality so that she could for the first time in her life explode with orgasm. Only with these potentially violent explosions could Mrs. C. ever again hope to experience the joy of living.

To face the fears of her catastrophic expectations, to cross the impasse and become responsible again, to confront the pain of having been dead so long, and then to undergo the tremors of emotional explosions and shed the totally clean character that had been the source of her identity, would perhaps be too much for Mrs. C. She would strongly prefer a psychotherapy that promised to improve her neurosis by letting her go back to being Mrs. Clean without having to wash all the time.

Assuming that Mrs. C. wanted more from treatment than to return to her former immature adjustment to life, a Gestalt therapist would ask her to begin by staying in the here and now. Of course, she couldn't do it. She would probably continually return to talking about pinworms or washing. She would insist on playing the helpless patient role and would let the therapist know how grateful she would be if the therapist could pull her out of her misery. Such maneuvers would be aimed at turning the responsibility for her miserable life over to the therapist. One of the most effective Gestalt exercises could be to instruct her to end all of her statements about her problems and her life with "and I take responsibility for it." If she could be encouraged and directed into really experiencing the possibility of being responsible for her neurosis, Mrs. C. might begin to experience some of the grief she must face over her wasted life.

A Gestalt therapist might also encourage Mrs. C. to use the empty chair technique to role-play her relationship to pinworms. She would first speak for the pinworms, which might well come on like Top Dog, and then respond with her present feelings toward the pinworms. As they yell out at her, "You must wash or we'll eat you up," she might be able to begin to experience her rage toward the pinworms for dominating her life. As she began to let more anger seep out, she would probably want to avoid, lest she be punished or rejected for being a naughty, angry person. She might begin to become more conscious of how childish her catastrophic expectations are. She might also become increasingly aware of just how much she has projected the responsibility for her problems onto the pinworms. It would also be important for the clinician to give Mrs. C. feedback about the variety of maneuvers she uses in order to get her therapist to take more direct control of her life.

As the Gestalt therapist refused to be manipulated into rushing in to rescue Mrs. C., she might begin to experience increasing anger toward the therapist, which would be a breakthrough from preoccupation with pinworms to feeling angry in the here and now. As she stayed with her fears over being angry, she would begin to realize that her catastrophic expectations were indeed her projections—her therapist would not hurt or reject her, and she would not get pinworms.

To own back so much of her disowned personality, Mrs. C. would probably have to participate in Gestalt dream work. Since almost all of her waking hours have been rigidly spent in obsessions and washing, her sleeping hours would be the only time in which her disowned self could be spontaneously expressed. While it would be difficult to force Mrs. C. to vividly attend to her dreams because of all the pain and grief that would come with awakening to memories of having once been a real person, the breakthroughs could be tremendous if she began to face how much she had given up for the security of washing. Probably only through Gestalt dream work could such an absolutely rigid, habitual character like Mrs. C. begin the cathartic process of reawakening to and reowning all the vital organismic aspects of her existence.

Future Directions

In retrospect, behavior was the favored content and focus of psychotherapy in the 1970s, and cognition was the favorite during the 1980s. In prospect, affect and emotion are probable winners in the late 1990s and the beginning of the next century. Adding affect into the therapeutic mix and facilitating emotional change will likely be major foci of psychotherapy practice, research, and training in the coming years, and this should reenerigize Gestalt. Instead of being avoided and controlled, emotions are increasingly recognized as organizing processes that enhance adaptation and problem solving (Greenberg, et al., 1993). Having regained "the mind" during the cognitive revolution in psychotherapy, mental health professionals will rediscover emotion after a 30-year drought since the 1960s heyday of Fritz Perls and the encounter movement.

We foresee Gestalt's continued influence in at least two spheres: psychotherapy integration and specific disorders/client presentations. Any satisfactory integrative or eclectic therapy must incorporate more than words and ideas. Whether they label it expressive, Gestalt, emotionally focused, experiential, affective, or emotional work, integrative practitioners seek methods to evoke emotions and to precipitate intense experiences. At the same time, emotional work is not always enough, and Gestalt therapists will increasingly seek other orientations—object relations, cognitive, and client-centered, in particular—to balance and complete their own perspective. Marcus (1976) anticipated many years ago this movement away from Gestalt therapy as an exclusive modality and the incorporation of other therapy systems. Back in 1976, contributors to the *Handbook of Gestalt Therapy* (Hatcher & Himelstein, 1976) were demonstrating the complementarity of Gestalt and other methods of psychotherapy. Gestalt therapists know that growth is by assimilation (Yontef, 1988).

In their review of research on the experiential psychotherapies, Greenberg and colleagues (1994, p. 533) wisely conclude that "Probably the most obvious trend that emerges from this review is the shift away from the practice of offering a uniform treatment to all clients and toward adapting experiential treatments to specific disorders or problems." Certain disorders and patient presentations would seem to virtually require experiential work along the lines suggested by Perls and other Gestaltists. Words and ideas alone are typically insufficient to heal the emotional ravages of chronic pain, personality disorders, sexual abuse, and posttraumatic stress disorders (PTSD). Conversely, there is a concomitant evolution in thinking that emotionally expressive work is not the treatment of choice for all people. Clients high in autonomy or reactance will probably respond negatively to more directive elements, and practicing Gestalt with them may partially explain the higher risk of negative effects. We will be increasingly able to "pick our moments" of using Gestalt work on the basis of clinical experience and research literature, such as the early but convincing demonstrations of the superiority of focused expressive therapy for overcontrolled patients. In doing so, we will have traveled full circle and returned to the population of reasonably healthy, oversocialized patients on whom Gestalt therapy was constructed and with whom Fritz Perls was so successful.

Suggestions for Further Reading

Daldrup, R. J., Beutler, L. E., Engle, D., & Greenberg, L. S. (1988). *Focused expressive psychotherapy: Freeing the overcontrolled patient.* New York: Guilford.

Gendlin, E. T. (1996). *Focusing-oriented psychotherapy: A manual of the experiential method*. New York: Guilford.

Greenberg, L. S., Rice, L. N., & Elliott, R. (1993). *Facilitating emotional change*. New York: Guilford.

Hatcher, C., & Himelstein, P. (Eds.). (1976). *The handbook of Gestalt therapy*. New York: Jason Aronson.

Mahrer, A. R. (1996). *The complete guide to experiential psychotherapy*. New York: Wiley.

Perls, F. (1969). *Gestalt therapy verbatim*. Lafayette, CA: Real People Press.

Perls, F. (1973). *The Gestalt approach and eye witness to therapy*. Palo Alto, CA: Science and Behavior Books.

Polster, E., & Polster, M. (1973). *Gestalt therapy integrated*. New York: Brunner/Mazel.

Wheeler, G. (1990). *Gestalt reconsidered: A new approach to contact and resistance*. New York: Gardner.

Zinker, J. (1977). *Creative process in Gestalt therapy*. New York: Brunner/Mazel.

Journals: *The Gestalt Journal; Journal of Humanistic Psychology*.

7

Interpersonal Therapies

Eric Berne

"DADDY, YOU SURE HAVE BEEN a lot nicer since you've been going to see that man," said Sara, the 12-year-old daughter. "Do you think I could go with you one week to talk with him, too?"

When Sara came in with her father to his psychotherapy session, she was eager to tell me how much better things were at home. She used to hide to avoid her dad's anger when he came home from work, but now she enjoyed being with him. Her father had always been extremely strict and stern and would use such put-downs as "stupid" and "dummy" when he corrected his daughter. Not only had his behavior led to problems with Sara's self-esteem and academic performance, but it had also been one of the major causes of arguments between her parents.

Conditions had improved markedly, however, since the father had begun reading *I'm OK—You're OK* (Harris, 1967) and participating actively in transactional analysis, and especially since the parents had come home from therapy and decided to play a game at dinner in which Sara and her 7-year-old sister would be the parents and the parents would play the role of the children. At first Sara was afraid to be her father, but once she got into the role she found herself imitating his angry silence and his stern reprimands. "Close your mouth when you're eating, stupid" or "Sit up in your chair, dummy," she would mimic. While these *role reversals* allowed all of the family members to see themselves more clearly, they also provided some hearty laughs together, including the normally somber father.

In our session together, the father was able to tell Sara how strict his own mother and grandmother had been when he was growing up. He did not have a father at home, and he grew up believing that it was natural for all parents to be rigid and punitive disciplinarians. He related to Sara that as she was getting more mature, he wanted to be able to relate to her more as an adult and less as a strict parent. Sara said that one of the things she had learned was that even when her father acted very strict at times, she could help by not responding as an angry child.

Sara went on to say that she really liked the I'm OK—You're OK ideas and the Parent–Adult–Child concepts but could not understand how a 12-year-old like herself could be a parent. Her mother quickly asked, "Do you think the way you boss your sister around all the time is your way of being a strict parent?" Sara laughed.

This chapter considers two of the many forms of psychotherapy identified as "interpersonal" in title or in content. We examine in detail the seminal theory and practice of transactional analysis, beginning with a sketch of its founder, Eric Berne. We then review in brief the newer and influential system known simply as "interpersonal psychotherapy."

A Sketch of Eric Berne

Eric Berne (1910–1970) first came upon the phenomenon of people relating as Parent, Child, or Adult when he decided to listen to his clients and not his teachers (Berne, Steiner, & Dusay, 1973). He had been practicing psychoanalysis for ten years and had learned to translate whatever clients were saying into the theoretical language he had gained from his teachers. Thus, when a client remarked, "I feel as though I had a little boy inside of me," Berne would typically have interpreted the little boy to mean an introjected penis, as Otto Fenichel did in a similar case. But instead of asking himself, "What would Otto Fenichel say in this case?" he asked the client what he thought about it. As it turned out, the client really did feel like a little boy, and this feeling was the most significant clinical fact in determining the course of the client's life. As therapy proceeded, Berne asked at an appropriate time, "Which part of you is talking, the little boy or the grown-up man?" (Berne et al., 1973, p. 371). At the moment of asking this question, transactional analysis was born.

Actually, Berne had been moving away from orthodox psychoanalysis for quite some time. He received his MD at McGill University in 1935 and completed his psychiatric residency at Yale from 1936 to 1941. He immediately began his training as a psychoanalytic candidate in New York, but this training was interrupted by an army stint from 1943 to 1946. During his military duty he began working with groups and became excited about the possibilities of group therapy, thus moving away from the strict one-to-one format of orthodox analysis.

After the war, he settled in Carmel, California, and resumed his psychoanalytic studies in San Francisco with Erik Erikson as his analyst. When he applied for membership in the psychoanalytic institute in 1956, he was rejected on the basis that he was not doing psychoanalysis. Because Berne readily agreed with the accusation, he dissociated himself from psychoanalysis and in 1957 presented his first paper on transactional analysis (TA).

Although this paper marked the formal introduction of transactional analysis, Berne had gradually developed his system during the previous decade. Beginning in the early 1950s, he had established a seminar group in Carmel in which he began to present his emerging theory and have it critiqued by the seven professionals who attended. By the time he published his first paper in 1958, the essence of his theory was already well developed.

In many ways, Berne was rather an unlikely candidate for establishing a new and popular system of psychotherapy. He was indeed creative and articulate, but he was also shy and lacking the charisma that characterizes many founders. Berne was also modest in his initial attempts to influence the thinking of other mental health professionals, as indicated by the small size of his initial seminar and the relatively slow pace at which he presented and published his theory.

Nevertheless, his influence increased markedly, from 40 members in his San Francisco seminars in 1958 to an international association six years later. Even the popularity of *Games People Play* (1964) was a surprise; Berne had written it primarily for professionals who were already manifesting an advanced interest in TA. Berne was actually afraid that the public success of his book might undermine his professional credibility. Instead, his theory continued to attract a growing number of professional advocates.

Berne's work, especially his writings and patients, formed the essence of his adult life. He spent every Tuesday and Wednesday with his private practice, consultations, and seminars in San Francisco and then flew back to Carmel, where he wrote and had a second practice. He seemed to derive a great deal of fun from going to the beach and dancing at the parties that typically followed the weekly seminars. For the most part, however, Berne seemed to prefer to be independent and relatively self-sufficient. Steiner (1974) believes that Berne had a *life script* that involved very strong injunctions against loving others and accepting the love of others. Like his father, a physician, Berne had chosen early in life a script involved with curing others. For Berne, this meant that his personal life was sacrificed to his professional life, with his loving relationships being relatively short-lived. Steiner speculates that when Berne died from a heart attack in 1970, he actually died from a broken heart because he was unable to let in enough of the strokes and love that others felt for him.

Theory of Personality

Everything in transactional analysis stems from the premise that human personality is structured into three separate ego states: *Parent*, *Adult*, and *Child* (PAC). These ego states are not theoretical constructs; they are phenomenological realities amenable to direct observation. When people are in the Child ego state, for example, they sit, stand, speak, think, perceive, and feel as they did in childhood. Behavior of the Child is impulsive and stimulus-bound rather than mediated and delayed by reason. Throwing temper tantrums, being irresponsible or irrational, and engaging in wishful thinking or daydreams are some of the expressions of the Child. At the same time, the Child is the source of spontaneity, creativity, humor, and fun and is thought to be the best part of the personality, because it is the only part that can truly enjoy life.

The Child ego state is essentially preserved intact from childhood. It is as if the Child has been recorded on a nonerasable tape in the brain and can be turned on live at any time. The Child is at most eight years old and can be as young as a newborn infant. The Child can be further differentiated into the *Natural Child*, which is the most emotional, spontaneous, and powerful expression of a child; the *Adapted Child*, which is the more obedient child molded to parental demands; and the *Little Professor*, which is the inquisitive and intuitive child who acts like a precocious adult.

The Parent ego state is also carried over essentially intact from childhood. The Parent is basically composed of behaviors and attitudes that are copied from parents or authority figures. Although much of the Parent is based on videotape-like recordings from childhood, the Parent can be modified throughout life as the person models new parental figures or changes as a result of actual experiences with parenting. When the Parent is in control, people use the language of controlling parents: "should," "ought," "must," "better not," and "you'll be sorry" predominate. Gestures like pointing a finger or standing impatiently with hands on the hips are other common expressions of the Parent.

The Parent is the controlling, automatic, limit-setting, and rigid rule maker of the personality, as well as the nurturing and comforting part of the personality. The Parent is also the repository of traditions and values and is, therefore, vital for the survival of civilization. In ambiguous or unknown situations, when adequate information is unavailable to the Adult, then the Parent is the best basis for decision making.

In a second-order structural analysis of the Parent, Steiner (1974) also differentiates between the *Nurturing Parent* and the *Pig Parent*. The Nurturing Parent acts out of genuine concern for others and provides support or protection when needed. This type of parent is potent and effective because of the respect it engenders in others. The warm but firm police officer is an example of such a Parent. The Pig Parent, on the other hand, is oppressive, acting not on the basis of what is best for others but out of anger and fear of others and an irrational need to control. This type of parent makes others feel not OK, engenders fear and hatred in others, and is thus at times called the Witch or the Ogre. The Pig Parent rules not out of respect but only because it has actual power over others in particular situations. Sara's father was an example of a person acting out this more derogatory and oppressive type of Parent.

The Adult ego state is essentially a computer, an unfeeling organ of the personality that gathers and processes data for making predictions and decisions. The Adult is a gradually developed ego state that emerges as the person interacts with the physical and social environment over many years. The Adult acts more clearly on the basis of logic and reason and is the best evaluator of reality because it is not clouded by emotion. The Adult can realistically evaluate not only the environment but also the emotions and demands of the Child or the Parent.

Because each ego state is a substructure of the ego, and because, as Hartmann (1958) has suggested, the ego is the adaptive function of the personality, each ego state is adaptive when used in the appropriate situation. The Parent, for example, is ideally suited when control is necessary, such as control of children, fears, the unknown, the Child, and undesirable impulses. The Child is ideally suited when creation is desired, such as the creation of new ideas or new life. The Child is also most adaptive for fun situations, such as parties or celebrations. The Adult is ideally suited when accurate prediction is necessary, such as deciding on a marriage, career, or budget.

The well-adapted personality, then, switches from one ego state to another depending on the needs of the present situation. Only one ego state can be in operation at a time. When a particular ego state is in control of the personality, it is called the *executive* and is said to be cathected, or imbued with the psychic energy necessary to activate muscles involved in behavior. The process of easily and voluntarily changing from one ego state to another is called *stabilization*; this is the sign of a healthy or stable personality.

Ego states provide the structure of the personality but not the motivation. Motivation for behaving comes from biogenetic drives for survival, such as hunger for food, but also from psychological drives, which Berne (1966) labels *stimulus hunger*, *recognition hunger*, *structure hunger*, and *excitement hunger*.

As early studies on stimulus deprivation demonstrated (for example, Hebb, Held, Riesent, & Teuber, 1961; Solomon, Kubzansky, Leiderman, Menderson, Trumbull, & Wexler, 1961), human beings can become highly disturbed if they are deprived of adequate amounts of incoming physical stimulation. One of the most important forms of stimulation needed for a healthy personality is *stroking*. For young children, stroking needs to be in the form of direct physical contact that comes through being held, soothed, and cuddled if they are to survive emotionally and physically (Spitz, 1945).

Although direct physical contact is the most nourishing form of stroking, adults can learn to get by with only the stimulation that comes from recognition. The need at times to be the center of another person's attention, to have our existence recognized by another human being, is especially obvious in children, who will settle for negative attention if that is the only way they can gain recognition. Although positive strokes such as smiles, greetings, applause, approval, and cheers are most valued, negative strokes such as frowns, cold looks, criticism, and disapproval at least satisfy the human hunger for recognition.

Structural hunger is the motive that develops out of the common human dilemma of deciding what to do with 8,760 hours a year. In some societies, all of this time is devoted to survival needs—to obtaining adequate sleep, food, and shelter. In most societies, however, people have surplus time and would have to be constantly deciding how to structure their time if social institutions were not available to help them order their lives. Religion, education, recreation, art, politics, marriage, and families are all designed, in part, to facilitate structuring the time at our disposal. Social leaders are those individuals who have special skills to help others structure their time. The most valued leaders are those who help to structure time in the most interesting and exciting ways, because the desire to avoid boredom, to have interesting and exciting hours, seems to be part of the human condition.

One of the most exciting ways to spend time is to exchange strokes with others. An exchange of strokes defines a *transaction*, and the hunger for strokes and for excitement makes human beings inherently social animals who are highly motivated to participate in social transactions. Transactions that are spontaneous, direct, and intimate can be exciting, threatening, and overwhelming. Such free and unstructured exchanges of strokes are generally avoided, especially in short-term social interactions, in favor of more structured and safer transactions.

The safest form of transaction is a *ritual*, which is a highly stylized interchange. There are informal rituals, such as greetings: "Hello, how are you?" "Fine, thank you, and how are you?" There are also formal rituals that become established as traditional ceremonies, such as weddings or funerals, which are entirely structured and predictable. Rituals convey very little information and constitute signs of mutual recognition.

The next safest form of social interaction is a work activity. Most work activities are highly programmed, not as bound by tradition and custom as rituals are, but by the intrinsic nature of the material with which the individuals are working. If the individuals are working together to build a car, then the most efficient structure is the assembly line. Participation in such work activities is typically geared to the Adult ego state of the workers.

Most leisure time is safely structured through pastimes. Pastime sharers are those with mutual interests, such as dog owners, Shriners, or people at weekend workshops. Although transactions in pastimes are more informal and individualized than rituals, pastimes are nevertheless designed to minimize the possibility of incidents that are too emotional and exciting. Pastimes allow people to structure their time in transactions that are fairly interesting but not too threatening.

The riskiest and most exciting transactions that are still structured are the *games people play*. A game is a complex series of ulterior transactions that progress to a psychological *payoff*—a feeling such as guilt, depression, or anger. In an ulterior transaction, communication appears to have not only an overt, social meaning but also a covert, psychological meaning. For example, if a woman asks a man, "Why don't you come by my place to see my collection of sculpture?" and the man responds, "I'd love to. I'm really interested in art," they may be having a simple, candid interchange between two Adults beginning to share a pastime. In a game, however, both players are also communicating a message at a different level. They may, for example, be exchanging Child-to-Child messages like "Boy, I'd really like to get you alone in my apartment" and "I'd like to hook up with you."

A game is able to progress because one player is pulling a *con*—that is, doing something other than what is on the surface, such as inviting the man to risk being alone in her apartment. For a con to work, the respondent has to present some type of weakness that gets *hooked*, such as vanity, greed, sentimentality, guilt, or fear. In this case the man's vanity is hooked, and he goes off to the apartment with great expectations.

For the payoff to occur, one of the players has to pull a *switch*. In this case, after a few drinks and sitting close on the couch listening to music, the woman still seems to be sending a seductive communication. The man's vanity convinces him to proceed, and he puts his hand on her leg, only to be rebuffed by a push away and an irate "What kind of woman do you think I am?"

The couple has just completed a hand of "Kiss Off" or "Indignation." Besides gaining mutual recognition, excitement, and some structured time together, there is also an emotional payoff for each. The woman is able to profoundly affirm her position in life that she is OK, while feeling angry toward men for not being OK, just as her mother always said. The payoff for the man is to feel depressed and thereby reaffirm his conviction that he is not OK.

People like these, who repeatedly seek payoffs of anger or depression, can be characterized as collecting *stamps*, like the trading stamps that people save. The color of the stamps depends on the feelings that are collected, such as "red stamps" for anger and "brown stamps" for depression. Collecting these stamps allows people to eventually trade in all of their stamps on a major emotional release, such as a hostile explosion or a suicide attempt.

Games also serve to reaffirm the life position that a person chooses very early in life. Based on experiences in the first few years of life, children make a precocious decision about how they are in life compared to others around them. The life position contains a summary conviction of how I am and of how others are. The four possible life positions are: (1) *I'm OK—you're OK*, (2) *I'm OK—you're not OK*, (3) *I'm not OK—you're OK*, and (4) *I'm not OK—you're not OK*. The first and universal position of children is to be OK unless the civilizing process helps to convince them that they are not OK. Or, as Berne believed, children are born princes and princesses, until their parents turn them into frogs (Steiner, 1974).

Adopting a life position at age 6 or 7 about being OK or not OK critically determines the life script that a person chooses. The decision that one is *Born to Win* (James & Jongeward, 1971), to act out a successful life plan, a get-on-with-it script, is consistent with a decision that one is indeed OK. Scripts calling for chronic failure or futility, getting-nowhere-with-it scripts, are much more likely to be selected by people who are convinced that they are not OK. The general tenor, then, of a script is made consistent with the life position a person chooses.

Many details of a life script are supplied by parental prohibitions, suggestions, and encouragements. "She argues like a lawyer," "He's such a helpful boy," "She definitely wants to be the queen bee," "You're going to go to hell" are parental statements that profoundly influence the development of particular scripts. Fairy tales and children's stories are also important sources of suggestions for a life script. A person's favorite myth or fairy tale, for example, is thought to reflect the person's original life script. A 25-year-old mother of two who was prepared to leave her third husband for a more exciting life on a lover's sailboat had prized the story of "Cinderella" throughout her childhood; now she was quite literally acting out the life script of a woman rescued from a miserable life by a man. While parental statements and childhood stories are important influences, the life script is still the creation of a young child who decides how best to act out a life position and to fulfill particular human hungers.

Theory of Psychopathology

Theoretically speaking, psychopathology can occur either at the intrapersonal level of personality, involving problems with the person's ego states, life position, or life script, or at the interpersonal level, involving transactional conflicts between the ego states of two or more people. Practically speaking, however, psychopathology is almost always a multilevel phenomenon entailing problems both within the personality and between personalities.

Difficulties within a person's ego states are *structural problems* of the personality. The most elementary structural problem is confusion, in which people are not capable of discerning their three separate ego states and slip from one state to another in a confused manner. A father, for example, who was removed from his home for almost killing his son, was talking in an Adult manner about the realistic conflicts he was having with his teenage son. As he was talking rationally about how the son at times talks back to his mother, he quickly became enraged and with a beet-red face said that he thought the best solution is to beat his son to a pulp. The father had little or no idea of how he was switching from his rational Adult to his self-righteous and irate Parent who demands total respect.

Another structural problem is *contamination,* in which part of one ego state intrudes into another. The Adult is the ego state most likely to be contaminated by prejudices of the Parent or myths and fantasies of the Child. A man cannot deal effectively with the realities of work, for example, if his Adult takes as fact the Child's fantasy that he is destined to marry a wealthy spouse who will rescue him from a lowly position. One such client bolstered his arguments for this rescue belief by going to a tea-leaf reader who insisted that he would soon be engaged to a wealthy woman.

Exclusion is the structural problem of people who rigidly hold to one ego state and shut out the other two. A husband who was almost always working and continually preached to his wife about how she should take care of the house and the kids was unable to find any fun or joy in life because his rigid Parent had successfully excluded both his Child and Adult from being expressed. On the other hand, the constant *Clown*, the prankster who is the life of the party but disgusts his wife because he can never be serious, exhibits a dominant Child that avoids the serious aspects of life by not giving expression to his Adult or Parent ego states.

Adoption of an unhealthy life position will obviously predispose people to live troubled lives. People who decide "I'm OK—you're not OK," to take one example, predispose themselves toward lives of crime and sociopathy. To exploit others, rob others, beat others, cheat others, or succeed at the expense of others is just further confirmation that the person was entirely correct in deciding "I'm OK and you're not." Who needs a conscience when I'm convinced that all I do is OK and anything that goes wrong must be the responsibility of those who aren't OK? This exploitive type of person need not be a criminal to act out this life position but can be the ruthless business executive who exploits others or the destructive lover who loves them and leaves them because that is all others are good for.

People who decide "I'm not OK—you're OK" are plagued with constant feelings of inferiority in the presence of those they judge as OK. Such a life position can lead to a life script that calls for withdrawal from others, because it is too painful to remain in their presence and be constantly reminded of not being OK. Withdrawal reaffirms the not-OK position but is even more self-defeating because it deprives the person of any chance of getting the adequate strokes from others that could lead to a belief of being OK. Withdrawn people may develop an elaborate fantasy life centered on wishes that if they become holy enough, wise enough, rich enough, or irresistible enough, then they will be OK. Failure to realize unrealistic fantasies can ultimately lead to the tragic resolution of institutionalization or suicide.

Withdrawal is not the only alternative that can follow from assuming "I'm not OK—you're OK." The person can write a counterscript based on lines borrowed from the Parent: "You can be OK if . . ." The person is then driven to achieve whatever contingencies the Parent demands in return for strokes. Be charming enough, submissive enough, helpful enough, entertaining enough, demands the Parent. The person is constantly looking to the Parent in others for strokes and approval, and such strokes can at least ease the pain of not being OK enough.

People who conclude "I'm not OK and neither are you" are the most difficult to reach. Why should they respond to others who aren't OK? What hope is there in life when neither oneself nor others are OK? These people simply survive, if they do not commit suicide or destroy others and themselves. The extreme withdrawal of schizophrenia or psychotic depression is their most common fate. They may regress to an infantile state in the primitive hope of once again receiving the strokes of being held and fed. Without intervention from caring others, the "I'm not OK—you're not OK" individual will live out a self-destructive life of intermittent institutionalization, irreversible substance abuse, senseless homicide, or tragic suicide.

Just as there are three basically unhealthy life positions, so too there are three basic life scripts that lead to self-destruction: (1) depression, or *no-love script*; (2) madness, or *no-mind script*; and (3) addiction, or *no-joy script* (Steiner, 1974).

The intensity of the no-love script varies in degree from the legion of lonely people who are in a constant, unsuccessful quest for a loving relationship to the smaller band of profoundly depressed people who are ready to call it quits because they are convinced they are unloved and unlovable. Basic training in lovelessness is provided early in childhood when parents provide injunctions against the free exchange of loving strokes. Strokes are controlled by a strict economy, as if love is a scarce commodity that can readily be depleted. Parental injunctions include: Don't give yourself strokes. Don't give your strokes away; trade your love for something valuable. Don't ask for strokes when you need them; love is not worthwhile if you have to ask for it. Don't reject strokes when you don't want them, even if the kisses, hugs, or compliments from some people seem oppressive and unhealthy. Acting out these injunctions from the Parent can result in such pathologies as the hypochondriac who can ask for strokes only by being sick; the modest neurotic who can never say anything good about him/herself; the miserably married partner who exchanges love for money, security, or status; and the easy make who never says no to the advances of anyone.

The no-mind script plagues those called mad and constantly lurks in the background for those who live in fear that someday they might go crazy. Mindlessness is also reflected in the lives of those who feel unable to cope with the world, those who get easily confused and have trouble concentrating, those who feel stupid or lazy, and those who have no willpower or mind of their own. Basic training in mindlessness comes from parental injunctions against thinking too much. Many women, for example, were traditionally discouraged from being logical, rational beings in order to eventually become unquestioning wives.

Parents give injunctions against thinking to protect themselves from not-OK feelings. Children who thought clearly might see the undeniable bigotry of their caretakers, might sense that their parents do not genuinely love each other, might challenge the sacred-cow teachings of their parents. To keep their children from seeing them accurately, parents discourage children from using their minds through such techniques as directly lying about the truth the child sees. For example, a mother brought her 12-year-old daughter in to see me because the girl was quite distressed over the belief that she was going crazy. The mother told me privately that the girl had been convinced, correctly, that the mother was having an affair with the carpenter, but the mother had convincingly lied to protect herself and the carpenter. Here the girl was afraid she was becoming paranoid, when her problem was that she was intuiting things too accurately. The mother was amazed at how quickly a dose of truth could remedy the daughter's emerging madness.

The no-joy script is the basic plan of those who decided early in life that it was better for them to shut out the joys and pleasures of their bodies. As adults, these kill-joys range in severity from those in need of a pill to sleep or caffeine to awake, to those in need of constant aspirins or antacids to shut out bubbling messages from within, to those in need of a fix or a fifth to survive in life.

In view of Western culture's long history of deciding that the body is not OK, it is understandable that many parents continue to proscribe experiencing and enjoying the body. In the process of shutting out their ability to spontaneously and freely experience their bodies, people also shut out one of the primary centers of joy in life. They lose one of the natural centers of living that is the birthright of the Natural Child. One of the apparent pleasures of drugs is that initially they shut out the Pig Parent that prohibits the pleasure of being body-centered. The catch is that as more drugs are needed to inhibit the Pig Parent, the person feels less joy and experiences more of the sickness that comes from introducing foreign substances into the natural body. Again, the body is experienced as not OK, and the person takes even more drugs to more fully close out the body. The payoff of feeling depressed from a hangover or withdrawal serves in part as a reaffirmation of the belief that the body and the person are indeed not OK.

The drama of tragic life scripts is heightened by the fact that patients eventually play each of the three roles that are part of the triangle of all drama: *the victim, the persecutor,* and *the rescuer* (Karpman, 1968). The script of the spouse of an alcoholic, for instance, begins with the spouse trying to rescue the poor drunk from self-destruction. Drama and excitement increase as the spouse becomes angry when rescue is not accepted and then turns to persecuting the drunk for not reforming. Eventually, the spouse's self-destructive script becomes apparent as the spouse ends up as a victim of the drunk's social, economic, and personal inadequacies.

To advance pathological scripts to their inevitably tragic conclusions, patients begin to play even heavier-handed versions of their typical games. An alcoholic who played "Kick Me," for example, may progress from playing "Kick me, I'm late again for dinner because I stopped at the bar" to "Kick me, I spent the check at the bar" to "Kick me, I lost my job." The payoff for the alcoholic comes in collecting brown stamps for depression and in reaffirming a position of not being OK. When enough feelings of depression are collected, the alcoholic can trade in his stamps and feel justified in killing himself, which is the required curtain call in his tragic life script (also see Steiner, 1971).

People are born princes and princesses until their parents turn them into frogs, according to Berne (Steiner, 1990). Innately healthy people write scripts early in life based on the negative or positive influences of those around them and spend the rest of their lives unconsciously making these scripts come true. The consequences of a negative script, as we have seen, can be disastrous—unless people make a conscious decision to change.

Theory of Therapeutic Processes

Transactional analysis typically begins with a *structural analysis,* through which patients become more fully conscious of ego states that were previously confused, contaminated, or excluded. Therapy then proceeds to transactional analysis, in which self-defeating transactions are made conscious, beginning with self-destructive games, leading to full awareness of the unhealthy life positions and life scripts that have been plaguing patients. With a curative increase in consciousness, clients are then able to choose which ego states to cathect at any particular time. With heightened awareness, they can also decide whether they will go on acting out tragic games, positions, and scripts or choose more constructive patterns of meeting their basic human hungers.

Consciousness Raising

The Client's Work. Consciousness raising begins as an educational process. Clients are expected to become well-informed about the language and concepts of TA, usually through *bibliotherapy* involving the books of Berne (1964, 1970, 1972), Harris (1967; Harris & Harris, 1990), James and Jongeward (1971), and Steiner (1971, 1974, 1990). If TA classes are available in the local community, then the client may be instructed to take a course in TA before beginning formal treatment. Education continues in psychotherapy, of course, as clients are taught to apply the concepts of TA to their own lives, beginning with becoming aware of which ego state is currently being expressed. As clients analyze their own lives in TA terms, they will frequently look to the therapist or group members for feedback regarding the accuracy of their self-interpretations.

As clients become better educated in TA and more aware of their own ego states, they are able to use their Adults to teach others how to analyze themselves. The client's work is usually a pattern of graduating from student to self-analyzer to teacher. As patients become more conscious of their own ego states, they can better analyze the complex transactions they enter into with others. They use their Adults to reflect on repeated patterns of conflict and to realize whether these conflicts are due to their own games or scripts or whether they are letting themselves become entangled in the games and scripts of others. Thus, the early stages of structural analysis depend more on the competence and assurance of the therapist, who teaches the client about relevant ego states, whereas the later stages of transactional analysis depend more on the work of the client.

At this later point in treatment, clients have almost all the relevant information regarding the overall patterns of their lives and must now use their Adults to inform the therapist about their personal games or scripts. For example, clients must provide accurate information to complete a script checklist (Steiner, 1967). This includes (1) the overall course of their lives, (2) whether their lives are to be OK or not, (3) when they decided on this life course, (4) the fairy tale hero or heroine that the life course is intended to emulate, (5) their counterscripts that allow them periods free from self-destruction, (6) the Parental injunctions against loving, thinking, or feeling joy, (7) the games that advance their courses, (8) the pastimes they use to structure their scripts, (9) the payoffs they seek in life, and (10) the tragic ending they expect from life. Clients must also use their Adults to confirm or disconfirm any hypothetical formulation the therapist may offer about the client's scripts or games.

The Therapist's Work. Because most psychotherapy patients are above all confused, the therapist's first task is to reduce confusion by providing patients with an accurate structural diagnosis of their problems. By analyzing emotional upsets in terms of conflicts among Parent, Child, and Adult ego states, therapists provide a clear and concise framework for understanding maladaptive behaviors. The structural diagnosis is both education, in that it teaches patients the basic concepts of TA, and feedback, in that it informs clients about the personal ways in which they express their own Parent, Child, and Adult. Besides reducing confusion, the structural diagnosis can be the starting point for reducing contamination, because the diagnosis will provide clarification and interpretation about which ego states are being contaminated by which other ego states.

To encourage clients to reduce their own confusion and contamination, the therapist frequently asks clients such questions as "What ego state are you in?" "Which part of you is talking now?" "Which part of you said that or made that gesture?" The clients then respond in terms of their own subjective awareness, which they can check against feedback from the therapist or other members in group therapy. If clients harbor doubts about the diagnosis proffered, the therapist will play back audio- or videotape recordings to help the client see or hear the behavior to which the therapist or group was responding. With such additional data, clients are usually able to become more clearly aware of each ego state.

Because the Adult is the least biased processor of information, the transactional analyst attempts to reduce confusion and contamination by hooking the Adult of the client into playing a central role in the analysis of ego states. Therapists hook the Adult of clients by communicating from their own Adult ego state to the Adult ego state of the client. Asking for information, for example, is a request from the Adult to the Adult. Because it is a principle of TA that the social response of a *transactional stimulus* (the request for information) is most apt to come from an ego state complementary to that from which the stimulus originated, clients are most likely to respond with communication from their own Adult. If therapists want clients to act as Adults, then they should themselves be Adults in their communication—a *complementary transaction*. If the therapist acts as a Parent and treats the patient as a helpless child, then the therapist should not be surprised if the client has trouble responding from an objective Adult state.

Exclusion can be counteracted by offering the client permission to become aware of and express an ego state that typically has been excluded. A therapist might encourage expression of the Child, for example, by giving a client the homework assignment of attending a folk music festival over the weekend and joining in the singing. Or the therapist may cultivate the appearance of the Child by encouraging the client to accept warm strokes from the group member toward whom the client feels closest. Because an ego state is usually excluded because of fear of injury or criticism, the client can feel freer to become aware of the risky Child once the therapist has provided a more protective and permissive setting.

Just as TA therapists can draw on complementary transactions to help clients, so too will they at times cross clients in order to help them become conscious of their reactions when crossed. A *crossed transaction* occurs when the ego state addressed by a communication is not the ego state that responds to the communication. If a client addresses a message to the therapist's Adult and the therapist responds from the Parent ego state, then the Adult-to-Adult communication is crossed by a Parent-to-Child response. Let's say that a client asks for information, an Adult-to-Adult transaction, such as, "Do you know if next month's TA lecture is open to the public? I have a few friends who would like to go." A complementary response would be an Adult sharing of the information about the lecture. To cross the client, however, the therapist might respond from Parent to Child by asking, "Can't you ever find out things for yourself?"

By crossing the client deliberately, the transactional analyst can elevate the client's awareness as to whether crossed transactions are met with anger, such as "Well, the hell with you," or withdrawal, such as a silent "Guess I'll never ask a question here again," or guilt, such as "I'm sorry for bothering you with my petty concerns." The therapist can encourage clients to become aware of constructive responses that need not threaten a relationship. The Adult seeking more information from the therapist, for example, would learn to respond to the angry therapist by asking, "Is there something bothering you today that I don't know about?" Before a therapist uses a deliberate crossed transaction to increase the awareness of a client, however, the therapist must be very confident that the therapeutic relationship is strong enough to weather it.

Becoming aware of the emotional impact of crossed transactions is part of the analysis of games patients play, because the switch in a game includes a crossed transaction. In the Kiss Off game, for example, the repartee that is occurring between the mutually attracted Child and Child is crossed when the woman switches to her Parent and asks accusingly, "What kind of woman do you think I am?" Because the emotional impact of such a switch is the key payoff of a game, it is absolutely critical that patients become conscious of how they cross transactions to elicit feelings. Much of the work in analyzing games involves confronting clients with the repetitious nature of their games and then interpreting the payoffs of the games and how they help advance the client's life script.

Clients can become fully aware of the meaning of their games only after becoming conscious of how their lives are following self-selected scripts. To help clients in the difficult task of script analysis, therapists can rely on the "20 questions" that Steiner (1967) uses in completing the script checklist. Asking clients to describe their favorite fairy tale or childhood story, for example, can help clients become more fully aware of when they decided on their life script and what mythical heroes they used as models for their lives.

Furthermore, therapists raise clients' consciousness of scripts through the technique of *script rehearsal* (Dusay, 1970). The therapist serves as director and actively sets the stage for a critical scene from a client's script. The "star" of the rehearsal is a patient with a pressing problem. The star is seated face to face with the costar, a group member who plays the other person most integrally involved in the scene, such as a spouse or sibling. Two other patients stand behind the star and represent the Parent ego states. Other patients sit around representing Child ego states, while one patient serves as the observing, computing Adult. The star and costar are directed to enact the scene involving the star's problem, and the other patients are directed to simultaneously express the ego states that they are assigned. The script rehearsal is enacted for ten minutes, followed by a ten-minute Adult-to-Adult discussion of the multilevel meaning of that scene.

Choosing

The Client's Work. In the process of becoming more fully conscious of their ego states, games, life positions, and life scripts, clients also become aware of an increase in volition. With a reduction in confusion or contamination, for example, clients are increasingly empowered to choose which ego state to cathect at any particular time. After expressing a previously excluded ego state in a session, clients can choose to express the same ego state outside the session. Once they become aware that their self-defeating life positions and scripts were originally decisions in childhood based on inadequate information, they can make more informed choices as Adults to live constructive, self-fulfilling lives.

Choices to radically change their lives need not be sudden, all-or-none decisions. Clients can, if they choose, use the therapeutic situation to try out new alternatives. They might risk giving up games in therapy in order to experience more intimacy with the therapist or group members, for instance. Clients can choose to try out new transactions, such as directly and honestly asking for strokes when they need them rather than using games to gain negative attention. Given the degree of freedom inherent in choosing, no one can predict the pace or place that clients will use to decide just how they will get on with the exciting process of life.

The Therapist's Work. Therapists actually encourage the volitional powers of patients right from the onset of treatment by making it a contractual arrangement. In the contract, the patient chooses which goals to work toward, and the therapist decides whether or not such goals fit within the therapist's value system. The therapist also lets clients know that they are free to renegotiate the contract at any time or to terminate therapy once the present contract is completed.

Later in the course of treatment, therapists aid the process of choosing by giving clients permission to use their time together to practice new alternatives. Therapists are also willing to provide strokes for clients risking more constructive lifestyles. For the most part, however, therapists recognize that choosing is a process that invariably falls mainly on the shoulders of clients, who are accepting responsibility for both the past and future courses of their lives.

One set of therapist interventions, known as *redecision therapy* (Goulding & Goulding, 1979), grew out of transactional analysis and Gestalt therapy in order to facilitate clients challenging their beliefs about themselves in the past. Clients are taught to listen to "Don't" injunctions which severely limit their choices: Don't be a child, Don't be important, Don't be close, Don't be successful, Don't grow, Don't trust, and certainly Don't be you. Once aware of these injunctions and confronted with choices, clients are freed to redecide who they are and who they want to be (Gladfelter, 1992; McClendon & Kadis, 1995).

Therapeutic Content

Although psychopathology is typically intrapersonal in origin, it is always interpersonal in expression. To allow the interpersonal manifestation of intrapsychic conflicts to become undeniably apparent, TA is most often carried out in groups. Even in a group format, however, the TA focus moves back and forth between problems occurring among group members and problems occurring within members.

Intrapersonal Conflicts

Anxiety and Defenses. Anxiety is a reaction of the Child ego state to a possible break in a Parent's injunction. Anxiety can be as overwhelming as the myriad terrors that children have experienced in the face of parental disapproval: fear of being beaten, abandoned, ignored, or insulted. The anticipation that parents might withhold all strokes, for example, can make the Child feel that psychological starvation is imminent. No wonder that patients can panic when their Child ego state reacts to a breach of injunctions from the Parent. The Parent, of course, is loaded with injunctions: "Don't laugh so loudly," "Don't eat too much," "Don't leave any food on your plate," "Don't talk," "Don't show anger," "Don't enjoy sex," "Don't give strokes," and "Don't accept strokes." Many people live in constant danger, then, that if they act directly on the basis of their human hungers, they will be overwhelmed by the panic of having broken at least one parental injunction.

Defenses have traditionally been analyzed as intrapsychic mechanisms that keep forbidden and thus dangerous desires from awareness and expression. Interpreting intrapersonal defenses of this nature is critical work in TA, to be sure, but equally critical are the interpersonal defenses used to avoid such dangerous desires as the wish to freely exchange strokes.

The games people play frequently serve defensive functions. People who are locked into mutual games have made unconscious deals to use games to avoid the risks of being intimate. A couple who find themselves bickering whenever one or the other feels like making love or feels like talking intimately is locked into the game of "Uproar." As long as they are fighting there is no risk of becoming truly intimate. What's more, neither person has to admit being terrified of being intimate; their only problem is that they cannot stop fighting.

Although the analysis and thus the removal of game playing are important parts of TA for many clients, it should be recognized that games, like any other defenses, may serve as the final barrier to psychosis and should not be attacked too quickly. A borderline couple, for example, may need to continue playing "Uproar" until each spouse's Adult ego state is decontaminated from a suspicious, paranoid Parent. Certainly the analysis of games should not become still another game engaged in at cocktail parties.

Self-Esteem. Enough has been said about the importance of life positions to recognize that one's sense of being OK is central to a healthy existence. What has not been said is that transactional analysts disagree on whether the original and universal life position is to be OK or not OK. Whereas Berne believed that children are born OK and should have a solid sense of esteem as their birthright, Harris (1967) suggests that people are born frogs until they transform themselves into princes or princesses. For Harris, "I'm not OK" is the original life position and developing a sense of esteem, a belief in being OK, is a central task of life for all people. Whether people are born with defects akin to original sin or whether parental injunctions help produce decisions about not being OK is an ongoing debate within TA circles. What is agreed upon, however, is that a majority of people in our society do emerge from childhood in a position of feeling not OK. Witness how long *I'm OK—You're OK* (Harris, 1967) was on the bestseller list.

People may be misled into believing that because their present problem with self-esteem, their not-OK position, was originally a decision in childhood, all they have to do to become OK is to decide as an Adult that they are indeed OK. Unfortunately, it is not that easy. Even with professional treatment, changing a life position comes only after considerable struggle to become aware of the ego states involved in the original decision about a life position, the games played to enhance a life position, and the script to which that position is intimately connected. To increase one's self-esteem by deciding to be OK involves a radical change in one's life script and one's transactions with the world. Feelings of genuine esteem and of being fundamentally OK accompany the awareness of having decided to live a more effective life.

Responsibility. Patients present to psychotherapy with confusion about the reasons their lives seem to be out of control. They are confused by their inability to sleep, to concentrate, to relax, to relate. They are confused by their own behavior, by why they so often seem unable to do what they really want to do: to exercise, to stop drinking, to quit arguing, overeating, or procrastinating. They are confused about their inability to communicate, even after 25 years of marriage. Most of all, they are confused about what to do with the mess they call their lives.

As long as psychotherapy systems continue to excuse people from accepting responsibility for lifestyle deficiencies, patients will continue to be confused over why their lives are a mess and what they can do about it. Transactional analysis gives people permission to experiment with a variety of new behaviors; but one thing TA will not accept is the old cop-outs that people use to avoid taking responsibility for their lives. Games such as "If it weren't for you" and "Look what you made me do" are prominent examples of cop-outs. The most common, however, is the *wooden leg game,* in which patients beseech others not to expect too much from them because they have a wooden leg. Wooden legs vary from being schizophrenic to being stupid, from being depressed to being lazy. Clients cry out to be excused because of countless deformities that they insist were externally imposed fates rather than self-selected destinies. The fact that clients choose their fates while still children is still no excuse from responsibility. At the same time, the fact that life positions and life scripts were chosen precociously can moderate the client's self-condemnation for having lived a self-destructive existence.

Interpersonal Conflicts

Intimacy and Sexuality. Lifetimes pass and intimacy is rarely known. We are among the fortunate few if we experience even 15 minutes of intimacy in a lifetime (Steiner, 1974). As a candid, game-free, mutual exchange of strokes without structure and without exploitation, intimacy may well be unattainable in the structured life scripts of most people. Those who have chosen early in life to demonstrate that either they or others are not OK have given up the option to be intimate. To let ourselves respond freely with others is to trust that they and we are OK.

Intimacy itself seems to be not OK for many people. The threat of intimacy comes in part from the many injunctions of the Parent to avoid freely taking or giving strokes. Free love continues to be taboo to the Parent in most people. There may, however, be an even more basic reason why intimacy seems so threatening. Intimacy brings with it the threat of being too stimulating and too exciting because it is too unstructured. Intimacy may be overwhelming because it threatens to bring chaos into the lives of people accustomed to the security of continual structure. People who hunger to structure their lives will settle for the strokes that come with rituals, pastimes, and games rather than risk the chaos involved in free encounters.

Sexuality can be as free from intimacy as is the rest of life. Society in the form of the Parent strives to impose structure on human sexuality by limiting sexual encounters to patterned relationships, such as engagement and marriage. Even within patterned relationships like marriage, where sexuality is permitted, people structure much of their sexuality into rituals, work activities, pastimes, or games (Berne, 1970). The ceremony of having sex three times a week following the 11:00 p.m. newscast, with five minutes of foreplay and five minutes of intercourse, is a pattern of lovemaking well known by many couples. Such patterns certainly can be pleasant and pleasurable, but they are seldom intimate. There are couples who still insist on structuring the "marital act" so that the man is always on top and the woman on the bottom—to do otherwise is to be abnormal or un-American.

Other couples accept sexuality as being all part of a day's work. These individuals see sexuality as a marital duty; they work to make sex as pleasant an activity as possible. Less-rigid couples will accept their sexuality as part of the great, all-American pastime. They share a mutual interest in each other and enjoy the chitchat that is part of lovemaking. They can't imagine a better pastime for a rainy day, but prefer not to risk the stormy emotions that could come with more adventuresome sexuality.

Some of the people who see their sexual lives as most intense and exciting are those whose sexual activities are just more games to play. These individuals enjoy the drama and emotional exploitation that come from such games as "They'll be glad they knew me," "Ain't it wonderful," "Look how hard I tried," and even "Now I've got you, you son of a bitch." Sexual games can advance a person's life position by proving, for example, that the opposite sex is really not OK or that one is irresistibly OK.

More spontaneous sexuality and deeper intimacy are for those who choose to break out of structured life scripts and risk security for excitement. The fact is, however, that many people do not need intimacy and sexuality to be OK, and a disservice is done if the suggestion is made that people are not OK unless they are sexual Olympians or emotional intimates. The quest for intimacy and freer sexuality may well be a luxury in a world in which all too many relationships are plagued by destructive games and self-defeating scripts.

Communication. Communication proceeds smoothly and satisfactorily as long as the transactions between two people are complementary. A complementary transaction exists if the response to a previous message is addressed to the ego state that was the source of the message and is emitted from the ego state to which that source addressed itself. A series of Adult-to-Adult, Parent-to-Parent, or Child-to-Child transactions are clearly complementary and lead to communications that result in a satisfying sense of being mutually understood. A mutual exchange of jokes or the kidding between the Child ego states of two people is an example of smooth and satisfying communication.

Crossed transactions occur when the ego state addressed is not the ego state that responds or when the ego state addressed responds back to an ego state different from the one that sent the message. A husband joking with his wife's Child is crossed when her Adult responds with the information that his kidding wasn't funny at all. Similarly, the transaction is crossed if the Child of the wife responds back to the husband's Parent rather than his Child, such as with a tearful response about how the husband is always picking on her.

The secret in helping couples with communication concerns is to help them become aware of their own ego states and how their ego states are crossing rather than complementing each other. If couples can learn to identify the ego state that was involved in a crossed transaction and can get back into the ego state that was being addressed, they can learn to participate in complementary transactions that, in principle at least, can lead to communication that proceeds indefinitely.

Hostility. Hostility is embedded not in any inherent impulse to destroy, but rather in the ulterior transactions between individuals who have decided that they or others are not OK. The ongoing hostility between people playing repetitive games on the order of "Uproar" is aimed not so much at destroying or hurting the other as at keeping the other from getting too close. Such hostility avoids the risks of intimacy while providing the more structured excitement of games. Hostility is especially exciting for those who collect red stamps to trade in on a big blowup. Beyond the cathartic release of emotion, they also enact the payoff of reaffirming their right to decide that others are not OK.

People in the racket of collecting angry feelings can also use their red stamps to enhance their life scripts. It they collect enough grudges, they can eventually have a hostile blowup big enough to justify a divorce or even a homicide, without having to feel any guilt or responsibility. Responsibility for hostility can begin only when angry people are willing to use the Adult within them to consider that maybe, just maybe, they were wrong to decide that others are not OK. Hostile people, however, tend to be self-righteous people who would rather attack others than attack the painful task of considering that their basic life positions are dead wrong.

Control. Control is an issue for parents and for the Parent in people. Individuals with a continual need to control are dominated, in their personality and their relationships, by the Parent within. These perennial Parents will have fewer problems in their relationships if the nurturant Parent is dominant and they are indeed concerned with the best interests of those they are attempting to control. A benign dictator is certainly easier to take than a Pig Parent, but even the protective Parent will wear thin with a partner who chooses to live life as an autonomous Adult.

Crossed transactions will be the rule as the Adult responds instead of the Child who is continually being addressed by the perennial Parent.

The perennial Parent is not the only source of control problems. People with little control over their own Child stimulate the Parent in others, urging others to step in to provide the controls that their own Adult and Parent are unable to provide. When others do respond as Parents, however, the Child is likely to rebel and to reject the controls. If people are to break out of relationships being destroyed by control conflicts, it is clear that both the Parent and the Child in the relationship will need to take responsibility for the part each plays in making control a central concern. In spite of what the self-righteous Parent or the naive Child might say, in control conflicts there are no innocent victims.

Individuo-Social Conflicts

Adjustment Versus Transcendence. The only fate that can possibly be transcended is a fate that is self-imposed. Self-defeating and self-destructive life scripts, not society, must be transcended. People prefer to believe, and are encouraged by social scientists to believe, that if they are losers it is only because the forces of society have been stacked against them. Although social forces urge many people to resign themselves to being losers in life, it is only when people take a stand against themselves—when they decide that society is OK and that they are not OK—that they begin to follow a loser's life script. Although the protective Parent would like to block the painful awareness that they have stacked the deck against themselves, that they are the joker in their own games, it is precisely through such painful self-confrontation that people can regain control over the scripted fates of their lives.

If patients decide to choose a winner's script, they need not be in constant conflict with society. They will be aware that it is only their rebellious Child who wants to be free from all restraints. The Parent within will understand the wisdom of traditions and conventions, will speak the language of control, and will help them adjust amicably to many of the authoritative forces of society. While their Adult may work to help make a more democratic and just society, the Adult is also unbiased enough to recognize that people can be winners even with the odds against them—as long as they do not continue to be against themselves.

Impulse Control. People are indeed overwhelmed at times by certain feelings, such as rage, lust, or a longing for food. They find themselves unable to keep from acting on these overwhelming feelings, even though it is not in their best interests to be controlled by them. Such people need to first track down and identify the feeling carefully and exactly (Holland, 1973). They can then become aware of the ego state that is cathected when the impulsive feeling occurs. They can also become aware that other structures of the personality are not engulfed by the impulsive feeling, and thus the feeling need not be overwhelming. Since the Child ego state is typically associated with impulsive feelings, the person can learn to control them by cathecting the Adult or Parent ego state when the impulsive feeling is threatening to get out of control.

Beyond Conflict to Fulfillment

Meaning. Meaninglessness is a symptom of psychological starvation. The loss of meaning is one of the major complaints associated with stroke deprivation, along with emptiness, a lack of deep feeling, a feeling of being unloved, a sense that life is not worth living, and a chronic case of boredom. Meaning is lost when people structure their lives with rituals, pastimes, and work activities low in stroke. Television and related pastimes that structure so much of a modern family's leisure merely pass the time with few strokes for the spectators. Much of modern work provides little excitement or recognition for the workers. When life's activities lack any nourishment other than structure, a person is left with a deep sense of being in a rut. Breaking out of a rut and finding more meaning in life entail choosing to restructure life with activities that satisfy the hunger for human strokes.

Ideal Individual. An ideal or stable individual is characterized by the freedom and flexibility to shift from one ego state to another, depending on the demands of a specific situation. As Adult, the stable person is realistic, rational, and responsible, avoiding games that are designed to shift the responsibility for life's problems onto others. As Parent, the stable person is a caring and cultured individual, who is committed to maintaining the most valuable traditions of the past. As Child, the stable person is spontaneous, joyful, and humorous, a delightful individual who is able to bring out the best in others.

The healthiest person will incorporate the judgment "I'm OK—you're OK" into life. The fundamental evil in life is to deny the worth of any human being, including oneself. Those judged to be not OK can be treated in immoral, not-OK ways. Lives of destruction and defeat demonstrate not only the pathology but also the immorality of deciding that any part of humanity is basically not OK.

Ideally, an aware person with the volition to act as Parent, Child, and Adult could dodge all of the destructive games that people play and could go through life without a commitment to any rigid life script. Practically, however, the best we should expect from structural and transactional analysis is people who can keep game playing to a minimum and who can choose to live constructive and caring scripts rather than the scripts of losers.

Therapeutic Relationship

The therapeutic relationship is part of both the content and the process of transactional analysis. The games that patients attempt to play with therapists, for example, are a critical part of the content that is to be analyzed. Clients who are consistently late or who fail to pay their bills may be playing "Kick me." The naive therapist may indeed relate with a kick rather than an analysis of the client's self-defeating games. At the same time, the relationship can be part of the process of therapy, as when the therapist relates as an Adult in order to hook and to strengthen the Adult of the client.

The Adult of the therapist is the ego state most often involved in transactions with the client. because consciousness raising is a rational process, the therapist relies on the Adult's rational abilities for processing clinical material. Psychotherapy is said to be under way when clients are willing to switch control of their lives from their own Parent to the therapist's Adult. The client will at first experience the therapist's rational control as being a function of the therapist's Parent. Eventually, clients will come to understand that the influence of the therapist is not the demanding, dominating force of a Parent, but rather that inherent in an Adult's ability to deal effectively with the world. Once clients decide that the Adult within them is as effective in interacting with the world as the Adult of the therapist is, then the client is ready to terminate.

In Rogerian terms, the therapeutic relationship is indeed unconditional in regard. The transactional analyst is convinced that patients are OK unconditionally rather than being OK only if they act in particular ways. Transactional analysts, however, rely more on rational processes for analyzing ego states, games, and scripts than on empathy for processing the critical information in treatment. Certainly therapists must be able to cathect their own Child or Parent to appreciate the feelings of the client's Child or Parent. Nevertheless, the cognitive process of the rational Adult is most effective in understanding the troubled structures and transactions of clients.

To be effective, transactional analysts must be genuine in therapy, because it is impossible to fake being an effective Adult, a humorous Child, or a caring Parent. Effective therapists are free to be genuinely spontaneous when they respond with the Child within them, but they certainly do not believe that the spontaneous reactions of the Child are the only genuine part of the human personality. Transactional analysts also believe in relating as equals with clients. The insistence on a therapeutic contract is an indication of the belief that therapist and client can relate as equals. The Adult of every individual is assumed to be equally effective in relating to the world, and one of the treatment objectives is to have the client relate on an Adult-to-Adult level as quickly as possible.

Patients are not the only potential game players in a transactional analysis. Although therapists should certainly be less apt to play games in their professional activities and personal lives than their clients, transactional analysts must be ever vigilant to enacting their own scripts at their clients' expense. "Burnout" is a typical racket system of professional helpers: give so much to everyone until it hurts and you can give no more to anyone (Clarkson, 1992). So are "Top Gun" games, in which therapists compete with one another in a hostile manner (Persi, 1992). Ongoing self-analysis and securing strokes away from the office are required to combat these and other therapist games.

Practicalities of Transactional Analysis

Group therapy is preferred, in part because it allows a greater number of transactions, including more troubled transactions, than might ordinarily occur with an individual therapist relating primarily as Adult. A typical group is composed of about eight members who meet once a week for two hours. Crisp beginnings and endings were preferred by Berne, so meetings traditionally begin and end promptly. Clients should be able to see the whole body of other members in order to pick up bodily cues that reveal Parent or Child ego states. A videotape recorder should be available to assist clients in analyzing their ego structures or transactions, although an audio recorder can serve some of the same purposes. A blackboard for diagramming ego states or crossed transactions is also recommended.

Many transactional analysts, of course, also offer individual, marital, and family therapies. They commonly integrate systems theory into TA when treating couples and families (Massey, 1989a, 1989b). The fees for TA generally follow the going rate for other types of psychotherapy in an area.

Transactional analysts hail from a full range of helping professions. The International Transactional Analysis Association (ITAA) offers categories of membership that correspond to certification levels: Regular Members are professionals who use TA but who are certified through another source; Certified Members are certified transactional analysts who have completed study in TA principles and passed written and oral examinations; and Teaching Members are teaching and/or supervising transactional analysts who have considerable experiences and expertise.

A Major Alternative: Interpersonal Psychotherapy

Interpersonal psychotherapy or *IPT* is a time-limited, empirically-tested treatment developed in the 1970s by the late Gerald Klerman, Myrna Weissman, and their colleagues (1984). Although originally launched as a research intervention for depression, IPT has evolved into a highly regarded and widely practiced clinical intervention for a range of behavioral disorders. In fact, when one speaks today of interpersonal therapy, the presumed reference is to Klerman and Weissman's IPT.

A Sketch of the Founders. Interpersonal psychotherapy is rooted in the interpersonal approaches of Harry Stack Sullivan and Adolph Meyer and is informed by the attachment theory of John Bowlby. The leading proponent of the *interpersonal school* of psychoanalysis, Sullivan (1953a, 1953b, 1970, 1972) was an influential American psychiatrist who found abnormal behavior to be rooted in impaired interpersonal relationships and believed that it could be ameliorated by an interpersonal variant of psychodynamic therapy. The therapist was to be a *participant-observer* in treatment, employing a mixture of reflectiveness and engagement in the therapy hour. Known for founding the interpersonal school and for his "psychobiological" approach, Meyer (1957) emphasized the patient's current psychosocial environment and posited that many forms of psychopathology represented misguided attempts to adjust to the environment, particularly under stressful circumstances or in a stressful environment. As mentioned in Chapter 2, Bowlby (1973, 1976) demonstrated that attachment in early life largely determines subsequent interpersonal relationships.

IPT was developed in the early 1970s as part of a collaborative research program on depression by Gerald L. Klerman, MD, in New Haven and then in Boston, and by his New Haven collaborators, Myrna M. Weissman, PhD, Bruce J. Rousaville, MD, and Eve S. Chevron. Their initial studies concerned the role of psychotherapy in relationship to the use of antidepressant medication in maintenance treatment of depressives after recovery from an acute episode. Several randomized trials of brief IPT were then undertaken for acutely depressed clients. The culmination of their research was their 1984 classic book, *Interpersonal psychotherapy of depression* (Klerman, Weissman, Rounsaville, & Chevron, 1984). The ensuing years have seen IPT thoroughly researched as a treatment for depression in all age groups and successfully applied to other mental disorders, particularly eating disorders and substance abuse (Klerman & Weissman, 1993).

Theory of Psychotherapy. Depression and other disorders occur within an interpersonal context. Interpersonal life affects mood (and all other human behavior), and mood affects how the individual handles his or her role (Markowitz, 1997).

The interpersonal approach to understanding depression reflects an undoctrinaire position that integrates the psychoanalytic emphasis on early childhood experiences with the cognitive-behavioral emphasis on current environmental stressors. This connection occurs in the following way (Halgin & Whitbourne, 1993): A person's failure in childhood to acquire the emotional nurturance, cognitive operations, and behavioral skills needed to develop satisfying relationships leads to despair, isolation, and resultant depression, as convincingly demonstrated in Bowlby's attachment research. Once a person's depression is established, it is maintained by poor social skills, overreaction to loss, and impaired communication, all of which lead to further rejection by others. Environmental stressors make a bad situation worse. For instance, a man predisposed to depression by early caregiver failures suffers the loss of his wife. In a prolonged grief reaction, he may become so distraught over an extended period of time that he alienates his friends and family members and thereby isolates himself. In time, a vicious cycle becomes established in which his behavior causes people to stay away, and because he is so lonely and miserable, he becomes even more difficult in interactions with others. Interpersonal disruptions, in this view, are both a cause and a result of depression.

Theory of Therapeutic Processes. Interpersonal psychotherapy acknowledges the profound impact of early developmental experiences on later interpersonal relations, but focuses on improving current interpersonal relations. Rather than reconstructing and analyzing the "there and then," IPT strives to restructure and improve the "here and now" of the interpersonal domain. Regardless of personality traits or biological vulnerability, depression occurs in a psychosocial and interpersonal context. What is essential for recovery from depression, then, is to examine the context associated with the onset of the depression and the possibility of renegotiating difficulties in current interpersonal contexts (Frank, 1991).

IPT is a short-term, present-oriented psychotherapy focused mainly on the patient's current interpersonal relations and life situations and, as such, can be best understood in comparison to other psychotherapies (Klerman, Weissman, Rounsaville, & Chevron, 1984).

IPT is:	IPT is not:
time-limited	long-term
focused	open-ended
current relationships	past relationships
interpersonal	intrapsychic
interpersonal	cognitive/behavioral
improving relationships	achieving insight
identifying assets	identifying defenses
learning how to cope	curing the problem

The clinical strategies of interpersonal psychotherapy occur in three phases of treatment, typically over 12 to 16 sessions. During the initial sessions of the first phase, four broad goals are accomplished. First, the therapist deals with the depression by reviewing symptoms, giving the syndrome a name, according the patient the "sick role," and evaluating the need for medication. Second, depression is related to the interpersonal context by determining the nature of interactions, clarifying expectations of significant others and whether these are fulfilled, and establishing the changes the patient desires in the relationships. Third, the major problem areas related to the current depression are identified. And fourth, the IPT concepts and contract are explained.

The second phase of IPT covers the intermediate sessions and directly addresses the primary problem area: grief, interpersonal disputes, role transitions, or interpersonal deficits. Only one or, at most, two of these problem areas are addressed. A number of problem areas will probably emerge, and these will be noted; however, the time restriction necessitates focusing on the most troubling area. The therapeutic strategies differ somewhat depending on which of these interpersonal problem areas has been targeted, but let us consider unresolved grief. The overarching goals of therapy are to facilitate the mourning process and to help the patient reestablish interests and relationships to substitute for what has been lost. Toward these goals, numerous strategies are employed: relating symptom onset to loss of the significant other, reconstructing the patient's relationship with the deceased, describing the sequences and consequences of events surrounding the loss, exploring associated positive and negative feelings, and considering possible ways of becoming involved with others.

Unlike other forms of psychotherapy, IPT has no ideological hesitation about the use of medications and makes no universal generalizations to all disorders. This integrative specificity probably originates in IPT's singular focus on clinical depression, which frequently requires adjunctive pharmacotherapy and which frequently presents quite differently than other psychological problems. The use of medication and the focus on depression stem, too, from the goals of treatment: symptom reduction and relationship improvement. Because of its brief duration and low level of psychotherapeutic intensity, IPT is not expected to have a marked impact on the enduring aspects of personality and character.

In the third phase, termination, similarly to other therapies, feelings about ending treatment are discussed, progress is reviewed, and the remaining work is outlined. As is also true of other intentionally brief therapies, the arrangements for termination are explicit and adhered to.

Therapeutic Relationships. Throughout the course of treatment, the therapist's role is one of patient advocate, not neutral commentator. The interpersonal therapist is active, not passive, at least in comparison to practitioners of long-term insight-oriented psychotherapies. The therapeutic relationship is not conceptualized as a manifestation of transference; patient expectations of assistance are seen as realistic, and interpretations of patient—therapist interactions are made only when they are disruptive to progress. Upon learning this stance, one of our colleagues summarized it as follows: "The interpersonal in IPT refers to analyzing the interpersonal origins of depression outside of psychotherapy, not to analyzing the interpersonal relationship in psychotherapy." In Rogerian terms, the therapeutic relationship in IPT is one of empathy and warmth, but not unconditional acceptance. The therapist conveys the message that depression is a problem to be resolved, not accepted, and is a temporary, not permanent, feature of the patient's personality.

Practicalities. IPT is designed to be conducted by mental health professionals of various disciplines who have attained a terminal degree in their profession and who have acquired at least two years of psychotherapy experience with ambulatory depressed patients. In addition, the IPT therapist should have a favorable attitude toward short-term treatment and interpersonal theory and, ideally, hold no rigid attachment toward any psychotherapy system. The techniques of IPT have been operationalized in a manual (Klerman, et al., 1984), which has fostered considerable research (see following sections) on this short-term treatment for clinical depression.

Brief Interpersonal Therapies

Transactional analysis can be conducted as either a lengthy or a brief psychotherapy. Berne tended toward a lengthy treatment consisting of psychoeducation, individual therapy, and group therapy involving several years. Contemporary versions of TA favor briefer treatment combined with methods culled from other systems of psychotherapy.

Interpersonal psychotherapy, by contrast, is definitely a time-limited treatment with a predetermined 12- to 16-week duration. By design, IPT is practiced as a weekly, face-to-face, present-oriented, and short-term therapy. Pragmatic interventions focusing on the current interpersonal context of a patient's life have been shown to facilitate recovery from the acute episode as well as to provide some protection against reemergence of symptoms (Frank & Spanier, 1995).

Effectiveness of Interpersonal Therapies

Turning first to transactional analysis, a review of the literature yields only a small number of controlled studies on TA's effectiveness. In their 1980 meta-analysis,

Smith, Glass, and Miller located eight controlled studies investigating transactional analysis. The average effect size for TA was .67—slightly larger than the average effect size of .56 found for placebo treatments, but slightly smaller than the average effect size of .85 for all psychotherapies. In their more recent meta-analysis on individual psychotherapy with adults, Grawe and associates (1998) located only four controlled studies covering 226 patients. They concluded that there was an insufficient number of treatment-to-control comparisons to reach any reliable statements about TA's effectiveness. Although some attention has been paid to child therapy in the TA literature (for example, Massey & Massey, 1989; Veevers, 1991), insufficient controlled research has been conducted on TA with children to make it into the meta-analyses (Weisz et al., 1987, 1995).

The emerging conclusions, then, are that transactional analysis has been consistently more effective than no treatment and usually more effective than placebo treatments in adult samples. Depending on the study and the interpretation of "differences," transactional analysis produces outcomes at best comparable to other forms of insight-oriented psychotherapy and at worst inferior to other forms of psychotherapy. A related conclusion is that transactional analysis has not been sufficiently evaluated in a large enough number of studies to reliably evaluate its relative efficacy.

By contrast, Klerman and Weissman's interpersonal psychotherapy has been thoroughly researched in the past decade but ironically is not yet included in the major meta-analyses because of its recent development. Klerman and Weissman (1991) summarized the results of IPT in six randomized clinical trials with depressed patients. In the treatment of acute depression, IPT was consistently more effective on a variety of outcome measures than the control treatments. Combined IPT and tricyclic antidepressant medication was more effective than either treatment alone. A one-year follow-up in one of the studies indicated that the positive benefit of IPT was sustained for most patients.

The effectiveness of IPT as a maintenance treatment has also been investigated. Since both tricyclic antidepressants and psychotherapy were efficacious in the treatment of acute depression, the questions became whether the treatments should be combined and what the role of psychotherapy might be in maintenance. In a well-constructed study, 150 acutely depressed outpatients who had responded positively to a tricyclic antidepressant (amitriptyline) received eight months of maintenance treatment with drugs alone, IPT alone, or a combination of the two. The findings showed that maintenance drug treatment alone prevented symptom relapse but did little for interpersonal functioning and that IPT alone improved social functioning and interpersonal relations but had little effect on symptom relapse. No negative interaction between the drugs and psychotherapy was found; on the contrary, the combination of medication and IPT was most efficacious, probably because of their differential effects (Klerman & Weissman, 1991). Of course, these results are limited in generalization to outpatients who had already responded to medication with symptom reduction in the past.

Additional research by Ellen Frank and colleagues (Frank, 1991; Frank, Kupfer, & Perel, 1989) has examined the prophylactic efficacy of interpersonal psychotherapy in depressed patients. IPT had a positive therapeutic effect in patients discontinued from medication at the outset of maintenance. After 18 months of maintenance, patients receiving IPT alone or IPT plus placebo survived, on average, 10 months longer without recurrence of depression than did those patients receiving occasional medical contact in conjunction with placebo. The median "survival" time was 61 weeks versus 21 weeks. The early data point to the value of IPT in maintaining treatment gains and protecting against early recurrence of depression.

The groundbreaking National Institute of Mental Health (NIMH) Treatment of Depression Collaborative Research Program evaluated the effectiveness of interpersonal psychotherapy, cognitive-behavior therapy, imipramine plus clinical management, and placebo plus clinical management for treating unipolar, nonpsychotic depressed outpatients (Elkin et al., 1989). This study, widely known by the less cumbersome title, *NIMH Collaborative Study*, was groundbreaking on many accounts. First, it was the first coordinated, multisite study initiated by the NIMH in the field of psychotherapy. Although the collaborative clinical trial model is frequently used in psychotherapy, it had rarely been employed in such a large study. Second, the sheer size of the undertaking—screening 560 patients, treating 239 of them, assessing their progress over 18 months, training 28 therapists, and coordinating four treatment conditions at three sites across the United States—was impressive in and of itself. Third, the NIMH Collaborative Study set a research standard for the precision and number of controls employed in comparative outcome research. These controls included standardized training for the therapists, careful monitoring of therapist adherence to the respective treatment manuals, rigorous screening of potential patients, appropriate use of multiple disorder-relevant outcome measures, and follow-up of clinical outcomes for 18 months posttreatment.

At termination, patients in all treatments showed significant reduction in depressive symptomatology and improvement in functioning. Aggregating across the battery of outcome measures, the three clinical treatments generally did best and the placebo treatment did worst. The percentage of "completer" patients judged to be recovered at termination on the Beck Depression Inventory was 70% for interpersonal therapy, 69% for imipramine, 65% for cognitive-behavior therapy, and 51% for the placebo treatment, which combined a pill-placebo with regular meetings consisting of support, encouragement, and if necessary, direct advice. On secondary analyses in which patients were dichotomized according to initial severity of depression, significant differences among the treatments were present only for the subgroup of patients who were more severely disturbed. Here, there was some preliminary evidence of the superiority of interpersonal therapy and strong preliminary evidence of the superiority of imipramine. In contrast, there were no differences among the three treatment groups for the less severely disturbed patients.

Although IPT was first introduced as a treatment for depression, it has been increasingly applied to other disorders as well. In eating disorders, for example, IPT targets interpersonal stress and current interpersonal relationships rather than dietary issues or body weight (Johnson, Tsoh, & Varnard, 1996). Binge eating often begins in the context of unsatisfactory interpersonal situations, and the anxiety from conflictual relationships often triggers binge eating, leading to a loss of control over food intake. In a controlled trial, IPT achieved equivalent effects in the reduction of binge eating and vomiting with over 90% reduction in symptomatology maintained at one-year follow-up. IPT was a bit slower in securing these positive results than cognitive therapy or behavior therapy (Fairburn, Jones, Pereler, Hope, & O'Connor, 1993); however, at long-term follow-up, the eating disordered patients treated with IPT fared better than those treated with behavior therapy (Fairburn, Norman, Welch, O'Connor, Doll, Pereler, 1995).

All told, the results from the NIMH Collaborative Study and other research strongly support the effectiveness of interpersonal psychotherapy for treating depressed outpatients. IPT uniformly outperforms no treatment and placebo therapy in both the acute and maintenance treatment of clinical depression. Whether or not this impressive record of success will hold for other disorders, as it has for depression and bulimia, remains to be seen.

Criticisms of Transactional Analysis

From a Behavioral Perspective

As an approach to theory and therapy construction, TA continues in the worst heritage of the clinical tradition. Concepts are carried over from clinical observations with total disregard to testing their scientific validity. Theoretical postulates are stated in totally untestable terms. Berne (1972, p. 415) himself was aware of this when he wrote, "Experimental validation of script theory is not possible with human beings." Is it possible with lower animals? Yet Berne and his followers (for example, Clarkson, 1991; Holland, 1973; Steiner, 1990) continue to write about script theory as if it were verified, let alone verifiable.

Like most insight-oriented psychotherapies, TA is presented as a universal treatment, appropriate for just about any problem the clinician might encounter. This specious universality is characteristic of therapies based on armchair philosophizing; specificity is characteristic of therapies based on scientific data. As psychosocial treatments become more scientific, we need to be able to specify which treatments work best with which problems under which conditions. TA may work best with hypothetical constraints like scripts, games, and ego states, but what about concrete disorders like phobias, obsessions, and depressions? To become scientifically respectable, TA must specify how constructs like Parent, Child, and Adult can be experimentally tested. To become clinically acceptable, TA must specify with which problems it works best and under what conditions. Otherwise, TA remains just another in a long line of psychotherapies for all seasons and all reasons.

From a Psychoanalytic Perspective

Transactional analysis attempts to translate the fundamental concepts of ego, superego, and id into the common-sense concepts of Adult, Parent, and Child. In the translation, TA loses the basic driving force of the personality, the instinctual drives of the id. The Child in TA becomes a neutralized concept, the innocent child of common sense, lacking the overwhelming hostility or sexuality that accounts for the prevalence of self-destruction. On one hand, TA would have us reject historical determinism and believe that people self-determine a loser's life through mistaken decisions at an early age. Their miserable lives are merely a mistake that can be readily reversed with a new decision. On the other hand, TA would have us believe that it is parents who transform children into frogs, which is a theory of historical determinism. But if it is parents who destroy the OK-ness of children, what destructive driving force is there in the parents that would lead them to transform their own children from prized princes and princesses into despicable frogs?

Somewhere along the line, a destructive force that sounds like the id rears its ugly head in spite of TA's repeated attempts to convince us that we are really OK. The truth of the matter is that something within us, either as children or as parents, is not OK, and we had better come to grips with that force, lest we go on reproducing lives of destruction and defeat.

From a Humanistic Perspective

Transactional analysis is faced with the Humpty Dumpty dilemma. Once you assume that human beings are broken into three separate parts, then all the king's horses and all the king's men will never put humanity back together again. Instead of the traditional dualism of Western thought, TA divides us into a tripartite personality that can never know the beauty of being whole. And it could get worse. If second-order structural analysis becomes established. the human personality will be fragmented even further, with 27 separate ego states currently the record (Steiner, 1974).

In an era when fragmentation and isolation due to modern role playing drive increasing numbers of human beings to seek treatment, how can we even think of using therapeutic terms like games and scripts? TA strengthens contemporary fragmentation by reassuring us that personality does indeed come in separate parts. Rather than recognize the phenomena of Parent, Child, and Adult as the social roles they are, TA would have us believe that these roles are the fundamental reality of human personality. Once stuck with this assumption of fundamental fragmentation, we can never hope to realize the holism essential to health.

From a Contextual Perspective

Transactional analysis and fellow interpersonal therapies fail to go far enough. Yes, they have appropriately extended the clinical focus from intrapsychic conflicts to interpersonal patterns, but they stop short of the family system and the sociopolitical context. When they're boiled down, the presumed determinants of interpersonal problems are still situated within the individual rather than within cultural structures and socialization. If we really want to look at games people play, how about looking at "spouse abuse," "children in poverty," "underpaid women in the workforce," "blame the minorities," and "government for and by wealthy white men." Let's analyze and modify those scripts!

From an Integrative Perspective

Presenting a psychotherapy in common language has the decided advantage of allowing nonprofessionals to appreciate and use the theory on their own. The popularity of TA suggests that people are taking advantage of its simple terms and trying to apply it to their lives. At the same time, formulating a theory of personality, psychopathology, and psychotherapy in the language of everyday life brings with it the risk of producing a system lacking depth. TA does indeed come through as a common-sense approach without the sophistication required to articulate the mysteries of the human condition. TA comes through as a theory too typically American in language to capture the breadth of human experience.

In fact, all too often TA sounds like a system of slick Madison Avenue slogans. "I'm OK—you're OK" sounds like a rating from an OK used-car lot. "Green stamps, red stamps, and brown stamps" imply that our deepest human feelings occur while waiting in a supermarket to collect bonus stamps. "Games people play" is a catchphrase more appropriate for daytime television than for tortured human transactions.

Everyday language is best suited for articulating everyday events. If we are attempting to explain (and rectify) the best and the worst of human pathology, then everyday language leaves us cold. If we are attempting to affirm our humanness and the best we can say is that we are OK, then we condemn ourselves to a devitalized existence. "How did you like your date?" "Oh, he's OK." "How did you like the movie?" "It's OK." Affirming ourselves by stating that we are OK is about as strong a stance as saying that a person is interesting or different. Saying OK is barely a position of commitment, let alone a life position on which we should base our sole existence. The problem with TA language and theory is that they are too common and too cognitive, too free from the depth and the passion that make existence exciting.

➤ A TRANSACTIONAL ANALYSIS OF MRS. C. ➤

Mrs. C. is locked into a mindless script that will result in madness and institutionalization unless an antidote is forthcoming. Her worst fear is that she has already gone mad. Her world threatens to reel out of control. In a desperate attempt to maintain structure in her life, Mrs. C. routinizes whatever she can until her life is nothing but a repetitive series of compulsive rituals. With mindlessness lurking in the background, Mrs. C. clings to her compulsions as if they represent sanity itself. She confuses structure with sanity, ritual with rationality.

The origins of Mrs. C.'s mindless script are found in her parental injunctions against thinking. "Shut up and do as I say" was her father's recurrent injunction against her attempts to speak or know her own mind. We can imagine that her mother discounted Mrs. C.'s efforts to be reasonable about dirt, disease, or sexuality, until she was left with a mindless terror of these natural phenomena. With such oppressive parents, Mrs. C. at some point made the critical decision in life that her parents knew better than she: they were right and she was wrong; they were OK and she was not OK.

From her loser's life position, Mrs. C. decided on a lifetime variation of the "poor little me" script. She was the helpless child, the victim of awful forces like disease and dirt, and she was desperately in need of a rescuer. Cinderella stories were her favorite fantasies. With the exclusion of her rational Adult ego state, she felt totally incapable of salvaging her own life. Her life was dominated by her helpless Child, who was terrified of relatively harmless parts of the world, and by her Pig Parent, who demanded total cleanliness, sexual nonresponsiveness, and nonassertiveness.

Mrs. C.'s counterscript operated sufficiently for a while after her husband had rescued her from tyrannical parents. For several years she seemed to lose herself in the role of parent, having one child after another, leaving herself little time to think. But early in life she had selected a script that was destined to leave her mindless. Chaos was bound to overwhelm her. Five children and a sixth on the way, an epidemic of Asian flu, and a threatening case of pinworms were enough to produce chaotic feelings that confirmed what she had decided long ago—namely, that she was not OK. Mrs. C.'s helpless Child took over, and she began again to cry out to the adults around her to rescue her from her fate.

In the "poor little me" script, however, the star cannot allow any permanent rescue unless the script is analyzed and rewritten. Mrs. C.'s initial therapists probably responded to her dramatic pleas to be rescued. As she failed to respond, the therapists most likely began to feel victimized by Mrs. C.'s mindlessness and became persecutors who labeled the ungrateful Mrs. C. as schizophrenic and suggested that she be hospitalized. Mr. C. had also joined in the dramatic triangle as a rescuer who valiantly awoke at 5:00 A.M. to rescue Mrs. C. from her morning shower. As Mrs. C. failed to be rescued over time, Mr. C. began to feel victimized by her relentless rituals until he, too, wanted to persecute her by having her institutionalized. Mrs. C.'s tragic life script was rapidly approaching the inevitable climax in which she would collapse into craziness. With obvious mindlessness, poor little Mrs. C. would be entirely helpless and in need of constant parenting from others.

Mrs. C.'s mindless script included a series of self-defeating games. She played a heavy hand of "Ain't it Awful"—ain't the pinworms awful, ain't my washing awful, and ain't my life awful, among them. "Look how hard I tried," she would lament. "I washed, and washed, and washed, and I went to therapy for years, and I'm still a hopeless case." Her "wooden leg" game would keep others from asking too much of her. In one way or another, she would say, "I'm a helpless, obsessivecompulsive handwasher on my way to becoming a mindless schizophrenic, so don't expect me to be an adequate Adult, a warm wife, a caring mother, or a successful patient."

Mrs. C. probably received most of her strokes from her family members and psychotherapists only when she was not OK. The hunger for recognition of six children could place a serious strain on the stroke economy of the C. household. As with so many traditional wives and mothers, abundant strokes would come only when she was on the edge of being in desperate trouble. Look at the special attention and care Mrs. C. received once she became a helpless neurotic. She could be sick with flu, pregnant, and caring for five other children and never receive much in the way of special attention. But Mrs. C. had decided as a child that strokes would come freely if she adopted a helpless, not-OK position in life.

Mrs. C.'s self-destructive life course would not be moving so smoothly and rapidly toward its ultimate end if Mr. C. were not so willing to play his part so well. He is locked into a script that calls for a superhuman effort of heroic rescue until he finally sacrifices himself on the alter of self-righteous martyrdom. He's OK—she's not. "If It Weren't for Her" is a convincing game he plays to advance his self-martyred script. Without involving Mr. C. in intensive TA, we can expect that he will continue, in subtle and not-so-subtle ways, to encourage Mrs. C. along her mindless course in life. His is a joyless script that is perfectly matched to a spouse who has chosen a life of mindlessness.

If the C.s are to avoid self-destruction, intensive structural analysis must be directed at the almost total lack of Adult functioning in their lives. The therapist's Adult must hook Mrs. C.'s excluded Adult if treatment is to have a chance of succeeding. At the same time, Mr. C. must be made aware that even his Nurturant Parent, who intends to help Mrs. C. through her compulsions, is in fact detrimental to her because it stimulates her helpless Child. Mr. C. must do all he can to cease and desist from any further rescue missions on his wife's behalf. She may threaten suicide or complain of dyscontrol, and yet he must not fall back into his pattern of rescuing his poor little wife. He should be encouraged to use his own Adult in times of stress to try to hook his wife's Adult to prevent her Child from becoming overwhelmed by irrational fears.

Mrs. C. also needs permission to ask for strokes when she feels OK rather than having to act not OK in order to receive recognition from her family. The therapist must give special attention to Mrs. C.'s strengths and let her know that strokes will be forthcoming even if she improves and not only if she deteriorates. With feedback and interpretations, Mrs. C. can be helped to become aware of how she felt the need to choose a mindless script early in life but that she need not continue on such a self-destructive course. Encouraging her to read books by Berne and Harris, for example, will encourage her to use her mind to help herself. Enrolling Mrs. C. in a TA group can help her discover not only that can she use her mind to improve, but that she also has the rational ability to help others improve themselves.

If Mrs. C.'s Adult can be hooked and if she can become aware of her mindless script, then she has a chance to reverse the pathological direction of her life. If she and her husband can both become aware of how involved they have been in a dramatic rescuer–victim–persecutor triangle, then they can both realize that rescuing Mrs. C. is about as helpful as giving heroin to an addict. Mrs. C. must learn to reject all attempts from others to rescue her, even if those others are mental health professionals. Her strokes can come from discovering with difficulty that she can direct her own life. She has to learn that, in spite of what her Pig Parents stated and in spite of what she decided early in life, she has the ability to be OK. She must decide that she will no longer be the helpless child. At the same time, she needs to be aware that regardless of what some mental health professionals might say, she is not a hopeless neurotic or an incurable psychotic. In the face of professional and parental pressures, Mrs. C. must learn that regardless of her troubled past she can still proudly affirm herself as being fundamentally OK.

Future Directions

After a public surge in the 1970s, transactional analysis has slowly faded as a prominent system of psychotherapy because of its arcane language and research inadequacy. Nonetheless, TA provided a strong impetus to interpersonal perspectives and is being supplanted by more scientific substitutes. The interpersonal variants of psychodynamic treatment (Chapter 2) and interpersonal psychotherapy are hot, but the prospects for TA are not.

The limited prospects for TA lie in its integration with other systems of psychotherapy. Transactional analysis is frequently combined with systems theory in couples/family treatment, redecision therapy fuses TA with Gestalt, and many transactional analysts find themselves associated with the existential/humanistic camp (Clarkson, 1991). TA's future path is integrative psychotherapy (Erskine, 1997; Special Issue of *Transactional Analysis Journal* on Integrative Psychotherapy, 1996).

Many features of Klerman and Weissman's interpersonal psychotherapy portend its increasing popularity. IPT has been clearly operationalized in treatment manuals; it has been rigorously evaluated in controlled research; it is short-term in nature; it has an underlying psychodynamic-interpersonal orientation attractive to many practitioners; it is applicable to acute as well as to maintenance treatment; and it is compatible with concurrent pharmacotherapy—all likely features of the immediate future of psychotherapy (see Chapter 15). It will also derive increasing popularity from its widening application to marital conflict, drug abuse, eating disorders, and adolescent depression (see Klerman & Weissman, 1993). Especially notable and distinctive are successful efforts to apply a briefer form of interpersonal therapy rendered by nurse practitioners to primary care patients, a large percentage of whom present with complaints directly related to anxiety, depression, and functional body ailments (Klerman et al., 1987). In this way, IPT can be offered to a wider audience than that presenting for formal psychotherapy.

IPT's efficacy compares favorably both to sophisticated pharmacotherapy and to psychotherapies with more elaborate theoretical underpinnings. Future challenges will be to broaden training opportunities in IPT, understand how (through what processes) interpersonal therapy exerts these salubrious effects, and to test its generalizability to other populations and other disorders (Frank & Spanier, 1995; Markowitz, 1997). In these ways, IPT can improve its impact and extend its scope to the interpersonal functioning of an enlarged share of humanity.

Suggestions for Further Reading

Berne, E. (1964). *Games people play*. New York: Grove.

Berne, E. (1972). *What do you say after you say hello*. New York: Grove.

Clarkson, P. (1991). *Transactional analysis psychotherapy: An integrated approach*. London: Routledge.

Harris, A. B., & Harris, T. A. (1990). *Staying OK*. New York: Harper & Row.

Harris, T. A. (1967). *I'm OK—you're OK*. New York: Harper & Row.

Kiesler, D. J. (1996). *Contemporary interpersonal theory and research*. New York: Wiley.

Klerman, G. L., & Weissman, M. M. (Eds.). (1993). *New applications of interpersonal psychotherapy*. Washington, DC: American Psychiatric Press.

Klerman, G. L., Weissman, M. M., Rounsaville, B. J., & Chevron, E. S. (1984). *Interpersonal psychotherapy of depression*. New York: Basic.

Sullivan, H. S. (1953). *The interpersonal theory of psychiatry*. New York: Norton.

Journals: *Psychiatry; Interpersonal and Biological Processes; Transactional Analysis Journal*.

8

Exposure and Flooding Therapies

Thomas G. Stampl

MEGAN WAS AFRAID that Roger had lost all tolerance for her sarcasm and criticism. He wanted a separation. He had tried to be patient while she struggled in intensive psychotherapy to understand the source of her hostility. He had tried to accommodate himself to her demands but was coming to believe that his efforts were futile. For a while it had helped to understand that much of her bitterness began in puberty when her alcoholic father threatened her if she refused to play with his penis and let him fondle her body. Roger understood her determination to never again submit to such degrading demands, but now he was feeling degraded by her constant cutting and unwarranted attacks. Both of them were seeking some relief from bitterness. Megan's marital therapist thought that implosive therapy might reduce her hostility enough to allow her marriage and her psychotherapy to continue.

When I asked Megan to imagine as vividly as possible the childhood sexual abuse, she had no problem picturing her father staggering into her room with a bottle in his hand and a sick smirk on his face. As he began grabbing at her breasts, she could feel the revulsion and the rage welling up inside herself. But instead of passively giving in, this time I had her imagine reaching for the bottle on the bed. As he bent over to take off his shoes, she used all of her strength to crack the bottle against his skull. Sinking to the floor, he was too dazed and too drunk to keep her from hitting him again.

When she saw his penis sticking out of his pants, she felt an urge to stand on her bed and jump feet first onto his penis, smashing it against the floor. As she became more engrossed in the scene, she leaped from her chair and began jumping, stamping her shoes against the floor, shouting, "I'll crush your cock, you filthy bastard. I'll squish you into slivers, you son of a bitch. You made me feel that all men are creeps. You made me feel like a creep if I let a man near me."

Repeated exposure to these implosive scenes allowed Megan to release her intense fear and hatred of men which, understandably, had generalized to her husband. Implosive work also enabled her to reenter marital therapy with her husband and eventually made it possible for them to begin anew in their marriage.

A Note on Exposure and Flooding Therapies

Directly confronting feared stimuli, such as Megan's sexual abuse, and activating intense emotions, such as Megan's rage, are the distinctive characteristics of a variety of therapeutic approaches known as *exposure and flooding therapies*. Following considerable attention given to these therapies in the 1970s, their clinical popularity waned in the 1980s, but they have been revived in recent years to combat a host of intransigent anxiety and trauma disorders. In this chapter, we will examine four of the most evocative and provocative of these therapies: character analysis; implosion; exposure; and EMDR (Eye Movement Desensitization and Reprocessing). This chapter sequence is intentional: it reflects their historical development (from past to present) and their theoretical predilections (from psychodynamic to behavioral/stimulus-specific).

As we shall see, these exposure and flooding therapies vary considerably in the procedures used to directly confront strong emotions: Reich's character analysis relies on manipulation of the body; implosive therapy presents a fantastic form of imagery; exposure offers both imaginary and actual confrontation to the fears; and EMDR promises desensitization by means of directed eye movements or hand taps. These approaches also vary considerably in their theoretical explanations of psychopathology and psychotherapy. Nevertheless, they share the common assumption that behavioral disorders can best be treated by exposing the patient to the emotional pain.

To keep this chapter to a manageable size, the sections on personality theory and therapeutic content have been omitted. Furthermore, we will group criticisms of the four therapies together to avoid redundancy.

Some critics have argued that Reich's character analysis should be omitted entirely from this book because there are few pure Reichians practicing today. And surveys of contemporary practitioners, as reviewed in Chapter 1, support their argument. However, as will soon be apparent, a host of popular therapeutic practices—analyzing resistance before transference, treating character problems, focusing on nonverbal communications, working with bodily actions and not just words, for example—are among Reich's lasting contributions. Furthermore, Reich is to many of the flooding therapies what Freud is to many of the insight therapies: the seminal thinker and courageous pioneer who spawned a new direction in psychotherapy, including Lowen's bioenergetics. For these reasons, we now turn our attention to the life and work of Wilhelm Reich.

Character Analysis

A Sketch of Wilhelm Reich

Wilhelm Reich (1897–1957) was one of the most controversial figures of the 20th century. Praised by Freud as a brilliant and effective analyst, he was later condemned by many Freudians as a dangerous and grandiose paranoid. Said to be caustic, suspicious, and irrational by some, he was praised by others, such as Neill (1958) of Summerhill, as one of their warmest, most relaxed, sincere, and capable friends. As a source of inspiration for many important innovations in psychotherapy, he unfortunately is remembered by all too many only for his mistaken notions that people could be cured of such illnesses as cancer and schizophrenia by lying in an *orgone box*, a metallic container surrounded by wood that was assumed to accumulate healing and life-sustaining "orgone" energy from the universe.

This complex man was born into a simple farming life in the German-Ukrainian part of the Austrian Empire. Unfortunately, his family life remained neither simple nor idyllic. Wilhelm discovered his mother having an affair with his tutor and told his father, who then confronted the wife. In response, she committed suicide. Reich's subsequent espousal of sexuality in all its forms may represent an attempt to compensate for the disastrous results of his own part in the family's triangle (McGoldrick & Gerson, 1985).

Working in harmony with nature, he came to believe and trust in what was natural. Serving in the Austrian army in World War I, however, he came to know the dark side of life as well. While still a medical student in 1920 at the University of Vienna, he became a member of the Vienna Psychoanalytic Society, a rare honor for so young a person.

Reich soon established himself as an expert on psychoanalytic technique. From 1924 to 1930, he headed an official seminar devoted to systematic case study of patients with whom traditional analysis had failed. Freud was sufficiently impressed with Reich's early contributions to include him in the inner circle of friends who met once a month in his home (Jones, 1957).

Gradually Reich's personal idiosyncrasies and theoretical positions brought him into increasing conflict with the elders of psychoanalysis. His first wife was a former patient, whom he later divorced to take up residence with another woman. His later admissions (Reich, 1967) to having had sexual affairs with some of his patients confirmed the rumors that were being spread in the analytic societies. Reich's continued commitment to a theory of complete sexual fulfillment, even for adolescents, became a source of anxiety to analysts, who were then finally attaining social respectability.

Reich himself could not accept Freud's emerging emphasis on a death instinct. Freud's hypothesis of a death instinct reflected a characteristic modern uncertainty about human nature (Robinson, 1969). Reich could not accept the notion that nature had burdened humanity with such an evil, destructive force. For Reich, the destructive forces in people were the result of the frustrations imposed by an oppressive society that prevented the full and free release of the life-giving and life-supporting orgasmic energies. Reich looked to a combination of Freudian analysis of personal repression and a Marxian analysis of social oppression for the solution to the human dilemma. Reich's personal and professional unorthodoxies, however, soon led to his dismissal from the International Psychoanalytic Society in 1934. His book, *The Mass Psychology of Fascism* (1970), led to his being unwelcome in the Communist party because he suggested that the authoritarian character of the working class was a major reason for Hitler's rise to power. In a matter of months, he lost most of his friends (Reich, 1953). He fled Germany in 1933 to escape from Nazism, only to be expelled from Denmark, Sweden, and Norway.

Coming to the United States in 1939, he believed he was finally free to continue his commitment to the personal and social liberation of humanity. Some say it was too late, that he had already sunk into madness and was preoccupied with paranoid delusions that included being able to see and capture the energy source of life, which he called the orgone (Cattier, 1971). Others (for example, Boadella, 1973) believe that his paranoid ideas, including his belief that the atmosphere was being poisoned by flying saucers, had become part of Reich's world view only after years of rejection, ostracism, and persecution for his life's work.

Certainly there was reason for Reich to feel persecuted when he was ordered to stand trial for violation of the Federal Drug Administration's (FDA) injunction against the sale of orgone accumulators across state lines. Refusing to cooperate with the courts, Reich was found in contempt of federal court and guilty of FDA violations. His orgone boxes were ordered destroyed, with some justification. The destruction of all of his writings, however, was a totally unconstitutional penalty that lends support to those who saw Reich's trial as motivated, at least in part, by a repressive system, which had fired 200 FDA agents in one month for being alleged subversives (Boadella, 1973). In 1957, Reich was totally ostracized from society when he was sent to Lewisburg Penitentiary for two years. He died in prison eight months later.

Theory of Psychopathology

Psychopathology can be prevented only through a sexual revolution that grants people their inherent right to be sexually free and fulfilled. Sexual repression is the core of pathology and must be attacked. There are, however, many forces both within and outside of people that resist the natural desire for sexual happiness and health. The outside forces are those of an authoritarian social system that exploits humanity. An oppressive society, however, cannot rule by social controls alone; it requires the cooperation of its people. The biggest threat to an oppressive society is sexually free people who, in the process of expressing their sexuality, experience a sensitivity and sociability toward others that would not allow them to tolerate the brutalization and degradation of the powerless. Those who will tenderly embrace humanity are those who have known the tenderness of a loving genital embrace.

At first Reich (1953) could not understand how the 400,000 ragged and starving unemployed people in Vienna could walk by wealthy shops and privileged citizens without attacking them. Social controls, such as the police, were not numerous or powerful enough to prevent a revolution of people in touch with the energy and the decency that would come from living out their natural sensuality. Authoritarian societies needed authoritarian personalities, he concluded. Pathological societies need pathological personalities. Inhuman oppression is internalized into neurotic repression through the social institution of the family.

The family believes its purpose is to develop moral character in its children, but its actual social purpose is to repress sexuality. The result is that families use parental power to build characters that are essentially antisexual and sick. When people are raised to automatically repress their own basic sexual humanity, they are preprogrammed to be cooperative robots that participate in their own oppression and that of others.

Built into the person is a pathological *character structure* that exists to maintain sexual repression and social oppression. To attack repression, then, is to attack a patient's very character. Since a patient's character represents a total lifestyle that determines not only symptoms but also work and family relationships, a patient can be expected to be highly resistant to efforts to analyze and liberate a total lifestyle. Reich (1945) identified six typical character structures that are seen most often in psychotherapy and that present the most difficult challenges to successful analysis: (1) the phallic-narcissistic male, who uses emotional lameness and intellectualization to repress strong emotions; (2) the passive-feminine male, who uses submission and an apparently cooperative "nice guy" facade to fight off the effects of therapy; (3) the masculine-aggressive female, who uses apparent toughness and rigidity to ward off feelings; (4) the hysterical female, who uses flirtatiousness and seductiveness to avoid real commitment to a profound sexual relationship; (5) the compulsive character, of either sex, who hides behind pride in self-control and perfectionism to avoid change; and (6) the masochistic character, who uses martyrdom and suffering as a way of repressing and investing sadism, and who resists health as another way of continuing to suffer.

The rigid character structures are a form of armor that binds frozen energy and prevents instinct expression. To analyze and liberate a patient's character threatens to release the emotional impulses that Freud had described so often—rage and a perverted, compulsive, dominating sexuality.

Most patients agree with Freud that these destructive impulses represent who they really are and thus resist any attempt to analyze and release such emotions. Reich, however, believed that destructive impulses result from repression of life's liberating libido. There is a monster below the social character, but it derives not from nature but from the unnatural process of authoritarian socialization that intends to destroy what is best in people—their life-giving and life-supporting sexuality.

The forces that Reich (1945) first found to be the causes and maintainers of psychopathology were (1) an oppressive and authoritarian society, (2) a repressive style of life, called character, and (3) a threatening group of hostile and perverted sexual impulses that result from repression of the child's naturally tender and loving sexuality. Later Reich (1951) came to believe that parents used their power to make repression part of the child's very body. If it is indeed the body the parents want to control, then the best method is to use power and fear to make children tense their muscles so much that their bodies become suits of armor that are too tight and too controlled to allow for the sheer abandonment needed for total orgasmic release.

To attack a patient's repression involves attacking the patient's muscular tension. Reich (1951) contended that there are *seven rings of muscular armor* that serve as repressive forces against full genital release. In this sense, psychotherapy becomes a matter of releasing each of these rings of muscular armor, beginning with the muscles at the top half of the head and moving down through each ring until the muscles circling the pelvis and genitals can be liberated. Only patients who have undergone body liberation can be truly free from neuroses and pathological character structures and become free to experience the full delights and values of being natural human beings.

Theory of Therapeutic Processes

As a Marxist, Reich (1953) was convinced that psychopathology could be prevented only through a revolution that established a nonoppressive, communist society. As a psychotherapist, however, he was not content to let people suffer until the revolution came. In 1929, he became one of the first community mental health workers by establishing several sex information and counseling clinics in Vienna. How far ahead of his time he was! Reich provided the young and unmarried with the latest birth control measures. Reich worked many hours without pay to raise the consciousness of the young and the poor regarding their sexuality and how they might attain greater sexual fulfillment. This work was primarily educational, providing the latest information that Reich and others had gathered in their therapy work.

Consciousness Raising. In terms of formal psychotherapy, Reich's (1945) first major contribution involved *character analysis*. He was extremely influential in establishing the rule in psychoanalysis that resistance must be analyzed first, before transference, and for Reich the first line of resistance was the client's character structure.

Reich originally followed the standard free association rule that the patient's job is to say everything that comes to mind without censoring feelings or fantasies. Patients provided information for analysis not only by what they said but, even more significant, by how they said it and by how they acted in the therapeutic hour. Reich (1953) was one of the first to sensitize clinicians to the significance of nonverbal communication. Patients could not help but provide information regarding their characteristic defenses. They might be too cooperative, appear to associate too smoothly, speak softly, smile frequently, or be submissive, stubborn, or seductive. Over time, their pattern of behaving in treatment became established as the first problem to be analyzed, since the real message behind such patterns is a determination to resist changing a style of life. The hardest work of patients is to stay with therapy even when they experience their very characters as being under attack.

Reich (1945) originally saw character analysis as a necessary preparation for psychoanalysis. Until patients are fully aware of how they use their typical patterns of responding as defenses, they are unable to ease up on their defenses and truly cooperate in the analysis of infantile conflicts. To help patients gain such awareness, the therapist must persistently employ confrontations and interpretations to provide patients with feedback about their most characteristic and pervasive forms of resistance.

For example, in treating a 25-year-old man with a few minor symptoms, Reich (1951) became aware that the patient assumed a self-confident, cool, and ironic bearing toward the world that communicated an attitude of being above it all and therefore unthreatened by others. In psychotherapy, this ironic and superior bearing came out most frequently as a smile that was neither warm nor friendly but rather a message of mockery. Reich continually confronted the young man with information concerning when the smile was occurring and how it was being used to keep treatment from having any real impact. He repeatedly interpreted the mockery that the smile was communicating toward the analyst and the analysis. Reich told his patient that he had no need to be afraid of laughing heartily and loudly at the analysis. From then on, the young man began to bring out his irony and mockery much more clearly. As his character defenses became more conscious, they also became less effective and allowed more infantile memories and emotions to surface. With such infantile material closer to the surface, Reich could then resort to the more passive role of the psychoanalyst engaged in interpreting the meaning of infantile conflicts.

Catharsis. It is not sufficient to make the unconscious conscious, to simply interpret the meaning of memories and dreams into conscious language. Clients must also experience and release the intense emotions contained in dynamic conflicts. With the analysis of *character armor*, emotions are inevitably expressed as the character structure is loosened and the frozen energy released. The emotions that are most likely to be experienced first are fear and rage toward the analyst for having attacked a character structure that has served as the source of security and esteem in the patient's life. As negative emotions are cathected and the patient undergoes a corrective emotional experience, the more intense sensual and sexual instincts begin to emerge. As the infantile sexual fixations are analyzed and released, patients are free to develop relationships in which they can express to the fullest this core of life, their genital sexuality.

As Reich (1951) developed into an even more independent theorist and therapist, he became convinced that character analysis must be accompanied by a more direct liberation of the body. Repression is tied up not only in one's characteristic patterns of behavior but also in the muscular knots of one's body. Body armor itself must be attacked with a manipulation that allows for the cathartic release of repression and emotion so that the energy of life can flow more freely through the body. With the addition of direct body work, Reich labeled his approach *vegetotherapy*, an unusual term designed to reflect the vital energies common to both plants and animals.

Since the body is both focus and locus of repression, the task of clients is to make their bodies available for therapeutic intervention. Clients disrobe and lie outstretched on a couch or bed to allow the therapist access to the rings of muscular armor that need to be attacked. Patients no longer free-associate or even speak unless they find at times that language is the best expression they can give to the emotions that are emerging as their muscular armor begins to dissolve. Otherwise, clients are free to scream, kick the couch, curse the therapist, or give any other ventilation to the overwhelming emotions that have been frozen in their muscular tensions. As each ring of armor and repression is liberated and the accompanying affects evoked, patients are able to own more fully the life that is their body.

The Reichian is not concerned with providing a relaxing massage or a sensational physical manipulation. The therapist's work on the tense muscle knots is guided at all times by the emotional functions of the muscle tensions. Using both theoretical training and interpersonal empathy, therapists recognize which emotions are locked into which muscles, such as murderous rage locked into the ocular muscles in the tense, glaring stare of the paranoid personality.

Usually the therapist attacks the rings of muscular armor in sequence, beginning at the top of the head and working down to the pelvic muscles. The therapist will stay with a muscle group until patients can express the tremendous rage that accompanies the pressure of parents having been on their backs. Beyond the release of muscle tension and the accompanying emotions, the clinician teaches patients a method of deep breathing that both reduces tension and refreshes the body. As patients come to breathe more freely and as they shed their body armor, they gain the capacity to abandon themselves to spontaneous and involuntary movements in therapy. Little by little the various sensations of warmth, of prickling in the skin, and of shuddering movements in the limbs and trunk begin to integrate into convulsive reflex movements of the whole body. Looked at as a whole, the body appears to be expanding and contracting in a pulsating manner. The client has become free to give total and involuntary release to the most pleasurable and energizing expression of life—the orgasmic reflex.

Therapeutic Relationship

Human beings are to be held in the highest regard, but it is the natural, genital human that is godlike, not the charade commonly known as character. Character structure represents what an oppressive society has demanded as the price of acceptance. We can no more love the oppressive defenses of neurotic individuals than we can prize the oppressive forces of an authoritarian society. We must care enough about real human beings to dedicate ourselves to the removal of both repression and oppression. Character and body armor must be attacked in order for the whole human being, who is so worthy of our highest regard, to emerge. Clients can and will direct their lives effectively and responsibly, but only after effective therapists have responsibly directed them in the therapeutic process of shedding characterological and bodily blinders. Similarly, a therapist should be available to enter into a genuine relationship with clients, but only after the clients have become free to be genuine.

Empathic relating has a special meaning in vegetotherapy. Empathy is a bodily experience that is sensed in the liberated bodies of therapists who are in physical contact with the tensions and emotions locked into the muscular armor of clients. Clinicians must trust in their own bodies to guide them in their physical work with clients.

Practicalities and Effectiveness

While Reich would have preferred mental health professionals to be trained in anatomy and physiology as well as in psychoanalysis, he would be much more concerned with their therapeutic experiences. A Reichian should undergo both character analysis and vegetotherapy to ensure that he or she is liberated both in behavior and in body. Reich (1951) also believed the use of intensive case seminars with supervision was essential to effective therapeutic training.

In practice, Reich seemed to emulate the psychoanalytic camp in conducting individual therapy with several sessions weekly. He claimed to be especially effective in treating neuroses and character disorders that were highly resistant to traditional analysis. Unlike classical analysts, he did not believe that therapy works best with verbal, intelligent, well-educated individuals but rather believed that such individuals frequently use their verbosity as an effective defense. As we have seen, he was willing to work with the poor and the oppressed.

Contemporary Reichians generally avoid the most controversial practices of Reich. For example, they generally have patients wear bathing suits or underwear, rather than be nude. They reject the notion that sex with clients can be justified but focus instead on helping clients become free to develop their own fulfilling sexual and intimate relationships outside of therapy.

Reviews of the literature failed to produce any controlled outcome studies on the efficacy of character analysis. Reich followed the Freudian example of intensive case studies as the means of validating his treatment.

Post-Reichian Therapy: Bioenergetics

Alexander Lowen (1910–   ) is the therapist and theorist most responsible for the survival, revival, and advancement of Reichian psychotherapy. Trained as a physician and psychoanalyst, Lowen underwent analysis and supervision with Reich. Lowen's concern was with the strictly therapeutic aspects of Reich's work, avoiding the political ramifications, in part because he believed that it was these commitments that led to Reich's destruction (Keleman, 1973).

The freedom to enjoy life can come only in a body that is fully alive, a body that allows the free flow of life's energy, *bioenergy*. Lowen is a strong voice against the antipleasure and antibody forces of society in his extensive private practice, his International Institute for Bioenergetics Analysis in New York, his nationwide workshops, and his numerous books on bioenergetics (Lowen, 1958, 1965, 1967, 1975, 1980, 1984).

For Lowen, psychopathology involves the repression and rigidification of life. For every rigidity of psychic functioning, there is a corresponding rigidity of metabolic organismic functioning. All psychopathology entails an arrest of full energy flow on both the psychological level of subject-world perceptions and the physiological level of internal channels of metabolic interaction (Brown, 1973). Rigidifications of the body and the self originate in the early conflicts between parent and child and eventually become the neurotic character structure and the muscular armor that Reich (1942, 1945) described.

Reich overlooked, however, two common clinical characters: the oral characters, who have trouble standing on their own two feet and who use dependency on the therapist to resist change; and the schizoid characters, who have restrictions in their breathing and living and who employ detachment from their bodies as defensive means of remaining detached from psychotherapy (Lowen, 1967). In his later years, Lowen (1984) has written about and worked with narcissistic characters, a complex character structure in which superiority and grandiosity are expressed in overdevelopment of the upper half of the body and relative weakness in the lower half.

All pathological characters, and especially schizoid and narcissistic characters, lack an adequate *grounding* in reality. Since character structure is established in childhood, it leads to an incomplete maturation of the ego, which represents the principle that effective living must be grounded in reality (Bellis, 1976). In more Freudian terms, patients have trouble with both the pleasure principle of finding adequate fulfillment for bodily desires and the reality principle of being well-integrated into the world. Whereas Reich emphasized giving free and full energizing to the autonomic part of the nervous system that controls sexual pleasure, Lowen gives equal emphasis to the cerebral cortex being fully energized.

Our fundamental grounding is in our bodies. "Apart from the body, life is an illusion" (Lowen, 1967, p. 758). We, as body, are the life process. To be well-integrated in our living reality is to have a well-integrated body. But, as Reich discovered, the bodies of troubled individuals are knotted layers of muscular armor that prevent the smooth, integrated flow of life's energy, *bio* energy. Muscular defenses also prevent the smooth, integrated flow of living in the world.

Bioenergetics entails the cathartic release of the body within the context of an analysis of the patient's infantile character structure. In other words, the physical work of therapy is not at the cost of the analytic work.

In the Reichian tradition, bioenergetics encompasses both consciousness raising and catharsis. Before there can be a free and full flow of feelings, clients must become aware of the chronic characterological and bodily tensions used to control feelings (Lowen, 1972, 1975). To become free of their infantile characters, patients must connect their present inhibitions with the past and become aware of the bodily impulses they were forced to repress by their behavioral and bodily inhibitions. In undergoing bioenergetic analysis, the main work of clients is to struggle to unblock their ears and hear clearly the interpretations of the therapist.

From the initial diagnostic reading of the body's behavioral performance, the bioenergetic analyst is trained to come to quick and decisive conclusions about the precise nature of the patient's psychological weaknesses. The analyst is highly didactic, informing patients they have a particular character structure as revealed by an analysis of the particular rigidities in their muscular armor. Patients are told, for example, that they have a tight jaw to hold back biting impulses or tense shoulders to refrain from hitting people. Once interpretations have been presented, it is the patient's responsibility to sense the tension in the jaw and the impulses to bite and be sarcastic. Although interpretations are based partially on feedback about a specific patient's experience, the interpretations are in large measure based on psychoanalytic and bioenergetic theory.

In bioenergetic body work, patients are more active than in vegetotherapy. They do not simply lie back and have their muscles manipulated. This occurs at times, but just as frequently, patients are asked to perform breathing and physical exercises designed to evoke intense emotions. Patients may be asked, for instance, to pit themselves against the world's field of gravity in such a way as to intensify their negative feelings against giving in or collapsing. They may be encouraged to arch their bodies off the ground by making contact with the floor with only their hands, head, and feet. After considerable struggle to stay up, they can experience the feeling of their bodies giving in to the inevitable, to the reality of life, as they tire and collapse to the floor. They can experience the fear or anger connected with giving in, and through analysis they can become aware that these and other negative emotions may be the result of early conflicts with parents who insisted on submission.

Gradually, patients may recognize that fears over giving in to reality may keep them from falling asleep or falling in love or surrendering to orgasmic reflex. Patients are also asked to practice exercises such as yelling or kicking and hitting the couch, both to release anger and to experience the inner ability to focus energy. These exercises may also evoke childhood memories of wanting to strike out against parents but dreading the thought. At the same time, they may help patients experience a sense of bodily grounding—that they can express their anger intensely and yet not go entirely out of control and attack the therapist, as they may have fantasized. Patients also practice proper breathing through exercises designed to release energy through a more natural breathing process.

Bioenergetic body work is not as systematic as vegetotherapy. The bioenergetic therapist works more spontaneously, working on the muscles that are currently providing the greatest resistance or those that contain the most emotions and energy. Or the therapist may not directly attack the body at any given moment but may turn to an exercise that might be more successful in releasing emotions and energy. The bioenergetic analyst encourages patients to surrender to the body, to let emotion and energy flow, and to trust the body as their direct link to reality (Keleman, 1971, 1973). The highly energized therapist is tuned to energy blocks and removes resistances to life through movements, muscular manipulations, or mental interpretations. With emotional release, patients discover a tremendous increase in bioenergy, the energy of life that flows within them and outside them. The release of emotions and energy is then grounded in the person's expanding awareness of reality—the reality they are willing to support and help create through the investment of their newfound energy.

With respect to practicalities, Lowen is similar in many ways to Reich, but differs in allowing patients to remain clothed or work in the nude, depending on their preferences. Besides individual therapy, he is also willing to perform bioenergetics with groups, especially in weekend workshops. He teaches a number of physical exercises that patients perform in the session and at home.

With respect to effectiveness, neither Lowen nor his students have conducted controlled outcome research on bioenergetics. In an extensive search of the published research literature in North American and Europe, Grawe and colleagues (1998) located only one controlled study on bioenergetics. Bioenergetic analysis is a psychotherapy system yet to be rigorously evaluated.

Implosive Therapy

A Sketch of Thomas Stampfl

Thomas Stampfl (1923–), the developer of implosive therapy, frequently asks his clients to imagine horrible scenes such as chopping up a child, eating lunch in a cesspool, or being devoured by rats, but relates as a personable, friendly, and warm individual. Early in his career he became convinced that avoidance is at the heart of psychopathology, and he developed his system of psychotherapy in order to help people face their most frightening memories, feelings, and thoughts.

Trained at Loyola of Chicago as a clinical psychologist, he was inspired by both the psychoanalytic content of psychopathology and the learning-theory processes of avoidance conditioning and extinction. While teaching at John Carroll University in Cleveland, he attempted to develop a treatment that would integrate psychoanalytic and behavioral therapy. When he moved to the University of Wisconsin at Milwaukee as director of clinical psychology, he principally concerned himself with documenting the behavioral foundation of implosive treatment. He was among the first behavioral researchers to demonstrate the efficacy of implosion in the laboratory and to apply it in the consulting room. Even in retirement, he is an influential proponent of this form of emotional flooding therapy, and his students, especially Donald Levis of the State University of New York, proudly carry the banner of implosive therapy forward.

Theory of Psychopathology

The symptoms and defense mechanisms that characterize psychopathology are learned *avoidance responses* that serve to reduce or minimize anxiety. Phobics avoid stimuli such as dogs, elevators, or heights; obsessive-compulsives may avoid dirt, disorder, or anger; schizophrenics may avoid close contact with people; hypochondriacs attempt to avoid disease. If troubled individuals did not use their symptoms and defenses to avoid these and other stimuli, they would be confronted with considerable anxiety that could take on panic proportions.

To understand how anxiety and avoidance responses are learned, we will do best to examine the challenging research on animal avoidance behavior. Animal research may initially appear irrelevant to human disorders, but we shall see that these studies serve as excellent analogues of human psychopathology and corrective interventions (Stampfl & Levis, 1973a, 1973b; Levis, 1993).

A dog can be conditioned to fear and flee from a buzzer that was previously neutral. If the dog is placed in a training cage and the buzzer is turned on, the dog will at first orient to the buzzer and then learn to ignore it. However, if the buzzer is followed by a painful or frightening event—say, an electric shock or a startling noise—a different response pattern occurs. When the buzzer and shock are both on, the animal will soon learn to escape the shock—by jumping over a barrier to the other side of the cage, for example. After several trials in which the buzzer and the shock are paired together, the animal learns to jump over the barrier as soon as the buzzer comes on in order to avoid the shock. If, following several trials of avoidance learning, the traumatic shock is terminated, the animal continues to avoid as soon as the buzzer begins. Solomon and Wynne (1954) reported that their dogs would avoid a buzzer for hundreds of trials, even though there was no chance of receiving another shock. The dogs were behaving as if they were buzzer phobics.

Mowrer (1947) employed a *two-factor theory of learning* to explain avoidance conditioning. The first factor is *classical* or *respondent conditioning*, through which the animal learns to fear the buzzer because it has been paired with shock. This conditioned fear is labeled anxiety. The buzzer becomes a conditioned stimulus capable of eliciting an automatic and autonomic conditioned response similar to fear. If the dog remains near the buzzer, the aversive anxiety increases in intensity. If the dog jumps over the barrier, the anxiety is reduced, and the dog's avoidance is reinforced by the powerful consequence of anxiety reduction. The second factor in learning to avoid is called *operant or instrumental conditioning* because it is instrumental in minimizing the dog's anxiety. The classically conditioned anxiety serves as the motivating or drive stimulus that activates the avoidance response, while the anxiety reduction provides the consequence necessary for reinforcement of the instrumental avoidance.

Applying this animal analogue to human disorders can inform us about the process by which people learn to avoid particular stimuli. For example, a 24-year-old man entered psychotherapy in order to overcome his dread of getting close to people, especially women. His traumatic childhood was punctuated by a hostile mother and an alcoholic, abusive father. He recalled multiple memories of physical and verbal abuse, such as the time he was talking jubilantly at breakfast about a field trip at school, when suddenly his mother grabbed his hair and pushed his face into the hot cereal because he was talking too loudly. He could never predict when he might get smacked in the back of the head or punished for showing anger, enthusiasm, or sadness. All he could predict was that when people were around, particularly his parents, he was more likely to face a frightening encounter. The stimuli that were conditioned to elicit anxiety were his parents specifically and, through the process of *generalization*, almost any person with whom he became emotionally involved. When he began to get close to someone, his classically conditioned anxiety would be elicited. When he then retreated and avoided interpersonal closeness, his anxiety would be reduced and his avoidance of people reinforced. Even though the new people he might approach would not shove his face into hot cereal or scream unpredictably, he was responding with anxiety and avoidance as if a shock were present in his environment.

This example also demonstrates that conditioning of disorders is often a more complex phenomenon than illustrated in the animal analogue. For one thing, when children are punished or frightened in their natural environment, there is not just one stimulus, such as a buzzer, being conditioned to elicit anxiety, but rather a complex series of stimuli. Humans are conditioned to experience anxiety in relation to the entire context in which anxiety was initially encountered—in this case, parents, adults, people, hot cereal, sitting at the breakfast table, feeling strong emotions, and openly expressing a feeling. Stampfl and Levis (Levis, 1966; Levis, Bouska, Eron, & McIlhon, 1970; Levis & Stampfl, 1972; Stampfl & Levis, 1973a, 1973b) returned to the laboratory to test the effects of conditioning animals to avoid a complex series of stimuli, such as dark walls, followed by a tone, followed by a flashing light. They found that a complex series of conditioned stimuli actually led to more effective avoidance conditioning; that is, it is learned more readily and is remarkably more resistant to extinction than when shock is paired with a single stimulus.

The conditioning of the shy young man reveals another important difference between human and animal conditioning. As in the animal analogue, the man was conditioned to fear and to avoid stimuli that were present in the environment at the time of punishment—namely, people. However, he was conditioned also to be anxious about what he was imagining or feeling at the time his parents hit him or yelled at him. Consequently, he became anxious even when he *imagined* exciting or emotional events, and he learned to avoid imagining or fantasizing such experiences. This is traditionally called *avoidance repression*. Defenses, then, can be seen to involve the cognitive avoidance of threatening thoughts, feelings, or fantasies by avoiding attending to the internal stimuli that elicit anxiety. When the young man repressed or avoided his anger, for example, he was reinforced by the reduction of anxiety that would be elicited by angry feelings.

Theory of Therapeutic Processes

If the cause of psychopathology is conditioned anxiety and avoidance, then the solution is to apply the most effective methods of extinguishing both avoidance and anxiety responses. *Extinction* is the gradual disappearance of the conditioned anxiety because it is no longer reinforced—in this case, no longer reinforced by avoidance. Implosive therapy was created in response to the single question of what intervention would faithfully reflect the operations of experimental psychologists when they subject lower animals to extinction procedures in the laboratory (Stampfl, 1976). Early on, research studies (for example, Baum, 1970; Black, 1958; Solomon, Kamin, & Wynne, 1953) documented that avoidance can be effectively extinguished if the animal is blocked from performing avoidance responses in the presence of anxiety-eliciting stimuli. We found (Schiff, Smith, & Prochaska, 1972) in our lab that as little as two minutes of blocking would produce almost total extinction of avoidance responding in rats. Although extinction of classically conditioned anxiety takes longer (Spring, Prochaska, & Smith, 1974), the anxiety could also be effectively extinguished by preventing the animal from avoiding.

When the animal is blocked in the presence of anxiety-eliciting stimuli, intense emotional reactions are evoked. The animal will scramble about the cage, climb the walls or attack the barrier, freeze in the corner, and shake, all followed by more scrambling. Soon the classically conditioned anxiety extinguishes, because there is no longer any shock or other unconditioned stimulus presented to reinforce the learned anxiety response. In the absence of anticipated punishment, such as shock, the animal learns to discriminate that the buzzer is not a painful stimulus, and it need not be avoided. On an animal level, this method of extinguishing anxiety by forcing the animal to remain in the presence of the conditioned stimuli is called *response prevention*. On a human level, the task for implosive therapy is to extinguish pathological anxiety by presenting clients with anxiety-eliciting stimuli while working to prevent them from avoiding them (Stampfl, 1970; Stampfl & Levis, 1967, 1973a, 1973b).

Catharsis. The client's task is to imagine as vividly as possible whatever stimulus scenes the psychotherapist describes and to experience as fully as possible the intense anxiety and other aversive emotions elicited by the scenes. Patients are instructed to stay with the frightening scenes even when they want to run, hide, and avoid. They are asked to continue to come back to psychotherapy, which they typically do because of the marked reduction in anxiety they experience even by the end of the first session.

The clients' work also involves putting themselves through the implosive scenes after the implosive therapist has presented the scenes the first time. Clients are to make the scenes even more anxiety- and emotion-evoking if possible. Also, in between sessions, they are to complete the extinction process at home by continuing to imagine any parts of the implosive scenes that are still eliciting anxiety. Clearly, this cathartic treatment demands a great deal of effort and cooperation from clients.

Implosive therapy may demand even more effort from the mental health professional. It is definitely one of the most emotionally draining therapies to conduct. Following a few evaluation sessions, the implosive therapist must construct stimulus scenes that evoke the maximum level of conditioned anxiety. Stimuli most directly related to the client's symptoms will be first in the series of anxiety-eliciting cues, such as bugs for a person with a morbid dread of bugs. When implosive therapists ask clients to vividly imagine scenes about bugs, they have the person imagine the bugs as close to them as possible, crawling on their arms, in their hair, sleeping with them in bed, under the covers, all over their bodies, with their bug eyes popping out, their antennas touching the client's lips, as they come mouth-to-mouth with each other.

More challenging for the implosive therapist is to construct scenes that have been repressed or cognitively avoided. These repressed stimuli are similar to what psychoanalysts refer to as the *dynamics of psychopathology*, such as repressed feelings of rage. These *dynamic cues*—or *hypothesized avoidance cues,* as they are also known—are assumed to be the conditioned stimuli that elicit the most anxiety. Dynamic cues are based on psychodynamic theories of psychopathology and on the therapist's clinical interpretations. Such cues include fears of losing control over hostile or sexual urges, anal impulses, fears of responsibility and facing one's conscience, and anxiety over anxiety itself. Implosive therapists use their full imaginations to create the most evocative scenes possible.

The implosive therapist instructs the client not to worry about whether the scenes are realistic or whether they make sense or even apply to the client. Clients are asked to imagine the scenes as if they were occurring in the present and to let themselves feel as fully as they can all the anxiety, anger, guilt, or other emotions that might be elicited by the stimuli being described.

As implosive scenes are presented, clients are observed for overt signs of anxiety, such as rapid breathing, sweaty palms, crying, gripping the chair, or curling up and covering their faces. When signs of anxiety are observed, the therapist uses this feedback to intensify or repeat the scene in order to elicit and thereby extinguish more anxiety. The polite person will typically terminate a discussion or image that another person finds objectionable; by contrast, the implosive therapist intentionally intensifies the image to make it more objectionable!

Implosive therapists also watch for signs that the client is trying to defend against the anxiety, in which case they try to block the avoidances or break through defenses by pushing the client even harder. An example of this occurred when one of my patients was being asked to watch her children die a slow and painful, but preventable, death. They pleaded for her to save them. I originally instructed her to imagine that she was yelling angrily at the children, "I won't help you. I don't want to help you." This evoked enormous anxiety and crying. When she was putting herself through the scene by overtly describing what was going on, she changed the scene and said, "I can't help you. You will have to die." At that point I interrupted to break through her denial of her angry wish by saying, "No, tell them you won't help them." When she no longer used her denial, her anxiety quickly intensified, as measured by increases in her blood pressure and heart rate (Prochaska, 1968).

As if that were not enough, the therapist must stay with a scene until the anxiety has been noticeably reduced and at least partly extinguished. If a session or scene were terminated while the client was highly anxious, the client could become even more sensitized to the conditioned stimuli and might increase his or her avoidance once the session had ended. The client could also have anxiety conditioned to the treatment setting and might avoid returning to therapy. Consequently, implosive therapists are trained to stay with scenes until the client is drained of most of the emotion connected with a particular scene.

Therapeutic Relationship

Theoretically, a relationship need not be developed, since anxiety-eliciting stimuli could be presented on tapes or films. Horror movies, to take an example, can be used for children and adults to confront their worst anxieties of death, violence, and the unknown, as well as to release aversive emotions through the dramatic effects of such scenes. However, these films can produce the opposite effect of increasing anxiety because the imagery is not repeated long enough or frequently enough for anxiety to be extinguished.

Practically, an abiding therapeutic relationship is essential, then, in order for clinicians to help clients stay with the threatening stimuli when they most want to run and to ensure that the most aversive stimuli are repeated and repeated until anxiety is markedly reduced. Obviously, the therapist must be able to engender trust in patients in order for them to continue to cooperate in treatment. Trust building is started at the beginning of the first evaluative session, as the therapist communicates a desire to understand and to assist the client in resolving unsettling problems.

Implosive therapists are not concerned with being genuine in therapy; they are concerned with being effective. They offer empathy only during the evaluation sessions to formulate clinical interpretations that lead to the development of effective scenes. During the treatment itself, it does not take empathy to observe the anxiety that clients experience during implosive scenes. Considerable regard is communicated to clients through the therapist's belief that clients are much stronger than they are usually given credit for being. Clients possess the strength and courage to confront the worst fears imaginable as long as they know that their intense anxiety is being elicited by psychotherapy and not by some unknown and uncontrollable inner source. Interestingly, it is typically other mental health professionals—not clients—who are most resistant to implosive techniques.

Practicalities

Implosive therapists must be trained to overcome their own socialized tendencies to avoid producing anxiety in other people. Their own conditioned anxieties must be extinguished so that they can effectively present very aversive stimuli. In our own experience, we found it necessary to implode ourselves on every scene before we could effectively present and stay with the scene with a patient.

In the past, most implosive therapists were trained to appreciate and use both psychoanalytic theory and learning theory. With increased emphasis now placed on the learning-theory foundations, the psychoanalytic content is minimized in the training process. If a therapist works only with symptom stimuli and assumes that dynamic cues are irrelevant or nonexistent, that therapist is technically doing what is called *flooding therapy* (Malleson, 1959; Rimm & Masters, 1974) rather than traditional implosive therapy.

Implosive therapists work primarily in the individual format because avoidance problems are assumed to be primarily intrapersonal. Implosive therapy generally lasts only 3 to 20 sessions. The sessions typically run longer than the standard 50 minutes, because damage could be done to clients by stopping a session on the hour when they are in the midst of experiencing intense anxiety. Implosive treatment requires relatively soundproof rooms in order to let clients emote fully. First-floor offices are also preferred, because people in an office below do not always appreciate a client stamping up and down on the floor above.

Effectiveness

In contrast to Reichian and Lowenian therapies, implosive therapy has been widely researched and its efficacy reported in meta-analyses. In an early chapter, Stampfl (1976) cites four controlled studies on the efficacy of implosive therapy with clinical patients. All four studies found that implosive therapy was superior to no treatment; in one study, implosion was more effective than desensitization and in one other study, the two treatments were equally effective.

Morganstern (1973) presented an early comprehensive review of the research on both implosive therapy and flooding therapy. Basically, his analysis indicated that flooding produced results comparable to those of imploding in which dynamic cues were included. The review further indicated that when implosion and flooding were compared with systematic desensitization, there were no consistent differences in the effectiveness of these treatments.

Several studies have demonstrated the efficacy of implosive therapy with combat veterans suffering from PTSD (see Keane, Fairbank, Caddell, & Zimering, 1989; Keane & Kaloupek, 1982). Cooper and Clum (1989) went further to examine the incremental effectiveness of imaginal flooding over standard psychotherapeutic and pharmacologic approaches in the treatment of combat-related PTSD. Seven male vets received 6 to 14 sessions of individual flooding therapy plus standard group therapy and pharmacotherapy; another seven male vets received the group therapy, pharmacotherapy, and individual meetings with a VA psychologist. Results indicated that the flooding did increase the effectiveness of the standard treatment; at termination and at follow-up, patients who had received the flooding experienced significantly fewer symptoms and reported improved sleep. For example, all seven of the flooded patients, but none of the patients in the standard, control group, experienced at least a 50% reduction in nightmares. Although the differences observed at termination were less pronounced at follow-up, there were still consistently positive indicators of the incremental effectiveness of flooding beyond that achieved by group treatment and medication.

The Shapiro and Shapiro (1982) meta-analysis on 143 controlled studies containing at least two treatment groups and one control group included 10 studies that evaluated flooding. The average effect size for all the studies was .93; the average effect size for flooding therapies was 1.12—a large effect in general, and a slightly larger effect than the other therapies to which it was compared.

Although many of the studies included in this meta-analysis were behavioral analogues conducted in the 1970s using student volunteers with minimal problems, the more recent, representative research leads to the conclusion that the efficacy of implosion and flooding has now also been satisfactorily demonstrated in actual patients suffering from debilitating symptomatology. Of course, this conclusion is limited to adults suffering from anxiety and trauma disorders. Implosive therapy has been shown to invariably outperform no treatment, consistently outperform placebo therapy, and generally perform in a comparable, if not superior, manner to alternative psychotherapies.

Exposure Therapy

Theory of Psychopathology

In the behavioral tradition, exposure therapists view anxiety as a conditioned response controlled by the two learning factors. Both respondent learning and operant learning are involved in the development and maintenance of behavioral disorders. Conditioning accounts for the acquisition of the fear, and extinction (or habituation) accounts for the fear reduction.

Freud coined the term *neurotic paradox* to describe this phenomenon: the failure of maladaptive anxiety to extinguish despite its self-defeating nature. The paradox is resolved by distinguishing between the short term and the long term. In the short-term, obsessive thoughts and compulsive rituals actually relieve anxiety by avoiding confrontation with feared situations. The obsessive-compulsive who washes his or her hands five times in a row or checks the door locks five times is being reinforced through anxiety reduction: "Whew! I avoided dirt and danger again." In the long term, however, such washing and checking invariably lead to more intense avoidance and more intense anxiety. Avoidance of an anxiety-producing situation, be it an exam, a confrontation, or a fear, brings relief immediately but more misery eventually.

Theory of Therapeutic Processes

The therapeutic strategy of exposure therapy is to reverse the reinforcement contingencies or the neurotic paradox: intentional, prolonged contact with the feared stimuli *(exposure)* and the active blocking of the associated avoidance behaviors *(response prevention)*. In the short term, patients will certainly experience increased anxiety, but through the process of *extinction*, they will with equal certainty experience reduced anxiety and avoidance in the long term.

Take, for example the ubiquitous fear that children develop toward large and unfamiliar dogs. The child will manifest anxiety—trembling, protesting, crying, sweating, among others—and resultant avoidance—turning away, leaving the area, refusing to enter the space occupied by the dog. To countercondition this fear, we could opt for several types of exposure therapy, as I (JCN) was forced to do when my son, Jonathon, developed a canine phobia resulting from a single unpleasant encounter with a stray dog.

One decision is whether to administer exposure in an intensive or graduated fashion. Jonathon could be exposed directly and immediately to the dog (intensive) or exposed slowly and incrementally (gradually) from the least feared to the most feared situation. In the former, we would place Jonathon directly next to an unknown dog which, of course, would precipitate intense arousal. In the latter case, we would slowly introduce Jonathon to the general area and take "baby steps" toward the dog.

A second decision is whether the feared dog is presented to Jonathon in his imagination (*imaginal*) or in the real situation (*in vivo*). In both cases, the feared stimulus can be presented in an intensive or gradual fashion.

Exposure methods varying on these dimensions of exposure medium and arousal level are accorded different names. Systematic desensitization, for instance, is at the extreme of imaginal and minimally arousing exposure (see Chapter 9). At the other extreme would be intense, in vivo exposure.

A third decision is how much we might block Jonathon's attempts to avoid the feared dog. Total *response prevention* would entail prohibiting the child from leaving the dog until practically all anxiety was eliminated, whereas partial response prevention would settle for less and allow the child to leave the dog following diminuation of anxiety.

All things considered, we decided to treat Jonathon with both imaginal and in vivo exposure in fairly intensive manner with partial response prevention. We taught Jonathon to relax and imagine dogs approaching him at home. Once he was able to comfortably do so, we ventured out to pet some neighborhood dogs, allowing him to pet them for a few minutes and then step away. The two-hour "treatment" was highly effective, despite the arcane jargon and the psychologist father. In fact, what we did closely resembled what most parents routinely do to overcome their children's fears.

In the exposure treatment of obsessive-compulsive disorder (OCD), the treatment target is the core, catastrophic fear that underlies the obsessions and compulsions. Each session is terminated after *habituation* (defined as 50% reduction in reactivity to fear-producing stimuli) is achieved. Response prevention is used to block compulsive rituals, such as washing, by instruction, encouragement, direction, persuasion, and other nonphysical means. Because the rituals serve an anxiety-reducing function, the patient must learn that the feared catastrophic consequences do not occur if the rituals are not performed (Turner, 1997).

Although imaginal and in vivo exposure treatments emerged from conditioning theories, more recent conceptualizations invoke the concept of *emotional processing* to explain fear reduction during exposure. Edna Foa and colleague (Foa &

Kozak, 1986; Foa & Meadows, 1997) suggest that exposure corrects erroneous associations and evaluations. This process of emotional processing requires the activation of the fear structure through the introduction of feared stimuli and the presentation of corrective information that is incompatible with the pathological elements of the fear structure. Thus, exposure reduces symptoms by allowing patients to realize that contrary to their mistaken ideas (Foa & Meadows, 1997):

- being in objectively safe situations that remind them of trauma is not dangerous;
- remembering the trauma is not equivalent to experiencing it again;
- anxiety does not remain indefinitely in the presence of feared situations or memories; and
- experiencing anxiety does not lead to loss of control.

The newer conceptualizations of therapeutic improvement evoke both desensitization and cognitive change.

In Foa's own exposure treatment for PTSD, both imaginal and in vivo methods are used and both desensitization and cognitive changes are expected. The early sessions entail a thorough assessment, education about common reactions to trauma, and *breathing retraining* (teaching clients to breathe calmly from the diaphragm). Repeated exposure to the trauma is achieved through imaginal exposure, which enhances the emotional processing, and then through in vivo exposure, which enables the client to realize that the trauma-related situations are not dangerous.

Similar processes are posited for the effectiveness of *cue exposure* in the treatment of addictive disorders. In substance abusers, cues related to alcohol use, such as the smell of beer or the sight of a vodka bottle, elicit conditioned responses, such as anticipated pleasure or physiological cravings. These conditioned responses are associated with a desire to resume substance abuse and a desire to avoid drug withdrawal. Repeated exposure to preingestion cues in the absence of substance use might lead to extinction of conditioned responses and maladaptive cognitions, thus reducing the likelihood of substance abuse in the future. Early results of cue exposure treatment for alcohol dependence are promising (Drummond & Glautier, 1994; Monti et al., 1993; Sitharthan, Sitharthan, Hough, & Kavanagh, 1997).

Therapeutic Relationship

In many ways an explosive therapist operates like an effective parent. Trust is engendered. Confidence is modeled, demonstrating that the feared stimuli, both real and imagined, will not hurt. There is also a parental insistence that helps the client remain in the presence of the feared stimuli, rather than running like a frightened child. The relationship reflects a form of tough love that says, "Don't run away from your problems. Soon you will master it and have a future free from conditioned fears."

Practicalities

The practice of exposure therapy generally parallels that of implosive therapy. Eight to 12 sessions, each 1—to 2 hours in duration, are the norm. Homework is assigned between sessions; the client is asked to conduct self-controlled exposure by, for instance, listening to an audiotape of a previous session or by imagining the feared situation while relaxing. Training is widely available from behavior and cognitive therapists experienced in the various types of exposure treatments.

Effectiveness

Exposure therapy has received considerable attention in controlled outcome studies for the treatment of anxiety and trauma disorders. In a representative study, Foa, Rothbaum, Riggs, and Murdock (1991) randomly assigned 45 rape victims with PTSD to one of four treatment conditions: stress inoculation training, prolonged exposure, supportive counseling, and wait list. Treatment consisted of 9 biweekly 90-minute individual sessions conducted by a female therapist. Multiple outcome measures were taken at termination and at 3 months posttreatment. All treatments produced improvement at termination and at follow-up. At termination, both stress inoculation training (reviewed in Chapter 9) and exposure produced significantly more improvement in PTSD symptoms than did support or wait list. At follow-up, however, prolonged exposure produced superior outcome in PTSD symptoms. The interpretation offered for this pattern of results was that prolonged exposure creates temporarily high levels of arousal, as patients are asked to repeatedly confront the rape memory, but leads to permanent change in the rape memory and hence results in more durable gains.

Indeed, in their review of exposure for combat-related PTSD, Frueh, Turner, and Beidel (1995) conclude that exposure is superior to wait-list controls and standard treatments. In particular, exposure results in decreased symptoms of intrusive images and physiological arousal. Treatment gains are generally maintained over time. In an independent review, Foa and Meadows (1997) similarly conclude that studies consistently support the efficacy of imaginal and in vivo exposure for the treatment of PTSD.

Two quantitative reviews have been conducted on the effectiveness of exposure with obsessive-compulsive disorder (OCD). In the first review (Abel, 1993), findings suggest that exposure with response prevention is more effective than serotonergic antidepressant medications, particularly in alleviating rituals. The literature also favors exposure in terms of side effects, dropout, and maintenance, while one advantage of drug therapy is that less time and effort are required by the therapist and patient. In the second review (Abramowitz, 1996), a total of 38 trials from controlled and uncontrolled trials were included in a meta-analysis. Results suggest that therapist-supervised exposure was more effective than self-controlled exposure and that the addition of response prevention to exposure was associated with better outcomes than no response prevention. In reducing anxiety, the combination of in vivo and imaginal exposure was superior to in vivo exposure alone.

In a meta-analysis of 34 treatment studies on panic disorder with agoraphobia (Cox, Endler, Lee, & Swinson, 1992), exposure therapy secured large, powerful effect sizes—1.34 to 3.42—across a variety of outcome variables. The treatment effects for the medication Alprazolam were also significant for most outcome variables, but exposure had the most consistent strong effect.

Graded exposure therapy is also generally recognized as one of the treatments of choice for specific phobias (Lazarus, 1991; Barlow, 1988). However, the superiority of exposure over alternative treatments, including supportive psychotherapy, is not nearly as overwhelming as commonly believed (Barber & Luborsky, 1991; Klein, Zitrin, Woerner, & Ross, 1983).

All in all, exposure therapy has acquitted itself well in the treatment of PTSD and the anxiety disorders. While it would be premature to hail it as the singular treatment of choice, exposure therapy certainly produces beneficial results, more so than no treatment, more so than several alternative therapies, and more so or comparable to leading medications.

EMDR

A Sketch of Francine Shapiro

The traumatic discovery that led to the 1987 development of Eye Movement Desensitization and Reprocessing (EMDR) began nearly ten years earlier. In 1979 Francine Shapiro was completing a doctorate in English literature at New York University and was enjoying success in that field. Then, right before launching into her dissertation on the poetry of Thomas Hardy, she was diagnosed with cancer. This devastating diagnosis led to a watershed in her life: searching for solutions to cancer and to its ravaging psychological effects. She left New York City, enrolled in a doctoral program in clinical psychology and serendipitously discovered in herself a method now widely used to treat other people's traumatic experiences (Shapiro, 1995).

While walking through the park one day, Shapiro stumbled onto the key of EMDR. She noticed that some disturbing thoughts she was having suddenly disappeared. When she brought these thoughts back to mind, they were not as upsetting or as valid as before. Fascinated, she paid close attention and noticed that, when disturbing thoughts came to mind, her eyes spontaneously started moving very rapidly back and forth. At that point, she started making the eye movements deliberately while concentrating on disturbing thoughts. Again, the thoughts disappeared and lost their charge. Later she experimented with this procedure with other people and found similarly positive results. Because the primary focus was on reducing anxiety in the behavioral tradition and because the primary method was directed eye movements, she called the new procedure Eye Movement Desensitization (EMD).

In response to several successful cases, published in 1989, she began training fellow clinicians and modifying the procedure. The result was the realization that the optimal procedure entailed simultaneous desensitization and cognitive restructuring of traumatic memories. This realization led her to rename the procedure Eye Movement Desensitization and Reprocessing (EMDR). More than just a change in name, this was a shift in perspective that would take EMDR beyond its original behavioral conceptualization as a desensitization treatment for anxiety to a new, integrative approach to psychotherapy (Shapiro, 1995).

Francine Shapiro, PhD, currently serves as the executive director of the EMDR Institute in Pacific Grove, California, an organization responsible for training and credentialing EMDR practitioners, and of the EMDR Humanitarian Assistance Program, an organization that coordinates disaster relief and provides free training worldwide. She and her associates have trained over 25,000 licensed clinicians in EMDR, making it one of the most rapidly disseminated psychological methods in recent history. Shapiro has written over 30 articles and book chapters on EMDR, as well as two books. The first, *Eye Movement Desensitization and Reprocessing: Basic Principles, Protocols, and Procedures* (Shapiro, 1995) is intended for the professional audience, whereas the second, *EMDR* (Shapiro & Forrest, 1997), brings this "breakthrough therapy" to a mass audience.

EMDR and Shapiro have been mired in intense controversy from the beginning, for several reasons. First, the early case histories indicated that EMDR could offer relief from PTSD in just a few lengthy sessions. This induced paradigm strain, if not downright incredulity, by promising therapeutic benefit in a substantially shorter period of time with PTSD and other disorders traditionally seen as recalcitrant to other forms of psychotherapy. Second, training in EMDR proceeded before several controlled outcome studies were available. Some saw this as offering a promising treatment for difficult disorders because little else was available; others saw it as irresponsible training in which dissemination far exceeded validation. Third, early EMDR training prohibited public distribution of precise EMDR methodology by requiring trainees to sign a statement agreeing that they would not train others in the use of the method. Shapiro and associates viewed this prohibition as recognizing that EMDR was an experimental treatment at the time and as enhancing quality control of the training; others viewed it as proprietorship and in violation of the public and open nature of scientific inquiry (Acierno, Hersen, van Hasselt, Tremont, & Meuser, 1994). And fourth, psychotherapy largely remains a male-dominated profession, especially in psychiatry and psychology. An assertive woman, a newcomer to the field controlling access to training and offering a paradigm-straining treatment with historically difficult patients, would certainly engender resistance.

Theory of Psychopathology

Humans possess an inherent physiological system geared to process information toward a state of mental health. The information processing system is intrinsic and adaptive. The assumption is that the system is configured to restore mental health in much the same way that the rest of the body is physiologically geared to heal when injured.

Briefly stated, psychopathology occurs when this information processing system is blocked. Traumatic life experiences set in motion a pathological pattern of affect, behavior, cognitions, sensations, and consequent identity structures. The pathological structures occur because the information is not processed; instead, the traumatic information is static, unresolved, fixed at the time it was stored during the disturbing event. These earlier, disturbing experiences are held in the nervous system in state-specific form. The trauma is, metaphorically speaking, "trapped" or "locked" in the neurophysiology.

Psychopathology persists beyond the time of the trauma because daily stimuli elicit the negative feelings and beliefs embodied in these traumatic memories and cause the client to continue to act in ways consistent with the trauma. In other words, the lack of adequate processing or resolution means that the client reacts emotionally and behaviorally in ways consistent with the trauma. Being held in a distressing, excitatory state-specific form, the trauma continues to be triggered by ongoing events and is expressed in nightmares, flashbacks, intrusive thoughts, and avoidant behavior. Megan, presented at the beginning of the chapter, intellectually knows that she is no longer a teenager forced to satisfy the sexual demands of an alcoholic father, but the trauma lives on and continues to dominate her adult interactions with her husband. She and her information processing are stuck in the past.

Traumatic memories are primarily responsible for pathological personality characteristics via a blockage in the information processing system. Accordingly, unblocking the system and transforming the memories will change personality characteristics.

Theory of Therapeutic Processes

The original conceptualization of EMD was one of desensitization according to the behavioral model; the evolved conceptualization of EMDR is that of the *accelerated information processing model.* Shapiro (1995) candidly acknowledges that the model is a working hypothesis; we do not yet know what transpires specifically at the physiological level of trauma.

Accessing the traumatic memories activates the information processing system, which then takes the information to adaptive resolution. This system not only transforms traumatic memories and disturbing information, but also concomitantly shifts feelings, thoughts, and sensations. Taken together, these constitute changes in identity. Megan, for example, will be asked to bring the traumatic experiences with her father into her mind, thus activating her information processing system. EMDR will accelerate her information processing toward health and resolution: substantial reduction in distress, followed by a "liberation" of her mature cognitions to think more rationally about the sexual abuse, and an eventual shift in her identity from a fearful, rageful victim to a resolved, mature woman. Desensitization and cognitive restructuring are by-products of the adaptive reprocessing taking place on a neurophysiological level.

The essential change process then is counterconditioning via desensitization and cognitive restructuring. Although consciousness raising and catharsis operate to some extent, they are not the central mechanisms of change in EMDR.

The eye movements have garnered the lion's share of attention, but EMDR actually consists of eight phases (Shapiro, 1995). The first phase involves taking a client history and planning the treatment. Clients unable to tolerate high levels of distress and clients without sufficient social support, for example, are not suitable candidates for the treatment.

The second phase encompasses preparation, in which the clinician introduces the client to EMDR procedures, explains the rationale, and prepares the client for possible between-session disturbance. The clinician briefs the client on the technical procedures, preferably in person and in a handout, and offers several metaphors for the experience itself. Two popular metaphors are train travel—riding on a train and looking out the window, just noticing the traumatic experiences and memories —and movie watching—sitting at the movies while watching the traumatic pictures on the screen. Both metaphors build in distancing from the traumatic experience itself and afford some self-mastery over the resulting emotions. Clients are expected to be proficient in self-soothing and relaxation before moving on to the desensitization proper. If they are not, then several sessions may be devoted to training and practice in various relaxation procedures.

In phase three, assessment, the EMDR clinician identifies the target and collects baseline data before desensitization. The client is asked to select one memory, typically the earliest or the worst, to work on in that session. Then he or she chooses a negative cognition that expresses a dysfunctional or unhealthy self-reference related to the traumatic experience. Megan, to take one example, might say "I am dirty," "I cannot love," or "I cannot let men close to me." The client then is asked to nominate a positive cognition that expresses a healthy or adaptive self-reference related to the trauma and that will later be used to replace the negative cognition during installation. Megan might nominate "I am worthwhile," "I can love again," or "I am in charge of my relationships." This positive cognition is assessed on a seven-point *Validity of Cognition (VOC) Scale*, where 1 is "completely false" and 7 is "completely true." Before treatment, most clients will, with their information processing system blocked, hold to the negative cognition and assess the positive congition as a 1, 2, or 3 (in the false range).

While holding the memory and negative cognition in mind, the client is asked to to give a SUD rating for how it feels right now. *SUD* is an acronym for *subjective units of distress*, where 0 is no distress or neutral and 10 is the highest distress imaginable. At predesentization, clients typically report a moderate to high level of distress, a SUD rating between a 5 and a 10.

This leads to the *desensitization* phase, the longest phase and the most arduous for the patient. She is asked to bring up the traumatic image, think of the negative cognition, and notice the feelings attached to it as she follows the therapist's hand with her eyes. The therapist generates eye movements from one side of the client's range of vision to the other as rapidly as possible without causing discomfort. Typically, the therapist holds two fingers upright, palm facing the client, approximately 12 to 14 inches from the client's face. Fifteen to 30 bilateral eye movements consitute a set, after which the therapist instructs the client to "blank it out" or "let it go" and to "take a deep breath."

The client describes her feelings, images, sensations, or thoughts with such purposefully broad prompts as "What do you experience now?" or "What comes up for you?" The client briefly describes her experience, say, "I see him coming after me" or "My chest is tightening up" or "Just very afraid and alone." The therapist refrains from empathic reflections or supportive comments, which would interfere with or delay the desensitization, and instead asks the client to "Go with that" or "Just think of that" as another set of eye movements is introduced.

Eye movements are only one means of activating the information processing system. Hand taps and repetition of auditory cues are widely used as alternate stimuli (Shaprio, 1995, 1997). Whatever the stimuli, the desensitization continues until near the end of the session or until the client reports a SUD rating of 0 or 1. Each target ordinarily takes several sessions to process fully.

The fifth phase of treament is called *installation* beacuse the objective is to install and increase the strength of the positive cognition. Once the SUD rating reaches 0 or 1, the client has obtained sufficient relief to allow a more realistic and adaptive cognition to emerge. The desired cognition is linked with the original memory by asking the client to hold the target and the positive cognition together in her mind's eye. Sets of eye movement (or alternate stimuli) are done to enhance the connection. This continues until the client reports a 6 or 7 (completely true) on the VOC Scale, which along with the SUD rating, comprises valuable outcome data on the procedure.

After the positive cognition is fully installed, the client is asked to perform a *body scan*, the sixth phase. She is asked to scan her body from head to toe and to identify any physical tension or discomfort. If some discomfort is located, this is targeted with successive sets until the discomfort is diminished or eliminated. If no discomfort is located, the clinician moves onto the final two phases: *closure* and *reevaluation*.

In closure, the client is returned to a state of emotional equilibrium, whether or not the desensitization is complete. The client is asked to maintain a log of distressing thoughts, images, or dreams that occur between sessions and is reminded to employ the self-soothing and relaxation exercises reviewed earlier in the treatment. In reevaluation, the clinician requests that the client review her experiences and success with the treatment process. This information guides and redirects future sessions.

These eight phases comprise the standard EMDR treatment. Protocols have been developed for specific populations and disorders, for example, children, phobias, grief, and somatic disorders.

In other cases, the client's processing will be blocked and the dysfunctional material will fail to reach resolution. When this occurs, the clinician employs the *cognitive interweave*: a proactive version of EMDR that deliberately interlaces clinician-derived statements with client-generated material, instead of relying solely on the client's spontaneous processing. Clients frequently require the clinician-initiated processing in four situations (Shapiro, 1995, p. 245): looping (repetitive thoughts that do not move and that block processing); insuffcient information; lack of generalization; and time pressures. The cognitive interweave is to be used sparingly, in cases where the client's own processing proves insufficient.

Therapeutic Relationship

The clinician-client relationship should be characterized by empathy, trust, and safety. A traumatized client has typically suffered for years in fear, embarrassment, and silence. Sharing the worst experiences of one's life takes extraordinary courage, and EMDR clinicians are taught to communicate their respect for this courage and the client's willingness to tolerate short-term distress for long-term relief. Although empathic, the EMDR therapist must refrain from providing empathic or supportive statements during the processing itself. To do so, as in other exposure treatments, can inhibit the patient's desensitization and retard his or her inherent tendency toward psychological self-healing.

The therapeutic relationship and treatment context must ensure client safety. EMDR confronts traumatic material and potentially encounters dissociation in clients. Building rapport, screening patients, teaching relaxation, preparing clients, reviewing a "stop signal" for them to suspend processing, and being available as necessary between sessions all create a safe haven for client and clinician alike.

Practicalities

EMDR sessions typically run 90 to 120 minutes to allow ample time for emotional reprocessing and a return to emotional equilibrium. The lengthier sessions occasionally pose difficulties in billing insurance companies, but the smaller number of sessions (4 to 6 for a single target) seems to compensate. EMDR has loudly advertised itself in managed care circles as a brief and comprehensive treatment for trauma disorders.

The EMDR Institute recommends two workshops and supervised practice for advanced competence in the approach. The two-day Level I workshop covers the basics, while the two-day Level II workshop addresses the cognitive interweave and advanced applications.

Probably more than in any other major system of psychotherapy, EMDR originators and practitioners have committed themselves to providing pro bono treatment and training in disaster areas. Through the EMDR Humanitarian Assistance Program, hundreds of clinicians have been trained for free and thousands of hours of EMDR have been rendered at token cost or no cost. EMDR has been taken all over the world to help victims of civil wars (e.g., Balkans, Northern Ireland), natural disasters (e.g., North Dakota floods, Florida hurricanes), and regional trauma (e.g., Oklahoma City bombing, San Salvador killings).

Effectiveness

The recent debate over the effectiveness of EMDR recapitulates the developmental history of validating many psychotherapy systems. First, the originator of the treatment and a few proponents publish uncontrolled case histories and issue early claims of magnificent outcomes not obtained by alternative therapies. Second, opponents immediately point to the paucity of rigorous, comparative outcome studies and publicly complain that the treatment enthusiasts have gone far beyond their data. Third, controlled outcome studies are gradually published that attest to the effectiveness of the treatment compared to no treatment or placebo but not to the purported superiority over alternative therapies. Fourth and finally, the detractors begrudgingly acknowledge that the treatment does work but not as well as originally claimed. Both sides then declare victory: the treatment originators are vindicated with a new, empirically-supported treatment and the early detractors are proud to have preserved the integrity of the scientific process.

As the dust settles on EMDR's outcome studies, we are left with the predicable end-state: originators concluding that it works quite well and detractors urging caution. Shapiro (1997, in press) reviews the results of 13 controlled studies, encompassing 250 patients, of EMDR in the treatment of trauma. In its ten-year history, EMDR has garnered more controlled research than other methods used to treat trauma. Research has demonstrated that the eye movements are only one form of useful stimulation and may not be required; in this regard, the "eye movement" in the "EMDR" title has proven unfortunate. EMDR clearly outperforms no treatment and has documented more positive effects than other methods that have been compared to it. However, insufficient research has been conducted to evaluate its effectiveness relative to other methods, such as exposure, implosion, and desensitization.

In contrast to Shapiro's rosy conclusions, other reviewers weigh in with more caution. Acierno and colleagues (1994) state that controlled experiments using objective and standardized measures have failed to support the efficacy of EMDR beyond that of its imaginal exposure component. They also articulate their concern that the clinical application of EMDR is rapidly increasing despite its lack of empirical validation. Similarly, Lohr, Tolin, and Lilienfeld (in press) reviewed 17 recent studies on the effectiveness of EMDR and conclude that its effects are limited largely or entirely to verbal report indices (for example, SUD ratings) and that the effects are consistent with nonspecific procedural artifacts.

In between these partisan reviews are more balanced conclusions. Boudewyns and Hyer (1996, p. 193), for example, are "of the opinion that EMDR could become an effective and useful psychotherapy technique, whatever the eventual merits and impact of the eye movements. EMDR applies the active treatment ingredient of exposure in a patient-acceptable manner." Dispassionate reviewers generally find the results of EMDR to be promising but mixed (Foa & Meadows, 1997). The APA Division of Clinical Psychology's Task Force on Promotion and Dissemination of Psychological Procedures (Chambless, 1998), for another example, lists EMDR as a "probably efficacious" treatment for civilian PTSD (along with exposure treatment and stress inoculation training), a step below a "well-established" effective treatment.

Criticisms of Exposure and Flooding Therapies

From a Behavioral Perspective

Character analysis evokes emotion all right: disgust and fear; disgust that 20th-century psychotherapists of the likes of Reich and Lowen would continue to spin their yarns with total disregard for validating evidence; fear that some unsuspecting students may mistake nonsensical notions such as an orgone box and seven rings of armor as fact rather than fantasy. If bioenergetics is to make it into the 21st century as a legitimate psychotherapy (or for that matter, into future editions of textbooks), then rigorous and comparative research on its effectiveness will be required.

Exposure therapy is rightly part of our behavioral tradition, and, of course, has considerable empirical verification. Let's call exposure therapy what it truly is—a behavior therapy method—and dissociate it from other pseudoscientific evocative therapies.

Implosive therapy, too, is based on a respectable theory and evidence regarding the extinction process. However, even implosive therapy is old wine in new bottles, a warmed-over version of Dollard and Miller's (1950) translation of psychoanalytic notions into learning terms. Because Stampfl has not demonstrated the validity of dynamic or hypothesized avoidance cues, he would do well to drop these unnecessary hypotheses and parsimoniously focus on only the stimuli that are clearly eliciting anxiety—namely, symptom stimuli.

While EMDR may or may not be an empirically-supported treatment, Francine Shapiro and her EMDR disciples got the proper sequence of treatment development backwards. A scientist first rigorously evaluates the effectiveness and safety of a new treatment, and then and only then trains fellow practitioners to use the method. By contrast, Shapiro proudly announces that 20,000 clinicians were trained in EMDR before the controlled outcome studies were complete. If you want to be accepted by the scientific community, then play by the established rules of science.

From a Psychoanalytic Perspective

Unfortunately, Reich became sexually fixated at an early stage of psychoanalysis. The mainstream of analysis matured into a discipline that recognized the central importance of ego processes in the production and treatment of psychopathology. Reich remained obsessed with the orgasm. Rather than considering orgasmic inhibition as one form of psychopathology, Reich continued to believe that the attainment of orgasm is the sine qua non of mental health. Even though analysts demonstrated in the 1930s that many neurotics and even some psychotics could attain orgasms and still remain disturbed, Reich was never one to let his cherished theories be disturbed by facts.

Reich idolized the autonomic nervous system and reduced humanity to a sexual energy machine (Brown, 1973). With the denigration of the cortical aspects of the nervous system, Reichian therapy degenerated into body manipulation aimed at releasing a reflex. Cognitive integration became less and less important. It is perhaps fitting that Reich's final form of treatment became so mechanical that the human sex machine was placed into a metal and wooden box in order to be energized by some fantastic orgone energy.

From a Humanistic Perspective

The eruption of emotion in exposure and implosion does not come from some intrinsically meaningful struggle within the person. Instead, exposure and implosion therapists evoke emotions from outside the person by artificial exercises and perverse imagery. Nor does the client play a central role in giving meaning to the feared scenes or events. The therapist imposes crass exercises upon clients, who are expected to bow to the therapists' sovereignty. Shades of *A Clockwork Orange*, the startling film in which behavioral reconditioning is employed to advance social improvement.

Exposure treatment brings into clear relief the philosophical conflict between "doing to" and "being with" in psychotherapy (Power, 1981). "Doing to" perfectly encapsulates the instrumentality and technology of exposure. We prefer "being with" trauma victims, witnessing and affirming their tortured experiences, instead of doing things to them. Anyone in the midst of crisis seeks a caring presence and a soothing attachment, not impersonal techniques and anxiety-intensifying assignments.

From a Contextual Perspective

Traumatized children and adults who predictably develop anxiety disorders require our compassion and respect. In implosive and exposure therapy, by contrast, they receive reactivation of the trauma and intensification of the anxiety. Exposure therapists may claim they do so only in the interest of client improvement, but the ends-justify-the-means argument is difficult to accept. The cure might be worse than the disorder.

At the very least, we should expect tons of therapist empathy with the victims' horrors and with the traumatic context producing the anxiety. However, the implosive therapists' empathy and sensitivity in these treatments are purposely employed to cultivate more frightening scenes for an anxiety-torn human. Trauma victims in search of sensitivity, support, and empowerment are provided more, higher-decibel pain. When there is no empathic and caring relationship between clinician and client, psychotherapy is not worth doing.

We should also expect implosive therapists (and other mental health professionals) treating victims of heinous crimes and unspeakable trauma to forcefully advocate for prevention of these crimes and trauma. Effective intervention is useful, of course, but don't we collude with a disturbed society by treating only the individual's symptoms rather than the social causes? Implosion is too little and too late in the causal sequence. Let's implode the citizenry and politicians with terror-filled images of war, rape, violence, poverty, and discrimination and then maybe we will address the underlying social causes, instead of mopping up after the carnage is done.

From an Integrative Perspective

EMDR has been advanced as a revolutionary integrative treatment that incorporates a number of theories and methods. The therapeutic emphasis on psychological self-healing and the client leading is consistent with client-centered therapy; the need to move toward psychological completion is compatible with psychodynamic therapy; imaginal exposure as a means of desensitization hails from behavior therapy; and the cognitive restructuring involving positive self-statements is a hallmark of cognitive therapy (Shapiro, 1995). EMDR is indeed much more than eye movements; it is an evolving, complex system of psychotherapy.

At least once a decade a miracle cure appears upon the therapeutic scene. Examples include hypnosis, character analysis, bioenergetics, desensitization, implosive therapy, primal scream therapy, and now EMDR. Professionals and laypersons can become mesmerized by such magic. The magic is in the eye movements, say hypnotists and EMDRists; the magic is in the bodily movements, say the character analysts and bioenergetics; or is it in the emotional bowel movements of implosive or primal scream therapy?

The real magic will emerge from scientific movements that seek to assess the most powerful processes of change that can be identified across psychotherapy systems. Is catharsis the key construct in explosive therapies? Or is the key construct the choice to face fears that we have avoided for too long? Or is extinction actually a function of counterconditioning as traumatic cues are paired with healthier responses like relaxation, eye or hand movements, or some other form of mastery?

As psychotherapists become more seasoned, they tend to become more integrative. It is encouraging to see such cognitive development within EMDR. Simple solutions for complex problems are not likely to stand the test of time or of science.

⏤ IMPLOSIVE THERAPY WITH MRS. C. ⏤

Mrs. C. is actively avoiding the conditioned stimuli of dirt and pinworms. Dirty underwear, dirt from the floors, and even thoughts of dirt or pinworms are stimuli that elicit anxiety. Because washing removes Mrs. C. from the presence of dirt or the possibility of pinworms, it reduces anxiety. Her compulsive hand washing is clearly an operant response that is instrumental in producing the powerful reinforcement of anxiety reduction.

Mrs. C. was originally classically conditioned to fear dirt and disease by an obsessive-compulsive mother. While details of her conditioning history are not given, we can imagine that dirt on her hands or clothes was probably paired with threats, castigations, slaps, or spanks, until the dirt automatically elicited anxiety. When punishment was administered, Mrs. C. would most likely be thinking about the dirt that got her in trouble, so that even thoughts of dirt were conditioned to elicit anxiety. In order to avoid further painful punishment from her parents, she learned to quickly wash her hands or to rigidly clean her clothes. Washing and cleaning would produce rapid reduction in anxiety, and Mrs. C. was thus becoming conditioned to be clean.

In an environment rewarding cleanliness, Mrs. C.'s rate of washing apparently remained within a normal range until the trauma of the pinworms. As far as Mrs. C. knew, her daughter's pinworms were an unconditioned aversive stimulus, something to be realistically feared. Her physician frightened her into boiling the family's clothes and bedding in order to avoid a pinworm plague. When Mrs. C. was informed of the frightening aspects of pinworms, she would have been thinking about pinworms, so the very thoughts of pinworms were conditioned to elicit anxiety.

Mrs. C. was especially vulnerable at this time to further conditioning. She was already anxious about her own and her family's health because they all had the Asian flu. Plague upon plague could raise her anxiety to intolerable levels. She would be eagerly seeking a response that could reduce her anxiety and avoid further disease. So when the physicians said washing was the answer, washing was her response.

The washing continued, however, even after the realistic threat was gone. The shock had worn off and the pinworms were gone, but her anxiety was not extinguished. Both her childhood anxieties and her recently conditioned fear of pinworms remained. Her hand washing was both stimulated by her anxiety over dirt and disease and reinforced by the reduction of anxiety. If she tried to remain in the presence of dirt or a scratching child without washing, her anxiety would increase markedly, almost to panic. When her anxiety level became unbearable, she would rush to wash, and her washing response would be even more strongly reinforced by the reduction of panic. Even thoughts of dirt or pinworms could elicit intense anxiety. Mrs. C. was now like a conditioned animal making avoidance trial after avoidance trial with no voluntary control over her conditioned anxiety or avoidance.

From implosive theory we would expect that dirt and pinworms are only part of a complicated context that elicits anxiety and produce avoidance. The nature of other avoidance cues can only be hypothesized. From her history we certainly see that she was conditioned to be anxious over any expression of anger, especially toward her father. She learned to repress or to avoid all expressions of anger. Accordingly, we might hypothesize that piles of dirty underwear or the sight of her daughter scratching her rear could precipitate aggressive thoughts or feelings. The avoidance of symptom stimuli—dirty underwear, for instance—could also serve as a means of avoiding such dynamic stimuli as anger toward her daughter.

Mrs. C.'s compulsive washing is probably controlled, then, by a complex series of anxiety-eliciting stimuli, including dirt, disease, and aggressive fantasies. The method of extinguishing her compulsive avoidance is to have her remain in the presence of each of the anxiety-eliciting stimuli. This method would, of course, evoke high levels of aversive emotion, and Mrs. C.'s natural response would be to avoid by washing or terminating treatment. The implosive therapist must work to keep her from avoiding. By remaining in the presence of these aversive stimuli, Mrs. C. would be flooded with fear, but soon the anxiety would begin to extinguish because there is no shock, no primary punishment, to reinforce the conditioned fear. The pinworms are gone; her parents will no longer hurt her. All she has to fear is conditioned fear itself, and that can be extinguished rapidly if she does not run.

Mrs. C. would first be asked to imagine symptom stimuli—say, scenes related to pinworms. Without regard to reality, she would be instructed to picture vividly that she is at home and is determined to conquer her compulsions. She enters the basement to do the laundry for the first time in years. As she gathers the filthy underwear, she smears a bit of feces on her hands and arms. She also senses something crawling on her arms. She is getting more and more anxious. She feels a desperate need to wash, so she drops the clothes and runs to the sink. As she turns on the faucet, there is no water. Instead, pinworms pour out, all over her hands and her arms, and she cannot wash them off. The worms begin burrowing into her skin; they are crawling in her ears; eating away at her eyes. Soon they cover her entire body and consume her flesh. Looking like a Swiss cheese with worms, she weakens and passes out on the pile of dirty underwear.

After this first scene, Mrs. C. is prepared for a scene that combines symptom and dynamic cues. She is ready for an anal picnic. In this session, she is with her husband and her parents on a picnic at a local park. As she is preparing the table, Mrs. C. feels the need to defecate. She walks to an outhouse, and as she goes to sit down, she notices that the hole is huge and she could fall in backward. The image panics her and she becomes lightheaded, beginning to pass out. She indeed falls backward and tumbles down into the deep, dark dung. As she struggles to the surface, she looks up in time to see her mother preparing to defecate on her. She yells out, and her mother is shocked to see her daughter playing in such filth. Her mother's scolding angers Mrs. C., so she throws a handful of dung into her mother's face, causing her to lose her balance and fall in. A similar sequence of events occurs with her father, but when her husband discovers that he is being left out, he grabs the paper plates and jumps in, exclaiming that they are not going to have a picnic without him!

To her disgust, Mrs. C. finds herself unable to resist selecting the tidiest turds for herself. As she bites into a tidbit, she can feel it crunching in her teeth and feels hair in her mouth. As the stuff sticks to her throat, she swallows some warm, yellow urine to wash it all down. Disgusting, but evocative!

Progressing in the series of avoidance cues, Mrs. C. is ready to attend to her anger and aggression. While some of her anger would be elicited toward her children, her father was the original stimulus that evoked both anger and anxiety over expressing anger. Therefore, a scene involving aggression toward her father should elicit maximum anger and extinguish maximum anxiety. Imagining herself as a 17-year-old, she arrives home 15 minutes late from a date. Her father is waiting up in his pajamas. He insists on knowing where she has been. When she tries to explain that they were delayed in the restaurant, he yells at her to shut up. She wants to explain that she did nothing wrong, but he smacks her and tells her to get in the kitchen and make him a sandwich. Anger begins to swell up within, as she tells herself, "Oh, I'd love to get even with him." In the kitchen she notices a hatchet near the basement door. She has the urge to pick it up, to really fix him this time. She puts a butcher knife in her belt and grabs the hatchet.

Her father is yelling for her to hurry up with his sandwich, and as she slowly approaches him saying, "Yes, Daddy dear, coming Daddy dear," she begins to raise the hatchet over her head. Her father's back is to her, and she can see the light glancing off his bald head. With the insults of her father and the indignities of her childhood running through her mind, she raises the hatchet higher and, with all her might, buries it in his scalp. With blood gushing down his face, her huge father somehow rises and starts coming toward her with his hands aimed at her throat. Backed into a corner, she pulls out the knife and jams it into his belly.

As she stands over him, he begs her to help him. "Like hell I will," she says. "You've bullied me long enough." She notices that his pajamas are open, and he is dying with a huge erection. So she pulls the hatchet out of his scalp and begins chopping away at the base of his penis, shouting, "You dirty bastard, you. I'll fix you good. You'll never rule me again." As he moans in pain, she pulls on his penis, stretching the last piece of skin until it snaps. Then, as if it were a bat, she takes his penis and smashes him in the face, saying, "That's for all the times you ridiculed me. That's for making me so afraid."

These implosive scenes, and others like them, are designed to evoke maximum anxiety and anger. As Mrs. C. becomes fully involved in the scenes, considerations of realistic detail fade into the background, as in an effective horror movie. Reality consists of her fears of pinworms, dirt, and the danger of anger. As the imaginary stimuli elicit increasing anxiety and anger, she becomes flooded with emotions. She wants to avoid them, but the therapist is there to break through her defenses, to urge her to feel as fully as she can, not to run but rather to face what she fears most. In facing her fantasies and feelings, Mrs. C. discovers that the shock has indeed worn off, the external danger is gone. And with the cathartic release and extinction of anxiety, the internal danger is also disappearing. The anxiety that has both stimulated and reinforced her constant washing is being extinguished. Mrs. C. will no longer experience the motivation to avoid thoughts of pinworms, anger, or hands that are a little dirty. After all, what is a little dirt on her hands after a picnic in a cesspool?

Future Directions

The pressing question for two of the emotional flooding therapies is whether they will have a future as separate psychotherapy systems. Reich's vegetotherapy has gone the way of his orgone box, and we suspect that Lowen's bioenergetics may not be far behind. Surveys of psychotherapists' theoretical orientations indicate that neither approach even makes a blip on the national scene (see Chapter 1), and surveys of psychotherapists' judgments about the soundness of treatments place bioenergetics (with primal therapy) as the most questionable therapy (Starker & Pankratz, 1996). Their permanent contributions—the emphasis on analysis of resistance, the value of abreaction, the manifestation of psychological conflict in the body—have been readily incorporated into other systems of psychotherapy. To have so many other psychotherapy systems recognize and incorporate your core practices is no mean feat, but one that jeopardizes your public and independent existence.

Probably the most optimistic prediction is that a return to Mother Earth and our natural bodies will rekindle a clinical interest in body work along the lines suggested by Reich, Lowen, and their followers. Coming back to our bodies may mean coming back to body-based therapies like those of Reich and Lowen. Environmentalism, vegetarianism, naturalism, and holism are popular trends consistent in spirit and in practice with enhanced attention to emotional and bodily release. Attention to our bodies will also manifest itself in endeavors outside psychotherapy; chiropractic care, deep massage, and nontraditional medicine will be perennial favorites in any culture that disowns the body and that ignores physical needs.

The most promising of this treatment genre are implosion, exposure, and perhaps EMDR. Based in theory, demonstrated in the laboratory, and now proven in the field, implosive therapy has experienced a resurgence in the treatment of intransigent anxiety-based disorders, such as the PTSD suffered by victims of sexual abuse and military combat. In fact, through the continuing refinement of implosive techniques by Donald Levis (1987, 1991, 1993) and others, as well as the positive evaluation of its efficacy, the prolonged exposure of implosive therapy is seen by many as one of the psychological "treatments of choice" for anxiety disorders (see Barlow, 1988; Marks, 1987; Noyes, 1991).

EMDR has been shrouded in such controversy that its future is not entirely clear. Several things seem certain: increasing numbers of clincans will be trained in the system; additional outcome research will evaluate its effectiveness compared to other mainstream therapies for trauma; future process research will examine the respective contributions of the various stimuli (eye movements vs. hand taps) and components (imaginal exposure alone vs. exposure with cognitive restructuring); and the controversy will continue until years of accumulated research and practice yield consensual conclusions.

Recapitulating Reich's struggles for recognition earlier in this century, the primary stumbling block to wider acceptance of the exposure and flooding therapies is attributable to therapist resistance. Although patients typically accept the procedure because they experience its benefits firsthand, many mental health professionals are reluctant to employ the anxiety-inducing techniques associated with exposure. Directly activating intense emotional expressions is too disconcerting for staid practitioners of "talk" therapy. The solution may lie in recognizing the truth in Reich's conviction that therapeutic breakthroughs require confronting pain encoded in memories and bodies; or in more contemporary lingo, no pain—no gain.

Suggestions for Further Reading

Boudewyns, P. A., & Shipley, R. H. (1983). *Flooding and implosive therapy*. New York: Plenum.

Foa, E. B. & Meadows, E. A. (1997). Psychosocial treatments for post-traumatic stress disorder: A critical review. In J. Spence (Ed.)., *Annual review of psychology* (pp. 449–480). Vol. 48. Palo Alto, CA: Annual Reviews.

Lowen, A. (1975). *Bioenergetics*. New York: Penguin.

Marks, I. M. (1987). *Fears, phobias, and rituals*. New York: Oxford University Press.

Olsen, P. (Ed.). (1976). *Emotional flooding*. New York: Human Sciences.

Reich, W. (1945). *Character analysis*. New York: Orgone Institute.

Shapiro, F. S. (1995). *Eye movement desensitization and reprocessing*. New York: Guilford.

Stampfl, T., & Levis, D. (1973). *Implosive therapy: Theory and technique*. Morristown, NJ: General Learning Press.

Journals: *Behavior Therapy; EMDRIA Newsletter; Journal of Behavior Therapy & Experimental Psychiatry; Journal of Traumatic Stress*.

9

Behavior Therapies

Joseph Wolpe

JUAN, A YOUNG SALESPERSON living the California dream, had developed a chronic case of claustrophobia that handicapped him in a variety of situations. When trapped in omnipresent traffic he would become panicky, which was leading him to avoid driving whenever he could. Elevators were aversive places that elicited anxiety and avoidance. Just sitting in a crowded airplane with no ability to exit quickly had become a nightmare for Juan, so flying was omitted from his response repertoire. Add in crowded restaurants, theaters, and churches, and you can see how limited Juan's California dream had become.

But Juan's biggest dread was going to the physician's office to receive a full medical exam. A crowded waiting room was bad enough, but Juan panicked about the prospect of having to enter an MRI machine. He knew that his family history placed him at high risk for serious cardiovascular disease and he should stay in close contact with his cardiologist, but Juan's anxiety and avoidance were preventing him from keeping appointments.

With an economic recession raging, Juan decided to give first priority to his driving phobia. It was keeping him from calling on customers, and he couldn't afford to lose any business. Working with a combination of systematic and in vivo desensitization, Juan was gradually able to extend the radius of his driving from only ten miles to the freedom to travel throughout California.

Juan then had the creative idea to construct an apparatus approximating an MRI machine—"closely confined like a coffin," he joked. Facing his fears both of confinement and of death, Juan practiced daily with his invention, using the deep muscle relaxation he had already learned. His wife and daughter teased him at times about retreating to his dark dungeon, but they also reinforced the gains they could see him making as he began moving freely into crowded conditions. "Why fear a crowd after you've spent time in a coffin?" Juan jested about his creative cure for claustrophobia.

A Sketch of Behavior Therapy

No single figure dominates behavioral approaches to psychotherapy the way Freud dominated psychoanalysis or Rogers represented person-centered therapy. Behavior therapists vary tremendously in both theory and technique; behavior therapy is less a monolithic structure than an ideographic approach that defies reduction to a few techniques. Traditionally, learning theory was seen as the ideological foundation for behavior therapy, although there was never agreement as to which learning theory (Pavlov's, Hull's, Skinner's, Mowrer's, or others) was at the core.

Although all behavioral approaches are unified in that they are principally derived from a learning theory, *behavior therapy* as a term can denote (1) a set of techniques, (2) the application of certain conceptual principles, and (3) the application of a methodological style (Jacobson, 1993; Jacobson & Margolin, 1979). However, the rapid proliferation of behavioral and cognitive-behavioral techniques during the 1970s and the 1980s defied any attempt to restrict the term to a unitary group of techniques. As a result, current usage of the term *behavior therapy* generally denotes conceptual behaviorism, methodological behaviorism, or an ill-defined combination of the two.

Conceptually, the framework of behavior therapy has been outlined frequently, as have its technical and theoretical differences with other systems of psychotherapy. Kazdin (1994), for instance, argues that the major characteristics of behavioral treatments are the primacy of behavior, the importance of learning, the directive and active nature of treatments, the importance of assessment and evaluation, and the use of persons in everyday life. In a longer list, O'Leary and Wilson (1987) cite the following among the core characteristics of behavior therapy:

- Most abnormal behavior is acquired and maintained according to the same principles as normal behavior.

- Most abnormal behavior can be modified through the application of social-learning principles.

- Assessment is continuous and focuses on the current determinants of behavior.

- People are best described by what they think, feel, and do in specific life situations.

- Treatment is derived from theory and experimental findings of scientific psychology.

- Treatment methods are precisely specified and replicable.

- Treatment is individually tailored to different problems and different people.

- Treatment goals and methods are mutually contracted with the client.

- Research evaluates the effects of specific therapeutic techniques on specific problems.

- Outcome is evaluated in terms of the initial induction of behavior change, its generalization to real-life settings, and its maintenance over time.

Although many of the concepts contained in these lists seem quite acceptable in today's light, they represent a radical departure from the medical model of psychopathology in general, and psychoanalysis in particular. For example, maladaptive behavior itself is seen as the problem that needs to be changed, rather than looking for some elusive underlying cause. No longer is troubled behavior seen as a symptom of some underlying disorder; rather, this medical notion is rejected in favor of the assumption that the symptom is the problem and is the appropriate treatment target for therapy, and that such treatment does not risk the substitution of new symptoms or the return of old symptoms.

These lists of core conceptual assumptions of behavior therapy also encapsulate the methodological focus: treatment is an empirical endeavor that must be tested and validated by the same rigorous, experimental procedures used in investigating any scientific question. Techniques cannot be assumed to be valid because they are derived from a favored theory. They must be validated under controlled conditions that use reliable and valid measures. *Baseline* levels of target behaviors need to be established before to therapy in order to determine whether or not the therapy is producing any change in the rate or intensity of responding.

Although behaviorists agree on approaching therapy as a data-based, experimental method, they disagree about just what the data or the experimental method should look like. Should the data be only overt responses that the experimenter/therapist can observe, for example, or are self-reports of subjective units of distress acceptable measures of anxiety? Should experimental designs be based on small-n (small-sample) procedures, in which a few clients are studied rigorously, or should techniques be validated through multigroup designs that include placebo and no-treatment control groups?

The point is that contemporary behavior therapy entails a vast array of techniques, a set of conceptual assumptions widely accepted but frequently debated, and a common methodological orientation with many possible methods for testing therapy. While divergence can be a source of confusion and ambiguity for students, it is also the source of some of the most creative work currently being carried out in psychotherapy. While appreciating the divergences among behavior therapists, we will nevertheless attempt to impose some clarity on this complex system by emphasizing three major thrusts within behavior therapy. We affectionately call these the "3 Cs" of behavior therapy: counterconditioning, contingency management, and cognitive-behavior modification. (Cognitive therapies per se are covered in the next chapter).

The first thrust we will survey is best represented by Joseph Wolpe's reciprocal inhibition or counterconditioning approach to therapy. Wolpe's approach has been based primarily on a respondent-conditioning explanation of anxiety-related behavior problems. Therapists utilizing counterconditioning techniques, including the stalwarts of systematic desensitization and assertiveness training, are most comfortable being called *behavior therapists*.

The second thrust has traditionally been labeled *behavior modification* and has focused on an operant conditioning approach to behavior disorders that is especially concerned with changing the contingencies that control behavior. With Skinner as a model, behavior modifiers have been particularly rigorous in validating interventions through well-controlled small-n designs, while being less concerned with theoretical explanations for effective techniques. In part because of the negative connotations that some politicians and some of the public have ascribed to the term behavior modification, the name *behavior analysis* is more often attached to this approach to therapy.

The third thrust has a less-clear heritage and a less-clear leadership but represents those behaviorists who are most willing to use cognitive explanations and cognitive techniques for producing behavior change. These therapists, known popularly as *cognitive behaviorists,* draw upon a diversity of procedures, including thought stopping, cognitive restructuring, and systematic problem solving. Psychotherapists who prefer the label *cognitive* to communicate their use of primarily cognitive and rational-emotive techniques will be considered in the following chapter. We freely admit, however, that the boundaries separating cognitive-behavior therapy from cognitive therapy are quite hazy, and that the distinctions may in fact be "academic" (as befits a textbook of this nature!).

Although the complex system of behavior therapy will be presented as three separate branches for simplicity's sake, it should be emphasized that most contemporary behavior therapists work with techniques and theories from each of these three viewpoints. Reflecting the multiple definitions and numerous techniques of behavior therapy itself, the members of the Association for the Advancement of Behavior Therapy (AABT) are a diverse lot. Eight percent categorize themselves as scientists, 60% as scientist-practitioners, and 32% as practitioners; in terms of theoretical labels, 27% characterize themselves as behavioral, 69% as cognitive-behavioral, and 2% as cognitive (Craighead, 1990). The point, again, is that behavior therapists are not particularly enamored of theoretical unity or technical purity but rather are driven to apply whatever methods are most effective and efficient in changing troubled behavior.

In an attempt to capture both the essence and the diversity of behavior therapies, we will modify the standard chapter outline we have been following. First, behaviorists have generally believed that environmental conditions are of much greater importance in controlling behavior than are internal personality traits (Mischel, 1968). Although many behavior therapists, especially in England, have at times talked in terms of traits, as a system behavior therapy has not been concerned with constructing a comprehensive theory of personality. Consequently, we will omit this section in the present chapter. Second, because the emphasis of behavior therapy has been on the processes of change rather than on the content to be changed, we will also omit the section on the theory of therapeutic content. We will consider, in turn, the theories of psychopathology and psychotherapy for each of the three thrusts of behavior therapy. Then we will examine the behavioral therapeutic relationship from a modeling perspective. The controlled outcome research on the various behavioral techniques will be presented in the section on effectiveness, followed by criticisms of behavior therapy. Finally, Mrs. C. will be analyzed through a comprehensive approach to behavior therapy that incorporates counterconditioning, contingency management, cognitive techniques, and the modeling view of the therapeutic relationship.

Counterconditioning

A Sketch of Joseph Wolpe

Joseph Wolpe's (1915–1997) book *Psychotherapy by Reciprocal Inhibition* (1958) is the most comprehensive approach to behavioral techniques based on counterconditioning processes. Wolpe came to a learning-based theory of therapy in a rather indirect manner. As a Jew raised in South Africa, he was influenced by his grandmother, who took on the responsibility of trying to make him into a pious believer. He read many Jewish writers, especially Maimonides. In his early twenties, he began investigating other philosophers, beginning with Immanuel Kant, moving to David Hume, and progressing through several other thinkers to Bertrand Russell. By the time his own intellectual journey was completed, his theistic beliefs had been replaced by a physical monism.

Because he viewed Freud as a rigorous materialist, Wolpe's view of humanity became increasingly more psychoanalytic during his middle twenties. He might have developed into a psychoanalytic psychiatrist except that he began reading the studies by Malinowski and others suggesting that Freud's theory did not fit some important facts. He was also struck by the fact that Russia, with a materialistic ideology, had rejected Freud in favor of Pavlov. Wolpe was impressed by Pavlov's research but found that he preferred the theoretical interpretations of conditioning in Hull's *Principles of Behavior* (1943).

In 1947, he began research on animal neuroses for his MD thesis at the University of Witwatersrand in Johannesburg. Working with cats, he paired a buzzer with a shock and classically conditioned anxiety to the buzzer. When the buzzer was on, the cats were inhibited from eating. Wolpe reasoned that if conditioned anxiety could inhibit eating, then maybe under the right conditions, the eating response could be used to inhibit anxiety. Since the troubled cats would not eat in their home cages, he began to feed them in dissimilar cages where their fear was much less. Wolpe thus began to countercondition the animals' anxiety by substituting an eating response for the anxiety response. By gradually feeding the cats in cages that were more and more similar to their home cage, he reduced their anxiety until they could eventually eat in their home cages. In a similar manner, he was able to use the eating response to inhibit anxiety to the buzzer.

Wolpe was now convinced that the use of such counterconditioning procedures could serve as the basis for a radically new approach to therapy. He began looking for responses in humans that could be used to successfully inhibit and eventually countercondition anxiety. As we will see, the use of deep relaxation to inhibit anxiety became the basis for systematic desensitization; the use of assertive responses to inhibit social anxiety became the basis for assertiveness training; and the use of sexual arousal to inhibit anxiety became the basis for new approaches to sex therapy. At the University of Witwatersrand, Wolpe met frequently with colleagues and students who were excited about this new and effective way to treat anxiety disorders. Arnold Lazarus and Stanley Rachman were among this group, and they helped to spread Wolpe's systematic desensitization to Great Britain and the United States, where Wolpe himself moved in 1963 (Glass & Arnkoff, 1992).

Wolpe surveyed the effectiveness of his counterconditioning approaches to treating behavioral disorders and reported success with 90% of more than 200 clients. His research with animals and his success with humans were reported in *Psychotherapy by Reciprocal Inhibition* (1958), and his work received considerable attention from clinical psychologists who had been trained in learning theory during their graduate education.

Wolpe continued his behavioral therapy and research program at the University of Virginia, Temple Medical School, the Eastern Pennsylvania Psychiatric Institute, and, at the time of his death, Pepperdine University as a distinguished professor of psychiatry. He was a central if somewhat controversial figure in helping to establish behavior therapy as a major movement in mental health through his writings, workshops, leadership in such groups as the Association for the Advancement of Behavior Therapy, and through establishing and editing the *Journal of Behavior Therapy and Experimental Psychiatry*. His influential text, *The Practice of Behavior Therapy*, is now in its fourth edition (Wolpe, 1990).

Theory of Psychopathology

Anxiety is the key to most behavior disorders. Anxiety is primarily a pattern of responses of the sympathetic nervous system when an individual is exposed to a threatening stimulus. Physiological changes include increased blood pressure and pulse rate, increased muscle tension, decreased blood circulation to the stomach and genitals, increased blood circulation to the large voluntary muscles, pupil dilation, and dryness of the mouth. These bodily changes are the basis of anxiety and can be elicited by such unconditioned stimuli as shock, a startling noise, or a physical beating.

Anxiety can also be learned. Learning is said to occur if "a response has been evoked in temporal contiguity with a given stimulus and it is subsequently found that the stimulus can evoke the response although it could not have done so before. If the stimulus could have evoked the response before but subsequently evokes it more strongly, then, too, learning may be said to have occurred" (Wolpe, 1973, p. 5). Thus, people can learn to respond with anxiety to any stimuli, including buzzers, dogs, people, sex, elevators, and dirt, even though these stimuli previously did not evoke anxiety. Through *classical,* or *respondent, conditioning,* a neutral stimulus, such as a dog, can be paired contiguously with a threatening stimulus, such as being bitten. The anxiety evoked by being bitten is associated with the sight of the dog, and the sight of the dog can become conditioned to evoke anxiety. Similarly, being threatened for sex play can make sex a conditioned stimulus that evokes anxiety, or being spanked for playing with dirt can result in dirt's being able to evoke intense anxiety. Even the thoughts associated with threatening stimuli, such as sexual thoughts, can become conditioned to elicit anxiety.

Through the process of *primary stimulus generalization*, stimuli that are physically similar to the original conditioned stimulus, such as other dogs, can also evoke anxiety. The more dissimilar a stimulus is to the original conditioned stimulus, the less anxiety the dissimilar stimulus will evoke. Thus, a puppy will elicit minimal anxiety because it is very dissimilar from the original large dog that bit the individual. Stimuli can be ranked on a gradient of similarity that constitutes a generalization gradient, or an *anxiety hierarchy,* that goes from the original stimulus, which evokes maximum anxiety, to a very dissimilar but related stimulus that evokes minimal anxiety. Human beings can also form hierarchies based upon similarities of internal effects through the process of *secondary,* or *mediated, generalization.* Thus, situations that are physically dissimilar, such as being turned down on a date, being made to wait, and missing a bus, can form a hierarchy or generalization gradient based on the internal response of feeling rejected. As a result of either stimulus or mediated generalization, most patients will report that their anxiety levels vary depending on the stimulus situations they are in. A person conditioned to fear authority figures may complain of physical upset at work where the boss is, for example, but report less anxiety at home, except when a spouse or child becomes bossy.

People who complain of constant, pervasive, or free-floating anxiety seem to be responding independently of any specific elicitor. Anxiety, however, is always the consequence of the elicitor; the problem for these patients is that they have been conditioned to fear stimuli that are omnipresent. One example was a client of mine who was constantly anxious, even when trying to sleep or shower, because he had been conditioned by severe parents to respond with anxiety to his own body, which is obviously omnipresent.

Anxiety is the primary learning problem in psychopathology. Once anxiety is established as a habitual response to specific stimuli, however, it can undermine or impair other aspects of behavior and lead to secondary symptoms. Sexual performance may be disrupted through an inhibition of sexual arousal; sleep may be disturbed by anxiety; tension headaches or stomach upsets may occur; irritability may increase; concentration, thinking, and memory may be impaired; or embarrassing tremors and sweating may occur. Over time, the chronic physiological reactions of anxiety may impair bodily functions and result in psychophysiological symptoms, such as ulcers and colitis. These secondary symptoms themselves may elicit anxiety because of their painfulness, their association with learned fears of physical or mental disorder, or simply their embarrassing social consequences. If these secondary problems produce additional anxiety, then new learning may occur, and a "vicious circle" is created that leads to more complicated symptoms.

Conditioned anxiety can produce responses that are acquired in order to avoid or terminate anxiety. Physical avoidance, such as phobias, may be learned because avoidance leads to the automatic consequence of terminating anxiety. Thus, some patients complain of having to avoid doctors, airplanes, elevators, or social gatherings. Other patients learn to terminate anxiety by consuming alcohol, barbiturates, narcotics, or other drugs.

Over time, the primary complaint is no longer anxiety but the phobias and drug abuse patients have developed in order to avoid anxiety. Of course, a drug habit itself can produce anxiety and can lead to further drug abuse in order to reduce the new anxiety, and the vicious circle goes on. The symptoms of patients are highly varied, ranging from sexual dysfunctions, to phobias, to psychophysiological complaints, to interpersonal difficulties, to drug abuse. The same patient may have several complaints that are not necessarily related in some supposed dynamic pattern. Thus, a patient may suffer from an elevator phobia and insomnia without the two being related, just as a medical patient may have a tremor that is entirely unrelated to a cold. The successful treatment of a phobia may have no effect whatsoever on the insomnia. Specific symptoms are the result of specific anxieties elicited by specific stimuli. Therefore, the successful elimination of a specific anxiety and a specific secondary symptom will not lead to new symptoms. *Symptom substitution* or symptom return is a theoretical myth of those who see all behavior as being interrelated by some common underlying dynamic pattern. What is common to most behavior problems is the presence of conditioned anxiety that is highly specific in both the stimuli that elicit it and the consequences that result from it. Successful treatment thus calls for successful, and at times successive, elimination of specific anxiety responses.

Theory of Therapeutic Processes

Because anxiety is learned through conditioning, it can be unlearned through counterconditioning. As Wolpe discovered in his research with "neurotic" cats, there are two critical tasks in effective counterconditioning. The first is finding a response that is incompatible with anxiety and that can be paired with the stimuli that evoke anxiety. The principle of *reciprocal inhibition* states that "if a response inhibiting anxiety can be made to occur in the presence of anxiety-evoking stimuli, it will weaken the bond between these stimuli and anxiety" (Wolpe, 1973, p. 17). With enough pairings of the anxiety-inhibiting response with the anxiety-evoking stimuli, the new, more adaptive response is eventually substituted for the maladaptive anxiety response. In oversimplified terms, do the opposite of the problem and the problem will disappear. Although there are many responses that can inhibit anxiety, the ones most frequently employed by behavior therapists are relaxation, assertion, exercise, and sexual arousal, all of which are associated with a predominance of parasympathetic nervous activity.

The second important task in counterconditioning relates to the fact that a strong sympathetic anxiety response is very likely to disrupt relaxation, assertion, exercise, or sexual arousal. Therefore, it is critical that counterconditioning begin with stimuli low on a generalization gradient or hierarchy. Stimuli low on a hierarchy, such as a small puppy versus a large German shepherd, will elicit much lower intensities of anxiety. Again, in oversimplified terms, begin with "baby steps" toward the eventual larger goal. With stimuli low on a hierarchy, deep relaxation, strong assertion, or another counterconditioning response will be able to clearly inhibit the anxiety response. By repeating such pairings with stimuli low on a hierarchy, the anxiety at each level is deconditioned. With the anxiety level receding, the pairings can proceed to stimuli higher in the hierarchy, until eventually the anxiety responses to the entire stimulus hierarchy can be deconditioned.

Systematic Desensitization. The principles of counterconditioning will first be illustrated by describing the techniques of systematic desensitization. Here progressive, deep-muscle relaxation is the predominantly parasympathetic response that is incompatible with anxiety. Borrowing from Jacobson (1938), therapists first teach clients how to relax the muscles throughout their bodies. Although behavior therapists vary their relaxation training to some extent, they all generally teach clients how to discriminate between when their muscles are tensely contracted and when they are fully relaxed. The therapist might begin by having clients grip the chair and focus on the tension in their forearms. Clients are then encouraged to relax their arms and to feel the contrast between the tension and the relaxation. Clients are encouraged to actively let go of the tension in their forearms until each fiber in their arms is relaxing. Clients are to learn that relaxing is an activity that can come under their control as they tightly tense each muscle group and then actively let their muscles relax. Some therapists encourage clients to relax a tensed arm, for example, by acting as if it were lead and letting the arm fall rapidly to their lap. Others encourage clients to relax slowly, feeling the sensations of tension gradually but fully leave the fibers of their muscles. Usually muscles are tensed for 10 to 20 seconds, followed by 10 to 20 seconds of relaxation. Each important muscle group in the body is tensed and relaxed, usually beginning with the hands and forearms, and then moving to the biceps and triceps. Next the muscles in the head, beginning with the forehead and moving down to the eyes, nose, mouth, and tongue, are tensed and relaxed. By moving step by step through the muscle groups, clients become more and more relaxed. Although Wolpe takes several sessions to train clients in progressive relaxation, most research reports have used only one or two sessions for teaching relaxation. Audiotaping the relaxation instructions while the therapist is taking the client through each muscle group or using a prerecorded tape can allow clients to practice muscle relaxation at home, between sessions.

The next step in desensitization is to construct an anxiety hierarchy that ranks stimuli from the most anxiety-arousing to the least anxiety-arousing. The hierarchy is frequently constructed along some stimulus dimension—time or space, for instance—as the stimulus situations move closer and closer in time to an anxiety-arousing situation, such as a job interview, or closer in space to a feared object, such as an elevator. The stimulus situations are imagined by the client and ranked from the least to the most anxiety-arousing. A typical hierarchy will have 10 to 20 stimulus scenes, spaced relatively equally along a 10- (or 100-) point scale from practically no anxiety elicited to intense anxiety elicited. The scenes are typically realistic, concrete situations related to the client's problem. Frequently, clinical patients will have more than one hierarchy to work on, although the greater number of specific anxieties they have, the less likely it is that desensitization will be effective.

Once the hierarchies have been constructed, clients are asked to think of one or two relaxing scenes, such as lying on the beach on a sunny summer day, that can be used to facilitate relaxation during the presentation of items in the hierarchy. Now the clients are ready to begin the actual desensitization. Once they are deeply relaxed, they are told that they will be asked to imagine a scene and that they should imagine it as clearly as possible and imagine only the scene that is presented. They are told that if they experience any anxiety at all, they should signal immediately by lifting their right index finger. The client signals when the scene is being clearly pictured and, if no anxiety is elicited, continues imagining the scene for ten seconds. If anxiety is elicited, then the client is instructed to stop imagining the hierarchy scene and go back to imagining the relaxing scene. Once clients report being clearly relaxed again, they are instructed to imagine the scene again. If a scene fails to elicit anxiety, then it is repeated at least once again before moving to the next item in the hierarchy. When a scene repeatedly elicits anxiety, the therapist can move back to the anxiety-arousing scene. If the scene continues to elicit anxiety, then clients need to be asked if they are adding stimuli to the scene. If they are not, then new items may need to be added to the hierarchy in order to allow the client to continue to progress. Usually a session is ended by having the client successfully complete a scene. The next session usually begins with the client imagining the last item that was successfully completed. A desensitization session typically lasts 15 to 30 minutes, with most clients finding it difficult to sustain both concentration and relaxation for more than 30 minutes. For clients with more than one hierarchy, a session will include scenes from each hierarchy rather than treating the separate hierarchies sequentially.

Once systematic desensitization is completed, clients are encouraged to test its effectiveness in a gradual manner. They are frequently instructed to use *in vivo desensitization*, in which they approach previously feared stimuli in real-life situations. They approach stimuli in the environment that were low on their hierarchies before confronting stimuli of greater intensity.

Systematic desensitization has been widely employed in clinical practice and has been subjected to a number of innovations. It has been successfully used in large groups, administered by computers, and abbreviated in length.

Implosion and exposure therapies share similar procedures with systematic desensitization, and many observers would place implosion and exposure in the behavioral camp. However, implosion typically entails full and immediate exposure to the disturbing stimulus, whereas systematic desensitization proceeds more gradually along the anxiety hierarchy. As a consequence, we consider implosion and exposure therapies in Chapter 8, separate from the behavior therapies.

Assertiveness Training. Whereas desensitization is the treatment of choice for phobias of nonhuman objects and situations and for anxieties evoked by the mere presence of people, assertiveness training is the choice for most anxieties related to interpersonal interactions. Candidates for assertiveness (or assertion) training include people who are afraid of complaining about poor service in a restaurant because of anxiety over hurting the waiter's feelings, people who are unable to leave a social situation when it is boring for fear of looking ungrateful, people who are unable to express differences of opinion because they are afraid others will not like them, people who are afraid to tell professors or authority figures that they do not like being left waiting because they are afraid the authority figures might get angry with them, people who are unable to ask for a raise or for a better grade because they feel inferior, and people who are unable to participate in competitive games for fear of losing. The meek will not inherit the earth. The meek will frequently find that all they inherit is bad feelings because they are inhibited by anxiety from standing up for their rights.

Assertiveness training is not just for the meek and shy, however. People who respond too often with inappropriate anger can frequently be helped by assertiveness training as they learn to have more effective control over social situations instead of feeling constantly frustrated and angry over not being able to influence others. Also, people who keep from expressing admiration, praise, or positive feelings because they might feel embarrassed can learn to be more positive through being more assertive. Assertive behavior is defined by Wolpe (1973, p. 81) as "the proper expression of any emotions other than anxiety toward another person." Accordingly, people who are characteristically passive or aggressive in interpersonal situations are appropriate candidates for assertion training.

Assertion and anxiety are to a considerable degree incompatible. Actively expressing admiration, irritation, and appropriate anger can inhibit anxieties over rejection, embarrassment, and possible failure. By learning to assert themselves in stimulus situations that previously evoked anxiety, patients begin to decondition anxiety by substituting an assertive response. As patients become more active and effective in their assertive behaviors, they are reinforced not only by the reduction of anxiety but also by their enhanced ability to be more successful in social situations. Individuals who have been inhibited by anxiety gradually become more effective as they remove anxiety through the counterconditioning effects of assertive responses.

The techniques of assertiveness training are varied, but almost invariably include teaching clients direct and effective verbal responses for specific social situations. Clients who, for example, feel irritated but are unable to say anything when people cut in front of them in line, are taught such responses as "This is a line, please go to the back of it," or "I and others here would appreciate your respecting the rules of waiting in line." Patients are also taught more assertive nonverbal expressions that can inhibit anxiety. Salter (1949) discusses facial talk that displays appropriate emotion when asserting, such as smiling when telling a spouse, "You look so lovely this evening!" Looking directly in the eyes when insisting that a person be on time for meetings communicates nonverbally a greater determination that others will not be allowed to violate one's right to be respected. Appropriate smiling, eye contact, and voice volume are nonverbal responses that can inhibit anxiety in social interactions.

Clients are encouraged to rehearse their new assertive responses both covertly and overtly. Covertly, clients distinguish between passive, assertive, and aggressive behavior and then imagine being more assertive in situations in which they were either passive or aggressive. Overtly, the clients rehearse assertion through role-playing interactions with the therapist or group members. The therapist may play a waiter or waitress while the client practices insisting both verbally and nonverbally that a steak be taken back because it was improperly prepared. The therapist can provide resistance to the client's assertions, such as saying, "I know the steak isn't quite right, but if I take it back the chef will be angry." Clients can then practice thinking on their feet, such as saying, "That's a problem for you and the chef to resolve. My concern is that I get what I ordered." The behavior rehearsals provide deconditioning of anxiety as well as preparation for clients to deal more effectively with adversaries that previously would have inhibited them.

As anxiety is reduced through role playing of assertive interactions, clients become more confident about their abilities to face real-life situations. Therapists then give graduated *homework assignments*, beginning with situations that are least frightening and are most likely to lead to successes for the client. Beginning with situations that are less anxiety-arousing is like starting at the bottom of an anxiety hierarchy in desensitization. As the anxiety in these less-threatening situations is effectively deconditioned through assertion, the person will usually experience less anxiety when preparing to assert in a more stressful situation. Beginning with too threatening a situation is likely to lead to failure, which will punish rather than reinforce the client's attempts to be more assertive. "Challenging but not overwhelming" is a phrase that captures just the right amount of difficulty.

Special care is needed when clients desire to be assertive in situations where assertion may lead to punishment. In the past, many behavior therapists used the rule of never encouraging assertive behavior when punishment is likely to follow. As Goldfried and Davison (1994) point out, however, such a rule encourages maintenance of the status quo for many people, including women, who traditionally have been derided for being aggressive when they were being assertive. Nevertheless, most clients and therapists desire to minimize the risk that the assertiveness of clients will evoke punishment, especially hostility or violence.

Using a *minimally effective response* reduces the probability that assertion will be met with hostility or other potentially punishing responses (Rimm & Masters, 1974). Thus, in expressing hurt or anger, clients should express the minimum negative emotion that is required to attain a desired goal. If the client's goal is not to be kept waiting by a professor, the client can knock on the door and with minimal irritation inform the professor that it is 2:00 and they have an appointment. A minimally effective response is less likely to evoke anger in the other person, and thus punishing consequences are less likely to occur. If a minimally effective response does not lead to the desired goal, then clients can be prepared to escalate their assertiveness and express more emotion and more determination to have their rights respected.

Although Wolpe's theory is still the leading explanation for the effectiveness of assertiveness training, current assertion trainers use techniques that involve more than counterconditioning. Many clients need to first reevaluate their attitudes toward what it means to be an effectively assertive person. For some, this involves personal empowerment methods, in which they realize their personal right to be assertive, and values-clarification techniques that help them reexamine such goals as trying always to be a nice, polite person. Smith (1975), for example, presents clients a personal bill of rights that challenges values suggesting that clients cannot be decent human beings while also being effectively assertive. For other clients, it is important to distinguish between being aggressive and being assertive. The therapist may role-play aggressive regimens in which part of the goal is to hurt the other person's feelings and contrast that with assertive behavior aimed at keeping others from violating one's personal rights.

Assertion training also entails operant conditioning as therapists reinforce clients for each attempt that is made to become more effectively assertive. Using the process of *shaping*, therapists reinforce clients' successive approximations to the finished goal of assertion. In the early stages, for instance, merely an increase in eye contact or an escalation in voice volume will be reinforced. Most assertiveness trainers also prefer conducting assertiveness training in groups so that group members can provide additional reinforcement for each other. The very process of giving effective reinforcement allows clients to practice being more effective in expressing positive emotions toward others.

Assertiveness training also involves a great deal of feedback, as clients are encouraged to become more cognizant of the verbal and nonverbal responses that fail to communicate assertiveness. Some therapists use videotapes, which allow clients to get direct feedback concerning such behaviors as failure to make eye contact or crouching over in a nonassertive manner. Other therapists rely on feedback from themselves or from group members to raise the client's awareness of what changes are needed to be more assertive. Once again, the practice of having group members give feedback allows for direct practice in being more assertive. Thus, the therapist can give group members feedback on how effective they were in providing direct feedback to another group member.

Modeling is another important technique used in assertiveness training. Either through role playing or through direct interaction with patients, the therapist is able to provide a model for more effective assertion. Most behavior therapists would agree that a minimal requirement for performing assertiveness training is that assertiveness trainers themselves be effectively assertive individuals.

The original assertiveness training has spawned a number of counterconditioning applications to interpersonal behavior. *Social skills training* includes but surpasses the behaviors originally taught in assertiveness training and has been extensively applied to individuals suffering from psychotic disorders or developmental disabilities (see Curran & Monti, 1982; Hollin & Trower, 1986). *Refusal skills training*, routinely taught in treatment programs for addictive and consumptive disorders, enables patients to politely but persistently refuse offers to partake of the troubling substance (see Marlatt & Gordon, 1985). And *communications skills training*, to take a final example, consists of instruction, modeling, practice, role play, and homework in fundamental communication skills, such as active listening and constructive negotiation (see Bornstein & Bornstein, 1986; Gottman, Notarius, Gonso, & Markman, 1976). Although all these procedures entail cognitive mechanisms of change, all received impetus from the counterconditioning paradigm: inappropriate social behavior is reciprocally inhibited by appropriate social behavior, accepting an abusive substance is incompatible with skilled refusal of it, and destructive arguments are counterconditioned by constructive communication.

Sexual Arousal. A final counterconditioning technique of behavior therapy to be considered is the use of sexual arousal to inhibit anxiety. Most contemporary forms of sex therapy either implicitly or explicitly use counterconditioning as an integral part of treating sexual dysfunctions, based on the seminal work of Helen Singer Kaplan (1974, 1987) and Masters and Johnson (1970). Wolpe (1958) was one of the first to report that sexual dysfunctions, such as male erectile disorder (impotence) and female sexual arousal disorder (frigidity), could be successfully treated with counterconditioning techniques.

Sexual arousal is primarily a parasympathetic response that can readily be inhibited by anxiety, which is primarily a sympathetic nervous system response. Given the negative attitudes toward sex that have traditionally prevailed in our society, it is not surprising that many people have been conditioned to respond to sexual situations with anxiety. If their conditional anxiety is intense enough, it will inhibit their sexual arousal. Reciprocally, sexual arousal can be used to inhibit the anxiety response, and through counterconditioning the sexual response can be substituted for the disrupting anxiety response.

Wolpe's (1958, 1973, 1990) approach to sex therapy is quite similar to his approach to in vivo desensitization. Clients are first asked to identify when in their approach to a sexual encounter they first feel anxiety. They are instructed to limit their sexual approaches to that point where anxiety begins. Obviously the partner's cooperation is important, because it can be extremely frustrating to have to stop just when genital caressing begins, or just after penetration occurs. Actually, in most cases anxiety is evoked when intercourse is about to begin, so the cooperative partner can still be provided a reasonable degree of sexual gratification through manual stimulation. It is essential, however, that the partner not mock or goad the inhibited spouse into progressing beyond the point at which anxiety begins. By stopping and just lying still or talking, the anxiety can subside and sexual arousal can intensify. Gradually the anxious person will find that more and more anxiety is being inhibited and counterconditioned by sexual arousal. Gradually the couple is able to move from lying in bed naked together, to caressing the nonerogenous areas of the body, to caressing genitals, to beginning intercourse, and continuing with intercourse to orgasm without anxiety.

Wolpe (1973) reports that his in vivo approach to sex therapy works best for male erectile disorders. For women who are more inhibited in their sexual response, he tends to begin with systematic desensitization and gradually reduces their anxiety to sexual images before proceeding to the in vivo form of sex therapy.

Although premier sex therapists on the order of Masters and Johnson (1970) and Kaplan (1974) include techniques that involve counterconditioning of anxiety, they would think it naive to hold that counterconditioning is the only process involved in effective sex therapy. The technique that these sex therapists use for reducing anxiety involves *sensate focusing*—literally, focusing on the sensations instead of the sexual act itself. In these exercises, partners take turns pleasuring each other, beginning with sessions in which the genitals and breasts are avoided and the rest of the body is caressed. The person being pleasured gives verbal or nonverbal feedback about what does and does not feel good. Once the couple is able to enjoy nonerogenous stimulation without anxiety, they give each other sensate pleasuring that includes genital caressing but with no demands to reach orgasm. If this step goes well, the couple is then able to proceed with sensate pleasuring that includes intercourse, but with no concern over reaching orgasm. With the gradual decrease in anxiety and marked increase in sexual arousal, couples are eventually able to participate in relatively free and gratifying sexual experiences.

Virtually all sex therapists also argue that other change processes are operative in successful sex therapy. Raising consciousness through educational techniques that involve giving clients the latest and most accurate sex information is important with many uninformed or underinformed clients. Increasing consciousness through communicating feedback about what each partner needs in order to be more fully aroused and to be orgasmic is also critical, such as the wife giving the husband feedback by guiding his hand as he gives her clitoral stimulation. Helping patients reevaluate their attitudes toward goal-oriented sex is important in helping them become free of performance anxiety. Just being free to enjoy the pleasure of the moment without worrying about whether intercourse or orgasm will follow allows for more spontaneous and uninhibited enjoyment of all that sexual pleasuring can mean, rather than reducing sex to only intercourse or only orgasm. Improving communication skills, such as the couple giving each other feedback about their feelings and about what they would like improved in their relationship, and addressing relationship conflicts, such as preventing indirect expressions of anger through sexual nonresponsiveness, can be also be accomplished in sex therapy.

Contingency Management

Theory of Psychopathology

Human behavior—whether adaptive or maladaptive—is largely controlled by its consequences. People are continually labeled pathological as if they are some strange breed of organism, when in fact their behavior can be explained by the same operant principles that account for most human behavior. Thus, maladaptive responses, such as painful head banging, are likely to increase in frequency if they are followed by reinforcements, such as special attention given only when head banging occurs. Conversely, maladaptive responses are likely to decrease in occurrence if they are followed by punishments—for example, withdrawing a special treat or introducing a noxious chore. Maladaptive behaviors are also likely to decrease in frequency when they are consistently unrewarded, and they will eventually extinguish if no reinforcement occurs.

Reinforcements and punishments that are made contingent upon particular responses will not only impact the probabilities of maladaptive behavior patterns already in existence but also the development of new responses. To illustrate the acquisition of a new maladaptive response, let me relate an experience I (JOP) had as an undergraduate out to have fun at a carnival. Walking along with a female friend, I was spotted by a barker who wanted me to try my luck at his gambling game. If he had told me that the eventual response he wanted was for me to plunk down my money as fast as I could get it from my wallet, I would have kept on walking. Over the years, however, he had learned something about the process of shaping behavior. Thus he began with a *prompt*, which included challenging me to win a big, furry $50 stuffed animal for my female friend. Responding to his prompt, I asked what I had to do to win, and he said just put 50 cents down and spin the wheel. When the wheel stopped, I had gained 450 points, which was more than half of the 800 points I needed for a prize. Winning points also gave me the opportunity to spin again, and this time I earned 100 additional points. The next spin was reinforced by 25 more points. When I failed to get any points on the next spin, he again used a prompt to encourage me to put down another 50 cents. After all, 675 points on one bet was certainly worth another try. This time my spin was followed by 50 points and then 10 points, and there was no way I could lose, he said. He had been *fading* the prompts, as my tendency to spin the wheel was becoming more reliable. Soon I was reaching for more money and winning 5 points here and 5 points there. My money, however, was going out faster than points were coming in. He had indeed shaped me into responding with rapid bets. Soon I lost the $19 in my wallet, and all I had to show for it was 785 points. As a psychology major, I went away shaking my head, thinking that B. F. Skinner had nothing on this carnival man, and Skinner's pigeons had nothing on me. No wonder compulsive gamblers are fond of saying that if you lose the first time out the Lord is on your side, and if you win big the first time out the Devil is on your side.

Maladaptive behavior does not take place in a vacuum. Some environment or stimulus situation sets the occasion for the behavior. A male patient beats up his wife at home almost every weekend but apparently treats her politely when in public. A woman client steals only in fancy stores but never in a discount store. The control that environmental stimuli can have over maladaptive behavior results, in part, from the fact that certain stimuli serve as signals that reinforcement is likely to follow a response when the response is emitted in that particular stimulus situation. These are called *discriminative stimuli*. Other stimuli serve to signal that reinforcement will not follow a response when made under these particular stimulus conditions. Hence, clients learn that aggressive behavior or stealing may be rein-forced in one situation and not reinforced, or even punished, in a different stimulus situation. A *behavioral,* or *functional, analysis,* then, consists of specifying the stimulus situations that set the occasion for the maladaptive behavior (*antece-dents*), operationalizing the behavior itself (*behavior*), and detailing the reinforce-ment contingencies that follow (*consequences*). This A → B → C sequence is known as the *behavior chain* and is the foundation for understanding and modify-ing contingencies.

Behavioral analysis indicates three categories of frequent problems: behavioral *excesses, deficits,* and *inappropriateness.* First, there are problems that involve an excess in responding, such as washing one's hands 30 times a day. The washing of hands per se is not maladaptive, but the washing of hands excessively can become maladaptive. Second are the behaviors that entail a deficit in responding, such as rarely interacting with people. Often with deficits the problem is a lack of learning, such as a failure of the social environment to teach the appropriate skills required for effective social interaction. In the early days, behavior therapists principally re-duced maladaptive behaviors rather than increased adaptive behavior, but in con-temporary practice, the two tasks have achieved a more reasonable balance.

The third type of problem involves responses that are inappropriate to a par-ticular situation or time, such as a patient of mine who occasionally drops his drawers in public. The problem here is not the rate or skill of disrobing, but the fact that the particular response is inappropriate to the particular situation. Fre-quently meant by "inappropriate" is that most adults would expect that the behav-ior in question would be performed in private or at a different place. We have been led to expect that in this particular situation the behavior would not lead to rein-forcement and might even be followed by punishment. For the person exhibiting the maladaptive behavior, however, the same situation seems to signal that rein-forcement is likely to occur. Either the person has failed to discriminate the stimu-lus situation accurately, such as a person who is acutely inebriated or profoundly retarded, or there is indeed a powerful reinforcement occurring that is not readily apparent to the observer.

What we frequently forget as observers is that reinforcement is entirely an indi-vidual matter, determined by an individual's particular reinforcement history. Thus, a reinforcing consequence for one of us—say, chocolate—might be a relatively neu-tral or even aversive consequence for another—as in the case of a nasty allergy to chocolate. A consequence can be judged to be a reinforcement only if it actually in-creases the probability that a response will be repeated, not merely if it appears to be pleasant. Inappropriate behavior is typically surprising and unexpected until we conduct an individual behavior analysis and discover what is in fact a reinforce-ment. Almost always, the heretofore bewildering behavior, such as masochistic pur-suit of pain, begins to make sense in light of the person's learning history.

Theory of Therapeutic Processes

Environmental contingencies are forever shaping, maintaining, and extinguish-ing our behavior and the behavior of patients. Behavior modification attempts to systematically control contingencies in order to shape and maintain adaptive behavior and to extinguish maladaptive behavior. Theoretically, the therapeutic process is straightforward: change the contingencies, and the behavior will change. Technically, effective contingency management involves the following six steps (Sherman, 1973):

1. State the general problem in behavioral terms, including the maladaptive responses and the situations in which they occur. This step is known as *operationalizing* the target behavior.

2. Identify behavioral objectives, which includes specifying target behaviors and whether the behaviors should be increased, decreased, or reinforced only when emitted in more appropriate situations, and what the acceptable level of performance of each target behavior is.

3. Develop behavioral measures and take *baseline measures* in order to be able to determine whether treatment is effective. Baseline measures show the rate of responses prior to the initiation of treatment. Multiple baselines are often taken, including measures of behaviors that are not targeted for change, in order to determine whether the changes in contingencies are specific to changes in the target behaviors.

4. Conduct naturalistic observations, which involve observing patients in their natural environments in order to determine what the existing contingencies are and thus what are effective reinforcements for a particular patient.

5. Modify existing contingencies, which involves specifying the conditions under which reinforcements are or are not to be given, what the reinforcements will be, and who will administer them.

6. Monitor the results by continuing to chart the rate of responses and comparing the results to baseline measures in order to determine the effectiveness of present interventions. Changes in treatment can then be made when necessary, and treatment can be terminated or stabilized when the behavioral objectives have been met.

The application of contingency management procedures varies somewhat according to the *who* and the *what*: who is most effectively able to control contingencies, and what type of consequence is being controlled. Contingency management procedures can thus be categorized according to (1) institutional control, (2) self-control, (3) mutual control or contracting, (4) therapist control, and (5) aversive control.

Institutional Control. This type of contingency management indicates that the managers of institutions are most effectively able to change the appropriate contingencies. In the past, hospitals for chronic psychiatric patients, training schools for delinquents, schools for developmentally disabled people, classrooms for troubled students, and the like frequently provided too few reinforcements. When they delivered reinforcements, the institutions often did so noncontingently. Thus, meals, television watching, recreation time, and field trips were given independent of the resident's daily behavior. Some reinforcements, such as special attention from the staff, often were given for maladaptive responses, such as self-abusive behavior or aggressive acting out. There was little incentive for residents to improve their living conditions, their hygienic habits, or their social behaviors, because most reinforcements were given independent of any effort the clients might make.

As operant principles began to be applied to maladaptive behavior, clinicians in charge of wards or troubled classrooms began to make reinforcements contingent on particular behaviors through the use of *token economies*. Tokens are symbolic reinforcers, such as poker chips or points on a tally sheet, that can be exchanged for items that constitute more direct forms of reinforcement, such as social outings, recreational activities, or personal items. An economy involves an exchange system that determines exactly what the tokens can be exchanged for and the rate of exchange, or how many tokens it takes to get particular items or privileges. The economy also specifies the target behaviors that can earn tokens and the rate of responding that is required to earn a particular number of tokens—for example, making one bed earns one token, and two tokens can be exchanged for a night at the movies.

Although it may sound simple to establish a token economy, it is truly complicated. Ayllon and Azrin (1968) articulate the multitude of rules that must be followed for an effective economy to work. Some of the more important considerations include staff cooperation and coordination, because the staff must be more observant and more systematic in their responses to clients than in a noncontingent system; adequate control over reinforcements, because an economy becomes ineffective if residents have access to reinforcements by having money from home or being able to plead an exception for movie night from a "nice-and-lenient" staff member; clear definition of behaviors to be changed, because any lack of specificity will provoke conflict as to what constitutes the criterion (as any parent knows about children making their beds!); and providing positive alternatives to problem behavior, because it is critical that residents be shown what actions they can take to help themselves, rather than relying on a negative set of eliminating responses. Perhaps most important, tokens must be gradually faded as problem behaviors are reduced and adaptive responses are established, because clients must be prepared to make the transition to the larger society. Using an abundance of social reinforcers along with token reinforcers helps prepare clients for fading, so that positive behaviors can be maintained by praise or recognition rather than by tokens. Also, encouraging patients to reinforce themselves, such as by learning to take pride in their appearance, is an important step in fading out tokens. All these and other procedures promote *generalization* of the adaptive behaviors to situations other than those in which the behaviors were learned and *maintenance* of the behaviors well into the future.

Self-Control. At the opposite extreme from institutional control is self-control. In order to serve as their own therapists, clients must be taught the fundamentals of the experimental analysis of behavior. They need to realize that self-control problems are not due to a paucity of mystical willpower or moral character but rather involve an inadequate appreciation of how a systematic manipulation of antecedents and consequences can change behavior. Clients must appreciate the ABCs of behavioral analysis, including the cardinal rule that immediate consequences exert greater control over behavior than do delayed consequences. Obesity, smoking, alcohol abuse, sedentary lifestyle, and procrastinating involve behaviors that have immediate positive consequences but long-term negative consequences.

Following an adequate baseline period that includes charting the antecedents that set the occasion for the maladaptive responses, clients can begin to redesign their environments. Obese patients, for example, can be taught self-control of eating behavior, which includes narrowing the stimulus situations for eating, from TV watching, newspaper reading, and visiting with friends to eating only at the table with the TV off. In beginning to narrow their eating responses to the table, clients reduce the number of occasions for overeating. Clients are also informed of the empirical findings of Schachter (1971), which demonstrate that for obese people the presence of food rather than hunger is the more important stimulus for eating. Clients can then restrict the availability of high-calorie foods in their environment.

Clients can also work to increase behaviors that are incompatible with eating—for example, hiking, biking, or lovemaking. The more hiking or lovemaking, the less likely they are to be eating. To increase their biking or hiking, they may make reinforcing activities, such as TV watching, contingent on an increase in hiking behavior. Clients should also reinforce themselves for avoiding fattening foods, such as allowing themselves to call a friend if they limit their calories at dinner. They can also inform their friends of their changes in eating behaviors so that friends or family can provide social reinforcement for avoiding overeating.

Appreciating the importance of shaping principles, clients should be careful to provide reinforcement for small improvements, such as studying for 10 minutes, rather than withholding reinforcement until their ideal goal is attained. Immediate reinforcement for studying should also be provided—say, going for a fruit juice or listening to a CD for 15 minutes—because the positive consequences of studying are quite delayed. Clients are also instructed to intervene early in the fairly long behavior chain that is terminated by the problem response, such as intervening when they are beginning to approach the refrigerator rather than trying to stop eating after the first potato chip is gone. Rather than testing their willpower by seeing if they can win the bet that they can eat just one, clients should realize that so-called willpower usually means intervening early rather than late in a chain of events that lead to trouble.

Mutual Control. This form of contingency management is indicated when two or more people in a relationship share control over the consequences that each wants. Couples, to take a prominent example, share control over many of the interpersonal consequences that each would like from the relationship. The most common form of mutual control of contingencies involves *contracting*. To form a contract, each person in a relationship must specify the consequences that he or she would like to have increased (O'Banion & Whaley, 1981). Each can then begin to negotiate what he or she would want in exchange for giving the consequences the partner desires. Stuart (1969) worked with four married couples who were in family court to get divorced. The couples shared the rather common complaint that the wife wanted more intimate talking while the husband wanted more frequent love-making. The couples then worked out contracts in which the husband would get a poker chip for each quarter hour of active talking that he engaged in with his wife. Once he had earned eight poker chips he would trade them in for a sexual encounter.

Needless to say, the rate of talking increased dramatically. At the same time, the wives were much more responsive to lovemaking. Some of the wives even acted out their fantasies of hustling by charging for sex, and the husbands would try to bargain them down to five or six chips when they were short on tokens. While some people might find this form of contracting artificial and unromantic, the couples in fact seemed to enjoy their talking and lovemaking more than ever, and each of the four couples was able to avoid divorce. What some people tend to dislike is that contracting makes explicit the *behavior exchange* theory of interpersonal relationships (Jacobson & Margolin, 1979), which holds that we interact in order to exchange reinforcements. As long as there is a fair exchange of reinforcements, people are likely to continue in a relationship and to feel relatively satisfied with the relationship.

Therapist Control. In outpatient psychotherapy, therapists ordinarily have little direct control over the daily environmental contingencies of their clients. Therapists can, however, control social reinforcers, such as attention, recognition, and praise, that occur in treatment. Therapists can take care to make their social reinforcers contingent on improvement in the client's behavior. Greenspoon (1955) was one of the first to demonstrate that verbal reinforcers can influence the types of responses emitted by clients, such as an increase in the number of "I" messages as a function of verbal reinforcement from the therapist. Effective therapists make a point of managing their own verbal and nonverbal reinforcements to make sure they are encouraging adaptive behaviors. All too often, therapists give special attention only to maladaptive responses, such as leaning forward and listening carefully when clients begin to express self-hatred.

Psychotherapists can gain greater control over contingencies by forming contracts with clients. A client can be required, for instance, to deposit $100 and to earn the money back through making appropriate responses, such as losing weight each week. A contingency contract in which the client earned 50 cents to $1 for each pound of weight loss adds to the effectiveness of a self-control package (Harris & Bruner, 1971). The therapeutic contract can also include a provision for response cost, such as the client's paying $2 for each pound gained. Even better, the $2 can be donated to the client's least favorite organization, such as the White Supremacists party or American Civil Liberties Union.

Of course, behavior therapists are not confined to their offices. As noted at the beginning of this chapter, behaviorists value direct observation and intervention in the patient's natural environment. Within the natural setting, therapists can help clients restructure the stimuli and consequences that are controlling their troubled responses. Working right in the natural environment has the decided advantage of not having to worry about generalization from the office to the client's home.

There need be no concern with transfer of training, because the training is done right in the troubled environment. When working with children, for example, the clinician can go into the home and train parents to function as therapist surrogates. Parents can be trained to manage contingencies more effectively by instituting a token economy, by contracting with their children, or through a more subtle use of social reinforcements made contingent on positive responses from the child while avoiding reinforcement of negative behaviors.

Aversive Control. There are rare times when the control of discriminating stimuli and the appropriate management of reinforcements fail to change the troubled behavior. At these times, the behavior therapist will carefully consider the use of aversive controls. Maladaptive behaviors traditionally labeled impulse-control problems—sexual deviations, alcoholism, smoking, and repetitive self-abuse, for example—may respond to aversive controls when more positive techniques have failed. This is an important point: any behaviorist worth his or her salt will only attempt aversive conditioning after multiple efforts at positive alternatives have failed. When aversive controls are applied within a contingency management paradigm, the emphasis is generally on the contingent use of *punishment.*

Punishment, in which an aversive consequence follows a particular response, has been minimized as a useful way of modifying behavior ever since Estes (1944) reported his research on punishment. Estes's studies indicated that punishment led to the suppression of the performance of a response but not to its unlearning. His conclusion was that a response could not be eliminated by punishment alone. Twenty years later Richard Solomon (1964) reviewed the laboratory work on punishment and concluded that punishment alone could indeed lead to new learning. Organisms can learn to avoid punishment through either active or passive conditioning. In active learning, the organism learns to do something, to make some alternative responses that will lead to the avoidance of punishment, as when a child learns to stop and look both ways before crossing a street in order to avoid punishment from a parent. Likewise, the organism can learn to simply passively avoid by not making a response that leads to punishment, as when a child learns not to cross the street at all in order to avoid punishment.

Ample research has outlined the conditions in which punishment can be most effective in producing powerful and lasting effects upon behavior. The guidelines for using punishment are as follows: Punishment should be *immediate*, because delay confuses the contingency and increases the person's anxiety. It should be *intense*, because the more aversive the punishment, the more effective it is. It should be *salient* to that person, along the same lines that reinforcement is individually defined. Punishment should be delivered *early in the behavioral chain,* to catch the problem early on before it intensifies. It should be delivered on a *continuous schedule*, which is more effective than an intermittent schedule of reinforcement, because intermittent reinforcement makes a response even more resistant to extinction. It should be provided across *all stimulus situations;* otherwise, the person learns to avoid responding in punished situations but not in unpunished situations. It should be delivered in a reasonably *calm manner,* so that the anger of the punisher is separated out from the punishment of the behavior. Finally, it should be accompanied by demonstration and reinforcement of *alternative, adaptive behaviors*, such as teaching a child to use restraint and assertive skills instead of smashing a younger sibling.

Let us illustrate the cautious use of aversive conditioning and apply the principles of punishment to a treatment case combining therapist control and aversive control. Susan was a profoundly retarded youngster but stood out because of her unnerving habit of smacking herself in the face with her fist. Four to five times a minute, 3,000 times a day, 1 million times a year, she hit herself. Susan's head banging had begun when she was around age 3. At first, anticonvulsants and tranquilizers had reduced it, but at age 7 she began to cry frequently. Her neurologist thought that perhaps her medication was excessive, so he reduced it on a trial basis. Unfortunately, her head banging intensified, and the crying remained the same. Increasing the medication and trying new drugs proved to be of no help. Other methods were just as fruitless, and out of a sense of desperation, the neurologist referred Susan to a clinic employing behavior modification when applicable (Prochaska, Smith, Marzilli, Donovan, & Colby, 1974).

We reviewed Susan's school records to discern what techniques other psychologists had tried in treating her head banging. Unfortunately, most of our ideas had already been tested and had failed, such as reinforcing an incompatible response like piano playing or trying to extinguish her head banging by paying no attention to it, while giving considerable attention to constructive behaviors. We also felt limited by the fact that baseline records indicated that Susan's rate of head banging seemed to remain quite stable across situations, including in an isolation room where she was unaware of being observed through a one-way mirror.

We decided to experiment with aversive conditioning. After wiring electrodes to Susan's legs and taking 15-minute baseline readings, we gave her a 2.5-milliamp shock each time she hit herself. It soon became apparent that the contingent shock was reducing the rate of head banging in the clinic. Systematic recordings even indicated some generalization to her school. Before long, however, we realized that Susan had begun to discriminate the stimulus that set the occasion for the shock. She would hit herself until the electrodes were attached, then she would stop. After a while, she even learned that she could hit herself without receiving a shock as long as her therapist wasn't watching her. Now there was no generalization outside of the clinic. We had been outsmarted by this supposedly profoundly retarded 9-year-old!

Realizing that a punishment paradigm of aversive conditioning could be effective only if given on a continuous schedule, we decided to purchase a remote-control shocking apparatus that would allow us to shock Susan any time of the day in any setting without her being able to discriminate where, when, or by whom she was getting shocked. On the first day of the remote conditioning, Susan hit herself 45 times compared to the usual 3,000 times. The next day it dropped to 17 hits, followed by 6 hits. Then the apparatus malfunctioned and began giving noncontingent shocks. Following repairs, it took only two days with a total of 12 shocks to bring Susan's head banging down to zero. For months she didn't hit herself. We decided to take the apparatus off her arm, and to our surprise she came over to us and wanted it back on. But we kept the apparatus off, and she went for months without hitting herself. In fact, for the next five years she hit herself approximately 250 times, compared with the 5 million hits she might have delivered without the aversive conditioning.

The logistics of aversive conditioning and the guidelines for effective punishment reveal why the punishment paradigm can become practically unworkable. With a 27-year-old exhibitionist, for example, it would be logistically impossible to have a therapist available whenever the client might come across a school bus. In Susan's case, it was possible to have someone available in all situations, but it obviously would become a highly expensive treatment if her parents had to hire someone to follow her with a remote-control device throughout her waking hours. One alternative with some patients is to train them to deliver their own shock immediately following a maladaptive response.

The use of painful punishers also raises important ethical and legal questions. In Susan's case, we spent two months convincing the Department of Mental Retardation that contingent shock was the best alternative available for treating Susan's self-abuse. In many cases, such as with prisoners, the use of aversive paradigms has been ruled illegal and thus is not available as an alternative. Thus, although we now know that the contingent application of aversive stimuli can be a powerful modifier of behavior, much needs to be done to resolve the practical, ethical, and legal issues involved in its use.

The use of *covert sensitization* as an aversive technique has raised fewer objections, in part because it has frequently been conceptualized as a self-control approach to modifying behavior. In covert sensitization (Cautela, 1967), conditioning is done through the use of covert stimuli and responses, such as thoughts and images. The client is first taught deep-muscle relaxation and then encouraged to imagine a scene that the therapist describes. A 30-year-old pedophile was asked to imagine approaching a 10-year-old boy to whom he was attracted. As he approaches the boy to ask him to come up to his apartment, he feels his stomach becoming nauseated. He feels his lunch coming up into his esophagus, and just as he goes to speak to the boy he vomits all over himself and the boy. People on the street are staring at him, and he turns away from the boy and immediately begins to feel better. He begins walking back to his apartment, feeling better and better with each step he takes. He gets back to his apartment, washes up, and feels great. After teaching this man the covert scene, we had him practice it overtly, including making vomiting noises and gestures. To make the scene even more vivid, we had him sit in his apartment window, and when he saw a boy on the street whom he would like to approach sexually, we had him go to the bathroom and stick his fingers down his throat and vomit as he imagined propositioning the young boy. Within two months, this chronic offender was no longer feeling the urge to approach young boys, and he had followed through on our assertiveness techniques for forming adult homosexual relationships.

Covert sensitization is usually conceptualized as a punishment paradigm in which an aversive scene follows the first response in a maladaptive chain of responses. Because the first response in a maladaptive chain is often a *coverant,* or covert operant response—such as thinking about approaching a stimulus—punishment rather than reinforcement of the coverant can lead to an increase in self-control over an impulsive chain of responses. Imagining turning away from a desired but maladaptive stimulus is a new coverant that gets reinforced. With practice, the punishment of a maladaptive coverant and the reinforcement of more adaptive thoughts and images can break up the automatic chain of responses that eventually leads to problems for the individual. Because covert sensitization works with thoughts and images, it could just as readily have been categorized with the cognitive-behavior therapies considered next.

Cognitive-Behavior Modification

Cognitive approaches to behavior change have been the most controversial alternatives for traditional behavior therapists. They contend that, by definition, cognitive techniques are incompatible with the traditional principles of behaviorism. Behaviorism was established as a radical alternative to mentalistic theories of psychology, which attempted to account for all human behavior in terms of cognitive constructs. Conditioning replaced cognition as the critical determinant of human behavior. Cognitive processes were not denied; they were viewed as less relevant to an effective analysis of behavior disorders.

However, as experimental psychologists conducted more rigorous research on cognitive processes, cognitive conceptualizations of behavior became respectable again. Most contemporary behavior therapists, as we saw in the survey results of the AABT membership, are comfortable with the incorporation of cognitive techniques and the label "cognitive-behavioral." They argue that once we go beyond treating children and retarded and psychotic individuals, we must take into account the cognitive processes that are critical in maintaining and changing complex adult behavior. Estes (1971, p. 23), a prominent learning theorist, states emphatically:

> For the lower animals, for very young children, and to some extent for human beings of all ages who are mentally retarded or subject to severe neurological or behavior disorders, behavior from moment to moment is largely describable and predictable in terms of responses to particular stimuli and the rewarding or punishing outcomes of previous stimulus response sequences. In more mature human beings, much instrumental behavior and more especially a great part of verbal behavior is organized into high-order routines and is, in many instances, better understood in terms of the operations of rules, principles, strategies, and the like than in terms of successions of responses to particular stimuli. Thus, in many situations an individual's behavior from moment to moment may be governed by a relatively broad strategy which, once adopted, dictates response sequences rather than by anticipated consequences of specific actions. In these situations it is the selection of strategies rather than the selection of particular reactions to stimuli which is modified by past experience with rewarding or punishing consequences.

Theory of Psychopathology

As a hybrid of cognitive and behavioral parentage, and a relatively recent hybrid at that, cognitive-behavioral theories of psychopathology and psychotherapy are less distinctive than either of their parental contributors. Some cognitive-behaviorists take their theories and techniques from the behavioral side and add a cognitive element, whereas others begin with the cognitive perspective of Albert Ellis or Aaron Beck and then throw in the behavioral element.

Lacking a consensual cognitive theory of psychopathology unique to behaviorists, we will adopt a cognitive model of maladaptive behavior that parallels the contingency model of maladaptive behavior. Thus, there are maladaptive behaviors that reflect a deficit in cognitive activity. Autonomic nervous system disorders, such as essential hypertension, tension headaches, and chronic anxiety, were traditionally assumed to be outside cognitive control because there is an inherent deficiency in psychological information available to the individual trying to control autonomic responses. With little or no feedback available, individuals are unable to use cognitive processes to gain voluntary control over disruptive autonomic responses.

Other problems are characterized by an excess of particular cognitive responses, as in the case of a hypochondriacal client who was constantly ruminating over the possibility of having cancer. Here the problem is that the same cognitive activity is occurring repeatedly and interfering with the client's ability to use cognitive processes to solve other problems and to relate effectively with the environment. In such cases, what is needed is a decrease in particular cognitive responses, such as a decrease in the frequency of thinking about cancer.

Perhaps the most common problem is the use of inappropriate or ineffective cognitive responses. For some clients this involves inappropriate labeling, such as a client who mislabels sex as dirty and then responds to a sexual encounter with disgust. Other clients develop cognitive expectancies that are mistaken, such as a graduate student who expected all people in authority to be harsh, cold, and condemning and thus had extreme difficulty in dealing with professors and supervisors in even the most routine matters. From a cognitive perspective, these clients are having trouble because they are not responding to the actual stimuli and consequences that occur in their environments. Instead, the clients are responding primarily to the labels and expectancies that are used to process environmental events. If their labels and expectancies are sufficiently inaccurate, then their behaviors are bound to be maladaptive.

At a more complex level, some clients have developed ineffective strategies for solving problems. In a rapidly changing society, it can be extremely important to be cognizant of the most effective methods for attacking common problems, such as dealing with an upsetting boss, handling one's budget in a time of inflation, solving the inevitable conflicts of marriage, and living with the anxieties of adolescents facing an uncertain future. If people learn ineffective strategies for approaching routine behavioral problems, they are likely to make serious mistakes that will lead to frustration, depression, and other emotional upsets. Clients, for example, who adopt a strategy of trying not to think about problems in hopes that they will go away, frequently wait until the problem is out of control before taking action. Other clients, who are frequently labeled overly dependent, may have adopted a strategy that involves rushing to an authority for the best solution. They may be unable to cope with even minor quandaries like what style of clothes to wear, what courses to take each semester, or how to study for an exam. These patients may do well when therapists give them specific directions on how to solve the particular quandary, but they are being reinforced in the short run for depending on a psychotherapist. What such clients actually need in the long run is more detailed information regarding the basic principles of effective problem solving.

Theory of Therapeutic Processes

If a patient's problem is the result of a deficit in information that precludes cognitive control over maladaptive responses, then the solution is to increase the client's awareness by providing the information necessary for cognitive control. If clients are not aware, for example, that their blood pressure is increasing, then there is obviously no way they can consciously prevent the increase. In the case of maladaptive responses within the autonomic nervous system, the necessary information could not be given to clients until an adequate technology was developed. With the development of instrumentation over the past 40 years, it has become possible to give clients ongoing feedback about specific physiological activity occurring within their body. These *biofeedback* techniques allow clients to become conscious of changes in their blood pressure, pulse rate, brain waves, dilations of blood vessels, and other biological functions. When clients are wired to a biofeedback apparatus, they can receive physiological information or biological feedback that offers an increase in cognitive control over autonomic responses. Despite the enormous attention it has received within the professional community, biofeedback has proven to be as effective or only slightly more effective than progressive muscle relaxation alone and, in addition, it is almost always used in conjunction for relaxation training (Miller, 1994; O'Leary & Wilson, 1987; Reed, Katkin, & Goldand, 1986; Silver & Blanchard, 1978). For this reason, we will not discuss the procedure or its effectiveness further apart from relaxation training.

Cognitive techniques for reducing the frequency of particular cognitions are varied, but the most developed is *thought stopping*. This technique begins with patients' verbalizing out loud their repetitive thoughts. At the beginning of the chain of thoughts, the therapist shouts "Stop!" thereby breaking the chain. Next the clients do not verbalize their thoughts, but signal with their hands when they are beginning to think their troubling thoughts. Again the therapist shouts "Stop!" Once patients attain the basics of the thought-stopping technique, they yell "Stop!" themselves when they begin to repeat their troubling chain of thoughts. Once the overt shouting is effective in stopping the repetitive chain of thoughts, clients begin to practice saying "Stop" to themselves whenever their excessive thoughts begin.

Thought stopping may prove to be more effective when combined with *covert assertion* (Rimm & Masters, 1974). With covert assertion, clients are taught to assert to themselves some thought that directly challenges their obsessive thoughts. A 22-year-old man who was obsessed with the thought that he was going crazy was taught that immediately after stopping his troubling thoughts, he was to assert to himself, "Screw it, I'm perfectly normal." At first, clients assert aloud, with considerable affect; then they are encouraged to assert to themselves constructive thoughts that challenge their repetitious ideas.

Several explanations can be given for the possible effectiveness of the combination of thought stopping and covert assertion. The thought stopping itself may follow a punishment paradigm in which the shouting and covert verbalizing of the word *stop* serve to suppress the repetitive chain of thoughts. The covert assertion may function as a counterconditioning technique by which the anxiety assumed to motivate the excessive thinking can be inhibited by a covert assertive response. The most cognitive explanation holds that both the thought stopping and the covert assertion serve as distractors. With these distractors available, clients are taught to consciously switch their attention from troubling, repetitive thoughts to more constructive thoughts.

When confronted with trying to change mistaken labels and expectancies, behaviorists frequently rely on techniques derived from Ellis's rational-emotive therapy and Beck's cognitive therapy, which are considered in more detail in the following chapter. Emotionally upsetting labels, including "awful" and "terrible," are challenged through cognitive restructuring techniques. So too are catastrophic expectations challenged, not only for the realistically low probability of their occurrence, but also for the exaggerated negative consequences that they are assumed to bring.

In adopting Ellis's basic techniques, some of the behaviorists have made important changes. Goldfried and Davison (1994), for example, describe *systematic rational restructuring*, which parallels systematic desensitization. In this approach, a hierarchy is constructed of increasingly more difficult situations with which a client is having trouble coping. Clients imagine the situations and construct how they would normally cope with the upsetting situation. Then they are asked to rationally reevaluate their responses in order to discover a more effective cognitive response to the situation. After coping successfully with an imaginary situation at one level, clients progress to situations further up the hierarchy. Systematic rational restructuring gives clients considerable practice in challenging their own upsetting labels and expectancies before having to face the heavier stress incurred in dealing with in vivo situations. Goldfried and Davison also report that with some clients it is critical that the therapist not try to change the client's cognition, because research indicates that some people will actively resist attempts by others to change them. They recommend that clinicians encourage clients to be as active as possible in challenging their own disruptive thinking rather than follow Ellis's model of the therapist as an active confronter.

In his *self-instructional training*, Donald Meichenbaum (1977, 1986) has made important contributions to cognitive-behavior modification (CBM). Besides working to reduce self-statements that produce maladaptive emotional responses, Meichenbaum also works with individuals to develop self-statements that facilitate self-control of overt verbal and motor behavior. Impulsive and aggressive children have been of special concern to Meichenbaum and his associates (Meichenbaum & Goodman, 1969, 1971; Meichenbaum, 1977). His early contributions laid the groundwork for the popular and manualized cognitive-behavioral treatments of childhood and adolescent disorders, especially attention-deficit, defiant, and impulsive disorders (for example, Barkley, 1987, 1991; Kendall, 1991; Kendall & Braswell, 1992).

To help impulsive children develop more adaptive cognitive controls, Meichenbaum draws on the theorizing of Russian investigators, particularly Luria (1961) and Vygotsky (1962). Luria postulates three stages in which children develop voluntary control over their behavior. In Stage 1, control is exercised by the verbal behavior of others, typically parents and other caregivers. In Stage 2, children repeat the overt speech patterns of parents to control their own behavior. Finally, in Stage 3, the child's behavior comes increasingly under the control of covert self-speech. As Meichenbaum (1977) points out, self-statements thus exert control over the individual's behavior in much the same way as statements coming from another person.

To help children develop better self-control through self-instruction, the therapist performs a task while talking out loud to him- or herself. The child then performs the task with guidance from the psychotherapist. Next, the child performs the task while giving self-instructions aloud. The child then whispers the self-instructions while going through the task. Finally, the child carries out the task employing covert self-instructions.

Meichenbaum and Goodman (1971, p. 117) illustrate what the therapist might say aloud at step 1 while copying line patterns.

> Okay, what is it I have to do? You want me to copy the picture with the different lines. I have to go slowly and carefully. Okay, draw the line down, down, good; then to the right, that's it, now down some more and to the left. Good, I'm doing fine so far. Remember, go slowly. Now back up again. No, I was supposed to go down. That's okay. Just erase the line carefully. . . . Good. Even if I make an error I can go on slowly and carefully, I have to go down now. Finished. I did it!

By internalizing constructive and deliberate self-statements, impulsive children can learn to instruct themselves to slow down when performing a task and to correct themselves without becoming angry or upset. Not only do these self-instructions replace irrational ideas that can lead to emotional upset, but they also provide cognitive coping skills for directing children in more adaptive behaviors.

Meichenbaum's (1986) CBM with adults also proceeds in three phases. The first phase, Conceptualizing the Problem, is concerned with helping patients understand the nature of their problems and enlisting their active collaboration in formulating a treatment plan. The second phase, Trying on the Conceptualization, helps clients explore, sample, and consolidate this mutual view of the problem behavior. With this preparatory work complete, in phase 3, Modifying Cognitions and Producing New Behaviors, the cognitive-behavioral therapist assists patients in modifying their internal dialogues and in enacting new behaviors to be performed in vivo. This third phase is designed to realign the ongoing reciprocal interactions among cognition, affect, behavior, and environment into more adaptive directions for the patient.

With children and adults these phases of CBM have been successfully applied most often in *stress inoculation therapy* (Meichenbaum, 1985, 1996). This treatment method is analogous to an inoculation in medicine wherein a small amount of an active virus is introduced into the body in order to mobilize a healthy response from the immune system. Instead of just learning to counter or control anxiety in stressful situations, individuals can develop covert cognitive coping skills and overt behavioral skills that can inoculate them against ongoing and future stressors. Previously anxiety-provoking events, such as school or work evaluations, public speaking, and interpersonal confrontations, can be reevaluated as challenges and learning opportunities. Such challenges can be mastered through a flexible combination of rational and behavioral skills rather than automatically construed as threats that must be avoided.

Another alternative to challenging mistaken cognitions has emerged from the social-psychological research on attribution theory. An *attribution* is an explanation for an observed event or an account of what caused something to happen. In their classic research on attributions, Schachter and Singer (1962) gave subjects injections of epinephrine and told one group that the emotional arousal they would experience could be attributed to the drug they were given. Other subjects were not informed of the effects of the drug and were placed in situations designed to evoke particular emotions, such as with a stooge modeling anger toward the experiment. Subjects who were able to attribute their arousal to the drug demonstrated less emotional responding than those who were not aware of the effects of the drug.

Misattributions can have devastating psychological effects. One couple presented for marital therapy complaining that the husband had been impotent for the first three years of their marriage. The problem began on their wedding night, with the usual tensions and conflicts. At the reception, the groom's friends insisted on buying him drinks. By the time the couple was in their hotel room, they were tired and tense, and he was more than a little tipsy. When they climbed into bed and he couldn't get an erection, the bride blurted out, "Oh, my God, I married a queer." Her attribution of his erectile dysfunction on that single, unrepresentative evening to homosexuality devastated their sexual relationship. If they had been able to attribute his trouble to situational stress and the acute effect of alcohol, they may have avoided a very troubled start to their marriage. Suffice it to say that the manner in which individuals perceive the causes of their disorder will significantly influence their psychological state and their expectations of the future of the disorder.

Working from attribution theory, Goldfried and Davison (1976, 1994) suggested several ways in which patients can be helped toward more accurate or more benign attributions. Clinical assessments, for example, are attributions made by clinicians, and the assessments can vary in the emotional upset they evoke. A client who attributes erectile dysfunction to unconscious conflicts over possible homosexual impulses may be relieved of considerable anxiety to learn that situational tension combined with alcohol can produce the observed problem. Clients with physical symptoms, such as a man with chronic headaches who is highly anxious because he attributes his headaches to a brain tumor, may be immensely relieved if he learns that the accurate attribution is that the headaches are due to anxiety over health. The expectations that clients have for future events can be dramatically changed if their attributions over past or present events are significantly altered.

Martin Seligman and associates (Abramson, Seligman, & Teasdale, 1978; Seligman, Abramson, Semmel, & vonBaeyer, 1979) have developed further the psychometric measurement and clinical treatment of maladaptive attributions. They have consistently identified three *attributional styles* of stability, internality, and globality (Peterson et al., 1982; Peterson & Villanova, 1988). Optimal performance and mental health are associated with a stable, internal, and global attributional style toward good events; that is, when positive events occur, we assign them a permanent, personal, and pervasive quality. The situation is reversed with bad events: optimal performance and mental health are associated with a temporary, external, and specific attributional style; that is, when dreaded events occur, we should think of them as temporary, atypical events caused by external forces. The resulting cognitive-behavioral therapy assists patients in modifying their pessimistic attributions and adopting "learned optimism" (Seligman, 1990).

Although there is considerable variation in how individuals solve problems, D'Zurilla and Goldfried (1971) report a remarkable degree of agreement on the operations involved in effective problem solving. The five stages of *problem-solving therapy* (Goldfried & Davison, 1976) can be taught to clients who need more effective strategies for approaching problems. They first educate clients in a philosophy that encourages independent problem solving. Their general orientation stage includes teaching clients that problems are a normal part of life with which they can cope. Clients are also encouraged to learn to identify problems early and to inhibit the tendency to respond to a problem with their first impulse. Emotional upsets, for example, can be identified not as a sign of pathology but rather as cues to shift attention to the problem situation that is producing the upset.

Defining and formulating the problem is the next stage. Clients are taught to define problems operationally in terms of the stimuli, responses, and consequences involved. Once all aspects of the problem situation have been defined concretely, clients are able to formulate the problem more abstractly, such as a conflict between two or more goals or between a goal and the available means to the goal. A student came to me, for example, for advice about whether she should drop out of college. She had just found out that her father was having an affair and her parents were planning to divorce. She was experiencing difficulties with concentration and studying, and was therefore contemplating dropping the remainder of her college education. In formulating her problem, it became evident that her major conflict right now was between her goal to advance herself and her desire to help her mother and younger siblings.

With the problem formulated, the next step is to generate alternatives. The client is encouraged to generate a range of possible responses to the situation. Principles of brainstorming (for example, Osborn, 1963) are encouraged during this stage: withhold criticism of any alternative; freewheeling is welcomed, the wilder the idea the better; the more alternatives the better, increasing the probability that effective ideas will occur; combine and improve alternatives into better ideas.

With a variety of alternatives generated, the problem then moves into the stage of decision making. Obviously, the person is trying to choose the best alternative from those available. Goldfried and Davison recommend two criteria: (1) the likelihood that the chosen alternative will indeed resolve the major issues of the problem, and (2) the likelihood that the person can indeed carry out the chosen strategy. The student, for example, might choose to stay in school while taking out a loan, and thereby help herself educationally and her family financially; however, a loan might not be available. Another of her alternatives—to live at home, work, and attend college part-time—might resolve her conflict and also be feasible.

Many people get bogged down in decision making when they should realize that very few decisions are irreversible. They need to make their best bet on one alternative and then move to the stage of verification, in which they begin to test the validity of their alternative. In taking action, such as moving home while continuing in college, the individual observes the consequences of her decision in order to verify its effectiveness. If the consequences of her action seem to match her expectation, then she has exited (Miller, Galanter, & Pribram, 1960) from her problem. If the consequences do not adequately match her expectations, then she can always return to an earlier stage, such as generating new alternatives or deciding on a previously discarded alternative. An awareness of the verification stage can be extremely helpful in moving people from decision making to action, because it assumes that if mistakes are made they can be corrected by reversing the problem-solving strategy.

The problem-solving approach is attractive for both professionals and patients in that it is easily learned and can be applied to a wide range of situations encountered in clinical practice. Broadly speaking, problem-solving therapy is applicable to those who generally cope well but are not doing so at present and to those with poor coping resources (Hawton & Kirk, 1989). For the second group, problem-solving therapy will probably involve longer-term intervention than with the first group.

Therapeutic Relationship

The importance of the therapeutic relationship in behavioral treatment varies according to the particular technique and clinician. With systematic desensitization, for example, the relationship is not nearly as consequential as in, say, cognitive-behavior modification; the former has been successfully applied in large groups and with a computer, whereas the latter emphasizes the active collaboration of patient and therapist. Similarly, the relationship assumes greater importance in some of the operant methods, especially if the therapist is using social reinforcement. Under such conditions, the more valuable the psychotherapist is to the client, the more effective a social reinforcer the therapist can be.

And behavior therapists can indeed be social reinforcers, leading to clients perceiving them as empathic and warm. The educational and collaborative nature of the therapeutic relationship leads to patient ratings on therapist empathy, understanding, and warmth generally comparable to other, relationship-oriented psychotherapies (Glass & Arnkoff, 1992). A case in point is the oft-cited Sloane et al. (1975) comparison of behavior therapy and psychoanalytic psychotherapy. From tape recordings, psychoanalytic therapists and behavior therapists were found not to differ on degree of warmth or positive regard. There were significant differences, however, on accurate empathy, genuineness, and depth of interpersonal contact. The behavior therapists were rated higher on each of these variables.

If there is any general value to the relationship, it is certainly not in terms of the criteria that Rogers suggested. The behavior therapist would do clients an injustice to pretend to be unconditional in positive regard, because social reinforcements, including positive regard, are in reality contingent. The behaviorist is less concerned with accurate empathy than with accurate observation, which is critical in determining both the rate of responding and the effectiveness of treatment. Nor is the therapist particularly concerned with being genuine; what clients need is a competent therapist, not one who is preoccupied with being authentic.

If there is any general value to a therapeutic relationship, it lies in establishing a secure precondition for psychotherapy and in therapist modeling. The behavior therapist must invoke sufficient credibility and trust and instill positive expectancies for clients to engage in the work expected of them during the session and in between sessions. The behavior therapist must also invoke the process of *modeling*—observational learning in which the behavior of the therapist (the model) acts as a stimulus for similar thoughts, attitudes, and behaviors on the part of the client (Perry & Furukawa, 1986). In assertiveness training, for example, the therapist serves very directly as a model who teaches clients to observe more effective methods of being assertive. Modeling is such a critical part of assertiveness training that therapists who are not genuinely assertive would probably not be competent as assertion trainers.

Modeling effects probably occur with most other forms of behavior therapy and cognitive-behavior modification as well. A desensitizer, for example, models a fearless approach toward phobic stimuli, teaching clients that such stimuli can be mastered if approached in a gradual and relaxed manner. We cannot envision a snake-phobic therapist successfully assisting a snake-phobic patient! The contingency contractor models a positive approach toward problem solving and teaches clients that conflicts can best be solved through compromise and positive reinforcement rather than through criticism and other forms of punishment.

Modeling can serve many important functions in changing behavior (Bandura, 1969; Perry & Furukawa, 1986). Through observation, clients can acquire new behaviors; for example, clients observe a competent asserter for the first time and then begin to acquire the essentials of effective assertion. Modeling can facilitate appropriate behaviors by inducing clients to perform behaviors that they are capable of performing but have not been performing in appropriate ways, such as expressing positive feelings toward a spouse after the therapist has been observed to express similar feelings.

Modeling can disinhibit behaviors that were previously avoided because of anxiety, as when clients learn to talk openly about sex because the therapist has been direct about sex. Finally, modeling can lead to vicarious and direct extinction of anxiety associated with a stimulus, as when children extinguish fear of dogs because they have observed the therapist's children having fun with dogs.

The essential point is this: considerable research demonstrates how beneficial modeling can be and also how modeling can be most effective. If behaviorists make therapeutic relationships a part of the process of change, then they must attend closely to what they are modeling and how effective a model they are becoming.

Practicalities of Behavior Therapy

Behavior therapists show considerable variation in the practical aspects of their work. Therapists using counterconditioning and cognitive-behavioral techniques are most likely to work in a traditional office setting. Treatment is typically conducted in an individual or, increasingly, a couples format. Many of the behavioral and cognitive-behavior techniques, including assertiveness training, relaxation training, and problem solving, are applied in a group format for the sake of cost-efficiency and group processes, including modeling, rehearsal, and group reinforcement.

Some behavior analysts are critical of therapists' staying in their offices; they suggest that interventions performed in the natural environment are not plagued with the same generalization or transfer-of-training problems as those performed in the office. Certainly when behavior therapists are managing contingencies on a larger scale, as with token economics, they work right in the environment of clients. Unfortunately, because of exaggerated fears of brave-new-world phenomena, behavior modification has been frowned upon in some environments, the most noteworthy being prisons under the influence of the federal government.

Behavior therapists and their cognitive-behavioral cousins are quite comfortable with technology as a part of treatment. The equipment can vary from a simple reclining chair for relaxation to remote-control aversive stimulators to complex biofeedback equipment. The most recent addition to the technology arsenal is the use of personal computers for collecting data and for administering treatments to clients in their home and work environments. Recent studies suggest that computer-based versions of self-control training can be quite effective for a variety of behavioral and addictive disorders (e.g., Hester & Delaney, 1997).

Behavior therapists continually test the limits of their techniques and consequently have worked with a wide range of clients, probably the widest range of any psychotherapy system. Counterconditioning has been used most often with verbal adults who would traditionally be labeled neurotic, psychosomatic, and character-disordered. Cognitive-behavioral techniques are most often used with adults and adolescents, although problem solving and self-instruction are employed extensively with children. Contingency management techniques have been applied to conditions that have been most difficult for verbal therapies, such as impulse-control problems, addictive disorders, children's dysfunctions, and the problems of severely retarded and psychotically regressed patients.

Behavior therapists represent the full range of mental health professions, but psychologists are two to three times more likely than members of other mental health professions to endorse behaviorism (Glass & Arnkoff, 1992). This is probably the case because they are more likely to have been trained in learning theories and in empirical research. Especially noteworthy is the role that experimental psychologists have played in the development of behavior therapy, because they traditionally have not been a direct part of any therapy system. The Association for the Advancement of Behavior Therapy (AABT) welcomes people from a diversity of backgrounds, although it encourages the independent practice of behavior therapy only by individuals with advanced degrees and special training in behavioral techniques.

Speaking of training, behavior and cognitive-behavior therapists are at the forefront of competency-based education in psychotherapy (Edelstein & Berler, 1987; Shaw & Dobson, 1988). The behavioral mandate is to demonstrate competency in scientifically established methods. Toward this end, behaviorists are heavily involved in creating *manualized treatments* and documenting *empirically-supported psychotherapies* for the purposes of enhancing professional training and treatment selection. The former is an attempt to operationalize the therapeutic procedures in a treatment manual, typically session by session, in such a way that other therapists can learn and replicate the procedures. The latter is an emerging trend, discussed in Chapter 15, to identify psychological interventions that have been empirically tested and supported as more effective than active placebos or alternative treatments and then to publicize the existence of those interventions to training programs (Task Force on Promotion and Dissemination of Psychological Procedures, 1995).

Personal therapy is not deemed a particularly valuable prerequisite for clinical work; in fact, only about one-half of behavior therapists report ever having experienced therapy themselves, a figure consistently the lowest among the theoretical orientations studied (Norcross, Strausser, & Missar, 1988). Interestingly and controversially, when behavior therapists do take their troubles to someone, that someone tends not to be a fellow behaviorist (Lazarus, 1971c; Norcross & Prochaska, 1984; Norcross, Strausser, & Faltus, 1988).

Brief Behavior Therapy

Behaviorists have always been committed to time-efficient, empirically-supported interventions. They were adherents of brief therapy before it became fashionable. In one study (Norcross & Wogan, 1983), behavior therapists reported seeing clients less frequently and for a shorter duration than psychotherapists of other persuasions; only 7% of their clients, on average, are seen for more than a year. Of course, particular clients will require more extensive treatment when warranted by their needs, not the therapist's theoretical orientation.

The entire movement in psychotherapy toward cost-efficiency is, in fact, old news to behavior therapists. As noted in the beginning of this chapter, the core characteristics of behavior therapy embody cost-efficiency: identify specific disorders, contract for treatment goals, apply empirically-validated methods, and evaluate the outcome. For these reasons, behavior therapists as a group are probably the most congenial to managed care insistence on short-term, problem-focused psychotherapy.

Effectiveness of Behavior Therapy

More controlled outcome research has been conducted on behavior therapy and cognitive-behavior therapy than on any other system of psychotherapy. About two-thirds of the outcome studies on psychotherapy with children and adolescents have been conducted on behavioral treatments (Kazdin, 1991; Weisz et al., 1987), and a majority of controlled outcome studies on psychotherapy with adults pertain to behavioral and cognitive-behavioral treatments (Grawe et al., 1998; Shapiro & Shapiro, 1982). It would take an entire book to review all the literature examining the efficacy of behavior therapy. Our plan in this section, therefore, is to summarize the findings of quantitative reviews and multiple meta-analyses on the effectiveness of behavior therapy. But first we briefly consider small-*n* research designs.

Small-*n* Designs

Our literature summary and meta-analytic reviews consider only controlled research using group designs. However, many behavior therapists have argued persuasively that there are legitimate research alternatives to the traditional multi-group design that uses placebo and/or no-treatment control groups. They argue that well-controlled case studies or studies with a small *n* can yield valid data when techniques such as multiple baseline or ABAB designs are used.

In the *multiple baseline design*, several of the client's behaviors (not just the behavior being directly modified) are measured initially. The therapeutic intervention is then introduced for one of the behaviors, while measurement of all the behaviors continues. If the intervention produces improvement in the target behavior but not in the other behaviors, it is argued that there is something about the specific relation between the target behavior and the environmental modification that has produced the improvement. The assumption is that other behaviors would have been equally subject to nonspecific effects, such as the passing of time and the relationship with the therapist. Although there is much to recommend this design, one problem with it is that we cannot say just what changes in the environment produced the changes. Was it changes in concrete contingencies, for example, or was it the result of experimenter demands or expectations?

A similar dilemma arises with ABAB types of designs. In the *ABAB (reversal) design*, the person receiving the treatment is measured repeatedly: before intervention (A); during the time when the intervention is in effect (B); during a subsequent period when the intervention is temporally discontinued (A); and again under the influence of the therapeutic intervention (B). The rationale behind this design is that if the subject's behavior improves during the periods when treatment is administered and is worse during the initial period and at any other time when treatment is withdrawn, then the treatment itself is presumed to be responsible for the change. Here again we cannot determine precisely what in the treatment package accounts for the behavior change. Was it the client's expectations, the therapist's special attention, the treatment itself, or another uncontrolled variable? Furthermore, most clients and therapists seek permanent changes from psychotherapy, not ephemeral effects that can be reversed as soon as treatment is removed.

Our point is this: Small-*n* designs are excellent vehicles for examining the efficacy of new procedures and are superb models for conducting clinical research when only a small number of patients are available. At the same time, however, small-*n* designs lack the power and control afforded by more traditional research designs. For these reasons, our review will not concern itself with the thousand-plus small-*n* studies published to date. Readers interested in additional examples are directed to the behaviorally oriented journals listed at the end of this chapter; those interested in the design itself are referred to Hersen and Barlow (1976) and Barlow, Hayes, and Nelson (1984).

Effectiveness of Behavior Therapy with Children

Weisz and colleagues (1987, 1995) have conducted two meta-analyses on the effectiveness of psychotherapy with children and adolescents. In 1987, their study statistically examined 108 well-designed studies with 4- to 18-year-old patients published between 1958 and 1984. Across various outcome measures, the average treated youngster was more improved after treatment than 79% of those not treated. Behavioral treatments proved more effective than nonbehavioral treatments regardless of client age, therapist experience, or problem type.

In 1995, Weisz and colleagues revisited the effects of psychotherapy with children and adolescents by conducting a meta-analysis on a new sample of 150 outcome studies published between 1983 and 1993. The overall effectiveness of therapy was again positive and effects were again more positive for behavioral than nonbehavioral treatments. Their results supported the specificity of treatment effects: Outcomes were stronger for the particular problems targeted in treatment than for problems not targeted.

The behavioral methods, number of treatment groups, and average (unweighted) effect sizes in the two meta-analyses were as follows (keep in mind that an effect size of .50 is considered medium and .80 a large effect in the behavioral sciences):

Behavioral method	# of groups		Effect size	
	1987	1995	1987	1995
Operant (e.g., reinforcement)	39	19	.78	.69
Desensitization/relaxation	17	31	.75	.70
Modeling	25	12	1.19	.73
Social skills training	5	23	.90	.37
Cognitive-behavioral	10	38	.68	.67
Multiple behavioral	10	35	1.04	.86

These effect sizes demonstrate superior effectiveness of various behavioral methods over no treatment, active placebo treatment, and alternative treatments.

The latter conclusion—the apparent superiority of behavioral treatments relative to nonbehavioral treatments—has been critically questioned. Shirk and Russell (1992) argued with some data that the reported differences may be due to (1) differences in methodological quality between behavioral and nonbehavioral treatment studies, (2) investigator allegiance effects favoring behavioral treatments, and (3) a lack of treatment representativeness among nonbehavioral treatments. However, careful analysis of the data (Weiss & Weisz, 1995a) and another meta-analysis (Weiss & Weisz, 1995b) found little support for either argument #1 or #2. However, with regard to #3, all partisans seem to agree that research evaluations of child therapy are unrepresentative of the real-life practice of child therapy. In particular, certain nonbehavioral forms of child therapy, such as play therapy and psychodynamic therapy, are not adequately represented in the research studies.

Looking specifically at cognitive-behavioral methods, Durlak, Fuhrman, and Lampman (1991) reviewed 64 overlapping studies on children 4 to 13 years old. The mean effect size was .56. After therapy, the average treated child was better off than 71% of control-group peers. Interestingly, children in Piaget's "formal operational" stage of thinking were more positively impacted by the cognitive-behavioral interventions (effect size = .92) than were children ages 5 to 7 (effect size = .57) or 7 to 11 (effect size = .55).

Effectiveness of Behavior Therapy with Adults

In their classic meta-analysis, Smith, Glass, and Miller (1980) located 101 controlled studies on systematic desensitization, 54 on behavior modification, and 34 on cognitive-behavior therapy. The mean effect sizes were 1.05, .73, and 1.13, respectively, all substantially better than the .56 effect size for placebo treatments.

Shapiro and Shapiro (1982) replicated the Smith, Glass, and Miller study with an improved design. They included only studies over a five-year period that contained at least two treatment groups and one control group. Most of the 143 studies evaluated behavioral therapies. The behavioral methods, number of treatment groups included in the analysis, and average effect sizes were as follows:

Behavioral method	# of groups	Effect size
Rehearsal and self-control	38	1.01
Covert behavioral	19	1.52
Relaxation	42	.90
Desensitization	77	.97
Reinforcement	28	.97
Modeling	11	1.43
Social skills training	14	.85

All of these effect sizes are considered large, and all are superior to those found for no treatment and placebo treatment. The differences among treatment outcomes have more to do with the problem type than with the psychotherapy system, but Shapiro and Shapiro (1982) concluded that their study revealed a modest but undeniable superiority of behavioral and cognitive methods and a corresponding relative inferiority of psychodynamic and humanistic methods.

Similarly, in their massive meta-analysis of controlled outcome studies, Grawe and colleagues (1998) report large and positive effect sizes for behavioral therapies. In 74 studies, covering 3,400 plus patients, statistically significant effects over control treatments were found for social skills training in 45 of the 61 comparisons. In 38 studies involving 1,556 patients, stress inoculation outperformed the control in 30 of the 39 cases. And in the 25 studies involving 775 patients, problem-solving therapy proved superior to control treatments in 27 of the 29 studies. When all was studied and done, the behavioral and cognitive-behavioral treatments were superior to client-centered and psychodynamic treatments in direct comparisons. As discussed briefly in Chapter 2, the clinical importance of these statistically significant differences remains controversial.

In an intriguing study, Bowers and Clum (1988) examined the relative contribution of specific and nonspecific treatment effects. Specifically, they conducted a meta-analysis of 69 studies comparing forms of behavior therapy with placebo control conditions to obtain an estimate of the incremental contribution of specific interventions to the nonspecific effects of placebo. Their comparison indicated that the specific effects of behavior therapies are twice as great as the nonspecific effects.

Effectiveness of Behavior Therapy with Couples and Families

Hahlweg and Markman (1988) used meta-analysis to determine the effectiveness of behavioral marital therapy (BMT) and behavioral premarital intervention (BPI). The intervention components included in these therapies were typically communication- skills training, problem-solving training, and modifying dysfunctional relationship expectations and attributions. The mean effect size for 17 marital therapy studies was .95 and for 7 premarital interaction studies was .79. These gains were generally maintained over time. Cross-cultural comparisons of behavioral marital therapy indicated equal benefits for couples in the United States and in Europe.

Dunn and Schwebel (1995) report converging conclusions in their more recent meta-analytic review of marital therapy outcome research. BMT obtained a mean effect size of .79, indicating that it produced significant changes in behavior, as compared with control couples.

The moderate to large effects found for behavioral family therapy are reviewed in Chapter 11 (Systemic Therapies). Suffice it to say here that behavioral family therapy has consistently demonstrated its superiority over no treatment and control treatment and, depending upon the review, occasionally over alternative, nonbehavioral forms of family therapy.

The effect sizes of behavioral marital and family therapy are in some respects faceless numbers and thus difficult to translate into improved behavior and recovered lives. Let us share the results of one controlled family therapy study demonstrating in concrete human terms what a large effect size means. Alexander and Parsons (1973) compared (1) contingency contracting-based family therapy ($n = 46$), (2) client-centered family therapy ($n = 19$), (3) psychodynamic family therapy ($n = 11$), and (4) no therapy ($n = 10$) in the treatment of adolescent delinquency. Results indicated that at a 6-month follow-up the contingency contracting group had a 26% recidivism rate, compared with 47% for client-centered therapy, 50% for no treatment, and 73% for dynamic family therapy. Tests of family interactions at the end of therapy indicated that the behavioral group talked more, showed more equality in terms of who talked, and were more willing to interrupt each other. In essence, this is what the faceless numbers of effect sizes tell us.

Effectiveness of Specific Behavioral Methods

Social Skills Training. Corrigan (1991) conducted a meta-analysis on 73 studies using social skills training in four adult psychiatric populations: developmentally disabled, psychotic, nonpsychotic, and legal offenders. The effect sizes were large across various outcome measures; patients participating in social skills training broadened their repertoire of skills, maintained these gains several months after treatment, and showed diminished psychiatric symptoms related to social dysfunctions. Consistent trends suggested that social skills training had the greatest effect on developmentally disabled groups and the least effect on offender groups.

Looking specifically at skills training for persons with severe mental illness, Dilk and Bond (1996) examined the effectiveness of various types of skills training, including social skills training, in 68 controlled studies. The overall effect size was medium (.40) at posttest and larger at follow-up (.56), which indicates that skills training was moderately effective to strongly effective in increasing skill acquisition and reducing psychiatric symptomatology. Interpersonal skills training resulted in a mean effect size of .30, assertiveness training in .40, and prevocational training in .73 for this chronic and recalcitrant population.

Stress Inoculation. A meta-analysis by Saunders, Drishell, Johnston, and Salas (1996) was conducted to determine the overall effectiveness of stress inoculation training devised by Meichenbaum (1985). The analysis was based on a total of 37 studies involving 1,837 clients. The overall effect size of .51 on performance anxiety and .37 on state anxiety revealed moderately powerful effectivness. Thus, stress inoculation treatment has been shown to be effective in reducing performance anxiety and decreasing state anxiety and far better than no treatment or control treatments.

Relaxation Training. Hyman, Feldman, Harris, Levin, and Mallory (1989) identified 48 experimental studies of nonmechanically assisted relaxation techniques used to treat a variety of clinical symptomatology. The effect sizes ranged from .43 to .66 for the treatment of health-related symptomatology, and were largest for nonsurgical samples with hypertension, headaches, and insomnia.

Self-Statement Modification. Dush, Hirt, and Schroeder (1983, 1989) performed separate meta-analyses on the effectiveness of self-statement modification with children and adults. The self-statement modification (SSM) was commonly oriented explicitly around the approach detailed by Donald Meichenbaum. For children, results of 48 outcome studies showed that self-statement modification surpassed no treatment and placebo treatment by roughly a half a standard deviation on average. The average effect, weighted equally by study, was .47. For adults, results of 69 studies showed that self-statement modification evidenced considerable gains beyond no treatment. The average effect size of .74 can be viewed as analogous to shifting the average treated client from the 50th percentile of control subjects to the 77th percentile. Alternative therapies shifted patients to the 67th percentile, on average (effect size = .49).

Behavioral Parent Training. Serketich and Dumas (1996) examined the effectiveness of behavioral parent training (BPT) to modify antisocial behavior in children through a meta-analysis of 26 controlled studies. The overall effect size of .86 indicates that the average child whose parents participated in BPT was better adjusted after treatment than approximately 80% of children whose parents did not.

BPT's large effects appear to generalize fairly well to both children's classroom behaviors and parents' personal adjustment. In the words of two reviewers of this literature, "perhaps no other technique has been as carefully documented and empirically supported as parent management training in treating conduct disorders" (Feldman & Kazdin, 1995, p. 4).

Effectiveness of Behavior Therapy for Specific Disorders

Obsessive-Compulsive Disorder. A handful of quantitative reviews have been published on the effectiveness of psychological treatment for obsessive-compulsive disorder (OCD). We will consider two of the recent meta-analyses.

In 1987, Christensen, Hadzi-Pavlovic, Andrews, and Mattick employed meta-analysis to integrate the research literature on the treatment of OCD. Antidepressants and behavior therapy both produced appreciable changes in symptomatology and attendant depression. The average effect size was 1.29 for tricyclic medication and 1.30 for exposure-based behavior therapy. The effects of the two treatments did not differ significantly, but both were superior to placebo treatments and to nonspecific treatment programs. Follow-up data were sparse for the medication, but the benefits of behavior therapy were stable at follow-up.

In 1994, van Balkom and associates reevaluated the enlarged literature (86 studies in all) and concluded that antidepressants, behavior therapy, and the combination of antidepressants and behavior therapy were significantly more effective than placebo treatment. On patients' self-ratings, the meta-analysis indicated that behavior therapy was significantly more effective than the antidepressants and that the combination of behavior therapy plus antidepressants tended to be more effective than the antidepressant medication alone. The overaraching finding of these and the other reviews is that behavior therapy, with or without adjunctive medication, is a premier treatment for OCD.

Migraine Headache. Holroyd and Penzien (1990) used meta-analysis to integrate the results from 25 clinical trials evaluating the effectiveness of propranolol and 35 clinical trials evaluating the effectiveness of relaxation/biofeedback training (2,445 patients, collectively). The meta-analysis revealed substantial, but very similar improvements in recurrent migraines treated with propranolol and relaxation/biofeedback training. In both cases, these treatments resulted in 43% reduction in migraine headaches when assessed by daily recordings and in 63% reduction when assessed by other measures. By contrast, placebo medication (14% reduction) and no treatment (essentially 0% reduction) were inferior to both propranolol and relaxation/biofeedback, which resulted in very similar outcomes.

Eating Disorders. Several quantitative reviews have evaluated the effectiveness of pharmacological and nonpharmacological treatments of bulimia nervosa and anorexia. Two meta-analyses (Hartman, Herzog, & Drinkman, 1992; Whitbread & McGowan, 1994) concerned the treatment of bulimia nervosa and reviewed overlapping studies, 18 in one study and 19 in the other. Results of the first study revealed that cognitive-behavior therapy (effect size=1.72) was the most effective and behavioral therapy (effect size=1.05) the second most effective treatment for reducing bingeing and purging among bulimics. These treatments outperformed pharmacological treatments, mostly antidepressants.

An independent review by Johnson, Tsoh, and Varnado (1996) on both bulimia and anorexia arrived at similar conclusions. Behavior therapy and cognitive-behavior therapy both outperform no treatment and control treatments. In the treatment of anorexia, behavior therapy has proven effective in promoting weight gain during hospitalization, and cognitive interventions at that point do not appear to augment the basic behavior therapy. In the treatment of bulimia, comparisons of pharmacotherapy and cognitive-behavior therapy suggest that psychotherapy alone is more effective than medication alone in reducing bulimic symptoms, and that behavior changes produced by psychotherapy endure at follow-up in contrast to medication where relapse rates are high. Dropout rates on medication are two to three times higher than those of cognitive-behavior treatments.

Hypertension. Linden and Chambers (1994) conducted a meta-analysis on the clinical effectiveness of various treatments for essential hypertension using 166 studies. Weight reduction (effect size =.57), physical exercise (effect size =.65), and individualized cognitive-behavior therapy (effect size=.65) were particularly effective and were of equal value to drug treatments in reducing systolic pressures. The individualized cognitive-behavior therapy was more effective than single-component behavior therapy, such as relaxation training, autogenic training, and biofeedback.

Anger Disorders. Tafrate, DiGiuseppe, and Goshtasbpour-Parsi (1997) recently conducted a meta-analysis on 41 studies testing the effectiveness of various behavioral and cognitive-behavioral treatments on adult anger disorders. The overall effect size of .71 indicated that these treatments clearly outperform no treatment and control treatments. They found the following effect sizes for the most common treatments: .60 for progressive muscle relaxation, .80 for anger/anxiety management training (a multi-component treatment relying heavily on relaxation training; Suinn & Richardson, 1971), .73 for systematic desensitization, .67 for self-instructional training, .81 for cognitive restructuring, .66 for problem solving, .80 for assertiveness training, and .72 for multi-component interventions. The dual conclusions are that behavioral treatments effectively reduce anger and that a variety of potent behavioral approaches are available.

Cigarette Smoking. Meta-analysis was used to cumulate the results of 633 studies of smoking cessation, involving over 70,000 subjects. Viswesvaran and Schmidt (1992) found that no treatment resulted in a 6% quit rate and that self-care methods produced a 15% quit rate on average. Both of these were significantly less effective than formal interventions. Among the most effective methods were smoke aversion (31% quit rate), other aversive techniques (27% quit rate), instructional methods in work sites (30% quit rate), and hypnosis (36% quit rate).

Insomnia. In an effort to identify effective psychological treatments for insomnia, Murtagh and Greenwood (1995) conducted a meta-analysis on 66 outcome studies. Generally, psychological treatments produced considerable enhancement of both sleep patterns and subjective experience of sleep. All of the active treatments, largely behavioral in nature, were superior to placebo therapies. Specifically, the following effect sizes were found at posttreatment: .81 for progressive muscle relaxation, .93 for other forms of relaxation, 1.16 for stimulus control, and .73 for paradoxical intentions. These are large and convincing effects, and the results demonstrate the value of behavioral treatments as effective alternatives to sleep medications, which can have negative side effects.

Nocturnal Enuresis. Houts, Berman, and Abramson (1994) provided a quantitative integration of research on the effectiveness of psychological and pharmacological treatments for nocturnal enuresis (children bed-wetting at night). At the end of treatment, an average of 57% of the children receiving psychological treatments ceased bed-wetting and 37% receiving pharmacological treatments ceased bed-wetting, compared to only 12% and 10% for placebo controls and no-treatment controls, respectively. Although both psychological and pharmacological interventions had outcomes superior to those observed in the control groups, children receiving psychological treatment were more likely to have stopped their bed-wetting at both posttreatment and follow-up than children given medications. The most successful treatment was that of the *urine alarm,* an old behavioral method of conditioning introduced in 1938 by Mowrer and Mowrer. A plastic pad underneath the child or a small sensor attached to the pajamas detects moisture from urination and starts an alarm to wake the child.

Criticisms of Behavior Therapy
From a Psychoanalytic Perspective

For a system priding itself on its empiricism, behavior therapy certainly is disappointing. In place of quality research, we get quantity. If numbers are good, then more numbers must be better. But what about the conceptual foundations of a problem that determine whether an experiment is even worth conducting? So what if desensitization can reduce a college coed's fear of spiders? Does that have anything to do with the devastating problems that therapists confront daily in their clinical practices? Who ever sees a snake phobic in a clinic? Most behaviorists would do themselves a service when planning a study if they asked the key clinical question for any outcome research—the so-what question. So what if having college students imagine vomiting in their lunches leads to a loss of a pound a week? So what if some of the loss lasts for four months? There is plenty of evidence that 85% of the people who lose weight through any means regain it within two years. How come only a tiny fraction of their studies use a two-year follow-up? Are the authors more concerned with completing a thesis quickly or rushing to publish than with establishing a useful treatment for clinical disorders? Perhaps behavioral researchers could use a little insight into the motives that lead to their voluminous but inconsequential research.

Behavior therapists would like us to believe that somewhere there are compelling data that demonstrate the consistent superiority of behavior therapy. But where are the data? Are they to be found in Paul's (1966) study using five sessions of insight therapy to treat the anxiety of students in a required speaking class? Send such students to Dale Carnegie! Certainly the classic study by Sloane, et al. (1975; reviewed in Chapter 2) provides little solace. Their rigorous comparison of comprehensive behavior therapy with brief psychoanalytic therapy found no significant differences between the therapies in effectiveness with outpatients. Even with time-limited therapy, the psychoanalysts held their own.

The results of number-crunching meta-analyses do occasionally—but not consistently—demonstrate the superiority of behavior therapy in terms of symptom relief. However, if one looks under the cover of behaviorists' "objective methodology," one discovers a preoccupation with short-term success and behavioral outcome measures that stack the cards in the behaviorists' favor. Even a prominent behaviorist like Alan Kazdin (1991) concedes that the purported superiority of behavioral methods begins to disappear when the type of outcome measure is controlled. The results of studies with nonclinical populations and nondiagnosable concerns certainly favor behavioral treatments, but what evidence is there of lasting recovery of genuinely disturbed people as the result of behavior therapy? Where are the controlled studies of behavior therapy with personality-disordered and multiple-problem patients? And where are the controlled studies on enhanced insight, improved object relations, deeper self-awareness—the things that matter most to people? Dig a little deeper, behaviorists.

What most of the behavior therapy research demonstrates is not the superiority but the superficiality of the behavioral view of humanity. Only such superficial thinking could account for hundreds of researchers wasting their time trying to substantiate clinically relevant therapies with normal college sophomores as clients. Researchers from other psychotherapy systems may at times be naive about methodology, but that is nothing compared to the behaviorists' naivete about psychopathology.

From a Humanistic Perspective

Examine the criteria for success in almost all the behavior therapy studies and it is apparent what is missing. Only a handful of studies clearly assessed the patients' feelings of general happiness and harmony as criteria for successful treatment. And guess what? Electric shock did not help homosexuals find happiness (Birk, Huddleston, Millers, & Cohler, 1971). What is missing from behavioral theory and therapy is a humane sense of values that can help us to decide what is a significant outcome for therapy. Significance in life is not determined by a .05 level of probability of changing symptoms. In an era when many people are suffering from a collapse in a sense of significance, behavior therapy strives only for symptom relief.

What behavior therapy offers to people seeking happiness and harmony in an alienating and dehumanizing world is a bunch of gimmicks and techniques. Do people who have been manipulated all their lives to believe that cigarettes can make them cool and attractive need to have hot smoke blown in their faces? Do people who overeat need to chart each bite of food to rid themselves of the boredom or the anxiety that gnaws away at them? Can thought stopping prevent middle-aged people from thinking that life is passing them by? Do we need people who are desensitized of all their anxiety, or do we need people who are anxious about all the insensitivity that surrounds them? Do we need to teach people to exchange poker chips to encourage talking, or should we learn how to help people find the intrinsic meaning that comes in sharing their most basic feelings? Alpha waves will not cure alienation. A gimmick a day will not keep the doctor away.

The dehumanizing technology of Western society that has removed people from their roots is no longer seen as a problem; it is now seen as part of the therapy. Does it not make us shudder to realize how readily patients and therapists alike can reduce themselves to fit a hollow and mechanical model of human beings? Have we become so alienated that we no longer realize that having smoke blown in our face or poker chips given in exchange for love is part of a much larger process of dehumanization? We create our cures to match the image of who we think we are and what we believe plagues us. The rise of behavior therapy reflects an image of humanity as directed by conditions outside our control. Is the solution to our contemporary problems to be found in submitting ourselves to even more mindless conditioning?

From a Contextual Perspective

Who defines what is adaptive and what is maladaptive behavior? Who and what has to change? Are behavioral techniques being used to encourage clients to conform to normative standards of the dominant social group? Are cultural norms appropriate for this particular client? In attempting to be explicit content-free methodologists, behaviorists risk becoming implicit content avoiders (Kantrowitz & Ballou, 1992). Psychotherapists invariably must make decisions about the appropriateness of target behaviors, treatment goals, and outcome criteria. Sure, clients should have a larger voice in making these decisions, but behaviorists can't simply wash their hands of the mutual responsibility and absolve themselves by insisting "It's the client's decision."

When the therapist's values are hidden from view, then implicit standards are used to determine what and who is in need of change. These nonconscious ideologies are likely to reflect mainstream, white, middle-class, heterosexual, masculine values. How many "rebellious" minority adolescents, "confused" homosexuals, "sexless" wives, and "misbehaving" children have been B-Modded at the behest of the "man of the house" in the name of value-neutral, content-free technology? Psychotherapy is an undeniably value-laden enterprise. Won't you at least come out and publicly endorse your values?

The behavioral focus on individual skill training can neglect social issues and support dominant group values (Kantrowitz & Ballou, 1992). Consider the ostensibly benign case of prescribing assertiveness training for a woman who has been sexually harassed in the workplace. On one hand, assertion training is an empirically supported intervention and one that will probably meet with the woman's approval. On the other hand, by focusing on a woman's skill deficits, neither aggressive sexuality nor boundary violations are addressed. Nor is the social norm of women's duty to protect themselves seriously questioned. The individual distress may be temporarily improved, but the social status quo is firmly protected.

In broader strokes, this is precisely the systemic complaint about behavior therapists: they fail to see that the entire family system, not the symptomatic person, is the therapeutic unit for achieving change. Ironically, the oft-touted "environmentalism" of behaviorism stops short of the family and the culture. A comprehensive treatment must alter the behavior patterns of both the individual and the system.

From an Integrative Perspective

Welcome to the club, behaviorists! Most people who are in this business long enough recognize that no one psychotherapy or single theory is complete enough to match the complexities of our clients. Certainly there is no unifying theory behind what is called behavior therapy. There are merely a series of techniques and a unifying commitment to determine which approaches work best with which types of problems. This sounds like classical eclecticism rather than classical conditioning. Even though prominent behaviorists such as Cyril Franks (1984) and Hans Eysenck (1970) criticized eclectics early on for muddying the therapeutic waters, the proliferation of new behavioral techniques without an integrating theory is certainly adding more to our complexity than to our clarity. Eclectics, however, have never had trouble living with ambiguity, even the ambiguity of a psychotherapy system that is supposedly united yet includes such diverse methods as desensitization, covert sensitization, biofeedback, rational cognitive restructuring, token economies, self-control, and problem solving. These techniques are about as alike as an eclectic's bag of tricks. Of course, there is really no criticism intended here. We don't mind being called behaviorists if you don't mind being called eclectics.

━ A BEHAVIORAL ANALYSIS OF MRS. C. ━

Mrs. C. is restricted by a broad range of maladaptive responses, so she will need a course of comprehensive behavior therapy if she is to regain a rewarding approach to life. First, she suffers from conditioned avoidance of dirt and disease. Her particular mode of avoiding is to wash excessively whenever she feels she has been in contact with conditioned stimuli, such as pinworms or dirt. Avoidance of these stimuli has also led to maladaptive behaviors, including avoiding cooking and caring for her children. She also avoids sexual relations, which may be related in part to her avoidance of dirt and disease, but is probably more related to her mother's modeling of avoidance and repugnance toward sex. Mrs. C. also has behavioral deficits in directly expressing her anger and in securing reinforcing and pleasant experiences.

Mrs. C.'s anxiety is pervasive and generalized, perhaps because it is elicited by stimuli such as dirt that are always present to some extent in the environment. Mrs.

C. learned an excessive fear of dirt and disease early in life from her mother's modeled behavior and attribution to them of exaggerated dangers. As an adult, Mrs. C. was further conditioned to be anxious about dirt because of the excessive dangers that both she and her physician apparently attributed to pinworms.

Mrs. C.'s interpersonal relations are characterized by excessive control, especially control of her family in order to prevent a plague of pinworms. Mrs. C. probably also receives considerable reinforcement by being the sick center of attention within the family.

The problems evoked by pinworms and dirt can best be treated by systematic desensitization and cue exposure, which in tandem are considered the behavioral treatment of choice for obsessive-compulsive disorders such as Mrs. C.'s. Training in deep relaxation would be followed by hierarchies made up of stimuli related to dirt and pinworms. Part of a hierarchy would include, for example, imagining buying brand-new underwear wrapped in cellophane, followed by touching brand new underwear, then approaching freshly laundered underwear, and moving toward picking up underwear that are basically clean though worn. Mrs. C. would be able to actually approach stimuli such as dirty underwear only after the automatic and uncontrollable response of anxiety is no longer elicited because it has been counterconditioned by desensitization. Over time, Mrs. C. can be exposed to a broad range of cues that elicit anxiety and avoidance, such as clean underwear, dirty underwear, piles of laundry, dirty loads, and washing machines. During such exposure sessions, Mrs. C. would be prevented from making her avoidance responses—for instance, washing or showering.

In a similar manner, in vivo desensitization and skill training would be employed to counter her lack of sexual responding and avoidance of sex. We would begin with sensate focusing, followed by the progressive steps of sexual therapy. Both Mr. and Mrs. C. would be encouraged to enjoy the pleasures of sensual touching with no performance demands. They could discover that such relaxing, sensual, and nondemanding conditions can become cues for sensual and sexual sensations without eliciting anxiety and avoidance.

Mrs. C.'s obsessive thoughts of pinworms can best be overcome by using thought stopping and covert assertion techniques to reduce the frequency of such thoughts. The thought-stopping procedures could be made part of a larger self-control package that would include self-reinforcements for thinking more positive thoughts—sensual thoughts or thoughts of being with her family, for instance. Whenever she switched from pinworms to planning a party, for example, Mrs. C. would reinforce herself with self-statements such as, "That's great! I'll take parties over pinworms any day" or "Doesn't it feel good getting free from pinworms?" After years of insight therapy, we may have to help Mrs. C. attribute her problems to her learning history instead of to unconscious forces that are threatening to overwhelm her.

Modifying Mrs. C.'s interpersonal behaviors will involve the whole family, because they have unwittingly reinforced her tendencies to dominate the family's interactions. We could experiment with family assertiveness training to help them stand up to Mrs. C.'s unreasonable demands and also to help her express her frustrations more directly. It would be important, of course, to include complimentary assertions as part of the training, since this family seems to rely heavily on negative rather than positive means of mutual control.

It will also be critical to teach the family reinforcement principles in order to help them reward Mrs. C. for constructive behaviors, such as cooking and playing with the kids, and to help them extinguish her maladaptive behaviors. Since Mrs. C. has spent so much of her time washing, it will not be enough simply to reduce her washing through desensitization. She could be left with a rather empty day, which could increase her depression. Thus, both the therapist and the family need to begin prompting and reinforcing constructive alternate responses that can replace the washing. These responses could include working, playing, relaxing, caring, and reconstructing a reinforcing approach to family and friends.

Throughout the course of this comprehensive treatment, the behavior therapist would be a model of assertion, self-reinforcement, and risk-taking. Mrs. C. would learn vicariously from the therapist's own interpersonal behavior, such as talking about dirt and disease without anxiety and avoidance, encouraging sensual pleasuring without shame or guilt, and taking charge of situations through assertion rather than symptoms. The therapist would also explain and model that consistent reinforcement of small steps gradually results in big strides toward extinguishing maladaptive responses and learning rewarding alternatives.

If Mrs. C. can learn to calm herself in the presence of dirt, assert herself when angry, pleasure herself and her husband, use self-control with her pinworm preoccupation, and gain reinforcements from her family for caring rather than cleaning, then she will have a chance to return to modes of responding that have some semblance of sanity. As it now stands, without an intensive and extensive program of behavior modification, Mrs. C. is at high risk of being punished for her failures by being sent to the state hospital.

Future Directions

Paralleling its growth over the past three decades, behavior therapy will continue to experiment and expand in the near future. Experimentation is deliberately used here in a double meaning: behavior therapists will rely on experimental methodology to determine which techniques work best with which disorders, and behavioral self-identity will experiment with its proper boundaries. By operating in the empirical tradition, behavioral work will necessarily become technically eclectic—using what works with a particular client with a particular disorder (see Chapter 14). But this will push the other question of experimentation: how "cognitive" can a behaviorist become before being relegated to the mentalistic heap or the cognitive camp? Several traditional behaviorists, B. F. Skinner (1990), Joseph Wolpe (1989), and Leonard Krasner (1988) among them, argue that the introduction of cognitive concepts unnecessarily dilutes and weakens the field. Younger behaviorists, as a rule, are more comfortable with both the identity of cognitive-behaviorism and the practice of cognitive techniques. In an AABT presidential address, W. E. Craighead (1990) maintains that "there's a place for us; all of us," but not all agree with him on who should be sitting at the table marked "behavior therapists."

Behavior therapy will expand in numerous directions, but we foresee three of particular significance and permanence. First, a wave of the future lies in the integration of pharmacotherapy and cognitive-behavior therapy. Medication can help control acute symptoms and allow patients to benefit more from psychosocial treatment. Conversely, cognitive-behavior therapy can help enhance medication compliance, reduce dropout and relapse rates, and interact with the medication to produce more comprehensive and synergistic changes (Agras, 1987; Glass & Arnkoff, 1992).

Second, as health care costs continue to rise and as mental health professionals become increasingly involved in health care, behavioral self-help, relaxation training, coping skills training, and self-management programs will be further integrated into health care practice. Much of this work will be conducted with traditional "behavioral medicine" disorders, such as headaches, chronic pain, asthma, tobacco smoking, hypertension, and obesity. But we will also witness behaviorally inclined clinicians routinely identifying, treating, and preventing medical problems that arise from poor health habits, such as poor compliance, excess fat consumption, and inadequate physical activity. Behavior therapy will surely move beyond the treatment of psychiatric problems into all branches of health care, including pediatrics and cardiology. Not too far in the future, behavioral coping strategies may well be routinely taught to assist in recovery from illness, in coping with chronic disease and its treatment, and in preparing for noxious medical procedures (Glass & Arnkoff, 1992; Taylor, 1990).

Third, the historical and explicit focus on behavior change in behavior therapy will be complimented by recognition of the value of acceptance (Wilson, 1996). Having made realistically sound and psychologically adaptive lifestyle changes, patients will need to accept what can probably not be changed—in their body shape, in their partners, in their physiological arousal, and the like. Clients will be given active strategies for facilitating acceptance, such as education, an accepting therapeutic relationship, cognitive restructuring, and self-affirmation. This is not to say that behavior therapists will settle for less, but that they are becoming more aware of what can and should be changed (Goldfried & Davison, 1994).

In answering the question "Where is behavior therapy heading?" Wilson and Agras (1992) address theoretical and technical developments. They contend that it is both inevitable and desirable that behavior therapy will continue to reflect theoretical developments in experimental psychology. Just as the field's early conceptual foundations were broadened in the 1970s to include cognitive and social-psychological theory, so too will behavior therapy be influenced by research in other areas, such as emotion and neuroscience. The experimental analysis of emotion and its complex interaction with cognition and behavior, in particular, will characterize the future (Rachman, 1991). The explosion of new techniques that marked the early growth of behavior therapy has passed; instead, progress will probably focus on refining and improving existing treatment methods, developing operationally explicit treatment manuals for different clinical disorders, and improving the ways in which treatment methods can be disseminated more broadly and implemented more efficiently. After three decades of explosive growth, behavior therapy will consolidate its gains, experiment with its self-identity, and expand more slowly, as befits one of the premier systems of psychotherapy today.

Suggestions for Further Reading

Barlow, D. H., & Cerny, J. A. (1988). *Psychological treatment of panic*. New York: Guilford.

Goldfried, M., & Davison, G. (1994). *Clinical behavior therapy* (rev. ed.). New York: Wiley.

Hawton, K., Salkovskis, P. M., Kirk, J., & Clark, D. M. (Eds.). (1989). *Cognitive behaviour therapy for psychiatric problems: A practical guide*. New York: Oxford University Press.

Jacobson, N. S. (Ed.). (1987). *Psychotherapists in clinical practice: Cognitive and behavioral perspectives*. New York: Guilford.

Kanfer, F. H., & Goldstein, A. P. (Eds.). (1991). *Helping people change: A textbook of methods* (4th ed.). Boston: Allyn & Bacon.

Kazdin A. E. (1994). *Behavior modification in applied settings* (5th ed.). Pacific Grove, CA: Brooks/Cole.

Masters, W., & Johnson, V. (1970). *Human sexual inadequacy*. Boston: Little, Brown.

Meichenbaum, D. (1977). *Cognitive-behavior modification*. New York: Plenum.

O'Leary, K. D., & Wilson, G. T. (1987). *Behavior therapy: Application and outcome* (2nd ed.). Englewood Cliffs, NJ: Prentice-Hall.

Turner, S. M., Calhoun, K. S., & Adams, H. E. (Eds.). (1993). *Handbook of clinical behavior therapy* (2nd ed.). New York: Wiley.

Wolpe, J. (1990). *The practice of behavior therapy* (4th ed.). Elmsford, NY: Pergamon.

Journals: *Advances in Behaviour Research & Therapy; Applied Psychophysiology and Biofeedback; Behavior Modification; Behaviour Research and Therapy; Behavior Therapy; Behavioral Assessment; Behavioural Psychotherapy; Child and Family Behavior Therapy; Journal of Applied Behavior Analysis; Journal of Behavior Analysis and Therapy* (electronic journal); *Journal of Behavior Therapy and Experimental Psychiatry; Journal of the Experimental Analysis of Behavior*.

10

Cognitive Therapies

Albert Ellis

"I NEVER THOUGHT I would like myself again," wrote Ros to her therapist. "When I got into that deep pit of depression, I didn't think I could find my way out. Everywhere I turned I saw darkness and dislike. My hair wasn't right, my clothes weren't right, my voice was too high, my height was too low. Oh, God was it awful, I couldn't escape from this self I couldn't stand. I'm afraid I can understand why someone could kill themselves in such a state. Who said 'Hell is other people'? In that place Hell is yourself and there seems to be no escape. The future is downhill; the past I messed up.

"It's still hard to believe I talked myself into that dark dungeon. Everywhere I turned I saw negative stuff. The old wine bottle wasn't just half empty; to me there wasn't a drop left. It's amazing what your mind can do to you.

"I really appreciate how you helped me find my way through my mental maze. It became fun trying to discover what I was telling myself to keep me down. Yes, it was depressing to have been divorced, but I couldn't focus on positive facts of still having my friends, my children, my writing, and my future. In the future I was constructing in my mind, the sun was never going to shine again.

"Thanks for helping me to use my writing as homework to straighten out my thinking. Before I came to see you, my writing sounded like Sylvia Plath—all darkness and despair. It's not that there's not a dark side of life—it's just that if all I think about is the dark side, then life becomes empty rather than full.

"One of the most helpful things about the work we did together is that I learned how to correct my own maladaptive cognitions. I learned how to search and destroy the automatic self-statement that said I was bad; situations were bad; the future was bleak; my biology was breaking down. As a writer, I appreciate how powerful words can be, but I never knew how we can create our own novel in our heads and then cast ourselves as the tragic characters destined to self-destruct.

"Just wanted to let you know that the new novel I'm writing in my mind is so much happier. It's not that everything is perfect. I still don't like my hair but that will probably always be an obsession with me, and I still am searching for a man to make my life more meaningful. I know I should think more independently but that's how women of my generation were raised to think. So sometimes I would rather change my situation than my thoughts about my situation. But at least I don't let the situations drag me down.

"Off to see my daughter in San Diego. Hope all is well with you."

—Ros

A Sketch of Albert Ellis

Albert Ellis (1913–) has been enthusiastically presenting and defending his rational approach to therapy since 1957, when he first demonstrated his innovative system at the annual convention of the American Psychological Association. Before that time, he had practiced various forms of psychoanalytic treatment, which he had learned while earning his PhD in clinical psychology from Columbia. From the late 1940s to the early 1950s, Ellis became increasingly dissatisfied with the effectiveness and efficiency of both classical analysis and psychoanalytic psychotherapy. He believed Freud was correct that irrational forces keep neurotics troubled, but he was coming to believe that the irrational forces were not unconscious conflicts from early childhood. Ellis had seen too many patients with incredible insights into their childhood and their unconscious processes who continued to keep themselves troubled. That something that Ellis saw was a continual reindoctrination of themselves in an irrational philosophy of life.

Ellis found free association to be too passive and historically oriented to seriously challenge patients' contemporary ideas about themselves and the world. He began to attack the clients' belief systems directly and pushed clients to work actively against their own irrational premises. Ellis found himself well suited to this rational approach to therapy. With his quickness of mind, clear and concrete articulation of abstract ideas, love of intellectual debate, hardheaded faith in the power of rational discourse, and excellent sense of humor for dissipating irrational anger or anxiety, Ellis (1957b) was able to demonstrate significantly greater effectiveness with his new approach than with his older, psychoanalytic approaches.

In 1959, Ellis established the Institute for Rational-Emotive Therapy in New York City as a nonprofit organization to provide adult-education courses in rational living, moderate-cost rational-emotive therapy for patients, and intensive training in rational-emotive therapy for professionals. The clinic has upwards of 20 therapists at any one time, and the Institute regularly offers workshops and seminars throughout the country.

In his workshops, as in his therapy sessions, Ellis is a directive therapist who goes right to the heart of an issue without mincing his words because someone might get anxious or upset. That is the other person's problem. Ellis's problem is to convince people to use their rational processes to create a life that maximizes the pleasure and minimizes the pain of existence. He is fond of stating "The purpose of life is to have a fucking good time," but Ellis is a long-term hedonist, not an irrational, short-term hedonist who indulges every momentary desire at the expense of long-term suffering. So I (JOP) once asked him, "If the purpose of life is to have a fucking good time, why is it that you haven't taken a vacation in 15 years?" Believing that Ellis was caught in an irrational contradiction between his philosophy and his life, I was surprised at how quickly he responded, "What is wrong with me really enjoying my work? I never said we all have to have a good time in the same way." Watching Ellis in action reveals a person who finds great pleasure in his profession.

Although now in his 80s, Ellis carries 70 patients a week and has patients scheduled from 9 A.M. to 11 P.M. All this, in addition to running a workshop every other weekend and publishing more than 500 articles and 60 books. He is indeed a tireless advocate for a rational-emotive approach to psychotherapy and to life.

In fact, Ellis continues to revise and expand his brand of cognitive therapy to this day. At a 1993 institute-sponsored conference entitled "A Meeting of the Minds" (Kernberg, Ellis, Person, Burns, & Norcross, 1993), he announced that he was changing the name of rational-emotive therapy (RET) to rational-emotive behavior therapy (REBT). Because the original name is still widely known throughout the world and because it communicates the distinctive "cognitive" element, we will continue to use the older name in this chapter.

Theory of Personality

A rational explanation of personality is almost as easy as ABC (Ellis, 1973; 1991b). At point A are the *Activating Events* of life, such as rejection by a lover or failure to get into a graduate program. Point B represents the *Beliefs* that individuals use to process the Activating Events in their lives. These Beliefs can be rational (rB), such as believing that the rejection was unfortunate and regrettable or that the failure was annoying and unpleasant. The Beliefs can also be irrational (iB), such as thinking "It was awful that I was rejected," "My lover shouldn't have left me," "I will never be loved again," or "How terrible it is that I didn't get into graduate school; they have prevented me from ever being successful." At point C, the person experiences the emotional and behavioral *Consequences* of what has just occurred.

Most people and many therapists have traditionally assumed that the critical emotional Consequences of personality development are a function of the nature of the Activating Events to which an individual has been subjected. That is, A leads directly to C. The more benign the agents and activities have been in early life, the healthier the personality will be; the more aversive the Activating Events, the more emotionally troubled the person. In traditional behavioral language, this is the stimulus–response (S–R) theory of personality development, which assumes that particular stimulus conditions produce particular responses in the organism.

As a cognitive theory, rational-emotive therapy points to processes within the organism as the critical determinants of personality functioning. In an S–O–R model, the way the organism processes stimulus events is critical in determining what responses are produced. In rational-emotive theory, it is not the stimuli, or Activating Events, that are crucial but rather the person's perceptions and interpretations of the events. That is, B leads directly to C. So a person who processes a rejection or a failure through a rational Belief may feel the appropriate Consequences of sorrow, regret, annoyance, displeasure, and a determination to change whatever can be changed to prevent a recurrence of the unfortunate events. Another person confronting very similar events but processing the Activating Events through an irrational Belief system can produce such inappropriate Consequences as depression, hostility, anxiety, or a sense of futility and worthlessness. The point is that individuals make themselves emotionally healthy or emotionally upset by the way they think, not by the environment; the "in here," not the "out there," actually determines our feelings. As the Stoics held 2,500 years ago (Ellis, 1973), there are virtually no legitimate reasons for rational people to make themselves terribly upset, hysterical, or emotionally disturbed.

People can avoid emotional disturbances if they base their lives on their inherent tendencies to be logical and empirical. Look at the progress we have made in the physical and biological sciences by keeping our assumptions about the world natural rather than supernatural or mystical. Empiricism and logic should be used to test our assumptions and develop a more effective construction to the nature of reality. How much more effective our relationship to ourselves and to others could be if we would rely on reason as our guide for living. Certainly reason is not god-like, and its limitations can disturb us at times, but there is no better basis for minimizing emotional disorders than to use rationality to process the personal and interpersonal events of our lives.

As rational human beings, we recognize that the world is not always fair, that unfortunate events will occur in all of our lives to a lesser or greater extent. We will at times, then, experience such valid emotions as sorrow, regret, displeasure, and annoyance. Realistically, we know we are imperfect and will always have our failures and faults, but we will rebel at the irrational idea that anyone can ever treat us as worthless just because we are imperfect. Accepting our tendencies to put our self-interests first, we will nevertheless be determined to change unpleasant social conditions along more rational lines, because we recognize that in the long run it is in our own self-interest to live in a more rational world.

In a more rational world, we would accept our natural predispositions to be self-preserving and pleasure-producing. We would be less likely to engage in such self-defeating activities as the short-term hedonism of smoking or overreacting, which provide immediate gratification at the expense of lessening our aliveness. We would actualize more of our desires to be creative, to use language effectively, to be sensuous and sexual, to love and be loved (Ellis, 1973). We would not fall into the irrational trap, however, of thinking of these natural desires as dire necessities. Being respected and valued by others, for example, would make life happier, but we would not conclude therefore that we must be approved by others. The emotionally healthy person can live in the delicate balance between caring enough about others to be effectively related but not caring so much about others as to become a prisoner of their approval.

Theory of Psychopathology

Just as human beings have a natural propensity to be uniquely rational and straight-thinking, so too humans have an exceptionally potent propensity to be crooked-thinking creatures (Ellis, 1973). Individuals differ in their inherent tendencies toward irrationality, and so in their tendencies to be more or less irrationally disturbed. Societies and families within societies also differ in their tendencies to encourage straight or crooked thinking, although unfortunately most societies rear their children in a manner that exacerbates their strong propensities to disturb themselves. But even the best of inheritances and the best of socialization cannot remove our susceptibility to being self-defeating and self-destructive.

There are no gods among us. In spite of perfectionistic and grandiose wishes to be gods, any of us at any time can fall victim to propensities to procrastinate, to make the same mistakes over rather than think things through anew, to engage in wishful thinking rather than responsible action, to be dogmatic and intolerant rather than probabilistic and open, to rely on superstition and supernaturalism rather than logic and empiricism, and to indulge in greedy, short-range hedonism that mistakes immediate gratification for a pleasurable life. The only difference between those labeled pathological and those labeled normal is the frequency and intensity with which they emotionally upset themselves by relying on irrational components of personality.

The psychopathologies of everyday life can be explained by the ABC formula of human functioning. In emotional disturbances, Activating Events are always processed through some irrational Belief. The most common irrational Beliefs are: (1) that basic human desires, such as to be sensual and sexual, are needs because we define them as needs, even though they are in fact merely preferences; (2) that we cannot stand certain events, whether it be having to wait in line, facing criticism, or being rejected, when in fact we can stand such events no matter how unpleasant they may be; (3) that our worth as a person is determined by our successes and failures or by particular traits, such as intelligence, as if the worth of a human being can be rated like performance traits; (4) that we must maintain the approval of parents or authority figures, as if our existence is dependent on them; (5) that the world should treat us fairly, as if the world can conform to our wishes; (6) that certain people are wicked or villainous and should be punished for their villainy, as if we can rate the lack of worth of a human being; (7) that it is awful or terrible when things do not turn out the way we would like them to be, as if an idea like awful is a definable term with any empirical referents; (8) that we would fail to act if we did not think things were awful or if we were not emotionally upset by anger or anxiety, as if we need to be emotionally disturbed in order to take rational actions that would make the world a more pleasant place; (9) that harmful things such as cigarettes or drugs can add to happiness in life or that such harmful things are needed, just because going without them may be unpleasant for a while; (10) that human happiness is externally caused and that people have little or no ability to control their feelings; (11) that one's past history is the all-important determinant of present behavior, as if something that once strongly affected one's life must affect it indefinitely; and (12) that beliefs learned as a child, whether religious, moral, or political, can serve as adequate guides for adulthood, even though the beliefs may be pure prejudices or myths (Ellis, 1972). Later in the evolution of RET, Ellis (1991a; Ellis & Dryden, 1996) recognized the rigidity of these original 12 irrational beliefs and distinguished between dysfunctional inferences and the core dogmatic musts from which they are usually derived.

What is common to these irrational Beliefs is a demanding and absolute mode of thinking that is characteristic of young children. Translating desires into needs, for example, is a style of thinking that makes a want into a must, a wish into a command. Preferences can be denied, but needs demand gratification. Needs are also more absolute and are assumed to be true for all people in all places. That we must succeed, must have approval, must be treated fairly, and must smoke or drink are all forms of immature demands. That there are people who are absolutely bad, events that are absolutely awful, and religious or moral teachings that are absolutely true reflect an authoritarian mode of absolutism that leaves no room for quibbling. Such absolute beliefs have a demanding quality about them, as if they are commands from God and are not open to question.

The irrational Beliefs (iBs) and dysfunctional attitudes (DAs) that constitute people's self-disturbing philosophies, then, have two main qualities (Ellis, 1991a). First, they have at their core rigid, dogmatic, powerful demands, usually expressed in the words *must, should, ought to, have to,* and *got to.* This is *musturbatory* thinking: "I absolutely must have this important goal unblocked and fulfilled!" Second, the self-disturbing philosophies, usually as derivatives of these demands, generate highly unrealistic and overgeneralized attributions. This is the *catastro-*

phizing inference: "If I don't have my absolutely important goal unblocked and ful-filled, then it's awful, I can't bear it, I'm probably worthless, and I'll never get what I want!"

Processing current Activating Events through absolute Beliefs will inevitably produce inappropriate or dysfunctional Consequences. These irrational Beliefs can produce such excessive upsetting consequences as anger over having to wait in line, self-pity over an unfair world, depression over parental disapproval, hostility to-ward wicked people, guilt over breaking a rule from a dogmatic morality, or futility over changing one's life. Just because emotional upsets occur daily in the lives of millions of people is no reason to accept the irrational illusion that such emotional disturbances are in any way healthy or necessary. Does extreme anxiety over final exams, for example, add anything to the education or happiness of students? Are the fitful sleep, the constant worry, the sweaty palms and armpits, and the stomach distress appropriate to facing a final, or are these symptoms more appropriate to someone going to war? Is the insistence that one must do "A" work on every exam the voice of a rational adult or the thinking of a scared child afraid of losing the ap-proval of parents?

Not only are emotional upsets unhealthy and unnecessary, but such emotions frequently interfere with performance by draining energy from learning and by producing emotional noise in the cognitive system that can interfere with thinking. Many students believe that it would be better to not be so anxious about exams, but they blame their anxieties on external events such as the exam or a competitive society. They fail to examine their internal beliefs about their own worth, the prob-able consequences of doing poorly on one exam, or the possibility of parental dis-approval. Some students become enraged over grading and evaluation procedures. They insist that tests are unfair and that grades should be dropped. Until the educa-tional world adapts to their demands, they refuse to compromise, either flunking out or getting by with the minimum. Other students become anxious about their test anxiety. They know anxiety frequently meets with social disapproval, so they become more anxious that people will know how anxious they are. They may con-demn themselves for being so anxious over an exam and end up feeling worthless and depressed.

When anxiety leads to more anxiety or depression leads to more depression, the original, inappropriate Consequence itself becomes an Activating Event that is evaluated by further irrational Beliefs as being awful or terrible, and this produces further disturbing emotional Consequences. The vicious cycle of emotional distur-bance can continue as people condemn themselves for being emotionally upset, then condemn themselves for continuing the condemning, then condemn them-selves for seeking psychotherapy, then condemn themselves for not getting better, then conclude that they are hopelessly neurotic and that nothing can be done (Ellis, 1973).

Theory of Therapeutic Processes

As long as patients (and psychotherapists) continue to focus on either the Activat-ing Events or the disturbing Consequences, little in the way of lasting help can be found. Yet traditionally, all too many therapists have focused on historical Activating Events, going from point A1 to A2 to A3, further and further back in the patient's history, as if anything in the past can be changed. Or clinicians have focused on releasing the anxious and distressed feelings, as if such emotional Consequences will dissipate into thin air just because they have been expressed. Once the ABCs of psychopathology are properly understood, it becomes clear that the proper route to changing distressing Consequences is neither through examining As nor by ventilating Cs; rather, it lies in directly modifying irrational Bs.

In RET, the ABC model of human disturbance is followed by D—the *Disputing* of people's irrational Beliefs when they feel and act in a self-defeating way. This process leads them to E, an *Effective new philosophy*—a sound and rational set of preferential beliefs (Ellis, 1991a). Thus, the therapeutic process is to identify the irrational beliefs causing the presenting symptoms, to dispute them vigorously, and to replace them with more rational beliefs that constitute, as a whole, an effective new philosophy of life. Clients and therapists work together to raise the clients' level of consciousness from a childish, demanding, and absolute style of thinking to the logical, empirical, and probabilistic style of processing information that characterizes the mature adult and the responsible scientist.

Before venturing into the specific therapeutic processes of rational-emotive therapy, we should note that RET has two major forms: general, or inelegant, RET, which is practically synonymous with cognitive-behavior therapy; and specialized, or elegant, RET, which adheres more precisely to Ellis's formulations. Ellis (1987a) lists nine ways in which specialized RET differs from cognitive behavior therapy. RET, for example, always employs psychoeducational techniques, includes a humanistic outlook, and differentially stresses profound philosophical change in addition to symptom removal. Although we appreciate the many points of convergence between RET and cognitive-behavior therapies, the following sections pertain to specialized rational-emotive therapy.

Consciousness Raising

The Client's Work. Because much of the consciousness raising in rational-emotive therapy is an educational process, the work of clients frequently resembles that of students. In the process of explaining their problems, clients are very quickly challenged to defend the Beliefs that underlie their emotional upsets. They are challenged to give evidence, for example, for the Belief that they must be popular in order to be happy. Clients soon learn that their favorite Beliefs and biases are not accepted by the teacher/therapist just because the client presents the belief in an absolute or demanding way. "Show me where it is written that you must be a success in order to feel good about yourself" is a common challenge to the dogmatism of clients. Clients soon become aware that they have important irrational beliefs that they cannot defend logically or empirically. They become aware that they are indeed upsetting themselves emotionally by insisting on such nonsense as the belief that just because they were the king of their family as children, they must be king of their companies in order to be happy. Such foolishness is met with impatience in rational-emotive institutes. Like honest and humble students, clients have a lot to learn about this business of living, but at the same time they are encouraged to maintain the appropriate belief that they have the human potential to be as rational and as clearheaded as the teacher/therapist.

One hour a week in therapy, however, is more like the tutorials of the British universities. If patients are to progress with any efficiency, they will ideally complete the homework that is assigned to them. Homework frequently entails reading some well-reasoned books and listening to some logic-driven audiotapes, especially those produced by Ellis and his associates. Homework may also include listening to and criticizing tapes of their therapy sessions, so that clients can come to recognize their own absolute or demanding Beliefs. Clients work to become aware of making "should" or "must" statements when statements of preference or desire would be more accurate.

If clients say they cannot stand to be rejected by the opposite sex, they will be given behavioral assignments to ask three different people out on dates to test the hypothesis that they can indeed stand rejection. This and similar assignments are instrumental in providing evidence to refute irrational beliefs to which patients cling tenaciously despite the absence of proof. Through such homework assignments, clients become irrefutably aware that their irrational Beliefs are not grounded in fact.

As clients become more skilled at consciously catching their own slips into childish cognitions, they can take turns teaching others in rational-emotive groups and seminars. One client will be called upon to analyze the underlying Beliefs that another client is using to produce emotional upset, or to criticize a fellow client's conclusion that failure to get a date this week proves that the client is a worthless worm. As many graduate students have discovered when they begin to teach, there is no better way to learn.

The Therapist's Work. Because the propensity to engage in crooked thinking is so profound, the rational-emotive therapist is prepared to use a multitude of cognitive, emotive, and behavioral techniques to teach clients to distinguish between mature, logical-empirical thought and the trouble-making foolishness that frequently passes for reason. The methods are both structured and unstructured, didactic and interpersonal.

The therapist begins in the first session to interpret the irrational Beliefs that are producing the clients' emotional complaints. The active therapist does not wait for patients to articulate all of their irrational premises. Being educated in rational-emotive theory and experienced with a variety of clients, the therapist can anticipate the nature of the underlying Beliefs based on the Activating Events and inappropriate Consequences. For example, rejection by a spouse (point A) followed by an incapacitating depression (point C) most likely involves the following irrational Beliefs: (1) The rejection is awful, (2) the person can't stand it, (3) she should not be rejected, (4) she will never be accepted by any desirable partner, (5) she is a worthless worm because she was rejected, and (6) she deserves to be condemned for being so worthless (Ellis, 1973).

Therapists need not be obsessive about the timing of interpretations. When they are confident that they understand the nature of the underlying Beliefs, they should present the information to the client directly and forcefully. Rational-emotive therapists are under no illusions that one well-timed interpretation will produce lasting insights. Interpretations and confrontations will be made over and over until clients become undeniably aware of their irrationalities.

Interpretations do not involve making conscious connections between present upsets and past events, but rather between present complaints and current beliefs that clients are using to upset themselves. In the process of giving clients feedback about their specific irrational Beliefs, therapists also teach the ABCs of rational-emotive therapy. Therapists also provide explicit information about the nature of scientific reasoning and how it can be used to solve personal problems. Through books, tapes, seminars, and frequent mini-lectures in therapy, clients are taught the essentials of rational-emotive theory. Of course, as with any theory, students tend to understand and accept rational-emotive theory more when it is made relevant to the explanation and solution of their personal problems.

In addition to providing interpretations and confrontations, therapists also raise the consciousness of clients to a more mature, rational level through refutations. As effective debaters, therapists can point out inherent contradictions between the clients' Beliefs or between Beliefs and actions. For example, the therapist shows clients that they can stand to be criticized even though it is uncomfortable; they do not die or go crazy or run out of the room just because the therapist has criticized one of their demanding Beliefs. If clients are deathly afraid of any homosexual desires and insist that homosexuals are bad, the therapist may counter with objective information about homosexuals. More frequently, the therapist puts refutations in the form of the common questions "What evidence do you have . . . ?" or "Where is it written that you must . . . ?"

Believing in active learning, therapists direct their clients to complete various homework assignments designed either to provide evidence to refute irrational hypotheses or to enable them to practice more rational thinking. Writing a paper on more effective means of finding a job can help a patient practice a more rational consciousness. Encouraging patients to get a massage can begin to refute the belief that they are not sensuous or that they cannot enjoy pleasure without guilt. Assigning perfectionists to wear two different colored socks or wrinkled slacks can help them to blow their own images and, in the process, practice their new insight that life can be a pleasure without having to be perfect.

Rational-emotive therapists use a multitude of techniques to encourage clients to become more rational in their emotions and behavior. Humor is a comparatively safe method for helping clients become aware of some of their foolishness. In treating anxiety disorders, Ellis might assign a patient to sing one of his rational humorous songs, such as this one called "Perfect Rationality" (Ellis, 1991b) to the tune of "Funiculi, Funicula" by Luigi Denza:

Some think the world must have a right direction,
And so do I! And so do I!
Some think that, with the slightest imperfection,
They can't get by—and so do I!
For I, I have to prove I'm superhuman,

And better far than people are!
To show I have miraculous acumen—
And always rate among the Great!
Perfect, perfect rationality
Is, of course, the only thing for me!
How can I ever think of being
If I must live fallibly?
Rationality must be a perfect thing for me!

Self-disclosure of the therapist's foibles can keep clients from falling back into the wishful thinking that anyone, including the psychotherapist, can be godlike. Encouraging the direct expression of embarrassing emotions is done not for the sake of emoting, but as the first step in clients' becoming fully aware of the emotional Consequences of their irrational Beliefs. The rational-emotive therapist is in many ways eclectic in technique, while maintaining a consistent and comprehensive theory of personality, pathology, and psychotherapy.

Contingency Management

Recognizing no absolutes, including his own theory, Ellis relies on other psychotherapy systems when his own approach reaches its limits. As a cognitive-behaviorist, he is especially receptive to behavioral interventions. Ellis has even at times characterized himself as a behavior therapist with a strong cognitive orientation, and the recent name change to rational-emotive behavior therapy underscores this conviction. As we saw in the previous chapter on behavior therapy, as behavior therapists move toward the cognitive direction, they in turn frequently incorporate the principles of rational-emotive therapy.

The Client's Work. If the client is failing to follow through on homework assignments in spite of therapist interpretations or exhortations, the client may be asked to make a contingency contract that seems workable for the client. A Democrat-hater, for example, might be required to give the therapist $100 and sign a contract that states that for each week the client fails to go on a date, the therapist will send a $25 check from the client to the Democratic National Commitee.

The Therapist's Work. Rational-emotive therapists also attempt to reduce the effects of contingencies by having clients reevaluate particular consequences. "What is the worst thing that can happen to you if you take a risk?" the therapist asks frequently, and "Is that consequence really awful or catastrophic or is it just inconvenient or unpleasant?" Consequences such as being laughed at, being turned down for a date, and not getting an "A" on an exam can be "deawfulized," and thereby defused as controlling Consequences. The therapist can deawfulize Consequences by having the group laugh at the client's foolishness, or having a female client assert herself by trying to convince a male in the group to kiss her. The therapist has clients confront the very Consequences that seem terrible so that they can reevaluate the Consequences and no longer be controlled by them. Similarly, the therapist can assign the client to imagine an expected Consequence ten times a day, until the imagined outcome no longer elicits much emotion; again, this can reduce the probable effects of contingencies. Finally, contingency controls are changed by having the client continue to ask, "But what is the objective probability that what I expect will really happen?" With a reevaluation of the objective probabilities that a particular consequence will occur, the client becomes more able to take the risks required to produce more pleasure in life.

Counterconditioning

In the interest of completeness, we should also note rational-emotive therapy's frequent use of counterconditioning procedures in the behavioral tradition. These largely follow the principles and procedures outlined in Chapter 9. Engaging in the healthy behaviors counterconditions, or reciprocally inhibits, the unhealthy behaviors; the obvious example in RET is that embracing rational beliefs interferes with holding irrational beliefs. In addition, Ellis and his associates routinely use rational-emotive imagery, rational role playing, and in vivo desensitization (see Maultsby & Ellis, 1974; Ellis & Dryden, 1996).

Therapeutic Content

Intrapersonal Conflicts

Psychological problems are intrapersonal in origin: individuals produce emotional problems within themselves by processing events through irrational belief systems. Therapy usually begins, therefore, with individual sessions focusing on the client's demanding thinking rather than on the relationship between client and therapist. Once clients are more conscious of their inappropriate cognitions, they are frequently placed in groups, which serve as a microcosm of the larger world and in which clients can practice reacting to criticism, rejection, or pleasure in more rational ways. In the groups, clients can also practice new behaviors, such as assertion, that follow from more logical attitudes toward life, and can practice teaching others to be more rational. Quite independent of how much of the psychotherapy is conducted in a group format, however, the focus is not on the relationships between group members but on the rational quality of their thinking, emoting, and behaving.

Anxiety and Defenses. Anxiety is an inappropriate consequence of irrational cognitions. When we examine the myriad of events about which people make themselves anxious, we see how widespread are irrational cognitions. Parents become unduly upset about their children's sexuality. Homosexuals are believed to be horrible, and communities become threatened by having a homosexual teacher in the schools. People tell themselves they must be perfect, then become anxious when confronted by criticism; they tell themselves they should be liked by everyone, then get tense when someone is angry with them. Such anxieties cannot be extinguished by desensitizing a person to a particular stimulus, but rather by disputing the irrational thoughts that a person has about stimulus events.

Defense mechanisms are examples of human irrational propensities. Projection is a clear example of people thinking that emotional upset is caused by external events. Repression is a reflection of the irrational belief that it is best not to think about unpleasant events. Probably the most common defense, rationalization reflects people's desire to convince the world that they are in fact reasonable human beings who have good reasons for behaving or feeling foolishly. To rational-emotive therapists, defenses are not to be protected; they are to be attacked. Confrontations, interpretations, and refutations can weaken these irrational forces and allow patients to become more rational and emotionally healthy.

Self-Esteem. There is no way that we can prove our worth as human beings. To base our esteem on an ability to achieve, to love, to be approved, to be honest, or even to be rational is to say that the value of the whole person is defined by the value of only a part of what that person is. To rate our worth by totaling the value of all our separate traits and performances—such as school grades, tennis scores, and academic degrees—represents a futile, irrational desire for a global report card that indicates where we stand in relation to the rest of the universe. Any grand conclusion about our worth or lack of worth is a self-defined identification that declares us on the team of the deity or the devil.

Self-acceptance is the key to being a natural and logical member of our own team. There is no empirical referent for self-worth, no objective criterion in the universe that can measure our worth. In fact, preoccupation with proving our worth can be a major interference in enjoying life. Self-acceptance, in contrast, is a logical and justifiable state. If self-worth is based on performances such as grades, for example, we can cause our moods to rise and fall with the latest exam rather than enjoy our education to the fullest. But when we adopt self-acceptance, we experience no dramatic rise and fall. When we can finally accept ourselves, warts and all, we can give up the elusive search for self-esteem and free up energy for the meaningful question of how we can most enjoy our entire life.

Responsibility. Clients can be held truly responsible for their troubled lives only if they have been instrumental in creating their personal problems. They cannot be responsible for how others treated them in childhood; they can be responsible only for how they currently construe their childhood. They cannot be responsible for their genetic makeup; they can be responsible only for choosing to rely on their propensities for reason over their propensities to be unreasonable. Clients can insist that their parents or their genes determined all that they are and can even bolster their beliefs with a variety of psychological theories. But this insistence provides only fleeting relief, the relief that comes with shirking any weighty responsibility, including the responsibility for creating a better life.

Accepting responsibility for one's own problems does not involve blaming oneself. Blame is just another expression of the tyranny of the should: "You shouldn't have been so foolish; you shouldn't have been so demanding." The fact is, patient, you have been foolish, demanding, and dogmatic, and you continue to be so as long as you engage in the irrational guilt that comes with blaming yourself and insisting that you should have been different in the past. The question is, "Are you willing to be mature and responsible enough right now to use your reason to find better alternatives for living? Or will you wallow in the guilt of self-blame or the resentment of parent-bashing? Feel regret and sadness if you will, but even more feel the excitement that can come with accepting the responsibility for a more reasonable and pleasurable life."

Interpersonal Conflicts

Intimacy and Sexuality. Surely love and intimacy can add to the good life. Not being islands, nearly all individuals find it enjoyable to love and be loved by significant others. It is reasonable to want to be able to relate well in interpersonal encounters. In fact, the evidence suggests that the better their interpersonal relationships, the happier people are likely to be. That is not to say, however, that love and intimacy are necessary for human existence. As soon as we define love as an absolute necessity, we become anxious, demanding, or dependent lovers. If we must have love, we become prone to try to possess those who provide essential nourishment, jealous if they turn their love toward others, and threatened that someone will come along and take away the love we cannot live without. The clinging-vine wife, the jealous husband, the possessive partner, and the insecure spouse are examples of people defining love as a necessity. In spite of popular religious beliefs, we need not deify love in order to appreciate it. Love is a human phenomenon that adds to the pleasure and joy of living, not an absolute that can justify our existence or sanctify ourselves.

Sex also requires no sanctification. Sex is not some dirty desire that can be justified only by procreation, marriage, or love. As an outspoken advocate of *Sex Without Guilt* (1958), Ellis was a rare rational voice for sexual freedom well before the sexual revolution began rolling in the 1960s. Recognizing that sex may be more enjoyable for many people when it occurs within an intimate relationship, it is still reasonable to ask, "Where is the evidence that sex and love must go together?" To insist that sex needs love to be good is apparently a human teaching that is really a moral wolf in sheep's clothing, a form of the old repressive morality that demands that sex be justified by some higher value than the purely intrinsic pleasure it produces. Sex can be just for fun. Sex can be the clearest expression of the natural propensity of people to be pleasure-producing. To be free to enjoy this profound pleasure is to ignore the irrational prohibitions of an antisexual society or the equally irrational demands of an achievement-oriented society that would judge the worth of individuals by the number of orgasms they achieve or the number of partners they have. Sex without guilt and without anxiety comes to those who are rational enough to express their natural sexual desires without concern for parental or performance demands.

Communication. Most of what are labeled communication problems are, in fact, thinking problems. People who communicate vague, boring, bizarre, repetitive, or contradictory messages are actually revealing the vague, boring, bizarre, repetitive, or contradictory character of their cognitions. Effective dialogue is rare because people who can think effectively are rare. If people are helped to become more rational in their style of thinking, they will generally also become more effective in their style of communicating. There are exceptions to this rule, of course, but they are relatively rare.

Many stutterers, to take one example, may think straight but have such desires to be perfect speakers that they are horrified at making the normal disfluencies of everyday speech. They cannot accept the hesitations, the "you knows," "ohs," and "ahs" of us mortal mouths. They end up self-consciously selecting the words over which they are least likely to stumble. As a result, they stop and stammer, recycle their sentences, and do a number of other things that result in even more disastrous disfluencies. They have to quit making demands on themselves to be ultrafluent and just start stumbling along like the rest of us.

Hostility. Hostility is the irrational consequence of (1) an inborn, biological tendency to become aggressive; (2) some unpleasant or frustrating event; and (3) a tendency to think crookedly about the event and a persistent refusal to work against this crooked tendency (Ellis, 1973). All three of these variables must be present for hostility to occur. Human beings are not just reflexive animals that react to frustration with aggression; otherwise, most of us would be hostile most of the time. Frustrating events are almost always available to us, because the world we live in obviously is a frequently depriving, restraining, unfair place. In order for us to erupt into rage, we have to focus on the frustrations around us; exaggerate the meanings of these events into something awful, horrendous, or villainous; and insist that such frustrations should not exist and that we can no longer stand their existence.

The hostile person demands the removal of all injustices, unfairness, and frustrations immediately. With such impossible demands, hostile persons upset themselves unnecessarily. They are like children throwing temper tantrums because their demands are not being met immediately. There is no law that says hostile people must continue with such unrealistic, immature demands. Because we cannot remove inborn tendencies to become aggressive or prevent all frustrations from occurring, our best alternative is to assist hostile people in construing frustrations as unfortunate and inevitable events, not major catastrophes they cannot tolerate.

Control. A need to control others is merely one expression of the irrational demand that the world conform to one's wishes. Tactics for gaining compliance from others include imposing the "tyranny of the should" on them and then trying to make them feel guilty if they do not act as we believe they should. This is a favorite tactic of parents, as they insist that their children should be polite, not talk back to them, be successful, and above all never disgrace the family name. Threatening to follow demands with anger is a less subtle controlling technique that works especially well with people who believe it is terrible to have someone angry at them.

Most controls work only if the people being controlled cooperate by allowing their irrational beliefs to respond: "You're right, I should feel guilty for not being polite." If the person responds rationally—"Don't make guilt; I have enough trouble disputing my own internal tyrannical shoulds without having to fight yours as well"—then the person attempting to control has his or her subtle irrational communications exposed by the light of clear thinking. The most effective counter-control method is to dispute the irrational demands of others by asserting one's own rationality.

Individuo-Social Conflicts

Adjustment Versus Transcendence. People who believe that they can in any real way transcend the restraints, injustices, and frustrations of society will inevitably make themselves emotionally upset. Fighting the inevitable is one of the foolish ways of creating hypertension, ulcers, anxiety, anger, or depression. The fantasy to fly like Icarus far above the world represents the grandiose beliefs of irrational people that they can somehow be more than mere mortals. Like Icarus, superhuman people eventually fall on their foolish faces.

Before we take on irrational forces in society, we had better first fight the irrational forces in ourselves. We have to first get our own heads on straight before we worry about setting straight the heads of state. To replace one set of irrational beliefs with demands that are equally irrational may be the history of much of the world, but it certainly is not progress. If we are to make significant strides toward making our communities more pleasant places to live, we will require a substantial number of people who are committed to solving social problems through logical and empirical methods rather than through the tired, old dogmatic demands that society must be more just and decent.

Impulse Control. Human beings are unique creatures who can make almost any desire into a seemingly uncontrollable impulse. The common desire to gain large sums of money without working can lead to a "need" to gamble. The desire for tasty foods can become an "irresistible impulse" to eat excessively, even though overeaters know obesity can be the consequence. Impulses to steal, smoke, or exhibit one's genitals are just some of the many ways that people can turn desires into self-destructive demands. Such short-term hedonists ignore the realistic long-term consequences of their actions by insisting "I should be able to eat all I want and not gain weight"; "I should be able to gamble against the odds and be a winner"; "I should be able to take what I want and not be punished." In reacting to such demands, most forces in society, including many systems of psychotherapy, foolishly attack the impulsive behavior rather than the stinking thinking that creates impulse-ridden characters.

Society can also define certain human desires as uncontrollable impulses and then use social forces to overcontrol individuals. Sex is a prime example. Western society has traditionally defined human sexuality as an uncontrollable, irrational impulse that must be repressed lest people become possessed by a demon that brings disease, unwanted pregnancies, and indecency. In fact, the irrational forces are the antisexual voices in society that have succeeded in suppressing the open dissemination of sex information, the free availability of birth control devices, and full access to humane health care that treats venereal infections like any other disease transmitted by people in close contact, not as a social disease or disgrace. That there are people who express their sexuality in irresponsible ways is not surprising in a society that has been so irresponsible in helping children to understand their sexuality as a natural desire that can be enjoyed fully within the context of a rational life. If we want to create a less impulsive and more human world, then the one impulse we want to attack is the tendency to engage in irrational thinking, whether that tendency occurs on an individual or a social level.

Beyond Conflict to Fulfillment

Meaning. If we are searching for some absolute meaning to life, we are bound to be disappointed. There are no absolutes except those we create. If by meaning we seek a belief that can justify our existence, forget it. The universe does not care that we exist; we do. If by meaning, however, we are looking for that which makes life more enjoyable, then we may be able to agree that it is best to maximize our pleasures and minimize our pains, since by definition pleasure is what we enjoy. The particular pleasure that we seek is an individual matter discovered by each person in the process of living. The important thing is that our pleasures come from desires, not demands. There surely is more joy in doing what we want to do rather than what we must do.

The rational person does not expect life to be a rose garden. The rational person knows that there are irritating thorns in each person's life but refuses to transform them into deathly ailments. In other words, mole hills remain mole hills— don't make unpleasant events any more unpleasant than they already are.

Meaning is, at bottom, a value system. Thus, effective therapists would do well to have a good philosophy of life. Psychotherapists should be prepared to discuss deeply philosophic questions with patients, if they expect to get very far. As Ellis has repeatedly noted, many popular therapies mainly seek to help patients *feel* better (minimize their presenting symptoms) rather than *get* better. Getting better involves making a profound philosophical change, which is intimately tied to examining, clarifying, and perhaps replacing values.

Questions of values may masquerade as purely practical questions of how to become less anxious or depressed. But as London (1964, 1986) has shown, behind such clinical requests are value judgments that it is better to be less anxious or depressed. There are those who believe that the best life requires suffering and deprivation. A therapist with such values might try to convince clients to cherish their depression rather than to extinguish it. Clients are looking for a better life, in which they are free from current symptoms and powerful enough to remove new symptoms, and effective therapists are prepared to present at least one alternative that has worked well for themselves.

Ideal Individual. The scientist is an excellent ideal for humanity because scientists are committed to the rational life, a life of applying logic and empiricism to solving problems. As Bronowski (1959) so elegantly argues, honesty and open communication are values inherent in science. True scientists welcome rational criticism of ideas and methods; they do not believe it is catastrophic if their favorite theories are eventually rejected for more elegant or effective explanations.

Scientists are fascinated, not frustrated, by what is inevitable. They recognize their own limits and do not expect that science can answer all the philosophical questions of life. At their best, scientists are hedonists who immensely enjoy their research into the unknown rather than puritans driven by demands that they must succeed. What other group of human beings can point to such accomplishments as a vaccine against the crippling of polio or the wonder of a man on the moon? The revolutionary discoveries of science are evidence for the value of a philosophy based on logic and empiricism.

Therapeutic Relationship

Practically the polar opposite of person-centered therapy, rational-emotive therapy concurs only with the Rogerian idea that the therapist demonstrates unconditional acceptance of clients, even while attacking many of the clients' irrational beliefs and self-destructive behaviors. Even when patients do not complete homework or come late for sessions, the RET clinician provides unconditional support of them as people. However, full acceptance of the client as a human does not mean that the therapist must demonstrate warmth or liking toward the client. Such warmth may feel good, but it is not necessary for successful treatment. Therapists try never to evaluate the client as a person, but they do evaluate the client's beliefs and behaviors.

Rational-emotive therapists are not particularly sympathetic with patient weeping or anger, but use such visible indications of upset to try to prove to patients the irrationality of their beliefs. Nor is accurate empathy with emotions particularly helpful; such empathy is frequently a form of commiseration that only encourages the person to continue feeling bad, sad, or upset. Rational therapists are quite empathic in the sense of listening closely in order to understand what clients are probably telling themselves to produce their upsetting emotions. Clients report feeling understood, not because the therapist is emoting with them, but because the therapist is bringing into awareness the cause of the client's problems.

Rational-emotive therapists are frequently genuine and open, directly revealing their own ideas, beliefs, and philosophy of life. They are also more willing than most to reveal some of their own foibles in order to dispute the client's belief that anyone, even a therapist, can be more than human. Transference feelings are challenged, not encouraged, because these represent yet more examples of clients' trying to demand that the world be something other than what it is.

A combination philosopher/teacher/scientist, the rational-emotive therapist views the therapeutic relationship primarily as a precondition for effective education. As long as the client remains willing to relate, the therapist can use hardheaded reasoning to teach the client how to actively dispute the irrational beliefs that are the root of emotional problems.

The vigorous challenging of the patients' irrational ideas (but not the patients themselves) has led some observers to take issue with Ellis's hard-line, directive approach. They advocate gentler models of cognitive disputation. Ellis (1987b) concedes the point but continues to believe that a forceful, debating style is often necessary, especially with resistant clients.

Beck's Cognitive Therapy

A Sketch of Aaron Beck. Like Albert Ellis, Aaron T. Beck (1921–) came to pioneer cognitive therapy from psychoanalytic origins. Trained as an undergraduate at Brown University and then as a medical student at Yale University, Beck was dissuaded initially from psychiatry because of the esoteric nature of psychoanalysis. He opted for neurology, but during his rotations, became intrigued by the dynamic psychiatrists and eventually moved to the Austen Riggs Center at Stockbridge, where he underwent a personal analysis and became enamored with cognition, derived from ego psychology then in vogue.

Convinced that psychoanalysis offered important insights into mental disorders, Beck undertook research to validate psychoanalytic hypotheses. However, his findings from experimental work on dreams and ideational material led him to discard most psychoanalytic notions. As good scientists do, Beck literally and figuratively followed the evidence away from psychoanalysis to formulate a cognitive theory and therapy for psychiatric disorders. Working simultaneously but independently from Ellis, he discovered that, by teaching patients to examine and test their negative ideas, their depression began to improve.

Over the past 35 years, Beck has created a system of psychotherapy known simply as *cognitive therapy* that has attracted enormous attention and that has prompted extensive research efforts. In order to implement his research, Beck developed a number of widely used instruments, including the Beck Depression Inventory, the Beck Anxiety Inventory, and the Scale for Suicide Ideation. His inital research and clinical focus was depression, spawning the classic *Cognitive Therapy of Depression* (Beck, Rush, Shaw, & Emery, 1980), but has broadened to anxiety disorders (Beck et al., 1985), substance abuse (Beck et al., 1993) , and personality disorders (Beck & Freeman, 1990). Acknowledging the salience of interpersonal as well as cognitive factors in emotional health, he wrote *Love Is Never Enough* (Beck, 1988), a mass-market book applying cognitive therapy to marriage and marital therapy.

Now into semi-retirement and over 45 years into his own marraige, Beck is University Professor Emeritus of Psychiatry at the University of Pennylvania and president of the Beck Center for Cognitive Therapy and Research in Bala Cynwyd, Pennsylvania. At the Center, he continues to teach and write, sometimes with the two of his four children who are psychologists. Known for his wisdom, warmth, and signature red bow tie, Aaron "Tim" Beck continues his prolific contributions to cognitive therapy.

Commonalities with RET. Although Beck developed his cognitive therapy independently from Ellis, there are numerous striking similarities in their approaches. First, both Beck and Ellis were originally trained in the psychoanalytic tradition and emigrated to a more contemporary-oriented, cognitive-focused psychotherapy as they became dissatisfied with the clinical theory and results of psychoanalysis. Second, Beck and Ellis share the goal of helping clients to become conscious of maladaptive cognitions, to recognize the disruptive impact of such cognitions, and to replace them with more appropriate and adaptive thought patterns. Third, both are rather eclectic in technique selection and empirical in theory revision, as is typical of cognitive-behaviorists in general. Fourth, both forms of cognitive therapy are problem-oriented, directive, and psychoeducational. And fifth, both Beckian cognitive therapy and Ellis's rational-emotive therapy view homework as a central and indispensable feature of treatment.

Theory of Psychopathology. Their respective theories of psychopathology converge in most important respects, although the vocabulary differs. In place of Ellis's irrational beliefs, Beck is more inclined to speak of maladaptive cognitions, dysfunctional attitudes, or in the case of his early research on depression, *depressogenic assumptions*. In their benchmark *Cognitive Therapy of Depression*, Beck and associates (1979) identify a number of common cognitive errors that cause depressed feelings. Several of these are presented in Table 10.1; note the tremendous overlap with the RET list of irrational beliefs.

Let us consider the case of one of our patients, a middle-aged small business owner, who consulted us for depression following the collapse of his business. His dysphoric feelings betrayed the entire litany of these depressogenic assumptions. "I'll never be able to run a successful company" (overgeneralizing). "All I can think about is this business failure. What else is there to my life?" (selective abstraction). "It's all my fault. I should have worked harder, not taken those two weeks of vacation last year, never purchased that expensive computer" (excessive responsibility). "All our neighbors and friends know I screwed up, and they're laughing at me behind my back" (self-references). And "It's all hopeless; there is nothing salvageable from the business" (dichotomous thinking).

Psychopathology originates in the client's preconscious or preattentive constructions of reality. These constructions reflect the operation of the client's cognitive organization, called *schemas*, in interaction with the current environment. As in RET, life events are interpreted through cognitive lenses or structures, which then lead to distressing thoughts and disturbing behaviors.

In cognitive therapy, the underlying cognitions are assumed to vary specifically with the behavioral disorder of clients, an idea known as *content specificity*. Different pathologies are related to different cognitive content. A paranoid personality, for example, holds core beliefs that motives are suspect, that one must look for hidden motives, and that trusting others is dangerous. The resultant behaviors are to accuse, counterattack, and be wary. The histrionic personality, by contrast, adheres to core beliefs that people are there to serve or admire me and that I can get by on my feelings. Their distinctive behaviors are to use dramatics, charm, temper tantrums, and crying. Each disorder, then, has a specific cognitive content.

Depression is related to a different pattern of ideas than is paranoia, hysteria, phobias, or obsessive-compulsive disorders. The basic ideation in depression has three themes, which Beck (1970) terms the *cognitive triad*: (1) Events are inter-

Table 10.1 Several Depressogenic Assumptions

Cognitive Error	Assumption
Overgeneralizing	If it's true in one situation, it applies to any situation that is even remotely similar.
Selective abstraction	The only events that matter are the failures, which are the sole measure of myself.
Excessive responsibility	I am responsible for all bad things, rotten events, and life failures.
Self-references	I am at the center of everyone's attention, particularly when I fail at something.
Dichotomous thinking	Everything is either one extreme or another (black or white, good or bad).

preted negatively. (2) Depressed individuals dislike themselves. (3) The future is appraised negatively.

These fundamental ideas are referred to by Beck as "rules." In contrast to Ellis, he does not view them as necessarily irrational. Instead, they are characterized as too absolute, too broad or extreme, or too arbitrary. Basic rules give rise to maladaptive self-verbalizations, or possibly visual images, which are experienced as automatic thoughts by clients. Much of therapy involves assisting clients in ferreting out *automatic thinking* and, ultimately, the basic rules and reevaluating those rules by testing them both logically and empirically.

Theory of Therapeutic Processes. In general, Beck (1976, p. 217) posits that the successful client passes through several stages in correcting faulty cognitions:

> First he has to become aware of what he is thinking. Second, he needs to recognize what thoughts are awry. Then he has to substitute accurate for inaccurate judgments. Finally, he needs feedback to inform him whether his changes are correct.

Although this sounds like a quote from Ellis, there are subtle but important differences between Beck's cognitive therapy and rational-emotive therapy.

Beck himself has delineated several of the salient differences between these two premier cognitive systems (Beck, 1976; Hollon & Beck, 1994). For one, Beck's therapy tends to emphasize the process of empiricism to a greater extent than does Ellis's RET; clients in cognitive therapy are encouraged to treat their beliefs as hypotheses to be tested by way of their own behavioral experiments. Whereas Ellis strives for a philosophical conversion based on rationality and logic, Beck encourages a reliance on the evidence to alter existing beliefs. For another, cognitive therapy tends to be more structured and precise than rational-emotive therapy. With depression, for example, Beck generally limits therapy to 20 hours. He adheres to treatment manuals specific to each disorder—depression (Beck et al., 1979), anxiety (Beck et al., 1985), and substance abuse (Beck, et al., 1993), among others. The cognitive therapist would also routinely administer brief symptom checklists, including the Beck Depression Inventory and the Beck Anxiety Inventory, before sessions to monitor the condition and progress of the patient. This structure encourages a problem orientation, discourages wasting time, and provides the client with a therapeutic rationale and direction.

Beck also distinguishes between therapeutic strategies designed to eliminate overt symptoms and those directed toward changing cognitions. As a leading authority on depressive disorders, Beck recognizes the need to sequence treatment goals. The first priority is to reduce severe symptoms such as suicidal impulses, insomnia, and weight loss. For symptom relief, Beck relies more on contingency management, structuring assignments in such a way that clients will succeed and be reinforced for their efforts. The first assignment might be simply to boil an egg. As the client begins to feel better, a more challenging assignment is given that can bring greater reinforcement, such as cooking a meal for the family. Interventions introduced early in therapy often include *activity scheduling*, in which specific daily activities are selected and evaluated strictly on the basis of how effectively they elevate mood. These activities are also rated by clients in terms of mastery and pleasure. Depressed clients who characteristically report that they can master nothing and enjoy nothing are thus confronted with feedback to the contrary. After symptoms begin to lift, then the focus of treatment shifts to underlying cognitions.

A key objective is to teach patients the method of *distancing*. They learn to deal with upsetting thoughts objectively, reevaluating them rather than automatically accepting them. Our depressed businessman was asked to examine the faulty logic behind his overgeneralization and to establish criteria for "similarity" to all other situations. When gently coaxed to do so, he rapidly realized that this was his first failure in a career of owning three successful enterprises. Likewise, clients are taught the *disattribution technique,* in which they disabuse themselves of the belief that they are entirely responsible for their plight. When asked not to automatically attribute all bad events to himself and to share the responsibility, our businessman quickly realized that the poor national economy, two new competitors in town, and production delays at one of his suppliers all certainly contributed to the demise of his business.

Three basic approaches to *cognitive restructuring*—modifying the thinking process—are to ask, in various ways, (1) What's the evidence? (2) What's another way of looking at it? (3) So what if it happens? Applied to the depressed businessman: Where is the evidence that you will never succeed again, that you were the only one responsible for the failure, that your neighbors are laughing at you? What's another way of looking at this event, this time in your life, this opportunity during a crisis? Using the *as-if technique,* the client is encouraged to think of himself *as if* he were rebuilding his business and becoming financially successful again. The as-if technique allows patients to restructure their cognitions in more positive directions, preparing them for more positive actions.

By becoming conscious of depressogenic assumptions and dysfunctional cognitions and by reevaluating these rules for living, clients begin to free themselves from debilitating expectations that they are doomed to depression and other forms of pathology. In the case of panic attacks, for instance, patients are taught to identify and modify their misinterpretations of bodily sensations. This entails a broad range of cognitive and behavioral interventions. Among the cognitive approaches are questioning patients' evidence for their misinterpretations, substituting more realistic interpretations, and restructuring their images. The behavioral procedures include inducing feared sensations (for example, hyperventilating or focusing attention on the body) in order to demonstrate the true cause of the panic attack, stopping safety behaviors (such as holding onto solid objects when dizzy), and practicing exposure to feared situations in order to allow patients to disconfirm their negative predictions about the consequences of their symptoms (Clark & Ehlers, 1993).

Therapeutic Relationship. In contrast to Ellis's direct confrontational style, Beck primarily uses a Socratic dialogue. Clients are led to make personal discoveries by a tactful progression of questions. This approach is described as *collaborative empiricism*: the participants are on a shared mission to determine from the evidence they gather which thoughts may be dysfunctional and which avenues they might pursue to enhance those thoughts. Therapeutic interactions are structured so that clients discover for themselves those thoughts that are inaccurate. A woman who thinks men will reject her if she expresses her positive feelings toward the feminist movement, for example, might be encouraged to test this hypothesis on her next date. Homework assignments are, for the most part, mutual decisions in which the patient is asked for ideas to test out the logic or to gather evidence.

The ideal type of therapist support will engender responsible dependency in a patient. The skilled cognitive therapist concurrently maintains the expert role in directing the course of treatment and yet insists that the patient be an active partner with commensurate responsibility for the implementation and ultimate success of the treatment. This dual stance is possible because it is the therapist who understands the general principles of cognitive therapy, but it is the patient who rapidly becomes the expert on how the application of the principles impacts his or her own functioning (Alford & Beck, in press). In this way, the cognitive therapist provides both support and direction.

Practicalities of Cognitive Therapies

As a no-nonsense approach in which active intervention begins in the opening intake interview, rational-emotive therapy is designed to be a short-term therapy that can teach the ABCs of emotional problems in one to ten sessions with most mildly to moderately disturbed patients. Once patients have the basic ABCs down, they are often placed in group therapy to further refine and practice the rational philosophy of living that they are applying to their problems (Ellis, 1992). Although rational-emotive therapy can be effective with a wide range of clinical problems, Ellis concedes that, as with almost all therapies, RET is most effective in treating mildly disturbed individuals or those with a single major symptom. Patients with greater inborn tendencies toward irrational thinking, such as borderline or psychotic individuals, can be helped, but therapy is longer-term, running at least a year.

Distinctive features of RET are the widespread use of bibliotherapy and public workshops. Ellis has been an extraordinarily prolific author, writing more than 60 books on a multitude of topics, and almost all clients are expected to read one or more of these books relevant to their presenting complaints. He has also probably been the most prolific workshop conductor in the history of psychotherapy, giving literally thousands of addresses, seminars, and workshops throughout the world. A unique feature of The Albert Ellis Institute in New York City is its almost-free ($5 a person) weekly meetings on Friday evenings that are open to present, past, or prospective clients or to people just interested in gaining some firsthand knowledge of rational-emotive therapy.

In form, the cognitive therapies are like most other therapies, with one-hour weekly individual sessions or two-hour group sessions as the norm. At the institutes, attempts are made to keep fees moderate, but in regular private practice, fees seem to follow the going rates in the community.

Both forms of cognitive therapy have been applied to clientele of various ages and disorders. As shown below in the section on effectiveness, cognitive and cognitive- behavioral therapies have proven successful with children, adolescents, adults, and older adults. In addition to the common neurotic disorders, Beck's cognitive therapy has been used to effectively treat bipolar disorders (Basco & Rush, 1996; Stuart & Bowers, 1995), psychotic disorders (Alford & Correia, 1994), paranoid disorders (Chadwick, Birchwood, & Trower, 1996), and borderline personality disorders (Layden, Newman, Freeman, & Morse, 1993). Both cognitive treatments are amenable to combination with psychotropic medication as indicated, and Beck was an early research pioneer in testing their separate and combined effects. RET and cognitive therapy have been applied to couples, to families, to sex therapy, to organizations, and to other complex systems (see Ellis & Dryden, 1996; Ellis, Sichel, Yeager, DiMattia, & DiGiuseppe, 1989; Epstein, Schlesinger, & Dryden, 1988; Freeman, 1983).

Training is widely available from Ellis's Institute of Rational-Emotive Therapy in New York City and Beck's Center for Cognitive Therapy and Research outside Philadelphia. Both facilities offer traineeships, postdoctoral fellowships, and continuing education opportunities, the latter offered regularly throughout the United States. Training is available to mental health professionals with terminal degrees in all disciplines; Beck's approach probably garners more attention in the psychiatric community and Ellis's in the psychological community given their respective disciplines. These cognitive therapies have now established themselves throughout the world; RET, for example, currently has eleven affiliated training institutes in the United States and another nine overseas.

Brief Cognitive Therapies

Cognitive therapies are generally short-term approaches due to their active, directive, and structured nature. Problems are diagnosed, goals are identified, principles of the cognitive model are taught, and homework experiments are designed in short order. Audiotapes, books, and handouts supplement the formal sessions. Manuals for Beck's cognitive therapy prescribe 12 or 16 sessions, spaced further apart as the patient recovers. Ellis's Rational Emotive Therapy—or its newest version, Rational Emotive Behavior Therapy—offers not only quick change but also "better, deeper, and more enduring" change in one to 20 session (Ellis, 1995).

Effectiveness of Cognitive Therapies

Rational-Emotive Therapy

The first outcome research was conducted by Ellis (1957b), who took closed case files and compared his own success using psychoanalysis, psychoanalytic psychotherapy, and rational-emotive therapy. He selected 16 cases from psychoanalysis, 78 from psychoanalytic psychotherapy, and 78 using rational-emotive therapy. His results were as follows:

Method	Considerable Improvement	Distinct Improvement	Little or No Improvement
Psychoanalysis	13%	37%	50%
Psychoanalytic psychotherapy	18%	45%	37%
Rational-emotive therapy	44%	46%	10%

Although Ellis concludes that these results demonstrate the superiority of RET over psychoanalysis, all he has shown is that he was more effective later in his career with his own psychotherapy than he was at the beginning of his career with Freudian analysis. Further, his study does not include a no-treatment control group, nor were the treatments administered at the same time or for the same length of time. His early work is more accurately seen as a comparative survey report in which he was the sole judge of outcome.

In the classic Smith, Glass, and Miller meta-analysis (1980) of 475 studies involving 25,000 patients, rational-emotive therapy produced an average effect size of .68 and cognitive-behavioral therapy a 1.13 effect size. This means that the average patient who receives RET is better off at the end of it than 75% of the persons who do not have treatment, whereas the average patient receiving cognitive-behavioral therapy is better off than 87% of those without treatment.

Between 1972 and 1988, at least 70 outcome studies have examined the effectiveness of rational-emotive therapy with various disorders and populations. Lyons and Woods (1991) conducted a meta-analysis on these studies, resulting in a total of 236 comparisons of RET to baseline, control groups, behavior therapy, and other forms of psychotherapy. The overall effect size for RET was .95, which translates into 73% of the treated patients demonstrating significant clinical improvement over those not receiving RET. This figure indicates that RET consistently outperforms control groups and no treatment. No general differences in outcome were found among behavior therapy, cognitive-behavior modification, and rational-emotive therapy. Effect sizes were highest when the therapists were experienced and when the treatment was lengthier, but there were no significant differences in effect size between those studies that used psychotherapy clients and those that used students as subjects.

Parallel conclusions about the efficacy of rational-emotive therapy were drawn in a meta-analysis of 28 controlled studies (Engels, Garnefski, & Drekstra, 1993). RET was shown to be superior to placebo and no treatment but equally effective in comparison with other types of cognitive and behavioral treatments. No support was found for the proposition that RET with a main or balanced emphasis on behavioral techniques is more efficacious than RET with a primarily or exclusively cognitive bent.

Rational-emotive therapy and associated cognitive therapies have also been found to be effective for older children and adolescents. In their meta-analysis of 150 outcome studies with children and adolescents, Weisz and colleagues (1995) found that the 38 treatment groups involving "cognitive/cognitive-behavioral therapy" produced an average effect size of .67, a moderately large impact. (You will recall that .20 is generally considered a small effect, .50 a moderate effect, and .80 a large effect.) The cognitive therapies also outperformed the nonbehavioral therapies, such as client-centered and insight-oriented. A separate meta-analysis of school-based studies of psychotherapy yielded similar conclusions: the cognitive/rational therapies produced a .43 effect size in individual therapy and a 1.03 effect size in group therapy, both superior to client-centered and human relations therapies (Prout & DeMartino, 1986).

Cognitive Therapy

Probably the most actively researched system of psychotherapy over the past decade has been cognitive therapy. We will approach this burgeoning literature by sampling the pertinent meta-analyses and quantitative reviews, beginning, as did Beck, with outcome studies on depression.

In 1983, Miller and Berman published a quantitative review of the research evidence on the efficacy of cognitive-behavior therapies with a variety of disorders. Analysis based on 48 studies indicated that cognitive-behavior therapies were superior to no treatment and to placebo treatment. However, at that time there was no firm evidence that cognitive-behavior therapies were superior to alternative psychotherapies.

In 1989, Dobson published a meta-analysis on the effectiveness of Beck's cognitive therapy for depression only. He identified 28 studies that used a common outcome measure of depression and made comparisons of cognitive therapy with other psychotherapy systems. The average effect size was quite high across various measures: the average cognitive therapy client did better than 98% of the untreated, control subjects. The results document a greater degree of change for cognitive therapy compared with no treatment, pharmacotherapy, behavior therapy, and other psychotherapies.

This conclusion is apparently correct, as far as it goes. A more comprehensive meta-analysis on psychotherapy for the treatment of depression by Robinson, Berman, and Neimeyer (1990) located 58 controlled investigations. Findings confirmed that depressed clients benefit substantially from psychotherapy, and these gains are comparable to those obtained with pharmacotherapy. Initial, uncorrected analyses suggested a superiority in the efficacy of cognitive and cognitive-behavioral therapies for depression, as found by Dobson (1989). However, once the effect of *investigator allegiance* was removed, there remained no evidence for the relative superiority of any single approach. That is, the apparent superiority of cognitive over other forms of therapy was largely, if not entirely, the result of the researcher's unintentional theoretical bias in such matters as construction of the study, selection of the sample and outcome measures, and differential expertise in the implementation of the psychotherapies consistent and inconsistent with the researcher's allegiance.

Revisiting the effect of investigator allegiance and cognitive therapy for depression, Goffan and colleagues (1995) reanalyzed the same 28 studies as Dobson (1989) and another set of 37 similar ones published from 1987 to 1994. Once again, about half the difference between cognitive therapy and other psychotherapies was predictable from the researcher's allegiance. However, comparable analyses from the newer set of studies showed no effect of investigator allegiance. The allegiance effect may be a historical phenomenon, perhaps the result of early reports being written by pioneers and advocates who delivered cognitive therapy more powerfully. Over time, the apparent magnitude of cognitive therapy's superiority over other treatments, particularly behavior therapy, has declined.

Two other meta-analyses looked specifically at the efficacy of cognitive therapies for depression among adolescents (Reinecke, Ryan, & DuBois, 1998) and older adults (Scogin & McElreath, 1994). Among adolescents, cognitive-behavioral therapy yielded an effect size of 1.02 at the completion of therapy and an effect size of .61 at follow-up. The results demonstrate that cognitive-behavioral therapy is more effective than no treatment or active placebo in treating dysphoric adolescents. Among older adults, the mean effect size for cognitive therapy versus no treatment or placebo was .85, a large and robust effect. The results indicated that cognitive therapy was reliably more effective than no treatment on self-rated and clinician-rated measures of depression. At the same time, again paralleling the conclusions of Robinson et al. (1990), cognitive therapy was equal in effectiveness to the other tested therapies in the treatment of geriatric depression.

Turning to the anxiety disorders, just as Beck and his associates did following their classic research studies on depression, we find considerable research on cognitive therapy. Quantitative reviews indicate that cognitive and cognitive-behavior therapies for anxiety are consistently more effective than waitlist and placebo control groups (Chambless & Gillis, 1993). Cognitive therapy's average effect size on generalized anxiety disorder was 1.69 and on social phobia was 1.00, both large by consensual standards. In both disorders, cognitive treatment gains were maintained or augmented at one- to six-month follow-up. For neither disorder, however, was cognitive therapy consistently more effective than behavioral treatments.

Despite the widespread acceptance of exposure therapy as the treatment of choice for obsessive-compulsive disorder, panic disorder, and social phobia, the empirical research shows that cognitive therapy holds its own here, too. In a meta-analysis on the controlled treatment outcome litearture for OCD, cognitive therapy proved to be at least as effective as exposure therapy (Abramowitz, 1997). A meta-analytic comparison of studies testing cognitive-behavior therapy and exposure therapy indicated that they are equally effective (Feske & Chambless, 1995). And a meta-analysis of treatment outcomes for panic found that the most effective treatment was a combination of cognitive restructuring and exposure (Gould et al., 1995).

In a review of five controlled trials of cognitive therapy in panic disorder, Clark and Ehlers (1993) found that 86% of the patients completed the cognitive therapy and that 82% of the patients were panic-free at follow-up. Both numbers were generally higher than those for alternative treatments, including supportive psychotherapy, relaxation training, and graded exposure alone.

Similarly positive results have been reported by Barlow and associates, whose *Panic Control Therapy* (PCT) includes elements of cognitive therapy, behavior therapy, and exposure therapy (Barlow & Lehman, 1996; Barlow & Spiegel, 1996). PCT consists of education about the nature and physiological aspects of panic, training in slow breathing, cognitive restructuring directed at negative cognitions related to panic, and repeated exposure to feared physical sensations associated with panic. As in many contemporary cognitive-behavioral treatments, the lines of distinction in PCT between behavior therapy, cognitive therapy, and exposure therapy are blurry and the best one can do is to describe it as cognitive-behavioral therapy.

Wilson and Fairburn (1993) reviewed the efficacy of cognitive treatment for eating disorders, especially the treatment of bulimia. Cognitive treatments have been shown to be consistently superior to waitlist controls in all six published studies of this kind and consistently more effective than antidepressant medication in all three published studies of that kind. The average reduction in purging was 79%, with 57% of the bulimics not purging at all at the end of treatment (Craighead & Agras, 1991). Therapeutic effects show good maintenance over time. Whether cognitive treatments are significantly more effective than alternative psychological treatments remains to be determined, as the comparative results were mixed.

In a review of treatment efficacy for anger disorders, Tafrate, DiGiuseppe, and Goshtasbpour-Parsi (1997) concluded that cognitive restructuring was one of the most effective therapies. The average effect size of .81 translates into 79% of the cognitive therapy patients experiencing less anger than those not treated at all.

Nor has the evaluation of cognitive therapy been limited to individual psychotherapy. Dunn and Schwebel (1995) meta-analytically examined the effectivness of cognitive-behavior marital therapy, defined as emphasizing overt attempts to identify and change partners' maladaptive cognitions concerning themselves, their partner, or the relationship. The three studies, involving a total of 74 couples, yielded mean effect sizes of .54 in terms of behavioral improvement in the relationship and .78 for cognitive improvements. Couples treated with cognitive therapy improved significantly more than untreated couples but did not improve more or less than couples receiving behavioral marital therapy or insight-oriented marital therapy.

A cardinal task of psychotherapy outcome research is to identify those particular disorders and patients for which a psychotherapy system is especially effective. A series of prospective studies by Beutler and colleagues (see Beutler, Engle, Mohr, et al., 1991; Beutler, Machado, Engle, & Mohr, 1993) identified differential effectiveness of Beck's cognitive therapy as a function of variation in patient coping style and defensiveness. Externalizing depressed patients improved more than internalizing depressed patients in cognitive therapy, whereas internalizing patients improved most in supportive, self-directed therapy. Low-defensive patients improved more in cognitive therapy as well. These results suggest that psychologically relevant patient characteristics can be used to differentially assign psychotherapy types; in this case, cognitive therapy was particularly valuable with externalizing coping styles and low resistance potential.

Criticisms of Cognitive Therapies

From a Behavioral Perspective

Although Ellis appropriately advocates the scientist as an ideal, he acts primarily as a rationalist and a philosopher. Of his hundreds of articles and books on rational-emotive therapy, only a handful report properly controlled, empirical experiments on its effectiveness. An examination of 41 published outcome studies revealed troubling figures: in 22 of the studies, no information was provided on whether manuals were used to guide treatment; in 23 studies, no information was provided in how well the treatment adhered to RET specifications; and only 3 of the studies reported formal assessment of the extent to which RET could be distinguished from comparison treatments (Haaga, Dryden, & Dancey, 1991). With such a widely practiced and touted therapy and with such a large number of RET publications available, it is difficult to rationalize how a therapist advocating empirical solutions to problems has produced so much dialogue and so little data. Perhaps Ellis is really more of an ethical philosopher preaching a set of hedonistic values based on belief than an empiricist teaching a theory tested by rigorous research.

What data are there, for example, to support the central assumption of Beck's cognitive therapy that behavior disorders are primarily a function of a person's beliefs about antecedent events rather than a function of the events themselves? Are we to believe that such traumatic events as being beaten by one's mother, molested by one's father, bereaved of both parents, rejected by peers, and ridiculed by teachers are less significant in producing emotional disturbances in children than are the beliefs that children possess about these events? Are we to believe that emotionally disturbed people are primarily victims of their own inherent tendencies to indulge in dysfunctional thinking rather than products of irrational environments? Placing the responsibility for emotional disorders on the individual winds up blaming the victim.

Finally, look at the data from your own studies. The hypothesis that the unique mechanism of action in cognitive therapy involves change in underlying cognitions (or schema) has *not* been supported by empirical studies. Instead, many therapies tend to produce cognitive change (Persons & Miranda, 1995). Further, in several studies, the therapist's focus on the impact of distorted cognitions on depressive symptoms does *not* correlate with outcome at the end of treatment (Castonguay et al., 1996). Don't confuse cause and consequence: the behavioral techniques, not the cognitive techniques, in cognitive therapy probably cause the consequence of improved thinking.

From a Psychoanalytic Perspective

Rational-emotive therapy replaces the irrational demands of a primitive and parental superego with demands from an attacking and authoritative clinician who teaches submissive patients to accept a questionable philosophy of life. Clients come to be cured, and instead they are converted. Using some of the oldest forms of brainwashing, of converting people to a new faith, rational-emotive therapists begin to attack and tear apart the patient's world view. Confronted by therapists adept in debate tactics, patients are made even more confused and anxious as their own explanations for their problems are characterized as foolish, irrational, and immature. As patients are made to feel defenseless by the relentless onslaught of the therapist ramming away at their ego processes, they become more vulnerable to whatever the therapist is selling. In place of old defenses, the rational-emotive therapist offers intellectualization and rationalization. The therapist offers a philosophical system that is glamorized as rational, logical, and empirical but is in reality a grand word game.

From a Humanistic Perspective

Where have the cognitive therapists been in the last half of the 20th century to not recognize that the problem for all too many people is that they cannot feel enough, rather than that they feel too much? Alienation, not emotional upsets, is the syndrome of our age. Alienation includes the inability of many people to experience the strong emotions that are part of being human. Emotions like horror, awe, terror, and anger may be unpleasant, but they are not inherently dysfunctional.

Yes, it may be irrational to feel awful about getting a C in a course rather than a B. But it is not inappropriate, irrational, or immature to feel awful about the deforestation and abuse of our planet. It may be irrational to become enraged over missing a bus, but it is not inappropriate to be outraged over children dying from preventable diseases. Too many people have lost the ability to be outraged over the continuing injustices of society. Let's not rationalize problems away; let's use our affect to fuel constructive change. Feel more, not less!

From a Contextual Perspective

The focus in cognitive therapies is obviously on thinking as opposed to other human processes. "Rational thinking" and the scientific orientation fit well with the preferred functions and processes of white male European-Americans. However, they may neither fit nor respond to the diverse ways of knowing of nonwhites, nonmales, and non-Europeans. Ways of knowing associated with some feminist and minority orientations—intuition, spirituality, and connection, to name a few— are ignored or devalued in cognitive treatments (Kantrowitz & Ballou, 1992). Cognitive therapists would have us believe that reliance on rational thinking is the be-all and end-all of effective human existence, but many feel and intuit otherwise.

One cornerstone of cognitive therapy is the notion that thinking is the primary determinant of one's feelings. In rational-emotive therapy, if you wish to alter distressing feelings and reactions, then you alter the belief system. But challenging beliefs does not fit well with some cultural and gender socialization patterns. Many Asians, for example, have been taught to create affective harmony and to avoid conflict. Must we pathologize these beliefs and challenge them simply because they do not fit cognitive therapy's narrow, rational framework? Indeed, the very terms of rational-emotive therapy—confronting, testing, challenging, disputing—force a stereotypically masculine view of beating inaccurate beliefs into submission and may reinforce a woman's sense of inadequacy.

We should also note, as we have in criticizing all the intrapsychic therapies, that cognitive treatment maintains the internal, mentalistic locus of psychopathology and psychotherapy. The problems with people and the way to fix them are located inside the individual's head, rather than out in the culture and in the world. Now that's an "irrational" idea!

From an Integrative Perspective

Cognitive therapies make the same mental mistake of many patients and many true believers—overgeneralization. Rather than assume a reasonable position that some patients distress themselves emotionally by thinking in demanding or absolute terms, cognitive therapies jump to the generalization that virtually all patients do so. Instead of positing that many patients will profit by modifying their "awfulizing" and "catstrophizing," cognitive therapists behave as though cognitive therapy is the treatment of choice for everyone. These overgeneralizations negate the tragic side of life and devalue the emotional side of humans. Reason can be used to help patients discriminate between truly tragic, catastrophic events in life and those unpleasant events that need not lead to emotional upsets.

Likewise, rational-emotive therapy overgeneralizes about the status of certain emotions. A case in point is the insistence that all anxiety is neurotic and self-induced. Such a universal generalization can encourage people to be anxious about being anxious rather than accepting some anxiety as healthy and authentic, such as anxiety over major decisions or death. In the areas of values and morality, rational-emotive therapy insists that all shoulds, oughts, and musts are immature and inappropriate. A value judgment that holds that a person must be clean and orderly to be decent may indeed be destructive. The generalization, however, that any moral imperative is foolish could be even more destructive of human morale. A judgment that Nazism was unfortunate or regrettable would have been less likely to inspire people to put their lives on the line than was the absolute belief that all that is decent in human nature demanded an end to the evil of Nazism.

— A RATIONAL-EMOTIVE ANALYSIS OF MRS. C. —

With her compulsive desire for order, Mrs. C. could appreciate an explanation of her problems that is as simple as ABC. She is already keenly aware of A, the activating event, which was the case of pinworms contracted by her daughter. She is equally aware of the C, personal and emotional consequences of that event—namely, her morbid dread of pinworms and her compulsive need to wash. Like most patients and even some therapists, however, Mrs. C. is relatively unaware of how B, her irrational belief system, has transformed an irritating and unfortunate case of pinworms into a catastrophe.

Mrs. C. may have difficulty accepting that she has actively produced and maintained her own miserable world. She has convinced herself that pinworms are in fact a terrible and awful event. She may, however, be able to appreciate how totally she has condemned herself for having allowed such diseases as the Asian flu and pinworms to infect her family. Mrs. C. may be able to agree that she does believe not only that the pinworms were terrible, but that she was horrible for letting them occur. What a worm she is for being such a careless mother: an ideal mother, a perfect mother, would never let such a terrible thing happen! But Mrs. C. failed to adequately protect her children from disease, and she believes she deserves to be condemned like a worthless worm. What a deserving target she is for pinworms: lowly, lousy, and loathsome. No wonder she feels so vulnerable to being infested by worms.

Mrs. C. has probably always had a strong propensity to think in absolutes, particularly the belief that she must be perfect in order to be worthwhile. Of course, her parents encouraged such irrational beliefs by their own absolutist demands that she be perfectly clean, free of disease and of desires. Nevertheless, Mrs. C. took to such teachings as if they were true because of her innate predisposition to think that perfection is possible. Her perfectionist beliefs were evidenced in her desire for perfect order as reflected in the alphabetical naming of her children and in her need to be clean even before her full-blown compulsions developed. Irrational thinking was clearly present throughout her life; all it took to produce undeniable pathology was a stressful activating event like a series of illnesses to set off her absolute, awfulizing tendencies.

Once Mrs. C. had processed the pinworm event through irrational categories of horrible, terrible, and catastrophic, she frightened herself into believing that she must do everything within her power to prevent a recurrence. She must work compulsively lest she or her family become recontaminated. We can predict, however, that she also engages in frequent self-condemnation for being so terribly compulsive. What a worm she is for always washing and never caring for her children! What a wife she is for always showering and never loving! The vicious cycle of self-condemnation will probably progress to condemning herself as a failure for not improving after years of psychotherapy, for wanting to kill herself, and for letting her family and her therapist down. What better evidence for her lack of worth than the fact that her husband and her therapist are prepared to condemn her to a life in the state hospital.

A closer look would probably reveal that Mrs. C. may well be psychotic and a probable candidate for hospitalization if effective outpatient treatment is not forthcoming. Like most patients diagnosed as severe neurotics (Ellis, 1973), Mrs. C. has many of the signs of a thinking disorder that is more characteristic of borderline or blatantly schizophrenic patients. For example, Mrs. C. has problems in focusing on a realistic solution to her problems because she is overfocused on pinworms. She perseverates as she thinks over and over and over again about pinworms. She also magnifies the dangers of pinworms entirely out of realistic proportions, becoming almost delusional in her belief that she is constantly surrounded by pinworms waiting to infest her.

An accurate diagnosis of Mrs. C. as an ambulatory psychotic would serve as a warning not to expect any psychotherapy to make her entirely free of pathology. Nevertheless, she and her family would be quite satisfied with having her return to her pre-pinworm level of compulsive adjustment. To make such a return, Mrs. C. will need to learn to dispute her intensely irrational belief system. She will have to learn that the pinworm event was catastrophic only because she defined it as such. As the rational-emotive therapist challenges her to think about the worst thing that could happen as a result of her OCD, she can begin to see that although such consequences would be irritating and unpleasant, they are by no means terrible or horrible.

Nor is Mrs. C. a worm because her daughter once had pinworms. Mrs. C.'s self-condemnation will need to be attacked repeatedly by the therapist until she can begin to recognize that nothing she has done or failed to do is deserving of such condemnation. She can go on condemning herself to a compulsive existence if she continues to engage in demanding, absolutistic thinking; or she can begin to rely more on what rational powers she possesses to work against the irrational beliefs that distort her world.

With strong propensities toward irrational thinking, Mrs. C. will have to work hard at disputing her emotionally disturbing beliefs. A variety of homework assignments is in order. For starters, Mrs. C. will be instructed to familiarize herself with basic tenets of RET by reading, for instance, *How to Stubbornly Refuse to Make Yourself Miserable about Anything—Yes, Anything!* (Ellis, 1988). She will be asked to review the tapes of her psychotherapy sessions to learn to identify her frequent use of such demanding concepts as *must, should, necessary, have to,* and *ought to.* She will be assigned to practice substituting more rational terms such as *want to, prefer to,* and *it would be better* for the many demanding things she tells herself. She may also be assigned to write a paper describing where it is written that a mother must keep her children free from any disease in order to be a worthwhile human being, as a means of challenging her self-condemnation. Her husband will also be given important homework assignments, such as reading *How to Live with a Neurotic* (Ellis, 1957a), so that he can begin to deal with her rationally rather than colluding with her neurosis.

Eventually, Mrs. C. may begin to deawfulize and thus defuse the possible consequences of pinworms. She may become more fully conscious of the fact that pinworms may be a pain, but they are not the worst of all possible fates; they may be unpleasant, but they are not catastrophic. The therapist will interpret how foolish beliefs have led Mrs. C. to continue to upset herself emotionally. Mrs. C. needs to become aware that the source of her problems is not pinworms, but rather the way in which she thinks about pinworms. Her problem is not her imperfections as a wife and mother, but rather what she believes her imperfections mean to her worth as a human being. Only if Mrs. C. can learn to actively dispute such irrational beliefs (and that is a big if) can she become free to enjoy some of life rather than waste herself away on foolish washing. Mrs. C. can find some joy in life if she learns to quit insisting on more order and perfection than the universe provides, when the best we can do is accept ourselves as imperfect beings who can live happily in an imprecise world.

Future Directions

Probably the safest prediction about cognitive therapy's direction is that it is moving up. Cognitive-behavioral therapies in general, and Beckian cognitive therapy in particular, are the fastest growing and most heavily researched orientations on the contemporary scene (Norcross, Alford, & DeMichele, 1992). Let us put it this way: if we were forced to purchase stock in any of the psychotherapy systems, cognitive therapy would be the blue-chip growth selection for the next five years.

Two reasons for cognitive therapy's current popularity—commitment to psychotherapy integration and dedication to empirical evaluation—will characterize its future as well. Since its introduction in the 1950s, rational-emotive therapy has become increasingly eclectic in methodology and content (Ellis, 1987b). RET clinicians adopt many types of techniques, particularly the active and directive ones, from disparate schools. Just as RET encourages patients to be skeptical and open-minded, so too in its own practice it abjures banning virtually any technique that may work at times (Ellis, 1987a; Ellis & Dryden, 1986).

Beck's version of cognitive therapy is equally committed to the cross-fertilization of psychotherapy systems. In fact, the construction and stance of his perspective have led some to describe it as an integrative therapy (Alford & Beck, 1997; Alford & Norcross, 1991; Beck, 1991a, 1991b). Cognitive methods are commonly blended into other therapies, as reviewed in Chapter 14; in fact, one particular integration with psychoanalytic therapy, known as *Cognitive Analytic Therapy* or *CAT*, is quite popular in Europe (Ryle, 1990, 1995). Cognitive therapies will continue to venture toward mutual enhancement with other approaches, especially affective and emotional restructuring (for example, Craighead, 1990; Goldfried, 1995) and interpersonal processes (for example, Safran & Segal, 1990). An increased understanding of tacit, nonconscious processing and the incorporation of techniques to access and resolve deeper experiences will bring cognitive therapy into closer contact with the psychoanalytic perspective (Westen, 1991).

The area of best-documented achievement for cognitive therapies to date has been the neurotic disorders, particularly unipolar depression and anxiety disorders. One of the major thrusts for psychotherapy in the future is the treatment of serious and chronic disorders, and cognitive treatments are currently being tested with patients suffering from personality disorders, substance abuse, and psychotic conditions (for example, Beck & Freeman, 1990; Beck et al., 1993; Ellis, McInerney, DiGiuseppe, & Yeager, 1988; Linehan, 1993; Wright, Thase, Beck, & Ludgate, 1992), and the results of these applications may be the acid test for cognitive therapies. The next five to ten years of research will afford a better evaluation of the strengths and weaknesses of cognitive therapy for conditions other than depression and anxiety (Beck & Haaga, 1992). Moreover, the ongoing dedication to examine the efficacy of cognitive therapy will keep it in good stead among the scientific, practitioner, and insurance communities in an era of short-term and problem-specific treatments.

Finally, both Ellis (1987a, 1987b) and Beck (Beck & Haaga, 1992) foresee a continued push of cognitive therapies into mass-media and self-help formats. In keeping with the drive toward cost-efficiency in health care, cognitive practitioners will build on the success of existing audiocasettes and best-selling books, such as Ellis and Harper's (1975) *New Guide to Rational Living*, Beck's (1988) *Love Is Never Enough*, and Burns's (1980) *Feeling Good: The New Mood Therapy*. Computer-administered cognitive treatments are already available (for example, Agras, Taylor, Feldman, Losch, & Burnett, 1990; Selmi, Klein, Greist, Sorrell, & Erdman, 1990), and these should proliferate during the next decade along with ownership of personal computers. Through these and other psychoeducational means, cognitive therapies will continue to share with the public at large the rational secrets of behavior change.

Suggestions for Further Reading

Alford, B. A., & Beck, A. T. (1997). *The integrative power of cognitive therapy.* New York: Guilford.

Beck, A. T., Emery, G., & Greenberg, R. L. (1985). *Anxiety disorders and phobias: A cognitive perspective.* New York: Basic.

Beck, A. T., Rush, A. J., Shaw, B, & Emery, G. (1979). *Cognitive therapy of depression.* New York: Guilford.

Beck, J. S. (1995). *Cognitive therapy: Basics and beyond.* New York: Guilford.

Ellis, A. (1973). *Humanistic psychotherapy: The rational-emotive approach.* New York: McGraw-Hill.

Ellis, A., & Grieger, R. (Eds.). (1986). *Handbook of rational-emotive therapy.* (Vols. 1–2). New York: Springer.

Ellis, A. , & Dryden, W. (1996). *The practice of rational emotive behavior therapy.* New York: Springer.

Freeman, A., Simon, K. M., Beutler, L. E., & Arkowitz, H. (Eds.). (1989). *Comprehensive handbook of cognitive therapy.* New York: Plenum.

Kuehlwein, K. T., & Rosen, H. (Eds.). (1993). *Cognitive therapies in action: Evolving innovative practice.* San Francisco: Jossey-Bass.

Linehan, M. M. (1993). Cognitive-behavioral treatment of borderline personality disorder. New York: Guilford.

Journals: *Cognitive & Behavioral Practice; Cognitive Therapy and Research; Journal of Cognitive Psychotherapy; Journal of Rational-Emotive & Cognitive-Behavior Therapy.*

11

Systemic Therapies

Virginia Satir

KATHY AND DAN HAILED from very prominent extended families. Historically, Kathy's family had been influential in government, while Dan's family were financiers. Kathy and Dan, however, were from branches of their families that were in decline. Dan's parents were plagued by alcohol abuse, as was Dan. Kathy's family of origin was plagued with a multitude of dysfunctions, including substance abuse, divorce, depression, and physical abuse. Kathy herself was troubled by depression and passivity. Though they were in their late thirties, both Kathy and Dan were stuck in their career development, unable to complete their graduate degrees. Their modest inheritances were rapidly disappearing. They each seemed to be stuck in a family system that was steadily deteriorating.

With the help of systemic therapy, Kathy and Dan were able to become more aware and to communicate more openly about how they were repeating patterns from their families of origin. Dan was grappling with rules against succeeding. Kathy was struggling with rules against being active and assertive. As part of her psychotherapy, Kathy traveled to different parts of the country to meet with her mother, sister, and brother. Instead of stepping into blame games, Kathy tried to communicate in a more objective and understanding manner. She was trying to complete the process of differentiating herself from her family of origin while remaining emotionally connected to family members.

Kathy was not surprised that she was becoming more active, less depressed, and more successful. She was surprised, however, that her brother took dramatic steps to get off drugs; her sister entered family therapy to work on stopping her physical and emotional abuse of her children; and her mother began to feel her long-standing depression lifting. From her graduate studies, Kathy knew how family members can deteriorate as one member improves in treatment. She was pleasantly surprised to discover that an entire family system could begin to improve as one member began to restructure her relationship to her family of origin.

The Context of Systemic Therapies

Systemic therapies maintain that individuals can only be understood within the social context in which they exist. Systemic therapies, themselves, can best be understood within the context in which they emerged. Although people have probably been examining and listening to family problems as long as there have been families, systemic therapy is truly a 20th-century development.

The decades of the 1950s and 1960s were seminal years for the development of systems therapies (see Broderick & Schrader, 1991, for a review). These decades witnessed the emergence of *General Systems Theory* in biology and *cybernetics* in computer science. Rather than follow the traditional scientific method of analyzing and reducing phenomena to their simplest elements, such as electrons, neutrons, and protons, General Systems Theory advocated studying the biological processes that lead to increasing complexity of organization of whole organisms (von Bertalanffy, 1968). Cybernetics advocated studying the methods of communication and control that are common to living organisms and machines, especially computer systems. In this chapter, we will first look at how systems are understood from these two perspectives and then see how this understanding has been applied to the study and treatment of troubled individuals, couples, and families.

To understand the functioning of whole organisms, we must study not only the separate parts of the organism but also the relationships among the separate elements. A *system* is defined as a set of units or elements that stand in some consistent relationship with one another. A system comprises not only separate elements but also the relationships among those units. A family system, for instance, comprises not only, say, four individuals but also the interrelationships among those four individuals and the entire context and rules of the family. Even the labels we give to individual members, such as parent and child, suggest consistent relationships between them.

Organization and system are virtually synonymous. A system is a set of organized units or elements. Principles of organization suggest that when elements are combined in a consistent pattern, an entity is produced that is greater than the additive sum of each of the separate parts. This is the concept of *wholeness*. A marital system, for example, cannot be broken down simply into two separate individuals. Not only are there two individual subsystems, but there is also a consistent relationship between the individuals that creates a marital subsystem. In this case, 1 plus 1 equals 3.

Systems are also organized in such a way that relationships among elements create *boundaries* around the system and each of its subsystems. In biological systems, the boundaries may be easily identifiable, such as a cell membrane or an animal's skin. In human systems, boundaries are frequently more abstract. The rules of relationships delineate boundaries. For example, the rules of monogamy help identify the boundaries of a traditional marriage; a spouse who is having an affair would be considered "out of bounds" or acting outside the rules of the relationship. Boundaries may be too permeable, with unclear rules about who can interact with whom and how. In incestuous families, for example, the boundaries between the parental subsystem and the child subsystem are unclear and permeable to the point of being pathological. Rules about incest are important in part because they help define healthy boundaries in family systems. Boundaries can also be too rigid, preventing adequate interactions among individuals in a system or between systems. Families with child abuse, for example, may be rigidly bound off from the larger social system and be unable to accept social support that could help prevent such abuse.

Systems are most often conceptualized as *hierarchically organized*. Systems are related one to another according to a series of hierarchic levels. Each system is seen as being made up of component subsystems of smaller scale; conversely, each system is a component part of a larger system. A family system, for example, comprises individual subsystems, a marital subsystem, a sibling subsystem, and a parental subsystem. The family system, in turn, is a component part of a larger neighborhood system, which is hierarchically related to even larger social systems, such as the community, the region, and the nation.

In order to function effectively, systems require methods for controlling or maintaining organization. Living systems have been characterized as dynamic steady states. Steady states reflect the condition of a system that is not changing over time. Systems theory emphasizes balance or stabilization within systems. Often this is mistakenly understood as rigidity—a sort of forced and inflexible structuring of behavior. Systems theory actually emphasizes controlled change, which allows the development of highly complex interactional patterns that increase rather than decrease options for the system. Control mechanisms allow elements to remain in dynamic interaction. These elements are able to relate meaningfully to each other because of an intricate and delicate series of control mechanisms. The control mechanisms keep the individual elements within an acceptable set of limits but also permit adaptation to occur.

Controlled adaptation is the key to meaningful change. Controlled growth leads to differentiation and development of tissues, organs, and individuals. Uncontrolled growth, like cancer, leads to the disorganization and even death of a living system.

The concept of *homeostasis,* or balance, explains how living systems control or maintain a steady state. Walter Cannon (1939), a physiologist, first described a set of mechanisms within the neuroendocrine system whose function was to maintain consistency of the internal environment of the organism, such as constant blood pressure, temperature, and water content. If changes in the organism start to exceed a set of safe limits, then control mechanisms in the hormonal and autonomic nervous system will be activated to help bring the system back into balance.

Family systems possess their own set of mechanisms whose primary purpose is the maintenance of an acceptable behavioral balance within the family. Families have been found, for example, to maintain surprisingly stable rates of speech interaction (Reiss, 1977). High interaction families maintain a high rate of speaking across sessions even though individual members vary a great deal in speaking across sessions.

The mechanisms that contribute to self-regulatory processes within the marriage or the family are analogous to servomechanisms in cybernetics (Wiener, 1962). *Servomechanisms* are automatic devices used to correct the performance of a mechanism by means of error-sensing feedback. *Feedback loops* are seen as the most important control mechanisms. Instead of two events' being related only in a linear, cause-and-effect fashion, two events can be related in a circular manner, characterized as either a positive or negative feedback loop.

In a positive feedback loop, an increase in any component part of the loop will, in turn, increase the next event in the circular sequence. In this type of sequence, deviations from the norm become amplified; thus, positive feedback loops increase deviations and serve as a self-destructing mechanism. Positive feedback loops set up a runaway situation that eventually drives the system beyond the limits or range within which it can function. Violent arguments in families, for example, can get out of control as anger in one spouse increases anger in the other, which in turn increases anger in a circular manner. Runaway rage can disrupt or even destroy a family's ability to function.

Negative feedback loops, in contrast, establish a balance among the deviations of different events within the loop. Negative feedback loops decrease deviations from the systems rules of relating and help maintain stability of marriage and the family. If one family member becomes angry, another may become sick. If the two deviations balance each other, the family can maintain a stable level of hostility in the system.

Living systems are characterized as *open systems*, which means that energy can be freely transported into, within, and out of the system. Information is the most important type of energy in living systems, because it is an energy that reduces uncertainty. Increases in information allow systems to be organized in more complex patterns. When information is packaged or programmed appropriately and efficiently, it has a powerful effect on a system's ability to function in a highly complex and well-organized manner. Communication involves the process by which information is either changed from one state to another, or moved from one point to another in space. Cybernetics serves as a model for how information can be transformed or transmitted effectively within marital and family systems.

These core concepts from General Systems Theory (GST) and cybernetics have served as the intellectual inspiration for innovative approaches to systems therapy. Because there is no single, unifying approach to systemic therapy, three major systemic approaches—the communication/strategic, the structural, and the Bowenian—will be presented. Inasmuch as these systemic therapies focus on patterns of relationships within systems rather than on individual personalities, the sections on theory of personality will be omitted. Each of the systems therapies does, however, have important things to say about the development and/or maintenance of psychopathology and how psychopathology in human systems can best be changed.

Over the years, the term *systemic therapies* has acquired multiple connotations. First, systemic, or systems, therapy can refer to a *therapy modality or format*. Like individual therapy or group therapy, systems therapy denotes meeting with the immediate system of consequence, typically a couple or family. Second, systemic therapy can refer to *treatment content or goal*. That is, the treatment deals with family systems content and works toward improving the family system. An individual is no longer the patient; the couple, the family, or another system is the patient. In this sense, it is quite possible to conduct systemic therapy without having the entire family present in the consulting room. As in our opening case of Kathy and as in the multigenerational family therapy of Murray Bowen, only one or two people may actually be in therapy, but the entire system is targeted for change. Third, systems thinking and systemic therapy can refer to a *paradigm shift* (see Kuhn, 1970). It represents a discontinuous break with past ideas of linear and intrapsychic causality; it is a revolutionary new way of thinking about psychotherapy and psychopathology. In this chapter, we will present systemic therapy primarily as a treatment content or goal and as a paradigm shift, and only secondarily as a therapy modality or format. Bear in mind, however, that the three meanings are frequently interrelated and not easily separable in practice.

Communication / Strategic Therapy

The communications approach to psychotherapy emerged from two interrelated organizations rather than from a single individual. The first organization was the

Double Bind Communications Project begun in 1952 by Gregory Bateson with Jay Haley and John Weakland as members of the project and Donald Jackson as consultant. The second organization was the Mental Research Institute (MRI) founded by Jackson in 1958 with Virginia Satir and Paul Watzlawick as two important members of the institute. The two organizations had unclear boundaries because Jackson participated in both projects. The Double Bind Project was located at MRI, and when the Double Bind Project terminated in 1962, Haley and Weakland joined MRI. It is not surprising that both of these organizations were founded in Palo Alto, California, which is part of the Silicon Valley, one of the world's foremost centers of computer science.

What these individuals shared in common was the assumption that communication is the key to understanding human behavior. The MRI group went so far as to assume that all behavior is communication. Just as we cannot not behave, so, too, we cannot not communicate. Communication, then, involves both verbal and nonverbal behaviors.

The Double Bind Project originally focused on how conflicting communications could produce symptoms of schizophrenia. Initial research on *double-bind communications* revealed important relationships between family dynamics and schizophrenic communications. In 1959, the project was divided into an experimental approach and a family therapy project. Family interactions were videotaped and attempts made to differentiate "schizophrenic" from "normal" communications. In the family therapy project, observations were made in natural settings, and various techniques based in part on communications theory were introduced. Over its ten-year existence, the project produced some 70 publications, reflecting the volume of creative work emerging from this research and therapy group (Sluzki & Ransom, 1976).

The staff at MRI was even more productive, publishing 130 articles and nine books during the period from 1965 to 1974. These writings described a format that focused on analysis of communication between individuals, and subsequently among family members. Interventions were then designed to change communication patterns between one individual and another and among all members of a family (Greenberg, 1977).

Gradually, the organization of these two groups began to change. Bateson's project ended in 1962, and he went on to advance a communication perspective on a broad range of human and animal behaviors until his death in 1980. Jackson died in 1968, ending a short but very creative career. Satir left to contribute to the human potential movement, which began in California and rapidly became a worldwide phenomenon; she later toured the country demonstrating and advocating for a humanistically oriented communication therapy, until her death in 1988. Haley relocated to the Philadelphia Child Guidance Clinic on the East Coast to participate with Salvador Minuchin in creating a vital center for systems therapy and then started his own Family Therapy Institute of Washington, DC, which he continues to codirect with his wife, Cloe Madanes.

Such a creative group of individuals would not be expected to leave behind a single, coherent theory of psychotherapy. They did, however, develop an innovative set of concepts for understanding psychopathology in systems and a set of therapeutic principles for helping systems change.

Theory of Psychopathology

Systemic therapists have frequently observed that decreases in psychopathology in one family member are often accompanied by increases in symptoms in another family member. Jackson, for example, treated a woman for depression and found that as her depression subsided, her husband began phoning to complain that his wife's emotional condition was worsening (Greenberg, 1977). The wife's continued improvement finally resulted in the husband's loss of his job and subsequent suicide.

Psychopathology is fundamentally an interactional process between or among family members, rather than an intrapersonal problem within one member. Psychopathology serves as a homeostatic mechanism to help families maintain an internal balance for family functioning. When a family is threatened, it can move toward balance though puzzling, psychotic, or other pathological behaviors. A family's status quo may be one in which the parents fight infrequently. When they do fight, if violence threatens to run out of control, a child can communicate concern by becoming symptomatic. These symptoms serve as a negative feedback loop that results in a halt in hostilities as the family develops a newfound concern with the *identified patient* (IP). But the entire system should be the patient, not merely the individual who has developed symptoms to help save the system.

A breakdown in family functioning occurs when the *rules of relating* become ambiguous. The rules of relationships provide a stable organization for family functioning. If the rules become ambiguous, the system becomes disorganized, and symptoms are likely to develop to restore order to the family. If the rules are clear, such as the rule that family members will not relate violently, then an argument between parents need not threaten the family's functioning, and a child will not have to develop symptoms to control a threat of violence.

The rules of relating in a family are best observed through the patterns of communication in the family. Who communicates to whom, how, and about what define the patterns of relationships that make up a family. Most families, for example, have a clear rule that when parents are communicating with each other in an angry manner, the children stay out of it. The spouse subsystem has clear boundaries or rules that prohibit children from becoming part of intimate arguments.

When communication patterns in families are unclear, then rules become more ambiguous and psychopathology is likely to develop. *Double-bind communications* are one of the most troublesome patterns of communicating because they involve two incompatible messages. A classic example of a double-bind situation is presented by Bateson, Jackson, Haley, and Weakland (1956, p. 259):

A young man who had fairly well recovered from an acute schizophrenic episode was visited in the hospital by his mother. He was glad to see her and impulsively put his arm around her shoulders, whereupon she stiffened. He withdrew his arm and she asked, "Don't you love me anymore?" He then blushed, and she said, "Dear, you must not be so easily embarrassed and afraid of your feelings." The patient was able to stay with her only a few minutes more and, following her departure, he assaulted an aide and was put in the tubs.

Verbally the mother is communicating a wish to be close to her son, but non-verbally her tightening communicates a wish to be distant. When the son with-draws, the mother contradicts her nonverbal message by asking, "Don't you love me any more?" The rules for relating are being communicated ambiguously at best. Are mother and son supposed to have a close or a distant relationship? The son clearly cannot win. If he relates closely, his mother tightens up. If he pulls back, she becomes upset. No wonder the son becomes confused, frustrated, and hostile.

Communication is a complex pattern of interactions that is frequently misun-derstood by psychotherapists, let alone clients. In their book *Pragmatics of Human Communication*, Watzlawick, Beavin, and Jackson (1967) conceptualize communi-cation in five axioms. First is the axiom already stated: it is impossible to not com-municate. Silence is obviously communication, though it is frequently ambiguous communication open to interpretation and to misunderstanding.

Besides transmitting information, communication also implies a commitment and defines the nature of the relationship. Communication contains both a report, which is the content of the message, and a command, which defines how the com-municators are to relate. Satir (1967) emphasizes that if the content and the com-mand are congruous, then the relationship is defined as harmonious. If the two lev-els of communication are incongruous, as when the mother conveys a verbal wish to be close and a nonverbal tightening that commands distance, the relationship is likely to be characterized by disharmony and pathology.

The third axiom states that the nature of a relationship is contingent upon how a communication sequence is punctuated. If a communication response can-not end with a period until the same person always has the last word, then such punctuation defines the person with the last word as having greater power in the relationship.

The fourth axiom states that human beings communicate both verbally and nonverbally. Verbal communication is clearest in terms of content but does not pro-vide much information about the relationship between the communicators. Non-verbal communication tells us more about the relationship but is still ambiguous about the nature of the relationship. For example, tears can be a sign of joy. The more families rely on nonverbal messages, the more ambiguous their relationships are likely to be and the more problems are likely to arise.

The fifth and final axiom states that all communication exchanges are either *symmetrical* or *complementary*, depending on the type of relationship. If equality exists and either party is free to take the lead, a symmetrical relationship exists. If one leads and the other follows, the relationship is complementary. Psychopathol-ogy can occur in either type of relationship.

In symmetrical relationships, competition can escalate into a runaway situ-ation as each struggles to have the last word in defining the nature of the relation-ship. Arguments can become endless. Pathology in symmetrical relationships is characterized by more or less open warfare, or a *schism,* as Lidz (1963) calls it.

Marital schism is defined as a state of severe chronic disequilibrium, discord, and recurrent threats of separation. One parent is constantly undercutting the other. The competition leads to parents' vying for the love of the children and the children in rivalry for the parents' affection. The rule that is being communicated in families with marital schism is mutual distrust and angry competition instead of cooperation.

Complementary relationships can rigidify and prevent adequate growth of family members. A parent who insists that a young adult relate as a child can disconfirm the young adult's sense of self as a person who should be able to relate more equally. Such disconfirmation can lead to symptoms of depersonalization, confusion, or aggressive acting out. In marital systems that have become rigidly complementary, one partner must always be in overt control and dominate the family. There is a lack of reciprocity, of give-and-take, between the partners, and the marriage and the family are skewed in the direction of the controlling partner (Lidz, 1963). The weak partner allows the domination so that continuation of the marital and family system is not constantly threatened, even if it means domination by irrational or pathological ways of behaving. The rule of these families is accommodation, even if it means compromising oneself away.

Theory of Therapeutic Processes

If psychopathology is primarily a function of unclear or hostile communication that results in ambiguous rules for relating, then psychopathology can best be modified by helping individuals in systems to communicate more clearly and constructively about the rules of their relationship. The emphasis in communication therapy is not on the content of the communication, but rather on the relationship-defining aspects of communication. The emphasis is not so much on what people communicate as on how they communicate. The focus is on *metacommunication*— that is, communication about communication. Since people can only relate through communication, if they change how the communicate, they also change how they relate.

Homeostatic mechanisms in families, however, make family systems resistant to change. If therapists are to be effective in changing the family's ingrained rules for communicating and relating, then they will need to intervene with a definite *strategy* (and thus are also known as *strategic* therapists) that is powerful enough to disrupt the family's rigid resistance.

Consciousness Raising. Among the communication strategic therapists, Jackson placed greatest emphasis on the importance of family members becoming more aware of the dysfunctional nature of their current rules for communicating and relating. Jackson assumed that before change is possible, the family must understand rule functioning. His emphasis on knowledge of family functioning resulted in his being labeled a cognitive communication therapist (Foley, 1974).

The client's task is not to develop historical insight into the family's rules of relating and communicating. The family's work is simply to relate in the here and now. Then, either by following the therapist's directives or by resisting such directives, they can begin to see how dysfunctional are their communication patterns and their rules for relating.

The first task for the Jacksonian therapist is to not become blinded by the content of communications. Focusing on a family's history, in particular, can be one of the quickest ways to miss how the family is interacting in the here and now. Since rules for relating are enacted in the present, the therapist's first task is to become more aware of who communicates to whom, about what, and how. In the initial sessions, the therapist will try to clarify the family's rules for functioning by asking about the family's expectations for each parent and about the role that each child plays in the family system. The therapist tries to open these areas up for clearer communication and, hopefully, for change.

Relabeling, or *reframing,* is a technique that is designed to make explicit the rules by which a family operates. As an example, Jackson (1967) cites a situation in which a mother and daughter are talking and the mother begins to cry. Because the daughter has been labeled as aggressive, she is assumed to be the cause of her mother's crying. The daughter even confirms this unwritten assumption by saying that she did not mean to hurt her mother. The therapist intervenes by relabeling the hurt as a "touching closeness." This technique takes away the negative motivation of an act and labels it in a positive way. Under the family's rules of communication, the daughter is perceived only as aggressive and hurtful rather than as trying to touch her mother in a close way. Family members may define a relationship between two people in a negative way for years, so that all communications between them are interpreted negatively. If the therapist can suddenly define the communication in a more positive way, the family can begin to see itself in a new way.

Another means of making the family aware of dysfunctional rules is to produce a runaway in the system by *prescribing the symptom.* If the problem is that the parents are being too punitive, the therapist would recommend that they be even more punitive as a means of regaining control. The parents then have the opportunity to discover just how they are relating to their children. As their punitive communications increase, they threaten to produce a runaway, or breakdown, in the system. The parents then have the opportunity to gain genuine insight into how dysfunctional their punitive actions are for the family's well-being.

A technique similar to prescribing the symptom is *reductio ad absurdum.* This technique takes the complaint to an absurd extreme so that a client can become aware of how dysfunctional it is to relate in a such a manner. If a mother is complaining about her daughter's aggressiveness, the therapist can commiserate with the mother regarding the daughter's acting out, emphasize the cross she has had to bear, suggest that anyone else would have been completely crushed by it, until finally the mother has to counter with "I didn't say it was *that* bad." In this way, the mother and the family come to realize that she is not as vulnerable to her daughter's acting out as she seems.

Choosing. Clients experience symptoms as being outside of their personal control. They are "helpless" when it comes to choosing whether to be free from symptoms or not.

Symptoms are especially likely to emerge in family systems characterized by double-bind communication patterns. Double binds cause individuals to develop a sense of having no choice. They're damned if they do and damned if they don't. Double-bind communications contain rules to relate in two incompatible ways—"Come close, but don't touch!" Double-bind communications help to create symptoms, in part because they leave the receiver with no choices for resolving incompatible or paradoxical communications.

Communication strategic therapists have been ingenious in liberating clients from double-bind situations and from symptoms by creating *therapeutic double binds*. When constructed correctly, these paradoxical techniques liberate clients by giving them two choices: to cooperate with the therapist's directives or to refuse to cooperate.

The client's work is simple: choose to follow the therapist's instructions, or choose to rebel. The therapist's task is more challenging. The therapist must create a paradox that will help liberate clients whether they chose to cooperate or refuse to cooperate with the therapist's directive. The directive is structured so that it (1) recommends continuing the very behavior the patient expects to change, (2) implies that acting out the symptomatic behavior will produce change, and (3) thereby creates a paradox because the patient is told to change by remaining unchanged.

Patients are thus put in an untenable situation regarding their symptoms. If they cooperate and choose to carry out their symptoms, they no longer have the experience of "can't help it"; the behavior becomes choice behavior rather than symptomatic or helpless behavior. If the clients resist the directive, they can do so only by not behaving symptomatically, which is the goal of therapy. Therapeutic double binds give clients two choices, both of which liberate them from symptomatic or helpless behavior.

A therapeutic double bind presupposes an intense therapeutic relationship that has a high degree of survival value and expectation for the patient (Watzlawick et al., 1967). In addition, it must be communicated in such a convincing manner that the client cannot dissolve the paradox by commenting on it. If the client says, for example, "You're trying to trick me," the paradox is dissolved.

In the case of a couple who argued constantly, Jackson reframed the argument as a sign of emotional involvement and told them that this apparent discord only proved how much they loved each other. He recommended that they continue their fighting in order to express their love. No matter how ridiculous the couple may have considered this interpretation—or perhaps because it was so ridiculous to them—they set about proving to the therapist how wrong he was. This was best done by stopping their arguing, just to show that they were not in love. The moment they chose to stop arguing, they found they were getting along much better (Watzlawick et al., 1967).

In another case, Jackson was trying to interview a bearded young man who believed he was God and remained completely aloof from other patients and the staff. The patient deliberately remained across the room from Jackson and ignored any questions or remarks. Jackson told the patient that his belief that he was God could be dangerous because he might let down his guard and neglect to check what was going on around him. But if he wanted to take this kind of chance, Jackson would go along with it. During this structuring of a therapeutic double bind, the patient became increasingly nervous and at the same time interested in what was going on. Should he choose to take the chance of being treated like God or not? The therapist then got down on his knees and presented the patient with a key to the hospital, saying that since he was God he would have no need for a key, but if he was indeed God, he deserved to have the key more than the therapist. The patient dropped his stony demeanor, came over to Jackson, and said, "Man, one of us is crazy."

Catharsis. Virginia Satir was unique among her Palo Alto colleagues in that she placed much more emphasis on feelings than did the others. She actually combined systemic theory with ego psychology and Gestalt theory. Satir agreed that troubled families need to communicate clearly. Most troubled families, however, have difficulty in communicating their feelings directly. If they cannot be clear about their feelings toward each other, they certainly would be more likely to have ambiguous rules for relating. Satir's (1967, 1972; Satir, Stachowiak, & Taschman, 1977; Satir & Baldwin, 1983) approach to systemic work, therefore, placed much more emphasis on helping families express their emotions and thereby change rules that prohibit relating on a feeling level.

The client's task is to begin to take the risk of communicating feelings more directly rather than indirectly through nonverbal actions. Clients first try to gain insight into which feelings they usually omit from their communications. *Blamers* usually omit feelings about the other person; *placaters* omit feelings about themselves; *super-reasonable* communicators omit feelings about the subject being discussed; and *irrelevant* communicators omit everything. Once aware of the pattern of communication they tend to use, clients then need to struggle to become more congruent communicators by expressing the emotions they usually eliminate.

The therapist first uses consciousness-raising processes to assist patients in becoming more aware of which patterns of dysfunctional communication they typically use. Through feedback and interpretations, the Satir therapist helps clients become aware of the meanings contained in both their verbal and nonverbal communications. As clients start to become aware of the deeper feelings that they are communicating only indirectly, the therapist encourages them to express their feelings more directly. Rather than communicating secondary feelings, such as anger or envy, the therapist would encourage clients to express the primary feeling of hurt. Secondary feelings such as anger can be dysfunctional for families, whereas expressions of hurt almost always help families to create more supportive and caring rules for relating.

Counterconditioning. Jay Haley is distinctive among the original MRI group for his therapeutic focus on power. Behind every communication is the command element or a struggle for interpersonal power. As he uses the term, a person who has achieved "power" has established him or herself as the one who determines what is going to happen. Power tactics are those maneuvers that people, including therapists, use to give themselves influence and control over their social world and so make that world more predictable.

In his classic (and controversial) book, *The Power Tactics of Jesus Christ and Other Essays*, Haley (1986) does not concern himself with the spiritual message of Jesus or his ideas, but with how Jesus organized and dealt with people. Jesus was the first leader to lay down a program for building a following among the poor and powerless. His basic tactic was to define the poor as more deserving of power than anyone else and so to curry their favor.

He was also an expert in the *surrender tactic*, reportedly used by certain beasts of the field and birds of the air. When two wolves are in a fight, for instance, and one is about to be killed, the defeated wolf will suddenly lift its head and bare its throat to the opponent. The opponent becomes incapacitated; he cannot kill as long as he is faced with this tactic. Although he is the victor, the vanquished is controlling his behavior merely by standing still and offering the vulnerable jugular vein. Throughout his public life, Jesus preached the use of the surrender tactic, turning the other cheek and forgiving those who wrong you. Becoming helpless in the face of authority almost invariably wins and frustrates the opponent.

This analysis of power in systems guides Haley's (1976, 1980, 1990) directive, problem-solving therapy, in which he tries to quickly grab the upper hand in the family system. His typical procedures include clarification, reframing, and a host of directives that function as fuzzy forms of counterconditioning in which family interactions are restructured to be incompatible with the old, pathological interactions. Having extensively studied the work of the famous hypnotherapist Milton Erickson, Haley (1973b) delivers two types of *directives*. Straight directives are given when the therapist wants the family to do what the directive says—for example, telling a disengaged and overly serious family to play a fun game for at least two hours. Paradoxical directives, based on the theoretical foundations laid by Don Jackson, are given when the goal is for the family to oppose the therapist—for example, the "winner's bet," in which the therapist bets misbehaving adolescents that they will continue their misbehavior. The therapist takes the position that adolescents cannot control their behavior, thus casting them in a therapeutic double bind.

Haley (1984) also developed *Ordeal Therapy*, a systemic twist to the behavioral process of contingency management for extremely resistant patients. Here the strategic therapist imposes an ordeal appropriate to the person who wants to change—an ordeal more severe than the problem. The main requirement of the assigned ordeal is that it cause distress equal to or greater than that caused by the symptoms. It is a variant of the paradox: the cure is worse than the illness.

In one case, a woman in her early thirties was suffering from extreme anxiety manifested by regular outbursts of perspiration. Haley's strategy was to contract for an activity that she would dislike so much that she would give up her anxiety rather than do it. The contract: If she was anxious enough during the day to perspire abnormally, then she was to awaken at 2:00 in the morning to wash and wax the kitchen floor. She had to repeat it every night—even though it was wasted energy devoted to her most hated chore—until she did not perspire. The success of the trick, so to speak, depends on the patient's not dissolving the paradox by realizing that it is a trick. The Haley-like therapist must also cultivate an enormously powerful image for the contractual ordeal to continue without the patient simply dropping out of treatment.

Therapeutic Relationship

Even though Satir was active and directive with families, she emphasized the importance of accurate empathy, positive regard, and genuineness in family systems. The therapist needs to relate in such a way as to help develop an atmosphere that is conducive to more congruent and functional communication. Functional communication requires an atmosphere in which anything can be discussed, anything can be raised, and there is nothing to hold a person back. This type of therapeutic context can best be developed in families when the therapist is able to relate to each family member in a caring, empathic, and congruent manner. Rather than be nondirective, however, the therapist needs to jump right in with the family and help direct them to the feelings that have been omitted from their incongruent communications (see Loeschen, 1997, for examples of Satir's relationship skills).

Haley, as we have said, concentrates on the command or power aspect of communications. The issue is which person is to govern the behavior of the other and so set the conditions for what sort of relationship they will have. Since the issue of who is in charge is critical to any relationship, it is also the central issue in a therapeutic relationship. In troubled systems, individuals avoid taking responsibility for defining the nature of their relationships. In a therapeutic system, it is necessary for the therapist to be responsible for defining the nature of the therapeutic relationship. The rule for relating is clear: the therapeutic relationship is organized hierarchically, with the therapist in charge and in control.

Giving directives is the means by which therapists can change the rules of relating and communicating in families. If a mother keeps intruding when a father and son are communicating, the strategic therapist can directly change this pattern by giving the mother a directive to stop intruding. Directives also serve to intensify the relationship between the therapist and family. By telling people what to do, the therapist becomes involved in the action and becomes important to the patients. Whether the family follows straight directives at home or resists paradoxical directives at home, the therapist remains in their lives throughout the week.

As a serious student of Milton Erickson, Haley (1973b) attempts to use direct and indirect techniques to control the therapeutic relationship. This is beautifully illustrated in the classic case of a bedwetting couple treated by Erickson.

Erickson told the couple that the absolute requisite for therapeutic benefits would be their unquestioning and unfailing obedience to the instructions given to them. Erickson then commanded the bedwetting couple to deliberately wet the bed before getting into it each night for a period of two weeks. At the end of this time, they would be given one night off and would sleep in a dry bed on Sunday night. On the following Monday morning, they were to throw back the covers when they saw a wet bed; then, and only then, would they realize that they would face another three weeks of kneeling and wetting the bed. There was to be no discussion or debate, only silence and obedience.

The outcome was that each night the couple, with considerable distress, wet the bed. However, two weeks later when they awoke on Monday morning, the bed was dry! They started to speak but remembered the order to be silent. That night, without speaking, they "sneaked" into a dry bed and did so for the next three weeks.

Did the couple choose to change their behavior, or were they following the injunctions of the therapist? Were they conscious of the use of paradox, or did the therapist have an indirect hypnotic control over their behavior? In Haley's view of therapy as a power struggle, the processes of change are not really important. What is important is the outcome—who won the battle.

Practicalities

Communication patterns can best be observed and modified when a full family system is present. Communication/Strategic therapists are flexible, however, and will work with marital subsystems or even an individual subsystem if necessary. Sessions usually last one or one-and-a-half hours, but the therapist expects the family to continue their work at home as the members struggle with the therapist's directives.

Because so much is communicated through nonverbal behavior, communication/strategic therapists find it very helpful to videotape sessions, especially for training of novice therapists. Family therapists in general, and communication/strategic therapists in particular, are at the forefront of videotaping, direct observation, and supervision through a one-way mirror. Videotaping also permits the sessions to be used for research on communication patterns in families.

Fees have at times been a tricky issue for systemic therapists. Most insurance policies are individual health programs that cover treatment for individual psychopathology but not marital or family problems. As a result, marital and family therapists can be forced to adhere to the ideology of an identified patient, if only for insurance reimbursement. Families also wonder if fees will be greater because more people are being seen in therapy. This is sometimes the case, but typically systemic therapists charge a standard fee per session regardless of whether a family, a couple, or an individual is being seen.

Structural Therapy

Salvador Minuchin (1922–) learned about the diversity and adaptability of families while growing up in a Jewish family in rural Argentina and while living in Israel, where families from all over the world converged to help build a new nation. He did not learn about the power that families have over psychopathology, however, until the early 1960s, when he was conducting psychotherapy and research with delinquent youths at the Wiltwyck School in New York. Minuchin had been trained as a psychiatrist in traditional psychotherapeutic techniques that were developed to fulfill the needs of verbally articulate, middle-class patients burdened by intrapsychic conflicts. The boys he was working with, however, were from disorganized, multiproblem, poor families. Improvements achieved through the use of traditional techniques in the residential setting of the school tended to disappear as soon as the children returned to their families.

Minuchin and others were looking for effective alternatives with delinquents at a time when psychotherapy was becoming liberated from its almost exclusive preoccupation with individual psychopathology. Family therapy emerged in the 1950s, and Minuchin and others at Wiltwyck began applying this new perspective to *Families of the Slums* (Minuchin, Montalvo, Guerney, Rosman, & Schumer, 1967). Approaching delinquency as a systemic issue proved more helpful than defining it as a problem of the individual. Minuchin and his colleagues recognized, however, that even family therapy was not a panacea for delinquency, because psychotherapy does not have the answers to poverty and other social problems (Malcolm, 1978).

In 1965, Minuchin became director of the Philadelphia Child Guidance Clinic, where he was able to develop structural family therapy with a wider cross-section of families. His *structural therapy* had considerable impact on diabetic and asthmatic children who were experiencing an unusually high rate of emergency hospitalizations because their conditions were being worsened by stress. Minuchin knew that he could not cure diabetes or asthma through family therapy, because these problems had a physical etiology. Minuchin believed that his model could best be tested with anorexia nervosa, because this eating disorder could be construed as due entirely to emotional factors (Minuchin, 1970). By working to change the structure of families, Minuchin claimed that he was able to cure more than 80% of children with anorexia nervosa, a syndrome that had traditionally been attributed to individual psychopathology.

Further expansion and refinement of structural therapy occurred throughout the 1970s, when Minuchin brought in Braulio Montalvo from Wiltwyck and Jay Haley from the MRI group. This work culminated in the classic *Families and Family Therapy* (Minuchin, 1974), a fully developed account of the structural way of understanding and treating families. In 1976, Minuchin stepped down from the politics and administration of directorship and concentrated on the training of family therapists. He now does so from The Minuchin Center for the Family in New York City (Colapinto, 1991), where he completed his ninth book, *Mastering Family Therapy: Journeys of Growth and Transformation* (Minuchin, 1997).

Theory of Psychopathology

Structural theory is more concerned with what maintains psychopathology than with its causes. By the time therapists see patients with symptoms, the causes of the problems are part of history. These historical causes frequently cannot be empirically determined and certainly cannot be changed. What can be changed are the contemporary factors that maintain psychopathology. Whether or not it is caused by the intrapsychic dynamics of the individual, psychopathology is maintained by the interpersonal dynamics of the system. Thus, we should be concentrating on pathological family structures rather than searching for pathological intrapsychic structures.

Pathological family systems can best be understood in contrast with healthy family systems (Minuchin, 1972). An appropriately organized family will have clearly marked *boundaries*. The marital subsystem will have closed boundaries to protect the privacy of the spouses. The parental subsystem will have clear boundaries between it and the children, but not so impenetrable as to limit the access necessary for good parenting. The sibling subsystem will have its own boundaries and will be organized hierarchically, so that children are given responsibilities and privileges consistent with age and gender as determined by the family's culture. Each family member is also an individual subsystem with a boundary that needs to be respected. Finally, the boundary around the nuclear family will also be respected, although the extent to which kin are allowed in varies greatly with cultural, social, and economic factors.

The boundaries of a subsystem are the rules defining who participates in the subsystem and how. The boundary of a parental subsystem is defined, for example, when a mother tells her older child, "You aren't your brother's parent. If he is playing with matches, tell me and I will stop him." Healthy development requires that subsystems in a family be relatively free from interference by other subsystems. The development of skills for negotiating with peers learned among siblings, for instance, requires noninterference from parents. Clear boundaries or rules help maintain freedom from outside interference.

The rules that govern transactions within a family, though not usually explicitly stated or recognized, form a whole—the *structure* of the family. In order for a family to change its structure, it must change some of its fundamental rules for interacting.

Two major types of family structures are pathological and need changing. The first is the *disengaged* family, which has excessively rigid boundaries. In the disengaged family, there is little or no contact between family members. There is a relative absence of healthy structure, order, or authority. Ties between family members are weak or nonexistent. The overall impression of this type of family is of an atomistic field. Family members have long moments in which they move as in isolated orbits, unrelated to each other. The family is disconnected. The mother in this group tends to be passive and immobile. She feels overwhelmed, has a derogatory self-image, experiences herself as exploited, and almost always develops psychosomatic and depressive symptomatology. The children in such families are at risk of developing antisocial symptomatology.

The second type of troubled family is the *enmeshed* family; its boundaries are diffuse. The distinguishing quality of enmeshed families is a "tight interlocking" of its members, such that attempts on the part of one member to change elicit immediate complementary resistance on the part of others (Minuchin et al., 1967). Enmeshment is essentially a weakening of the boundaries that allow family subsystems to function. Because the boundary between nuclear family and families of origin is not well-maintained, in-law problems are likely to develop. The boundary separating the parents from their children is crossed frequently in improper ways, such as incest. The roles of spouse and parent are insufficiently differentiated, so that neither the spouse subsystem nor the parental subsystem can operate. The children are not differentiated on the basis of age or instructional level, so that the sibling subsystem cannot contribute properly to the socialization process. Finally, individual boundaries are not respected, so that individual subsystems are not able to develop adequate autonomy and identity. An anorexic adolescent, for example, may be able to assert autonomy only by saying no to the family's demands to eat.

Families are open systems that continually face demands for change. These demands may come from changes in the larger environment, such as the death of a family friend. Demands may also come from developmental changes in the family, such as the birth of a baby or a child's attaining adolescence. Healthy families respond to demands for change by growth on the part of each individual in the family, each subsystem within the family, and the family as a unit. Dysfunctional families respond to demands for change in pathological ways, as when the mother in a disengaged family becomes more depressed or a child acts out. Usually one family member develops symptoms and becomes the identified patient, even though the basic problem is the family's inability to grow and adapt to change.

Theory of Therapeutic Processes

Given that symptoms emerge and are maintained in family structures unable to adapt to environmental or developmental demands, the goal of therapy is to restructure families in order to free the members to grow and relate in nonpathological patterns. Because the structure of a family reflects the rules for interacting that govern the family, changing a family's structure involves changing its rules for relating. This typically entails changing the system's boundaries from rigid or diffuse to normal, from disengaged or enmeshed family to a healthy family.

Consciousness Raising. Minuchin (1974) shares a view of consciousness that is unique to systems theorists: consciousness is not just an intracerebral process, but also includes extracerebral events that occur within the individual's context. Individuals think and feel and exist within social contexts, and the events they experience in the family are important aspects of consciousness. If the family context transforms to a higher level of development, then the individual's consciousness will also be raised. Members of disengaged families, for example, are likely to perceive the social world as structured like an atomistic field, with disconnected people revolving in their individual orbits. To conceive of people as interrelated and interdependent is against the family rules. By participating in a family context that begins to change and become more engaged, the individual becomes mindful of how people are inherently related.

The client's work in this process is relatively simple: to attend the family sessions and be attentive in the sessions; to give feedback to the therapist when asked about changes that might be desired; and to perceive changes in relationship patterns as they occur in the family context. In a classic case with an anorexic girl, Minuchin (1974) asked the attentive adolescent about the family's rule against closed doors. Would she like to close her door in order to have more privacy? The girl said that indeed she would. She was thus helping the structural therapist to become more aware of the need to develop clearer boundaries around individual subsystems in this enmeshed family. By perceiving others in the family context beginning to close their doors, including the parents closing their bedroom door for the first time, the clients could begin to see how a family can function better by having better boundaries.

In structural therapy, the therapist does much of the work. The therapist is active and directive. In order to direct actions in an appropriate way, however, the therapist must become conscious of the structure and the rules that govern a particular family. The therapist's attention is focused on the here and now, because family rules can best be perceived by observing who interacts with whom and how. Some of this increased awareness the therapist shares overtly with clients; other aspects are best perceived by changing the family context. The therapist will almost routinely reframe a presenting problem, for example, so that the family members can become more conscious of how symptoms are system events rather than individual events.

Minuchin (1974, p. 1) illustrates *reframing* in an opening session with Mr. Smith, who has been hospitalized twice for agitated depression, his wife, 12-year-old son, and father-in-law. Minuchin asks, "What is the problem?" and Mr. Smith says, "I think it's my problem." "Don't be so sure. Never be so sure," Minuchin says. "Well, I'm the one that was in the hospital," Mr. Smith responds. "Yeah, that still doesn't tell me it is your problem," says Minuchin. "Okay, go ahead. What is your problem?" Minuchin asks. "Just nervous, upset all the time . . . seem to be never relaxed," Mr. Smith responds. "Do you think you are the problem?" asks Minuchin. "Oh, I kind of think so. I don't know if it is caused by anybody, but I'm the one that has the problem," says Mr. Smith. "Let's follow your line of thinking. If it would be caused by somebody or something outside of yourself, what would you say your problem is?" asks Minuchin. "You know, I'd be very surprised," says Mr. Smith. "Let's think in the family who makes you upset?" asks Minuchin. "I don't think anybody in the family makes me upset," says Mr. Smith. "Let me ask your wife, okay?" Minuchin replies.

Instead of focusing on the individual, Minuchin focuses on the person within the family context. He is beginning to help the family become aware of how symptoms are systemic issues rather than individual problems. Reframing the problem in this way will help family members raise their consciousness from a strictly individualistic ideology to a systemic perspective.

Frequently, reframing is used to interpret the role that symptoms play in maintaining homeostasis or balance within a family. To the parents of a girl who had been hospitalized for a psychotic break, Minuchin expressed his concern that when they returned home with their daughter, she would go crazy again (Malcolm, 1978). The reason she would go crazy was to save their marriage. The psychotic symptoms were thus interpreted as the means by which a good daughter could help her family stay together, rather than the weakness of a bad daughter who falls apart. Interpretations through reframing help each of the family members become more aware of how symptoms are an integral part of the family's functioning.

The therapist will encourage a family to enact family transactions rather than describe them. In *enactments*, the therapist explicitly directs family members to engage in a particular activity, such as "Discuss with your mother your curfew time and try to come to a decision." More dramatically, the therapist may arrange an anorexic lunch and have food brought to the session so the family can enact how they dine with an anorexic in their midst. Enacting transactional patterns helps family members experience their own reactions with heightened awareness. Enactment also allows therapists to see family members in action, and it is through such observations that the therapist becomes aware of the family structure.

Choosing. Structural therapy is relatively unique in that it emphasizes the process that we have labeled *social liberation*. Social liberation is the process whereby a social system is changed in such a way as to create more alternatives for healthy responding. The more alternatives in a system, the greater the freedom individuals have to choose responses conducive to their own growth. Structural therapists emphasize restructuring of family systems as the means by which subsystems in the family can become freer to respond and relate in healthier patterns.

The client's commitment to help liberate the system from pathogenic rules begins with a formal or informal contract to participate in therapy. The contract includes rules of how often the family will meet, who will attend, how long sessions will last, and the initial goals of therapy. Implicitly, the family is also choosing to let an outsider, the therapist, join their system. Once therapy is under way, clients need to find the courage to try alternative ways of relating that the therapist recommends. Restructuring assignments in the session and as homework can produce stress, because the assignments transgress rules that have bound the family together. By cooperating with such assignments, however, family members participate actively in creating a new set of rules that permit them to relate in a family that can foster growth rather than illness.

It would not be farfetched to characterize the structural therapist as a freedom fighter committed to liberating a social system from destructive patterns of relating. As for other freedom fighters, the first task of the structural therapist is to join the system in order to change it from within. But that is no small task, because family systems have boundaries designed to exclude outsiders. Minuchin uses the common term *joining* to denote a host of specific techniques for entering a family system by engaging its members and subsystems. The therapist must learn to speak the language of the family, using its own metaphors and idioms. The therapist must also join all of the various subsystems in the family, lest the therapist be seen as the parents' agent or the children's agent. When joining with the parents, the therapist will speak the language of responsibility; when joining the sibling subsystem, the therapist will speak the language of rights.

Like anthropologists who join new social systems, systemic therapists must initially accommodate themselves to the rules of the system. If the family is hierarchically structured across four generations, the therapist might address the great-grandmother first. This type of *accommodation* involves maintenance of the family subsystems through planned support of the family structure. The therapist also accommodates to the family through tracking the context of the family's communication and behavior, by asking questions for clarification, making approving statements, or asking for amplification of certain points. Another accommodation technique is *mimesis*, which is imitating or miming important communication or behavior patterns of the family. In a jovial family, for example, the therapist becomes jovial; in a family with a restricted communication style, the therapist's communication becomes sparse.

Once the therapist and family have joined, they have in fact created a new therapeutic system. The therapist is the leader of this system, as expressed through the therapist's becoming more active and directive. The therapist's use of reframing, for example, communicates that the family will function at a systems level rather than focus on one identified patient. In the process of joining the family, the therapist avoided confrontation, lest the therapist risk being excluded by powerful subsystems of the family. Once all parties are joined, however, the therapist can risk confronting and challenging the patterns and rules of the system.

Marking boundaries is one of the techniques the therapist uses to restructure the family. Like a good leader, the structural therapist has created a psychopolitical map of the family terrain. The therapist needs to have an accurate idea of who relates to whom and how. Then the therapist can begin to give assignments that will redraw the boundaries along healthier lines. If mother and daughter relate like siblings, for example, the therapist may put the mother in charge of the daughter's activities for a week. If the boundary that delineates an individual is not respected, the structural therapist may ask each person to think and speak only for her or himself. If a clear boundary does not exist around a couple who spend all their time parenting, the therapist may ask them to go away together for a weekend without children.

The structural clinician can keep the therapeutic system functioning at home by assigning tasks for homework. The mother who follows through on her homework of supervising her daughter's activities for a week is responding at home to the healthier therapeutic system rather than to the old rules of relating that defined mother and daughter as sisters.

The use of enactment in the sessions not only increases consciousness about current patterns of relating, but also permits the therapist to change patterns of relating in the here and now. The therapist may, for example, use a *blocking technique* that breaks up the usual communication patterns. Daughter may be blocked from communicating to father through mother and asked to relate to father directly. If mother and father consistently avoid clear boundaries around them by having a child sit between them, the therapist can block such transactions by directing the child to change seats with mother or father.

The therapist may use an exaggerated imitation of the family's actual style in order to point out a dysfunctional pattern. In a family with an overcontrolling mother who yells at her adolescent daughter, the therapist might yell louder. Manipulating such moods can force the mother to soften her interactions and thereby give the daughter more autonomy.

The therapist may also use symptoms to promote changes. Minuchin gives the example of a family in which the apparent problem is the child's stealing. The stealing is interpreted as a reaction to ineffective control by the parental subsystem, and thus the child is instructed to steal from his father. This technique relocates the symptoms in an immediate situation that mobilizes the parents to set better controls (Minuchin, 1974).

By accommodating and joining and then confirming, blocking, and challenging the family's patterns of interacting, the structural therapist is liberating the family from destructive rules of relating. In the process of helping a family restructure itself, the therapist frees its members from transactions that have created symptoms of psychopathology.

Therapeutic Relationship

The structural therapist has a unique way of relating to clients. The joining process certainly includes accurate empathy, warmth, and caring. But once a therapeutic system has been created, the therapist relates as an authoritative leader. The therapist acts like a psychopolitician, advocating for the benefit of each of the family members against a social system that has developed a destructive structure. The therapist joins with each of the family subsystems to overthrow a set of rules that prevent the members from relating within and across clear and healthy boundaries.

Without a therapeutic relationship based on joining techniques, the therapist would be impotent in trying to help families liberate themselves from enmeshed or disengaged transaction patterns. The relationship alone, however, cannot produce structural changes in family systems. The therapist must be willing to challenge, confront, block, and disrupt a homeostatic system. Only by using techniques that cause disequilibrium can the family therapist give troubled families greater freedom to restructure themselves along healthier lines.

Practicalities

The format of therapy should be consistent with the function of therapy. If the goal is to observe how a family structures itself in space, then the whole family should be present. The room should be large and flexible enough to allow family members to sit initially wherever they choose, thereby revealing the family's rules. The therapist must also be flexible enough to restructure the seating as a means of restructuring the family. The practicalities of many therapies, such as the seating arrangements of clients, are part of the process of understanding and changing the structure of families.

A therapist who is attempting to strengthen the boundaries of the spouse subsystem may request to see only the parents for a session or two. If a therapist is trying to restructure a multigenerational family, then it is most practical to have all generations present, rather than have the clients simply talk about the grandparents. In practice, structural therapy has been used most often with families in which a child or adolescent is the identified patient. Such families are usually more willing to come in as a full family than are families in which an adult member is identified as the patient.

Structural therapy is designed as an active, short-term treatment that initiates the processes that help families become restructured. By releasing family members from their stereotyped positions, this restructuring enables the system to mobilize its underutilized resources and to improve its ability to cope with stress and conflict. The structural therapist is encouraged to limit participation to the minimum necessary to set in motion the family's natural helping resources.

It may happen that, as a result of structural intervention, the family is helped not only to change but also to *metachange*; that is, in addition to overcoming its current crisis, the family will enhance its ability to deal with future events without external help (Colapinto, 1991). This high level of achievement is of course desirable, but more modest and practical accomplishments are still valuable. Families may well need to come back for help at times of future crises. This prospect, however, is more practical, natural, and economical than the protracted presence of a therapist accompanying the family for years.

Bowen Family Systems Therapy

The audience was expecting Murray Bowen (1913–1990) to present a theoretical paper as part of a symposium at a professional convention. Instead, Bowen (1972) presented a "convention shattering" procedure that he had used to change his own family of origin.

Bowen was part of a large extended kin group that had dominated a small southern town for many generations. At the symposium in 1967, Bowen revealed how he had intruded into most of the dominant triangles of his immediate family by means of a surprising strategy. He sent off letters that told various relatives about the unpleasant gossip that others were circulating about them. He signed these letters with endearing salutations such as "Your Meddlesome Brother" or "Your Strategic Son." He also announced an impending visit. Bowen then arrived as heralded, to deal with the predictably indignant reactions of his relatives. The effect on the family was dramatic. Many closed-off relationships were reopened. And once the initial fury against Bowen had subsided, his intervention created a warm climate of better feelings all around.

Bowen's intervention with his family of origin grew out of the family systems therapy he had been developing over the previous two decades. After serving as an army physician in World War II, he had trained at the Menninger Clinic in Topeka, Kansas. Like many of the early systems theorists, he was particularly enthusiastic about trying to understand and treat schizophrenia. It was not new to conceptualize schizophrenia as emanating from an unresolved symbiosis between mother and child. It was a radical innovation at a psychoanalytic center such as Menninger's, however, to actually bring the mother into the clinical picture as part of the investigation and treatment of schizophrenic patients.

Bowen's clinical work was followed by five years of family research, from 1954 to 1959, at the National Institute of Mental Health (NIMH) just outside Washington, DC, Bowen began by having a small group of schizophrenic patients and their mothers live together on a hospital ward. After a year of individual therapy for both patients and mothers, fathers were included and the family was treated as a single unit rather than treating individuals in the unit (Bowen, 1978).

Feeling that the NIMH was not particularly supportive of his new approach, which flew in the face of conventional intrapsychic psychotherapy, Bowen relocated a few miles away to Georgetown University, where he remained until his death. Here, Bowen (1978) formulated his cerebral and deliberate approach, known as *family system therapy*, and here he completed detailed multigenerational research with a few families, including one case going back more than 300 years. Noting that one could spend a lifetime on only a few such family studies, Bowen made the seminal decision that his own family was most accessible for such a multigenerational study. From this study and the intervention with his own family, Bowen (1978; Kerr & Bowen, 1988) became convinced of the importance for both clients and therapists of differentiating themselves from their families of origin.

Theory of Psychopathology

Emotional illness arises when individuals are unable to adequately differentiate themselves from their families of origin. *Differentiation of self* is the ability to be emotionally controlled while remaining within the emotional intensity of one's family. Differentiation of self reflects the extent to which one can think objectively about emotionally loaded issues within the family.

Fusion is the phenomenon that interferes with differentiation of self from family. Fusion refers to two aspects of immaturity. First, there is the fusion of feeling and thinking when objective thinking is overwhelmed by emotionality and becomes its servant. What results then is rationalization or intellectualization to justify the acting out of emotional immaturity. Second, fusion refers to the absence of boundaries or the lack of individuality between two or more individuals, as in the case of symbiotic relationships.

Fusion in families results in an *undifferentiated family ego mass*, which is a quality of "stuck togetherness." Fusion leads to a conglomerate emotional oneness that exists in all levels of intensity. The more threatened or insecure a family feels, the more they tend to fuse. The more stressed or distressed individuals feel, the more they seek the security of oneness that results from family fusion. Chronic distress can produce emotionally ill individuals who are unable to differentiate themselves from their family. They remain stuck forever in the family, and the family is stuck around them.

Fusion between any two people, such as a husband and wife, relieves tension by involving vulnerable third parties who take sides. Fusion thus gives rise to *triangulation*. Dyads are inherently unstable because they inevitably result in periods of insensitivity, abrasiveness, or withdrawal. The party who feels offended or rejected will attempt to triangulate a parent, child, neighbor, or lover for support. Triangles are much more stable relationships; they are, in fact, the basic building blocks in any emotional system. Triangles can make differentiation from the family difficult because the parents need a child to maintain a stable system or because a child needs a parent for support against others. In marital conflicts, the most common triangles lead to in-law problems, affairs, or child problems.

Triangles in a state of calm consist of a comfortable twosome and an outsider. One of the classic triangles of this type is the close mother and child with a passive, withdrawn father. The favored position is to be a member of the close twosome rather than the odd one out. When tension mounts in the outsider, the predictable move is to try to form a twosome with one of the original members of the twosome, leaving the other one an outsider. Thus, the foci within the triangle shift from moment to moment and over long periods of time, as each member jockeys for a comfortable position. In this case, if father tries to get close to his child, the mother is likely to react with upset lest she be the odd one out.

When the triangle is in a state of tension, the outsider position becomes the preferred position. From this comfortable position the person can say, "You two fight and leave me out of it." In a state of tension, if it is not possible to shift the focus within the triangle, the members of the original twosome will form another triangle with a convenient family person, such as another child. In periods of very high tension, a system will triangle in more and more outsiders. A common example is a family in crisis that uses the triangle system to involve neighbors, schools, police, and mental health professionals as participants in the family problem. If the family is successful in getting others involved, then they can revert to a more comfortable homeostasis and let the outsiders fight.

Rather than resolve triangles through self-differentiation, most people use *emotional cutoff* to cope with their unresolved attachments to their parents. The cutoff consists of denial and isolation of the problems when living close to the parents, or physically running away, or a combination of the two. Whatever the pattern, the person yearns for emotional closeness but is allergic to it. People who use intrapsychic cutoff mechanisms to tolerate living closer to the parents generally function better. Those who put physical distance between themselves and the parents—the infamous "geographic cure"—tend to blame parents and act out immaturity impulsively in relationships. When problems develop in their own marriage or nuclear family, they tend to run from these as well. The emotional cutoffs keep triangles intact and block further differentiation, so that the more severe the cutoff, the more severe the pathology that is likely to develop in new relationships.

Triangles tend to occur across generations, because a parent or child is often the most available and vulnerable person to be brought into a marital conflict. If a wife is experiencing considerable discomfort about her marriage, she can regain homeostasis or balance in her marriage by projecting her anxieties onto a child. A *family projection process* pulls the parents together by creating a preoccupation with the child's problem. The child who is most vulnerable to this projection is the child who is emotionally closest or most fused with the parents. This child will tend to be the person who develops symptoms for the family. This child will also have little chance of differentiating an adequate self, because the family needs the child to maintain homeostasis in the parents' relationship. If the child becomes unstuck and matures through psychotherapy, for example, then the parents' marriage will be at risk of deterioration.

Because triangles typically occur across generations, severe psychopathology can develop from a *multigenerational transmission process*. A child who has been triangulated can emerge from the family with a lower level of self-differentiation. This child is likely to marry someone of a similar differentiation level, and their children are likely to have even lower levels of differentiation. Finally, after multiple generations, a child can emerge with such a low level of differentiation that a severe pathology, such as schizophrenia, is almost inevitable. Rather than an individual process, psychopathology is almost always a multigenerational transmission process.

Theory of Therapeutic Processes

Because emotional illnesses arise from an inadequate differentiation of self from the family emotional system, the goal of Bowenian treatment is to increase differentiation of self. Because triangles interfere with differentiation of self, successful therapy will involve detriangulation of family members. Rather than work on all possible family triangles, the therapist has the advantage of knowing that a family is a system of interlocking triangles. Thus, change produced in one triangle will cause change in all the triangles.

A nuclear family is formed as the result of the fusion of a husband and wife. Accordingly, they are the most important members who need to increase their differentiation of self, even if it is a child who is manifesting symptoms for the family. Bowen (1978), therefore, preferred to work with the marital subsystem rather than have the children present in therapy. He indicated, however, that successful therapy is possible by working with only one individual member who is motivated to mature. When there is finally one member of a troubled triangle who can control his or her emotional responsiveness and not take sides with the other two, while still staying in constant contact with the other two, the emotional intensity within the twosome will decrease and both will move to a higher level of differentiation. Unless the triangulated person can remain in emotional contact, however, the twosome will triangle in someone else. By helping only one member to become more differentiated and detriangulated, a therapist can help an entire family system to change.

Consciousness Raising. Differentiation of self involves the ability to think objectively about emotionally loaded issues in the family. Clients can begin to think more objectively about themselves and their families by developing their powers of observation more profoundly. Observation involves the ability to step back from an emotional interaction and perceive the events from an emotional distance. Observation helps control automatic and autonomic reactions.

When two or more members of a family system are present, such as spouses, the work of each patient is to observe what the other person is communicating. Observation can allow clients to become more objectively aware of what others are communicating rather than being busy building an emotional rejoinder. Clients working alone can learn to use these same powers of observation as part of their homework. When they are home, their work is to observe the role they play in family triangles and to observe the typical emotional reactions they exhibit in each triangle. Observation not only leads to an objective perspective but helps develop a unique perspective that is different from the perspective of family members who are too caught up in the family drama to see themselves and others clearly.

When two or more family members are present, the Bowenian therapist's work includes keeping the emotional system sufficiently toned down to allow clients to process issues objectively without undue emotional reactions. The therapist is active with constant questions, first to one spouse and then to the other. The therapist will then ask the listening client to share his or her thoughts and observations about what was just communicated. Encouraging spouses to communicate directly to each other will only encourage them to react emotionally rather than objectively.

The therapist also uses education to teach clients about how family systems function and dysfunction. This education begins by helping clients become more aware of each other's family history and the role each played in the history of his or her family of origin. Often the therapist will create a *genogram,* a family tree of sorts, that illustrates the relationships of family members across several generations. The genogram will illustrate which family members were close, which were cut off, and which were conflicted. This genogram can then be used to teach clients about triangles and how they interfere with differentiation of a more autonomous self.

Family system therapists emphasize observations rather than interpretations as the means to a more objective and differentiated level of consciousness. Interpretations are directed more at the "why" of family interactions. Why people act the way they do is not open to direct observation, and interpretations about the motives of others tend to be subjective and emotional. Observations focus on the who, what, when, and where of family relationships, which are more objective, observable facts.

Choosing. Patients can liberate themselves from the family system by choosing to respond in a more autonomous fashion. Autonomy involves responding from an "I" position rather than reacting from a "We" position. The "I" position is developed in part from what "I" observe to be factual rather than what "We" as a family know to be true. It takes courage, however, to choose to respond differently from the family ideology, because the individual risks the wrath or rejection of family members, just as Bowen risked the fury of his family when he chose to respond differently.

Choosing to respond autonomously does not mean returning to the family of origin and blaming one's parents or siblings for personal problems. That sort of blaming is just another emotional reaction to the family system that will stimulate the blamed relative to triangle in a third party for support. Autonomous responding is not intended to blame or to change the other person. The differentiating person chooses the "I" position to communicate "This is what I think or believe" and "This is what I will do or not do," without imposing my values or beliefs on other family members. The "responsible I" assumes responsibility for one's own experiences and comfort and leaves emotional and intellectual space for others to create their own happiness. A reasonably differentiated person is capable of genuine concern for others without expecting something in return. The togetherness forces of family fusion, however, treat differentiation as selfish and hostile.

People who choose to be different in significant ways from their families must be willing to respond reasonably rather than react emotionally to the predictable forces against differentiation. The predictable steps in the family reaction to differentiation are: (1) "You are wrong." (2) "Change back." (3) "If you do not, you will be criticized, be ostracized, or be guilty of driving your parent or partner crazy."

The therapist's task is to respond autonomously to family forces rather than re-act emotionally. The therapist chooses to remain differentiated rather than be trian-gulated into the family system. The therapist is differentiated enough to respond reasonably to clients' attempts to make the therapist feel guilty, angry, anxious, or overly responsible. The therapist responds from a well-differentiated "I" position rather than a "We" or "You" position.

When clients are ready to risk more autonomous responses in their families of origin, the therapist functions more like a coach or consultant. The therapist helps the client to clarify that the goal in such responding is to differentiate oneself, not to blame or change others. The goal is not to win in a confrontation or to impose an interpretation, but simply to enhance one's differentiation. Clients can be re-minded that they can choose to respond differently in their family regardless of whether others change or not. Responding differently can indeed liberate relatives to change, but that is their responsibility, not the client's. Like a good coach, the therapist will check on the progress clients have made between sessions in their re-lationships to their family of origin.

Therapeutic Relationship

The Bowenian relationship is important as much for what the therapist does not do as for what the therapist does. Effective therapists do not allow themselves to be triangulated into family relationships. Even though spouses will use all types of conscious and nonconscious maneuvers to triangle the therapist into reacting emotionally, the differentiated therapist consciously chooses to respond reasonably. Unlike some family therapists who dive right into the family system to create strong emotional transference reactions, the Bowenian therapist prevents a trans-ference reaction by maintaining an objective "I" position. Entering a triangled rela-tionship with spouses may indeed allow them to reestablish a homeostasis that re-moves symptoms, but it does nothing to help them establish differentiated selves that can prevent future symptoms. The Bowenian therapist, in sum, acts as a model of autonomous, responsible, and differentiated behavior despite the inevitable at-tempts to ensnare the therapist in triangles and emotions.

By maintaining an "I" position, the family system therapist does relate in a genuine manner, which allows clients to differentiate their own beliefs and actions from the therapist's. The therapist relates in a calm, relaxed, and interested style that communicates caring, without trying to establish the unconditional positive regard that is more conducive to family fusion than self-differentiation. Finally, the Bowenian therapist depends on the powers of observation and objective thought rather than empathy to try to understand what is going on in troubled families.

Practicalities

Bowen's family therapy is much more flexible than those systemic theories that insist on having all family members present. Actually, the more family members that are present, the more difficult it is to detriangulate the parents, because the energy and emotions can shift from one triangled child to the next. Thus, Bowen (1978; Kerr & Bowen, 1988) himself preferred to work with the spouses or with one motivated parent, rather than with the children present. Other Bowenian therapists, however, will work with entire families as part of their practice. Robert Aylmer (1978), a former president of the Society for Family Therapy, estimates that about 25% of his systemic practice is with entire families, 25% with spouses, and 50% with individuals.

Family system therapists will typically see clients once a week for 45 to 60 minutes at the beginning of treatment. Once clients have become more conscious of their family's functioning and their role in that system, sessions will shift to alternate weeks or even monthly sessions. Spacing of sessions allows clients more adequate time for doing their homework of observing their family of origin and responding autonomously rather than reacting emotionally while in the context of their family. Differentiation of self is a lengthy and often painful process before people can become more autonomous adults in the presence of their parents.

Psychotherapy can certainly facilitate this process. It is recognized, however, that many clients are seeking simple relief from symptoms rather than differentiation of a self. Therapy will thus be briefer with many clients, but it will take several years of well-spaced sessions to complete a genuine growth process.

More so than other systems theorists, Bowen was a strong proponent of individual and family of origin therapy for the therapist. Because therapists must avoid becoming triangulated by the togetherness forces of the clients' systems, it is essential that Bowenian therapists participate in personal therapy designed to differentiate themselves more fully from their own family of origin.

Brief Systemic Therapy

Systemic therapies are, in theory and practice, designed as active, short-term treatments that initiate the change process. By teaching communication skills, by restructuring relationships, and by reassigning power, therapy enables the system to mobilize its underutilized resources and to improve its ability to cope with stressors. Structural and strategic therapists are encouraged to limit participation to the minimum necessary to set in motion the family's natural helping resources. Communications therapy was originally developed with schizophrenic families and would typically be long-term, lasting a year or two. By contrast, the MRI's newer Brief Therapy (Segal, 1991) and Haley's (1976) problem-solving therapy are short-term endeavors, lasting just a few weeks or months.

Early on, the Mental Research Institute group developed and evaluated a brief form of communication/strategic therapy, which they call MRI Brief Therapy (Weakland, Fisch, Watzlawick, & Bodin, 1974; Segal, 1962). Although this approach is based on communications theory as presented by Watzlawick, Beavin, and Jackson (1967), there are some important changes in practice. Brief Therapy is a ten-session, generic model of problem formation and problem resolution (Segal, 1991). Treatment is oriented toward solving specific problems and changing symptoms rather than necessarily changing systems (Watzlawick, Weakland, & Fisch, 1974). Although case formulation is based on a systemic perspective, treatment often involves a single individual. Finally, communication changes are made primarily by changing behavioral interactions between members of a family system. In short-term follow-ups of 97 cases seen for an average of seven sessions, Weakland et al. (1974) found that 40% reported complete relief of the presenting complaint, 32% reported significant improvement, and 28% failed to improve.

All in all, systemic therapies have been pioneers in brief therapy and remain highly compatible with the contemporary emphasis on time-limited psychotherapy.

Effectiveness of Systemic Therapies

Overall Effectiveness

The value of conventional research methodologies in assessing the effectiveness of systemic therapies is widely contested in some circles. Although many defend the importance of empirical evaluation, some critics argue that most therapy research designs reflect the assumptions of logical positivism, which are antithetical to the principles of systems thinking itself. According to those who espouse the *"new epistemology"* (epistemology being the study of how we know), the assumptions of the scientific method are incompatible with the following underlying assumptions of systemic therapy (Goldenberg & Goldenberg, 1996):

- Multiple viewpoints exist regarding what constitutes reality and change (rather than a single, objective reality).

- Multiple causalities account for most events (not simple, linear, treatment-causes-improvement sequences).

- The entire system should be the unit of study (rather than changes in individuals or smaller units to ensure rigor).

- The therapist should be searching for systemic connections (not explanations based on linear causality).

For better or worse, however, the "new epistemologists" have not published outcome studies using their own guidelines, so we are left to consider the published research conducted in the conventional manner.

At least a dozen reviews on the general effectiveness of family therapy have been published. The reviews center on the format of family therapy, rather than the theoretical orientation of systemic therapy, but they are nonetheless of direct relevance. We will consider six of these reviews, considered in chronological order and selected for their thorough method and balanced conclusions.

In 1978, Gurman and Kniskern extensively reviewed 200, mostly uncontrolled studies on the outcomes of both marital and family therapy. They found that in outpatient marital and family therapy, 76% of cases improved and 24% did not—figures strikingly reminiscent of those usually reported for individual therapies. Further, 73% of the studies directly comparing marital/family therapy with individual or group therapy favored marital and family therapy; the remaining 27% found no differences. The overall conclusions were that:

- Family therapy is at least as effective as, and possibly more effective than, individual therapy for a wide variety of problems, both apparently "individual" difficulties and more obviously family conflicts.

- For certain clinical goals and problems (such as treating anorexia, juvenile delinquency, and sexual dysfunction), systems therapies are the treatment of choice.

- Couples benefit most from treatment when both partners are involved in therapy, especially when they are seen conjointly.

- Individual therapy for marital problems is an ineffective treatment strategy and one that appears to produce more negative effects than alternative approaches.

- Therapist relationship skills exert a major impact on the outcome of systemic therapies, regardless of the theoretical orientation of the treatment and clinician.

In 1987, Hazelrigg, Cooper, and Borduin published a meta-analysis of 20 rigorously controlled investigations that included families as the subject population, included a control group, and reported detailed results of the statistical analyses performed. The results showed that family therapy has a positive effect on patients, compared with no treatment, as measured by both family interactions and behavior ratings. Approximately 68% of the people receiving no treatment showed less favorable functioning than did the average person receiving family therapy. When family therapy was compared to alternative treatments (such as individual or group therapy), the results also demonstrated the relative effectiveness of family therapy. Depending on the type of outcome measure and the length of follow-up, family therapy was at least as effective as, and often more effective than, alternative treatments. In the six studies using recidivism as a follow-up measure of treatment effectiveness, family therapy proved to be more effective than alternative treatments.

In 1993, Shadish and colleagues conducted a meta-analysis of 163 randomized trials (including 59 dissertations) on family and marital psychotherapies. The average effect size was .51 or .61, depending upon how one codes nonsignificant findings. These figures imply that a family or marital therapy client on average was better off than 70% or 73% of no-treatment control clients. These figures also translate into a treatment success rate of 62% or 65% in marital and family therapies compared to 38% or 35% in control groups. When the results of marital and family therapy are compared to individual therapy within the same study, the differences in outcomes were small and nonsignificant. Shadish, Ragsdale, Glaser, and Montgomery (1995, p. 348) advance the conclusion of "for now, a tie." When the results of different forms of marital and family therapy are compared, only modest theoretical orientation differnces emerged. All treatment types examined had positive effect sizes except humanistic (Satir or person-centered therapies). Careful analyses indicated that behavioral family therapy outperformed humanistic, eclectic, and unclassified family therapies but not the structural and strategic approaches.

In 1995, Dunn and Schewebel conducted a meta-analysis of 15 controlled marital therapy outcome studies. Their study did not examine any family therapy studies but did contain many of the marital studies analyzed by Shadish and colleagues (1993). They concluded that all three types of marital therapy examined in their study—behavioral marital therapy, cognitive-behavioral marital therapy, and insight-oriented marital therapy—had a mean effect size of .73, a moderately large impact. All three types of marital treatment were clearly more effective than no treatment at all.

Two more recent meta-analyses examined the effectiveness of family treatment for substance abuse disorders. In 1995, Edwards and Steinglass conducted a meta-analysis on 21 controlled studies of family-involved therapy for alcholism. Family therapy was definitely effective in motivating alcoholics to enter treatment; in fact, alcoholics whose family members were involved in therapy entered treatment at rates ranging from 57% to 86% across the four studies as compared with rates from 0% to 31% in the control groups. Once the alcohol abuser entered treatment, family therapy was only marginally more effective than individual therapy.

In 1997, Stanton and Duncan performed a meta-analysis on 15 studies, involving 1,571 cases, involving couples and family therapy for drug abuse. Clients receiving couples or family therapy manifested significantly lower drug use after treatment than did clients in nonfamily therapy. Family therapy was shown to be as effective for adults as for adolescents and to be a cost-effective adjunct to methadone maintenance. The meta-analytic evidence favored family therapy over (a) individual psychotherapy, (b) peer group therapy, and (c) family psychoeducation for the treatment of drug abuse.

A final point before closing this section is that the outcome literaure on marital and family therapies (MFT) is comparatively large and quite impressive —". . . therapists and researchers should be pleased with the state of the MFT outcome research literature. It is generally as good or better than outcome research in most other areas of psychotherapy, and it demonstrates moderate and often clinically significant efffects" (Shadish et al., 1995, p. 358).

Communication / Strategic Therapies

Most of the communication therapists have not been involved in systematic assessments of their treatments. In an evaluation of her therapy approach, for example, Satir (1982) reported that she had treated closed to 5,000 families of nearly every shape, form, nationality, race, income group, religious orientation, and political persuasion. Although she believed that her approach had been generally useful to her clients, she indicated that she had done no formal research on her effectiveness. In fact, the few direct evaluations on the Satir approach have yielded nonsignificant effect sizes (Shadish et al., 1993).

Shadish and associates (1993) located only three controlled trials of strategic therapy, but the average effect size was a respectable .61. In their review of the effectiveness of family therapy for drug abuse, Stanton and Shadish (1997) found favorable evidence for the effectiveness of both Jay Haley's strategic therapy and Duncan Stanton's structural-strategic therapy in treating substance abusers. However, the effectiveness of general strategic therapy remains uncertain with schizophrenic and psychosomatic disorders, two conditions which it purports to treat successfully (Gurman, Kniskern, & Pinsof, 1986).

Although not restricted in use to strategic therapies, paradoxical interventions have received some research attention. Shoham-Salomon and Rosenthal (1987) examined the effectiveness of paradoxical interventions in psychotherapy by means of a meta-analysis of 12 data sets. Overall, paradoxical directives were as effective as, but not more effective than, typical or straight directives. However, paradoxical interventions showed relatively greater effectiveness one month after treatment termination and with more severe cases. An open question is whether positive connotation/positive reframing is more or less effective than symptom prescription: one meta-analysis (Shoham-Salomon & Rosenthal, 1987) found reframing more effective than symptom prescription, whereas another meta-analysis (Hampton & Hulgus, 1993) found that symptom prescription produced greater treatment effects than reframing.

Structural Therapy

During the 1970s, Minuchin and his colleagues published a series of clinical survey studies on four disorders in children: labile diabetes, anorexia nervosa, chronic asthma, and psychogenic abdominal pains. Very impressive gains were reported: for example, at follow-up, 88% of the treated diabetic children were judged to be recovered, meaning there had been no hospital admissions for acidosis after treatment and/or diabetic control had become stabilized within normal limits (Rosman, Minuchin, Liebman, & Baker, 1978). In another example, 86% of child and teenage anorexics, treated for between 2 and 16 months, were found at follow-up to have achieved normal eating patterns and a normal body weight (Rosman et al., 1978).

As with most uncontrolled research, these findings are difficult to evaluate or trust. The surveys were generally cumulative, with later reports including cases from previous surveys. In some reports (for example, Minuchin, Baker, Rosman, Liebman, Milman, & Todd, 1975), it sounds as if these impressive effects with anorexia are due entirely to structural therapy. In other reports (for example, Liebman, Minuchin, Baker, & Rosman, 1975), the treatment for anorexia nervosa is described as an integration of structural therapy and behavior modification. Contingency control processes were used in such a way that the anorexic children could earn activity privileges in the hospital or at home only by gaining weight. Because these are survey studies, it is impossible to determine how much of the outcome is due to behavior therapy compared to structural therapy. Further, the absence of placebo control groups, no-treatment groups, or an alternative family therapy makes it unclear what is producing these impressive results in these and related surveys.

Controlled outcome studies yield more definitive and trustworthy evidence of effectiveness, but suprisingly few controlled studies on structural therapy have been conducted (Gurman et al., 1986; Shadish et al., 1993). Structural therapy has been thoroughly tested in the family treatment of substance abusers; depending on one's definition of structural therapy, it has been evaluated in between two and five studies with this difficult population (Stanton & Shadish, 1997). And the results are quite encouraging: structural therapy has been shown to be definitely superior to no treatment and probably superior to individual treatment for drug abusers. However, its effectiveness is still untested in schizophrenia, affective disorders, anxiety disorders, and marital problems, as well as childhood conduct disorders (Gurman et al., 1986).

Bowen Family Systems Therapy

To our knowledge—and to others' (for example, Gurman et al., 1986; Friedman, 1991; Shadish et al., 1993)—there have been no controlled outcome studies on the Bowenian approach to treatment. One study has been conducted on an adaptation of Bowen systems therapy for drug abuse, using a combination of both family and individual sessions (see review by Stanton & Shadish, 1997). The effectiveness of Bowen's family system therapy is thus largely untested.

Criticisms of Systemic Therapies

From a Psychoanalytic Perspective

Structural therapy is another in a long series of attempts to construct simple solutions for complex problems. It is simplistic, for example, to assume that all of psychopathology is maintained by structured relationships in current family living. What about more severely disturbed adults, like many borderline personalities, who live alone? What is the structural therapist going to do for a person who needs help in developing relationships, not restructuring them? Remember that roughly three-quarters of patients receive individual psychotherapy (Norcross, Prochaska, & Farber, 1993). What does structural therapy have to offer to the majority of clients? There are only so many ways that a therapist and client can restructure their seating arrangements. What structural relationships is the therapist going to observe, map, and rearrange with individual patients?

Simplistic also is the belief that the history of the family, patients' developmental histories, and their internal dynamics can simply be ignored. Just join the family and let the action begin. But the family never becomes aware of how problems developed, nor will they necessarily understand how the problems disappeared. All that is clear is that they were joined by a benign parent figure who rearranged the furniture and used metaphors about open and closed doors to settle boundary disputes. It certainly can shake things up and probably even help, but what happens when the family faces its next developmental crisis? There has been no systematic attempt to help the family gain insight into either the causes or the cures of their problems. No wonder the family is likely to have to return for more restructuring (or is it reparenting?) from an all-knowing mental health professional.

From a Behavioral Perspective

Bowen is pouring old wine into new bottles. The old wine is his psychoanalytic heritage; the new bottles are multigenerational families. Key concepts have a distinctly Freudian flavor. Differentiation of self from family fusion sounds like differ-entiation of ego from id. The goal of having intellect control emotions sounds like the goal of having the ego control the id. Triangles are seen as the source of psycho-pathology; this sounds similar to the oedipal conflict as the key to psychopathol-ogy, with mother, father, and child in conflict. No wonder some psychoanalytic theorists claim Bowen as one of their own.

In therapy, Bowen is prepared to continue the same kind of archeological expe-dition that psychoanalysis favors. Psychoanalytic therapists, at least, would only take the patient back to birth; Bowen is prepared to dig back through previous gen-erations for further clues to contemporary problems. Unlike communications and structural therapists, Bowenian therapists don't stop when symptoms go away. They continue to restructure multigenerational relationships in search of an autonomous self, just as psychoanalysts restructure the psyche in search of an autonomous ego.

Like psychoanalysts, Bowenian therapists cannot serve as objective guides for such archeological expeditions unless they have also undergone the almost intermi-nable training process of differentiating the self from the family of origin. Lest therapists be at risk of becoming triangulated in therapy (acting out the counter-transference?), they need to undergo intensive therapy themselves.

Bowen tries to bridge two theoretical perspectives, psychoanalysis and systems theory, without appreciating that neither has a solid foundation in scientific re-search. The result is a shaky structure that has not undergone the rigorous tests of controlled experimentation. The result is also a theory that is shaky as to whether it is grounded in principles and practices of individuals or systems. Look, for exam-ple, at how Bowen prefers to work with individuals instead of having the whole family present. Even when Bowen works with couples, he doesn't focus on their communications or structural relationships but rather has each spouse communi-cate individually to the therapist.

Furthermore, how can a true systems theorist believe in an autonomous self? Systems theorists are determinists who assume that an individual component is de-fined and controlled by the organized system of which it is a part. Bowen's thesis would seem to stand systems theory on its head. Instead of the whole being greater than the sum of the individual parts, Bowen would have us believe that an individ-ual can be greater and stronger than the sum of the whole family's forces.

From a Humanistic Perspective

Communication/strategic therapists present us with too many paradoxes. First they create a theory based on how systems stay the same. Then they recommend this theory to help people change. Concepts of wholes, hierarchies, homeostasis, and feedback loops explain how systems maintain a stable relationship, not how they change. This theory teaches therapists to expect resistance and encourages pes-simism about the potential that families have for change. As a result, families have to be tricked into changing rather than being treated with respect. Paradoxically, it may be the therapist's technique that encourages resistance rather than the system's rules. Who wouldn't resist being treated like God, being told to deliberately wet one's bed, or having one's complaints reduced to absurdities? Such therapists can produce the very resistance they have been taught to expect. When such tricks work, the therapist is so clever; when they fail, the family is at fault.

Why should we believe that marital and family systems are so stable, when marriages are disintegrating at unprecedented rates? Communication and strategic theories may have been appropriate to the stable 1950s but not to the rapid changes of the second millennium. Change is the norm today, not stability. Future shock includes distress from too much change and too little stability in our social systems (Toffler, 1970). Less therapeutic disruption, fewer tactics and tricks, and more therapist genuineness and support will foster the greater stability required of contemporary families.

Do individuals matter in these families, or are they just mindless elements controlled by the rules of the system? Systemic therapists see the woods, but miss the trees. Who is responsible for these rules—the system, or the individuals in the system? And who will be responsible for changing the rules? Haley (1976, 1986) recognizes this paradox, but unfortunately he winds up delivering power to the therapist rather than according power to the clients. In power struggles, processes of change don't matter, only the outcome—does the therapist win the struggle? This ethos sounds dangerously close to the ends justifying the means. But how else can you justify using such manipulative techniques as prescribing symptoms, placing patients in double binds, and assigning them ordeals? These techniques make for good theater of the absurd, but they fail to create a humane system for the troubled individuals, couples, and families of our day.

From a Contextual Perspective

The "fathers" of family systems therapies were just that—fathers with a masculine bias. With the exception of Virginia Satir, the pioneers of family therapy were white men trained originally in the 1940s and 1950s in the psychoanalytic tradition and inbred with a male-dominated orientation to psychotherapy. In her influential *The Family Interpreted: Feminist Theory in Clinical Practice*, Deborah Luepnitz (1988) provides a feminist critique of the major approaches to family therapy.

Murray Bowen's perspective has much of value to feminists, but his concept of "differentiation" smacks of the politics of rational man. Bowen describes the differentiated person as "autonomous," "being-for-self," and "intellectual," while the poorly differentiated person is characterized as "seeking love and approval," "being-for-others," and "relatedness." What is valued in Bowen's system are those qualities for which men are socialized; what is devalued are those for which women are socialized. As is true of practically all social and philosophical schools from Socrates onward (Lloyd, 1984), Bowen elevates reason as a principle, associating it with men and their activities, and devalues emotion, associating it with women and their activities.

Bowen also repeats the cultural biases that minimize the father's role and over-implicate the mother's in explaining children's problems. Mothers, we are told, "overinvest" in their children because of their inability to separate from their own mothers. Entire families are hospitalized, but fathers disappear from the case accounts. Being an expert in genograms does not ensure that one person on the genogram will not be made a villain (Luepnitz, 1988).

Minuchin, similarly, tends to unbalance and restructure the family through the mother. Mothers are the overinvolved ones, and they are the family members generally in need of change. Luepnitz's (1988) analysis of Minuchin's writings and videotapes leads her to conclude that he treats the peripheral fathers with much greater deference and much less pressure to change. Watching Minuchin's taped demonstrations, especially the one entitled "Taming Monsters," reminds her of the pervasive description of mothers in the "adequate" American family: obese, overwhelmed with responsibility, without access to the outside sources of activity and self-esteem that fathers have. Then to top it off, structural therapists tell the mothers that they must change! Structural family therapy may well recapitulate the mother-blaming of the larger social order.

The communications and strategic approach seeks to perfect the unexamined life. The assumptions that action often precedes understanding and that changing patterns is more important than insight are not necessarily congenial to women and other oppressed groups. The dualism between action and insight is unfortunate, because women frequently seek both in psychotherapy and because empowerment typically entails some form of awareness. Assigning ordeals, intervening paradoxically, and employing tactics without mutual insight begin to feel a lot like social control, even if they are designed to be therapeutic.

Underlying most systems theory is a single normative model for healthy family functioning that transcends all class, cultural, and ethnic differences. In a pluralistic society such as the United States, it is a constant struggle to help people understand that there is richness and strength in diversity, including diversity of family forms. After an intensive study of healthy families, Lewis, Beavers, Gossett, and Philips (1976) decided to title their book *No Single Thread,* implying that they had discovered no single structure in the ways these families functioned. Yet many family therapists continue to theorize about Ozzie-and-Harriet models of the family that include well-bonded spouse, parental, and sibling subsystems. The U.S. Census finds that less than 5% of the nation's households matched the stereotype of a working father, a nonworking mother, and two children. What about the large number of single-parent families, child-free families, extended families, cohabitating couples, gay-couple families, blended families, immigrant families? Inclusive theorizing and inclusive practice are required for pluralistic societies.

From an Integrative Perspective

Systems therapies are very useful additions to the psychotherapist's repertoire as long as they are kept within reasonable bounds. For example, strategic therapists have created paradoxical interventions that can prove valuable with highly resistant individuals, couples, or families. But most clients cooperate in treatment, and imposing a paradoxical intervention on these patients undermines the sanctity of the therapeutic alliance and perpetuates the image of therapists as manipulative control freaks. Structural therapy lacks an adequate theory and technique for dealing with intense resistance but would appear to be helpful with families motivated to help a child in crisis with psychosomatic stress or anorexia. Bowenian therapy, on the other hand, seems better suited for young adults who are experiencing problems in the process of separating from their families of origin. Some form of systems-informed family therapy is certainly indicated for alcohol and drug abusers. Within such bounds, systemic therapies can become part of a more comprehensive approach to change.

Systemic therapies are out of bounds, however, when they try to construe every problem as a systems problem. It is true that in some cases, improvement in one family member can be accompanied by a worsening in another family member. However, it is even more often the case that when one family member recovers from substance abuse, anxiety, depression, or other forms of psychopathology, the whole family system improves. Just as the specter of symptom substitution threatened therapists for generations, systemic positions would make us believe that patient substitution—in which symptoms shift from one family member to another—is the rule rather than the exception. But there is no research to suggest that patient substitution is any more frequent than the old bugaboo of symptom substitution.

— A SYSTEMIC ANALYSIS OF THE C. FAMILY —

For six years, individually oriented psychotherapists attempted to treat Mrs. C. out of context. Mrs. C. was treated as an isolated event, even to the extent of being removed from the family for a year in a psychiatric hospital. Blinded by the traditional ideology that psychopathology is an individual event, previous mental health professionals were unable to see how her symptoms were developed and maintained in a pathological family system.

The marital subsystem is characterized by a complementary relationship in which Mrs. C. speaks or acts and Mr. C. reacts. The entire family is skewed in the direction of Mrs. C.'s symptoms. Her obsession with cleanliness dominates the family's rules for relating. It is not surprising that Mrs. C.'s family of origin was skewed in the direction of her domineering father.

The family system is also characterized by enmeshment. Unclear boundaries abound, as Mrs. C. runs around with bare breasts in front of her teenage sons. The children have no space in their own home into which they can invite their friends. The boundaries between Mr. and Mrs. C. are lost when he participates in the washing rituals. Mr. C. arises at 5:00 A.M. to yell out "Right arm, Martha; left arm, Martha." And yet only Mrs. C. has been identified as a patient. *Folie à deux!* The entire family lets silverware and underwear lie around the house until it looks like a dump. Yet only Mrs. C. is going to be dumped in the state hospital. *Folie à famille!*

What threatened this family to the extent that it could regain balance only by developing puzzling and pathological behaviors? The family history suggests that the family health care system was threatened by a runaway of pinworms, Asian flu, and a sixth pregnancy. Apparently the family was unable to grow and adapt to the changes imposed by this crisis. The family physician prescribed washing, and Mrs.

C. washed and washed until she became the identified patient. But were other family members able to grow to help meet the tremendous demands on the family? Was Mr. C., for example, able to grow into a more complete parent to help with the burdens of five children, illness, and an infestation of pinworms?

The boundaries of this enmeshed family were becoming too permeable. The boundaries had already been permeated by pinworms and a foreign influenza. The system's preoccupation with cleanliness seemed to communicate a need to establish clearer boundaries. Mrs. C., for example, was becoming entirely enmeshed in her children's health and hygienic concerns, just as her father had been enmeshed in her personal concerns. In a desperate attempt to clarify her personal boundaries, Mrs. C. would scrub her skin; Mrs. C. was trying to keep clean the skin that defines the physical boundaries of herself as an individual.

The C. family became organized around a set of compulsive rules for relating. Perhaps because there were so many children in the family already, these rules forbade any neighbor children from crossing the literal boundaries of the home. Mr. and Mrs. C. were able to relate as a couple in the intimacy of their bedroom primarily around the compulsive shower. The shower also set limits on Mrs. C.'s availability for relating to her children in the morning. She also set limits on her concerns by communicating only about their health and hygiene and not about friends and feelings.

For ten years, the compulsive rules for relating served to cleanse and clarify many of the boundaries in the family. With the older children entering adolescence and adulthood, however, these rules were too rigid and constrictive to respond to the children's increasing needs for autonomy, intimacy, and privacy. In trying to restructure itself, the family was threatening to remove Mrs. C. from the boundaries of the home. In return, she threatened suicide.

The C. family is clearly in need of a powerful agent from outside the system who can join with the family to restructure their communication patterns and rules for relating. The entire family should be seen, including Mrs. C.'s parents if necessary. The therapist would first have to join with each of the subsystems in the family. With the children, the therapist would speak the language of greater autonomy and responsibility. The therapist might help the children to communicate a goal of being able to invite a friend to visit within the bounds of their own room. The therapist would help open new areas of communicating, such as rules about dating, curfews, and working outside the home.

Once the systemic therapist had joined the family to create a new therapeutic system, she or he would begin to liberate the family from dysfunctional rules and structures by producing disequilibrium. Of course, there is no rigid way of restructuring a family system. A rigid set of rules for relating in therapy could present the paradox of substituting one compulsive set of rules for another. The therapist would relate in a flexible manner, responding more freely to pathological communications or structures than the family members respond. If the family insists on defining the problem as Mrs. C.'s problem, for example, the therapist will be able to reframe the compulsive symptoms into systems language. The compulsive rules of cleanliness can be reframed positively as an expression of the family's desire to stay healthy together. Reframing the symptoms can produce cognitive disequilibrium that helps the family become more aware of how the symptoms have served the family.

The therapist can help liberate the family from compulsive rules by prescribing alternative ways of relating, both in the sessions and at home. If Mrs. C. keeps her physical distance from her children in the sessions, the therapist may take a younger child's hand and say, "Come on, let's give Mama a big hug to show her we love her." As part of the concern about staying healthy together, the therapist may give the parents a homework assignment to spend one evening together cooking their children a big, healthy meal. This assignment could help to create better boundaries around the parents and could help the children to perceive them as more equal rather than complementary.

If the C.s prove to be particularly resistant to restructuring, the systemic therapist can always call on paradoxical techniques for liberating the family. The therapist may prescribe the symptom—say, a two-hour shower in the morning. The rationale would be that the shower is one of the best ways that Mrs. C. has for communicating her concern with staying clean for the good of her family. Also, the morning shower is one of the best ways that Mr. C. has of showing his concern for his wife. Since the shower is one of the best ways they have for cooperating together as a couple, a long, leisurely, warm shower is just what the doctor ordered.

Of course, prescribing a long morning shower would serve as a therapeutic double bind. This assignment would give Mr. and Mrs. C. two choices: to cooperate or not to cooperate with the assignment. If they choose to cooperate, then they are choosing to carry out their symptoms. The symptoms would no longer be out of control, because they would no longer have the experience of "I can't help it— I must wash, or I must keep track of my wife's washing." If they choose not to cooperate, then they are choosing not to carry out their symptomatic behavior. Either way, they begin to liberate themselves from a pathologically structured way of relating.

Future Directions

Systems theory remains an alternative to conventional wisdom rather than a part of it. The clinical concepts and therapeutic strategies associated with it are not yet considered part of the mainstream. At the same time, we and others find unambiguous signs that the systemic perspective is moving toward paradigmatic parity with more conventional and established perspectives, such as the psychodynamic, humanistic, behavioral, and cognitive traditions (Coyne & Liddle, 1992) . The future of systemic therapies is thus filled with expanding opportunities, but it must temper past claims and pursue new directions.

Part of the expansion is likely to lie in the continuing application of systems theory to areas beyond the treatment of the nuclear family system. One of these areas is, paradoxically, the individual patient: to treat both the psyche and the system within the context of individual psychotherapy (Torgenrued & Storm, 1989). Another area of expansion (and the title of a journal) is *family systems medicine*, in which family medicine and family therapy are integrated. The family treatment of substance abuse, as we have seen, is a particularly promising, as is family therapy with clients suffering from dementia, cardiovascular disease, and unipolar depression (Pinsof, Wynne, & Hambright, 1996). Systems theory will continue to be applied to larger social systems as well, such as organizations and communities (McDaniel, Hepworth, & Doherty, 1992; Senge, 1992).

Another promising direction is the use of a consensual diagnostic system for dysfunctional families. Traditional diagnostic schemes, such as the DSM-IV (American Psychiatric Association, 1995), locate the source of the disorder within the individual and neglect the relational context. No standard classification scheme for dysfunctional relationships has emerged and, as a consequence, systems therapists and their patients have been hampered by a variety of clinical, legal, and insurance difficulties. However, the authors of the DSM-IV have agreed to further study scales for the assessment of relational functioning for possible inclusion in the next edition of the DSM. Equally important, several organizations joined forces to compile a comprehensive typology of family diagnosis. Kaslow's (1996) monumental *Handbook of Relational Diagnosis and Dysfunctional Family Patterns* summarizes the typologies and provides the next steps for a truly interactional system of clinical diagnosis.

Within systemic therapy, there has been a decided breakdown of schoolism and a movement toward integration. In large surveys of family therapists, between one third and one half describe their theoretical orientation as eclectic; systemic therapy is far from monolithic (Jensen, Bergin, & Greaves, 1990; Rait, 1988). The growing contact between systems therapies and psychotherapy integration could have any of three results: harmony at any price, mutual repulsion, or an extended dialogue (Coyne & Liddle, 1992). So far, an extended dialogue has ensued (Goldenberg & Goldenberg, 1996; Pinsof, 1995).

In the past, systemic therapy had been like a car cruising on automatic control with the driver comfortably seated in the lotus position. Family therapy rested on the normative concepts of gender relationships and idealized conceptions of family relationships. Gender bias was "cruising" along by exaggerating gender differences or ignoring them (Hare-Mustin, 1987). But no more. In the future, an indisputable direction of systemic therapies will be the creation of gender-sensitive and culture-relevant treatments (for example, Boyd-Franklin, 1989; Carter, 1989; Gopaul-McNicol, 1991; McGoldrick, Giordano & Pearce, 1996).

In terms of training, equivalency training will gradually give way to a requirement of academic marital and family training. In the past, most family therapists have been trained in the disciplines of psychology, psychiatry, or social work and then attended postdegree training programs or advanced workshops to satisfy the Association for Marriage and Family Therapy (AAMFT) or a state licensure/certification board that they were qualified family therapists. But now the once-open doorways to AAMFT membership and state certification have become almost impassable for most professionals without a degree from a family therapy program. The wisdom of this change has been hotly debated, but it appears that family therapy as a profession will become similar in its exclusiveness to psychology, medicine, and other professions. At the same time, the technique and theory of systemic therapy will become a standard part of psychology and psychiatry training, even if their graduates are not fully recognized as "family therapists."

As a result, family therapy will be increasingly perceived as a separate and distinct profession. Psychologists, psychiatrists, and social workers will become less involved in family therapy organizations (but still conduct marital and family therapy), as the path to becoming a "family therapist" gradually but relentlessly narrows (Gurman & Kniskern, 1992). Ironically, perhaps, most of the field's founders would be unable to qualify as family therapists, as defined by the 21 states that have licensure or certification.

As is true of most psychotherapy systems, which mature from adolescence into adulthood, systemic therapies, once the radical and innovative pioneers, have now become rigid and institutionalized in terms of training and credentialing. Nonetheless, they continue to embody the paradigm shift to systems thinking as a whole new way of conceptualizing human problems and their resolution.

Suggestions for Further Reading

Bowen, M. (1978). *Family therapy in clinical practice*. New York: Jason Aronson.

Goldenberg, I., & Goldenberg, H. (1996). *Family therapy: An overview* (4th ed.). Pacific Grove, CA: Brooks/Cole.

Gurman, A. S., & Kniskern, D. P. (Eds.). (1991). *Handbook of family therapy* (Vol. 2). New York: Brunner/Mazel.

Haley, J. (1976). *Problem-solving therapy: New strategies for effective family therapies*. San Francisco: Jossey-Bass.

Hoffman, L. (1981). *Foundations of family therapy: A conceptual framework for systems change*. New York: Basic.

Luepnitz, D. A. (1988). *The family interpreted: Feminist theory in clinical practice*. New York: Basic.

Mikesell, R. H., Lusterman, D., & McDaniel, S. H. (Eds.). (1995). *Integrating family therapy: Handbook of family psychology and systems theory*. Washington, DC: American Psychological Association.

Minuchin, S. (1974). *Families and family therapy*. Cambridge, MA: Harvard University Press.

Satir, V. (1967). *Conjoint family therapy*. Palo Alto, CA: Science and Behavior Books.

Watzlawick, P., Weakland, J. H., & Fisch, R. (1974). *Change: Principles of problem formation and problem resolution*. New York: Norton.

Journals: *American Journal of Family Therapy; Contemporary Family Therapy; Family Process; Family Therapy; Family Therapy Networker; International Journal of Family Psychiatry; International Journal of Family Therapy; Journal of Family Psychology; Journal of Family Psychotherapy; Journal of Feminist Family Therapy; Journal of Marital and Family Therapy; Journal of Psychotherapy and the Family; Journal of Sex and Marital Therapy; Journal of Systemic Therapies; The Family Journal*.

12

Gender- and Culture-Sensitive Therapies

with Mary C. Sweeney

OUR DUTCH COLLEAGUE, Dr. Sjoerd Colijn, shared the following anecdote at a professional conference in an effort to demonstrate the presumptive error of importing one culture's system of psychotherapy into another. With the kind permission of his entire family, we present this illuminating incident as a sage warning against culture-insensitive therapy.

In 1974, when I had just started my studies at the University of Amsterdam, my family of origin, including me, had family therapy for about six months. These were the early years of family therapy; my family felt very unfamiliar and uneasy in the therapy situation, but endured this ordeal with Calvinist equanimity. Looking back, I am confident that the therapists felt just as unfamiliar and uneasy and just put up with the situation as well. Careful maneuvering by the therapists and cautious cooperation by my family resulted in the idea the we were making progress, even though all of us felt quite uncertain.

At that time, the American family therapy pioneer Carl Whitaker visited Europe and was invited to do live demonstration sessions in the Netherlands with several families. My family was selected. The therapy language was English; the children translated for each other.

It was a memorable session. No careful maneuvering this time; within an hour Carl Whitaker turned our family upside down. One family member was identified as "the crucified of the family," another member's motives were interpreted as "driven by the fear of death," and my parents were made aware of the "benevolent but suffocating regime" they had imposed upon our family. I managed to escape the wrath of this vengeful god, as all of my family felt it then, by being completely occupied in translating for my brother and sister.

One session later we informed the therapists of our decision to terminate. We met only mild resistance on their part.

The point I want to make is that even though American culture and Northern European culture are not very dissimilar, the cultural gap between the two turned out to be very large indeed. Carl Whitaker may be a wonderful family therapist, and from his point of view he must have made some very well-designed interpretations. The validity of his assumptions were probably affirmed in his mind by the turmoil of our family. But the interpretations he gave, however true, we did not understand; the interventions he made, however adequate within his therapy system, only aroused fright and shock; the way he made contact with us, whatever he wanted to convey, was experienced as disrespectful. His therapy felt to us like balancing on the brink of chaos. From the point of view of a Dutch upper-middle-class family, there was no way that this session could have been helpful.

A Sketch of Sociopolitical Forces

Modern psychotherapy was created by white European men in their own image. Since its earliest beginnings in Europe, psychotherapy has emphasized white male society's definition of healthy mental states and has largely ignored the needs of the diverse populations it professes to serve. Most psychotherapy research, practice, and training have been conducted by men, even though women have comprised the majority of clients.

Psychotherapy was originally envisioned as a universal, transcultural process: one size or type would fit all potential patients. However, it was soon discovered that psychotherapy was created by humans to solve human problems and that any product of human ingenuity is by definition *cultural*. Psychotherapy is inescapably and inextricably bound to a particular cultural framework (Wohl, 1989). Traditional therapies—based on white, middle-class, male assumptions—are increasingly seen as inappropriate for addressing the problems of minority and oppressed groups, such as African Americans, Asian Americans, Latino/Hispanic Americans, and women.

The late 1960s witnessed a growing realization that racial minorities' and women's concerns were being neglected in the mental health field. This interest was spurred in large part by the 1964 Civil Rights Act and the Women's Rights Movement. Both the American Psychological Association (APA) and the American Association for Counseling and Development (AACD) recognized the need to develop policies and to establish committees to work with racial and ethnic minority groups more effectively. Training conferences recommended that conducting psychotherapy without gender and cultural sensitivity be declared unethical. In 1978, the President's Commission on Mental Health examined, for the first time, the effectiveness of psychotherapy for ethnic minorities.

Changing demographics signal the need for cultural awareness in all pursuits, but especially those as rooted in interpersonal relations as psychotherapy. At present, African Americans comprise about 12% of the U.S. population. The poverty rate is increasing among this group, and the unemployment rate is alarmingly disproportionate. The Asian American population of the United States has doubled since the 1970s: it now comprises 3% and will grow to 10% at mid-century. Latino/Hispanic Americans are currently the second-largest and fastest-growing minority group in the United States. One in four Americans already defines himself or herself as a member of an ethnic minority. If current trends in immigration and birth rates persist, people of color will no longer be the minority, but the majority, by the year 2050 (Henry, 1990; U.S. Bureau of the Census, 1990).

As minority groups continue to immigrate to the United States, they face the harsh reality of a land that generally does not speak their native language and that embraces cultural norms vastly different from the ones they may have experienced. Social changes such as these often lead to stress and culturally induced psychopathologies that traditional psychotherapy is ill-equipped to handle. Thus, as the population of the United States becomes more diverse, the practice of psychotherapy must follow suit or be left by the wayside. In other words, the *browning of America* changes not only people of color, but also the institution of psychotherapy.

At the same time that cultural sensitivity was making inroads into the psychological community, awareness of the lack of appropriate psychotherapeutic services for women was coming to the fore. Fed by societal changes propelled by the cross-cultural movement, the human rights movement, and the wider availability of opportunities not limited by gender, women began to demand that psychotherapy alter its discriminatory nature and take appropriate steps to offer services specifically for and by women.

Female psychotherapists across the nation began dialogues that both reflected and ignited the feminist therapy movement. In the 1970s, these women joined together to form a number of feminist mental health organizations, including the Association for Women in Psychology. Inspired by such events as the ongoing Women's Rights Movement and the United Nations Decade of the Woman (1976–1985), feminist therapy has grown by leaps and bounds since its early beginnings. Feminist therapy continues to be based on the belief that women share many of the characteristics of oppressed people. The key to a healthy individual lies in recognizing the negative effects of a male-dominated society on women's self-concepts and on establishing a more egalitarian power balance with men.

In addition to the sociopolitical forces driving the development of gender-aware and culture-sensitive therapies, these psychotherapies have themselves undergone historical evolution. Comas-Diaz (1992) outlines four developmental stages of psychotherapy with ethnic minorities and women. The first stage involved a *reactive* position: the efficacy of psychotherapy for oppressed populations was questioned and examined. The second stage, characterized by an *inquisitive* position, entailed active clinical and analogue research that demonstrated that women and people of color could indeed benefit from psychotherapy. The third and current stage endorses a *revisionist* position, in which the field moves beyond the question of effectiveness and examines the process variables of race, gender, and culture in psychotherapy as well as the ethnicity/gender interaction. The immediate future will probably involve an *integrative* position, one that comprehensively addresses the daily reality of minority individuals. The multiple interactions of race, culture, biology, gender, class, sexual orientation, religion, and other variables will all become critical considerations in the development of new, integrative theoretical models.

A framework for gender-aware and culture-sensitive psychotherapy can be based on one of two models (Comas-Diaz, 1992). The first model consists of developing gender- and culture-specific psychotherapies for each patient group: Native Americans, Asian Americans, African Americans, Latino/Hispanic Americans, women, and men, to name a few. This transforms psychotherapy by replacing or adapting culture-specific theories and techniques to the unique sociocultural reality of each group. The second model consists of developing generalized cross-gender and transcultural therapeutic skills that are applicable across a wide array of groups. Although a promising model, cross-cultural therapy is relatively new and untested. As a consequence, our coverage in this chapter will follow the more widely established and practiced models of gender-specific and culture-sensitive therapies.

Feminist Therapy

Of late, there has been confusion and backlash over the use of the term *feminist* (Faludi, 1991). We will use the term descriptively and accurately as defined in the dictionary: a person who believes in and/or advocates the principle that women should have political, economic, and social rights equal to those of men.

Theory of Personality

Feminist psychotherapy has its roots, paradoxically, not in psychology, but in the philosophy of the women's movement of the 1960s. As a result, it has no consensual theory of personality. Nonetheless, a distinctive emphasis common to feminist theory is the assertion that a person's identity is profoundly influenced by prevailing environmental pressures, such as gender roles and gender-based discrimination. These factors influence cognitive structures and behavior patterns.

Nancy Chodorow (1989) has proposed that psychological differences between the genders are due mainly to the fact that children are raised primarily by women. A little girl's identity is founded on a sense of continuity in her relationship with her mother. She internalizes the personality messages her mother sends out and attempts to incorporate them into her own behavioral repertoire. In contrast, a little boy's identity is formed through a discontinuity in his relationship with his mother. He learns to give up his identification with his mother and becomes masculine through his relationship with his father. Chodorow (1978) asserts that mothers connect more with their daughters and separate from their sons and that this produces a "division of psychological capacities" between girls and boys. Because girls learn to be affiliative and nurturant from their mothers, they grow up motivated for motherhood. Boys, however, because they actively avoid emulating their mothers, never learn to be nurturant. They typically model the aggressive, power-seeking nature of older male role models.

Power inequalities and gender-role expectations shape the cognitive structure from the moment a child comes into the world. From the first day of life, a child is constantly bombarded with messages of gender expectations. Consider an illustrative study by Smith and Lloyd (1978): mothers of first-born infants were presented with a previously unknown 6-month-old infant dressed in "gender-appropriate" or "cross-gender" clothing and instructed to play with the infant for ten minutes. The results indicated that only the infant dressed as a girl was first offered a doll to play with, while only the infant dressed as a boy was first offered a hammer or a rattle. The infant dressed as a boy was also encouraged to be more physically active than the infant dressed as a girl.

Girls are typically expected to be sweet, sensitive, and docile, while boys are expected to be strong, stoic, and brave. Girls are socialized to cultivate attractiveness to men, and males are socialized to view women as objects of consumption (Luepnitz, 1988). As Meth and Pasick (1992) observe, "Gender politics are deeply imbedded in the fabric of American society and, thus, over the course of our psychological and social development, profoundly influence how we see ourselves as men and women" (p. 5). Gender-role expectations are deeply ingrained in adult personality.

Theory of Psychopathology

Most psychological distress is environmentally induced, and "cultural determinism" is the basis for the self-destructive actions. Pathology occurs when the social structure is so rigidly defined that people are not permitted to grow and change and when relationships between individuals are unbalanced, as is the case with power inequalities between men and women. Distress is emphatically not solely the result of intrapsychic conflicts, but more likely the result of social and political factors. In fact, the term *psychopathology* is generally avoided in the feminist literature because it smacks of an underlying medical and intrapsychic perspective; words such as *distress, pain,* or *problem* are preferred.

Definitions of normality and identification of psychopathology frequently reflect male-centered bias. While the predominant categorization of mental disorders, the American Psychiatric Association's (1995) DSM-IV, describes clusters of real symptoms, it also represents the dominant attitudes of its membership (80% plus male) and overvalues stereotypically male behaviors of autonomy and control (Nikelly, 1996). Dependent personality, self-defeating personality, and passive-aggressive personality are offered in the DSM-IV as female-predominant mental disorders, not as coping behaviors resulting from disadvantaged positions and exploitive situations that women cannot easily escape. But the DSM-IV fails to consider exaggerated male traits as pathological. Where are the delusional dominating personality disorder, the greedy personality disorder, and the macho personality disorder?

Gender socialization shapes not only the prevalence but also the expression of distress. The prevalence rates of various behavioral disorders differ between the sexes (Robins et al., 1984). Congruent with sex role stereotyping that leads women to internalize distress and men to externalize it, men have higher lifetime prevalence rates for externalizing disorders, such as alcohol and drug abuse and antisocial personality disorder, whereas women show a higher prevalence of affective, phobic, obsessive-compulsive, and panic disorders—largely internalizing problems.

A multitude of interrelated sociopolitical factors place women at higher risk for these forms of behavioral distress. A short and incomplete list would include sex role stereotyping, gender-role expectancies, role strain and conflict, sexual trauma, and gender-related economics.

Messages from the larger culture are relayed routinely through the media (including television, magazines, and movies), through school-based sexism, through religious institutions, and through sexist language. These media instill in young children messages about gender inequality, stereotyped sex role behavior, and negative self-values. Textbooks generally depict little girls as passive and fearful, while little boys are adventurous and daring. Curriculum choices often encourage girls to pursue courses in home economics, while boys are encouraged to pursue courses in math and science. Teachers attribute the failures of girls to lack of competence, but attribute the failures of boys to lack of effort (Worell & Remer, 1992).

These social messages are facets of internalized oppression; the external messages become a part of how we think and feel. Little girls are scolded for wanting to play with trucks and trains, the so-called "boy toys," and told that their self-worth rests primarily on being pretty and proper. Girls are rarely encouraged to pursue activities that require autonomy or skill; they are told to play "dress up" and "house," while little boys are encouraged to play astronaut or police officer. At an early age, girls begin to devalue themselves and their true desires as they begin to conform to the expectancies of the larger society. Seidenberg (1970, p. 134) states, "No woman will treasure fame or glory she can achieve at the price of being called unfeminine. This below the belt blow sends most women into despair."

Gender-role conflicts and expectancies often generate a false sense of self. Women are forced to accept the "gender rules" that society stipulates as necessary for women to be widely accepted by men. Women are expected to always be a lady, to never swear, hit, or get angry. They should strive to please men and, above all, never act more intelligent or beat a man at a game. The unquestioning acceptance of these rules leads women to adopt roles they might not care to undertake if they were given a choice. After years of living a life that is false and unfulfilling, a woman's reservoir of anger, frustration, and resentment builds and is often expressed through self-destructive behaviors.

Omnipresent sex role stereotyping limits the potential of all human beings. When individuals are forced to conform to gender-role expectancies, they fail to achieve—or even try to achieve—skills or interests in areas outside of their gender borders. Individuals, especially women, who subscribe to a traditional sex role orientation have a higher incidence of depression and anxiety, lower self-esteem, and more social withdrawal than women who do not strictly adhere to traditional female roles and expectancies (Worell & Remer, 1992).

Ms. A. came to therapy with an ultrafeminine appearance and not a hint of any so-called masculine traits (Lerner, 1988). She had never gone through a "tomboy" stage and had avoided aggressive play her entire life. She seemed to be a model of domesticity and femininity. Lately, her boyfriend and the feminist subculture had been pressuring her to become more liberated, but when she tried to change her appearance, even slightly, to include more masculine aspects, such as wearing jeans, she began to have feelings of depersonalization and unreality. Through psychotherapy, it became evident that Ms. A. maintained her sexual identity primarily through strict conformity to behaviors ascribed to her sex that were clearly differentiated from those ascribed to men.

Women's distress also stems from stresses created by society's lack of support for their changing roles. As women have entered into new roles, they have developed a greater sense of self and independence, but the reluctance of society to change with them has hampered their success. Women in new work roles face poor child care options, husbands who are unwilling to become coequal in parenting and household responsibilities, and few employers willing to establish flexible shifts and job-sharing positions. The challenge of trying to balance work with a traditional household role leads many women to develop role overload and role strain. *Role strain* involves conflicting demands from different roles. For example, a woman may work during the day, come home and care for her family in the evening, and then attend school at night. She has four distinct roles to perform (worker, mother, wife, and student) and the strain of having to adequately perform all these roles is tremendous. *Role conflict* involves roles clashing with each other, as when elements involved in being a good mother begin to conflict with elements of being a student. The pressures of one role will begin to take over and inhibit an individual from performing the duties of other roles. With conflict over "abandoning" children to day care settings, many women feel that they are being forced to choose between being a good mother and having a meaningful career. The fire fueling this guilt is associated with the messages society sends to women about proper child-rearing practices.

Mother-blaming, or mother-bashing, portrays mothers as responsible for all the problems of children. Psychology contains no concept of "acceptable" or praiseworthy behaviors for mothers (Caplan, 1989). If the family appears to be warm and loving, it is enmeshed, and this is invariably considered to be the mother's fault. There is also a double standard in describing mothers and fathers. Mothers are described according to how they are, while fathers are described by what they do; if both parents behave in the exact same manner, the mother's behavior is described as "cold," while the father is "just that way."

Sexual trauma is another major contributor to psychopathology among women. Women who have experienced sexual violence as a child or as an adult see the world through different eyes than those who have not. They frequently express feelings of alienation, of being out of step with others, and of psychological distance (Walker, 1990). Violence against women is horribly common, and its devastating consequences can haunt women for the rest of their lives. Approximately one-fourth of American women may have experienced some form of childhood sexual abuse. A history of childhood sexual abuse has often been found in adult women who suffer from eating disorders, substance abuse, posttraumatic stress disorder, and various dissociative disorders.

Women who have experienced sexual trauma are victimized twice—once during the act, and again by society, the medical profession, and the law. About 60% of rapes are acquaintance rapes (Worell & Remer, 1992), but the men who commit this crime are frequently let off the hook. Blaming women for rape is a way of denying the violent and traumatizing nature of the crime. Holding women responsible for rape by inferring that they broke the rules of society (the rules being to protect yourself at all times) keeps many women from reporting the act and also prevents them from experiencing the feelings of anger and loss at the violation. It is estimated that only 20% of rapes are reported; of those reported, only 10% of the perpetrators are found guilty. Instead, the victims are made to feel guilty, and their bottled-up rage manifests itself in pathological symptoms—depression, denial, anxiety, sleep disturbances, low self-esteem, and sexual dysfunctions, to name a few.

The lower economic status of women adds to the formation and maintenance of distress. Women continue to be clustered in lower-paying, lower-status, traditional sex role occupations (Worell & Remer, 1992); there is a distinct economic disadvantage to being female. The "feminization of poverty" is a pithy phrase that captures the realization that single and divorced women and their children constitute an increasing proportion of poor people, especially in the United States (Goldberg & Kremen, 1990). High gender wage gaps, low social welfare benefits, and expectations that women have primary child care responsibilities all conspire to keep women in economically fragile and thus less powerful and more distressed positions.

As a result of centuries of dependence on men, women are typically paid less than men and are usually well below men in income level. The average female worker is just as well-educated as the average male worker (median schooling of 12.6 years), but a woman makes only 76 cents for every dollar a man earns when they both work full-time year-round (U.S. Bureau of Labor Statistics, 1997). Women comprise 80% of clerical workers, but only 40% of managers and administrators (U.S. Department of Labor, 1997). Society continues to value men in the workplace, as evidenced in the salary and power differentials between men and women. Money does not guarantee mental health, but it does offer a buffer against the strains of life.

The workplace, in general, is a harsh setting for women. Between 40% and 90% of all working women have been sexually harassed, depending on the definition (Worell & Remer, 1992). Harassment and the acceptance of harassment by a male-dominated society leave women feeling powerless and with lowered self-esteem. It also reinforces the view of women as sex objects and denies that they are intelligent, contributing individuals.

Many career women suffer when they choose to have a child: their companies assign them to the so-called "mommy track," and suddenly promotions and important assignments begin to disappear (Paludi, 1992). Also hindering mobility and advancement is the glass ceiling—a term used to describe the subtle barrier that women and minorities face in their climb up the corporate ladder. Although women can see the top of the hierarchy and are informed that with patience and persistence they can reach the apex, they rarely do. The *glass ceiling* prevents women from moving into the top management positions; only 3.6% of board directorships and 1.7% of corporate officerships in Fortune 500 companies are held by women (VonGlinow & Krzyczkowska-Mercer, 1988).

Whatever the pathology, a cure becomes possible only when the cause is discovered. From the feminist viewpoint, the cause of dysfunctional behavior is principally related to gender, not through genes or chromosomes, but through the gender socialization processes, expectancies, and discrimination. Corrective actions are thus frequently informational and political in nature.

Theory of Therapeutic Processes

Consciousness Raising. Consciousness raising is a vital part of feminist psychotherapy. In order for a woman to escape the oppressive thumb of the male-dominated culture, she must first realize the negative impact these values and expectations have had on her life. It is important for her to understand how sociopolitical and interpersonal forces influence her behavior. Men face less discrimination, less harassment, and to a certain extent, less rigid role expectations than women. Both sexes are subject to gender-role expectations, but women often receive the more severe punishment if they refuse to acquiesce in role expectations (Hyde, 1991).

Women need to differentiate between what they have been taught is socially acceptable and what is actually healthy for them. Millions of women were raised to be "good girls"—docile and submissive—but later learned that such a passive style contributes to behavioral deficits and emotional distress. Women taught to be interpersonally passive instead of assertive, for instance, are likely to experience more depression, eating disorders, and sexual conflicts than their assertive counterparts (McGrath, Keita, Strickland, & Russo, 1990).

Consciousness raising helps uncover the underlying purposes of behaviors. Women come to realize that they often do not do things because they truly want to, but rather because society expects them to act in certain ways. Connections between external situations and psychological problems often surface when a woman realizes that the reason she feels unfulfilled is because she has rarely done anything just for herself, that her actions have always been in response to the expectations of others.

Consider the case of Ms. J., a 30-year-old woman married to a financially successful husband and the mother of a young daughter (Lerner, 1988). She came for therapy complaining of depression, stating that her life was "going nowhere." Ms. J. described her husband as a "brilliant workaholic" who engaged in repetitive cycles of distancing and dominating the family. He had not "allowed" her to work until their daughter entered kindergarten. The client was now bored and unfulfilled with her current job and wanted to return to graduate school, but she feared that her husband would never be able to tolerate her competence or her involvement in anything that excluded him. In keeping with the dictates of culture and the prescribed complementarity of marriage, the client had dutifully underfunctioned, putting aside her own ambitions in order to bolster her husband and preserve harmony.

Consciousness raising about possible sex bias and sex role stereotyping in the *therapist* is the beginning of the therapist's work. Most mental health disciplines have adopted principles related to sex role bias. Table 12.1 lists 13 guidelines for therapy with women promulgated in the 1970s by the American Psychological Association (American Psychological Association, 1975, 1978). Responsible psychotherapists are enjoined to routinely examine their own practice and language for gender stereotypes and to raise their own consciousness about the characteristics of psychotherapy.

Feminist therapists have a variety of options regarding consciousness raising. One task is to be a client's supporter, to encourage her in whatever she feels would be beneficial for her, but also to educate her on sexist social methods and individual cognitions. Therapists explain to clients the unfair expectations they have been socialized to accept and encourage them to evaluate the influence of social roles and norms on their problems. Through the use of self-disclosure and mutual support, therapists encourage clients to become more self-directed and autonomous. In consciousness raising, a feminist therapist can both educate and understand, something that is often difficult to accomplish in traditional psychotherapies.

Feminist therapists walk a tightrope: they demonstrate how women are subject to expectations and limitations imposed by a sexist society, but they also reinforce the idea that women must not accept the role of the passive victim. Too little or too much toward either side will probably retard improvement.

Therapists liberally refer clients to groups that endorse feminist principles and that aid in the therapeutic process. Women's groups, domestic abuse groups, assertiveness training, power analysis, and sex role analysis are just a sampling of the variety of educational groups that are based on feminist therapy principles. Power analysis groups are designed to increase women's awareness of the power differential existing between men and women and to empower women to have influence on the interpersonal and institutional externals in their lives. Similarly, sex role analysis groups are designed to increase women's awareness of how the sex role expecta-

Table 12.1 Guidelines for Therapy with Women

1. The conduct of therapy should be free of constrictions based on gender-defined roles, and the options explored between client and practitioner should be free of sex role stereotypes.

2. Psychologists should recognize the reality, variety, and implications of sex-discriminatory practices in society and should facilitate client examination of options in dealing with such practices.

3. The therapist should be knowledgeable about current empirical findings on sex roles, sexism, and individual differences resulting from the client's gender-defined identity.

4. The theoretical concepts employed by the therapist should be free of sex bias and sex role stereotypes.

5. The psychologist should demonstrate acceptance of women as equal to men by using language free of derogatory labels.

6. The psychologist should avoid establishing the source of personal problems within the client when they are more properly attributable to situational or cultural factors.

7. The psychologist and a fully informed client mutually agree upon aspects of the therapy relationship such as treatment modality, time factors, and fee arrangements.

8. While the importance of the availability of accurate information to a client's family is recognized, the privilege of communication about diagnosis, prognosis, and progress ultimately resides with the client, not the therapist.

9. If authoritarian processes are employed as a technique, the therapy should not have the effect of maintaining or reinforcing stereotypic dependency of women.

10. The client's assertive behaviors should be respected.

11. The psychologist whose female client is subjected to violence in the form of physical abuse or rape should recognize and acknowledge that the client is the victim of a crime.

12. The psychologist should recognize and encourage exploration of a woman client's sexuality and should recognize her right to define her own sexual preferences.

13. The psychologist should not have sexual relations with a woman client nor treat her as a sex object.

Adapted with permission from Guidelines for Therapy with Women, copyright © by the American Psychological Association (1978).

tions of society adversely affect them and also to understand the ways in which men and women are socialized differently in society.

Consciousness-raising groups are an integral component of feminist therapy. These groups, initially an outgrowth of the women's movement, involve groups of women who meet regularly to discuss their lives as women. They share information about their lives and identify common threads in their experiences. A woman who is being abused by her husband may become involved in a consciousness-raising group and subsequently discover that several other members of the group have also been abused. The knowledge that she is not alone in her predicament may help the woman feel less isolated; moreover, group members' experiences and advice may prompt her to seek the help she desperately needs. Women come to understand that their experiences with discrimination and violence are not isolated incidents involving only themselves, but are universal experiences of women.

Bibliotherapy involves the client's learning about herself and her environment through reading. Reading books and articles relevant to therapeutic issues educates the client and reduces the knowledge differential between the therapist and the client. Popular examples are books related to assertion, sexual abuse, women's health, codependency, workplace discrimination, relationship issues, and family-of-origin concerns.

Choosing. Genuine choice is often a difficult concept for clients to understand. After being trapped in a repressed lifestyle for years, the idea that they can choose to live and grow without the heavy weight of a gender-role albatross around their neck is both fascinating and frightening. The forces of society are strong, and old cultural norms are difficult to break. Once the client comes to understand the impact that society has had on her life, she usually develops a genuine desire to adapt to a healthier lifestyle.

Society, however, does not acclimate quickly or easily to "rocking the boat" and will resist her efforts. Through the process of choosing how to change, the client will probably face many obstacles, such as discrimination, hatred, and discouragement, including discouragement from family and friends who feel that the client was "fine just the way she was," which usually means submissive and dependent.

Two major choices a client faces are the degree of change she wants to accomplish and whether she can achieve her goal without the support of her family. The power a woman gains in changing her life may not be worth the pain of alienating her family in the process. Getting a prize, even the prize of power, may be worthless unless you have important people in your life to share it with.

In short, choosing in feminist therapy means choosing power and choosing how to use it. A woman who realizes the impact that society has upon her can use the power of her knowledge to change. She can choose to remain powerless and dependent, or she can choose to use her power to change both herself and society.

The feminist therapist encourages the client to make choices that will change her life for the better—not just to settle for what others are willing to give her, but to go out and fight for what she is truly entitled to. The therapist and the client agree upon the parameters of treatment. Ideally, the therapy is free of constrictions based on gender-defined roles, and the options explored are free of sex role stereotypes (Table 12.1). By empowering clients, therapists help them develop greater self-esteem, self-confidence, and power. To choose something, rather than just passively accept current conditions, requires power, and power is what the therapist seeks to instill in clients. The term *empowerment* captures the essence of this process. Choosing is ultimately the responsibility of the client, but helping the client develop the power and the skill to choose wisely is in the hands of the therapist.

Social Liberation. The change process known as social liberation entails increasing alternatives for social behaviors. These include advocating for the rights of oppressed populations, empowering clients to change their lifestyles, and making policy interventions.

The sociopolitical context of clients' lives and the interconnectedness of their "inner" world and their "outer" world are often ignored in traditional psychotherapy (Gerber, 1992). But through feminist therapy, clients come to realize the significance of the statement *The personal is political.* This feminist motto essentially means a commitment to using individual understanding about oneself as a basis for understanding the oppression of all women. Traditional sex role socialization limits the potential of people; this motto represents the feminist viewpoint that the source of psychopathology is not intrapsychic, but rather social and political in nature. The intrapsychic influences on distress pale in comparison to the broader social and political forces that hold women captive in stereotyped expectancies and gender discrimination. The focus in therapy, therefore, must be to change the unhealthy external situation and the messages that have been internalized by many women.

Feminists have reconceptualized many behaviors traditionally viewed as personal—as simple interactions between individuals—and reconceptualized them as expressions of political power (Hyde, 1991). When a woman is sexually harassed in the workplace or is raped in the park, society tends to view these acts as personal, individual acts—one person acting against another. Feminist therapy, however, views these actions not only as personal attacks, but also as political expressions of men's power over women. The sexual assault not simply a personal attack against that one woman; it is an act of power directed against all women by men who feel entitled to demean, humiliate, and abuse women.

By reflecting on their own experiences of discrimination, lack of power, and male domination, women come to understand that oppression does not affect only them; it affects everyone in society, women and men alike. Clients come to understand that to be truly free, they must work at it the rest of their lives. Just because they have come to realize the effects of oppression, it does not disappear. Women need to become involved with the political process, to work to change the attitudes and discriminatory actions of society. It is not enough merely to understand that women have unequal power and that many problems stem from the control society imposes on them; women must join together to liberate all members of society from gender expectations and harmful stereotypes that label people without first trying to understand them.

Feminist therapists teach and help women to undergo a "revolution from within" and a "revolution from without." Traditional therapies focus only on internal, individual psychological changes. Feminist therapy endorses this essential change but combines it with external, collective, and political transformations. A woman assisted in recovering from a sexual assault, for instance, may be encouraged to extend the healing process through co-leading therapy groups for assaulted women, volunteering at a women's resource center, educating the public about sexual abuse, or lobbying in the state capital for a bill protecting victims.

The feminist therapist seeks to help women understand the need to continue fighting for their rights and to be a positive role model for involvement. Toward this end, therapists themselves form and join groups to initiate social change. Feminist therapists testify in court on behalf of clients, testify in legislatures on behalf of all women, advocate for adequate welfare and child care, and participate in a myriad of social, political, and psychological activities to free women from abuse.

The content of therapy is based on understanding the sociopolitical determinants of inequality, but understanding inequality is not enough. Therapists seek to help women strive to achieve equality, not only for themselves, but for all individuals in society. The therapeutic imperative is to aid clients in their personal struggles for equality and power and also to be active politically to reform the system. Feminist therapists understand that both the internal and external conditions a client faces are inextricably intertwined and that to change one condition, a change in the other must either come first or follow shortly behind.

At the same time, feminist therapists attempt to educate and liberate fellow mental health professionals. In the past two decades, feminists have brought the attention of all psychotherapists to "the problems of violence and abuse in the family, to the strains of gender roles in a changing culture, to the ethics of practice and boundary violations, to precision and care in the application of diagnostic labels, to consideration of the need for fair and unbiased evaluations of all parties in marital and custodial disputes, and to the need for clients to have power over their actions and relationships" (Brown & Brodsky, 1992, p. 56).

Therapeutic Content

Anxieties and Defenses. Anxiety is a woman's natural reaction to the forces of sexism, discrimination, poverty, and violence that have kept her in a subservient position. Anxiety also results, in part, from the conflict between the desire to expand life experiences beyond those traditionally available to women and the need to maintain the ties and strength that women receive from their group identity. The limiting nature of society increases women's distress and provokes their defensive reactions. This natural anxiety can stereotype women as unassertive, weak, and dependent, but when women fear walking alone or must constantly be on guard against discriminatory practices, anxiety and defenses must be viewed as acceptable forms of coping.

Self-Esteem. A large part of women's self-esteem is based upon maintenance of and interactions in relationships. A woman feels a great sense of satisfaction and fulfillment when the relational aspects of her life are in place, when she feels loved and accepted for who she is and who she wants to be.

In a broader context, women often view society as a collection of relationships. The nature of these relationships shapes self-esteem of the group as a whole. Many theorists view women's relational style as healthier than men's, but when unhealthy relationships arise, they can lead to low self-esteem and maladaptive behaviors among women.

For centuries, men have ingrained in women the belief that attractiveness, not character, is their most important attribute; women, in turn, strive not to fulfill their own needs and desires, but the desires of men. These beliefs are crippling to women's self-esteem. What woman wants to hear that no matter how intelligent she is or how good she is at her job, the only thing that really matters is looking good and finding a husband? These messages inhibit many women from striving to achieve their highest potential, which in turns leads to feelings of guilt and inadequacy.

In general, women tend to underestimate their abilities, whereas men tend to overestimate theirs (Worell & Remer, 1992). The tendency for women to make statements such as "I just don't have the ability" and "I can't" stems mainly from societal expectancies. Society tends to attribute women's success to luck and men's success to skill—a damaging stereotypical message that cultivates a sense of inferiority, which in turn leads to low self-esteem and a negative attitude toward the self.

Responsibility. Many women feel a sense of responsibility for everyone but themselves. They put the needs of others (children, family, co-workers, supervisors) above their own. Women must come to appreciate the need for personal responsibility—to be happy and well-adjusted themselves. Responsibility involves understanding the importance of making time for oneself, nurturing the self in order to be better able to nurture others. Women have to realize that in order to truly love and support others, they must first learn to love and respect themselves.

Women must also come to accept responsibility for helping to break the cycle of oppression and powerlessness. Responsibility rests on the shoulders of all women to understand the negative impact of society and work for change. Women must understand the full meaning of the motto "The personal is political," appreciating the need to free not only themselves but all people from the bonds of stereotypes and oppression.

Intimacy and Sexuality. Women face a distorted sense of intimacy and sexuality stemming from the fact that women are seen, and react to being seen, as sexual objects. For many women, being sexual is also a way of being and of relating to men (Jordan, Kaplan, Miller, Stiver, & Surrey, 1991). Male-dominated society equates sex with intimacy. Although women can typically establish intimate friendships with other women, it is difficult to establish these intimate bonds with men. Men have been socialized to view women as sexual objects of consumption, and these stereotyped expectancies are hard to break.

Communication. Communication problems between the sexes exist because men and women have not learned to "speak the same language." Sometimes it seems as if men are speaking in Chinese while women are speaking in Russian, and there is no translator available to straighten out the mixed messages and confusion. Men tend to express their anger, whereas women tend to express their pain and needs. These two communication styles lead to a paucity of genuine communication.

To communicate effectively, men and women must be willing to learn to really listen to each other, to stop thinking only of themselves and their needs, and to open themselves up to the other's communication style. Many women must learn to express anger and frustration effectively; in turn, many men must learn to communicate the whole gamut of feelings and needs.

Control. Central to the issue of control is the issue of power. Who holds the power, and how do they use it? The current power base of society rests in the hands of men, as it has for centuries. This power imbalance both reflects and perpetuates male domination of society. Men perpetuate myths about women that undermine their self-confidence, distort their attributes, and in essence, keep them relatively powerless in society. Women internalize this lack of control in many ways, including a lack of self-confidence, acceptance of abuse, and the feeling of dyscontrol over their lives. Conditions of worth imposed on women dictate that women are not supposed to be powerful; they should be meek and deferential to men. If women express a desire for power and control, they are labeled as unfeminine and scorned by the male-dominated society. Women must work to gain power to put them on an equal footing with men, because to gain power is to gain the self-confidence and control that are necessary to lead a healthy, productive life.

Adjustment Versus Transcendence. The goal of feminist therapy is to enable the client to change the social, interpersonal, and political environment at the root of psychological problems. Simply adjusting to an oppressive society helps neither the client nor society; "adjustment" to a sexist society *is* the problem. In order for both the self and society to advance, we must transcend—go beyond what we already know and accept—to a higher level where stereotyping and biases are eliminated. Through achieving personal and social power, women will discover that adjusting to social expectations is not likely to result in the contentment they desire. They must learn to live life for themselves, to move beyond the traditional and restricting conditions of society, and to exercise their newfound power to help free others caught in the web of society's control.

Ideal Individual. The ideal individual, woman or man, is one who is in touch with feelings and needs, is self-nurturant, and is interdependent. Interdependence involves the sharing and caring of two independent people. The ideal person possesses self-esteem and power, but doesn't use these to control others. The ideal individual has progressed to a higher level of social and self-awareness and works toward the improvement of society as a whole.

Some feminist theorists have suggested that the ideal individual would represent an Aristotelian mean, an equal balance of stereotypically male and female characteristics, a concept known as *androgyny*. An androgynous individual possesses a large and flexible behavioral repertoire and exhibits a range of psychological characteristics depending on the situation. Androgyny has been prescribed by many as a way for women to become liberated from traditional gender-role traits and lead more fulfilling lives. Androgynous individuals tend to be more independent, flexible, and higher in self-esteem than stereotypically "feminine" women (Bem, 1975, 1977).

There are arguments against androgyny as a prototype for the ideal individual, however. By valuing an androgynous personality, society is setting up new expectancies, an ideal that is incredibly demanding. Now people must be successful not only at their own prescribed gender role, but also at another. As Hyde (1991, p. 119) puts it, "In the good old days, a woman could be considered reasonably competent ('successful') if she could cook well. To meet new standards and be androgynous, she not only has to cook well, but also has to repair cars." Some feminists also argue that to become androgynous, women must add "masculine" traits to their behavior patterns, thus making women become more like men. Instead of urging women to emulate selected stereotypically male traits in an attempt to curry favor in a male-dominated society, society should learn to value qualities that women already possess.

Therapeutic Relationship

The client-therapist relationship in feminist therapy is characterized by two Es: empowerment and egalitarianism. *Empowerment* is the process whereby therapists help instill power, both social and individual, in the client. The power balance between the sexes in society is alarmingly disproportionate. For centuries, men have possessed the power advantage over women, from physical strength to academic and vocational advantages; women always seem to come in second in a two-gender race. Constantly being the "second sex" (de Beauvoir, 1961) is psychologically harmful, and women have come to internalize these messages.

Women are entitled to power, and the therapeutic relationship models and provides it. When women are taught to achieve power and to use it appropriately, many psychopathologies linked to poor self-esteem will disappear. Through the therapist's own understanding of power and use of self-disclosure, the therapeutic dyad is able to transfer power to the client and serve as a role model for interactions outside of the office.

The second hallmark of the therapeutic relationship is *egalitarianism*—a comparatively equal relationship between the therapist and the client. Equalizing power will be manifested in many ways: reducing the knowledge discrepancy between the participants, generating mutual goals, increasing the clinician's self-disclosure, and demystifying the process of therapy. Reducing the discrepancy includes valuing the client's perspectives and insights just as highly as the therapist's. This respect leads a woman to greater self-esteem and a feeling of confidence. Since therapy is a cooperative relationship, goals are mutually generated by the therapist and the client. Self-disclosure reduces the role distance and the power differential between the parties and aids in developing a trusting relationship. Because feminist therapy often focuses on sensitive women's issues, such as rape, sexual harassment, and physical changes, therapist self-disclosure is a vital component in establishing trust, communication, and a sense of understanding. By sharing beliefs and experiences, the therapist conveys to the client her willingness to become involved and serves as a positive role model for the client.

Therapy is a demystifying process. Feminist therapy is a way of being, believing, and understanding; it is a perspective that allows fluidity, acknowledges interconnectedness, and encourages exploration. "Feminist counseling attempts to avoid dogma, rigidity, and jargon. It is concerned with making the counseling process accessible and comprehensible, rather than mystifying and mysterious" (Walker, 1990, p. 73). Behaviors are not labeled, but are evaluated through mutual sharing and communication.

The egalitarian relationship is centrally important in feminist therapy—first, because it minimizes the social-control aspects of therapy and, second, because it does not reproduce the power imbalances women face in society. Its importance is reflected in the APA's Guidelines for Therapy with Women (Table 12.1, item 9): "If authoritarian processes are employed as a technique, the therapy should not have the effect of maintaining or reinforcing stereotypic dependency of women." By becoming involved in a relationship in which their opinions and feelings are validated, women will come to expect and enact this type of relationship with others. The end result will be enhancement of their power and self-esteem.

Above all, the therapeutic relationship in feminist therapy is characterized by a deep, personal, two-way communication between the therapist and the client regarding feelings, ideas, problems, and most of all, how to start solving problems. In the humanistic tradition, the ideal relationship is one of mutual respect, sharing, empathy, and equality.

Practicalities

Feminist therapy is consumer-oriented from the start. Clients are encouraged to shop around until they find a therapist they relate to comfortably. More than most practitioners, feminist therapists are inclined toward lower-cost sessions and sliding fee scales to make their services available to a larger proportion of the population. Feminist therapists also expect and invite clients and their families to ask questions about the types of services they will receive. *Empowered consent* means that the client gains access to knowledge that the clinician possesses regarding, for example, risks and benefits of psychotherapy, the right to refuse any method, the ability to seek a second opinion, and the right to terminate treatment at any time. The distinctive emphasis on women's groups and bibliotherapy contributes to the demystification of psychotherapy and the value of social liberation.

Feminist therapists require additional gender-awareness training in mental health. Appreciation of gender issues in treating women requires understanding not only how girls and women are raised but also how psychosocial services respond to them (Walker, 1990). Courses should be offered in gender and sex role development, gender analysis of contemporary society, issues and techniques in counseling women, and practice with feminist supervision of cases involving women's issues.

A final practical issue is the gender of the psychotherapist. Almost all self-identified feminist therapists are female. Controversy abounds on whether male therapists can practice feminist therapy or merely profeminist therapy (Ganley, 1988).

Effectiveness

Little controlled outcome research has been conducted on feminist therapy. It is not included in the various meta-analyses on the effectiveness of psychotherapy.

Available research suggests that female therapists, first, and therapists of the patient's gender, second, facilitate the treatment *process*, especially if these therapists present a nonstereotypic sexual viewpoint (Beutler, et al., 1986). Enhanced empathy and increased satisfaction are commonly observed in same-gender dyads as compared to opposite-gender dyads. However, same-gender therapeutic relationships have not consistently produced differential *outcomes* (Orlinsky & Howard,

1980). That is, there are few observable effects of therapist gender or patient/therapist matching on treatment effectiveness (Bowman, Scogin, Floyd, & McKendree-Smith, 1997).

Traditional outcome studies on the efficacy of feminist therapy may be more difficult to conduct than in other therapy systems because most evaluation research examines remission of symptoms, which is only a small part of the feminist therapy agenda. Feminist therapists are interested in changes in decision making, attitude, flexibility, and social advocacy. For example, Ballou (1990) concludes that studies using methodology that accepts the reality of the experience of the respondent find consciousness-raising (CR) groups have an enormous impact on female participants. Researchers who ask women to report experiences, or who have participated themselves, using self-reports and participant observation, have found significant changes in social/political awareness, vocational interests, attitudes, self-perception, sex roles, and ego strength. However, no significant changes are typically found on standardized measures of symptom reduction.

Psychotherapy for Men

Traditional psychotherapy was designed by men primarily to treat women. It thus reflects male assumptions about female personality development. In recent years, feminist psychotherapists have enumerated the flaws in these assumptions and offered correctives. The next task is to design therapy for men based on an accurate understanding of male personality development (Levant, 1990).

The feminist movement, while intended primarily to further the cause of women, also sparked the realization that men are negatively affected by gender-role expectations and that they, too, experience role strain. Brannon and David (1976) summarize four stereotypes of "true masculinity": (1) *No sissy stuff*: A truly masculine person avoids anything remotely "feminine." (2) *The big wheel*: A masculine person is successful and looked up to; he is the breadwinner of the family. (3) *The sturdy oak*: Masculinity involves exuding confidence, strength, and self-reliance. (4) *Give 'em hell*: A masculine person is aggressive and daring.

In order to conform to societal stereotypes, men must achieve or exceed these standards or accept the consequences of "failure." Uncritical acceptance and achievement of these expectations is a burden for men, but so also is the risk of being unmasculine and therefore ostracized. To negotiate between these two perils, men frequently hide their feelings behind a facade of toughness, resistance, and sometimes violence.

The privileged position of men in Western cultures has been, at once, a blessing and a curse. Historically, men have enjoyed advantages in education, ownership, politics, employment, and power. At the same time, this masculine gender role entails inhibition of emotional expressiveness, reliance on aggression and control, as well as obsession with achievement and success (Eisler & Blalock, 1991). Many male problems—domestic violence, rampant homophobia, objectification of women, neglect of health needs, and detached fathering, to name a few—are unfortunate by-products of the typical male socialization (Levant & Pollack, 1995)

This male gender role complicates psychotherapy. Men find it very difficult to seek help because to do so would be to admit weakness, further threatening self-esteem. Socialization also begets difficulty in identifying and expressing emotions, a condition known as *alexithymia*. Men are often genuinely unaware of their emotions. In the absence of such awareness, men tend to rely on their cognition and try to logically deduce how they should feel (Levant, 1990).

Treating men in therapy can be an arduous process. Men often fear intimacy, and the therapeutic relationship is certainly an intimate one. Men are typically reluctant to admit to their problems and share them with the therapist. For instance, one of our male clients repeatedly protested at the slightest hint of empathy, declaring "I'm a big guy and don't need anyone holding my hand or feeling sorry for me." Attempts at empathic resonance were rejected as "unmasculine."

Male-sensitive therapy seeks to help men understand the strong connections between beliefs about gender and problematic behaviors. Through treatment, men come to recognize emotional needs, identify sources of beliefs, and recognize that these beliefs were not freely chosen but can be changed nonetheless. Men aim to change their "reality" about the meaning of masculinity to more functional and healthy ideals. For example, "real men" can express positive and vulnerable feelings, can be more openly nurturant in their relationships, can acknowledge needs for interdependence and security, and can learn alternatives to physical or intellectual responses.

In recent years, increasing awareness of the special psychological concerns of men have opened up new discussions about treating men in psychotherapy. The Society for the Psychological Study of Men and Masculinity (SPSMM), as one organizational force, promotes the critical study of men and advances male-sensitive treatment. A deluge of recent books has focused on male issues in psychotherapy (e.g., Brooks, 1995; Meth & Pasick, 1992; Scher, Stevens, Good, & Eichenfield, 1987; Fine, 1988; Levant & Pollack, 1995), and the emerging male-sensitive treatments acknowledge their historical debt to feminist scholarship for articulating the profound and pervasive impact of gender, on women and men alike.

Culture-Sensitive Therapy

Theory of Personality

Culturally sensitive psychotherapy is based on the premise that there is no single, universal theory of personality. One's culture and development are the major determinants of personality; each distinct culture includes norms, events, and expectancies that shape both the group and the individual.

The European American culture highly values individual choice, self-sufficiency, and most especially, independence. These values, however, are not embraced by all ethnic groups. Many non-European children are raised with an emphasis on harmony and family reliance. Asians, for example, raise their children to be interdependent within the family unit and expect group members to subordinate their individual needs to the needs of the family and society. Likewise, many African

Americans are raised in extended family units and feel strong kinship bonds and a sense of "we-ness" with members of their group. Many of these cultural characteristics are not shared with members of the dominant culture; thus, group personality characteristics differ among cultural groups, just as they differ among individuals within each group.

The notion of a single theory of personality, then, is antithetical to the pluralistic and variable nature of culture. Each subpopulation within a culture may share defining or delimiting features, but a universal theory of personality does not exist. We require multiple perspectives rooted in, and sensitive to, particular cultures.

Theory of Psychopathology

The expression and manifestation of psychopathology are often culturally determined. The *Diagnostic and Statistical Manual of Mental Disorders* (DSM-IV; American Psychiatric Association, 1995) enjoins the clinician to take into account the individual's ethnic and cultural context in diagnosing psychopathology and provides a glossary of culture-bound syndromes. Table 12.2 outlines several disorders believed to be culture-bound. Another example is *kitsunetsuki,* which occurs in areas of rural Japan; victims believe they are possessed by foxes and are said to change their facial expressions to resemble them. Culture-bound disorders are not restricted to rural and non-Western regions; anorexia, for example, is an eating disorder that predominantly affects American girls and young women.

To the extent that we can generalize beyond specific cultures, psychopathology among culturally diverse populations can stem from a number of personal and social factors. These include discriminatory conditions, inadequate coping mechanisms, family influences and stresses, societal expectations, and economic hardships. Discriminatory conditions faced by many minority-group members, such as racial/ethnic prejudice, have precipitated high levels of stress and a loss of self-esteem and cultural pride. The path to psychopathology can begin when immigrants first step off the boat. Immediately, they are bombarded with discriminatory messages from the dominant culture: European American values should be revered. Racial and ethnic discrimination, rarely experienced in their native lands, lower immigrants' self-respect and create new stresses.

Ethnic stereotypes abound in the United States. "African Americans are stupid; they only excel in athletics." "Asian Americans are super-smart and subservient." Stereotypes such as these trap minorities in a cycle from which they must struggle to escape. They begin to develop negative attitudes about themselves and their cultural group, and these beliefs often become self-fulfilling prophecies. As minority-group members become engaged in trying to fit into society's all-American image, they may become disconnected from their cultural group and fail to establish a healthy sense of group identity. In trying to fit in, they ultimately fall out of important relationships.

Failure to be accepted by American standards can be devastating: not only have the individuals been rejected by a group they desperately want to join, but they no longer have a reference group to turn to for support. This double rejection can precipitate maladaptive behavior, including drug and alcohol abuse, gang

Table 12.2 Unusual Behaviors Considered to Be Culture-Bound

Disorder	Culture	Description
Amok	Malaya	Characterized by sudden, wild homicidal aggression; usually found in males who are rather withdrawn and quiet prior to onset. Stress, sleep deprivation, extreme heat, and alcohol are among the precipitating conditions.
Anorexia nervosa	Western nations	Preoccupation with thinness produces a refusal to eat. Occurs most frequently among young women.
Ataques de nervios	Caribbean nations	Impulsivity, dissociation, and communication disturbances of brief duration, following a stressor. Seen primarily in Spanish-speaking people.
Latah	Malaya	Repetition of the actions of others, negativism, and compulsive use of obscene language; precipitated by the word *snake* or by tickling. Occurs most frequently in middle-aged women of low intelligence who are subservient.
Susto	Mexico and Central America	A frightening event causes the soul to leave the body, resulting in depression and somatic symptoms. Ritual healings call the soul back to the body.
Taijin kyofusho (TKS)	Japan	An intense fear of offending or hurting other people through being awkward in social situations or because of an imagined physical defect.
Windigo	Algonquin Indian hunters	A hunter, usually a man, becomes anxious and agitated, convinced that he is bewitched. The fear centers on being turned into a cannibal.

Based on Carson & Butcher (1992); Oquendo, Horwath, & Martinez (1992); American Psychiatric Association (1995).

membership, and physical and sexual abuse, as well as psychological manifestations such as depression and anxiety. For example, Native Americans on reservations disproportionately abuse drugs and alcohol, and their suicide rate is twice the national average (Sue & Sue, 1990). Substance abuse among Native Americans may be related to the need to release frustration, counter boredom, and escape responsibility.

Psychopathology stems not only from the dominant culture, but also from family responses to that new culture. Non-natives often face a wealth of problems with language, customs, gender, and social-role hierarchies. Males often deal poorly with the loss of respect, income, and social standing resulting from immigration, whereas women generally have an easier transition and acculturation process. Female immigrants are more likely to find employment than males, and this role reversal is difficult for many males to accept. Conflicts often begin to surface on the home front.

Children of immigrants also face hardships that frequently manifest themselves in psychopathological conditions. Problems faced at home are often mirrored in problems at school. Language difficulties, especially when parents refuse to learn English, force children to act as interpreters for their family and place enormous responsibility on them. Conflicts occur over acculturation: children may want to do things the "American way," refusing to learn or continue to speak their parents' native language or to participate in cultural traditions and customs. This rebelliousness is often viewed by minority parents as disrespect, and they blame American society for their family problems.

Individuals are torn between remaining loyal to their family of origin and cultural group, on the one hand, and desiring to experience new ways of thinking and acting, on the other. In general, the difficulties of older minority clients stem from *acculturation* problems, such as role reversal, downward mobility, and discrimination, while younger clients experience conflict with their family over lack of cultural flexibility. The problems of adults usually manifest themselves in psychosomatic complaints, whereas children's problems are more likely to take the form of acting out behaviors and substance abuse (Ho, 1992).

Psychopathology is also evident in minorities whose ancestors immigrated centuries ago. Many African Americans trace their roots to the slave trade of two or three hundred years ago. Yet the past still haunts them. Discrimination and prejudice rarely disappear; they simply change form. Overt discrimination changes to more subtle, indirect forms of intolerance. Derogatory comments and prejudice haunt millions of African Americans daily. They may have internalized these messages for years, and they may pass them on to each new generation in a continuous cycle of low self-esteem and self-hatred. As the discrimination continues, the stereotypes impede some members of minorities from breaking out; instead, they begin to idolize white culture and denigrate their own. This produces conflict with their own cultural group and often generates interpersonal conflicts and identity crises.

Neither extreme seems to cut it. On the one hand, African Americans who try to fit into white cultural norms of success may be labeled "Uncle Toms" or "Oreos" (black on the outside and white on the inside), even to the point of being outcast from black society. On the other hand, adult African Americans who assert their own heritage through dress, language, and customs may not make it in a white-dominated employment world. The "damned if you do" (acculturate) and "damned if you don't" (separate) dilemma inevitably prompts conflict. No healthy balance is achieved.

Atkinson, Morten, and Sue (1989) outline a model of racial/cultural identity development that encapsulates pathological origins and the corrective process. In stage 1, the *conformity* stage, minority-group members have a deprecating attitude toward themselves and their group and a discriminatory attitude toward others of different minority groups. The individual highly values the characteristics of the dominant culture. In stage 2, *dissonance*, minority-group members are caught in a conflict between appreciating and depreciating themselves and their group, and also the values of the dominant society. Stage 3, *resistance and immersion*, is characterized by an appreciating stance toward oneself and one's own minority group, conflicts between empathy for other minority groups and culture-centrism, and a depreciating attitude toward the dominant culture. In stage 4, *introspection*, individuals become concerned about the basis of their attitudes. And in stage 5, *inte-*

grative awareness, individuals learn to appreciate themselves, their minority group, and different minority groups, and are able to confer selective appreciation on the dominant culture.

Psychological distress also stems from economic hardships—less money, poor schooling, inadequate child care, lack of affordable housing, and expensive health care, to name just a few. Poverty is a major risk factor for chronic mental and behavioral problems.

Theory of Therapeutic Processes

Consciousness Raising. Since many of the problems minority clients face stem from the adverse impact of the majority culture's expectations, an essential aspect of culture-sensitive therapy is for patients to come to understand how the dominant culture has shaped their views about themselves and their culture. Often clients must face the truth about themselves—that they hold the norms of the dominant culture in high esteem and denigrate aspects of their own culture, denying their heritage and family group. Eventually, clients come to realize that by turning their backs on their culture, they have alienated themselves and have lost important cultural-group support.

In a case presented by Sue and Sue (1990), a young female college student of Chinese descent presented for psychotherapy suffering from a severe depressive reaction manifested in feelings of worthlessness, suicidal ideation, and an inability to concentrate. The patient had little contact with members of her own race, outside of her family, and she openly expressed scorn for anything Chinese. She was hostile toward Chinese customs and especially Chinese men, whom she described as introverted, passive, and sexually unattractive. She dated only white men, to the disappointment of her family, but her most recent relationship had ended because of her boyfriend's parents' objections to her race. Although she was not completely conscious of this, the client was having increasing difficulty with denying her racial heritage. The breakup of her relationship had made her realize that she was Chinese and not fully accepted by all segments of society. At first she had denounced the Chinese for her present situation, but later much of her hostility was turned back onto herself. Feeling alienated from her own subculture and not fully accepted by American society, she experienced an identity crisis, resulting in feelings of worthlessness and depression. As this case demonstrates, consciousness raising must help clients understand the devastating effects of prejudice; only then can they begin to rectify cultural alienation.

Consciousness raising may also entail assisting patients in recognizing how their cultural conditioning impedes their acceptance of psychological treatment and implementation of change. In responding to domestic violence, for instance, some Mexican women will not seek help because they believe their situation is God's will. Under the same circumstances, some Southeast Asian women may be afraid to confide in their counselors because Hmong tradition requires that, in times of conflict, clan elders must be consulted first. Battered African American women may have been socialized to believe that seeking psychological help is only for whites (Mitchell-Meadows, 1992). In such situations, a culturally sensitive therapist can help women become aware of the potentially detrimental influences of socialization on their functioning.

Culturally sensitive consciousness raising has a dual function, for therapists as well as client. First, therapists must understand and come to terms with their own feelings and attitudes about racism and a client's culture. To help patients come to terms with their ethnic identity, therapists must be comfortable discussing their own cultural biases. For example, a therapist may say to a client, "I appreciate your letting me know when I say subtle things in an insensitive way, not realizing I am being biased."

Second, therapists assist clients to consciously identify their individual styles of dealing with racism and to recognize modes that are unhealthy and insufficient. Sue and Sue (1990) illustrate this process in a case in which a recently divorced black medical student came to therapy complaining of stress-related migraine headaches. He felt that the racist environment of his medical school and one professor in particular were responsible for his problem. He wanted to confront the professor directly and accuse him of racism, but knew that doing so could lead to his dismissal from school. Therapy revealed that the patient's choice of strategy was partially related to unresolved feelings of anger over his recent divorce, and the resultant bitterness and vulnerability had overdetermined his choice to confront the professor. As the client began to understand the impact of his divorce, he was able to consider a wider range of options and decided it would be better to file a complaint with the minority affairs office. Although the tension between the client and his professor remained high, the client felt that he had chosen the best option, enabling him to remain in school.

Catharsis. Suppressed anger over discrimination and cultural alienation often comes to the surface once patients comprehend the negative impact of the dominant culture—the culture they once held in such high esteem—on their belief system and interpersonal relationships. It is important that minority clients express this anger and begin to recognize that their anger is a normal and justified response. Whether it be an immigrant angry at her loss of status and cultural support or an African American resentful of racial discrimination and internalization of the dominant culture's messages about self-worth, the healthy expression of anger is a vital aspect of therapy. Consciously coming to terms with their pain and unhealthy responses is a necessary first step for people establishing new patterns of coping.

The primary goal of the therapist, in this respect, is to facilitate the client's expression of affect, working through of antagonism, and redirection of anger into appropriate channels. If the therapist is of a minority background, he or she can often serve as a positive role model in teaching the client how to cope with discrimination and anger. Minority therapists can share with clients their own feelings and methods of coping with discrimination. For example, a black therapist who had a difficult time dealing with the effects of employment discrimination can share his or her experiences with clients facing similar circumstances.

A therapist from a dominant cultural background can model positive attitudes toward racial diversity and multiculturalism. White therapists can attempt to learn as much as they can about the culture and nature of the clients they are working with. By showing respect and a genuine interest in learning about and under-standing other cultures, they display the type of positive attitude and acceptance of others they want to encourage in clients.

Choosing. Once patients have acknowledged their anger, they must choose how to express and channel their new-found energy appropriately. One of the most critical choices clients face is how to integrate their sense of self with their cultural group. Clients face choices regarding how much to integrate, how to accomplish integration, and how to achieve healthy relationships in the face of social and cul-tural expectations. Ethnic clients must learn to make conscious, deliberate choices about these matters, choices that are compatible with their own values and goals, not only those valued by dominant society.

An African American history professor expressed his anger in therapy about not being free to just be a professor. "You whites can just worry about what's best for your career, but I'm expected to care about what's best for all blacks, not just what is best for me. I worked all my life to be free to immerse myself in history. But if I'm not heavily involved with black students, black faculty, and black studies, I feel guilty and afraid I'll be seen as a traitor. Do you even have these problems as a white professor?" No, I had to admit that, as a white male, I have the privilege of just caring about my profession if that is what I choose to do.

Immigrants face choices regarding how to incorporate cultural traditions and roles with the norms of their new country. Clients must choose how much they want to acculturate into their new society and determine how they can blend as-pects of both cultures without losing important aspects of each. The basic choice for such clients comes down to how to live in a healthy, comfortable balance. This, of course, is easier said than done. If we don't have healthy roots, it's hard to grow.

As patients face decisions regarding the balance between acculturation and re-tention of minority-group traditions, therapists concentrate on assisting them in dealing with their confusion and uncertainty about the future. Some clients may choose not to rejoin the minority group, and their feelings of pain and guilt must be addressed. The therapist can assist clients in working through these feelings and support their decisions. Other clients may decide that they would like to rejoin their cultural group, but fear rejection. In these instances, the therapist will work with the client in planning ways to reintegrate with their cultural group and handle rejection if it occurs. The African American professor had to deal with anger both from some white colleagues whom he could no longer see as often and from black colleagues who wondered where he had been so long.

The culturally sensitive therapist will assist other clients to achieve a bicultural identity and help them learn to deal effectively with the cultural and societal back-lash resulting from their choices. Clients need to become aware of the pros and cons of their decisions and how their lives will change. Cooperative planning and mutual problem solving give patients a sense of self-esteem and empowerment.

Therapeutic Content

Anxiety and Defenses. Anxiety about cultural norms and a healthy degree of acculturation is the root of many minority clients' psychological distress. When clients are unable to blend their cultural norms with prevailing norms, anxiety often manifests itself in defensive actions and maladaptive behaviors.

Anxiety takes many forms in diverse cultural contexts. Physical symptoms and complaints, such as headaches and, especially among Latino/Hispanics, visions, are a common and culturally acceptable means of expressing psychological conflict. Many patients of various ethnic backgrounds, including Asians and Hispanics, complain of headaches and pain when faced with emotional crises. Many groups believe that physical problems cause emotional disturbance, and once the physical symptom is treated, the emotional symptoms will also disappear. In many cultures, it is far more acceptable to be physically ill than emotionally unstable. Anxiety also surfaces as acting-out behavior, especially among minority adolescents and family scapegoats.

Self-Esteem. A major focus in culturally sensitive therapy is lowered self-esteem among minority clients. Racial/ethnic discrimination has had a ripple effect for centuries, trapping each new generation in a web of stereotypes and self-fulfilling prophesies. How can people who for generations have internalized messages about being incompetent and unmotivated be expected to emerge unscathed and psychologically sound? When minorities are constantly bombarded with messages that the White, dominant culture is best, they begin to uncritically accept these messages and denigrate both themselves and their own cultural group—a process known as *internalized racism*. Minorities often begin to idolize the dominant culture and see their own culture and themselves as inferior, resulting in self-esteem difficulties.

Intimacy and Sexuality. Intimacy—or, more specifically, the loss of intimacy—is a key issue in culturally related problems. Intimacy lies in the deep bonds of family and cultural groups, not only between two lovers. When these bonds are broken, owing mainly to the influence of the dominant culture, an individual feels not only the loss of familial support, but also a loss of self. Reestablishing the bonds of intimacy, or coming to terms with the loss of it, is crucial to reestablishing the sense of self and self-esteem.

Views of healthy sexuality differ among cultural groups. The safest generalization is that there is no single acceptable perspective on sexuality. Many Latinos/Hispanics are traditionally raised in a macho, male-dominated social world, while many African American relationships focus on the strength of the woman. Sexual customs must be recognized and viewed from the perspective of the culture they reflect; they cannot be judged solely from the dominant European American point of view.

Communication. Communication problems can occur both between the dominant culture and minority cultures and within minority groups. The focus of communication difficulties between cultural groups is on expectancies, biases, and prejudicial messages. There must be a distinction between healthy, meaningful communication and communication that is false and destructive, such as racial and ethnic slurs. Communication can be good or bad, depending on the context; communication fails when differences between individuals, and individual minority groups, overshadow their similarities.

Communication difficulties within cultural groups, especially within families, manifest themselves in misunderstandings and resentment when communication between individuals and their cultural group is lost. Gaps in communication can only be corrected when group members try to understand the needs of those individuals who want to experience a lifestyle and people different from the one in which they were raised. Individuals must also appreciate the values and opinions of the group into which they were born. Only when the lines of two-way communication remain open can both parties reach mutual understanding and respect.

Hostility. Hostility among minorities is the expected reaction to years of discrimination, abuse, and loss of self-esteem. Whether it is the Los Angeles riots in response to white police officers' being acquitted of beating an African American motorist or an uprising among Haitian immigrants denied entrance into the United States, anger is a natural reaction to oppression and powerlessness. Problems occur when hostility builds and is expressed in maladaptive behaviors. Acting out hostility is one of the things that is destroying too many young minority-group members. Yet we have to hear and understand their cry: "No justice, no peace." How to express anger and outrage without destroying self or others is an issue that many in the majority never have to face. Validating anger and outrage without encouraging destructive hostility can be a delicate balance for clients and therapists alike.

Control. For many minorities, the task is not only how to control anger and hostility, but also how to stop being controlled by others, especially being controlled by the biased messages of society. Biased messages control cognitions and actions, preventing minority-group members from achieving their potentials. The resolution of issues of control, both intrapersonal control of hostility and structured control of social rewards, rests on establishing greater freedom and opportunities for individuals and groups.

Adjustment Versus Transcendence. Many minority-group members have never fully adjusted to society, so it is even harder for them to transcend it. In Maslow's hierarchy, one must meet security and belongingness needs before achieving self-actualization and transcendence.

To transcend, minority-group members will learn how to avoid internalization of prejudicial messages and to acquire self-esteem. They must not merely adjust to societal conditions, but transcend to a level of positive self-worth not dictated by society. If this means a need to separate at times, then separate they must.

Impulse Control. One negative stereotype is that particular minority groups have frequent problems with impulse control. The fact is that the majority of all groups are law-abiding citizens who control impulses just fine. But we should not be surprised that impoverished people who are discriminated against are more likely to act out anger and outrage. We should not be surprised that young people may act out fantasies to be important, successful, or well-off if they have few opportunities to live out their fantasies. Yet psychotherapists need to help individuals appreciate that indiscriminate acting out of impulses is ultimately self-defeating and self-destructive. Validating the feelings behind such impulses while helping to find more valuable and valid activities for enhancing oneself is the therapeutic key.

The Ideal Individual. In the context of cultural differences, we cannot subscribe to the myth of a single ideal individual. Rather, the ideal cognitive framework is one in which minority individuals accept themselves for what they really are. Ideal individuals learn to disregard messages that are false and to view the dominant European American culture for what it truly is—another lifestyle, not the paragon of virtue. Minority individuals respect their own culture and feel free to live life in the manner they see fit; they are in control, but not controlled. Above all, the ideal individual understands that being culturally different is a source of values allowing all to experience different cultures and life in its grand diversity.

Therapeutic Relationship

The establishment of an abiding therapeutic relationship is one of the most challenging aspects of culturally sensitive treatment. Often, minority clients feel more comfortable with a psychotherapist from their own ethnic background. A same-culture therapist can serve as a positive role model and can genuinely empathize with the problems and concerns of the minority client. However, with so many diverse cultural groups, it would be impractical to expect that there would be a psychotherapist readily available to match each patient's cultural background. Therapists, therefore, often find themselves working with clients from cultural backgrounds radically different from their own. This can be a source of problems for both the client, who may feel misunderstood by the therapist, and the clinician, who may struggle to come to understand the client's cultural framework and the need to change therapeutic strategies to fit the client's individual needs.

Ideally, the treatment strategy is culturally consistent with the patient's expectations and background. One of the American Psychological Association (1991, 1993) guidelines for working with ethnic minority clients is the responsibility to be cognizant of relevant research and practice issues related to the population being served. The Asian values of reserve, restraint of strong feelings, and subtleness in approaching problems, for example, may come into conflict with Western therapist expectations of openness, psychological-mindedness, and assertiveness (Leong, 1986). Other guidelines instruct therapists to respect a client's religious and spiritual beliefs and to be mindful of the differing roles of family members, community structures, and hierarchies within the client's culture, as these will profoundly affect the therapy process. Many Asian Americans, to continue our example, prefer more structured and directive strategies that emphasize the central role of family (Leong, 1986).

The clinician acts as a guide for minority clients in pursuit of clarifying both their personal and cultural identity. As the guide, the therapist must take into account the client's cultural perceptions and therapy expectations. Asian Americans, as we have noted, ordinarily expect the therapist to take an active, directive role in therapy. But members of other groups may expect the opposite from their therapeutic guide.

Preparation and collaboration are two keys. It is essential that therapists prepare clients for psychotherapy by explaining what will happen in the context of therapy, what is expected of the client, and what the therapist will provide. This straightforward approach to the therapeutic relationship is one of the most effective ways of building trust and conveying to the client the sense of cooperation and mutual respect.

The relationship is also characterized by collaboration in that clients are involved at each stage of therapy in mapping out goals and planning strategies. Incorporating aspects of the client's culture into treatment shows the therapist's respect and interest in that culture. Part of working in minority cultures is to collaborate with traditional healers, such as shamans and curanderos, whose indigenous practices profoundly impact the clients' belief systems (American Psychological Association, 1993). Other clients, such as American Indians, may present to the clinic with their entire families who accompany them to provide support. Collaboration in this case may be to render treatment centered on the family and the whole community.

Practicalities

The practice of culture-sensitive therapy cannot be reduced to universal prescriptions any more than identical treatment strategies can be applied to clients of all racial and ethnic heritages. The length, format, and cost will depend on the needs of the particular client(s) in interaction with the expectations and knowledge of the therapist.

Nonetheless, one common practice is to acquaint beginning clients with the respective roles of patient and therapist and the nature of the psychotherapy enterprise. These procedures, which fall under the heading of *pretreatment patient preparation*, take a variety of forms, including direct instruction, informational interviews, modeling, film presentations, and role playing. Many patients hold unrealistic expectations about the goals and processes of psychotherapy and may be uncomfortable with the nature of mental health treatment; pretherapy orientation is designed to clarify these expectations and to define a more accurate and comfortable role for the client. Evidence for the positive impact of this preparation is quite plentiful (Levine, Stolz, & Lacks, 1983; Lorion, 1978; Orlinsky & Howard, 1986). Similar positive treatment consequences accompany efforts to prepare therapists for disadvantaged and minority clients, although these efforts are far less common. In practice, the upshot is for culture-sensitive therapists and their clients to engage in mutual exploration of role expectations and treatment structures.

As with gender-aware therapy, culture-sensitive therapy demands training beyond the mainstream of contemporary American thought. Students must have educational experiences that generate sensitivity and appreciation of the history, current needs, strengths, and resources of minority communities (Lopez et al., 1989). Courses covering this content should have a consciousness-raising component, an affective component, and a knowledge and skills component. Students are expected to acquire knowledge of the particular cultures of patients they will be treating, of course, but in addition they should develop an awareness of interethnic relationships, racism, and the historical, political, social, and psychological context in which cultural groups have functioned. With this background, even when therapists cannot articulate the cultural *content* of each patient, they can demonstrate the *process* of cultural sensitivity and respect. Indeed, early research reviews examining both the indirect and direct linkages between cross-cultural training of therapists and their subsequent psychotherapy outcomes suggest that an empirical case can be made for diversifying the training curriculum (Yutrzenka, 1995).

Part and parcel of this broader training curriculum is attracting more ethnic minorities to the psychotherapy profession. Ethnic minorities provide a dimension and a viewpoint that act as a counterbalance to the forces of misinterpretation (Sue & Sue, 1990). The end result will be a more inclusive, pluralistic profession characterized in principle and in personnel by gender and sociocultural awareness (Bronstein & Quina, 1988).

Effectiveness

Conclusions reached in reviews of the literature on race and ethnicity effects in psychotherapy appear to reflect the race of the reviewer (Abramowitz & Murray, 1983). White reviewers tend to minimize the effects of ethnic differences, while ethnic minority reviewers tend to emphasize findings in which differences are found.

Three robust conclusions can be drawn, however. First, most racial and ethnic minorities are underserved in the mental health arena (President's Commission on Mental Health, 1978). Studies show that Asian Americans and Latino Americans, in particular, underutilize mental health services (Sue, Zane, & Young, 1994). Second, the evidence supports preferences for ethnically similar therapists by members of racial minority groups (Abramowitz & Murray, 1983; Atkinson, 1985). A meta-analysis of relevant studies showed that ethnic minorities definitely tend to prefer ethnically similar counselors over European American counselors (Coleman, Wampold, & Casali, 1995). Third, the available research findings fail to demonstrate that ethnic minority therapists achieve differential treatment outcomes (Atkinson, 1985; Sue, 1988). Neither strong, comparative studies nor weaker, naturalistic studies have consistently found differences in treatment outcomes as a function of patient/therapist ethnic matches (Beutler, Crago, & Arezmendi, 1986).

Few controlled studies have been conducted in the United States on the effectiveness of psychotherapy in the treatment of culturally diverse populations. Based on the limited evidence, Sue and colleagues (1994) conclude that:

- In no studies have African American clients been found to exceed white American clients in terms of favorable treatment outcomes. Some investigations have revealed no ethnic differences, and some studies have supported the notion that outcomes are less beneficial for African Americans.

- Research is inadequate to address the question of the effectiveness of psychotherapy with Native Americans.

- Any conclusions about the effectiveness of treatment for Asian Americans would be premature given the limited data (only four outcome studies).

- Insufficient controlled studies have been performed to test scientifically the assumption that mainstream psychotherapies are less effective with Latinos.

A meta-analytic review on the effectiveness of psychotherapy with Latinos in the United States produced positive results (Navarro, 1993). A total of 15 published and unpublished studies were identified, with the majority of therapeutic interventions (57%) being conducted in the Spanish language. All treatments showed positive effects beyond no-treatment controls, and the average effect sizes were similar to those reported for mainstream psychotherapies. While Latinos clearly benefit from culturally sensitive psychotherapy, it remains to be seen if they benefit as much as white Americans.

Criticisms of Gender- and Culture-Sensitive Therapies

From a Psychoanalytic Perspective

Criticize feminist and culture-sensitive therapies? Are you kidding? Politically correct forces have made such criticisms academically dangerous. Everyone knows that feminist and culture-sensitive therapies are on the side of justice, equality, diversity, and all that is good and right. In the name of overthrowing a socially oppressive system, they have substituted an academically oppressive system. Psychology has been replaced by victimology. People do not participate in producing their pathologies. Individuals are strictly victims of abusive, restrictive stereotypes and discriminatory social systems, including families, schools, governments, and corporations. All of these social institutions have conspired to keep women and racial minorities down.

This world view is a little paranoid. If it weren't for all those outside forces controlling me and coercing me, I would be free to be happy, healthy, and successful. If we are participating in producing our own problems, then we can participate in discovering our own solutions. But if we are victims of social oppression, then can we ever be free short of a social revolution? Such social analysis certainly has a proper place in academia. But is it appropriate for feminists to advance their political ideology in the name of psychotherapy?

From a Behavioral Perspective

Science is the search for universal laws applicable across remarkably diverse conditions. Contextualists would deny that such universal principles exist. They maintain that all truths are contextual. But is calculus any less valid in Africa than in Europe where it was developed? Do the laws of physics vary from culture to culture, or are there universal truths of electronics and mechanics that can be applied by any person in any place? Does each person in each culture have to construct his or her own principles of physics? What chaos we would have if such constructivism were true.

Psychology as a science also involves the search for universal principles of behavior. Is there any evidence that principles of contingency control hold in some cultures but not in others? Certainly cultures differ in terms of what behaviors they reinforce or punish. But if they do not reinforce prosocial behaviors and punish antisocial behaviors, there will soon be no culture. If minority patients have been conditioned by the dominant culture to adopt behaviors that are self-defeating or self-destructive, then they had best apply principles of contingency control, counterconditioning, and stimulus control in order to counter their conditions and control their contexts.

And, at the risk of sounding gender or culturally *in*sensitive, where are the experimental data showing that feminist and multicultural treatments effect client improvement more than current behavior therapy? Contextual sensitivity may represent social progression, but the lack of solid outcome research represents scientific regression.

From a Humanistic Perspective

Values of equality, diversity, and justice evoke compassion. But if we want diversity, what's wrong with individuality? Why does an individual's gender, racial, or ethnic group confer identity more than does personality? A humanistic society and a humanistic psychology hold that all individuals are uniquely and inherently valuable. No two people are the same. But a group psychology threatens to treat all members of a group the same. In the name of diversity, individuals can lose their identity.

That is what happened in so many Soviet societies that were based on a single value system. For the sake of equality and social justice, many other values, including individual freedom, were sacrificed. If all individuals have unique potentials, and if all individuals are free to fulfill their individual potentials, then ultimate outcomes will not be equal. But if inequalities can only emerge from an unjust system, then individual differences must be denied. And individual freedoms must be denied. In the name of anti-oppression, these socialist systems constructed, and still construct, some of the most oppressive institutions in the history of humanity.

One of the grand experiments of the 20th century was to construct cultures that would ensure that everyone had equal outcomes. These experiments were based in part on the belief that all psychopathology was the result of an unjust society. Almost all pathology was seen as the result of oppressive poverty. What were the results of these grand experiments? Yes, it is true that no groups had to live in desperate poverty. But was there any less alcoholism? Was their any less depression? Was there any less oppression? Was there any greater happiness? Was there more self-actualization? In the search for social solutions to individual pathologies, these grand experiments ended up producing sick societies.

From an Integrative Perspective

How can we help patients become free from oppressive ideologies if we are dogmatic? How can we empower individuals to be autonomous adults by convincing them that they are victims? How can we help clients affirm their uniqueness if we treat them as part of a group? You want to know the ultimate context: eclecticism. It posits that the context for every individual, male, female, African, Asian, Latino, or Anglo, is unique. And each psychotherapy needs to be individually constructed to best match the needs of a particular person. In some cases, this involves helping individuals become free from social oppression. In other cases, it means helping them become free from mental obsessions. In yet other cases, it involves treatment of biological depression. When will we learn that no single system has a stranglehold on the truth? Not feminism, not constructivism, not empiricism, not even eclecticism.

Theoretical humility can enhance our humanity. Therapeutic pluralism can best prepare us to treat every individual uniquely. As therapists, we know we cannot predetermine what is right for any individual. No therapist has the omnipotence or the omniscience to decide what is the best way for clients to restructure their lives. Why should we believe we have such wisdom to decide what is the best way to reconstruct entire societies? Of course, we can and should advocate for social changes that we believe will benefit oppressed people, and obsessed people, and depressed people. However, we must do it with the humility of knowing we just might be mistaken and someone else just might have a better solution. Just because justice is on our side doesn't mean that truth is.

Finally, feminist therapy and theory have been developed by and with white women. In the honest acknowledgment of two leading feminists (Brown & Brodsky, 1992, p. 3): "Currently, feminist therapy theory is neither diverse nor complex in the reality it reflects. It has been deficient from the start in its inclusiveness of the lives and realities of women of color, poor or working class women, non—North American women, women over sixty-five, or women with disabilities." A truly comprehensive and contextual psychotherapy must integrate the needs of all people, men, women, and children, not only adult mainstream women.

― A FEMINIST ANALYSIS OF MRS. C. ―

For most of this century, women like Mrs. C. were treated out of context—not the context of marriage and family—but rather the larger social context that dictated roles that women could play and rules for feminine behavior. Individual psychopathology was seen as the villain, and there was little appreciation of how women could be victims of a rigid and restrictive society.

Take Mrs. C.'s frigidity, for example. How many men have ever been diagnosed as frigid? Is this because women are weaker in their sexuality? Or is it because women have historically been more oppressed sexually? Look at Mrs. C.'s father, waiting up for her after a date to question her as if she were accused of a crime. He even had the gall to follow her on a date as if she were a chattel that he had the right to control. Would a father dare to do that to his son? Would he even think to do that to a son?

With a father so preoccupied with his teenage daughter's dating behavior, we must wonder about the possibility of incestuous activity. For most of this century, incestuous concerns were supposed to be a function of childhood fantasy—until feminists pulled the covers off of a dreadful reality. Millions of children, particularly girls, were discovered to be victims of sexual abuse. Psychotherapy would certainly need to explore the real possibility that Mrs. C., like all too many female clients, was using symptoms to cover over traumatic memories. Mrs. C.'s preoccupation with cleanliness may have been related to early experiences in which she was made to feel dirty and bad. How would one wash away the trauma of having one's innocence soiled and spoiled by abusive behavior?

Of course, Mrs. C.'s preoccupation with keeping her house clean from germs and worms represents the stereotype that a woman's work is never done. Do men ever have compulsions related to housework? Men frequently have aversions to housework but rarely compulsions. When did Mrs. C.'s compulsions get out of control? When her 1-year-old daughter developed pinworms and the physician ordered Mrs. C. to boil everything—on top of the housework, the child care, the flu, and the pregnancy. Most people still don't realize that only a couple of cultures in the world will allow anyone to have exclusive child care responsibilities for more than five or six hours. It's emotionally too exhausting. No wonder Mrs. C. broke down. She insisted on functioning effectively in a dysfunctional social system.

Did she ever get relief? One child after another, from A to E. Who wouldn't be likely to fail? When it came to having so many children, was she doing her Catholic duty? When it came to having sex, was she doing her wifely duty? When was Mrs. C. ever free? Not as a young child; not as a blossoming teenager; not as a young mother; not as a mature wife. Perhaps in the privacy of her shower, she experienced a place free from demands of others, free from control by others. But whatever pleasure she might have sought from the sensation of warm water caressing her body was soon controlled by rituals as rigid and restrictive as the roles she played as daughter, mother, and housewife.

Mrs. C. doesn't need another therapist to tell her what's wrong with her. She certainly doesn't need another man to tell her what to do. Mrs. C. needs the freedom of feminist therapy to raise her consciousness about coercive controls that defined her as a daughter, as a mother, as a housewife, and as a dental hygienist. But when was she ever free to be a woman outside the narrow confines of these stereotypical female roles?

Mrs. C. doesn't need to be told what to do. She needs to be empowered by a sensitive female psychotherapist to do what *she* wants to do. She will gradually discover her authority and soon speak in her own voice. Mrs. C. will discover how she can begin to take control of her life through personal strength rather than social weakness. If she is sick of excessive housework, for example, she can choose to say no. If she is angry over being controlled by men—her father, her husband, her previous psychotherapist, or her physician—she can be empowered to restructure her relationships rather than controlling herself through compulsions. Like all too many women, Mrs. C. needs to be free to control her life through hidden strengths rather than overlearned weaknesses. An egalitarian women's group or an assertion training group in addition to individual treatment would enhance both her consciousness and her skills.

Once Mrs. C. begins to struggle to win back her body and her self, to break out of roles and rules too small for her soul, don't be surprised if such healing is resisted by her husband, her children, her parents, and her priest. Who knows what a liberated woman might choose to do? They no doubt want her free from her neurosis. But do they want her free from the roles and rules that make her a predictable, sacrificial, and controllable woman?

What if Mrs. C. decides that to be healthy and whole she needs to be on her own—something she has never experienced? Will she be accused of abandoning her children, opposing her church, dumping her husband? Repressive forces may well exert themselves and tempt Mrs. C. to believe that there are only certain roles she is free to play. Feminist theory recognizes that if women are to become free from internalized cultural conflicts, then psychotherapy must help facilitate social change as well as self-change. The personal will also be political for Mrs. C.

Future Directions

Although there have been numerous theoretical shifts in the history of psychotherapy, all of these have maintained a white, male, Western European common denominator. In the future, the populations that traditional psychotherapy forgot will not settle for androcentric, monocultural treatments. The demographic avalanche and the ensuing pluralistic nature of American society make gender-sensitive and multicultural therapies virtually inevitable. The future must include increasing cultural literacy and gender sensitivity if psychotherapy is to remain relevant for anyone except the ever-smaller White, middle-class population for whom it was traditionally targeted.

Following the *integration* stage in the evolution of gender- and culture-sensitive therapies, *pluralism* is likely to dominate (Comas-Diaz, 1992). Pluralism will become the social blueprint, infusing diversity and flexibility into psychotherapy constructs. Existing paradigms will not only be questioned, but modified or replaced by pluralistic ones that are less ethnocentric and more inclusive. Many extant "universal" principles of human behavior will be perceived as examples of cultural myopia or cultural imperialism (Comas-Diaz, 1992). Pluralism will manifest itself in a broadening definition of psychological health, expanding models of explanation and healing, a widening conceptualization of family dynamics, therapist language, and metaphor. Mainstream assumptions of normative behavior in terms of independence, internal locus of control, and assertiveness, for instance, will be complemented by other culturally rewarded behaviors of interdependence, fate, and social obligation. The impending cultural revolution and increasing heterogeneity of people will create a pluralistic perspective that transforms psychotherapy into a more inclusive and relevant field.

One step toward an inclusive psychotherapy is to broaden the meaning of culture to embrace sexual orientation, chronological age, physical appearance, and other salient dimensions of personal identity and social life. These are frequently subject to the same prejudice and oppression as gender; the homosexual, the elderly, and the disabled suffer as well. In organizing the multitude of factors to be considered in culturally responsive practice, Hays (1996) constructed an acronym that forms the slightly misspelled word *ADRESSING:*

Age and generational influences

Disability

Religion

Ethnicity

Social Status

Sexual orientation

Indigenous heritage

National origin

Gender

In the future, practitioners will indeed be "adressing" the complex interweave of these multiple factors in their assessment and treatment of heterogeneous clients. Although the content of each category is dissimilar, there are many commonalities relating to acculturation-separateness, inclusion-exclusion, and power-oppression.

A pressing challenge for the 21st century will be to create training programs with sufficient attention to racial/ethnic diversity. Professional organizations have formally acknowledged that ethnicity, culture, and gender impact on behavior and have required that practitioners take these factors into account when working with diverse populations; however, systematic evidence that this is routinely being accomplished is nonexistent. Cultural pluralism is not yet reflected in students, faculty, curriculum, or research of psychotherapy training programs (Highlen, 1994). Of course, attracting more ethnic minorities to the helping professions will bring the browning of America to the heart of psychotherapy. A Delphi poll of experts in cross-cultural counseling revealed predicted increases in all areas related to training and preparation (Heath, Neimeyer, & Pedersen, 1988).

In addition to training needs, Brown and Brodsky (1992) foresee three new tasks and a continuing process in the future of feminist therapy. The new tasks are (1) to develop a central, organizing theory of feminist theory for understanding human behavior and development; (2) to more fully address the needs of men, children, families, elders, and people with disabilities; and (3) to cultivate training and practice standards for feminist therapists through inclusionary, consensual models. The continuing process is to act as a powerful gadfly, moving the mainstream away from destructive dominant sexist paradigms toward new visions shaped by feminist analysis. In the words of Brown and Brodsky (1992, p. 56), feminist therapy

> will always be a voice for the least powerful and most oppressed in our cultures; we will always be a source of irritation to whatever complacencies about their good intentions that our colleagues may develop about their work with women and members of other disenfranchised and at-risk groups. We will continually challenge mainstream theories and practices to be more inclusive of human diversity, more questioning of their assumptions, more willing to scrutinize their need to be paternalistic with functioning adult clients.

This perpetual focus, this process of gender-aware and culture-sensitive therapies, will likely presage their contributions in years to come.

Suggestions for Further Reading

Brown, L. S., & Root, M. P. P. (Eds.). (1990). *Diversity and complexity in feminist therapy*. New York: Haworth.

Comas-Diaz, L., & Greene, B. (Eds.). (1994). *Women of color: Integrating ethnic and gender identities in psychotherapy*. New York: Guilford.

Comas-Diaz, L., & Griffith, E. H. (Eds.). (1988). *Clinical guidelines in cross-cultural mental health*. New York: Wiley.

Dudley, G. R., & Rawlins, M. R. (Eds.). (1985). Psychotherapy with ethnic minorities. [Special issue]. *Psychotherapy, 22*(2s).

Meth, R. L., & Pasick, R. S. (1992). *Men in therapy: The challenge of change*. New York: Guilford.

Pedersen, P. (Ed.). (1985). *Handbook of cross-cultural counseling and therapy*. Westport, CT: Greenwood.

Rosewater, L. B., & Walker, L. E. A. (Eds.). (1985). *Handbook of feminist therapy*. New York: Springer.

Scher, M., Stevens, M., Good, G., & Eichenfield, G. A. (Eds.). (1987). *Handbook of counseling and psychotherapy with men*. Newbury Park, CA: Sage.

Sue, D. W., & Sue, D. (1990). *Counseling the culturally different: Theory and practice*. (2nd ed.). Somerset, NJ: Wiley.

Worell, J., & Remer, P. (Eds.). (1992). *Feminist perspectives in therapy: An empowerment model for women*. New York: Wiley.

Journals: *Cultural Diversity and Mental Health; Hispanic Journal of Behavioral Sciences; Journal of the Asian American Psychological Association; Journal of Gay and Lesbian Psychotherapy; Journal of Men's Studies; Journal of Multicultural Counseling and Development; Journal of Multicultural Social Work; Psychology of Women Quarterly; Women & Therapy.*

13

Constructivist Therapies: Solution-Focused and Narrative

Insoo Kim Berg

DIANE HAD BEEN DUMPED; unceremoniously and unexpectedly dumped by her longtime boyfriend in the middle of her senior year in high school. How could he! And dumped for a good friend of hers! Her heart felt like it had been ripped out and thrown on the floor. She alternated between grief and rage, one moment sobbing and unable to get out of bed and the next moment fantasizing some murderous payback. How could he! Her first true love, her first sexual partner, her first soul mate.

To make matters worse, Diane's mother seemed as upset as she was. Her mother tried to be supportive and comforting; after all, she was a talented psychotherapist committed to lengthy, insight-oriented work. Yet Mom hinted darkly to Diane at home and to me in the referral call of "relational vulnerabilities" and "emotional traumatization" resulting from this breakup. The mother/therapist was expecting months, perhaps years, of weekly intensive psychotherapy to address the roots of the problem.

But Diane wanted to dig out of her crisis, not dig into the archeology of her emotional life. When I (JCN) asked her to describe her goals for psychotherapy, she immediately replied, "Not to let this jerk spoil the rest of my senior year. To get back my life." When I invited her to imagine that tonight, after our first session, she went back home and fell asleep and a miracle happened that solved the problems that brought her to psychotherapy, what would she notice that would be different? Diane had her answer ready: "I would get up happy in the morning, planning my day, looking forward to basketball practice, and thinking about my friends." Diane knew the path to her health and how to proceed.

Despite her mother's expectations of months of ponderous psychotherapy, Diane finished her work in just four sessions. She had cried enough in the week between being dumped—which she rechristened "liberation day"—and our first appointment. She called on her considerable skills and resources as a college-bound student to develop a plan to get her life back. Return to basketball, return to friends she had perhaps neglected because of her beau, and most important, return to her own interests and identity, separate from her boyfriend. She consumed the best-seller *Reviving Ophelia* (Pipher, 1994) in one night, declaring that she too had totally lost her self in a relationship, like far too many adolescent women.

After four sessions in pursuit of solutions, not problems, Diane felt empowered to direct her recovery and to mobilize her resources. At the close of our final session, just two months after we initially met, Diane turned to me and said, "We've really surprised Mom. She was pissed at first that we decided to only meet every two weeks; if she had her way, you would have seen me twice a week. But much as I love her, sometimes the patient knows what's best for her, not the therapist. And sometimes therapy doesn't have to be so long. I proved that to myself and to Mom."

In this chapter, we cover two newer entries onto the psychotherapeutic scene which we shall collectively know as *constructivist* (Neimeyer, 1993; Neimeyer & Mahoney, 1995). These therapies share three common features: each is a new "brief" therapy, often averaging only 4 or 5 sessions; both focus on change and resources as opposed to the causes of problems; and each emphasizes the client's unique, subjective perspective or self-constructed narrative as contrasted with an "objective" or consensual reality. Consistent with the brief nature of these therapies, this chapter will be relatively brief. We begin with solution-focused therapy and then examine narrative therapy.

A Sketch of the Construction of Theories and Therapies

The major philosophical struggle on college campuses pits *constructivism* against *empiricism*. Constructivism's core claim about knowledge is that the knower does not—indeed cannot—under any circumstances attain knowledge of a reality that is objective or independent of the knower (Held, 1995). Reality is not out there to be found; reality is constructed inside each of us. We cannot attain knowledge of how the world really is. All knowledge is relative to the construct, culture, language or theory that we apply to particular phenomenon. We cannot know patients and their problems purely and directly: we can only know our interpretations of patients and their problems. Different theories, different languages, and different cultures result in very different perceptions of the same client and the client's condition.

Witness Mrs. C., for example. Each therapy system in this book can make a compelling case for its particular construction of Mrs. C and her obsessive compulsive disorder. Mrs. C., herself, actively participates in constructing her own reality. Her reality is filled with threatening things, like underwear, that need to be avoided.

Empiricism holds that given the correct scientific methods, we can discover reliable and valid knowledge about Mrs. C. and her obsessive-compulsive condition. Applying scientific methods can result in an adequate knowledge of the reality in which Mrs. C. was socialized, the real causes of her condition and consequently, the best solutions for helping her overcome her obsessive-compulsive behaviors. At this point in history we may not have developed all of the scientific technologies we need, such as psychological tests and interpersonal interviews, to reach scientific agreement on the causes and cures for the case of Mrs. C. But we are progressing toward such scientific means for knowing the reality of such complex cases.

Constructivists counter that science is just another social construction. Different scientists at different times in history, studying in different cultural contexts, have constructed very different theories of reality. The diversity of theories in this book is not a temporary condition that will disappear as the science of psychotherapy progresses. The diversity of theories is a permanent condition reflecting the complexity and individuality of each client and each knower (McNamee & Gergen, 1992). Our clients are truly open to a diversity of alternative interpretations. That is part of what protects their individuality (Held, 1995). They cannot be reduced to a set of universal laws or principles that can account for the uniqueness of personality and psychopathology.

People are like great poems. Each of us who interacts with a person or a poem perceives something different. Literary critics have constructed a multitude of meanings and interpretations for a single poem, such as T. S. Eliot's "The Waste Land." When asked if he meant all of these interpretations when he wrote the poem, Eliot responded "I didn't then, but I do now."

Such *postmodern* literary criticism has swept the humanities by storm. The sciences resist, insisting that knowledge in science is a result of validation and replication not interpretation.

Is psychotherapy a science or an art? Is knowledge about personality, psychopathology, and psychotherapy based on a reality that we can discover? Or are therapists always left with knowing only the language, the theory and the "reality" that they and their clients construct and interpret together?

Given the growing popularity of constructivism in the academy, it is not surprising that a growing number of therapies based on constructivism are emerging from the postmodern movement. In this chapter we will explore two of the most influential therapies based on *social constructivism*: Solution-Focused Therapy and Narrative Therapy.

Solution-Focused Therapy

Theory of Personality and Psychopathology

Solution-focused therapy begins with refreshing assumptions. People are healthy. People are competent. People have the capacities to construct solutions that can enhance their lives. Psychotherapy can help people enhance their lives by focusing on solutions rather than problems.

Theories of personality and psychopathology fundamentally focus on causes rather than solutions, problems from the past rather than changes in the future. There is a long-standing belief that therapists and patients need to know the causes of troubling behavior before they can find solutions for changing such behavior. However, as constructivism has demonstrated, we can never know the real causes of people's problems. We can construct alternative interpretations. We can apply different theories of personality and psychopathology in attempts to explain people's problems. But we can never know the "reality" of personality and psychopathology. There are respected empiricists, such as many behavior therapists, who reject the entire domain of personality and psychopathology. After a century of searching, personality theories have been able to account for very little of human behavior.

Furthermore, precious little evidence exists to support the belief that constructing causes leads to better solutions. Not knowing the causes of breast cancer doesn't keep oncologists from curing breast cancer. *Why* someone became a drinker 25 years ago (e.g., peer pressure) can have little to do with *how* the individual is going to change now.

Change is happening all the time. People quit smoking or drinking every day. People overcome depression and anxiety every day. The fact is most problems get solved without psychotherapy, further attesting to individuals' competencies. And few people who solve problems on their own have theories of personality and psychopathology.

What replaces past causes of problems like personality and psychopathology in solution-focused therapy? What is the force that can help people, including therapists, shift from a problem-oriented endeavor to a solution-focused enterprise? If the answers are not to be found in the past, then what is left is the present and the future.

What can pull people into a healthier and happier future? Healthier and happier goals. We cannot change our past; we can change our goals. Better goals can break us out of stuck places and can lead us into a more fulfilling future. Rather than learning all types of personality characteristics and psychopathology categories, what effective brief therapists need to know are characteristics of therapeutic goals.

Here are criteria for constructing well-defined goals (Berg & Miller, 1992; Walter & Peller, 1992):

- *Positive*. Rather than have negative goals such as "I am going to get rid of drinking, depression or anxiety," the goals should be positive. The key word here is *instead*. *Instead* of drinking, being depressed or anxious, what positive things are you going to do? A simple therapeutic question for setting goals is: "What will you be doing *instead?*"

- *Process*. The key word here is *how*. "*How* will you be doing this healthier or happier alternative."

- *Present*. Change happens now, not yesterday and not tomorrow. The key phrase here is *on track*. A simple question to help is, "As you leave here today, and you are *on track*, what will you be doing differently or saying differently to yourself?" Today, not tomorrow.

- *Practical*. "How attainable is this goal?" The key word is *attainable*. Clients who want their spouse, employer, parent or teacher to change are seeking unattainable solutions and will set themselves up for more problems.

- *As specific as possible*. "How specifically will you be doing this?" Global, abstract, or ambiguous goals, such as "spending more time with my family," are not nearly as effective as: "Specifically I will take a 15-minute walk with my wife each evening," "I will volunteer to help coach my daughter's soccer team," or "I will take my son golfing with me on Saturdays."

- *Client control*. "What will *you* be doing when the new alternative happens?" The key word is *you*, the client, because *you* have the competency, the responsibility and the control to make better things happen.

- *Client language*. Use the clients' words for forming goals rather than the therapist's favored theoretical language. "I am going to have weekly adult telephone conversations with my father" is more effective than "I am going to resolve my Oedipal conflicts with my father."

In place of personality and psychotherapy, in place of problems and the past, psychotherapy proceeds in the present guided by specific positive goals constructed in the client's language and under the client's control.

Theory of Therapeutic Processes

Given that people can be stuck repeating past patterns because they focus too much of their time and energy on their problems, the goal of therapy is to shift the focus as readily as possible onto solutions in the present that will sustain healthier and happier goals in the future. *Problem talk* maintains a problem focus, so therapeutic change will involve a shift to *solution talk*.

Consciousness Raising. Too many clients enter therapy preoccupied with problems. "I'm depressed all the time." "I can't control my drinking." "My spouse and I are always fighting." "I'm a worry wart." "I can't sleep." The natural response would seem to be to ask "Why? Why are you depressed? Why is your drinking out of control? Why are you and your partner always fighting?"

Therapists could apply their favorite theories to construct answers to these causal questions. But is that helpful? They could help clients become even more conscious of their problems and the multitude of past experiences that may have contributed to their problems. Constructing elegant explanations for events in the past might allow clients and therapists to feel better, but will the clients live better?

Solution-focused therapists help clients become more conscious of the *exceptions* to their problem patterns (Miller, Hubble & Duncan, 1996). "When are the times when you don't feel depressed?" "Oh, when you go to church, and when you play golf, and when you listen to your favorite music." Raising awareness about such exceptions can begin to create solutions.

"When have you been most in control of your drinking?" "Oh, when you attended Alcoholics Anonymous (AA) regularly, and when you were most in touch with your spirituality, and when you were around people who cared about you." Are there any clues in such increased consciousness as to how controls over drinking could be reconstructed?

Rare are clients who have no exceptions to their times of trouble. For those who are having special difficulty focusing on more positive exceptions to their problems, their therapists can ask the *miracle question*. "If by a miracle, you found yourself free from your problems overnight, how would things be different?" Constructing in imagination exceptions to a problem-filled world can help clients become more conscious that their current reality need not be their only reality. The miracle of therapy can be to help clients transform their imagined reality into practical and specific goals that they can attain.

Choosing. The goals we choose determine the future we live. As clients become more conscious of current exceptions to a problem-filled life, they can choose to create more of those exceptions. The client who entered therapy focused on a life filled with depression can choose to participate in more church functions, play golf more often, and listen to more favorite music, specifically uplifting music. The client who was focused on alcohol problems could choose to focus on alcohol solutions with immediate goals such as daily AA attendance, reading religious and inspirational materials, and initiating more socializing with people who care about him.

Here are four guides to therapeutic choices (Walter & Peller, 1992):

1. If it works, don't fix it. Choose to do more of it.
2. If it works a little, choose to build on it.

3. If nothing seems to be working, choose to experiment, including imagining miracles.

4. Choose to approach each session as if it were the last. Change starts now, not next week.

Here are pathways for constructing solutions (DeShazer, 1985, 1988, 1994).

- *Goal focus.* Therapy begins by focusing on goals in the present that can construct a better future. "What is your goal in coming here?" The therapist frames treatment around goals in the present rather than problems from the past. "What brings you here?" is an opening that is much more likely to encourage clients to continue to focus on problems.

- *Problem focus.* If the client responds by talking about problems and complaints, the therapist is understanding and empathic. But once the problem story is told, the therapist is prepared to shift the focus.

- *Solution focus.* "When the problem is solved what will you be *doing* differently?" Is the client ready to begin *doing* a small piece of it now? If so, start the change immediately.

- *Exception focus.* "How is what you will be doing differently happening some now?" or "When isn't the problem happening?" These are known as *exception-finding* questions that build on the client's strengths.

- *Choice or spontaneity.* Are the problem-free events occurring by choice, deliberately, intentionally? Or are these healthier and happier times occurring spontaneously, accidentally, or unpredictably?

If the exceptions are perceived as already under the client's control, then specific goals can be constructed that encourage the client to choose to do more of what helps. If the exceptions are seen as more spontaneous, such as friends dropping by, then the focus is on finding out how such events can occur, such as inviting your friends to stop by.

If the client responds to any of these question by saying "I don't know," the therapist should let the client know that is a good sign. This process is new to the client. It will help the client to think differently and to begin constructing alternatives that may not have been imagined before.

- *Small changes lead to larger changes.* Follow-up sessions build on the gains and the goals that are constructed early in therapy. As one of my clients said, "Changing me is like turning an ocean freighter rather than a speed boat. Slowly, gradually at first. But once I have a new direction, there's no holding me back."

- *Each solution is unique.* Just as each client is a unique individual, so too is each solution unique. Therapists need to be prepared to be surprised. Here is one creative solution constructed by an elderly women living alone in the center of a city. To help free herself from depression, she joined three churches: Catholic, Baptist, and evangelical! She received three times as much social support, had three times as much social opportunities, and much less empty time to get depressed. The fact that most people construct their lives around only one denomination, didn't prohibit her from being ecumenical.

- *Solutions evolve out of conversations.* Whether it is from self-talk or talking in therapy, solutions emerge from dialogues. If therapy encourages us to talk about our same old problems that we know all too well, then we are likely to remain our same old self. Change begins in talking about solutions. If therapy is to be brief, then therapeutic dialogues should focus on solutions as soon as possible.

- *Language is our reality.* Show us a therapist whose language is filled with technical terms about personality and psychopathology, and we will show you a therapist who is prepared to do long-term therapy that repeats the past. Show us a client who begins to talk about practical and personal goals in the present, and we will show you a client whose reality is changing.

Therapeutic Relationship

Because solution-focused therapy is designed to be brief, the therapist plays a more active role in shifting the focus as quickly as possible from problems to solutions. The therapist gently but persistently guides clients in exploring their strengths and building solutions. Once the focus is on solutions, the client is much more in charge. Clients are the experts on what goals they want to construct. The goals are always unique to each client and are constructed by the client to create a better future.

Solution-focused clinicians are expert on the process and structure of therapy; helping clients construct their goals within frameworks that can produce successful solutions. The fundamental relationship, then, is like a multidisciplinary collaboration between experts. Each expert, the client and the therapist, contributes to co-constructing a shared solution.

Practicalities

As with multidisciplinary teams collaborating to create solutions to problems, the therapeutic relationship lasts only as long as needed to construct an acceptable solution. Remarkably few therapeutic sessions are scheduled. Time is not wasted on indexing every psychopathology or researching every etiology. In this time-effective therapy, the search is on as soon as possible for solutions.

Solution-oriented treatment is designed to start, not finish, the solution process. As collaborator, the client is competent to continue implementing the solution long after therapy has ended. Starting therapy in such a time-effective manner limits the tendency of clients to become dependent on the expert therapist who can divine the causes of their disorders and apply the best therapeutic solutions within therapy sessions.

Solution-oriented therapy is indeed brief. The average number of sessions hovers between three and five. A study of 275 clients presenting for services at the Brief

Family Therapy Center in Milwaukee resulted in the following distribution by length of treatment (DeJong & Hopwood, 1996):

Number of Sessions	Number of Cases	Percent of Cases
1	72	26%
2	80	29%
3	47	17%
4	31	11%
5	20	7%
6	10	4%
7 or more	15	6%

As seen, more than 80% of patients came for 4 or fewer sessions with an average of only 2.9 sessions.

Solution-focused therapy has been applied to virtually all behavioral disorders and in all therapy formats. The brief focus is particularly valued for the treatment of mild problems and adjustment disorders (Araoz & Carrese, 1996) but has also been recommended for "chronic mental patients" (Booker & Blymyer, 1994; Webster, Vaughn, & Martinez, 1994). The fundamental concepts—using what is already working, emphasizing existing strengths, speaking in solution language, and listening to client beliefs—are applied to inpatient settings with patients historically treated as incompetent. Although solution-focused therapy was initially launched as a family therapy at the Mental Research Institute in Palo Alto, California (see Chapter 11) and at the Brief Family Therapy Center in Milwaukee, Wisconsin, it is now also widely practiced in the individual format.

Narrative Therapy

While solution-focused therapists hold that clients construct their future by using goals they choose in the present, narrative therapists assert that clients construct their past by stories they tell in the present. The past can be changed by constructing new *narratives* or stories. Witness how the history of the United States is being changed by narratives written by and about women, native Americans, and African Americans whose stories were once omitted from our history.

A realist or an empiricist might want to argue that one cannot change the reality of the past. What was, was. Naive answer, reply the narratives. Recognize that "what was" is what history books tell us. You can know history books, but you cannot know history. And history books are being rewritten as more and more people claim their freedom to tell their stories.

Narrative therapists are anti-realists (Held, 1995). They believe there is no objective reality that exits behind our stories. The "reality" in which we exist is our stories. His-tory and her-story is the reality of each client—unique, personal, subjective, and fortunately open to change.

Theories of Personality and Psychopathology

Theories of personality and psychopathology are the stories that psychotherapists tell about their clients. Unfortunately such theories can also be the stories that therapists impose upon their clients (McNamee & Gergen, 1992). Such theoretical impositions or interpretations can be oppressive at best and destructive at worst. For too many decades male therapists tried to convince women that they were plagued by "penis envy." Women's "Herstory" had to do with problems relating to "voting envy," "career envy," "salary envy," "political power envy," and sexual abuse. For too long childhood sexual abuse was interpreted according to the dominant theory that held that such events were childhood fantasies based on the child's wish fulfillment to have sex with a parent. The professional story about gay and lesbian individuals was that they were DSM disorders: sexual deviants.

No wonder narrative therapists reject empirical theories of personality and psychopathology. It is professional arrogance for therapists to believe that they can tell people who they are. Clients must be free to tell us who they are and who they want to be. Theories are oppressive; they seek to impose one perspective on all people. Theory masquerading as reality is equally oppressive. There is no reality; there are only stories we tell about reality.

Empirical reality is said to be objective, fixed in time, so that we can eventually all come to know the same reality. Would that mean that once the truth is known about what a healthy personality is, for example, we would all strive to be the same person? Such psychological cloning of humans should be seen as being unethical as biological cloning of humans. What the world needs is diversity, not identity. Even identical twins do not have the same identity, the same personality. Each has her or his unique story to tell, just as each client has her or his unique story to tell. If we are to protect the freedom and individuality of our clients, then we start by rejecting an imperial empiricism that would seek to impose the same reality on us all.

One of the wonders of narratives is that they are open, ongoing, never ending. Historical narratives and scientific narratives are open, ongoing, and changing. As our stories change, so too do we change. Look at how radically our society has changed as more women, minorities, and other oppressed people have had emerging opportunities to tell their stories.

If you want to know your identity, the reality of who you are, don't turn to someone else's theory. Turn to the next chapter in your own story.

In place of theories of personality and psychopathology, narrative therapists encourage us to rely on *stories* (White & Epston, 1990, 1994). Narrative therapists, like fine literary critics, can help us to construct new meanings and new interpretations about who we are, who we have been, and what we can become.

Theory of the Therapeutic Process

Given that our experience of problems is a function of the stories we have constructed, then resolution of our problems emerges from deconstructing our old stories and constructing new ones. Therapeutic narratives must be more consciously constructed as liberating stories.

Consciousness Raising. First we need to become conscious of how much of our story has been constructed from the *dominant discourses* in our families and societies (McNamee & Gergen, 1992). Who are the powerful people who tell us how to think and feel about life and about ourselves? Whose language defined sex as bad and high grades as good? Whose stories said that being spontaneous was dangerous and being controlled was safe? Who constructed the reality in which children with high energy and enthusiasm would be diagnosed and drugged for Attention Deficit Hyperactivity Disorder (ADHD), because they couldn't sit still for long hours in boring classes? Whose dominant discourses declared that people who prefer their own company and their own imagination over superficial social discourse are introverted, withdrawn, or antisocial?

In the past, powerful people had the privilege of editing our experiences. Perhaps some of them were strong enough to impose meaning on our lives, such as "I'm a weakling; I'm a coward; I'm shy; I'm ugly; I'm a sex object; I'm a problem."

In the presence of a narrative therapist we can become aware that when it comes to constructing the story of our lives, we have the *privileged position* (White & Epston, 1990, 1994). No predetermined theoretical interpretations are imposed on our personal experiences. No damaging diagnoses will reduce us to a schizophrenic, a bipolar, an obsessive-compulsive, a sexual deviant, an addict, or an ADHD. Only therapeutic discourses occur in which we have the privileged position of being both reader and author of the text of our lives.

As we begin to retell our story the psychotherapist can help us to perceive ourselves from multiple perspectives. Who in the past would not be surprised that we are getting better and doing better? Was our life always this way? Or were there important changes and stages? As we begin to perceive a changing world in the past we can begin to perceive the possibilities for a changing world in the future.

But first we must become aware of how powerful our Problem has become. As in dramatic story telling it helps to have a villain and a victim. Personifying the problem helps put it in perspective as an oppressor that demands much of our time and energy and sense of self (White & Epston, 1990, 1994). My Depression is a demon that demands that I listen to sad music, attend depressing dramas, read absurd existential fiction, and tell sad stories. My Addiction insists that I go out late at night to clubs where controls are checked at the door and people get high on suds, sex, and seduction. My Procrastination requires that I am late for every paper and performance and that I rebel against other people's rules by putting off their wishes as long as I possibly can.

By mapping the influence of this key character in our life, we can read more clearly how determined we have been by the description, the demands and the discouragement of our Problems. But we can also look for unique and unexpected outcomes. When were the occasions when we resisted the Problem's invitation to become part of it? What were the occasions where we were the hero or heroine, when we in fact or fantasy defeated our Demon? When were the times we were free from our Problem, where we escaped the dominance and oppression of the Problem? Were we then like the fox in the Russian poem who escaped from the Soviet cage roaming free in a world that he did not know, in a world that frightened him by being so novel and new? Did we retreat back to the comfort and security of that small cage? Did we escape from freedom, from the responsibility of having to author a novel life?

Choosing. Are we prepared to plot an alternative story? Just as there have been plots against us, to suppress our sexuality or to oppress our originality, so too can we construct plots in our favor. We can choose to overthrow dominant discourses with own voice, our own words, our personal privileged perspective. Keeping a journal, for example, is a choice that asserts that our words matter, our experiences are meaningful. Writing letters to our parents without having to worry about mailing them can free us to give meaning to parts of us that have been omitted for too long. The adult in us, the assertive one in us, the angry one or the forgiving one, might emerge when we are telling it like it is or like it was.

Countering. To construct a new story we need new words, new images, and new meanings (Friedman, 1993). To counter our chronic construction, narrative therapy encourages the use of poetic and picturesque language. As our language becomes richer, our experience becomes richer. As our words have multiple meanings, our lives have more meaning. If our lives are too empty, too narrow, too common, too restricted, or too devitalized, it is because our language is too limited.

In narrative therapy, clients can experience aspects of themselves that they never expressed before. A broader range of emotions—anger, excitement, joy, sadness, and outrage—and counter the same old drab, dreary, monotone meaning that is so depressing. Excitement, anticipation, frustration, and wonder are words that can substitute for the tight, repetitive, burdened language of the worry wart. One of the clearest signs that one's self is changing is that one's words are changing, but one should not substitute technical or scientific terms that have little personal meaning for worn-out words from the past that only have problem meanings.

Not only does narrative therapy encourage clients to experience a sense of authorship in the telling and retelling of their life stories but it also allows them to star in their newly constructed narratives. They are free to rehearse in therapy sessions, where all the anxieties of acting and speaking anew can occur in a safe and accepting place. However, clients are encouraged to launch their performances on other stages: with more accepting friends at first, then with employers or parents who have been experienced as part of the Problem.

One client's parents were taken aback when she began to share some of the rich dialogue that she had written to them in unmailed letters. She not only talked about her old story, when she had to be "oh so perfect" in her dress, her manners, her homework, and her language. Now she expressed herself in a less-than-perfect style, stammering and stopping at times, loud and emotional at other times, colorful and off-color at other times. After one particularly moving soliloquy expressing her estrangement from herself and her father, her parents actually broke into light applause and into tears. They were changing too.

Therapeutic Relationship

Ideally, each therapeutic relationship is unique: constructed by a particular client and a particular clinician conversing together in a particular time, place, and context (McNamee & Gergen, 1992). The relationship unfolds in their dialogue; it is not predetermined by generic principles based on a standard theory of personality, psychopathology, or psychotherapy. Only in this manner of relating can the client's particularity and individuality be respected and protected.

Ideally, nothing more need be said. But in practice, if there are no general guiding principles, then there is nothing that can be taught or learned. Nothing can be generalized from one client to another or even one session to another. The continuity in therapy is constructed from the story clients tell. The narrative therapist's general contribution is to gently guide clients into constructing new editions of their stories that are less limiting and more liberating. Teaching the tools of literary criticism is what therapists can contribute to the "reality" of a story. Therapists can help clients construct novel narratives that flow into a freer future. If we want to appreciate the richness of relationships between therapists and clients, then we need to listen to and interpret the multiple meanings of their dialogue.

Although there is no universally correct therapeutic attitude, therapists do strive for what has been called *narrative empathy* (Omer, 1997). Unlike external empathy, which describes the client from the outside and from the point of view of theory, narrative empathy attempts to construe and express the inner emotional logic of the client's problem patterns. The criterion of an empathic narrative is that it elicits from the client the response "That's me!"

Practicalities

In light of the uniqueness of each therapeutic relationship it could seem impossible to describe any common practices for narrative therapy. Unlike solution-focused therapy, the length of narrative therapy can vary considerably. There is a preference for brief therapy but there is no theory that requires that the co-construction of narratives be a brief process. In practice, sessions are in fact structured by the therapist with the standard 50-minute session being the rule rather than the exception. But therapy can overflow the rigid boundaries of this rule because clients continue the narrative process in the journals or letters they write. Clients are also expected to pay for their sessions with real money.

Effectiveness of Constructivist Therapies

The newer solution-focused and narrative therapies have patterned themselves after the older clinical tradition in favoring a few surveys and therapist testimonials instead of controlled outcome studies. The leading theorists and practitioners have been far more invested in therapeutically applying their procedures than in empirically researching their effectiveness. Leading texts devote only one or two pages to outcome research, and then to the same unpublished outcome study carried out at the Brief Family Therapy Center (BFTC) in Milwaukee, Wisconsin (DeJong & Hopwood, 1996). As the new psychotherapy on the block, constructivist therapy research is in its infancy.

The two outcome studies on solution-focused therapy to date are uncontrolled in design and were not published in peer-reviewed journals. Nonetheless, the findings convey some sense of the typical practices of the treatment.

In the 1988 unpublished study, Kiser contacted 164 clients of the BFTC 6, 12, and 18 months after termination of therapy. Using nonstandardized measures, the indications were of highly successful outcomes: 66% of clients stated that they met their goals and 15% said they had made significant improvements within an average of 4.6 sessions. When clients were contacted at 18 months, the success rate had increased to 86% (quoted in DeJong and Hopwood, 1996).

Similar success was reported in a thoughtful, yet uncontrolled, study of 275 clients who presented for treatment at BFTC in 1992 and 1993. Most of the clients were seen by one of the solution-focused therapists employed by BFTC, although a few clients were seen by trainees supervised by senior solution-focused therapists listening behind a one-way mirror. Fifty-seven percent of the clients were African American, 5% Latino/Hispanic, 3% Native American, and 36% white. Over half were unemployed, and the majority were referred by public welfare agencies.

DeJong and Hopwood (1996) employed two outcome measures. The first intermediate measure involved the *scaling question* asked by the therapist at each session: "On a scale of one to ten, where ten is 'the problems you came to therapy for are solved' and one is 'the problems are the worst they've been,' where are they now on that scale?" On this measure, 26% showed no progress or worsened, 49% showed moderate progress (defined as 1 to 3 points higher on the scaling question), and 25% showed significant progress. The second measure was obtained by contacting the clients by telephone following treatment and asking whether their treatment goals was met. The data showed that 45% of contacted clients (50% of the total) said their treatment goals was met, and an additional 32% said some progress was made toward that goal. The remaining 23% replied that no progress was made. In such an uncontrolled study, of course, we have no reliable comparisons of how many of these clients would have reported success without psychotherapy, with longer therapy, or with another type of therapy.

Criticisms of Constructivist Therapies

From a Behavioral Perspective

Let us tell you a story about two women who suffered from a morbid dread of developing breast cancer. Several relatives of each woman had died of breast cancer. Personal acquaintances had developed breast cancer. As successful career women, they had delayed having children until their mid-thirties. Each coped with their anxiety and depression by drinking and eating too much and exercising too little. Facing forty, they found their fears increasing and their coping abilities decreasing.

Nan consulted a narrative therapist and told her story. She interpreted her text as having been written primarily by a society that would use science to scare women who placed higher priority on developing careers than on having children. Bad things like breast cancer would happen to such women, especially those who drank too much and dieted too little. With the help of her therapist, Nan co-constructed her own story in which a woman was free to fulfill her career first and would not be punished for delaying having children. In this construction, how she coped was her own business, as long as it did not violate anyone else's rights. She finished narrative therapy with a fresh appreciation of her power to tell her story free from fears and negative consequences. Four years later Nan died of undiagnosed late-stage breast cancer.

Ann consulted a behavior therapist who prescribed the research-validated methods of desensitization and exposure to reduce her morbid dread. The therapy prepared Ann to face her fears, in part by going for regular mammograms. Ann also learned from the scientific literature that alcohol abuse, high-fat diets, and sedentary lifestyles increased risks for breast cancer and many other chronic diseases. With the help of her therapy, Ann developed healthier habits for coping with emotional distress. She finished behavior therapy doing her best to reduce her risks from breast cancer and other chronic diseases. Two years later Ann was diagnosed with early stage breast cancer that was successfully treated with surgery and chemotherapy.

From a Psychoanalytic Perspective

If you do not have a theory of psychotherapy that can do justice to the complexities and challenges of personality and psychopathology, then the solution is simple. Deny the reality of personality and psychopathology. Poof—the problem disappears!

Proof? That's another problem that disappears with postmodernism. Only modernists believe in the privileged position of rationalism and empiricism: that through reason and experimentation we can differentiate between reality and fantasy. Postmodernists in the guise of constructivist therapists would have us regress to infantile narcissism. Reject the reality principle! Overthrow the ego! Reason, cognition, and objectivity have no privileged place in helping us or our patients determine what is real and what is not.

Reality is oppressive and it keeps us from being free to fulfill every fantasy. That was the common complaint from many clients fixated on wish-fulfilling fantasy. Now we are hearing the same complaint from clinicians seduced by the fantasy that they can fix a lifetime of psychopathology in a brief time. Instant gratification is available for everyone—clients, clinicians, and managed care organizations.

But there are solutions even simpler than psychotherapy. Pharmacotherapy is super-efficient at constructing a pill for every problem. Personality and psychopathology are deconstructing and dissolving in a brief solution-focused therapy. Next to go will be the psychotherapy itself—deconstructed and dissolved by the reality (or is it the fantasy?) of pharmacotherapy. We can begin constructing this brave new world free from personality, psychopathology, and psychotherapy by putting Prozac in the public water supply or Zoloft in all diet sodas.

From a Humanistic Perspective

We applaud postmodernism's purpose of attempting to protect individualism from the oppression of totalitarianism. Certainly the 20th century has repeatedly witnessed the political and personal pathology that can be imposed on people in the name of reality. Whether that reality is constructed from fascism or communism, racism or sexism, colonialism or imperialism, the results are the same. Privileged people in power who dominate the discourse can impose their universal truths on everyone. If we construct a theory or a science in which one size fits all, then you had better fit in. Otherwise the powers that be can diagnose you as a misfit—a personality disorder, a political prisoner, or simply a problem. How you get treated is up to them. They can label you or libel you, imprison you or hospitalize you, shock you or drug you, and most of all alienate you. Alienate you from yourself if you buy into their social construction, or alienate you from society if you reject their reality.

The challenge for the postmodern clinician is how to protect the particularity of this special person existing in this particular place and time. The problem is that in place of the oppressive generality of the universal truths of science, narrative therapists are left with a single tool. This is the tool of interpretation derived from a literary criticism that holds that each particular reader is free to give new meaning to a text—a poem, a play, or any performance. With this metaphor in mind each individual is deconstructed, discovering what meaning is missing from their dominant discourse. Then a new play or performance is co-constructed through conversations between the client and the clinician.

However, let's examine how de-humanizing this new construction can be. Poems don't feel pain, people do. Words don't worry, women do. Metaphors don't miss emotions, men do. Theories don't make life-enhancing or limiting decisions, individual clients and clinicians do. Language is not responsible for how we live. What is so liberating about becoming adult is that we can now take responsibility for what we say and what we think and what we do. We can learn what was once a foreign language, if we choose. We can live in what was once an alien culture, if that is what we want. In our living, learning, and changing, we are not limited by only one tool of knowing. As creative and constructive as literary criticism can be, it has no privileged position helping me to know who I am and who I will become.

We are reminded again of Abraham Maslow's metaphor that if our only tool is a hammer, then we will treat everything and everyone like a nail. So please don't try hammering away at my real problems as if they were simply poems, merely metaphors or temporary texts. If you don't have a way of knowing who I am as a real person, then I don't want to know who you are as a psychotherapist.

From an Integrative Perspective

Who says that we must choose between constructivism and empiricism, words and numbers, art and science? As a scientist and a therapist, I have both ways of knowing. Art is the source of my inspiration. Science is the source of my validation.

Plays, poetry, painting, and music can all create a deeper and richer appreciation of humanity. Theater, for example, so often makes real the personal and interpersonal struggle of individuals to break out of self-defeating patterns and problems. The images used in poetry and paintings can give new insights into the darker side of ourselves that are often hidden from direct observation. Music gives voice to such a broad range of emotions that we can all experience if we open our ears. These are wonderful ways of knowing and expressing that can enrich our lives and our work with others.

At the same time, our lives and our work can be equally elevated by discovering scientific principles that can be generalized across problems and across people. Behavioral methods and cognitive therapies, for example, relieve suffering around the world—quite independent from the question of who told that therapeutic story first in which language. Our search for valid principles for progressing through the stages of change, for another example, has enabled us to construct treatment programs that can reach many more people than previously possible (see Chapter 15). Such generalizable principles permit us to approach clients with confidence that we know something special that can help them change.

We don't have to act like "know-nothings" who must discover everything anew with each particular person. Of course, we need to be open to understanding what is of special importance to each individual client, and what particular changes would most enhance their lives. However, if we do not have any generalizable knowledge to share, then each client is reduced to trial-and-error learning, which is inefficient and ineffective. Each client would have to reinvent the wheel of change. We in psychology and in education have known for decades that guided learning is so much more efficient and effective than trial-and-error learning. Clinical ethics dictate that we listen to both our clients and our science.

We can assign a privileged position to those in the arts and humanities who have special talents for constructing a multitude of interpretations for humanity. We can also assign a privileged position to those in the sciences who have the ability to conduct research and test theories. Their scientific methods allow us to reject even our favorite interpretations in favor of alternatives that meet our toughest tests of validation. But no theory, literary or scientific, can meet the test of absolute certainty. As Nietzsche warned, we should not be misled by those who would substitute certainty for truth. Science has the privileged position of telling us what is most probably valid given all that we know to date.

Unfortunately, in psychotherapy we often don't have enough scientifically valid knowledge that can be generalized to a particular person or problem. We are thrown back for now to relying on theoretical interpretations. The privileged position here is the professional and personal perspective of clinician and client struggling together to understand and modify particular problems. Their perspectives are likely to be most valid and most helpful when they are informed by the best that the art and science of psychotherapy has to offer.

— A NARRATIVE ANALYSIS BY MRS. C. —

Mrs. C. has told and retold her story too many times. Before therapy, during therapy, and after therapy she repeated her preoccupation with pinworms. Her psychoanalytic therapy just kept going backward in time, obsessively paying attention to every detail of her disease. Seeking to uncover the hidden causes of her disorder deep in her childhood memories, her therapists were missing the forest for the trees. Mrs. C.'s discourse was her disorder.

The more Mrs. C. focused on her childhood, the more she repeated the dominant discourses that were so demanding, disrupting and discouraging. "Be clean! Be cute! Pick that up. Put that down. Eat your peas. Slowly. Be home on time. Behave! Be good. Be healthy. Be careful! Be neat. Be prompt. Be still."

In narrative therapy it would not take Mrs. C. long to discover who had held privileged positions in her past: her patriarchal parents, her pastor, and then her psychotherapists. Her parents and her pastor were obvious, with all of their demands based on predetermined categories of how a good child, a good American, and a good Christian should behave. Her psychotherapists were more subtle, but soon Mrs. C. could see that they were repeating the same pattern of imposing their predetermined categories on her: obsessive-compulsive neurosis; anal-stage fixations; conflicts over toilet training; defenses against sexual and aggressive impulses; and the laundry list went on. The language had changed, but the meaning was the same. Some privileged person—like a parent, pastor, or psychotherapist—had the power to tell her story. Their paternal, religious, or psychological constructs took precedence over Mrs. C's personal experience. She had no right to interpret their behavior because it was all benign; they were only doing it for her own good.

A narrative therapist would refuse to impose any predetermined meaning on Mrs. C. She doesn't need a detached, theoretical formultation of herself written by a psychotherapist; she deserves a lived, personal story written by herself. She would be encouraged to construct her own story. What fits? What feels good? What was missing from the old stories? Mrs. C. would begin to deconstruct the dominant discourse. What meanings were missing? What was the hidden text covered and controlled by all the cleaning? Where's the joy? Where is the fun? No spontaneity. No ripping up. No running around. No desires, just demands. No decisions, just disruptions. Startled, Mrs. C could discover that what was missing from such discourse was her self, her soul.

Her therapist would encourage Mrs. C. to accept the privileged position of being at the center of her own life. No one needed to tell her what to do, to tell her story and determine what it meant and how it must unfold. Mrs. C. could become free to be the author of her own existence.

In her daily journal Mrs. C. could begin to write in her own words the multiple meanings that had been omitted, washed away by the dominant discourse; the joy of having her first child; the lust that had gotten lost along the way.

She might decide that her soap opera show had run its course. It had lost its vitality. For too long she had tried too hard to buy into what her privileged parents were promoting: "Be clean; be good; behave." She could decide to experience a much fuller range of stories—from comedy to drama; from mystery to history. Mrs. C. might decide to enroll in courses at her local university. Here she could see the world from multiple perspectives. What better way to revitalize her life, to fill the void, than to bring art and music into her existence? What fun it could be to go to the football games with her family! After all, when it came to constructing her own life, she felt like a freshman.

Mrs. C. could come to understand why such a curriculum is called "liberal arts." For her, they could be liberating arts. If she had received such an education earlier in her life, she might have seen through her parents' privileged position. She might have realized that their way of constructing life was only one of many. Then she could have been free earlier to begin authoring her own existence.

Fortunately, Mrs. C. could discover that it is never too late to reconstruct the world and her self. Combining constructs from across continents and across ages, ideas, emotions, and insights from different religions and different philosophies could all enrich and enhance her life. Mrs. C could shift her focus from a profound preoccupation with problems and pathologies to a liberating awareness of how open and ongoing is history and humanity. No longer would Mrs. C. need to be fixated on the past; by creating her own narrative she could perceive from her privileged position how open and ongoing is her story and her self.

Future Directions

Constructivism is one of the dominant discourses in academics, and psychotherapies based on it should thus continue to grow in popularity and diversity. Indeed, the use of "constructive" words (words beginning with "construct") nearly doubled in the psychological literature between 1974 and 1994 (Mahoney, 1996). In this chapter we have explored two of the leading examples of constructivist therapy. The gender- and culture-sensitive therapies presented in Chapter 12 are additional alternatives constructed specifically for women, men, and racial/ethnic minorities. Theoretically there is an unlimited number of therapies that can be created from a constructivist perspective.

One of the future challenges for the constructivist movement will be to articulate criteria for choosing what therapies to teach and to practice from a growing diversity of approaches. One problem is that predetermined criteria for choosing the most promising approaches can run counter to a constructivist philosophy. Are there any general principles of psychotherapy to be taught or to be applied? If each approach is optimally constructed by a particular trainer working with a particular trainee, then teaching these therapies will be done in the context of an apprenticeship or partnership rather than in a classroom or training clinic.

In academia the security of tenure and the principle of academic freedom gives faculty the right to teach and write whatever they choose. No predetermined criteria are imposed on their classroom curricula or their research agendas. In the health care system, however, there is no such security or autonomy. Increasingly, managed care organizations are requiring criteria such as scientific outcomes and evidence-based practices. Science, along with business, is becoming a dominant force in health care. Narrative and solution-focused therapists are likely to confront a limiting future that will test their philosophical assumptions. They will need to produce hard empirical data demonstrating that constructivist clinicians can produce cost-effective outcomes with real clients with DSM disorders. The alternative will be to construct practices not covered or controlled by insurance and health care systems.

In the meantime, the philosphical appeal of constructivism, its popularity in academia, and the brevity of solution-focused therapy are likely to appeal to clinicians helping clients develop solutions and rewrite their life stories in an era of short-term psychotherapy.

Suggestions for Further Reading

Berg, I. K., & Miller, S. D. (1992). *Working with the problem drinker: A solution-focused approach*. New York: Norton.

DeShazer, S. (1985). *Keys to solution in brief therapy*. New York: Norton.

DeShazer, S. (1994). *Words were originally magic*. New York: Norton.

Friedman, S. (1993). *The new language of change*. New York: Guilford.

Held, B. S. (1995). *Back to reality: A critique of postmodern theory in psychotherapy*. New York: Norton.

Hoyt, M. F. (Ed.). (1998). *The handbook of constructive therapies*. San Francisco: Jossey-Bass.

Miller, S. D., Hubble, M. A., & Duncan, B. L. (Eds.). (1996). *Handbook of solution-focused brief therapy*. San Francisco: Jossey-Bass.

Neimeyer, R. A., & Mahoney, M. J. (Eds.). (1995). *Constructivisim in psychotherapy*. Washington, DC: American Psychological Association.

Walter, J. L., & Peller, J. E. (1992). *Becoming solution-focused in brief therapy*. New York: Brunner/Mazel.

White, M., & Epston, D. (1990). *Narrative means to therapeutic ends*. New York: Norton.

Journals: *Constructive Change; Journal of Constructivist Psychology*.

 **14** # Integrative and Eclectic Therapies

Arnold Lazarus

FOR SOME STUDENTS, every exam threatens to overwhelm them with anxiety. No matter how hard they study, they can't be confident. They can't relax. They are convinced that their dreaded anxiety will interfere with their performance. And it usually does. Their debilitating test anxiety can interfere with clearly under-standing the exam questions, or it can disrupt retrieval of the correct answers. No matter how bright they are, they almost always perform below their potential.

Highly test-anxious students have trouble sleeping before an exam. The day of a big exam, they may have trouble eating. Their intestinal tracts may act up. One of their worst fears is that they will block entirely on an exam and will feel abso-lutely foolish when they turn in a test that is barely begun. When test anxiety be-comes so aversive and debilitating, very talented students can drop out of college to escape what one student called "a fate worse than death."

To help such students, we compared two treatments for test anxiety. The first was traditional *systematic desensitization* that paired deep muscle relaxation with images of exam situations that become increasingly stressful. Over time, these stu-dents learned to counter highly anxious reactions to images of exams with deep muscle relaxation. The second was a novel and integrative treatment called *dy-namic desensitization*. This therapy combines the counterconditioning principles of behavior therapy with images from a psychodynamic interpretation of test anxiety.

According to the psychoanalytic perspective, debilitating test anxiety is rooted in early childhood experiences in which mistakes or failures were met with parental criticism and threats of rejection or other forms of loss of love. Children who are dependent on their parents' approval are not free to fight back against what they perceive as their parents' demands for perfection. To express their anger would be to risk corporal punishment, emotional abuse, and the possibility of rejection. As students grow older, every exam becomes a test of their self-worth. Every exam threatens to prove their parents' harsh judgments that they are not bright enough, not careful enough, not good enough. Any ambiguity on an exam, the slightest un-fairness in wording or grading, can threaten to overwhelm them with anger toward the teacher/parent who is just waiting to make them look bad.

In dynamic desensitization, students learned to vividly imagine a series of evaluative situations in which they make a mistake, are berated by a parent or teacher, and are overwhelmed with anxiety and anger that bursts out, resulting in both humiliation and physical retribution from parental figures. In essence, this therapy integrates behavioral change processes and psychoanalytic content.

We were not surprised to find that both forms of desensitization were effective in significantly reducing debilitating test anxiety. In fact, there were no differences between the treatments in terms of immediate effectiveness. We were pleased to dis-cover, however, that the dynamic desensitization led to significantly more generali-zation to a broad range of evaluative situations. Not only were students in this integrative therapy better able to cope with demanding exams, but they were also more relaxed in other situations where they felt they were being evaluated, such as meeting new people, giving a speech, going out on a date, and starting a new job. These students were helping us to enhance the integration movement, which seeks innovative methods of combining powerful processes and appropriate content from psychotherapy systems traditionally viewed as theoretically and clinically incompatible.

A Sketch of Integrative Motives

Psychotherapy integration is motivated by a desire to look beyond the confines of single-school approaches to see what can be learned—and how clients can benefit—from other approaches. The objective of doing so, not yet fully realized, is to enhance the effectiveness and efficiency of psychotherapy. The integration "movement," as it is now called, is characterized by a spirit of open inquiry and a zest for transtheoretical dialogue (Norcross & Arkowitz, 1992).

Rivalry among theoretical orientations has a long and undistinguished history in psychotherapy, dating back to Freud. In the infancy of the field, therapy systems, like battling siblings, competed for attention and affection in a "dogma eat dogma" environment (Larson, 1980). Clinicians traditionally operated from within their own particular theoretical frameworks, often to the point of being blind to alternative conceptualizations and potentially superior interventions.

As psychotherapy has matured, the ideological cold war has abated and integration has emerged as a climate of opinion. The debates across theoretical systems appear to be less polemic, or at least more issue-specific. The theoretical substrate of each system is undergoing intensive reappraisal, as psychotherapists acknowledge the inadequacies of any one system and the potential value of others (Norcross & Newman, 1992).

Integration as a point of view has probably existed as long as philosophy and psychotherapy. In philosophy, the third-century biographer, Diogenes Laertius, referred to an eclectic school that flourished in Alexandria in the second century. In psychotherapy, Freud consciously struggled with the selection and integration of diverse methods. In fact, as early as 1919, Freud introduced psychoanalytic psychotherapy as an alternative to classical analysis, recognizing that the more rarefied approach lacked universal applicability and that many patients did not possess the requisite psychological-mindedness (Liff, 1992).

Even the Iron Curtain isolating Eastern Europe and the governments there imposing a single system of treatment (Pavlovian conditioning) could not stop psychotherapy integration. From 1950 until 1968 in Czechoslovakia, Ferdinand Knobloch (1996; Knobloch & Knobloch, 1979) created an integrated approach combining various theories, as well as embracing individual, group, and family modes of treatment. Inspired by the therapeutic community, this integrated psychotherapy predated many contemporary approaches and foreshadowed several contemporary principles of psychotherapy.

Although the notion of integrating various therapeutic approaches has thus intrigued mental health professionals for more than 75 years, it is only within the past 15 years that integration has developed into a clearly delineated area of interest. Indeed, the temporal course of interest in psychotherapy integration, as indexed by both the number of publications (Arkowitz, 1992a, 1992b) and the development of organizations and journals (Goldfried & Newman, 1992), reveals occasional stirrings before 1970, a growing interest during the 1980s, and rapidly accelerating interest from 1985 to the present.

The recent and rapid increase in integrative psychotherapies leads one to inquire "Why now?" At least eight interacting, mutually reinforcing motives have fostered the development of integration (Norcross & Newman, 1992):

- *Proliferation of therapies.* Which of 400-plus therapies should be studied, taught, or bought? The hyperinflation of brand-name therapies has produced narcissistic fatigue: "With so many brand names around that no one can recognize, let alone remember, and so many competitors doing psychotherapy, it is becoming too arduous to launch still another new brand" (London, 1988, pp. 5–6). This might also be called the Exhaustion Theory of Integration: the cynical but accurate observation that peace among warring schools is the last resort.

- *Inadequacy of any single theoretical system for all patients and problems.* No single system has cornered the market on utility. Underlying the ecumenical spirit is the stark realization that narrow conceptual positions and simple answers to major questions do not begin to explain the evidence in psychotherapy. Clinical realities have come to demand a more flexible, if not integrative, perspective (Kazdin, 1984).

- *External socioeconomic contingencies.* Psychotherapy has experienced mounting pressures from not easily disregarded sources such as government policy makers, informed consumers, insurance companies, and national health insurance planners. Without some drastic changes, psychotherapists stand to lose prestige, customers, and money. As Mahoney (1984) put it, there is something to be said for having the different therapies "hang together" rather than "hang separately."

- *Growing popularity of short-term, problem-focused treatments.* The brief, problem focus has brought formerly different therapies closer together and has created variations of different therapies that are more compatible with each other. Integration, particularly in the form of eclecticism, responds to the pragmatic time-limited injunction of "whichever therapy works better—and quicker—for this patient with this problem."

- *Opportunities for therapists to observe and experiment with various treatments.* The establishment of specialized clinics for the treatment of specific disorders—sexual dysfunctions, obsessive-compulsive disorders, depression, and eating disorders, to name only a few—have afforded exposure to other theories and therapies, and stimulated some to consider other orientations more seriously. Psychotherapy treatment manuals have also induced an informal version of "theoretical exposure": previously feared and unknown therapies were approached gradually, anxiety dissipated, and the previously feared therapies were integrated into the clinical repertoire.

- *Recognition that therapeutic commonalities play major roles in determining therapy outcome.* As discussed in Chapter 1, only about 15% of outcome variance is generally accounted for by specific techniques (Beutler & Clarkin,

1990; Lambert, 1992), and many have found that therapeutic success can be best predicted by common elements of psychotherapy, such as properties of the patient, the working alliance, and facilitative qualities of the therapist.

■ *Identification of specific treatments of choice.* At the same time as the field has come to appreciate the potency of therapeutic commonalities, research has also identified specific treatments of choice for certain disorders and patients. Controlled outcome research generally finds cognitive therapy and interpersonal therapy most effective for depression; behavior therapy most effective for phobias, panic disorders, and childhood aggression; systemic therapy for marital conflict, and so on (Lambert & Bergin, 1992). We can now selectively prescribe different treatments—or combinations of treatments—to particular patient problems.

■ *Development of professional societies for integration.* The development of professional networks has been both a consequence and cause of interest in psychotherapy integration. Several organizations, principally the Society for the Exploration of Psychotherapy Integration (SEPI), have brought together integration enthusiasts through conferences, networking, and journals. Integrationists and eclectics now have a professional home.

These motives speak to the entire field of psychotherapy moving toward integration. But what motivates individual therapists to embrace eclecticism or integration? From a personal-historical perspective, Robertson (1979) identifies six factors that facilitate the acquisition of an eclectic or integrative stance. The first is the lack of pressures in training to adopt a doctrinaire position and the absence of a charismatic figure to emulate. The second factor, which has been substantiated by survey findings (see Norcross & Newman, 1992, for a review), is length of clinical experience: as therapists encounter complex clients and problems over time, they may be more likely to reject a single theory as too simple. A third factor is the extent to which doing psychotherapy is making a living or making a philosophy of life; Robertson asserts that eclecticism is more likely to follow the former. In the words of several distinguished scientist-practitioners (Ricks, Wandersman, & Poppen, 1976, p. 401):

> So long as we stay out of the day to day work of psychotherapy, in the quiet of the study or library, it is easy to think of psychotherapists as exponents of competing schools. When we actually participate in psychotherapy, or observe its complexities, it loses this specious simplicity.

The remaining three factors are personality variables: an obsessive-compulsive need to give order to all the interventions of the therapeutic universe; a maverick temperament to move beyond some theoretical camp; and a skeptical attitude toward the status quo.

Technical Eclecticism or Theoretical Integration?

There are numerous pathways toward the integration of the psychotherapies (Mahrer, 1989c). The three most popular routes at present are technical eclecticism, theoretical integration, and common factors (Arkowitz, 1989; Norcross & Grencavage, 1989). Although all are intent on increasing therapeutic efficacy, efficiency, and applicability by looking beyond the confines of single-school approaches, they do so in rather different ways and at different levels.

The *common factors* approach, as we discussed in Chapter 1, seeks to determine the core ingredients that different therapies share in common, with the eventual goal of creating more parsimonious and efficacious treatments based on those commonalities. This search is predicated on the belief that commonalities are more important in accounting for therapy outcome than the unique factors that differentiate among therapies. One way of determining common therapeutic principles is by focusing on a level of abstraction somewhere between theory and technique. This intermediate level of abstraction, known in the transtheoretical model as a *change process*, is a heuristic that implicitly guides the efforts of experienced therapists. Goldfried (1980, p. 996) argues:

> To the extent that clinicians of varying orientations are able to arrive at a common set of strategies, it is likely that what emerges will consist of robust phenomena, as they have managed to survive the distortions imposed by the therapists' varying theoretical biases.

In specifying what is common across disparate orientations, we may also be selecting what works best among them.

Since we have already introduced common factors in Chapter 1 and will consider them again in Chapter 15, we shall devote the remainder of this chapter to technical eclecticism and theoretical integration.

Technical eclecticism is the least theoretical but should not be construed as either atheoretical or antitheoretical (Lazarus, Beutler, & Norcross, 1992). Technical eclectics seek to improve our ability to select the best treatment for the person and the problem. This search is guided primarily by data on what has worked best in the past for others with similar problems and similar characteristics. Eclecticism focuses on predicting for whom interventions will work: the foundation is actuarial rather than theoretical.

Proponents of technical eclecticism use procedures drawn from different sources without necessarily subscribing to the theories that spawned them, whereas the theoretical integrationist draws from diverse systems that may be philosophically incompatible. For technical eclectics, no necessary connection exists between metabeliefs and techniques. "To attempt a theoretical rapprochement is as futile as trying to picture the edge of the universe. But to read through the vast amount of literature on psychotherapy, *in search of techniques*, can be clinically enriching and therapeutically rewarding" (Lazarus, 1967, p. 416).

The term *eclecticism* has acquired an emotionally ambivalent, if not negative, connotation for some clinicians because of its allegedly disorganized and indecisive nature. Indeed, it is surprising that so many clinicians admit to being eclectic in their work, given the negative valence the term has acquired (Garfield, 1980).

But these accusations of being "wishy-washy" should be properly redirected to *syncretism*—uncritical and unsystematic combinations (Norcross, 1990; Patterson, 1990). Such haphazard "eclecticism" is primarily an outgrowth of an accumula-

Table 14.1 Most Frequent Combinations of Theoretical Orientations

Combination	1986		1976*	
	%	Rank	%	Rank
Cognitive and behavioral	12	1	5	4
Humanistic and cognitive	11	2		
Psychoanalytic and cognitive	10	3		
Behavioral and humanistic	8	4	11	3
Interpersonal and humanistic	8	4	3	6
Humanisti and systems	6	6		
Psychoanalytic and Interpersonal	5	7		
Systems and behavioral	5	7		
Behavioral and psychosomatic	4	9	25	1

*Percentages and ranks were not reported for all cominbations in the 1976 study (Garfield & Kurtz). Table adapted from Norcross and Prochaska (1988).

tion of pet techniques and inadequate training, which produce an arbitrary, if not capricious, blend of methods "by default." Eysenck (1970, p. 145) characterizes this indiscriminate smorgasbord as a "mish-mash of theories, a hugger-mugger of procedures, a gallimaufry of therapies," having no proper rationale or empirical verification. This muddle of idiosyncratic clinical creations is the opposite of effective psychotherapy, which is the product of years of painstaking clinical research and experience. Rotter (1954, p. 14), years ago, summarized the matter as follows: "All systematic thinking involves the synthesis of pre-existing points of view. It is not a question of whether or not to be eclectic but of whether or not to be consistent and systematic."

In *theoretical integration*, two or more psychotherapy systems are integrated in the hope that the result will be better than the constituent therapies alone. As the name implies, there is an emphasis on integrating the underlying *theories* of psychotherapy along with therapy techniques from each. The various proposals to integrate psychoanalytic and behavioral theories illustrate this direction, as well as grander schemes to meld all the major systems of psychotherapy.

Psychotherapists combine literally all available theories in creating their clinical hybrids. When 113 self-identified integrative psychotherapists rated their use of six theories (behavioral, cognitive, humanistic, interpersonal, psychoanalytic, systems), the resulting 15 dyads were each selected by at least one therapist (Norcross & Prochaska, 1988). The most common combinations are shown in Table 14.1, along with the findings of a similar study conducted ten years previously (Garfield & Kurtz, 1977). The modal combination in the late 1970s was psychoanalytic-behavioral; in the late 1980s, the three most popular combinations all involved cognitive theory (see Alford & Norcross, 1991, and Beck, 1991b, for related accounts).

Theoretical integration entails a commitment to a conceptual creation beyond a technical blend of methods. The goal is to create a theoretical framework that

Table 14.2 Eclecticism versus Integration

Eclecticism	Integration
Technical	Theoretical
Divergent (differences)	Convergent (commonalities)
Choosing from many	Combining many
Applying what is	Creating something new
Collection	Blend
Applying the parts	Unifying the parts
Atheoretical but empirical	More theoretical than empirical
Sum of parts	More than sum of parts
Realistic	Idealistic

synthesizes the best elements of two or more approaches to therapy. Integration, however, aspires to more than a simple combination; it seeks an emergent theory that is more than the sum of its parts and that leads to new directions for practice and research.

How, then, do these two strategies differ? A National Institute of Mental Health (NIMH) Workshop (Wolfe & Goldfried, 1988) and two studies (Norcross & Napolitano, 1986; Norcross & Prochaska, 1988) have summarized the distinctions between integration and eclecticism. These are shown in Table 14.2.

The primary distinction between eclecticism and integration is that between empirical pragmatism and theoretical flexibility. Integration refers to a commitment to a conceptual or theoretical creation beyond eclecticism's pragmatic blending of procedures. To take a culinary metaphor, the eclectic selects among several dishes to constitute a meal; the integrationist creates new dishes by combining different ingredients. A corollary to this distinction, rooted in theoretical integration's early stage of development, is that current practice is largely eclectic; theory integration represents a promissory note for the future. In the words of Wachtel (1991, p. 44):

> The habits and boundaries associated with the various schools are hard to eclipse, and for most of us integration remains more a goal than a constant daily reality. Eclecticism in practice and integration in aspiration is an accurate description of what most of us in the integrative movement do much of the time.

We now examine one exemplar of theoretical integration and one of technical eclecticism—namely, Paul Wachtel's integrative psychodynamic-behavior therapy and Arnold Lazarus's multimodal therapy.

Integrative Psychodynamic-Behavior Therapy

A Sketch of Paul Wachtel

Paul L. Wachtel (1940–   ) authored the 1977 classic, *Psychoanalysis and Behavior Therapy: Toward an Integration,* that many believe ushered in an era of sophisticated attempts at theoretical integration. He was formally trained at the graduate and postgraduate levels in psychoanalytic psychotherapy and operated largely from this traditional perspective in his early years, but gradually incorporated behavioral and systemic perspectives into his practice.

An early integrative influence was John Dollard, who taught Wachtel his first psychotherapy course at Yale and was his first therapy supervisor, and who coauthored *Personality and Psychotherapy: An Analysis in Terms of Learning, Thinking, and Culture* with Neil Miller in 1950. This seminal contribution went beyond an attempt to translate psychoanalytic concepts into behavioral language to a synthesis of ideas about neuroses and psychotherapy from the two perspectives in order to create a more unified theory. Dollard and Miller's (1950, p. 3) objective—"The ultimate goal is to combine the vitality of psychoanalysis, the rigor of the natural science laboratory, and the facts of culture"—anticipated Wachtel's own substantial and evolving body of work.

His 1977 integrative classic began, ironically, in an effort to write a paper portraying behavior therapy as "foolish, superficial, and possibly even immoral" (Wachtel, 1977, p. xv). But in preparing his paper he was forced for the first time to really look at what behavior therapy was and to think carefully about the issues. When he actually observed some of the leading behavior therapists of the day, including Joseph Wolpe and Arnold Lazarus, much to his astonishment he realized that the particular version of psychodynamic therapy toward which he had been gravitating dovetailed to a surprising extent with what a number of behavior therapists were doing. Wachtel's experience in this regard reminds us that separate and isolated theoretical schools perpetuate caricatures of other positions, thereby avoiding basic changes in viewpoint and expansion in therapy practice. Integration typically occurs only after "desegregation" and interaction occur.

In short, Wachtel found many sources of dissatisfaction with standard psychoanalytic accounts and several strengths in the behavioral perspective. Psychoanalysis overemphasized the causal role of early experiences, overplayed the role of insight as the agent of change, undervalued the process of extinction as a major source of change, and devoted insufficient attention to the role of social skills. Behavior therapy introduced the possibility of active intervention, highlighted the role of context in determining human behavior, and emphasized empirical validation of concepts and procedures. The psychodynamic influence has remained considerable in his thinking, so much so that he still occasionally describes his approach as "integrative psychodynamic therapy," but the compatibility of his interpersonal version of psychodynamic therapy with the social-learning version of behavior therapy is the distinctive feature of his theoretical integration.

Wachtel continues to expand and articulate his integration in his positions as distinguished professor of psychology at the City University of New York, cofounder of the Society for the Exploration of Psychotherapy Integration (SEPI), and workshop leader on several continents. The scope of his perspective has been enlarged in more recent years to include broader systemic forces (*The Poverty of Affluence*, 1989, and *Family Dynamics in Individual Psychotherapy* with Ellen Wachtel, 1986) as well as continued attention to the principles of therapeutic communication (Wachtel, 1993).

Theory of Personality and Psychopathology

The centrality of anxiety is a common emphasis of both the psychoanalysts and the behaviorists. To be sure, there are major differences between the two viewpoints in formulating and treating anxiety. But these differences can be recognized as complementary, rather than contradictory. Bridges can be built to connect the chasms that separate them. Moreover, by distinguishing between the original assumptions of psychoanalysis and behavior therapy and their evolving practice, more commonalities can be discovered. These are Wachtel's (1977, 1997) integrative strategies.

What is particularly characteristic of the psychoanalytic perspective is its emphasis on the persisting influence of certain childhood wishes and fears *despite* later experiences that might be expected to alter them. Repression prevents the desire or fantasy from "growing up," from changing over the course of development. This is the "timeless unconscious" or, as Wachtel (1977) calls it, the *woolly mammoth* view of psychopathology—once trapped in ice, it stays perfectly preserved forever.

This classical Freudian view of the role of the past in present functioning presents a major obstacle to any effort to reconcile the psychoanalytic and behavioral approaches. But if one reevaluates the conception of the historical dimension in creating the neurosis, then more behavioral explanations (and interventions) of anxiety can be employed. Wachtel tries to do precisely this in arguing against the woolly mammoth view. We are not unalterably frozen in time; we do modify and act on the original fantasy and wishes.

Must neurosis be locked-in remnants of the past that can be changed only by gradually uncovering layer after layer of intrapsychic structure? Or can the presence of these primitive inclinations be accounted for by the way the patient is currently living? And might these inclinations change if the way of living is changed? By arguing in the affirmative to the latter two questions, Wachtel offers an active and interpersonal alternative to classic psychoanalytic thought. It draws heavily on the formulations of Karen Horney, Harry Stack Sullivan, and Erik Erikson. In contrast to the psychoanalytic metaphor of treatment as peeling an onion, Wachtel views it as an unfolding and self-creating process.

Wachtel maintains that the primitive demands that are seemingly unresponsive to reality turn out, on closer and more subtle inspection, to *be* responsive to reality and *not* to be completely cut off from the ego's perceptual contact with reality. That is why helping people to change the way they live can lead to changes in these seemingly out-of-touch-with-reality intrapsychic attitudes.

An anxiety-ridden, 30-year-old chef whose mother had died when he was an infant had a clinging, passive-dependent relationship with his wife. He looked to her to tell him what to wear, what to eat, what to cook, and what to do in his spare time. This pattern had been tolerable until they had their own children. Now with two young ones hanging on her, the wife was increasingly impatient with what she called her "third child." He was panicky that she was pushing him away, criticizing his clinging, and demanding that he grow up and share the parenting. Was his problem buried deep within his oral-stage psyche with a schema of women who would abandon him unless he held on for dear life? Or was his problem apparent in his repeated pattern of clinging to his wife for parenting and nurturing? Wachtel would find the answers in the parallel between the client's unresolved intrapsychic conflicts and his current interpersonal behaviors.

Conflicts that dominate a person's life can be understood as following from, as well as causing, the way he or she lives. Intrapsychic conflicts create problematic behavior; problematic behavior creates intrapsychic conflicts. This ongoing etiological process is known as *cyclical psychodynamics*. A person's meek and self-denigrating lifestyle, for instance, may be caused by repressed rage. But a meek and self-denigrating lifestyle may also generate rage. It's a vicious, self-perpetuating cycle.

The patient's current way of living both stems from and simultaneously perpetuates his or her problems. But how are these connections, these continuities, between past and present to be construed? The traditional psychoanalytic imagery is archeological—layer after layer of residue in hierarchical fashion. The traditional behavioral view emphasizes the conditioning process of generalization from one event to another. Wachtel conceptualizes the connection between past and present as a cyclical recreation of interpersonal events. To invoke Piaget's notion of *schema*, we assimilate new experiences into older schemata—more familiar ways of viewing and thinking about things. New people and new relationships thus tend to be approached in terms of their similarity to earlier ones.

The core of neurosis is the anxiety invoked and maintained by the client's cyclical psychodynamics. A young woman presents for therapy with a developmental history filled with enormous conflict over sexual activity. This internal conflict has led to considerable anxiety over sexual relationships and inhibitions in learning the everyday social skills involved in approaching a man who interests her. She is caught in a vicious cycle in which intrapsychic conflicts generate anxiety over sexual arousal, which then leads to avoidance of sexual situations. Hence, she is awkward and ineffective in speaking with men; hence, her anxiety intensifies over sexual arousal. Such a cyclical pattern, repeated countless times, is likely to be far more responsible for her current fear of men than exotic symbolic representations of her anxiety that finally "emerge" in her analytic sessions.

Theory of Therapeutic Processes

That interpersonal events perpetuate neurosis implies a need for active intervention on the part of the therapist in order for neurotic patterns to change. The cyclical psychodynamic view attaches value to direct intervention in the patient's day-to-day problems in living. Wachtel moves away from the psychoanalytic notion that interpretation is the "pure gold" of psychotherapeutic interventions and from the largely unsupported claim that lifting repression and imparting genuine insight will automatically give way to behavior change. Interpretive efforts aimed at insight into origins or even current motives are but one of many ways of disrupting the destructive circle of events.

The immediate therapeutic implication is, in the title of a published collection of Wachtel's (1987) essays, to combine *Action and Insight*. Actions and insights are mutually facilitative; ways of approaching and understanding clinical phenomena that exclude one or the other are not fully satisfactory. "To put it differently, who we are cannot be separated from what we do; fundamental personality change requires fundamental change in how we handle the events of our daily lives" (Wachtel, 1987, p. vi). It is not a matter of action or insight, or of one first and then the other, but of both or neither.

True to the spirit of Wachtel's message of synergy among the processes of change, we will consider together his use of the action process of counterconditioning and the insight process of consciousness raising.

The Therapist's Work. The integrative psychodynamic-behavioral therapist adopts a clinical style that has both dynamic and behavioral points of view. Dynamically, much of the interpretive work is similar to that of the psychodynamically oriented therapists, as presented in Chapter 2. Behaviorally, much of the counterconditioning and skills training is akin to that of behavior therapists, as summarized in Chapter 9. But putting them together produces a synergistic integration, an emerging whole, superior to either alone.

In the treatment of a self-diagnosed case of "test anxiety," Wachtel (1991) combined systematic desensitization, imagery, and insight-oriented work to help "John" overcome his anxiety. The cyclical psychodynamic perspective led the therapist to see as relevant, and as part of a larger pattern, a number of features of John's experience of a licensure test. His concerns about status and humiliation led him to avoid studying and to treat the exam lightly. This, in turn, produced additional anxiety brought on by the unacknowledged sense of being underprepared and by failures on previous administrations of the test. The failures, in turn, heightened his test anxiety and further threatened his status, leading to still further avoidance and more compensatory actions to appear cavalier about the entire matter.

The therapy attended, sometimes alternately and sometimes simultaneously, to John's concerns about status, his shame about those concerns, his need to expose himself to the test-taking cues that generate anxiety, his behavioral avoidance, his study habits, and several other considerations in a complex weave of interventions. Insights from "psychoanalytic" exploration informed the process of systematic desensitization and the metaphors for the imagery procedure, and the results of these two "behavioral" procedures fueled new and deepened insights.

Such a seamless theoretical integration of two historically rival theoretical approaches requires another type of therapist work: building bridges across the chasm that separates psychoanalysis and behaviorism and piercing the stereotypes that obscure significant commonalities between them. Quite apart from acquiring the technical competencies to conduct each form of therapy, the integrative therapist must complete the arduous mental work of finding the perspectives mutually enriching and complementary, not irreconcilably contradictory.

Consider the behavioral methods of systematic desensitization and assertiveness training. Although there are real and important differences between psychodynamic treatment and systematic desensitization, they are not as hard and fast as typically thought (Wachtel, 1977). If one looks past the dogmatism and rhetoric to what experienced behavior therapists actually do, there are some striking similarities.

Gradual exposure to increasingly threatening images and fantasies characterizes both behavioral and dynamic work. It is usually impossible to proceed directly to the original occurrence of the symptom. Even if one could recapture it, such a direct assault on the target has little therapeutic effect. Rather, Freud found that he had to proceed gradually and systematically back from recent occasions until the original event was finally recalled and tolerated. This is, conceptually and methodologically, very similar to systematic desensitization. Under the rubric of "dosing the anxiety," "timing of interpretations," and "allowing the patient to set the pace," dynamic therapists are trained to create conditions just like systematic desensitization. "Wild analysis" and "flooding"—in which clients are confronted prematurely with repugnant images—are generally frowned upon. Psychoanalysts and behaviorists, then, emphasize in practice the same effective components of relaxation, hierarchical and gradual approach, exposure to anxiety cues, and client willingness to trust the therapist and explore fears.

Similarly, endorsement of the essential components of assertion training are shared by behaviorists and psychodynamicists—if they choose to openly examine each other's practices. Specific deficits are identified, in-session "training" is provided, therapist modeling and patient rehearsal are emphasized, and then gradual entries into the real world are encouraged. Assertiveness training becomes in vivo desensitization (Wachtel, 1977).

In the past decade, Wachtel (1997) has extended cyclical psychodynamics to the relational world. This extends treatment from the largely intrapsychic world of clients to the larger context in which they live. A fuller, richer therapy results from bringing significant others into the consulting room, employing active systemic methods, and facilitating action in the real world.

The tasks of the cyclical psychodynamic therapist, in summary, are to employ interventions traditionally associated with psychoanalytic, behavioral, and to a lesser degree, systemic approaches, and to do so in a manner that renders them mutually facilitative and their effects synergistic. Both technical competence and integrative commitment are required to meld insight and action.

The Client's Work. Although some psychotherapists find the integrative burden too technically or theoretically onerous, clients typically accept the combination of action and insight quite naturally. Conflicts and inhibitions that typically are at the core of the patient's problems lead regularly to specific behavioral deficits, and patients, as a rule, are interested in both understanding the origins of their difficulties and taking concrete steps to correct them. Probably the only differential expectation in cyclical psychodynamics is that patients, with the guidance of the therapist, repeatedly translate insight into action and action into insight. Beyond this, the client's work at any moment will depend specifically on the nature of the "behavioral" or "psychodynamic" intervention.

Therapeutic Content

The cyclical psychodynamic approach to theory and practice developed as an integrative effort to incorporate the observations and concepts of diverse perspectives into a coherent conceptual view. The theoretical synthesis attempts to encompass a full range of observations addressed by its contributory sources and to provide a context for a wide range of clinical interventions (Wachtel & McKinney, 1992). As an integrative effort, the approach does not prescribe specific or unique therapeutic content. Rather, it is a way of looking at, and working with, clinical phenomena in a new and more inclusive fashion.

The recurrent "content," if one can call it that, is the pervasive role of vicious cycles in initiating and maintaining anxiety. Cyclical psychodynamics places primary emphasis not on the fixation of traumatic experiences but on the vicious cycles set in motion by those experiences and on the ways those cyclical patterns persist into the present. This emphasis on circular processes, both intrapsychic and interpersonal, provides a key to bringing together the individual psychodynamic and family systems approaches (Wachtel & Wachtel, 1986) and to integrating the characterological emphasis of psychoanalytic approaches and the situational emphasis of behavioral approaches (Wachtel, 1977).

Therapeutic Relationship

Psychotherapy is, first and foremost, a human relationship (Wachtel, 1990). The cultivation of the real relationship and analysis of the transference speak to Wachtel's psychodynamic underpinnings, but his interpersonal and integrative variant departs from traditional psychoanalytic perspectives in important ways, principally in the need for more active intervention.

To use Wachtel's phrase (1983; published in Wachtel, 1987), "You can't go far in neutral." He addresses the numerous limitations of the classic analytic stance of therapeutic neutrality and the attendant avoidance of prescriptive action. Minimal intervention typically begets minimal change. The dangers involved in "muddying the waters of transference" and in "contaminating the field" are outweighed by the lost opportunities for creative and direct intervention.

A more positively affirmative stance and more behaviorally active relationship are required. The therapeutic relationship is viewed as both a precondition of change and a process of change and, depending on the presenting problem, perhaps also as a content to be changed (such as shyness). Empathy, genuineness, and respect are combined with in-session behavioral interventions such as imagery, systematic desensitization, and assertiveness training and with between-session "homework."

The prevailing emphasis on neutrality in some psychotherapeutic camps has also incurred Wachtel's (1983) wrath because many interpretations are unwittingly cast in an accusatory or destructive manner. In his book, *Therapeutic Communication*, Wachtel (1993) addresses principles of respectfully and collaboratively conveying information to the patient. In the treatment of John's test anxiety, discussed previously, the inquiry into his status concerns—concerns that were initially disavowed vigorously—began by addressing his parents' concerns and proceeded only gradually to inviting John to explore his own conflicts in that area. That exploration was undertaken in a way that enabled John to examine those concerns in a manner that permitted him to maintain his self-respect. The path toward acknowledging and assuming responsibility for those concerns led initially through an early disavowing of responsibility (it was his parents' hang-up). This strategy of enabling people to recognize and take responsibility for their experiences by initially placing the responsibility elsewhere is known as *externalization in the service of the therapy*. It is one of several strategies developed to ensure that provision of interpretations and information enhances, rather than diminishes, the client's self-esteem and the therapeutic relationship.

Practicalities

As an integrative perspective, as opposed to a distinct "school" of psychotherapy, cyclical psychodynamics has relatively little to say about the practicalities of learning and conducting psychotherapy. The typical duration of treatment is probably longer than a "pure" behavior therapy but shorter than a "pure" psychodynamic treatment for the same patient. The approach has been almost exclusively applied to individual, outpatient treatment of neurotic disorders, although the underlying principles have also been applied to family contexts and social criticism (Wachtel & McKinney, 1992).

Effectiveness

The clinical experiences of Wachtel and other analytically oriented clinicians personally attest to the value of blending more active, behavioral observations with psychodynamic psychotherapy. There is also a significant body of research, largely in social and developmental psychology, that supports the basic tenets of cyclical psychodynamics, including expectancy effects, self-fulfilling prophecies, and disconfirmation of pathogenic expectations (see Wachtel & McKinney, 1992, for a review). However, controlled research and comparative outcome studies on this perspective have not been conducted.

Reviews of the psychotherapy literature also fail to locate any controlled outcome studies on the effectiveness of other forms of theoretical integration (Glass, Victor, & Arnkoff, 1992; Grawe et al., 1998). The one exception, described as "the most thoroughly tested model" of integration (Glass et al., 1992, p. 17), is the transtheoretical model, which is reviewed in Chapter 15.

Multimodal Therapy

A Sketch of Arnold Lazarus

Arnold A. Lazarus (1932–) approached technical eclecticism from the behavioral tradition, quite a different origin than that of Wachtel. Lazarus was born, raised, and educated in South Africa, where he earned his PhD in 1960 from the University of the Witwatersrand in Johannesburg under the tutelage of the behavior therapy pioneer Joseph Wolpe. His dissertation, "New Group Techniques in the Treatment of Phobic Conditions," examined the efficacy of systematic desensitization in groups and employed objective measures for assessing phobic avoidance.

Although his early training and practice were in "pure" behavior therapy, his treatment results and follow-up studies showed that although behavioral interventions frequently produced impressive headway the gains were often not maintained. As early as the late 1950s, Lazarus (1956, 1958) emphasized that problems are best tackled within a broad-spectrum frame of reference and called for a synthesis of various psychoeducational, psychotherapeutic, and pharmaceutical measures. In 1967, he briefly propounded the virtues of *technical eclecticism* (as opposed to theoretical integration) and specifically recommended the addition of cognitive interventions to the behavioral armamentarium. By this time, he was forcibly distinguishing his broad-spectrum behavior therapy from narrow-band behavior therapy (Lazarus, 1966b, 1971a).

But even extending behavior therapy with cognitive interventions proved incomplete and unsatisfactory for Lazarus. Scrutiny of his case notes revealed that clients with situational crises or circumscribed problems obtained positive results, but people suffering from obsessive-compulsive disorders, panic attacks, addictions, and other self-destructive tendencies did not. The search for additional interventions led him past behavior and cognition to imagery, sensory, and affective domains. As a result, in 1973 Lazarus introduced a distinctive approach termed *multimodal therapy* to emphasize comprehensive coverage of all the modalities (for example Lazarus, 1973, 1976). His evolution from a pure behavior therapist to an eclectic therapist continues to this day, as he incorporates new techniques into the multimodal repertoire and as he experiments with such notions as matching his therapeutic stance to the individual needs of the client.

Previously located at Stanford, Temple, and Yale universities, Lazarus has found a permanent home at the Graduate School of Applied and Professional Psychology at Rutgers University, where he holds the title of distinguished professor. His scholarly output is prolific: more than 200 articles and chapters and 16 books, including his classic *The Practice of Multimodal Therapy* (1981/1989a). He offers workshops throughout the world and, in national surveys, is regularly cited by his peers as one of the most influential psychotherapists. His interpersonal charisma, inculcated in his early South African/English upbringing, and his feisty temperament, forged in his early boxing experiences, coalesce into a powerful and persuasive voice for technical eclecticism.

Theory of Personality and Psychopathology

Predictably, the multimodal theory of personality is broad and inclusive. We are the products of a complex interplay of our genetic endowment, social-learning history, and physical environment. Lazarus addresses the genetic role in the etiology of affective and schizophrenic disorders and the inborn differences among people in sensory thresholds. The social-learning triad—classical conditioning, operant conditioning, and vicarious conditioning/modeling—accounts for some disorders, but the majority of clinical disorders seem to emanate from perceived associations rather than actual conditioning. Departing from a pure behavioral perspective toward a more phenomenological and cognitive viewpoint, Lazarus reminds us that people rarely respond automatically to the "out there" (external stimuli), but respond instead to the "in here" (internal cognitions) representations of stimuli. While recognizing the existence of a multitude of forces in personality development, the multimodal position underscores the impact of the biological substrate and of learning history broadly conceived.

In matters of personality, we should subscribe to *Occam's razor*—entities should not be multiplied unnecessarily and the simplest of competing theories is preferred. Lazarus (1997) has submitted that we do not have to look beyond seven factors that shape and maintain human personality: associations and relations among events; modeling and imitation; nonconscious processes; defensive reactions; private events; metacommunications; and physical thresholds. But even here, we do not require a precise, accurate explanation of personality and psychopathology to remedy them.

By the same token, the multimodal approach views psychological disturbances as resulting from numerous, poorly understood influences. Psychopathology is typically a product of one or more of the following: conflicting or ambivalent feelings and reactions, misinformation, missing information, maladaptive habits, biological dysfunctions, interpersonal inquietude, issues pertaining to negative self-acceptance, external stressors, and existential concerns (Dryden & Lazarus, 1991; Lazarus, 1989b, 1992).

Consider the apparently simple case of specific phobias. The psychoanalytic view, as demonstrated in Freud's well-known study of phobic 5-year-old "Little Hans," holds that phobias nearly always have unconscious significance and usually result from the displacement of hostile or erotic impulses. The behavioral view, as exemplified by Watson and Rayner's (1920) case of the 11-month-old "Little Albert" rendered fearful of furry objects, holds that phobias nearly always have their origins in conditioning and are usually compounded by subsequent avoidance behavior. The psychological formulations embodied in the benchmark cases of Little Hans and Little Albert are insufficient for multimodal therapy. The dichotomy between the psychoanalytic and behavioral views has retarded clinical progress. More complex conceptualizations and multimodal treatments are required for phobic—and other—behavioral disorders (Lazarus, 1991).

Multimodal therapy, characteristic of other eclectic approaches, is principally concerned with the remediation of psychopathology, not with explaining it. Behind every technical eclectic is a vague or inclusive theory of personality. We now turn to the content and process of change, a shift in clinical attention that eclectics heartily endorse.

Therapeutic Content

A central premise of multimodal therapy is that patients are troubled by a multitude of specific problems that should be remedied with a similar multitude of specific techniques. Unlike psychotherapists in some other systems, the multimodal therapist neither dictates the particular content to be treated nor forces the client's problems onto a Procrustean bed. (You may recall that Procrustes was the legendary Greek innkeeper who placed unsuspecting guests onto a single-size bed and then trimmed or stretched guests to fit the bed.) Rather, the task of the multimodal therapist is to comprehensively and systematically assess the patient's specific deficits and excesses. The multimodal assessment template is the BASIC I.D.:

B = Behavior
A = Affect
S = Sensation
I = Imagery
C = Cognition
I = Interpersonal relationships
D = Drugs/biology

This acronym serves to specify the content for psychotherapy and to guide the therapist in selecting specific and effective interventions for each.

A point Lazarus repeatedly emphasizes is that all modalities but one can be dealt with directly in treatment. Affect can only be worked with indirectly because one cannot elicit or change emotions directly. Affect can be accessed and affected only through behavior, sensation, imagery, cognition, interpersonal relationships, and drugs/biological processes. Although many people seek therapy because they *feel* bad, "the multimodal position is that the most elegant and thorough way of reducing anxiety, lifting depression, and assuaging guilt is to eliminate the specific and interrelated dysfunctional patterns" on the other modalities (Lazarus, 1992, p. 239).

Theory of Therapeutic Processes

In many systems of psychotherapy, the postulated change processes drive the selection of the therapeutic content. That is, the "how" of therapy intentionally or unintentionally determines the "what" of therapy. In multimodal therapy, in contrast, the patient's problems, as catalogued through the multimodal assessment on each domain of the BASIC I.D., in large part determine the change processes to be employed. For this reason, we have departed from our usual chapter outline to address therapeutic content first and therapeutic processes second.

The technical eclecticism of multimodal therapy leads to a wide array of available mechanisms of change. The specific mechanisms operating in a given case depend on the selected techniques, which in turn depend on the patient's particular problems. Cutting across all patients and problems, some of the main hypothesized mechanisms of change include the following (Lazarus, 1992, p. 238):

Behavior: Positive reinforcement; negative reinforcement; punishment; counterconditioning; extinction

Affect: Acknowledging, clarifying, and recognizing feelings; abreaction

Sensation: Tension release; sensory pleasuring

Imagery: Coping images; change in self-image

Cognition: Cognitive restructuring; heightening awareness; education

Interpersonal relationships: Modeling; developing assertive and other social skills; dispersing unhealthy collusions; nonjudgmental acceptance

Drugs/biology: Identifying medical illness; substance-abuse cessation; better nutrition and exercise; psychotropic medication when indicated

This partial listing of available change mechanisms in multimodal therapy overlaps to a great extent with the ten processes of change discussed in Chapter 15. Feedback, education, corrective emotional experiences, stimulus control, self-liberation, counterconditioning, reevaluation, and contingency management are all prominently represented (although Lazarus does not always use these exact terms). Missing are social liberation and dramatic relief, the two change processes least frequently employed across the psychotherapies (see Chapter 15). But even here, Lazarus has on occasion reported techniques in his published case histories that incorporate these processes—empowering patients and referring them to organizations devoted to advocating for their social rights in the case of social liberation, and promoting intense and draining catharsis in the case of dramatic relief.

Rather than redundantly summarizing here all the change processes used by multimodal therapists, we refer you to the previous chapters in which the respective processes have been defined and illustrated. Counterconditioning and contingency management are most expertly handled by the behavior therapists, cognitive restructuring by the cognitive therapists, helping relationships by the person-centered therapists, and so on. This is in keeping with the multimodal maxim of borrowing any intervention from any theoretical framework when indicated in a particular situation.

The Client's Work. The work of the client, like that of the therapist, depends to a large degree on the nature of the problem and on the type of procedures employed. The treatment is personalized and goal-directed, the person being the client (not the therapist) and the goals largely those of the client. If imagery is one of the techniques selected, then the patient will be instructed in deep relaxation, visualize the scene, relay the experiences to the therapist, and collaborate on some visualization scenes to practice between sessions. If assertiveness training is mutually selected as the treatment of choice, then the client will be asked to engage in active role-playing, perhaps purchase and read an assertion book, and attempt some homework assignments prior to the next appointment.

Multimodal therapy is an active and comparatively demanding therapy, but it should be far less demanding on the client than on the therapist (Dryden & Lazarus, 1991). The skillful clinician will pace treatment according to the capacities and objectives of the individual client. Clients typically don't feel overwhelmed, but some therapists do (Dryden & Lazarus, 1991).

The Therapist's Work. When properly executed, a day of multimodal therapy is mentally and behaviorally exhausting for the clinician. Psychotherapists who offer very similar technical interventions, relationship stances, and therapy formats to virtually all of their patients have it comparatively easy. But customizing all these elements, in each and every case, demands additional mental energy and considerable clinical competence.

The multimodal therapist obtains information from initial interviews and a comprehensive life history inventory (Lazarus & Lazarus, 1991) and then creates a *Modality Profile*–essentially, a BASIC I.D. chart listing the patient's problems by modality and the indicated intervention for each problem. If additional information is desired or if treatment impasses occur, then a second-order BASIC I.D. assessment will be performed. In addition to the modality profiles, another multimodal assessment procedure is the use of *structural profiles*, which are quantitative ratings across the BASIC I.D. Seven-point ratings (1 being the lowest and 7 the highest) are made by clients on each modality; for Behavior, to take the first one, clients are informed "Some people may be described as doers—they are action oriented, they like to busy themselves, get things done, take on various projects" and then asked "How much of a doer are you?" These ratings are then depicted on a graph.

Having compiled this clinical information, the multimodal therapist proceeds, in consultation with the patient, to select the therapeutic procedures and postures indicated for this particular case. Obviously, the therapist's work will depend on the type of procedures and postures elected. A "Glossary of Principal Techniques" employed in multimodal therapy (Lazarus, 1989a) contains no less than 39 interventions—and those are only the *principal* ones! The therapist's task in implementing Gendlin's (1981) focusing technique as opposed to, say, paradoxical strategy or thought blocking will be quite different indeed.

The primary basis for technique selection is outcome research attesting to that technique's effectiveness. The treatment of bulimia, for example, usually calls for a structured and active program of therapy that involves response prevention and cognitive restructuring. However, the technique must be accommodated to the idiosyncratic characteristics of each individual. If response prevention proves unsuccessful or unacceptable to the patient, then the empty chair technique or imagery or literally dozens of other interventions will be considered. Selecting a therapy technique is a science, but implementing it is an art.

In working with a young woman who had developed a cat phobia after watching a grisly television program in which feline monsters were possessed by the devil, Lazarus (Dryden & Lazarus, 1991) initially opted for standard desensitization, an extensively researched and laboratory-based procedure of having the client relax while visualizing cats in the distance getting closer and closer to her. But in this case it did not work. Lazarus recalled a specific technique drawn from neuro-linguistic programming (NLP) that seemed relevant, even though he considers NLP to be theoretically unsound and scientifically untenable. The technique consists of imagining the feared object and shrinking it down to a tiny little size that you can then crush. In this case, the procedure fit the patient perfectly, and it worked splendidly. As a technical eclectic, Lazarus could employ an NLP technique without subscribing to the entire theory behind it.

To recapitulate: the work of the multimodal therapist is to conduct a multimodal assessment, determine the treatments of choice, and customize the therapeutic relationship to the needs of that particular client.

Therapeutic Relationship

Multimodal therapy regards the patient–therapist relationship as the soil that enables the techniques to take root—not as the principal means to the end (Lazarus & Fay, 1984). In this respect, multimodal clinicians, like their behavioral colleagues, view the therapeutic relationship as a precondition of change in practically all cases and as a content to be changed in only those cases in which a specific interpersonal style (such as assertion deficits or anger excesses) is identified as problematic in the interactions between the patient and therapist during their sessions. A warm, caring relationship is the context for change, but only rarely the central process of change. Far more often, patients require alleviation of maladaptive behaviors, faulty cognitions, and other problems throughout the BASIC I.D. with coping-skills training.

Lazarus (1991, 1993) has been particularly critical of the notion that genuine empathy, therapist congruence, and positive regard are the necessary and sufficient conditions for constructive personality change, as Rogers (1957) has suggested. For one thing, the empirical research supports neither the necessity nor sufficiency of these facilitative conditions (see Chapter 5). For another thing, offering the identical, unitary (or unimodal) therapeutic relationship to all clients flies in the face of a personalized, custom-made psychotherapy. In Lazarus's (1993) words: "They [militant client-centered therapists] do not stop to consider when, and under what circumstances, and with whom, a focused didactic or pedagogic stance should be employed, or when a sphinx-like guru might be made to order" (p. 404). And: "How is it that one of the first things we all learn in Psychology 101 is that individual differences are paramount, that everyone is unique, but when it comes to treating patients, some seem to assume that they all come from identical molds?" (p. 406).

The multimodal therapist attempts to modify his or her participation in the therapeutic process in order to offer the most appropriate relationship for that particular client, as opposed to fitting the person to the treatment. In his *Behavior Therapy and Beyond*, Lazarus (1971a, p. 38) asserts that a therapist's empathy, warmth, and genuineness often facilitate progress, but "one should remain on the lookout for individual exceptions to these general rules—e.g., those cases who react adversely to warmth or empathy and require distant, impartial interaction." He emphasizes the virtues of sagacious referrals and the value of matching, when possible, a therapist's relationship stance to individual patients.

The notion of the *authentic chameleon* is often invoked. A flexible repertoire of relationship styles and stances is required to suit different client needs and expectations. This would include the therapist's level of informality or formality, the degree to which the therapist discloses personal information, the extent to which the therapist initiates topics of conversation, and in general, when and how to be directive, supportive, or reflective. "The only don'ts to which we subscribe are (1) Don't be rigid and (2) Don't humiliate a person or strip away his or her dignity" (Lazarus, 1989b, p. 129).

The markers that guide the clinician's interpersonal stances are the client's readiness for change and resistance level (Lazarus, 1993). In treating a young woman who was exceedingly timid and offended by loud and pushy people, for instance, he would almost whisper and be excessively polite. But in dealing with a middle-aged woman who described herself as "a wife, mother, homemaker, and part-time legal secretary in that order," he would respond with friendly banter and jesting. Consider his recollection (Lazarus, 1993, p. 405) of his first session with this challenging, brusque woman, who looked him up and down upon entering his office:

PATIENT: Why do you have graves outside your office?

LAZARUS: (surprised and responding in Rogerian style) I have graves outside my office?

PATIENT: Look outside the window, dummy!

LAZARUS: (Looking outside his office window to the two new flower beds which had been installed alongside the front walk) Well, since you ask, I have just buried one of my clinical failures in one grave and the other is earmarked for you if you turn out to be an uncooperative client.

Two very different relationship stances, but both apparently therapeutic for the clients involved. The authentic chameleon changes color and blends into various contexts, but admittedly no creature has an infinite range of different hues and shades. If the therapist's style differs markedly from the patient's expectations, positive results are unlikely. When the therapist is unable or unwilling to match relationship stances to individual clients, Lazarus openly advocates judicious referral.

Practicalities

It is decidedly difficult to generalize about a personalized psychotherapy that seeks to tailor-make psychological treatment for each unique patient. The recurrent answer to questions about the length, format, and cost of multimodal therapy is in the subtitle of a series of conversations with Lazarus (Dryden & Lazarus, 1991): "It depends."

The average length of multimodal therapy with patients experiencing disorders of moderate severity seems to be about 40 sessions, less than a year of weekly sessions—more or less; it depends. More than most psychotherapy systems, the multimodal approach employs and combines different formats—individual, marital, family, group—with various populations—inpatients, outpatients, children, and older adults. Specialized sex therapy and pharmacotherapy are also offered, as indicated in a given case, relatively often.

Following from his technical eclecticism, Lazarus endorses clinical training that culls effective methods from many sources. This demands that the therapist be continually on the lookout for efficacious procedures, independent of their "theoretical baggage," and that the therapist be aware of the research on psychotherapy outcome. More demanding still, the multimodal therapist is committed to acquiring competence in a wide array of technical interventions and relationship stances. Mentally and emotionally exhausting indeed!

Fascination with abstruse theorizing and relentless commitment to certain theories undermine the breadth of effective eclectic therapy. Psychoanalytically inclined trainees, for one example, spend too much time exploring mental conflicts rather than promoting action. Family systems aficionados are prone to see the entire woods but not the individual trees. And rigidly cognitive trainees, for a final example, continue to dispute, challenge, and explain when getting nowhere instead of switching modalities.

Training is available from many dedicated and systematic eclectics, as well as several multimodal therapy institutes around the country. Personal therapy is not mandatory except in those instances in which the therapist's personal problems are likely to interfere with accurate assessment and effective treatment.

Effectiveness

Several dissertations and a few published articles have examined the clinical utility of multimodal therapy's suppositions and constructs (see Lazarus, 1992, for a review). Lazarus himself has conducted several outcome and follow-up inquiries on patients receiving multimodal treatment, but no controlled comparative investigations have been published to date. Multimodal therapy tries to incorporate state-of-the-art research findings into its open framework, in contrast to yet another "system" of psychotherapy, but whether scanning the field for better assessment and treatment methods "augments clinicians' overall effectiveness remains an empirical question" (Lazarus, 1992, p. 255).

In broader strokes, the outcome research on eclectic psychotherapy comes in three guises. First and most generally, the entire body of empirical research on psychotherapy informs eclectic treatment selection. A genuine advantage of being an eclectic is the vast amount of research attesting to the efficacy of psychotherapy and pointing to its differential effectiveness with certain types of disorders and patients. Of course, this research only translates into improved outcomes if the psychotherapist is aware of, and adheres to, the research conclusions.

Second, some controlled outcome research has been conducted on psychotherapy crudely characterized as "eclectic" or "mixed." In their comprehensive review of the adult literature, Grawe and colleagues (1998) located 22 controlled studies covering 1,743 patients treated with diverse therapies described as eclectic: either explicitly no school connection or multiple combinations of methods. In 9 of the 13 comparisons, the eclectic therapy outperformed the control treatment in terms of symptom relief and in 4 of the 6 comparisons in terms of subjective well-being. In their comprehensive meta-analysis of the child literature, Weisz and his colleagues (1995) located 20 controlled studies on mixed treatments, which produced a respectable effect size of .63, a moderate to large effect. The interpretative problem, however, is that we possess little sophisticated understanding of what these multifarious treatments represent. Perhaps the only conclusions that can be reliably drawn are that coherent "eclectic" and "mixed" psychotherapies outperform no treatment and that these treatments are insufficiently compared to other systems of psychotherapy.

Third and more specifically, ongoing programmatic research supports the effectiveness of disciplined eclectic approaches that prescriptively match different treatments to different people. An exemplar of *prescriptive matching* is Beutler's (1983, 1992; Beutler & Clarkin, 1990) *systematic eclectic psychotherapy*. All the patient qualities that predict differential effectiveness have not yet been determined, but considerable research conducted by Beutler and colleagues indicates that certain patient variables point to certain treatments, which if applied, enhance the success of psychotherapy (see Beutler & Clarkin, 1990; Gaw & Beutler, 1995; Norcross & Beutler, 1998). For example, a person's externalizing coping style differentially predicts a favorable response to symptom-focused interventions and contraindicates the use of insight interventions. High resistance, for another example, specifically indicates the use of nondirective, self-directed, and even paradoxical interventions. And a low degree of patient social support predicts the value of interpersonally focused and family therapies. All of these research-supported prescriptive matches improve the effectiveness and efficiency of psychotherapy.

Brief Integrative and Eclectic Therapy

Time-limited treatment and psychotherapy integration are definitely simpatico. Virtually every form of brief therapy advertises itself, in comparison to its original long-school, as active in nature, collaborative in relationship, and eclectic in orientation (Budman, 1981; Hoyt, 1995). Indeed, one of the propelling forces of the integration movement, as we have seen, was the ascendency of brief therapies and the resultant pressure to do more (and better) in 6, 12, or 24 sessions with a variety of clientele. Brief therapy and integrative therapy share a pragmatic and flexible outlook that is quite opposite from the ideological one that characterized the previous school-domination in the field (Omer, 1993).

The clinical realities of brief therapy have come to practically demand a flexible, if not downright eclectic, orientation. In one study of 294 American therapists, for instance, the prevalence of eclecticism/integration as a theoretical orientation nearly doubled as a function of employment in settings favoring brief, problem-focused psychotherapy (Austad, Sherman, & Holstein, 1991).

Lazarus (1989, 1997; Lazarus & Fay, 1990) has written specifically about brief multimodal psychotherapy. On the opening page of his recent book on brief therapy, he immediately "cuts to the chase"—an appropriate line given his topic—and inquires: "Anyone can offer brief therapy, but is it possible to provide a course of short-term but comprehensive psychotherapy? My explicit answer is 'Often, yes.'" (Lazarus, 1997, p. 1). The ensuing book outlines exactly how this can be achieved, according to a concise multimodal formula. First, determine whether there are significant problems in each of the BASIC I.D. modalities. Second, in concert with the client, select three or four pivotal problems that require specific attention. Third, if so indicated, have the patient receive a physical examination and psychotropic medications. Fourth, whenever possible, apply empirically validated methods of treatment to the specific problems.

Effective brief therapy depends far less on the hours you put in than on what you put into those hours. Trying to accomplish "more with less" places significant demands on the eclectic clinician to rapidly and systematically identify problems, cultivate a therapeutic relationship, and intervene with specific methods. This description probably applies to all brief therapies in general, but definitely applies to brief multimodal therapy in particular.

Criticisms of Integrative and Eclectic Therapies

From a Psychoanalytic Perspective

Wachtel's integrative psychodynamic-behavioral therapy only has the first half right. His insistence on adding behavioral interventions bespeaks his impatience with the necessarily gradual alteration in historically situated intrapsychic conflicts. If he seriously expects us to employ behavioral methods, then he must definitely demonstrate, in repeated clinical cases, that their addition contributes anything over and above what we achieve with psychodynamic therapy alone. Keep the original faith!

Lazarus is a cognitive-behaviorist, pure and simple. His methods are too active, too technical, and too dismissive of historically situated conflicts and insight-oriented contributions. He delights in bashing classic psychoanalysis in his writings and workshops. Enough said; see our criticisms of cognitive and behavior therapies for details.

From a Behavioral Perspective

Wachtel's integrated psychodynamic-behavioral therapy only has the second half right. His insistence on retaining psychoanalytic metapsychology bespeaks his acceptance of inefficient means to alter environmentally maintained behavioral problems. If he seriously expects us to employ psychoanalytic methods, then he must definitively demonstrate, in controlled outcome studies, that their addition contributes anything over and above what we achieve with behavior therapy alone. Make a clean break with the psychoanalytic psychobabble!

Lazarus anticipated our future early on by augmenting narrow-band behavioral procedures with cognitive interventions. But by contemporary standards, he is a cognitive-behavioral therapist in the guise of a technical eclectic. Take away the BASIC I.D. assessment template and the structural profiles, and you have a self-professed empiricist in the social-learning tradition. Welcome home, Arnie!

Eclecticism usually means that therapists beg, borrow, and steal from the leading systems of psychotherapy. Eclectics rarely do create new therapeutic interventions or theoretical constructs. To the extent they are creative at all, it is in the way they put together their bag of tricks rather than in creating new concepts that others can borrow.

Although eclectics are proficient at employing other people's techniques, they have performed little empirical research on *any* of their grand integrative creations

(Lambert, 1992; Mahalik, 1990). More controlled research and clinical specificity are needed. We applaud the general thrust of combining the most efficacious techniques without regard to their theoretical parentage, but the proof of the pudding is in the eating. Keep cooking, and call us when you have something worth consuming.

From a Humanistic Perspective

In title and deed, Wachtel's psychodynamic-behavioral hyphenated hybrid completely disregards humanistic and existential contributions. Combining two theories is barely integrative. We are open to combining theories and methods (for example, Goldfried, 1982; Thoresen, 1973; Wandersman, Poppen, & Ricks, 1976), but any genuine integration must undoubtedly embrace at least portions of the third force.

For us, psychotherapy is an encounter between two people in a helping relationship; for Lazarus, psychotherapy is more a technical enterprise. His clients disappear in his case presentations, partitioned into segments by the BASIC I.D. and then repaired in segments with precise surgical interventions. Nowhere do we have a sense of the person of the client, of how the segments fit together or what sort of functioning whole they constitute (Davis, 1990). The therapeutic relationship is the constant bedrock of our work, but Lazarus's "authentic chameleon" sounds as valid as a genuine phony.

From a Contextual Perspective

As each psychotherapeutic door opens, another closes. There are always trade-offs in the service of psychotherapy integration. In recommending action along with psychic exploration, Wachtel closes off some avenues to deeper meaning and intention. In bringing cognitive, affective, and sensory factors into the behavioral purview, Lazarus reduces his appeal to measurable objectives and environmental contingencies (Messer, 1992).

Integration also brings with it another problem. A clinical technique is not a disembodied procedure that can be incorporated wholesale from one context to another without consideration of its psychotherapeutic surround. Does an effective technique in one psychotherapy system lose something in the translation and transportation into another system? Does it take on different nuances of meaning and intention in the new context? Would not much of the supportive research on a technique in the previous context need to be reconducted on its efficacy in the new context? Most contextualists think so (Messer, in Lazarus & Messer, 1991).

And finally, as is so often the case with new movements, psychotherapy integration is male-dominated and empiricism-preoccupied. While we applaud Wachtel and Lazarus for conducting marital/family therapy and for recognizing systemic forces, there is little appreciation of culture-sensitive and gender-aware issues in the integration movement. You want therapeutic integration? Then find methods to integrate the oppressed and disenfranchised into the wealthy resources of our society.

That will solve some real problems. Otherwise, you are only including theories and techniques while excluding major groups of people.

⎯ A MULTIMODAL ANALYSIS OF MRS. C. ⎯

Complex cases such as Mrs. C. require a comprehensive and individualized psychotherapy. The breadth and multitude of her problems make her an ideal candidate for a multimodal approach.

We begin by constructing a modality profile that identifies specific excesses and deficits on the client's BASIC I.D. Throughout therapy, we will return to this profile, a list that directs therapeutic interventions and enables ongoing treatment evaluation. At the beginning of therapy, most of the BASIC I.D. information will be obtained from the initial interview and from the Multimodal Life History Inventory (Lazarus & Lazarus, 1991) completed and returned by the client before her second interview. These give rise to a detailed modality profile, which would include the following:

> *Behavior:* Compulsive washing; not cooking and caring for children; physically unkempt; tends to withdraw and isolate herself; avoids dirt
>
> *Affect:* Anxiety (especially in the presence of dirt and disarray); depression; underlying and unexpressed anger; fear of being institutionalized; periodic hopelessness
>
> *Sensation:* Out of touch with her body; nervous; panicky if prevented from washing or in the presence of dirt
>
> *Imagery:* Vivid pictures of parental censure and paternal control; images of pinworms contaminating the C. family; pictures herself being hospitalized; "going crazy" when unable to engage in rituals
>
> *Cognition:* Intrusive thoughts about pinworms; dictatorial demands about cleanliness; perfectionistic; catastrophic thinking; "I'm hopeless and might as well kill myself"
>
> *Interpersonal relations:* Excessive attempts to control others; marital tensions; avoids sexual encounters; withdrawn from most friends; alienates her children and their friends; resorts to compulsive rituals when confronted
>
> *Drugs/biology:* Probably out of shape; no mention of regular exercise; may require pharmacotherapy for depression and anxiety

The life history questionnaire would also probably indicate that Mrs. C. favors an aggressive, action-oriented therapy that can save her marriage and avoid hospitalization at the state psychiatric facility. Let us presume she responds that her first treatment goal is to reduce her washing time and her closely related avoidance of dirt. Her expressed preferences and the modality profile—not the therapist's intransigent predilections or a global diagnosis of obsessive-compulsive disorder—furnish a blueprint for personalized and immediate treatment strategies.

When a client such as Mrs. C. experiences problems in almost all spheres of functioning, the more modalities therapy can impact, the more positive and efficient will be the outcome. With such deeply entrenched disorders, it is doubtful that Mrs. C. would recover to her premorbid level of functioning without a personalized broad-based program.

Where to start? With a problem to which the client accords high priority and for which we have demonstrably effective interventions. The research indicates that her affect, imagery, and behavior problems evoked by pinworms and dirt can best be remedied through a combination of gradual response prevention and systematic desensitization followed by in vivo desensitization. First, Mrs. C. will be trained in deep relaxation that she can apply during her anxious moments. She can practice the relaxation response at home with audiotapes. Once this is achieved, we will create hierarchies composed of stimuli related to dirt and pinworms. Part of a hierarchy would include, for example, imagining buying brand-new underwear wrapped in cellophane, followed by touching brand-new underwear, then approaching freshly laundered underwear, and moving toward picking up underwear that are basically clean though worn. Mrs. C. will be able to actually approach dirty underwear and limit her washing time only after her anxiety is no longer elicited because it has been counterconditioned by desensitization. With this newfound relaxation response at her disposal and with increasing confidence in her behavioral control, she will begin, step by step, to reduce the amount of time she spends in her daily shower.

Having sharply curtailed her anxiety and attendant rituals, we move on to her irrational cognitions. The available research and Mrs. C.'s preferences point to cognitive restructuring in the rational-emotive tradition as the treatment of choice. A self-help book devoted to identifying and disputing cognitive distortions, such as *Don't Believe It for a Moment! 40 Toxic Ideas That Are Driving You* Crazy (Lazarus, Lazarus, & Fay, 1993), would be recommended as a homework assignment between therapy sessions. Mrs. C.'s lowered self-esteem and assertion deficits would suggest a therapeutic relationship more supportive, gradual, and collaborative stance than Ellis might employ.

After several months of weekly or biweekly hard-working therapy sessions, Mrs. C. is slowly coming alive behaviorally and cognitively. But her other modalities are still impaired, and we will probably tackle them simultaneously—ever alert to the client's preferences and expectations, of course. Her paucity of sensual sensations and avoidance of sex can best be treated with sensate focusing, followed by the progressive steps of sexual therapy. Didactic information, perhaps in the form of readings from Masters and Johnson's books, will be used to counteract the myths she has inherited from her parents. Some of the sex therapy will occur in the context of conjoint marital sessions, which will also address her controlling style of family interactions. We can experiment with family assertiveness training to help other family members stand up to Mrs. C.'s unreasonable demands and also to help her express her frustrations more directly.

Depending on her response to the foregoing interventions, we will certainly consider the possibility of a referral for an antidepressant medication, which research has found useful with many patients suffering from similar problems. This is especially true if she is unable to learn deep relaxation or respond to cognitive therapy.

Multimodal therapy, then, aims at combining the most efficacious psychotherapeutic, didactic, and psychopharmacological interventions available for this patient in this situation. We try to impact across modalities in helping her acquire a variety of constructive modes of responding. If Mrs. C. desensitizes herself to dirt, learns to use the relaxation response and realistic thinking as alternatives, asserts herself when angry, and pleasures herself and her husband, she will gradually return to a more rewarding life. In place of obsessive ruminations fostered by passive psychoanalytic musings, she will develop healthier functioning directed by active, multimodal interventions.

Future Directions

By all accounts, one or more variations of psychotherapy integration will represent the psychotherapeutic Zeitgeist of the 21st century. The confluence of forces that has fostered the emergence of the integration movement in the past decade, reviewed earlier in this chapter, will continue to exert enormous pressure toward intertheoretical cooperation and cost-efficient treatment. The limitations on insurance reimbursement for psychotherapy and the impact of managed health care—arguably the most radical change ever in the delivery of mental health services (Austad & Berman, 1991)—will favor short-term, integrative, and prescriptive practice.

The theoretical integrationists and technical eclectics diverge slightly at this juncture as to how the integrative trend will (or should) manifest itself. In broad strokes related to psychotherapy as a whole, integrationists such as Goldfried and Castonguay (1992) predict increasing consolidation and rapprochement of theoretical orientations, incorporation of concepts and findings from cognitive science, and the combination of psychotherapy and pharmacotherapy. In narrower strokes related to integration per se, they foresee prominent attention to the extent to which crucial change processes are common or unique to different approaches, more reliance on empirical findings in creating integrative approaches, and continued consciousness raising about integration for those who continue to work within a given orientation. While maintaining their respective theoretical identities, more psychotherapists will acknowledge the limitations of their own paradigms and will experiment with other methods, thus becoming "de facto integrationists" (Goldfried & Castonguay, 1992, p. 8).

Technical eclectics predictably foresee that the limitations of theoretical integration will be more fully realized in the future and that specific treatments of choice for selected clinical disorders will become standard practice. Clearly delineated and preferred treatments will be routinely implemented for many syndromes and problems, including bulimia nervosa, focal phobias, pain management, panic disorders, enuresis, sexual disorders, and stress-related complaints, among others. Psychological therapies, according to eclectics such as Lazarus, Beutler, and Norcross (1992), will be matched increasingly not only to clinical diagnoses but also to client variables, such as reactance level, coping style, stage of change, and situational contexts.

Another probable direction is the deliberate attempt to individualize or customize the therapeutic relationship to individual clients. Instead of offering the identical or similar interpersonal stance to all patients, eclectic therapists will thoughtfully tailor it to the particular person and problem. One way to conceptualize the issue, paralleling the notion of "treatment of choice" in terms of techniques, is the therapeutic "relationship of choice" in terms of interpersonal behaviors (Norcross, 1993; Norcross & Beutler, 1998). Different strokes for different folks, so to speak. This will extend the scope of eclecticism beyond its historical connotation of only selecting techniques to individualizing relationship stances.

As eclecticism matures, it will invariably become "institutionalized" and reified as yet another competing therapeutic "school" instead of the open system it was intended to be. Whether or not eclecticism can successfully navigate between the perils of haphazard syncretism, on the one side, and the dangers of ideological institutionalization, on the other, will largely determine its continuing contribution to psychotherapy in the forthcoming millennium.

Suggestions for Further Reading

Ammerman, R. T., Last, C. G., & Hersen, M. (Eds.). (1993). *Handbook of prescriptive treatments for children and adolescents.* Boston: Allyn & Bacon.

Arkowitz, H., & Messer, S. B. (Eds.). (1984). *Psychoanalytic therapy and behavior therapy: Is integration possible?* New York: Plenum.

Beutler, L. E., & Clarkin, J. (1990). *Systematic treatment selection: Toward targeted therapeutic interventions.* New York: Brunner/Mazel.

Pinsof, W. M. (1995). *Integrative problem-centered therapy.* New York: Basic.

Lazarus, A. A. (1989). *The practice of multimodal therapy* (rev. ed.). Baltimore: John Hopkins University Press.

Lazarus, A. A. (1997). *Brief but comprehensive psychotherapy: The multimodal way.* New York: Springer.

Norcross, J. C., & Goldfried, M. R. (Eds.). (1992). *Handbook of psychotherapy integration.* New York: Basic.

Wachtel, P. L. (1977). *Psychoanalysis and behavior therapy: Toward an integration.* New York: Basic.

Wachtel, P. L. (1997). *Psychoanalysis, behavior therapy, and the relational world.* Washington, DC: American Psychological Association.

Journals: *Evidence-Based Mental Health; Integrative Psychiatry; Journal of Psychotherapy Integration.*

15 Comparative Conclusions: Toward a Transtheoretical Therapy

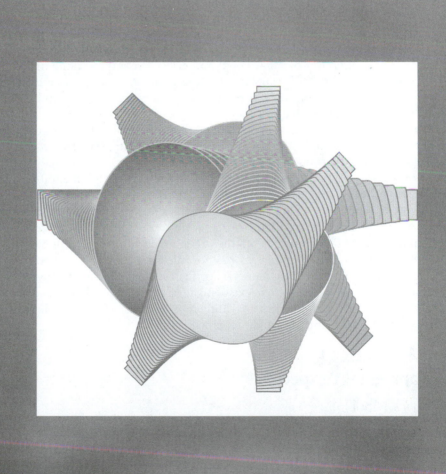

THE TRANSTHEORETICAL MODEL BEGINS with a comparative analysis of the major systems of psychotherapy within the integrative spirit of seeking the best that each has to offer. As you read—and as we wrote—the preceding chapters, we recognized that each psychotherapy system has brilliant insights into the human condition. Each system provides a logical, coherent, and compelling construction for understanding human function and dysfunction, once we accept its core assumptions. Most of the systems are inspiring and, we hope, encourage deeper exploration of the theory and its interventions. Applying each system to the same complex case of Mrs. C. indicates how differently and yet convincingly each can explain and treat the same troubled individual. All of the systems provide practical insights that can be useful within a more integrative model of therapy.

Each system also had its shortcomings, however. Most were much more rational than empirical in construction. None consistently demonstrated in controlled research a superior ability to predict how people would respond in therapy or a superior ability to help people change as a result of psychotherapy across all behavioral disorders. Many systems focused on theories of personality and psychopathology (*what* to change) rather than processes of change (*how* to change). And, of course, with the exception of multimodal and eclectic therapies, none of the psychotherapy systems provided templates for the integration of profound insights and beneficial methods from diverse therapies into a more coherent and comprehensive model of behavior change.

The net result is an acute confrontation with the dilemma of choosing the type of psychotherapist we might become or the type of psychotherapist we might consult. What further structure can we provide for such a diverse, if not chaotic, discipline? For starters, we must realize that the way we structure and integrate psychotherapy cannot at this time depend entirely on empirical research that demonstrates the consistent superiority of one system of psychotherapy over another. As seen throughout this book, research has revealed only a few robust differences in outcome among the evaluated mainstream therapies; in the words of London (1988, p. 7), "Meta-analytic research shows charity for all treatments and malice towards none." Nor can a purely rational analysis of the theoretical morass provide a definitive answer. At this point in the development of clinical knowledge, the manner in which we structure and integrate psychotherapy systems is largely an imposition of our own intellectual and ethical development.

Developmental Perspectives

Perry's Model

Given the pluralistic nature of knowledge, dedicated individuals will structure knowledge according to the particular forms that characterize their current level of cognitive development. Let us examine William Perry's (1970) model of intellectual and ethical development to see how it applies to the personal view that we are likely to take toward the diverse theories of psychotherapy.

Based upon longitudinal research on the development of Harvard undergraduates, Perry (1970) derived a cognitive stage theory of intellectual and ethical development. He identified nine different stages, each representing a qualitatively different mode of thinking about the nature of knowledge. Since several of Perry's stages are primarily transitional, we will focus only on the four stages that represent the most contrasting structures that students impose on knowledge. These four stages of intellectual and ethical development can be summarized as follows:

Dualistic→Multiplistic→Relativistic→Committed

Dualists. In the dualistic stage, the world is seen in polar terms: right/wrong, truth/error, good/bad. Dualistic students are likely to expect that in this final chapter the authors as authorities will reveal which single theory of therapy is correct. Dualistic students view themselves as receptacles eagerly waiting to receive the truth.

Dualistic therapists believe they have had the truth revealed to them. Dualists are the *true believers* who think that a particular therapy system is correct and all others are in error. Data are of little concern because the true system of psychotherapy is already assumed to be known and data would only document the obvious.

Dualistic therapists can be found in any system of psychotherapy. True-believing analysts, behaviorists, humanists, or eclectics are the result not of the structure of their theoretical system, but rather of the structure of their own intellects.

Multiplists. As students develop, they come to accept that diversity and uncertainty in an area such as psychotherapy do exist. At first the diversity is seen as unwarranted confusion that comes from poorly qualified authorities. "Psychotherapists don't know what the hell they're doing" may be a common complaint of these students. Later, diversity and uncertainty are seen as legitimate, but only as temporary in the development of our knowledge. The multiplistic therapist thinks that at some point in the future a particular theory of therapy will be proved correct. Multiplists are the *true bettors* who are convinced that investing their energies in one therapy will pay off in the future when it is eventually proven to be correct.

Relativists. Students in the relativistic stage of intellectual development view knowledge as disconnected from the concept of truth and absolute correctness. Diversity and uncertainty are not temporary. The very nature of knowledge is that it is contextual and relative. The truth about therapy is that it is pluralistic, with a variety of valid alternatives. Relativists are the *true eclectics.*

The validity of psychotherapy systems is relative to particular issues. Some eclectics see the form of therapy as being relative to a patient's specific conflicts or symptoms. Other therapists see the utility of therapy systems as relative to the patient's personality, while others assume that the value of any therapy is relative to the therapist's personality. Their system of choice is that which best fits their personality. Other eclectics see the treatment of choice as relative to the client's values, so that a therapy should be matched to values or goals.

Given the relativistic nature of knowledge, the eclectic thinks that no single psychotherapy theory will ever be found to be the best or the most correct. Some developing psychotherapists find this relativism to be tremendously disconcerting. The old guidelines of right/wrong and true/false are lost, and the therapist can be faced with an alienating experience of being lost and alone in a chaotic world of psychotherapy. Such therapists are usually judged to have a low tolerance for ambiguity, although more accurately they have a low tolerance for relativity. The ensuing existential anguish and sense of alienation can precipitate a retreat to the more secure stages of dualism or multiplism.

Although the relativism of eclecticism is a highly respectable, scholarly position, one problem is that the psychotherapist is an activist, not only a scholar. Seeking to prescriptively match psychotherapies with symptoms, personalities, or values is truly an important task of our time. But what does the relativistic therapist do when confronted with a particular patient in need of assistance? The data are not always in on which therapies work best with which types of problems or patients. There are some established "treatments of choice," of course, such as behavioral methods for focal phobias, systemic therapy for marital conflict, and cognitive or interpersonal treatment for moderate depression (Lambert, 1992). But for now the eclectic is frequently left with decisions on the basis of clinical folklore, much of which may well be fact, but some of which is surely folly.

Given the knowledge explosion in the therapeutic domain, does anyone seriously believe that any therapist can expect to master all the available theories and techniques of psychotherapy? Many therapists who reach the stage of intellectual relativism begin to comprehend the necessity of becoming oriented in a relativistic world through personal commitment.

Committed Therapists. The dilemma for the ethical psychotherapist is maintaining intellectual integrity while making a commitment to a personal approach without the security of adequate data in all situations. Realizing that the empirical evidence is not always convincing and that there is little consensus on a paradigm for studying or doing psychotherapy, the clinician is free to make a commitment to a theoretical system that is based on an ethical position—a position of values. The ethical therapist moves beyond the realm of knowing to the realm of acting by affirming, "This is the approach to humanity that I would love to see valid, and I commit myself to trying to validate it." An ethical commitment brings with it a passion to master the particular approach, to improve it, and to evaluate it.

The ethical therapist is not a dogmatic absolutist. The commitment flows out of an undeniable relativism and entails a humility that derives from the awareness that other therapy systems may be equally valid for other individuals. The psychotherapist is prepared to refer clients to other approaches when it is apparent that the client is not going to make a commitment to the therapist's most valued alternative. By contrast, the dualistic therapist will work to convert the client in the name of truth, righteousness, and all that is good.

Committed therapists form a community of dedicated professionals who realize that, at this point in our intellectual development, the questions we share are more important than the answers we give. That is, they are centrally concerned with questions of what is the best way to be in psychotherapy; what is the most valuable model we can provide for our clients, our colleagues, and our students; and how we can help our client attain a better life. As intellectual relativists, we know can we provide no absolute answers to such questions. We value the fact that colleagues are committed to actualizing other alternatives that we ourselves have not chosen.

Werner's Model

Werner's (1948; Werner & Kaplan, 1963) organismic-developmental theory is also instructive for conceptualizing psychotherapists' development of a mature integrative stance (Kaplan et al., 1983; Rebecca, Hefner, & Oleshansky, 1976). In the first of three developmental stages in learning new information, one perceives or experiences a global whole, with no clear distinctions among component parts. All systems of psychotherapy are uncritically grouped into the catchall category of "therapy." Unsophisticated laypersons and untrained undergraduates probably fall into this category.

In the second stage, one perceives or experiences differentiation of the whole into parts, with a more precise and distinct understanding of components within the whole. Obsessive comparisons and precise contrasts among psychotherapy systems are prized. However, one no longer has a perspective on the whole, and consequently loses the "big picture." Many psychotherapy courses, textbooks, and formally educated practitioners fall into this category.

In the third stage, the differentiated parts are organized and integrated into the whole at a higher level. Here, the unity and complexity of psychotherapy are appreciated. Both the valuable differences and the essential similarities among the schools are recognized. Few psychotherapists have successfully reached this summit, but many more are scaling the slope.

The Transtheoretical Model

The transtheoretical model strives to surpass the relativism of eclecticism through a commitment to creating a higher-order theory of psychotherapy that, in Werner's terms, appreciates the unity *and* the complexity of the enterprise. Transtheoretical therapists make an epistemological commitment more than an ethical commitment. The commitment is predicated on the belief that the current relativism can be transcended by discovering or constructing concepts that cut across the traditional boundaries of the psychotherapies.

In the committed integrative spirit, we set out to construct a model of psychotherapy and behavior change that can draw from the entire spectrum the major theories—hence the name *transtheoretical*. We were guided by a number of criteria for the model. First, as we have emphasized throughout the text, a sophisticated integration will respect both the fundamental diversity *and* the essential unity of psychotherapy systems. The valuable and occasionally unique contributions of the major systems of psychotherapy must be preserved; reducing all systems to their least common denominator removes their richness and applicability. Second, the model should emphasize empiricism, in that the fundamental variables must be measurable and validated; why bother with a new model if it is never tested or if it does not produce more compelling guidelines or outcomes than those already available? Third, we sought a model that could account for how people change without therapy as well as within therapy, since the majority of people with clinical disorders do not seek professional assistance (Veroff, Douvan, & Kulka, 1981a, 1981b). Fourth, the model should prove successful in generalizing to a broad range of human problems, including physical health as well as mental health problems. Fifth and finally, the transtheoretical model should encourage psychotherapists to become innovators, not simply borrowers from other systems. The integrative model to which we aspire must provide guiding structures for practice and core principles for a comparative analysis and, at the same time, must remain flexible to encourage therapist choice and the addition of new therapy systems and research developments.

Processes of Change

The first dimension involves the processes of change. Processes are the covert or overt activities that people engage in to alter affect, thinking, behavior, or relationships related to particular problems or patterns of living. Initially the processes were the theoretically derived principles used in this book's comparative analysis of leading systems of psychotherapy (Prochaska, 1979). They were then modified empirically based on research on how people attempt to change an addictive behavior with or without professional treatment (DiClemente & Prochaska, 1982; Prochaska & DiClemente, 1983).

The following ten processes of change have received the most empirical support to date:

Consciousness raising

Catharsis/dramatic relief

Self-reevaluation

Environmental reevaluation

Self-liberation

Social liberation

Counterconditioning

Stimulus control

Contingency management

Helping relationship

We have suggested in this book that the major psychotherapies diverge much more in terms of the content to be changed than in the processes used to change that content. Divergences in content are a function of the multitude of personality theories rather than of a multitude of change processes constituting the essence of the therapeutic endeavor.

A summary of the change processes advocated by psychotherapy systems shows more convergence than would appear when we are distracted by the content of therapy. Table 15.1 demonstrates where each of the major therapeutic systems fits according to the salient processes of change.

One thing that becomes quickly apparent from Table 15.1 is that the change process with the greatest agreement is consciousness raising. Compared with other processes of change, three times as many therapies include an expansion of consciousness as a central factor in behavior change. Unless major theorists have really missed the mark, this table indicates that considerable research needs to go into exploring just which specific techniques are most effective in helping people to process information that was previously outside awareness. One research strategy is for clinicians to join forces with educators who are equally concerned with discovering the most effective means of helping to increase the awareness of students.

The transtheoretical analysis embodied in Table 15.1 reveals how much therapeutic systems agree on the processes producing change (the how) while disagreeing on the content to be changed (the what). In other words, different orientations do not dictate the specific interventions to use as much as they determine the therapeutic goals to pursue (Beutler, 1983). A consensus on treatments of choice, then, will be attained only when we agree on the target problem to be treated and on the kinds of evidence to be accepted for successful psychotherapy (Mahrer, 1991).

Consider the psychological treatment of specific phobias. Freud (1919), the intrapsychic master, stressed that if the analyst actively induced the patient to expose him/herself to the feared stimulus, "a considerable moderation of the phobia" would be achieved. This observation predates the contemporary consensus on the superiority of exposure and response prevention in alleviating phobic behavior (see Chapter 8). The existing evidence points to the necessity of reducing phobic anxiety and avoidance through exposure to the feared object; this approach, in its many forms, is considered the treatment of choice (Barlow & Beck, 1984; Barlow & Wolfe, 1981). Freud readily understood the process of reducing phobic behavior, but he decided that the desirable content of psychoanalysis—the therapeutic goal— was to make the unconscious conscious (Norcross, 1991).

Table 15.1 also indicates that psychotherapy systems have largely ignored the impact of common or nonspecific factors in producing change. Anywhere from 10% to 40% of change can be attributed to expectation or placebo (see Chapter 1 and Lambert, 1992). Our assumption is that the critical process of change in placebo groups is that clients have chosen to change. They have made a commitment to change, as affirmed by their continuing attendance at placebo sessions. The placebo sessions provide a public forum for them to make their commitment known, and it is generally believed that a public commitment is more likely to be lived up to than is a private decision.

From this point of view the critical question becomes: Just what change processes do people use to solve their own personal problems? Psychotherapists should not be so arrogant as to believe that people do not solve psychological problems without professional assistance. One strategy of our research program is to study

Table 15.1 Summary of Psychotherapy Systems According to the Change Processes Assumed to Be the Essence of Therapy

Consciousness raising

1. *Feedback*
  Psychoanalysis
  Psychoanalytic therapy
  Psychodynamic therapy
  Adlerian therapy
  Existential therapy
  Logotherapy
  Reality therapy
  Person-centered therapy
  Motivational interviewing
  Gestalt therapy
  Bioenergetics
  Rational-emotive therapy
  Cognitive therapy
  Transactional analysis
  Communication/strategic
    therapy
  Structural therapy
  Bowenian therapy
  Solution-focused therapy
  Narrative therapy

2. *Education*
  Psychoanalysis
  Adlerian therapy
  Logotherapy
  Transactional analysis
  Rational-emotive therapy
  Cognitive therapy
  Behavior therapy
  Bowenian therapy
  Self-control therapy
  Feminist therapy
  Culture-sensitive therapy
  Multimodal therapy

Catharsis

1. *Corrective emotional experience*
  Psychoanalytic therapy
  Person-centered therapy
  Gestalt therapy
  Bioenergetics
  Implosive therapy
  Satir's family therapy
  Culture-sensitive therapy

2. *Dramatic relief*
  Gestalt therapy

Conditional Stimuli

1. *Counterconditioning*
  Behavior therapy
  Rational-emotive therapy
  Cognitive therapy
  EMDR therapy
  Exposure therapy
  Multimodal therapy
  Solution-focused therapy

2. *Stimulus control*
  Behavior therapy
  Multimodal therapy

Contingency control

1. *Reevaluation*
  Adlerian therapy
  Rational-emotive therapy
  Cognitive therapy
  EMDR
  Multimodal therapy

2. *Contingency management*
  Rational-emotive therapy
  Behavior therapy
  Multimodal therapy

Choosing

1. *Self-liberation*
  Adlerian therapy
  Existential therapy
  Logotherapy
  Reality therapy
  Motivational interviewing
  Transactional analysis
  Behavior therapy
  Communication/strategic
    therapy
  Bowenian therapy
  Feminist therapy
  Culture-sensitive therapy
  Multimodal therapy
  Solution-focused therapy
  Narrative therapy

2. *Social liberation*
  Adlerian therapy
  Structural therapy
  Feminist therapy
  Culture-sensitive therapy

Therapeutic relationship
  Psychoanalytic therapy
  Adlerian therapy
  Existential therapy
  Person-centered therapy
  Motivational interviewing
  Gestalt therapy
  Communication therapy
  Structural therapy
  Feminist therapy
  Culture-sensitive therapy

people who successfully change their problem behaviors on their own. We will soon see how research on self-changers and therapy changers has provided data and concepts for developing the transtheoretical model.

In fact, our studies indicate that people in the natural environment use many different processes of change to overcome problems (Prochaska, Norcross, & DiClemente, 1995). Most psychotherapy systems, however, emphasize only two or three processes. One of the positions of the transtheoretical model is that therapists should be at least as cognitively complex as their clients. They should be able to think in terms of a more comprehensive set of processes and be able to apply techniques to engage each process when appropriate.

Stages of Change

The optimal use of change processes involves understanding the stages of change through which people progress. The stages are the second dimension of change that we discovered empirically (Prochaska & DiClemente, 1982). When we tried to assess how frequently people applied the change processes in self-change and therapy change, people kept saying that it depended on what point in the course of change we were talking about. At different points they used different processes. In their own words, our psychotherapy patients and self-change volunteers were describing the phenomena we now call *stages of change*.

Stages of change had not been identified in any of the major systems of psychotherapy. These stages are a relatively unique contribution from the integrative tradition.

As currently understood, the stages of change represent specific constellations of attitudes, intentions, and behaviors related to an individual's status in the cycle of change. They provide a temporal dimension, in that change is a phenomenon that unfolds over time. Each stage reflects not only a period of time but also a set of tasks required for movement to the next stage. Although the time an individual spends in each stage varies, the tasks to be accomplished are assumed to be invariant.

Change unfolds over a series of five stages: precontemplation, contemplation, preparation, action, and maintenance. What follows is a description of each stage and the tasks to be accomplished to progress to the next stage.

Precontemplation is the stage at which there is no intention to change behavior in the foreseeable future. Many individuals in this stage are unaware or underaware of their problems. As G. K. Chesterton once said, "It isn't that they can't see the solution. It is that they can't see the problem." Families, friends, neighbors, or employees, however, are often well aware that the precontemplator has problems. When precontemplators present for psychotherapy, they often do so because of pressure from others. Usually they feel coerced into changing by a spouse who threatens to leave, an employer who threatens to dismiss them, parents who threaten to disown them, or judges who threaten to punish them. They may even demonstrate change as long as the pressure is on. Once the pressure is off, however, they often quickly return to their old ways.

Even precontemplators can *wish* to change, but this is quite different from intending or seriously considering change in the foreseeable future. Items that are used to identify precontemplation on a continuous stage-of-change measure include "As far as I'm concerned, I don't have any problems that need changing" and "I guess I have faults but there's nothing that I really need to change" (McConnaughy, Prochaska, & Velicer, 1983). Resistance to recognizing a problem is the hallmark of precontemplation.

Precontemplators are not considering altering their behavior in the foreseeable future and, as a consequence, engage in little change process activity. In order to move ahead, they need to acknowledge or "own" the problem, increase awareness of the negative aspects of the problem, and accurately evaluate self-regulation capacities.

Contemplation is the stage in which people are aware that a problem exists and are seriously thinking about overcoming it but have not yet made a commitment to take action. People can remain stuck in the contemplation stage for long periods. In one of our self-change studies, we followed a group of 200 contemplators for two years. The modal response of this group was to remain in the contemplation stage for the entire two years without ever moving to significant action (Prochaska & DiClemente, 1984; DiClemente & Prochaska, 1985).

The essence of the contemplation stage is communicated in an incident related by Benjamin (1987). He was walking home one evening when a stranger approached him and inquired about the whereabouts of a certain street. Benjamin pointed it out to the stranger and provided specific instructions. After readily understanding and accepting the instructions, the stranger began to walk in the opposite direction. Benjamin said, "You are headed in the wrong direction." The stranger replied, "Yes, I know. I am not quite ready yet." This is contemplation: knowing where you want to go, but not being quite ready yet to go there.

Contemplators, then, are evaluating options. To move forward in the cycle of change, they must avoid the trap of obsessive rumination for years—what we call "chronic contemplation"—and make a firm decision to begin to take action. These small steps of preliminary action lead them into the next stage.

Preparation is a stage that combines intention and behavioral criteria. Individuals in this stage are intending to take action immediately and report some small behavioral changes, such as smoking five fewer cigarettes or delaying their first cigarette of the day for 30 minutes longer than precontemplators or contemplators (DiClemente et al., 1991). Although they have made some reductions in their problem behaviors, individuals in the preparation stage have not yet reached a criterion for effective action, such as abstinence from smoking, alcohol abuse, or heroin use. They are intending, however, to take such action in the very near future. On a continuous measure, they score high on both the contemplation and action scales.

Like anyone on the verge or cusp of momentous actions, individuals in the preparation stage need to set goals and priorities. In addition, they need to dedicate themselves to a specific action plan they choose. Often they are already engaged in change processes that would increase self-regulation and initiate behavior change.

Action is the stage in which individuals modify their behavior, experiences, and/or environment in order to overcome their problems. Action involves the most overt behavioral changes and requires a considerable commitment of time and energy. Modifications of a problem behavior made in the action stage tend to be most visible and receive the greatest external recognition. People, including professionals, often erroneously equate action with change. As a consequence, they overlook the requisite work that prepares changers for action and the important efforts necessary to maintain the changes following action.

Individuals are classified as being in the action stage if they have successfully altered a problem behavior for a period of one day to six months. Successfully altering a problem behavior means reaching a specific criterion, such as abstinence. With smoking, for example, cutting down by 50% or changing to lower tar and nicotine cigarettes are behavior changes that can help prepare people for action, but they do not satisfy the criterion for successful action. On a continuous measure, individuals in the action stage endorse statements such as "I am really working hard to change" and "Anyone can talk about changing; I am actually doing something about it." They score high on the action scale and lower on the scales assessing the other stages of change. Modification of the target behavior to an acceptable criterion and significant overt efforts to change are the hallmarks of action.

People in the action stage require the skills to use the key action-oriented change processes, such as counterconditioning, stimulus control, and contingency management, to interrupt habitual patterns of behavior and adopt more productive patterns. They become aware of the pitfalls that might undermine continued action, whether these are cognitive (abstinence violation expectations), behavioral (apparently irrelevant decisions), emotional (exacerbation of stress or depression), or environmental (lack of reinforcement or spousal support) in nature. In this way, they will acquire effective strategies to prevent lapses or slips from becoming complete relapses.

Maintenance is the final stage, in which people work to prevent relapse and consolidate the gains attained during action. Traditionally, maintenance has been viewed as a static stage. However, maintenance is a continuation, not an absence, of change. For chronic problems, this stage extends from six months to an indeterminate period past the initial action. For some behaviors, maintenance can be considered to last a lifetime. Being able to remain free of the chronic problem and/or to consistently engage in a new incompatible behavior for more than six months is the criterion for considering someone to be in the maintenance stage. On the continuous measure, representative maintenance items are "I may need a boost right now to help me maintain the changes I've already made" and "I'm here to prevent myself from having a relapse of my problem." Stabilizing behavior change and avoiding relapse are the hallmarks of maintenance.

As is now well known, most people taking action to modify addictions do not successfully maintain their gains on their first attempt. With smoking, for example, successful self-changers make an average of three to four action attempts before they become long-term maintainers (Schachter, 1982). Many New Year's resolvers report five or more years of consecutive pledges before maintaining the behavioral goal for at least six months (Norcross & Vangarelli, 1989). Relapse and recycling through the stages occur quite frequently as individuals attempt to modify or cease addictive behaviors.

Because relapse is the rule rather than the exception with problems such as addictions, we found that we needed to modify our original stage model. Initially we conceptualized change as a linear progression through the stages; people were sup-

Figure 15.1 The Spiral Pattern of Change

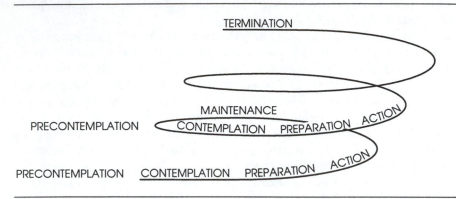

posed to progress simply and discretely through each step. Linear progression is a possible but relatively rare phenomenon with chronic disorders, like the addictions.

Figure 15.1 presents a spiral pattern that illustrates how many people actually move through the stages of change. In this spiral pattern, people can progress from contemplation to preparation to action to maintenance, but many individuals will relapse. During relapse, individuals regress to an earlier stage. Some relapsers feel like failures—embarrassed, ashamed, and guilty. These individuals become demoralized and resist thinking about behavior change. As a result, they return to the precontemplation stage and can remain there for various periods of time. Approximately 15% of smokers who relapsed in our self-change research regressed back to the precontemplation stage (Prochaska & DiClemente, 1984).

Fortunately, this research indicates that the vast majority of relapsers—85% of self-changers, for example—recycle back to the contemplation or preparation stage (Prochaska & DiClemente, 1984). They begin to consider plans for their next action attempt, while trying to learn from their recent efforts. To take another example, fully 60% of unsuccessful New Year's resolvers make the same pledge the next year (Norcross, Ratzin, & Payne, 1989; Norcross & Vangarelli, 1989). The spiral model suggests that most relapsers do not revolve endlessly in circles and that they do not regress all the way back to where they began. Instead, each time relapsers recycle through the stages, they potentially learn from their mistakes and can try something different the next time around (DiClemente et al., 1991).

Termination of a problem occurs when a person no longer experiences any temptation to return to troubled behaviors and no longer has to make any efforts to keep from relapsing. Obviously, termination of treatment and termination of a problem are not coincidental. Psychotherapy frequently ends before serious problems terminate entirely. Consequently, it is expected that, for many clinical disorders, clients will return for booster sessions, most often when they feel they may be slipping back from previous gains. Also, because treatment terminates before most problems have reached their termination, clients tend to experience considerable anxiety and distress over the termination of therapy. Patients have been dependent on the psychotherapist for help in coping with problems that may have improved significantly but are by no means completely overcome.

Individuals who seek our professional assistance do not arrive at our doorstep in the identical stage of change. We have reported many clinical examples in which clients enter psychotherapy at various stages and how this can affect the progress of therapy (DiClemente, 1986; Prochaska & DiClemente, 1984, 1986). Patients entering treatment programs at two different outpatient psychotherapy clinics and at a large outpatient alcoholism treatment center demonstrated a variety of profiles on the stages-of-change scale (McConnaughy, DiClemente, Prochaska, & Velicer, 1989; DiClemente & Hughes, 1990). The type of screening and the particular demands made by the treatment program can influence the numbers of people in different stages who present for help, but it is unlikely that any program would be able to recruit clients only from one stage unless it preassessed stage of change as a selection criterion. For most practitioners and programs, patients represent a rather heterogeneous group in terms of readiness to change.

A patient's pretreatment stage of change is an important determinant of prognosis. The further along clients are in the stages of change at the beginning of therapy, the more quickly they can be predicted to progress. When therapy involves two or more clients working together, as in marital therapy, then therapy can be expected to progress most smoothly when each of the clients is at the same stage of change. If one spouse is ready for action while the other has not contemplated what change will mean, then treatment will be difficult at best. The therapist is then in the difficult position of being damned by one spouse for moving too slowly or resisted by the other for moving too quickly. With family therapy, it is almost axiomatic that some of the family members will be in different stages. Perhaps this is one reason why homeostasis as a source of resistance has been such a key concept in systemic perspectives. Getting all family members to the same stage of change at about the same time is no small challenge.

Representative Studies

A number of research studies have been conducted to examine the clinical utility and predictive validity of the stages-of-change construct. We will review here the results of a selection of representative studies.

The amount of progress clients make following intervention tends to be a function of their pretreatment stage of change (for example, Prochaska & DiClemente, 1992a; Prochaska, Norcross, Fowler, Follick, & Abrams, 1992). This has been found to be true for brain-impaired patients in rehabilitation programs (Lam, McMahon, Priddy, & Gehred-Schultz, 1988), panic-disordered patients receiving anti-anxiety medication (Beitman et al., 1994), cardiac patients undergoing counseling (Ockene et al., 1992), and Mexican Americans enrolled in community programs for smoking cessation (Gottlieb, Galavotti, McCuan, & McAlister, 1990). This strong stage effect applies immediately following intervention, as well as 12 and 18 months afterward (Prochaska, DiClemente, Velicer, & Rossi, 1993).

In another study, we examined the percentage of 570 smokers who were not smoking over an 18-month period as a function of the stage of change before random assignment to four home-based programs. The amount of success was directly related to the stage they were in before treatment (Prochaska & DiClemente,

1992a). To treat all of these smokers as if they were the same would be naive; yet that is what we have traditionally done in many of our treatment programs.

If clients progress from one stage to the next during the first month of treatment, they can double their chances of taking action during the initial six months of the program. Of the precontemplators who were still in precontemplation at one month follow-up, only 3% took action by six months; of the precontemplators who had progressed to contemplation at one month, 7% took action by six months. Similarly, of the contemplators who remained in contemplation at one month, only 20% took action by six months; of the contemplators who had progressed to the preparation stage at one month, 41% attempted to quit by six months. These data demonstrate that treatment programs designed to help people progress just one stage in a month can double the chances of participants' taking action on their own in the near future (Prochaska & DiClemente, 1992a).

Another study (Medieros & Prochaska, 1993) demonstrated that the stages of change can predict who remains in psychotherapy. For some time clinicians have known that approximately 30% to 40% of patients terminate psychotherapy prematurely; however, the characteristics of these "dropouts" have not been reliably known. Premature termination from a variety of psychotherapies was predicted using variables traditionally among the best predictors of therapy outcome—including client characteristics, such as demographics, and problem characteristics, such as duration and intensity—but these variables had zero ability to predict therapy dropouts. When the stages and processes of change were used, 93% of the premature terminators—as opposed to therapy continuers and early but appropriate terminators—were correctly identified. The stage profile of the 40% who dropped out of therapy was that of precontemplators. The stage profile of the 20% who terminated quickly but appropriately was that of people in the action stage. The stage profile of the therapy continuers was similar to that of contemplators.

A person's stage of change provides prescriptive as well as proscriptive information on the treatment of choice. Action-oriented therapies may be quite effective with individuals who are in the preparation or action stage. These same programs may be ineffective or detrimental, however, with individuals in the precontemplation or contemplation stage.

An intensive action- and maintenance-oriented smoking cessation program for cardiac patients was highly successful for those patients in action and ready for action. This same program failed, however, with smokers in the precontemplation and contemplation stages (Ockene, Ockene, & Kristellar, 1988). Patients in this special-care program received personal counseling in the hospital and monthly telephone counseling calls for six months following hospitalization. Of the patients who began the program in the action or preparation stage, an impressive 94% were not smoking at six-month follow-up. This percentage is significantly higher than the 66% nonsmoking rate of patients in similar stages who received regular care for their smoking problem. The special-care program had no significant effects, however, with patients in the precontemplation and contemplation stages. For patients in these stages, regular care did as well or better.

Independent of the treatment received, there was a clear relationship between pretreatment stage and outcome. Patients who were not smoking at 12 months included 22% of all precontemplators, 43% of the contemplators, and 76% of those in action or prepared for action at the start of the study.

Integration of Stages and Processes

One of the most helpful findings to emerge from our research is that particular processes of change are emphasized during particular stages of change. The integration of stages and processes of change can serve as an important guide for psychotherapists. Once a patient's stage of change is evident, the therapist would then know which processes to apply in order to help that patient progress to the next stage of change. Rather than apply the change processes in a haphazard or trial-and-error manner, therapists can begin to use them in a much more systematic and efficient style.

Table 15.2 diagrams the integration between the stages and processes of change (Norcross, Prochaska, & DiClemente, 1995; Prochaska & DiClemente, 1982, 1992b). Specifically, the table shows the change processes used most often during the five stages of change. Let us now review how this integration can systematically direct the conduct of psychotherapy.

During precontemplation, individuals use change processes significantly less than people in any other stage. It was found that precontemplators process less information about their problems; spend less time and energy reevaluating themselves; experience fewer emotional reactions to the negative aspects of their problems; are less open with significant others about their problems; and do little to shift their attention or their environment in the direction of overcoming their problems. In treatment, these patients are labeled resistant or defensive.

What can help people move from precontemplation to contemplation? Table 15.2 suggests that several change processes are most helpful. First, *consciousness raising* interventions, such as observations, confrontations, and interpretations, can help clients become more aware of the causes, consequences, and cures of their problems. To move to the contemplation stage, clients have to become more aware of the negative consequences of their behavior. Often we have to first help clients become more aware of their defenses before they can become more conscious of what they are defending against. Second, the process of *dramatic relief* (or catharsis) provides clients with helpful affective experiences, such as those used in Gestalt interventions like the empty chair. These experiences can release emotions related to problem behaviors. Life events can also move precontemplators emotionally, such as the disease or death of a friend or lover, especially if such events are problem related.

Clients in the contemplation stage are most open to consciousness raising interventions, such as observations, confrontations, and interpretations. Contemplators are much more likely to use bibliotherapy and other educational interventions. As clients become increasingly more aware of themselves and the nature of their problems, they are freer to reevaluate themselves both affectively and cognitively. The *self-reevaluation* process includes an assessment of which values clients will try to actualize, act upon, and make real, and which they will let die. The more central

Table 15.2 Stages of Change in Which Change Processes Are Most Emphasized

Stages of Change				
Precontemplation	Contemplation	Preparation	Action	Maintenance
Consciousness raising				
Dramatic relief				
Environmental reevaluation				
	Self-reevaluation			
		Self-liberation		
			Contingency management	
			Counterconditioning	
			Stimulus control	

problem behaviors are to their core values, the more their reevaluation will involve changes in their sense of self. Contemplators also reevaluate the effects their behaviors have on their environment, especially the people they care about most.

Movement from precontemplation to contemplation, and movement through the contemplation stage, involves increased use of cognitive, affective, and evaluative processes of change. To better prepare individuals for action, changes are required in how they think and feel about their problem behaviors and how they value their problematic lifestyles.

Preparation indicates a readiness to change in the near future and incorporation of valuable lessons from past change attempts and failures. Preparers are on the verge of taking action and need to set goals and priorities accordingly. They often develop an action plan for how they are going to proceed. In addition, they need to make firm commitments to follow through on the action option they choose. In fact, they are often already engaged in processes that would increase self-regulation and initiate behavior change (DiClemente et al., 1991). Individuals typically begin by taking some small steps toward action. They may use counterconditioning and stimulus control processes to begin reducing their problem behaviors. Counterconditioning involves learning to substitute healthier alternatives in conditions that normally elicit problems, such as learning to relax instead of smoking in certain stressful situations. Stimulus control involves managing the presence or absence of situations or cues that can elicit problems, such as not stopping at a bar after work. Addicted individuals may delay their use of substances each day or may control the number of situations in which they rely on the addictive substances.

As they prepare for the action stage, it is important that clients act from a sense of *self-liberation*. They need to believe that they have the autonomy to change their lives in key ways. Yet they also need to accept that coercive forces are as much a part of life as is autonomy. Self-liberation is based in part on a sense of self-efficacy (Bandura, 1977, 1982)—the belief that one's own efforts play a critical role in succeeding in the face of difficult situations.

Self-liberation, however, requires more than merely an affective and cognitive foundation. Clients must also be effective enough with behavioral processes, such as *counterconditioning*, *contingency management*, and *stimulus control*, to cope with those conditions that can coerce them into relapsing. Therapists can provide training, if necessary, in behavioral processes to increase the probability that clients will be successful when they do take action.

Just as preparation for action is essential for success, so too is preparation for maintenance. Successful maintenance builds on each of the processes that has come before, and also involves an open assessment of the conditions under which a person is likely to be coerced into relapsing. Clients need to assess the alternatives they have for coping with such coercive conditions without resorting to self-defeating defenses and pathological responses. Perhaps most important is the sense that one is becoming more of the kind of person one wants to be. Continuing to use counterconditioning, contingency management, and stimulus control is most effective when it is based on the conviction that maintaining change maintains a sense of self that is highly valued by oneself and at least one significant other.

To sum up: We have determined that efficient behavior change depends on doing the right things (processes) at the right time (stages). We have observed two frequent mismatches in this respect. First, some clients (and clinicians) appear to rely primarily on change processes most indicated for the contemplation stage—consciousness raising, self-reevaluation—while they are moving to the action stage. They try to modify behaviors by becoming more aware, a common criticism of classical psychoanalysis: insight alone does not necessarily bring about behavior change. Second, other clients (and clinicians) rely primarily on change processes most indicated for the action stage—contingency management, stimulus control, counterconditioning—without the requisite awareness, decision making, and readiness provided in the contemplation and preparation stages. They try to modify behavior without awareness, a common criticism of radical behaviorism: overt action without insight is likely to lead to temporary change (Prochaska, DiClemente, & Norcross, 1992).

Competing systems of psychotherapy have promulgated apparently rival processes of change. However, ostensibly contradictory processes can become complementary when embedded in the stages of change. Specifically, change processes traditionally associated with the experiential, cognitive, and psychoanalytic persuasions are most useful during the precontemplation and contemplation stages. Change processes traditionally associated with the existential and behavioral traditions, by contrast, are most useful during the action and maintenance stages.

Levels of Change

At this point in our analysis, it may appear that we are restricting our discussion to a single, well-defined problem. However, as we all realize, reality is not so accommodating, and human behavior is not so simple. Although we can isolate certain symptoms and syndromes, these occur in the context of complex, interrelated levels of human functioning. The third basic element of the transtheoretical approach addresses this issue. The *levels of change* represent a hierarchical organization of five distinct but interrelated levels of psychological problems that can be addressed in psychotherapy. These levels are:

1. Symptom/situational problems
2. Maladaptive cognitions
3. Current interpersonal conflicts
4. Family/systems conflicts
5. Intrapersonal conflicts

Historically, psychotherapy systems have attributed psychological problems primarily to one or two levels and have focused their interventions on these levels. Behavior therapists have focused on the symptom and situational determinants, cognitive therapists on maladaptive cognitions, family therapists on the family/systems level, and psychoanalytic therapists on intrapersonal conflicts. A critical point in treatment occurs when psychotherapists and patients agree as to which level they attribute the problem to and which level (or levels) they are willing to mutually target as they work to modify the disorder.

What is the key level of content for psychotherapy? The answer obviously depends on the therapists's preferred theory of personality and psychopathology and/or the client's preferred theory of problems. As an integrative model, transtheoretical therapy appreciates the validity of each level. How critical each level is can vary for different clients even when they are presenting the same symptoms.

Consider, for example, three cases of vaginismus (Prochaska & DiClemente, 1984). Case A recovered by simply focusing on the symptom/situational level and changing the situations under which the couple had sexual encounters. Case B, a difficult success, clearly had current interpersonal problems of communication and control that contributed to the maintenance of vaginismus. Case C, a failure, appeared to have critical involvement of family/systems conflicts, with the young woman experiencing her sexuality as still under the control of her mother's rules.

Given five different levels of change, how can psychotherapists proceed systematically across them? In the transtheoretical model, we prefer to intervene initially at the symptom/situational level because change tends to occur more quickly at this more conscious and contemporary level of problems. The further down the hierarchy we proceed, the further removed from awareness and the present the determinants of the problem are likely to be. That is, "deeper" levels involve more unconscious and historical conflicts contributing to the disorder. Thus, we predict from the transtheoretical model that the deeper the level that needs to be changed, the longer and more complex psychotherapy is likely to be.

What's more, the further removed in history are the determinants of the problem, the greater resistance there will be to trying to change those determinants. One of the reasons for increased resistance is that deeper attributions tend to be more threatening to self-esteem than are more surface attributions. It is more threatening, for example, to believe that vaginismus is due to hostility toward men and a desire to emasculate them than to believe that the anticipation of painful intercourse elicits fear and involuntary circumvaginal muscle contractions. One of the guidelines of the transtheoretical model is to use the least threatening attributions that can be justified, because our clinical formulations have the potential for producing damage in their own right.

These levels, it should be emphasized, are not independent or isolated; on the contrary, change at any one level is likely to produce change at other levels. Symptoms often involve intrapersonal conflicts; maladaptive cognitions often reflect family/system beliefs or rules. In the transtheoretical approach, therapists are prepared to intervene at any of the five levels of change, though the preference is to begin at the highest and most contemporary level that clinical assessment and disciplined judgment can justify.

Putting It All Together

In summary, the transtheoretical model sees therapeutic integration as the differential application of the processes of change at specific stages of change according to the identified problem level. In colloquial terms, we have identified the basics of *how* (processes), *when* (stages), and *what* (levels) to change. Integrating the levels with the stages and processes of change provides a model for intervening hierarchically and systematically across a broad range of therapeutic content. Table 15.3 presents an overview of the integration of levels, stages, and processes of change.

Three basic strategies can be employed for intervening across multiple levels of change. The first is that of *shifting levels*. Therapy would typically focus initially on the client's symptoms and the situations supporting the symptoms. If the processes could be applied effectively at the first level and the patient could progress through each stage of change, psychotherapy could be completed without shifting to a deeper level of analysis. If treating only the symptoms was not effective enough, then therapy would shift to a focus on maladaptive cognitions that are supporting the symptoms. The processes of change would be applied to cognitive content with the goal of progressing through each stage of change. If progress was not sufficient at the cognitive level, then therapy would shift to current interpersonal conflicts. The processes would now be applied at an interpersonal level, with the goal of progressing through each stage of change. The same pattern of successfully progressing through the stages or shifting levels would be followed until the client had sufficiently improved or until the deepest, least conscious, and most resistant intrapersonal conflicts had been analyzed. This strategy of shifting from a higher to a deeper level is illustrated in Table 15.3 by the arrows moving first across one level and then down to the next level.

The second strategy is to focus on *key levels*. There are certain clear-cut cases in which a high degree of consensual validation would emerge among clinicians regarding the causes of a client's problems. If the available evidence is unambiguous and points to one key level of causality, then the psychotherapist would work first and foremost at this key level of intervention. These cases are relatively easy to formulate once the clinical data are in, though that does not mean that they are necessarily easy to treat.

Table 15.3 Levels × Stages × Processes of Change

			Stages of Change		
Levels	Precontemplation	Contemplation	Preparation	Action	Maintenance
Symptom/situational	Consciousness raising				
	Dramatic relief				
	Environmental reevaluation				
		Self-reevaluation			
			Self-liberation		
				Contingency management	
				Counterconditioning	
				Stimulus control	
Maladaptive cognitions					
Interpersonal conflicts					
Family/systems conflicts					
Intrapersonal conflicts					

The third alternative is the *maximum-impact* strategy. With complex clinical cases, it is sometimes clear that variables at every level are involved as a cause, an effect, or a maintainer of the client's problems. For maximum impact, interventions can be created that engage the patient at each and every level of change. This creates a synergy of change interventions. The maximum-impact strategy will be illustrated in the transtheoretical analysis of Mrs. C.

As should now be evident, the length of psychotherapy varies according to both the stage and the level of change, as well as how hard and how well clients work between sessions. Clients who enter treatment prepared to take action can have brief but successful therapeutic experience, typically in six to ten sessions. The more defenses patients have to work through and the less successful work they have been able to do before entering treatment, the longer the course of psychotherapy is likely to be, typically ranging from 6 to 24 months.

It follows, then, that clients with problems at the situational and cognitive levels can typically expect comparatively brief treatment. For patients saddled with disorders more deeply embedded in the context of a dysfunctional family of origin or a pathogenic intrapersonal history, psychotherapy will typically be of longer duration. Problems that develop in a current interpersonal relationship are usually of more moderate duration, averaging about 12 months. Problems that are multilevel in origin usually necessitate longer treatment.

Hopefully, psychotherapy research will progress to the point where we will know that a specific level of intervention is most effective with particular types of patients afflicted with particular disorders. Research already suggests that about half of the patients with focal phobias can be effectively helped by modifying the situational determinants of their phobias. Research does not suggest, however, what to do with the 50% of phobic patients who drop out or fail to progress at the situational level (Barlow & Wolfe, 1981). Until more clear-cut research is available for guiding therapeutic interventions with specific disorders, the transtheoretical model provides an efficient and effective guide for various client presentations.

Theoretical complementarity and integration are the keys to synthesizing the major systems of psychotherapy. Each theoretical persuasion has a place, a differential place, in the "big picture" of behavior change. Table 15.4 illustrates where leading systems of therapy fit best within the integrative framework of the transtheoretical model. Depending on which level and which stage we are working at, different therapy systems will play a more or less prominent role. Behavior therapy and exposure therapy, for example, have developed specific interventions at the symptom/situational level for clients who are ready for action. At the maladaptive cognition level, Ellis's rational-emotive therapy and Beck's cognitive therapy are most indicated for clients in the preparation and action stages.

The transtheoretical model does not exclude, a priori, any system of psychotherapy. Ours is an open framework that allows for incorporation of new and innovative interventions, as well as inclusion of existing therapy systems that research or clinical experience suggest are most efficacious for clients in particular stages at particular levels of change.

A prominent psychotherapy missing from Table 15.4 is Rogers's person-centered therapy. His system has been most eloquent in articulating and demonstrating

Table 15.4 Integration of Psychotherapy Systems within the Transtheoretical Model

Levels	Stages of Change				
	Precontemplation	Contemplation	Preparation	Action	Maintenance
Symptom/situational	Motivational interviewing				Behavior therapy EMDR and exposure
Maladaptive cognitions		Adlerian therapy		Rational-emotive therapy Cognitive therapy	
Interpersonal conflicts	Sullivanian therapy	Transactional analysis		Interpersonal therapy (IPT)	
Family systems/conflicts	Strategic therapy	Bowenian therapy		Structural therapy	
Intrapersonal conflicts	Psychoanalytic therapy	Existential therapy			

the importance of the therapeutic relationship as a critical process of change. Our own thinking and research on the helping relationship has been heavily influenced by the client-centered perspective even though we do not rely only on client-centered techniques for developing the therapeutic alliance. Thus, Rogers's influence on the transtheoretical approach cuts across levels of change.

Prescriptive Matching

One of the central themes of psychotherapy is determining empirically driven means to prescriptively match treatments to clients, thereby enhancing the efficacy, efficiency, and applicability of psychotherapy (Norcross & Freedheim, 1992). Much of therapy research has traditionally been dedicated to determining if one type of therapy is a better match for a specific problem than is an alternative therapy. Such horse-race contests have resulted in a disappointing abundance of ties (Beutler, 1991; Luborsky, Singer, & Luborsky, 1975; Smith, Glass, & Miller, 1980; Stiles, Shapiro, & Elliot, 1986). After nearly 50 years of research, we are only partially able to specify which type of treatment is best for which type of client with which type of problem under which type of conditions.

The transtheoretical model offers a unique means of treatment matching: match to the client's stage and level of change. If troubled people vary in their readiness to take action on their disorders, then treatments should vary in terms of how much action they demand of clients. Behavior modifiers have been ingenious in their ability to develop action-oriented interventions, but these action-oriented interventions may be appropriate only for the small percentage of people who are prepared for action at any given time.

A patient and therapist each working at different stages is a prescription for resistance. If the therapist is action-oriented and the client is a precontemplator, then the client will experience the therapist as insensitive and coercive, like a parent pressuring change when the client isn't convinced that change is needed. Conversely, if the patient is prepared to take action and the therapist relies almost exclusively on consciousness raising and self-reevaluation processes, the client will experience treatment as moving much too slowly while the therapist may perceive the client as acting out.

Similarly, clients who believe that immediate situational changes will improve their symptoms are likely to be resistant to spending much time becoming more conscious of their childhood. Clinicians who depend heavily on situationally focused techniques, such as desensitization, may experience resistance from patients who are convinced that their phobias are rooted in much deeper levels, which they want to understand. A client who was being treated with systematic desensitization for a social phobia by one of our graduate students complained, "It seems to me that the therapy you are using is like treating a cancer with aspirin."

If therapists can only work effectively at one level of change, then they had better have the luxury of selecting patients who match that level. In choosing a psychotherapist, clients are often implicitly seeking someone who works at a level that they believe is most relevant to their problems. This is a leading reason why some clients prefer behavior therapists, while others seek psychoanalytic therapists, and still others seek interpersonal or family therapists. A transtheoretical therapist can potentially be trained to match the needs of a much broader range of clients. Such therapists would need to have adequate training in the theories and techniques appropriate to each level. What we don't know with certainty at this point is what constitutes adequate training to facilitate behavior change at each level (Alberts & Edelstein, 1990; Andrews, Norcross, & Halgin, 1992; Beutler, et al., 1987).

Therapists who are well matched to a client's stage and level of change are likely to experience the therapeutic process as progressing reasonably smoothly. Of course, patients can become stuck in a stage, but at least the psychotherapist is aware of not contributing to the stagnation. A case in point: Many patients stuck in the contemplation stage tend to substitute thinking and reflecting for acting. They can be very comfortable with clinicians who prefer contemplation-oriented processes such as consciousness raising and self-reevaluation. But encouraging such clients to go deeper and deeper into more levels of their problems can be iatrogenic; that is, the treatment itself can produce negative outcomes, such as feeding into their problems of being "chronic contemplators." At some point, action must be taken. But a therapist who has not been trained to use action-oriented processes effectively might prefer to avoid action in the same way that chronic contemplators avoid action. After years and years of archeological expeditions into the deepest levels of personality, such clients may yell out like the character on the cover of *The New Yorker* magazine: "Help, I'm being held captive in psychotherapy!"

The Transtheoretical Relationship

In general, the transtheoretical psychotherapist is seen as an expert on change—not in having all the answers, but in being aware of the critical dimensions of change and being able to offer some assistance in this regard. Clients have potential resources as self-changers that must be tapped in order to effect a change. In fact, clients need to shoulder much of the burden of change and look to the therapist for consultation on how to conceptualize the problem and ways to free themselves to move from one stage to the next (Prochaska & DiClemente, 1992b).

As with any interactive endeavor, rapport must be built in order to accomplish the work. However, the type of therapeutic relationship should be tailored to the stage and level of change being addressed.

The therapist's stance at different stages can be characterized as follows. With precontemplators, often the role is like that of a *nurturing parent* joining with a resistant and defensive youngster who is both drawn to and repelled by the prospects of becoming more independent. With contemplators, the role is akin to a *Socratic teacher* who encourages clients to achieve their own insights into their condition. With clients who are in the preparation stage, the stance is more like that of an *experienced coach* who has been through many crucial matches and can provide a fine game plan or can review the person's own plan. With clients who are progressing into action and maintenance, the psychotherapist becomes more of a *consultant* who is available to provide expert advice and support when action is not progressing as smoothly as expected. As termination approaches in lengthier treatment, the transtheoretical therapist is consulted less and less often as the client experiences greater autonomy and ability to live a life freer from previously disabling problems.

In some ways, this sequence of stances parallels the changing roles that effective parents play as their children grow through stages of personal development. In this sense, psychotherapists would use the evolving countertransference as clients progress through stages of intentional change. Like parents, psychotherapists should not strive to be perfect role models but "good enough" guides who can help clients through the complexities of changing.

The amount of structure that needs to be provided in a given case also varies with the client's stage of change. Precontemplators need much more help in getting started and dealing with defenses. Contemplators love to engage in consciousness raising and self-reevaluation processes and can typically do much of the within-session work with minimal structure. Once it comes to taking action, clients vary in how much direction they seek from treatment. Those who have become demoralized about their ability to maintain changes usually look to the therapist for guidance on how they can be more effective in their next action attempt. Other clients can be quite creative in applying behavioral processes to modify their situations, cognitions, interpersonal relationships, family/systems, and intrapersonal conflicts.

Effectiveness of Transtheoretical Therapy

Over the past 20 years, the transtheoretical model has generated vast amounts of data about how people change on their own and in psychotherapy. As reviewed earlier, the amount of positive change is a function of a person's pretreatment stage of change. This has been found repeatedly for both self-initiated and treatment-facilitated change across a broad range of behavioral disorders.

The only controlled outcome research to date on the transtheoretical model involves efforts to facilitate smoking cessation. A transtheoretical therapy (TTT) action manual was tested in studies with smokers, many of whom had tried unsuccessfully to quit on their own during the past two years. These studies included a comparison of the TTT materials with the sophisticated American Lung Association (ALA) action manual, which has been accepted as the "gold-standard" manual for smoking cessation (Glasgow & Rosen, 1978) under both self-administered (manual) and therapist-administered (clinic) conditions.

Results of these studies were encouraging. At the four-week posttest, the percentage of subjects who had taken action in the TTT clinic groups was much higher than in the ALA clinic groups (58% v. 23%). At the six-month follow-up, 17% of the TTT clinic subjects reported they were not smoking, compared to only 3% of the ALA subjects. At a second site, 42% of the TTT clinic group were not smoking at six months, compared to 6% for the ALA group. In the self-administered manual studies, 38% of the TTT manual subjects reported taking action in the past month, compared to only 17% of the ALA manual subjects.

A special mission of transtheoretical therapy is to impact the 99% of the waking week that clients spend between psychotherapy sessions. One way to do this is to create home-based interventions that permit people to work as wisely on their problems at home as they do when under the expert guidance of therapists at a clinic. In health psychology, we have created computer-driven expert systems that provide feedback about which stage people are in and which of the change processes they are underutilizing, overutilizing, or utilizing appropriately. This theory-based and computer-driven expert system has been found to produce a success rate 2.5 times that of the best home-based program for smoking cessation (Prochaska, DiClemente, Velicer, & Rossi, 1993).

The transtheoretical model holds considerable promise for describing, predicting, and explaining changes in a broad range of disorders. To date, the similarities in variables related to changing a diversity of problems have been more striking than the differences. While people vary a great deal in the etiology, severity, and topology of their dysfunctions, they may be remarkably similar when it comes to modifying a broad range of psychological disorders.

Research has been highly supportive of the core constructs of the transtheoretical approach and the integration of the stages, processes, and levels. Longitudinal studies affirm the relevance of these constructs for predicting premature termination and treatment outcomes. Comparative outcome studies attest to the potential of stage-matched interventions to outperform the best alternative treatments available. Population-based studies support the importance of developing interventions that match the needs of individuals at all stages of change (see Prochaska, Norcross, & DiClemente, 1995, for a review).

— A TRANSTHEORETICAL ANALYSIS OF MRS. C. —

Mrs. C. entered psychotherapy stuck in the contemplation stage. The six years she spent in psychoanalytic psychotherapy had increased her consciousness about her obsessive-compulsive patterns and personality. She had spent considerable time reevaluating her life. Intellectually, she appreciated how much her life had gotten out of control; but emotionally, it still felt right to protect herself and her family from dirt and disease. As is often the case with obsessive-compulsive clients, Mrs. C. isolated much of her affect from her intellect when reevaluating her self and her symptoms.

Obsessive-compulsive patients are especially prone to getting stuck in the contemplation stage (Prochaska & DiClemente, 1982). They prefer to believe that if they keep thinking enough about an issue, eventually the problem will be resolved or enough information will be found that points to a perfect solution to a perplexing problem. They are seeking certainty as to the causes of their symptoms, when probability is the best that can be provided. Obsessives, like Mrs. C., hate to admit that there can be serious limits to thinking and that many dysfunctions can only be changed by commitments that go beyond reason. The fear of facing the irrational can keep obsessives seeking sufficient information for years, as they shift from one theory to another or from one therapist to another. Of course, some therapists are also afraid of making commitments to action without an obsessive understanding of their clients' problems.

Mrs. C. was feeling coerced into action. Her environment was threatening to force changes on her. Her psychotherapist had given up and had decided to terminate treatment. Her family was also giving up on her. Mrs. C. took an overdose of aspirin to express the depression and anger she felt over the rejection that would come with the alternative of being placed in a psychiatric hospital.

Her alternatives for action, then, were to work with me, to go to the hospital, or to follow through on suicide. We hoped Mrs. C. would be able to identify with our efforts as potentially the most liberating alternative rather than feeling entirely coerced into cooperating. The fact is that if she felt entirely coerced, she really wouldn't be able to cooperate and would resist being changed by someone trying to control her.

At what level should we try to help Mrs. C. change? Mrs. C. is clearly a complex case. At the symptom and situational level, dirt and disease evoke compulsive handwashing that is apparently reinforced by reduction in anxiety. At the cognitive level, Mrs. C. believes that she needs to be perfectly clean in order to be perfectly safe and secure. Her maladaptive cognitions include perseverating about pinworms and magnifying the dangers of pinworms entirely out of realistic proportions. She seems to believe that even thoughts or images of dirt and pinworms are awful and unbearable. She also seems to believe that things around her will go out of control if she does not keep up her compulsive rituals.

At the interpersonal level, Mrs. C. has mixed relationships at best. She relates ambivalently to her children, as she struggles to protect them from dirt and disease. Her relationship to her husband has deteriorated to the point where it lacks intimacy or sexuality. Their only significant interaction is Mr. C.'s participation in her morning shower ritual. Mrs. C. is in conflict over caring for her family or controlling her family.

At the family/systems level, Mrs. C. is still heavily influenced by her mother's rules to be ultraclean and careful about dirt and disease. She comes from a family in which she was dominated by her parents but was not free to acknowledge anger and resentment toward their coercive control.

At the intrapersonal level, she appears to be defending against , in psychoanalytic terminology, classic anal impulses. Urges to play with her anus and its products are counteracted by doing the opposite, a reaction formation that entails being perfectly clean. She has trouble letting go, as she hoards cheap jewelry and other junk. She lives a highly constricted life in which she overcontrols her feelings, her sexual urges, and her aggression. To let go of her defenses in the slightest would threaten to drive Mrs. C. crazy.

With the transtheoretical model, we have the option of beginning psychotherapy at the symptom/situational level and shifting to deeper levels, if necessary. We can also intervene at a key level of change if one of the levels is clearly the key to her problems. Or we can use the maximum-impact strategy and attempt to produce changes at each level. With a complex case like Mrs. C., where there are multilevel problems, a maximum-impact strategy is preferred.

Even though I (JOP) treated Mrs. C. as a psychology intern long before transtheoretical therapy was developed, it is intriguing to realize how much my early integrative style anticipated my later theorizing. With Mrs. C., for example, psychotherapy involved multilevel interventions. Treatment also included a range of change processes that were appropriate for a client moving into action. (Were Mrs. C. to present for treatment today, she would also undoubtedly receive one of the new anti-obsessive medications).

At the symptom/situational level, treating Mrs. C. as an inpatient enabled the psychotherapist to exert greater influence over stimulus situations that controlled her symptoms. Because her handwashing at home was immediate and automatic, she had little voluntary control over washing. As an inpatient, she would have to sign in at the nurses' station before she could wash and sign in again after completing her washing. This gave an accurate count of her compulsive washing and would serve as feedback about the effectiveness of our treatment. The signing in also served as a delay during which the nurses could use counterconditioning to help Mrs. C. cope with her anxiety, such as talking about it or encouraging her to relax by playing cards, knitting, or watching television. The delays also allowed Mrs. C. to begin to use self-liberation and make more conscious decisions to wash or to resist washing. If she resisted washing, the staff could then use contingency management and reinforce Mrs. C. for not washing. As therapy progressed, the signing in also served as a stimulus control procedure that controlled how often and how long Mrs. C. could remain in washing situations.

A helping relationship was enhanced by meeting twice a week in more client-centered, supportive sessions. In these sessions, Mrs. C. could share the many thoughts and feelings generated by her hospitalization and treatment. These sessions also helped Mrs. C. identify with therapy, as she experienced her therapist as caring rather than coercive. The more Mrs. C. identified with psychotherapy, the more she relied on self-liberation, as she committed herself more fully to taking action to overcome her chronic compulsions.

The comprehensive treatment also entailed implosive sessions three times a week. The implosive scenes described in Chapter 8 affected almost every level of Mrs. C.'s problems. The first scene, for example, encouraged Mrs. C. to face such situations as dirty underwear filled with pinworms. The anal picnic scene would impact on several levels simultaneously, ranging from symptom stimuli of dirt and disease to intrapersonal desires to act out anal impulses. We also introduced challenges to maladaptive cognitions of having to be perfectly clean in order to be safe and secure and family/systems themes related to rebellion against parental dominance over toilet training.

The third scene impacted upon interpersonal conflicts, especially Mrs. C.'s ambivalence toward her children. She imagined her children being infected by pinworms because of her carelessness. In the middle of the night, she heard her children complaining to her as they were being bothered by pinworms. Mrs. C. ignored their pleas and went to bed feeling free at last from having to care for her children.

The interpersonal level was also addressed by the psychotherapist's meeting with the family for biweekly sessions. The family members needed to express the considerable anger and resentment toward Mrs. C. that had accumulated over the years. For a while it looked as though Mrs. C. might not be able to return home, because four of the children were adamant about not wanting her back. As the anger dissipated, however, Mr. C. and the older children were able to help the younger children reevaluate their mother, because they shared memories of how Mrs. C. was before she became obsessed. Individual sessions with Mr. C. also helped him to remember the warm feelings that had been buried under all the frustration and resentment.

The family/system conflicts of Mrs. C. were most intensely affected by the fourth scene, in which she imagined sinking an ax into her father's bald head. Besides the scenes described in Chapter 8, Mrs. C. also confronted what psychoanalysts would describe as oedipal conflicts with a father who waited up for her after dates. Of course, these scenes could also impact upon intrapersonal conflicts, as Mrs. C. imagined releasing some of her most taboo impulses of sex and aggression.

Another scene was directed at intrapersonal conflicts over losing control and going crazy. She imagined running around the house nude, wrecking the house, and then being shipped back to the clinic for disposition. At the clinic, a full staff meeting was held with the family members present. After discussing all the terrible things that Mrs. C. had done, the director asked if anyone from the clinic or the family had anything good to say about her. Silence was the only response. Again the question was asked, and again no one spoke. Finally, Mrs. C. was sent to the state hospital in a panel truck and placed in an isolated room with a sign on her door: "Hopeless Case: No Visitors Allowed." This scene, in addition, assisted Mrs. C. in confronting some of her situational anxieties regarding relapse after returning home from the hospital.

The final implosive sessions involved real unwashed underwear that Mr. C. had brought from home. Mrs. C. had to reach into the bag with her eyes closed and handle the dirty underwear. This in vivo exposure helped Mrs. C. confront not only situational stimuli but also her maladaptive cognitions that magnified out of all proportion the dangers of dirty underwear.

By the end of Mrs. C.'s six-week stay in the clinic, the sign-in sheets indicated a dramatic decrease in the frequency and duration of her washing compulsion. The biggest change came after the fourth implosive scene, in which Mrs. C. was to imagine physically attacking her father. During this session, Mrs. C. was in a psychophysiological lab and was wired to seven different channels for measuring aspects of anxiety. As the session progressed, Mrs. C. reported that she was having trouble with the scene. She could imagine the scene all right, but she was not able to feel emotions as she had in previous scenes. Recognizing her reaction as a form of defensive isolation, I told her to really let go, to strike out with her hand and tell him what a bastard he was, to tell the son of a bitch she was glad he was suffering as he had made her suffer. Suddenly she began hacking away at the table and swearing, sobbing, and shaking. The seven anxiety channels all went off the recording paper, as Mrs. C. opened up for the last 15 or 20 minutes of the session. She then went up to her room and, with a nurse present, continued to relive the scene for over an hour with considerable affect expressed. The next morning, she again relived the scene until she felt emotionally drained.

Mrs. C.'s Outcome

After this intensive course of treatment, Mrs. C. looked and felt considerably better. She now reported being able to pick up such things as a ball of yarn off the floor. She could accept a drink of soda from the same can from which a hippie-type youngster had been drinking; previously she would not even get near such an unclean person. Her showers and handwashing responses were down to average times, and Mrs. C. was ready to return home.

Fortunately, Mrs. C.'s family had been willing to use stimulus control to change their environmental conditions, both for their own sakes and for Mrs. C.'s. They had been painting, repairing, and redecorating the house, which had come to look like a city dump. On her first weekend home, Mrs. C. joined right in and directed the discarding of all the junk she had retained for years. Her children and their friends formed a long line, and Mrs. C. handed them boxes of dresses, towels, and assorted items to be picked up by the trash truck. Mrs. C. genuinely enjoyed the sense of freedom of being able to let go.

To our surprise, she was also able to let go sexually with her husband more than she ever had in her life. The first day home, they went up to their bedroom in the daytime, which they had never done before, and really enjoyed making love. Mr. C. blurted out spontaneously, "This isn't the girl I married!" A few months later, Mrs. C. experienced her first orgasm at the age of 47.

The family was amazed at Mrs. C.'s newfound freedom. The kids reported her doing things they could never imagine, such as getting down on the floor and playing with them or picking up a cookie off the new rug, brushing it off, and eating it. She was cooking special meals, helping with the cleaning, and allowing her children to have their friends over.

Mr. C. said that he was amazed by his wife's improvement but also troubled because he had always thought of himself as better adjusted than she was, whereas now she seemed healthier. I offered him some implosive sessions, but he declined with a smile, saying he could learn to adjust all right.

After some initial enthusiasm at being home and feeling good, there were the predictable setbacks. Mrs. C. was generally more tense at home than in the clinic. Part of her anxiety derived from trying to give to six children after having been withdrawn from them for so long. She was especially troubled by the guilt she felt over the emotional problems she believed she had helped cause in her second son. Even though her son was receiving psychotherapy, Mrs. C. still felt that her guilt was authentic, and all she could do was continue her commitment of trying to be available emotionally to her children when they needed her.

Mrs. C. experienced some trouble limiting her morning shower to five minutes. She felt much more anxious in her shower at home, which had been the scene of so many repetitions of her irrational ritual. So I went to the house and imploded Mrs. C. in her shower (while she was fully clothed, of course).

Mrs. C. also experienced a mild depressive reaction when I left the clinic and our therapeutic relationship was terminated. My supervisor, who continued to see her on a monthly basis, half-jokingly suggested to me that her dramatic improvement seemed to be the result of her having fallen for me and thus trying very hard to please me. I told him that his explanation sounded an awful lot like a "transference cure" explanation for a behaviorist like himself!

The last I heard of Mrs. C. was two years posttermination. She was continuing to function much more autonomously. Her morning shower was occasionally giving her problems, but what empowered her most was a new job that would not tolerate her being late. There was no denying that Mrs. C. could still be characterized as an obsessive-compulsive personality, but her needs for cleanliness and neatness were more under self-control. She had regained sufficient autonomy to reassert the commitment she had made many years before: to share her life with her family rather than wasting it in a compulsion to wash.

The Future of Psychotherapy

In this concluding section, we extract and amplify important trends in psychotherapy as we enter the 21st century. We begin by reviewing the results of a Delphi poll completed by 75 preeminent authorities on psychotherapy (Norcross, Alford, & DeMichele, 1992). Then, by integrating converging developments articulated in the preceding chapters and in other sources (e.g., Freedheim, 1992; Norcross, 1992), we sketch ten emerging themes for psychotherapy practice.

Delphi Poll

The volatile and impermanent nature of the psychotherapy discipline has created a pressing need for both professional and lay people to identify trends that will affect service delivery, research programs, clinical training, and policy decisions. However, Yalom (1975, p. 204) has cautioned that only a truly intrepid observer would attempt to differentiate evanescent from potentially important and durable trends in the field. Furthermore, as Ekstein (1972) has warned, many predictions in the uncertain world of psychotherapy tend to be self-fulfilling prophecies or magical wish-fulfillments.

For these reasons, we attempted to secure the consensus of a panel of experts, representing commitments to diverse orientations, and to elicit their prediction of what *will happen,* not what they personally would like to happen (tempting as that might be). We were principally concerned with the "big picture" or "megatrends" confronting the discipline as it enters a new millennium.

We employed a sensitive forecasting method—the Delphi poll—to predict the future of psychotherapy in the United States for the next ten years. Named in honor of the ancient oracle, Delphi polling structures a group communication so that the process is effective in allowing a group of individuals, as a whole, to deal with a complex problem. A panel of experts answers the same questions at least twice. In the first phase, the experts answer the questions anonymously and without feedback. In subsequent phases, the experts are provided with the names and views of the entire panel and given the opportunity to revise their predictions in light of the group judgment (Linstone & Turoff, 1975).

Consistent with the commonly held notion that "two (or more) heads are better than one," the Delphi poll takes systematic advantage of multiple and interactive expert perspectives (Dalkey & Helmer, 1963; Moore, 1987). The particular virtues of Delphi methodology are (1) that it consistently provides the closest answer to extremely difficult questions compared to other prognostication techniques; (2) the responses from the second phase are typically less variable and hence less ambiguous than those of the first; and (3) group consensus has been found to be more accurate than individual expert opinion (Ascher, 1978; Linstone & Turoff, 1975).

These 75 intrepid observers first forecasted the extent to which specific therapeutic interventions and techniques would be increasingly or decreasingly employed over the next ten years. Of the 33 therapeutic interventions, 14 obtained mean ratings between "remain same" and "slight increase." In ascending order of predicted increase, they were as follows: confrontation, therapist self-disclosure, biofeedback, accurate empathy, reassurance, relaxation techniques, behavior modification, bibliotherapy, expressing support/warmth, teaching/advising, computerized therapies, behavioral contracting, imagery and fantasy, and self-control procedures. Eight obtained a mean rating between "slight increase" and "moderate increase": assertion/social skills training, in vivo exposure, cognitive restructuring, communication skills, homework assignments, audio/video feedback, problem-solving techniques, and self-change techniques.

Of the 11 interventions expected to be decreasingly employed over the next ten years, 6 were given mean ratings between "remain same" and "slight decrease" and 5 between "slight decrease" and "moderate decrease." In ascending order of predicted decrease, these were as follows: paradoxical interventions, hypnosis, systematic desensitization, cathartic methods, analysis of resistance, transference interpretation, emotional flooding/implosion, free association, and aversive conditioning.

Among therapy formats/modalities, seven out of nine were predicted to increase in the future. Those predicted to increase were individual therapy, group therapy, conjoint family therapy, marital/couples therapy, crisis intervention therapy, psychoeducational classes for specific disorders, and short-term therapy. Those predicted to decrease were network therapy and long-term therapy. Long-term therapy's predicted decrease was 3.4 points below that of short-term therapy (the modality predicted to increase the most of all).

The composite predictions on the fate of 14 theoretical orientations are shown in Table 15.5. As shown in the table, seven were predicted to increase and seven to decrease. Those predicted to increase, in ascending order of increase, were feminist, behavioral, psychobiological, theoretical integration, cognitive, technical eclecticism, and systems/family systems. Predicted to decrease were humanistic, psychodynamic/neo-Freudian, client/person-centered, existential, neurolinguistic programming, psychoanalytic, and transactional analysis.

These experts' composite ratings portend "what's hot and what's not" as we enter the 21st century. In terms of interventions and modalities, the consensus is that psychotherapy will become more directive, psychoeducational, present-centered, problem-focused, and briefer in the next decade. Concomitantly, aversive, relatively unstructured, historically oriented, and long-term approaches are predicted to decrease. In terms of therapy formats, individual, couples, family, and

Table 15.5 Composite Predictions of Theoretical Orientations of the Future

Orientations	Mean*	SD
Systems/family systems	5.32	1.10
Technical eclecticism	5.23	0.97
Cognitive	5.15	0.93
Theoretical integration	5.01	0.93
Psychobiological	4.96	1.04
Behavioral	4.70	0.95
Feminist	4.21	1.14
Humanistic	3.53	1.06
Psychodynamic/neo-Freudian	3.47	1.01
Client/person-centered	3.22	0.83
Existential	3.15	0.93
Neurolinguistic programming	2.80	1.15
Psychoanalytic	2.68	0.87
Transactional analysis	2.37	0.82

*1 = great decrease, 4 = remain the same, 7 = great increase.
Adapted from Norcross, Alford, & DeMichele (1992).

group therapy are seen as continuing their upward swing, but the huge transformation is expected in the length of therapy: short-term is in, and long-term is on its way out. In terms of theoretical orientations, integrative, eclectic, systems, and cognitive persuasions will thrive, but classic psychoanalysis, humanistic, and existentialism will not. The latter, however, will probably continue to exert significant influence through integrative and eclectic psychotherapies.

Emerging Directions

By immersing ourselves in the content of this book and the psychotherapy literature, we have been able to discern several nascent directions for the future of psychotherapy. Several of these themes represent a continuation of contemporary trends, while others portend a future discontinuous with our past. There is little need here to amplify directions that are widely recognized as having "come of age," such as psychotherapy integration and brief therapy. Instead, we choose to give voice to ten newer directions.

1. Industrialization of Mental Health Care. We begin our whirlwind tour of the future of psychotherapy by addressing the rhinoceros in the living room: managed care. Managed care now covers 75% of the Americans who attain their health benefits through their jobs and the percentage is slowly increasing.

It would be inaccurate to lump all managed care into a monolithic entity, so let us broadly frame the concern as "industrialization." Following are the common mechanisms of managing psychotherapy:

- restricting access to treatment (e.g., only "medically necessary" services for Axis I disorders)
- limiting the amount of psychotherapy (e.g., 4 to 12 sessions)
- using lowest cost providers (e.g., master's- and baccalaureate-level therapists)
- implementing utilization review (e.g., after 5 or 6 sessions)
- approving primarily short-term, symptom-focused psychotherapies
- shifting to outpatient care (e.g., only hospitalize if suicide attempt)
- referrals through gatekeepers (e.g., only through primary care physicians)
- restricting patient's freedom of choice in providers and treatments

Health care is manifesting the two cardinal characteristics of any industrial revolution (Cummings, 1986, 1987). First, the producer—in our case, the psychotherapist—is losing control over the services as this control shifts to business interests. Second, practitioners' income are decreasing because industrialization requires cheap labor.

In our recent study of clinical psychologists, we discovered that 75% accept some managed care patients and 25% accept none. In fact, the median percentages of managed care patients in psychologists' caseload expanded tenfold —from 5% to 50%—from 1993 to 1997 (Norcross, Karg, & Prochaska, 1997). These are the footprints of a rhinoceros tramping across the landscape of psychotherapy.

While we do not subscribe to the Cassandran prophecies of the demise of psychotherapy, we recognize that in the new millennium, psychotherapy will increasingly be performed in the public marketplace by subdoctoral professionals for briefer intervals and according to practice guidelines. Some clinicians will find opportunities in the transformation, while others will curse the change, but all will be profoundly influenced by these socioeconomic forces.

2. Practice Guidelines. Insurance carriers are increasingly turning to *practice guidelines* to determine which psychotherapies to approve and fund. Professional associations and government agencies are issuing such guidelines in order to foster evidence-based practice by educating clinicians about the research base for clinical practice. The American Psychiatric Association has promulgated eight published practice guidelines, on disorders ranging from schizophrenia to anorexia to nicotine dependence. The American Psychological Association's Division of Clinical Psychology has identified empirically supported psychological interventions for adults and has begun to publicize the existence of these treatments to fellow psychologists and training programs. A succession of task forces has constructed and elaborated a list of empirically validated, manualized treatments for specific disorders based on randomized controlled studies which pass muster for methodological rigor (Chambless, 1998). In the case of OCD, like Mrs. C.'s, exposure with response prevention is listed as a "well-established treatment" and cognitive therapy and relapse prevention are listed as "probably efficacious treatments."

The movement toward proactive guidelines has been widely lauded and widely condemned; we do not wish to enter the debate here except to point out that such guidelines favor cognitive-behavioral treatments, which have been subjected to far more empirical research than other therapies, and manualized treatments, which are frequently a requirement for consideration. The point is this: however controversial, practice guidelines are growing in number and influence. Clinical practice in the new millennium will be expected to adhere to them—for better and for worse.

3. Self-Help Resources. Converging forces will contribute to the proliferation of self-help organizations, self-change materials, and psychoeducational groups for specific disorders. One force is managed care: brief professional treatment means that adjunctive and ancillary methods must be incorporated to secure sufficient gains. A second force is their widespread availability and lower costs. Another force is their effectiveness. In a review of the empirical evidence on the rate at which neurotic patients improve on their own, without professional treatment, Lambert (1976) found that a median of 43% of people demonstrate improvement. Gould and Clum (1993) conducted a meta-analysis on the effectiveness of 40 self-help studies that used no-treatment, waitlist, or placebo comparisons as control groups. The effect size for self-help treatments was nearly as large as therapist-assisted interventions within the same studies. Fears, depression, headache, and sleep disturbance were especially amenable to self-help approaches. In another meta-analysis (Cuijpers, 1997) involving six studies comparing bibliotherapy (with no or minimal therapist contact) to waitlist, the mean effect size for bibliotherapy was .82, a large effect indeed.

For multiple reasons, then, people in their natural environments and psychotherapists in their consulting rooms recommend self-help and self-change resources. In any given year, for example, 87% of surveyed therapists recommend a self-help/support group to patients and 85% recommend a self-help book (Clifford, Norcross, & Sommer, 1998). As was evident in our experts' forecast of the future, mental health professionals will provide clients with information to change on their own and recommend "do-it-yourself" therapies. In fact, according to the Delphi poll, self-help groups are destined to flourish more than any other psychotherapy provider.

4. Technological Applications. Psychotherapy has been relatively immune from the information revolution: Two people speaking to each other in the privacy and immediacy of the consulting room remains the prototypical format. But the information age will soon dramatically change psychotherapy in the forms of computer-assisted treatment, telepsychotherapy, virtual reality treatment, and on-line counseling. In place of, as the old saying goes, psychotherapy only needing two people, an office, and a box of tissues, in the 21st century we might only require two people and a computer.

The unique features of computers will prove advantageous in treating behavioral/mental disorders in multiple ways. Computer tools may reduce the cost of treatment, improve access to psychotherapy, provide psychoeducation, promote self-monitoring, rehearse coping skills, store and display data, provide outcome measures, and function reliably without fatigue (Wright & Wright, 1997). Computer-assisted psychotherapy has been readily accepted by patients, and the early research has demonstrated its effectiveness.

Computer technology has enabled *virtual therapy,* the use of virtual reality as a therapeutic intervention in the treatment of anxiety disorders. Patients are immersed in computer-generated environments using a head-mounted display that covers their eyes. This treatment provides controlled, safe exposure in which the patient can be introduced to anxiety-producing situations, such as heights, air flight, and open spaces. The results of controlled research are promising (Glantz et al., 1996; Lamson, 1997) and presage increased experimentation.

At the same time, we fully expect the emergence of psychotherapy by telephone, videotelephone, and videoconferencing. This has been labeled *telepsychotherapy:* psychological treatment conducted by a therapist at a location different from the patient's through bidirectional communication technology supporting real-time interactivity in the audio, audiovisual, or text modalities (Kaplan, 1997). Imagine conducting psychotherapy from around the country or around the world at any hour of the day—that's what live, on-line counseling services now offer on the Internet. Although fraught with ethical and logistical concerns, various types of telepsychotherapy are destined to proliferate. The information revolution will assuredly arrive in psychotherapy.

5. Pluralism. One of the remarkable events of modern society is how quickly professions change and diversify. Only 100 years ago, a veritable wink of the eye in a historical sense, psychotherapy was practiced almost exclusively in an individual format by medically trained men in independent practice from a psychoanalytic perspective in Vienna. This textbook on contemporary psychotherapies underscores the burgeoning pluralism of the psychotherapeutic scene.

Consider the expanding host of settings for the practice of psychotherapy: private practice, universities, psychiatric hospitals, child and family guidance centers, schools, work sites, HMOs, community mental health centers, prisons, the military, and so forth. Each setting provides differing patient populations, and thus influences views on the best means for facilitating psychological and behavior change. Broader availability of psychotherapeutic services also begets pluralism of another sort: creation of psychotherapeutic interventions and theories for a fuller range of behavioral dysfunctions (VandenBos, Cummings, & DeLeon, 1992).

Additionally, pluralism is evident in the range of therapy providers and formats. The entire chapter on gender- and culture-sensitive therapies begins to counterbalance historical androcentric and white biases. Going beyond the critique of psychotherapy as male-centered and culturally insensitive, these perspectives document new concepts and methods predicated upon a pluralistic perspective. Although initially dominated by psychiatrists and psychoanalysts, psychotherapy is now primarily conducted by nonmedical and nonpsychoanalytic clinicians. Psychologists outnumber psychiatrists as health service providers, and clinical social workers outnumber both combined. Where individual therapy once dominated, recent research (for example, Norcross, Karg, & Prochaska, 1997) and the foregoing chapters demonstrate that the majority of psychotherapists routinely conduct marital/couples and conjoint family therapy.

Pluralism must be reconciled, of course, with client benefit and empirical validation. While applauding theoretical innovation and creative application of a variety of research designs, Strupp and Howard (1992) remind us of the scientific requirement to demonstrate the relative efficacy of these new approaches. Uncritical acceptance is not prized. This view is embodied in the distinction between informed pluralism and uninformed faith. As the Maharasi of Jaipur was once reported to have said: "Keep an open mind; an open mind is a very good thing. But don't keep your mind so open that your brains fall out."

6. *Prescriptionism.* Abraham Maslow was fond of repeating the adage, "If you only have a hammer, you treat everything like a nail." The history of psychotherapy has repeatedly confirmed this observation. Sad to say, the preponderance of contemporary clinicians probably still reach for their favorite tool when confronted with puzzling problems. It is all too common for clinicians to recommend the identical treatment—their treasured proficiency—to virtually every patient who crosses their paths (Norcross, 1985a).

In the future, psychotherapy providers will become discriminating craftworkers who go beyond subjective preference, institutional custom, and immediate availability to predicate their treatment selection on patient need and comparative outcome research. That is, they will develop and employ an expanded toolbox instead of senselessly "hammering away" at anything remotely similar to a nail.

Prescriptionism is concerned with that elusive, empirically driven match among patient, disorder, and treatment (Norcross, 1991). With increasing refinement in the categorization of disorders and more precise delineation of change strategies, further advances in prescriptive treatment are likely. At that point, effective therapy will be "defined not by its brand name, but by how well it meets the need of the patient" (Weiner, 1975, p. 44). In other words, the question will no longer be "Does it work?" but rather "Does it work *best* for this client?"

The need to match patient and treatment has been recognized from the beginning of psychotherapy (Frances, 1988). As early as 1919, Freud introduced psychoanalytic psychotherapy as an alternative to classical analysis on the recognition that the more rarefied approach lacked universal applicability and that many patients did not possess the requisite psychological-mindedness (Liff, 1992). He referred the majority of so-called "unanalyzable" patients for a psychotherapy based on direct suggestion. The subsequent evolution of psychoanalytic work was, in part, refinement on the basis of differential patient need.

Clinical wisdom and empirical research indicate a slowly expanding number of prescriptive matches. Different rates of response to different psychotherapy procedures are predicted by patients' coping style and reactance levels, for example. Ongoing research (for example, Beutler, Engle, Mohr, et al., 1991; Beutler, Mohr, Grawe, Engle, & MacDonald, 1991) has found, among diagnostically homogeneous groups, that directive treatments are more effective than nondirective ones with low-resistance patients. Treatments focusing most explicitly on overt behavior are differentially effective over internally focused approaches with clients with externalizing coping styles.

Among the more important achievements of psychotherapy research is the demonstration of the differential efficacy of a few therapies with specific disorders. These include behavior therapy for specific symptoms and childhood aggression, systemic therapy for marital conflict, and cognitive and interpersonal therapies for depression. This desideratum of specificity has enormous potential implications for the future, including development of more focused therapeutic strategies, provision of sharper answers to the question of what psychotherapy can do for particular patients, and generation of optimal matches among therapists, patients, and treatments.

The emerging theme of prescriptionism—also known as differential therapeutics, treatment matching, and the specificity factor—will complement, rather than replace, the "common factors" approach. The fact that disparate therapy methods sometime secure comparable outcomes, the "equivalence paradox" (Stiles, Shapiro, & Elliott, 1986), supports the immense power of therapeutic commonalities, but does not preclude specific effects of certain psychotherapies. The nascent consensus on the specific versus common factors controversy is that it is not either/or, not a dualism. We have begun to transcend the dichotomy and progress toward combining the power of commonalities and the pragmatics of specificity. The emerging direction is for the potency of therapeutic commonalities to be accentuated by matching strategies.

7. Therapeutic Alliance. The two previous themes, we predict, will converge to produce a renewed but modified emphasis on the therapeutic alliance. Pluralism will contribute a heightened sensitivity to the interpersonal relationship and remind us that the value of a clinical intervention is inextricably bound to the relational context in which it is applied; prescriptionism will remind us that a unitary therapeutic relationship cannot suffice for diverse clients and will mandate that therapists tailor interpersonal stances and styles to fit the unique needs of individual clients.

Specific delineations among therapeutic technique, strategy, and relationship are nearly impossible in practice, as all three are interwoven in the contextual fabric of psychotherapy. Hans Strupp (1986) has offered an analogy to illustrate the inseparability of the constituent elements of psychotherapy: Suppose you want a teenage son to clean his room. One technique for achieving this is to establish clear standards. Fine, but the effectiveness of this technique will vary depending on whether the relationship between you and the boy is characterized by warmth and mutual respect or by anger and distrust. This is not to say that the technique is useless, merely that how well it works depends on the context in which it is used.

There is virtual unanimity among the contributors and reviewers of the outcome research that the therapist–patient relationship is central to positive change. Moreover, strong consensus is arising that a facilitative therapeutic alliance is a common, transtheoretical feature (Grencavage & Norcross, 1990). A unique and early article published by a number of psychoanalytic psychotherapists, for example, reported their intensive observations of two leading behavior therapists (Arnold Lazarus and Joseph Wolpe) for a week. Klein, Dittman, Parloff, and Gill (1969) found that the therapeutic relationship exerted far more power in behavior therapy than had previously been recognized. Behavior therapists and other clinicians who previously slighted the curative power of the therapeutic relationship are now emphasizing it to a far greater extent than in the earlier literature (Glass & Arnkoff, 1992). The current emphasis on the therapeutic relationship in cognitive therapy and psychotherapy integration is likely to grow as well.

A similar trend is evident in psychoanalytic practice and research. A decisive shift involving a relative deemphasis on interpretation and insight and increasing emphasis on the therapist–patient interaction (see Chapter 2) reflects a growing awareness of contextual and relational influences. Concomitant shifts are also visible in the reconceptualization of transference and countertransference to reflect a more interactional, two-person view of the treatment. Working from a time-limited psychodynamic perspective, Luborsky (1992) reviewed eight studies and discerned significant positive correlations between the alliance measured in the early sessions and the outcome of treatment, an impressively consistent pattern in a field fraught with nonsignificant and contradictory findings.

Systematic studies on relational "matchmaking" in psychotherapy (for example, Talley, Strupp, & Morey, 1990) will examine the commonly shared perception among therapists of feeling better suited to deal interpersonally with some patients than with others. The accumulating empirical literature will then be able to generate prescriptive matching decisions for use of interpersonal as well as technical interventions in specific circumstances (Norcross, 1993).

8. Relapse Prevention. Although psychotherapy is typically effective in the short-run, relapse is the most common, long-term outcome in the treatment of addictions and serious mental disorders. In a classic review of outcome literature on alcoholics, heroin addicts and habitual smokers, relapse curves across these different substances showed a strikingly similar pattern. Within three months of treatment completion, nearly two-thirds of all patients had relapsed, with a majority of these relapses occurring within the first month following treatment termination (Hunt, Barnett, & Branch, 1971). Early treatment approaches focused on changing behavior but not necessarily on maintaining those changes over time. This resulted in a "revolving door" or "recycling" in which treatment completers returned to treatment following each relapse (Roberts & Marlatt, 1998).

As a result of the ubiquity of relapse, increasing emphasis has been placed on the maintenance stage. *Relapse Prevention* (RP) offers an alternative to the revolving door through an integration of behavioral skills training, cognitive interventions, and lifestyle changes (Marlatt & Gordon, 1985). Although initially developed for alcoholics and drug addicts, the principles of RP have been adapted to other behavioral disorders.

Relapse prevention is a self-management training program designed to enhance the maintenance stage of the change cycle. With skills training as the cornerstone, RP teaches clients how to:

- understand relapse as a process;
- identify high risk situations;
- learn how to cope with cravings and urges to engage in the addictive behavior;

■   reduce the harm of relapse by minimizing the negative consequences and learning from the experience; and

■   achieve a balanced lifestyle, centered on the fulcrum of moderation (Roberts & Marlatt, 1998).

Reviews of the accumulating research on RP yield encouraging findings in the treatment of problem drinkers, tobacco smokers, substance abusers, depressed patients, and obese people (Carroll, 1996; Wilson, 1996). At the very least, relapse prevention was found to be more effective than no-treatment controls. At the most, several relapse prevention outcome studies revealed a delayed emergence of effects: patient receiving relapse prevention did better than patients receiving alternative treatments at follow-up (Carroll, 1996).

With the advent of mandated brief therapy and with the high prevalence of recycling, psychotherapists in the future will regularly attend to maintenance strategies and will frequently train patients in relapse prevention.

9. Population-based Interventions. In the new health care system, all projections are that opportunities will shrink for doctoral-level psychotherapists as psychotherapy providers since the bulk of psychotherapy will be performed by master's- and baccalaureate-level professionals. Those same projections indicate, however, that psychotherapists will increasingly be asked to serve as supervisors, researchers, administrators, and consultants with regard to service provision to individual patients and, equally important, as experts in population-based interventions. A revolution in the science and practice of behavioral health could meet huge unmet needs and create magnificent positions for mental health professionals. This revolution will entail a shift from the action paradigm to a stage paradigm (described earlier in this chapter), from case management to population management, from a biomedical focus to a behavioral health focus, and from reactive to proactive practice.

Over 50% of health care costs are due to behaviors (Prochaska, 1996). Smoking, alcohol abuse, obesity, depression, and stress are the most costly conditions in our society. They are costly to individuals, their families, employers, communities, and health care systems. Yet, as behavior health is currently practiced, less than 10% of these conditions are treated effectively. Most often these problems are undiagnosed or misdiagnosed, untreated or mistreated.

In a population-based program, we would proactively reach out and assess the needs of an entire population in a health care organization and determine what stage of change they are in. Then we would match therapeutic interventions to their stage of change. We would apply a step-care approach, starting with the least costly help, such as self-help resources. If these work, great. If not, we would step up to a more intensive treatment, for example technological applications such as multimedia interactive programs delivered over the Internet. If more help is needed we could add telephone counseling. Face-to-face psychotherapy would be saved for the most complicated cases, such as individuals with multiple diagnoses, for example smoking, alcoholism, and major depression. Such population-based, behavior health interventions would transform our health care systems by emphasizing disease prevention and health promotion and by treating the behavioral causes of chronic diseases, not just the biological symptoms.

10. Psychotherapy Works! The controlled outcome research reviewed in the preceding chapters consistently attests to the effectiveness of those psychotherapies rigorously evaluated to date. Whether one prefers to rely on the over 1,000 individual studies or the dozens of meta-analyses, well-developed psychological interventions have meaningful, positive effects on the intended outcome variables (Lipsey & Wilson, 1993). At the end of the psychotherapy, the average treated person is better off than 80% of untreated people. In a series of intriguing comparisons between the effects of psychotherapy and the effects of biomedicine, Rosenthal (1990, 1995) has convincingly demonstrated that the typical magnitudes of psychotherapy are of great practical importance, rivaling and exceeding the magnitude of effect often found in biomedical breakthroughs.

A case in point is the treatment of clinical depression. Popular belief holds that antidepressant medications, particularly the selective serotonin reuptake inhibitors, are plainly the most potent treatment for depression. But, in fact, there is no stronger medicine for depression than psychotherapy (Antonuccio, 1995; Antonuccio, Danton, & DeNelsky, 1994). The preponderance of available scientific evidence shows that psychotherapy, particularly cognitive-behavioral and interpersonal therapies, are generally as effective or more effective than medications in treating depression, especially when patient-rated measures and long-term follow-ups are considered. This is not to devalue the salutary impact of antidepressants; rather, it is to underscore the reliable potency of psychotherapy (Munoz et al., 1994).

Nor is this to say that nothing more needs to be researched; on the contrary, we must all do better and must all better understand the active ingredients of successful psychotherapy. The proper agenda for the next generation of psychotherapy research is to investigate which treatment variables are most effective, the mediating causal processes through which they work, and the therapist characteristics that maximize improvement. Determining what works for whom—the prescriptive mandate —is also part of the research agenda (Ross & Fonagy, 1996). The question is no longer whether it works, but how it works and how it can be made to work better (Lipsey & Wilson, 1993).

To reiterate the future direction: Providers, consumers, policymakers, and payers alike will increasingly come to recognize the considerable science supporting the efficacy of psychotherapy. The science of effect sizes and probability values, we must remember, translate into vital human statistics: happier and healthier people.

In Closing

Psychotherapy has a short history but, we are confident, a long and prosperous future. Concerned as we are about the possibility of Draconian cuts in funding for mental health services, we are equally excited about psychotherapy in the future. Exactly how that future will look in 25 years, or even in 10, is not easy to predict.

In some ways, we hope that human behavior will remain as mysterious as it often is, but that the wondrous effects of psychotherapy will become more predictable and increasingly widespread.

The creative and committed psychotherapist, like the Roman god Janus, must look simultaneously forward and backward (Rothenberg, 1988). In the Janusian tradition, we hope our efforts in this book have captured the sizable knowledge from our past and have embodied our enthusiastic pursuit of the future.

Suggestions for Further Reading

Gabbard, G. O. (Ed.). (1995). *Treatments of psychiatric disorders.* (2nd ed.). Washington, DC: American Psychiatric Press.

Hoyt, M. F. (1995). *Brief therapy and managed care.* San Francisco: Jossey-Bass.

Mahoney, M. J. (1991). *Human change processes: The scientific foundations of psychotherapy.* New York: Basic.

Nathan, P. E., & Gorman, J. M. (Eds.). (1988). *A guide to treatments that work.* New York: Oxford University Press.

Norcross, J. C. (Ed.). (1992). The future of psychotherapy [Special issue]. *Psychotherapy, 29*(1).

Prochaska, J. O., & DiClemente, C. C. (1984). *The transtheoretical approach: Crossing the traditional boundaries of therapy.* Homewood, IL: Dow Jones—Irwin.

Prochaska, J. O., DiClemente, C. C., & Norcross, J. C. (1992). In search of how people change: Applications to addictive behaviors. *American Psychologist, 47,* 1102–1114.

Prochaska, J. O., Norcross, J. C., & DiClemente, C. C. (1995). *Changing for good.* New York: Avon.

Rosenblatt, A. D. (Ed.). (1991). *Psychotherapy in the future* (GAP Report #133). Washington, DC: American Psychiatric Press.

Ross, A. & Fonagy, P. (1996). *What works for whom? A critical review of psychotherapy research.* New York: Guilford.

Appendix:
An Alternative Table
of Contents

1. Defining and Comparing the Psychotherapies: An Integrative Framework (all of Chapter 1)

Defining Psychotherapy. The Role of Theory. Therapeutic Commonalities. Processes of Change: *Consciousness Raising; Catharsis; Choosing; Conditional Stimuli; Contingency Control*. Initial Integration of Processes of Change. Therapeutic Content. The Case of Mrs. C. Suggestions for Further Reading.

2. Therapeutic Relationship

3. Consciousness Raising—Feedback

4. Consciousness Raising—Education

In Psychoanalytic Therapies (pp. 38–39). In Adlerian Therapy (pp. 78–79). In Existential Therapy (pp. 108–109). In Person-Centered Therapy (pp. 143–145). In Gestalt Therapy (pp. 172–174). In Transactional Analysis (pp. 210–212). In Interpersonal Therapy (pp. 211–212). In Cognitive Therapies (pp. 328–329). In Bowen Family Systems Therapy (pp. 382–383). In Feminist Therapy (pp. 407–408). In Culture-Sensitive Therapy (pp. 422–423). In Multimodal Therapy (p. 475). A Transactional Analysis of Mrs. C. (pp. 229–231). A Systemic Analysis of Mrs. C. (pp. 394–396).

5. Catharsis

In Person-Centered Therapy (pp. 145–146). In Gestalt Therapy (pp. 174–177). In Reichian Therapy (pp. 241–243). In Implosive Therapy (pp. 249–251). Implosive Therapy with Mrs. C. (pp. 266–269). A Gestalt Analysis of Mrs. C. (pp. 193–195).

6. Choosing—Self-Liberation

In Adlerian Therapy (p. 80). In Existential Therapies (pp. 109–111). In Communication/Strategic Therapy (pp. 366–368). In Bowenian Family Therapy (pp. 383–384). In Feminist Therapy (p. 410). In Culture-Sensitive Therapies (p. 424). In Solution-Focused Therapy (pp. 442–444). An Existential Analysis of Mrs. C. (pp. 128–130). A Narrative Analysis by Mrs. C. (pp. 453–455).

7. Choosing—Social Liberation

In Adlerian Therapy (p. 80). In Transactional Analysis (p. 213). In Structural Therapy (pp. 376–378). In Feminist Therapy (pp. 410–412). In Culture-Sensitive Therapy (p. 424). A Feminist Analysis of Mrs. C. (pp. 432–434).

8. Self-Reevaluation

In Cognitive Therapies (pp. 331–332). A Rational-Emotive Analysis of Mrs. C. (pp. 351–354).

9. Stimulus Control

In Behavior Therapy (pp. 272–273; 277–279). In Multimodal Therapy (pp. 467–469). A Behavioral Analysis of Mrs. C. (pp. 316–318).

10. Counterconditioning

In Exposure Therapy (p. 254). In EMDR (pp. 259–261). In Behavior Therapies (pp. 275, 285). In Cognitive Therapies (p. 332). In Multimodal Therapy (pp. 475). A Multimodal Analysis of Mrs. C. (pp. 483–485).

11. Contingency Management

In Behavior Therapies (pp. 285–295). In Cognitive Therapies (pp. 331–332). A Behavioral Analysis of Mrs. C. (pp. 316–318).

12. Effectiveness of the Psychotherapies

In Psychoanalytic Therapies (pp. 55–66). In Adlerian Therapy (p. 87). In Existential Therapies (pp. 125–126). In Person-Centered Therapy (pp. 154–156). In Gestalt Therapy (pp. 190–191). In Interpersonal Therapies (pp. 224–227). In Exposure and Flooding Therapies (pp. 243; 252–253; 256–257; 262–263). In Behavior Therapies (pp. 305–313). In Cognitive Therapies (pp. 345–349). In Systemic Therapies (pp. 386–390). In Feminist Therapy (pp. 416–417). In Culture-Sensitive Therapies (pp. 429–430). In Constructivist Therapies (pp. 449–450). In Integrative Psychodynamic-Behavior Therapy (p. 471). In Multimodal Therapy (pp. 479–480).

13. Future Directions in Psychotherapy

In Psychoanalytic Therapies (pp. 66–67). In Adlerian Therapy (pp. 91–92). In Existential Therapies (pp. 130–131). In Person-Centered Therapy (pp. 160–162). In Gestalt Therapy (pp. 195–196). In Interpersonal Therapies (pp. 231–232). In Exposure and Flooding Therapies (pp. 269–270). In Behavior Therapies (pp. 318–319). In Cognitive Therapies (pp. 354–355). In Systemic Therapies (pp. 396–398). In Gender- and Culture-Sensitive Therapies (pp. 434–435). In Constructivist Therapies (pp. 455–456). In Integrative and Eclectic Therapies (pp. 485–486). In Psychotherapy General (pp. 519–528).

14. Comparative Conclusions: Toward a Transtheoretical Therapy (all of Chapter 15)

Developmental Perspectives. The Transtheoretical Model. Processes of Change. Stages of Change. Integration of Stages and Processes. Levels of Change. Putting it All Together. Prescriptive Matching. The Transtheoretical Relationship. Effectiveness of Transtheoretical Therapy. A Transtheoretical Analysis of Mrs. C. Mrs. C.'s Outcome. The Future of Psychotherapy. Suggestions for Further Reading.

Topics Missing in this Course Organization

A Sketch of the Founder
Theory of Personality
Theory of Psychopathology
Therapeutic Content
Criticisms of the Psychotherapies

References

Abel, J. L. (1993). Exposure with response prevention and serotonergic antidepressants in the treatment of obsessive compulsive disorder: A review and implication for interdisciplinary treatment. *Behaviour Research and Therapy, 31,* 463–478.

Abraham, K. (1927). The influence of oral eroticism on character formation. In K. Abramson (Ed.), *Selected papers.* London: Institute for Psychoanalysis and Hogarth Press.

Abramowitz, J. (1996). Variants of exposure and response prevention in the treatment of obsessive-compulsive disorder: A meta-analysis. *Behavior Therapy, 27,* 583–600.

Abramowitz, J. (1997). Effectiveness of psychological and pharmacological treatments for obsessive-compulsive disorder: A quantitative review. *Journal of Consulting and Clinical Psychology, 65,* 44–52.

Abramowitz, S. I., & Murray, J. (1983). Race effects in psychotherapy. In J. Murray & P. Abramson (Eds.), *Bias in psychotherapy.* New York: Praeger.

Abramson, L. Y., Seligman, M. E., & Teasdale, J. D. (1978). Learned helplessness in humans: Critique and reformulation. *Journal of Abnormal Psychology, 87,* 49–74.

Acierno, R., Hersen, M., van Hasselt, V. B., Tremont, G., & Meuser, K. T. (1994). Review of the validation and dissemination of Eye-Movement Desensitization and Reprocessing. A scientific and ethical dilemma. *Clinical Psychology Review, 14,* 287–299.

Adams, D. B. (1992). The future roles of psychotherapy in the medical-surgical arena. *Psychotherapy, 29,* 95–103.

Adler, A. (1917). *Study of organ inferiority and its physical compensation.* New York: Nervous and Mental Diseases Publishing.

Adler, A. (1929). *Problems of neurosis.* London: Kegan Paul.

Adler, A. (1931). Compulsion neurosis. *International Journal of Individual Psychology, 9,* 1–16.

Adler, A. (1936). The neurotic's picture of the world: A case study. *International Journal of Individual Psychology, 3,* 3–13.

Adler, A. (1964). *Social interest: A challenge to mankind.* New York: Capricorn. (Original work published 1929)

Agras, W. S. (1987). So where do we go from here? *Behavior Therapy, 18,* 203–217.

Agras, W. S., Taylor, C. B., Feldman, D. E., Losch, M., & Burnett, K. F. (1990). Developing computer-assisted therapy for the treatment of obesity. *Behavior Therapy, 21,* 99–109.

Alberts, G., & Edelstein, B. (1990). Therapist training: A critical review of skill training studies. *Clinical Psychology Review, 10,* 497–511.

Alexander, F., & French, T. M. (1946). *Psychoanalytic therapy.* New York: Ronald.

Alexander, J., & Parson, B. (1973). Short-term behavioral intervention with delinquent families: Impact on family process and recidivism. *Journal of Abnormal Psychology, 81,* 219–225.

Alford, B. A., & Beck, A. T. (in press). Therapeutic interpersonal support in cognitive therapy. *Journal of Psychotherapy Integration.*

Alford, B. A., & Beck, A. T. (1997). *The integrative power of cognitive therapy.* New York: Guilford.

Alford, B. A., & Correia, C. J. (1994). Cognitive therapy of schizophrenia: Theory and empirical status. *Behavior Therapy, 25,* 17–33.

Alford, B. A., & Norcross, J. C. (1991). Cognitive therapy as integrative therapy. *Journal of Psychotherapy Integration, 1,* 175–190.

American Psychiatric Association. (1994). *Diagnostic and statistical manual of mental disorders* (4th ed.). Washington, DC: Author

American Psychological Association. (1975). Report of the Task Force on Sex Bias and Sex-Role Stereotyping in Psychotherapeutic Practice. *American Psychologist, 30,* 1169–1175.

American Psychological Association, Task Force on Sex Bias and Sex-Role Stereotyping in Psychotherapeutic Practice. (1978). Guidelines for therapy with women. *American Psychologist, 33,* 1122–1123.

American Psychological Association. (1991). *Guidelines for psychological practice with ethnic and culturally diverse populations.* Washington, DC: Author.

American Psychological Association. (1993). Guidelines for providers of psychological services to ethnic, linguistic, and culturally diverse populations. *American Psychologist, 48,* 45–48.

Ammerman, R. T., Last, C. G., & Hersen, M. (Eds.). (1993). *Handbook of prescriptive treatments for children and adolescents.* Boston: Allyn & Bacon.

Anchin, J., & Kiesler, D. E. (Eds.). (1982). *Handbook of interpersonal psychotherapy.* New York: Pergamon.

Anderson, E. M., & Lambert, M. J. (1995). Short-term dynamically oriented psychotherapy: A review and meta-analysis. *Clinical Psychology Review, 15,* 503–514.

Anderson, W. (1974). Personal growth and client-centered therapy: An information-processing view. In D. Wexler & L. Rice (Eds.), *Innovations in client-centered therapy.* New York: Wiley.

Andrews, J. D., Norcross, J. C., & Halgin, R. P. (1992). Training in psychotherapy integration. In J. C. Norcross & M. R. Goldfried (Eds.), *Handbook of psychotherapy integration.* New York: Basic.

Ansbacher, H. L., & Ansbacher, R. R. (Eds.). (1964). *Superiority and social interest.* New York: Viking.

Antonuccio, D. O. (1995). Psychotherapy for depression: No stronger medicine. *American Psychologist, 50,* 450–452.

Antonuccio, D. O., Danton, W. G., & DeNelsky, G. Y. (1994). Psychotherapy for depression: No stronger medicine. *Scientist Practitioner, 4*(1), 2–18.

Araoz, D. L., & Carrese, M. A. (1996). *Solution-oriented brief therapy for adjustment disorders.* New York: Brunner/Mazel.

Arkowitz, H. (1989). The role of theory in psychotherapy integration. *Journal of Integrative and Eclectic Psychotherapy, 8,* 8–16.

Arkowitz, H. (1992a). A common factors therapy for depression. In J. C. Norcross & M. R. Goldfried (Eds.), *Handbook of psychotherapy integration.* New York: Basic.

Arkowitz, H. (1992b). Integrative theories of therapy. In D. K. Freedheim (Ed.), *History of psychotherapy: A century of change.* Washington, DC: American Psychological Association.

Arkowitz, H., & Messer, S. B. (Eds.). (1984). *Psychoanalytic therapy and behavior therapy: Is integration possible?* New York: Plenum.

Ascher, W. (1978). *Forecasting.* Baltimore: Johns Hopkins University Press.

Atayas, V. (1977). *Psychology and education of beyond adjustment.* Unpublished manuscript, University of Rhode Island Counseling Center.

Atkinson, D. R. (1985). A meta-review of research on cross-cultural counseling and psychotherapy. *Journal of Multicultural Counseling and Development, 13,* 138–153.

Atkinson, D. R., Morten, G., & Sue, D. W. (1989). A minority identity development model. In D. R. Atkinson, G. Morten, & D. W. Sue (Eds.), *Counseling American minorities* (pp. 35–52). Dubuque, IA: W. C. Brown.

Austad, C. S., & Berman, W. H. (1991). *Psychotherapy in managed health care: The optimal use of time and resources.* Hyattsville, MD: American Psychological Association.

Austad, C. S., & Hoyt, M. F. (1992). The managed care movement and the future of psychotherapy. *Psychotherapy, 29,* 109–118.

Austad, C. S., Sherman, W. O., & Holstein, L. (1991). *Psychotherapists in the HMO.* Unpublished manuscript.

Ayllon, T., & Azrin, N. (1968). *The token economy: A motivational system for therapy and rehabilitation.* New York: Appelton-Century-Crofts.

Aylmer, R. (1978). *Family systems therapy.* Workshop presented at the University of Rhode Island, Kingston.

Azrin, N., & Holz, W. (1966). Punishment. In W. Honig (Ed.), *Operant behavior: Areas of research and application.* New York: Appleton-Century-Crofts.

Bachrach, H. M., Galatzer-Levy, R., Skolnikoff, A., & Waldron, S. (1991). On the efficacy of psychoanalysis. *Journal of the American Psychoanalytic Association, 39,* 871–916.

Ballou, M. B. (1990). Approaching a feminist-principled paradigm in the construction of personality theory. In L. S. Brown & M. P. P. Root (Eds.), *Diversity and complexity in feminist therapy* (pp. 23–40). New York: Hawthorne.

Bandura, A. (1969). *Principles of behavior modification.* New York: Holt, Rinehart & Winston.

Bandura, A. (1977). Self-efficacy: Toward a unifying theory of behavior change. *Psychological Review, 84,* 191–215.

Bandura, A. (1982). Self-efficacy mechanism in human agency. *American Psychologist, 37,* 122–147.

Bandura, A., & Menlove, F. (1968). Factors determining vicarious extinction of avoidance behavior through symbolic modeling. *Journal of Personality and Social Psychology, 8,* 99–108.

Barber, J. P., & Luborsky, L. (1991). A psychodynamic view of simple phobias and prescriptive matching: A commentary. *Psychotherapy, 28,* 469–472.

Barber, S. L., Funk, S. C., & Houston, B. K. (1988). Psychological treatment versus nonspecific factors: A meta-analysis of conditions that engender comparable expectations for improvement. *Clinical Psychology Review, 8,* 579–594.

Barker, R. T., & Barker, S. B. (1996). An Adlerian approach to managing organizational change. *Individual Psychology, 52,* 181–192.

Barkley, R. A. (1987). *Defiant children: A clinician's manual for parent training.* New York: Guilford.

Barkley, R. A. (1991). *Attention-deficit hyperactivity disorder.* New York: Guilford.

Barlow, D. H. (1988). *Anxiety and its disorders.* New York: Guilford.

Barlow, D. H., & Beck, J. G. (1984). The psychological treatment of anxiety disorders: Current status, future directions. In J. B. W. Williams & R. L. Spitzer (Eds.), *Psychotherapy research: Where are we and where should we go?* New York: Guilford.

Barlow, D. H., & Cerny, J. A. (1988). *Psychological treatment of panic.* New York: Guilford.

Barlow, D. H., Hayes, S. C., & Nelson, R. O. (1984). *The scientist practitioner: Research and accountability in clinical and educational settings.* New York: Pergamon.

Barlow, D. H., & Lehman, C. L. (1996). Advances in the psychosocial treatment of anxiety disorders. *Archives of General Psychiatry, 53,* 727–735.

Barlow, D. H., & Spiegel, D. A. (1996, July). *Panic-control therapy.* Paper presented at the 10th World Congress of Psychiatry, Madrid, Spain.

Barlow, D. H., & Wolfe, B. (1981). Behavioral approaches to anxiety disorders: A report on the NIMH–SUNY, Albany, research conference. *Journal of Consulting and Clinical Psychology, 49,* 448–454.

Barth, J. (1967). *The end of the road.* New York: Doubleday.

Barton, A. (1974). *Three worlds of therapy.* Palo Alto, CA: National Press Books.

Bateson, G., Jackson, D., Haley, J., & Weakland, J. (1956). Toward a theory of schizophrenia. *Behavioral Sciences, 1,* 251–261.

Basco, M. R., & Rush, A. J. (1996) *Cognitive-behavioral therapy for bipolar disorder.* New York: Guilford.

Baum, M. (1970). Extinction of avoidance responding through response prevention (flooding). *Psychological Bulletin, 74,* 276–284.

de Beauvoir, S. (1961). *The second sex.* New York: Bantam.

Beck, A. T. (1967). *Depression: Clinical, experimental, and theoretical aspects.* New York: Harper & Row.

Beck, A. T. (1970). The core problem in depression: The cognitive triad. In J. Masserman (Ed.), *Depression: Theories and therapies.* New York: Grune & Stratton.

Beck, A. T. (1976). *Cognitive therapy and the emotional disorders.* New York: International Universities Press.

Beck, A. T. (1988). *Love is never enough.* New York: Harper & Row.

Beck, A. T. (1991a). Cognitive therapy: A 30-year retrospective. *American Psychologist, 46,* 368–375.

Beck, A. T. (1991b). Cognitive therapy as *the* integrative therapy. *Journal of Psychotherapy Integration, 1,* 190–194.

Beck, A. T., Emery, G., & Greenberg, R. L. (1985). *Anxiety disorders and phobias: A cognitive perspective.* New York: Basic.

Beck, A. T., & Freeman, A. (1990). *Cognitive therapy of personality disorders.* New York: Guilford.

Beck, A. T., & Haaga, D. A. F. (1992). The future of cognitive therapy. *Psychotherapy, 29,* 34–38.

Beck, A. T., Rush, A. J., Shaw, B, & Emery, G. (1979). *Cognitive therapy of depression.* New York: Guilford.

Beck, A. T., Wright, F. D., Newman, C. F., & Liese, B. S. (1993). *Cognitive therapy of substance abuse.* New York: Guilford.

Beck, J. S. (1995). *Cognitive therapy: Basics and beyond.* New York: Guilford.

Beitman, B. D. (1986). *The structure of individual psychotherapy.* New York: Guilford.

Beitman, B. D. (1989). Why I am an integrationist (not an eclectic). *British Journal of Guidance and Counselling, 17,* 259–273.

Beitman, B. D. (1992). Integration through fundamental similarities and useful differences among the schools. In J. C. Norcross & M. R. Goldfried (Eds.), *Handbook of psychotherapy integration.* New York: Basic.

Beitman, B. D. (in press). Pharmacotherapy and the stages of psychotherapeutic change. *Annual Review of Psychiatry.*

Beitman, B. D., Beck, N. C., Deuser, W. E., Carter, C. S., Davidson, J. R. T., & Maddock, R. J. (1994). Patient stage of change predicts outcome in a panic disorder medication trial. *Anxiety, 1,* 64–69.

Bellis, J. (1976). Emotional flooding and bioenergetic analysis. In P. Olsen (Ed.), *Emotional flooding.* New York: Human Sciences.

Bem, S. L. (1975). Sex-role adaptability: One consequence of psychological androgyny. *Journal of Personality and Social Psychology, 31,* 634–643.

Bem, S. L. (1977). On the utility of alternative procedures for assessing psychological androgyny. *Journal of Consulting and Clinical Psychology, 45,* 196–205.

Benjamin, A. (1987). *The helping interview.* Boston: Houghton Mifflin.

Berg, I. K., & Miller, S. D. (1992). *Working with the problem drinker: A solution-focused approach.* New York: Norton.

Bergin, A. E., & Lambert, M. J. (1978). The evaluation of therapeutic outcomes. In S. L. Garfield & A. E. Bergin (Eds.), *Handbook of psychotherapy and behavior change* (2nd ed.). New York: Wiley.

Berne, E. (1964). *Games people play.* New York: Grove.

Berne, E. (1966). *Principles of group treatment.* New York: Oxford University Press.

Berne, E. (1970). *Sex in human loving.* New York: Simon & Schuster.

Berne, E. (1972). *What do you say after you say hello.* New York: Grove.

Berne, E., Steiner, C., & Dusay, J. (1973). Transactional analysis. In R. Jurjevich (Ed.), *Direct psychotherapy* (Vol. 1). Coral Gables, FL: University of Miami Press.

Beutler, L. E. (1983). *Eclectic psychotherapy: A systematic approach.* New York: Pergamon.

Beutler, L. E. (1991). Have all won and must all have prizes? Revisiting Luborsky et al.'s verdict. *Journal of Consulting and Clinical Psychology, 59,* 226–232.

Beutler, L. E., & Clarkin, J. (1990). *Systematic treatment selection: Toward targeted therapeutic interventions.* New York: Brunner/Mazel.

Beutler, L. E., & Consoli, A. J. (1992). Systematic eclectic psychotherapy. In J. C. Norcross & M. R. Goldfried (Eds.), *Handbook of psychotherapy integration.* New York: Basic.

Beutler, L. E., & Crago, M. (Eds.). (1991). *Psychotherapy research: An international review of programmatic studies.* Washington, DC: American Psychological Association.

Beutler, L. E., Crago, M., & Arezmendi, T. G. (1986). Research on therapist variables in psychotherapy. In S. L. Garfield & A. E. Bergin (Eds.), *Handbook of psychotherapy and behavior change* (3rd ed.). New York: Wiley.

Beutler, L. E., Engle, D., Mohr, D., Daldrup, R. J., Bergan, J., Meredith, K., & Merry, W. (1991). Predictors of differential and self-directed psychotherapeutic procedures. *Journal of Consulting and Clinical Psychology, 59,* 333–340.

Beutler, L. E., Engle, D., Shoham-Salomon, V., Mohr, D. C., Dean, J. C., & Bernat, E. M. (1991). University of Arizona: Searching for differential treatments. In L. E. Beutler & M. Crago (Eds.), *Psychotherapy research: An international review of programmatic studies.* Washington, DC: American Psychological Association.

Beutler, L. E., Machado, P. P. P., Engle, D., & Mohr, D. (1993). Differential patient treatment maintenance among cognitive, experiential, and self-directed psychotherapies. *Journal of Psychotherapy Integration, 3,* 15–30.

Beutler, L. E., Mahoney, M. J., Norcross, J. C., Prochaska, J. O., Sollod, R. M., & Robertson, M. (1987). Training integrative/eclectic psychotherapists II. *Journal of Integrative and Eclectic Psychotherapy, 6,* 296–332.

Beutler, L. E., Mohr, D. C., Grawe, K., Engle, D., & MacDonald, R. (1991). Looking for differential treatment effects: Cross-cultural predictors of differential psychotherapy efficacy. *Journal of Psychotherapy Integration, 1,* 121–141.

Bibring, E. (1954). Psychoanalysis and the dynamic psychotherapies. *Journal of the American Psychoanalytic Association, 2,* 745–770.

Binswanger, L. (1958a). The case of Ellen West. In R. May, E. Angel, & H. Ellenberger (Eds.), *Existence.* New York: Basic.

Binswanger, L. (1958b). The existential analysis of school of thought. In R. May, E. Angel, & H. Ellenberger (Eds.), *Existence.* New York: Basic.

Binswanger, L. (1963). *Being-in-the-world: Selected papers of Ludwig Binswanger.* New York: Basic.

Birk, L., Huddleston, W., Millers, E., & Cohler, B. (1971). Avoidance conditioning for homosexuality. *Archives of General Psychology, 25,* 314–323.

Black, A. (1958). The extinction of avoidance responses under curare. *Journal of Comparative and Physiological Psychology, 51,* 519–525.

Boadella, D. (1973). *Wilhelm Reich: The evaluation of his work.* London: Vision.

Bohart, A. C. (1993a). Experiencing: The basis of psychotherapy. *Journal of Psychotherapy Integration, 3,* 51–67.

Bohart, A. C. (1993b). The person-centered therapies. In A. S. Gurman & S. B. Messer (Eds.), *Modern psychotherapies.* New York: Guilford.

Bohart, A. C., & Greenberg, L. S. (Eds.). (1997). *Empathy reconsidered: New directions in psychotherapy.* Washington DC: American Psychological Association.

Bolling, M. Y. (1995). Acceptance and Dasein. *Humanistic Psychologist, 23,* 213–226.

Booker, J., & Blymyer, D. (1994). Solution-oriented brief residential treatment with "chronic mental patients." *Journal of Systemic Therapies, 13*(4), 53–69.

Bornstein, P. H., & Bornstein, M. T. (1986). *Marital therapy: A behavioral-communications approach.* New York: Pergamon.

Boss, M. (1963). *Daseinanalysis and psychoanalysis.* New York: Basic.

Boss, M. (1983). *Existential foundations of medicine and psychology* (2nd ed.). New York: Jason Aronson.

Boudewyns, P. A., & Hyer, L. A. (1996). Eye Movement Desensitization and Reprocessing as treatment for post-traumatic stress disorder. *Clinical Psychology and Psychotherapy, 3,* 185–195.

Boudewyns, P. A., & Shipley, R. H. (1983). *Flooding and implosive therapy.* New York: Plenum.

Bowen, M. (1972). On the difference of self. In J. Framo (Ed.), *Family interaction: A dialogue between family researchers and family therapists.* New York: Springer.

Bowen, M. (1978). *Family therapy in clinical practice.* New York: Jason Aronson.

Bowers, T. G., & Clum, G. A. (1988). Relative contribution of specific and nonspecific treatment effects: Meta-analysis of placebo-controlled behavior therapy research. *Psychological Bulletin, 103,* 315–323.

Bowlby, J. (1969). *Attachment and loss: Vol. 1. Attachment.* New York: Basic.

Bowlby, J. (1973). *Attachment and loss: Vol. 2. Separation, anxiety and anger.* New York: Basic.

Bowlby, J. (1977). The making and breaking of affectional bonds. I. Aetiology and psychopathology in light of attachment theory. *British Journal of Psychiatry, 130,* 201–210.

Bowman, D., Scogin, F., Floyd, M. & McKendree-Smith, N. (1997, August). *Effect of therapist sex on the outcome of psychotherapy: A meta-analysis.* Poster presented at the annual convention of the American Psychological Association, Chicago, IL.

Boyd-Franklin, N. (1989). *Black families in therapy: A multi-systems approach.* New York: Guilford.

Bozarth, J. D. (1984). Beyond reflection: Emergent modes of empathy. In R. E. Levant & J. M. Shlien (Eds.), *Client-centered therapy and the person-centered approach.* New York: Praeger.

Bozarth, J. D. (1991). Person-centered assessment. *Journal of Counseling and Development, 69,* 458–461.

Brannon, R., & David, D. S. (1976). The male sex role: Our culture's blueprint of manhood, and what it's done for us lately. In D. S. David & R. Brannon (Eds.), *The forty-nine percent majority.* Reading, MA: Addison-Wesley.

Broderick, C. B., & Schrader, S. S. (1991). The history of professional marriage and family therapy. In A. S. Gurman & D. P. Kniskern (Eds.), *Handbook of family therapy* (Vol. 2). New York: Brunner/Mazel.

Bronowski, J. (1959). *Science and human values.* New York: Harper & Row.

Bronstein, P., & Quina, K. (Eds.). (1988). *Teaching a psychology of people: Re-*

sources for gender and sociocultural awareness. Washington, DC: American Psychological Association.

Brooks, G. R. (1995). The centerfold syndrome: How men can stop objectifying women and achieve true intimacy. San Francisco: Jossey-Bass.

Brown, L. S. (1990). The meaning of a multicultural perspective for theory building in feminist therapy. Women and Therapy, 9, 1–21.

Brown, L. S., & Ballou, M. (Eds.). (1992). Personality and psychopathology: Feminist reappraisals. New York: Guilford.

Brown, L. S., & Brodsky, A. M. (1992). The future of feminist therapy. Psychotherapy, 29, 51–57.

Brown, L. S., & Root, M. P. P. (Eds.). (1990). Diversity and complexity in feminist therapy. New York: Haworth.

Brown, M. (1973). The new body psychotherapies. Psychotherapy: Theory, Research and Practice, 10, 98–116.

Brown, N. O. (1959). Life against death. Middletown, CT: Wesleyan University Press.

Buber, M. (1958). I and thou. New York: Charles Scribner.

Budman, S. H. (Ed.). (1981). Forms of brief therapy. New York: Guilford.

Budman, S. H., & Gurman, A. S. (1988). Theory and practice of brief therapy. New York: Guilford.

Bugental, J. F. T. (1965). The search for authenticity. New York: Holt, Rinehart & Winston.

Bugental, J. F. T. (1976). The search for existential identity. San Francisco: Jossey-Bass.

Bugental, J. F. T. (1987). The art of the psychotherapist. New York: Norton.

Bugental, J. F. T. (1990). Intimate journeys: Stories from life-changing therapy. San Francisco: Jossey-Bass.

Bugental, J. F. T. (1991). Outcomes of an existential-humanistic psychotherapy: A tribute to Rollo May. The Humanistic Psychologist, 19, 2–9.

Bugental, J. F. T., & Bracke, P. E. (1992). The future of existential-humanistic psychotherapy. Psychotherapy, 29, 28–33.

Burns, D. D. (1980). Feeling good: The new mood therapy. New York: William Morrow.

Burns, D. D., & Nolan-Hoeksema, S. (1992). Therapeutic empathy and recovery from depression in cognitive-behavioral therapy: A structural equation model. Journal of Consulting and Clinical Psychology, 60, 441–449.

Camus, A. (1956). The rebel: An essay on man in revolt. New York: Knopf.

Cannon, W. (1939). The wisdom of the body. New York: Norton.

Caplan, P. J. (1989). Don't blame mother. New York: Harper & Row.

Carkhuff, R. (1969). Helping and human relations: A primer for lay and professional helpers (Vols. 1–2). New York: Holt, Rinehart & Winston.

Carroll, K. M. (1996). Relapse prevention as a psychological treatment: A review of controlled clinical trials. Experimental and Clinical Psychopharmacology, 4, 19–36.

Carson, R. C., & Butcher, J. N. (1992). Abnormal psychology and modern life (9th ed.). New York: Harper Collins.

Carter, B. (1989, July/August). Gender-sensitive therapy. Family Therapy Networker, pp. 57–60.

Castonguay, L. G., Goldfried, M. R., Wiser, S., Raue, P. J., & Hayes, A. M. (1996). Predicting the effect of cognitive therapy for depression: A study of unique and common factors. Journal of Consulting and Clinical Psychology, 64, 497–504.

Cattier, M. (1971). The life and work of Wilhelm Reich. New York: Horizon.

Cautela, J. (1967). Covert sensitization. Psychological Reports, 74, 459–468.

Cautela, J. (1977). The use of covert conditioning in modifying pain behavior. Journal of Behavioral Therapy and Experimental Psychiatry, 8, 45–52.

Chadwick, P., Birchwood, M., & Trower, P. (1996). Cognitive therapy for delusions, voices, and paranoia. New York: Wiley.

Chambless, D. L. (1998). Empirically validated treatments. In G. P. Koocher, J. C. Norcross, & S. S. Hill (Eds.), *Psychologists' desk reference*. New York: Oxford University Press.

Chambless, D. L., & Gillis, M. M. (1993). Cognitive therapy of anxiety disorders. *Journal of Consulting and Clinical Psychology, 61*, 248–260.

Champney, T. F., & Schulz, E. M. (1983). *A reassessment of the effects of psychotherapy*. Paper presented at the 55th annual meeting of the Midwestern Psychological Association, Chicago, IL. (ERIC document ED237895).

Chodorow, N. J. (1978). *The reproduction of mothering: Psychoanalysis and sociology of gender*. Berkeley: University of California Press.

Chodorow, N. J. (1989). *Feminism and psychoanalytic theory*. New Haven: Yale University Press.

Christensen, H., Hadzi-Pavlovic, D., Andrews, G., & Mattick, R. (1987). Behavior therapy and tricyclic medication in the treatment of obsessive-compulsive disorder: A quantitative review. *Journal of Consulting and Clinical Psychology, 55*, 701–711.

Clark, D. M., & Ehlers, A. (1993). An overview of the cognitive theory and treatment of panic disorder. *Applied and Preventive Psychology, 2*, 131–139.

Clarkson, P. (1991). *Transactional analysis psychotherapy: An integrated approach*. London: Tavistock/Routledge.

Clarkson, P. (1992). Burnout: Typical racket systems of professional helpers. *Transactional Analysis Journal, 22*, 153–158.

Clifford, J. S., Norcross, J. C., & Sommer, R. (1998, February). *Autobiographies of mental patients: Psychologists' uses and recommendations*. Paper presented at the 69th annual meeting of the Eastern Psychological Association, Boston.

Cohen, J. (1977). *Statistical power analysis for the behavioral sciences*. New York: Academic Press.

Colapinto, J. (1982). Structural family therapy. In A. Home & M. Ohlsen (Eds.), *Family counseling and therapy*. Itasca, IL: Peacock.

Colapinto, J. (1991). Structural family therapy. In A. S. Gurman & D. P. Kniskern (Eds.), *Handbook of family therapy* (Vol. 2). New York: Brunner/Mazel.

Colby, K. (1951). On the disagreement between Freud and Adler. *American Imago, 8*, 229–238.

Coleman, H. L. K., Wampold, B. E., & Casali, S. L. (1995). Ethnic minorities' ratings of ethnically similar and European American counselors: A meta-analysis. *Journal of Counseling Psychology, 42*, 55–64.

Comas-Diaz, L. (1992). The future of psychotherapy with ethnic minorities. *Psychotherapy, 29*, 88–94.

Comas-Diaz, L., & Greene, B. (Eds.). (1994). *Women of color: Integrating ethnic and gender identities in psychotherapy*. New York: Guilford.

Comas-Diaz, L., & Griffin, E. H. (Eds.). (1988). *Clinical guidelines in cross-cultural mental health*. New York: Wiley.

Combs, A. W. (1988). Some current issues for person-centered therapy. *Person-Centered Review, 3*, 263–276.

Cooper, N. A., & Clum, G. A. (1989). Imaginal flooding as a supplementary treatment for PTSD in combat veterans: A controlled study. *Behavior Therapy, 20*, 381–391.

Corrigan, P. (1991). Social skills training in adult psychiatric populations: A meta-analysis. *Journal of Behavior Therapy and Experimental Psychiatry, 22*, 203–210.

Cox, B. J., Endler, N. S., Lee, P. S., & Swinson, R. P. (1992). A meta-analysis of treatments for panic disorder with agoraphobia: Imipramine, alprazolam, and in vivo exposure. *Journal of Behavior Therapy and Experimental Psychiatry, 23*, 175–182.

Cox, B. J., Swinson, R. P., Morrison, B., & Lee, P. S. (1993). Clomipramine, fluoxetine, and behavior therapy in the treatment of obsessive-compulsive disorder: A meta-analysis. *Journal of Behavior Therapy & Experimental Psychiatry, 24*, 149–153.

Coyne, J. C., & Liddle, H. A. (1992). The future of systems therapy: Shedding myths and facing opportunities. *Psychotherapy, 29*, 44–50.

Craig, E. (1988). Daseinanalysis today: A brief critical reflection. *Humanistic Psychologist, 16*, 224–232.

Craighead, L. W., & Agras, W. S. (1991). Mechanisms of action in cognitive-behavioral and pharmacological interventions for obesity and bulimia nervosa. *Journal of Consulting and Clinical Psychology, 59*, 115–125.

Craighead, W. E. (1990). There's a place for us, all of us. *Behavior Therapy, 21,* 3–23.

Craske, M. G., Brown, T. A., & Barlow, D. H. (1991). Behavioral treatment of panic disorder: A two-year followup. *Behavior Therapy, 22,* 289–304.

Crits-Cristoph, P. (1992). The efficacy of brief dynamic psychotherapy: A meta-analysis. *American Journal of Psychiatry, 149,* 151–158.

Crits-Christoph, P., & Barber, J. P. (Eds.). (1991). *Handbook of short-term dynamic psychotherapy.* New York: Basic.

Cuijpers, P. (1997). Bibliotherapy in unipolar depression: A meta-analysis. *Journal of Behaviour Therapy and Experimental Psychiatry, 28,* 139–147.

Cummings, N. A. (1986). The dismantling of our health system: Strategies for the survival of psychological practice. *American Psychologist, 41,* 426–431.

Cummings, N. A. (1987). The future of psychotherapy: One psychologist's perspective. *American Journal of Psychotherapy, 61,* 349–360.

Curran, J. P., & Monti, P. M. (Eds.). (1982). *Social skills training.* New York: Guilford.

Daldrup, R. J., Beutler, L. E., Engle, D., & Greenberg, L. S. (1988). *Focused expressive psychotherapy: Freeing the overcontrolled patient.* New York: Guilford.

Dalkey, N., & Helmer, O. (1963). An experimental application of the Delphi method to the use of experts. *Management Science, 9,* 458.

Davanloo, H. (Ed.). (1978). *Basic principles and techniques in short-term dynamic psychotherapy.* New York: Spectrum.

Davanloo, H. (Ed.). (1980). *Short-term dynamic psychotherapy.* New York: Jason Aronson.

Davis, J. (1990). Contribution to "The Wallflower." In N. Saltzman & J. C. Norcross (Eds.), *Therapy wars.* San Francisco: Jossey-Bass.

DeJong, P., & Hopwood, L. E. (1996). Outcome research on treatment conducted at the Brief Family Therapy Center, 1992–1993. In S. D. Miller, M.A. Hubble, & B. L. Duncan (Eds.), *Handbook of solution-focused brief therapy* (pp. 272–298). San Francisco: Jossey-Bass.

Denes-Radomisli, M. (1976). Existential-Gestalt therapy. In P. Olsen (Ed.), *Emotional flooding.* New York: Human Sciences Press.

DeShazer, S. (1985). *Keys to solution in brief therapy.* New York: Norton.

DeShazer, S. (1988). *Clues: Investigating solutions in brief therapy.* New York: Norton.

DeShazer, S. (1994). *Words were originally magic.* New York: Norton.

DiClemente, C. C. (1986). Self-efficacy and the addictive behaviors. *Journal of Social and Clinical Psychology, 4,* 302–315.

DiClemente, C. C., & Hughes, S. (1990). Stages of change profiles in outpatient alcoholism treatment. *Journal of Substance Abuse, 2,* 217–235.

DiClemente, C. C., & Prochaska, J. O. (1982). Self-change and therapy change of smoking behavior: A comparison of processes of change in cessation and maintenance. *Addictive Behaviors, 7,* 133–142.

DiClemente, C. C., & Prochaska, J. O. (1985). Coping and competence in smoking behavior change. In S. Shiffman & T. A. Wills (Eds.), *Coping and substance abuse.* New York: Academic Press.

DiClemente, C. C., Prochaska, J. O., Fairhurst, S. K., Velicer, W. F., Valesquez, M. M., & Rossi, J. S. (1991). The process of smoking cessation: An analysis of precontemplation, contemplation, and preparation stages of change. *Journal of*

Consulting and Clinical Psychology, 59, 295–304.

Dilk, M. N., & Bond, G. B. (1996). Meta-analytic evaluation of skills training research for individuals with severe mental illness. *Journal of Consulting and Clinical Psychology, 64,* 1337–1346.

Dinkmeyer, D. C., Dinkmeyer, D. C., Jr., & Sperry, L. (1990). *Adlerian counseling and psychotherapy* (2nd ed.). Englewood Cliffs, NJ: Prentice-Hall.

Dobson, K. S. (Ed.). (1988). *Handbook of cognitive-behavioral therapies.* New York: Guilford.

Dobson, K. S. (1989). A meta-analysis of the efficacy of cognitive therapy for depression. *Journal of Consulting and Clinical Psychology, 57,* 414–419.

Dollard, J., & Miller, N. (1950). *Personality and psychotherapy: An analysis in terms of learning, thinking, and culture.* New York: McGraw-Hill.

Dostoevski, F. (1963). *Crime and punishment.* New York: Dodd & Mead.

Dreikurs, R. (1947). The four goals of children's misbehavior. *Nervous Child, 6,* 3–11.

Dreikurs, R. (1948). *The challenge of parenthood.* New York: Duell, Sloan & Pearce.

Dreikurs, R. (1950). Techniques and dynamics of multiple psychotherapy. *Psychiatric Quarterly, 24,* 788–799.

Dreikurs, R. (1959). Early experiments with group psychotherapy. *American Journal of Psychotherapy, 13,* 882–891.

Dreikurs, R., & Stoltz, V. (1964). *Children: The challenge.* New York: Meridith.

Drummond, D. C., & Glautier, S. (1994). A controlled trial of cue exposure treatment in alcohol dependence. *Journal of Consulting and Clinical Psychology, 62,* 809–817.

Dryden, W., & Lazarus, A. A. (1991). *A dialogue with Arnold Lazarus: "It depends."* London: Open University Press.

Duan, C., & Hill, C. E. (1996). The current state of empathy research. *Journal of Counseling Psychology, 43,* 261–274.

Dublin, J. O. A. (1975). Gestalt therapy, existential-Gestalt therapy, and/versus "Perls-ism." In E. Smith (Ed.), *The growing edge of Gestalt therapy.* New York: Brunner/Mazel.

Dublin, J. O. A. (1981). Bio-existential therapy. *Psychotherapy, 18,* 3–10.

Dudley, G. R., & Rawlins, M. R. (Eds.). (1985). Psychotherapy with ethnic minorities [Special issue]. *Psychotherapy, 22*(2s).

Dunn, R. L., & Schewebel, A. I. (1995). Meta-analytic review of marital therapy outcome research. *Journal of Family Psychology, 9,* 58–68.

DuPont, N. (1975). *Effects of induced expectancy and systematic desensitization on test anxiety in therapy, pseudo-desensitization, and control group subjects.* Unpublished doctoral dissertation, University of Rhode Island, Kingston.

Durlak, J. A., Fuhrman, T., & Lampman, C. (1991). Effectiveness of cognitive-behavior therapy for maladapting children: A meta-analysis. *Psychological Bulletin, 110,* 204–214.

Dusay, J. (1970). Script rehearsal. *Transactional Analysis Bulletin, 9,* 117–121.

Dush, D. M., Hirt, M. L., & Schroeder, H. E. (1983). Self-statement modification with adults: A meta-analysis. *Psychological Bulletin, 94,* 408–422.

Dush, D. M., Hirt, M. L., & Schroeder, H. E. (1989). Self-statement modification in the treatment of child behavior disorders: A meta-analysis. *Psychological Bulletin, 106,* 97–106.

D'Zurilla, T., & Goldfried, M. R. (1971). Problem solving and behavior modification. *Journal of Abnormal Psychology, 78,* 107–126.

Edelstein, B. A., & Berler, E. S. (Eds.). (1987). *Evaluation and accountability in clinical training.* New York: Plenum.

Edwards, D. G. (1982). *Existential psychotherapy: The process of caring.* New York: Gardner.

Edwards, D. J. A. (1990). Cognitive-behavioral and existential-phenomenological approaches to therapy: Complementary or conflicting paradigms? *Journal of Cognitive Psychotherapy, 4,* 105–120.

Edwards, M. E., & Steinglass, P. (1995). Family therapy treatment outcomes for alcoholism. *Journal of Marital and Family Therapy, 21,* 475–509.

Eisler, R. M., & Blalock, J. A. (1991). Masculine gender role stress: Implications for the assessment of men. *Clinical Psychology Review, 11,* 45–60.

Ekstein, R. (1972). In quest of the professional self. In A. Burton (Ed.), *Twelve therapists: How they live and actualize themselves.* San Francisco: Jossey-Bass.

Elkin, I. E., Shea, T., Watkins, J. T., Imber, S. D., Stotsky, S. M., Collins, J. F., Glass, D. R., Pilkonis, P. A., Leber, W. R., Docherty, J. P., Fiester, S. J., & Parloff, M. B. (1989). National Institute of Mental Health Treatment of Depression Collaborative Research Program: General effectiveness of treatment. *Archives of General Psychiatry, 46,* 974–982.

Ellenberger, H. (1958). A clinical introduction to psychiatric phenomenology and existential analysis. In R. May, E. Angel, & H. Ellenberger (Eds.), *Existence.* New York: Basic.

Ellenberger, H. (1970). *The discovery of the unconscious: The history and evolution of dynamic psychiatry.* New York: Basic.

Ellis, A. (1957a). *How to live with a neurotic.* New York: Crown.

Ellis, A. (1957b). Outcome of employing three techniques of psychotherapy. *Journal of Clinical Psychology, 13,* 344–350.

Ellis, A. (1958). *Sex without guilt.* New York: Grove.

Ellis, A. (1972). Rational-emotive therapy. In R. Jurjevich (Ed.), *Direct psychotherapy: 28 American originals* (Vol. 1). Coral Gables, FL: University of Miami Press.

Ellis, A. (1973). *Humanistic psychotherapy: The rational-emotive approach.* New York: McGraw-Hill.

Ellis, A. (1987a). Integrative developments in rational-emotive therapy (RET). *Journal of Integrative and Eclectic Psychotherapy, 6,* 470–479.

Ellis, A. (1987b). Rational-emotive therapy: Current appraisal and future directions. *Journal of Cognitive Psychotherapy, 1,* 73–86.

Ellis, A. (1988). *How to stubbornly refuse to make yourself miserable about anything—yes anything!* Secaucus, NJ: Lyle Stuart.

Ellis, A. (1991a). Rational-emotive treatment of simple phobias. *Psychotherapy, 28,* 452–456.

Ellis, A. (1991b). The revised ABC's of rational-emotive therapy. *Journal of Rational-Emotive and Cognitive-Behavior Therapy, 9,* 139–172.

Ellis, A. (1992). Group rational-emotive and cognitive-behavioral therapy. *International Journal of Group Psychotherapy, 42,* 63–80.

Ellis, A. (1995). *Better, deeper, and more enduring brief therapy.* New York: Brunnel/Mazel.

Ellis, A., & Dryden, W. (1996). *The practice of rational emotive behavior therapy.* New York: Springer.

Ellis, A., & Grieger, R. (Eds.). (1986). *Handbook of rational-emotive therapy* (Vols. 1–2). New York: Springer.

Ellis, A., & Harper, R. A. (1975). *A new guide to rational living.* North Hollywood, CA: Wilshire Books.

Ellis, A., McInerney, J. F., DiGiuseppe, R., & Yeager, R. J. (1988). *Rational-emotive therapy with alcoholics and substance abusers.* Elmsford, NY: Pergamon.

Ellis, A., Sichel, J., Yeager, R., DiMattia, D., & DiGiuseppe, R. (1989). *Rational emotive couples therapy.* New York: Pergamon.

Engels, G. L., Garnefski, N., & Drekstra, R. F. W. (1993). Efficacy of rational-emotive therapy: A quantitative analysis. *Journal of Consulting and Clinical Psychology, 61,* 1083–1090.

Epstein, N., Schlesinger, S. E., & Dryden, W. (Eds.). (1988). *Cognitive-behavioral therapy with families.* New York: Brunner/Mazel.

Erikson, E.H. (1950). *Childhood and society*. New York: Norton.

Erskine, R. G. (1997). *Theories and methods of an integrative transactional analysis*. San Francisco: TA Press.

Estes, W. (1944). An experimental study of punishment. *Psychological Monographs*, 57 (Whole No. 263).

Estes, W. (1971). Reward in human learning: Theoretical issues and strategic choice points. In R. Glaser (Ed.), *The nature of reinforcement*. New York: Academic.

Eysenck, H. J. (1970). A mish-mash of theories. *International Journal of Psychiatry*, 9, 140–146.

Fairbairn, W. (1952). *An object-relations theory of the personality*. New York: Basic.

Fairburn, C. G., Jones, R., Peveler, R. C., Hope, R. A., & O'Connor, M. (1993). Psychotherapy and bulimia nervosa: Longer-term effects of interpersonal psychotherapy, behavior therapy, and cognitive behavior therapy. *Archives of General Psychiatry*, 50, 419–428.

Fairburn, C. G., Norman, P. A., Welch, S. L., O'Connor, M. E., Doll, H. A., & Peveler, R. C. (1995). A prospective study of outcome in bulimia nervosa and the long-term effects of three psychological treatments. *Archives of General Psychiatry*, 52, 304–312.

Faludi, S. (1991). *Backlash: The undeclared war against American women*. New York: Craun.

Feldman, J. M., & Kazdin, A. E. (1995). Parent management training for oppositional and conduct problem children. *The Clinical Psychologist*, 48 (4), 3–5.

Feldman, L. B. (1992). *Integrating individual and family therapy*. New York: Brunner/Mazel.

Fenichel, O. (1941). *Problems of psychoanalytic techniques*. Albany, NY: Psychoanalytic Quarterly.

Fenichel, O. (1945). *The psychoanalytic theory of neurosis*. New York: Norton.

Ferguson, E. D. (1996). Adlerian principles and methods apply to workplace problems. *Individual Psychology*, 52, 270–287.

Feske, U., & Chambless, D. L. (1995). Cognitive behavioral versus exposure only treatment for social phobia: A meta-analysis. *Behavior Therapy*, 26, 695–720.

Fine, R. (1988). *Troubled men: The psychology, emotional conflicts, and therapy of men*. San Francisco: Jossey-Bass.

Fisher, S., & Greenberg, R. P. (1996). *Freud scientifically reappraised: Testing the theories and therapy*. New York: Wiley.

Foa, E. B., & Kozak, M. J. (1986). Emotional processing of fear and exposure to corrective information. *Psychological Bulletin*, 99, 20–35.

Foa, E. B., & Meadows, E. A. (1997). Psychosocial treatments for post-traumatic stress disorder: A critical review. In J. Spence (Ed.), *Annual review of psychology* (pp. 449–480). Palo Alto, CA: Annual Review.

Foa, E. B., Rothbaum, B. O., Riggs, D. S., & Murdock, T. B. (1991). Treatment of post-traumatic stress disorder in rape victims: A comparison between cognitive-behavioral procedures and counseling. *Journal of Consulting and Clinical Psychology*, 59, 715–723.

Foley, V. (1974). *An introduction to family therapy*. New York: Grune & Stratton.

Fonagy, P., & Target, M. (1996). Predictors of outcomes in child psychoanalysis: A retrospective study of 763 cases at the Anna Freud Centre. *Journal of the American Psychoanalytic Association*, 44, 27–77.

Forfar, C. S. (1990). Personal communication to the authors.

Frances, A. (1988, May). *Sigmund Freud: The first integrative therapist*. Address to the fourth annual meeting of the Society for the Exploration of Psychotherapy Integration, Boston.

Frank, E. (1991). Interpersonal psychotherapy as a maintenance treatment for patients with recurrent depression. *Psychotherapy*, 28, 259–266.

Frank, E., Kupfer, D. J., & Perel, J. M. (1989). Early recurrence in unipolar depression. *Archives of General Psychiatry*, 46, 397–400.

Frank, E., & Spanier, C. (1995). Interpersonal psychotherapy for depression: Overview, clinical efficacy, and future directions. *Clinical Psychology: Science and Practice*, 2, 349–369.

Frank, J. D. (1961). *Persuasion and healing: A comparative study of psychotherapy.* New York: Schocken.

Frank, J. D. (1973). *Persuasion and healing* (rev. ed.). Baltimore: Johns Hopkins University Press.

Frank, J. D., & Frank, J. (1991). *Persuasion and healing* (3rd ed.). Baltimore: Johns Hopkins University Press.

Frankl, V. (1963). *Man's search for meaning.* New York: Washington Square Press.

Frankl, V. (1967). *Psychotherapy and existentialism: Selected papers on logotherapy.* New York: Washington Square Press.

Frankl, V. (1969). *The will to meaning.* New York: New American Library.

Frankl, V. (1978). *The unheard cry for meaning.* New York: Simon & Schuster.

Franks, C. (1984). Can behavior therapy find peace and fulfillment in a school of professional psychology? *The Clinical Psychologist*, 28, 11–15.

Freedheim, D. K. (Ed.). (1992). *History of psychotherapy: A century of change.* Washington, DC: American Psychological Association.

Freeman, A. (Ed.). (1983). *Cognitive therapy with couples and groups.* New York: Plenum.

Freeman, A., Simon, K. M., Beutler, L. E., & Arkowitz, H. (Eds.). (1989). *Comprehensive handbook of cognitive therapy.* New York: Plenum.

French, T. M. (1933). Interrelations between psychoanalysis and the experimental work of Pavlov. *American Journal of Psychiatry*, 89, 1165–1203.

Freud, S. (1919). Turnings in the ways of psychoanalytic therapy. *Collected papers* (Vol. 2). London: Hogarth.

Freud, S. (1923). *The ego and the id.* London: Hogarth.

Freud, S. (1925). Character and anal eroticism. *Collected papers.* London: Institute for Psychoanalysis and Hogarth.

Freud, S. (1930). *Civilization and its discontents.* New York: Norton.

Freud, S. (1937/1964). Analysis terminable and interminable. In J. Strachey (Ed.), *Complete psychological works of Sigmund Freud.* London: Hogarth.

Freud, S. (1959). The question of lay analysis. In J. Strachey (Ed.), *The standard edition of the complete psychological works of Sigmund Freud* (Vol. 20). London: Hogarth.

Freud, S. (1965a). *Interpretation of dreams* (J. Strachey, Trans.) New York: Avon. (Original work published 1900)

Freud, S. (1965b). *New introductory letters on psychoanalysis* (J. Strachey, Trans.). New York: Norton. (Original work published 1933)

Friedman, E. H. (1991). Bowen theory and therapy. In A. S. Gurman & D. P. Kniskern (Eds.), *Handbook of family therapy* (Vol. 2). New York: Brunner/Mazel.

Friedman, S. (1993). *The new language of change.* New York: Guilford.

Frueh, B. C., Turner, S. M., & Beidel, S. M. (1995). Exposure therapy for combat-related PTSD: A critical review. *Clinical Psychology Review*, 15, 799–817.

Gabbard, G. O. (Ed.). (1995). *Treatments of psychiatric disorders* (2nd ed.). Washington, DC: American Psychiatric Press.

Ganley, A. L. (1988). Feminist therapy with male clients. In M. D. Douglas & L. E. Walker (Eds.), *Feminist psychotherapies: Integration of therapeutic and feminist systems* (pp. 186–205). Norwood, NJ: Ablex.

Garfield, S. L. (1980). *Psychotherapy: An eclectic approach.* New York: Wiley.

Garfield, S. L. (1986). Research on client variables in psychotherapy. In S. L. Garfield & A. E. Bergin (Eds.), *Handbook of psychotherapy and behavior change* (3rd ed.). New York: Wiley.

Garfield, S. L. (1992). Eclectic psychotherapy: A common factors approach. In J. C. Norcross & M. R. Goldfried (Eds.), *Handbook of psychotherapy integration*. New York: Basic.

Garfield, S. L., & Bergin, A. E. (Eds.). (1993). *Handbook of psychotherapy and behavior change* (4th ed.). New York: Wiley.

Garfield, S. L., & Kurtz, R. (1977). A study of eclectic views. *Journal of Clinical and Consulting Psychology, 45,* 78–83.

Gaw, K. F., & Beutler, L. E. (1995). Integrating treatment recommendations. In L. E. Beutler & M. R. Birren (Eds.). *Integrative assessment of adult personality* (pp. 280–319). New York: Guilford.

Gay, P. (1990). *Reading Freud.* New Haven: Yale University Press.

Gendlin, E. T. (1981). *Focusing* (2nd ed.). New York: Bantam.

Gendlin, E. T. (1996). *Focusing-oriented psychotherapy.* New York: Guilford.

Gerber, L. (1992). Intimate politics: Connectedness and the social-political self. *Psychotherapy, 29,* 626–630.

Gill, M. M. (1994). *Psychoanalysis in transition: A personal view.* Hillsdale, NJ: Analytic Press.

Gladfelter, J. (1992). Redecision therapy. *International Journal of Group Psychotherapy, 42,* 319–334.

Glantz, K., Durlach, N. I., Barnett, R. C., & Aviles, W. A. (1996). Virtual reality (VR) for psychotherapy: From physical to social environment. *Psychotherapy, 33,* 464–473.

Glasgow, R. E., & Rosen, G. M. (1978). Behavioral bibliotherapy: A review of self-help behavior therapy manuals. *Psychological Bulletin, 85,* 1–23.

Glass, C. R., & Arnkoff, D. B. (1992). Behavior therapy. In D. K. Freedheim (Ed.), *History of psychotherapy: A century of change.* Washington, DC: American Psychological Association.

Glass, C. R., Victor, B. J., & Arnkoff, D. B. (1992). Empirical research on integrative and eclectic psychotherapies. In G. Stricker & J. R. Gold (Eds.), *Comprehensive handbook of psychotherapy integration* (pp. 9–26). New York: Plenum.

Glasser, W. (1975). *Reality therapy.* New York: Harper & Row.

Glasser, W. (1984). *Control theory: A new explanation of how we control our lives.* New York: Harper & Row.

Glover, E. (1925). Notes on oral character formation. *International Journal of Psychoanalysis, 6,* 131–154.

Goffan, E. A., Tsaousis, I., & Kemp-Wheeler, S. M. (1995). Researcher allegiance and meta-analysis: The case of cognitive therapy for depression. *Journal of Consulting and Clinical Psychology, 63,* 966–980.

Goldberg, G. A., & Kremen, E. (Eds.). (1990). *The feminization of poverty: Only in America?* New York: Praeger.

Goldenberg, I., & Goldenberg, H. (1996). *Family therapy: An overview* (4th ed.). Pacific Grove, CA: Brooks/Cole.

Goldfried, M. R. (1980). Toward the delineation of therapeutic change principles. *American Psychologist, 35,* 991–999.

Goldfried, M. R. (Ed.). (1982). *Converging themes in psychotherapy: Trends in psychodynamic, humanistic, and behavioral practice.* New York: Springer.

Goldfried, M. R. (1995). *From cognitive-behavior therapy to psychotherapy integration.* New York: Springer.

Goldfried, M. R., & Castonguay, L. G. (1992). The future of psychotherapy integration. *Psychotherapy, 29,* 4–10.

Goldfried, M. R., Castonguay, L. G., & Safran, J. D. (1992). Core issues and future directions in psychotherapy integration. In J. C. Norcross & M. R. Goldfried (Eds.), *Handbook of psychotherapy integration.* New York: Basic.

Goldfried, M. R., & Davison, G. (1994). *Clinical behavior therapy* (rev. ed.). New York: Wiley.

Goldfried, M. R., & Newman, C. (1986). Psychotherapy integration: An historical perspective. In J. C. Norcross (Ed.), *Handbook of eclectic psychotherapy.* New York: Brunner/Mazel.

Goldfried, M. R., & Newman, C. (1992). A history of psychotherapy integration. In J. C. Norcross & M. R. Goldfried (Eds.), *Handbook of psychotherapy integration.* New York: Basic.

Goldfried, M. R., & Safran, J. D. (1986). Future directions in psychotherapy integration. In J. C. Norcross (Ed.), *Handbook of eclectic psychotherapy.* New York: Brunner/Mazel.

Good, G. E., Gilbert, L. A., & Scher, M. (1990). Gender aware therapy: A synthesis of feminist therapy and knowledge about gender. *Journal of Counseling and Development, 68,* 376–380.

Gopaul-McNicol, S. A. (1991). *Working with West Indian families.* New York: Guilford.

Gordon, T. (1970). *Parent effectiveness training.* New York: Peter Wyden.

Gordon, T. (1974). *Teacher effectiveness training.* New York: Peter Wyden.

Gottlieb, N. H., Galavotti, C., McCuan, R. S., & McAlister, A. L. (1990). Specification of a social cognitive model predicting smoking cessation in a Mexican-American population: A prospective study. *Cognitive Therapy and Research, 14,* 529–542.

Gottman, J., Notarius, C., Gonso, J., & Markman, H. (1976). *A couple's guide to communication.* Champaign, IL: Research Press.

Gould, R. A., Buckminster, S., Pollack, M. H., Otto, M. W., & Yap, L. (1997). Cognitive-behavioral and pharmacological treatment for social phobia: A meta-analysis. *Clinical Psychology: Science and Practice, 4,* 291–306.

Gould, R. A., & Clum, G. A. (1993). A meta-analysis of self-help treatment approaches. *Clinical Psychology Review, 13,* 169–186.

Gould, R. A., Otto, M. W., & Pollack, M. H. (1995). A meta-analysis of treatment outcome for panic disorder. *Clinical Psychology Review, 15,* 819–844.

Goulding, M. M., & Goulding, R. L. (1979). *Changing lives through redecision therapy.* New York: Brunner/Mazel.

Grawe, K., Donati, R., & Bernauer, F. (1998). *Psychotherapy in transition.* Seattle: Hogrefe & Huber.

Greenberg, G. (1977). The family interactional perspective: A study and examination of the work of Don D. Jackson. *Family Process, 16,* 385–412.

Greenberg, L. S. (1995). *Process experiential psychotherapy.* Washington, DC: American Psychological Association.

Greenberg, L. S., Elliott, R., & Lietaer, G. (1994). Research on experiential psychotherapy. In A. E. Bergin & S. L. Garfield (Eds.), *Handbook of psychotherapy and behavior change,* (4th ed., pp. 509–539). New York: Wiley.

Greenberg, L. S., & Goldman, R. L. (1988). Training in experiential therapy. *Journal of Consulting and Clinical Psychology, 56,* 696–702.

Greenberg, L. S., & Johnson, S. M. (1988). *Emotionally focused therapy for couples.* New York: Guilford.

Greenberg, L. S., Rice, L. N., & Elliott, R. (1993). *Facilitating emotional change.* New York: Guilford.

Greenson, R. R. (1967). *The technique and practice of psychoanalysis* (Vol. 1). New York: International Universities Press.

Greenspoon, J. (1955). The reinforcing effect of two spoken sounds on the frequency of two responses. *American Journal of Psychology, 68,* 409–416.

Grencavage, L. M., & Norcross, J. C. (1990). Where are the commonalities among the therapeutic common factors? *Professional Psychology: Research and Practice, 21,* 72–378.

Grissom, R. J. (1996). The magical number. 7±2: Meta-analysis of the probability of superior outcome in comparisons involving therapy, placebo, and control. *Journal of Consulting and Clinical Psychology, 64,* 973–982.

Guisinger, S., & Blatt, S. J. (1994). Individuality and relatedness: Evolution of a fundamental dialectic. *American Psychologist, 49,* 104–111.

Gurman, A. S., & Kniskern, D. P. (1978). Research on marital and family therapy:

Progress, perspective, and prospect. In S. L. Garfield & A. E. Bergin (Eds.), *Handbook of psychotherapy and behavior change* (2nd ed.). New York: Wiley.

Gurman, A. S., & Kniskern, D. P. (Eds.). (1991). *Handbook of family therapy* (Vol. 2). New York: Brunner/Mazel.

Gurman, A. S., & Kniskern, D. P. (1992). The future of marital and family therapy. *Psychotherapy, 29,* 65–71.

Gurman, A. S., Kniskern, D. P., & Pinsof, W. M. (1986). Research on the process and outcome of marital and family therapy. In S. L. Garfield & A. E. Bergin (Eds.), *Handbook of psychotherapy and behavior change* (3rd ed.). New York: Wiley.

Haaga, D. A., Dryden, W., & Dancey, C. P. (1991). Measurement of rational emotive therapy in outcome studies. *Journal of Rational Emotive & Cognitive Behavior Therapy, 9,* 73–93.

Hahlweg, K., & Markman, H. J. (1988). Effectiveness of behavioral marital therapy: Empirical status of behavioral techniques in preventing and alleviating marital distress. *Journal of Consulting and Clinical Psychology, 56,* 440–447.

Haley, J. (1973b). *Uncommon therapies: The psychiatric techniques of Milton Erickson, M.D.* New York: Norton.

Haley, J. (1976). *Problem-solving therapy: New strategies for effective family therapies.* San Francisco: Jossey-Bass.

Haley, J. (1980). *Leaving home.* New York: McGraw-Hill.

Haley, J. (1984). *Ordeal therapy.* San Francisco: Jossey-Bass.

Haley, J. (1986). *The power tactics of Jesus Christ and other essays* (2nd ed.). Rockville, MD: Triangle.

Haley, J. (1990). *Strategies of psychotherapy* (2nd ed.). New York: Norton.

Halgin, R. P., & Whitbourne, S. K. (1993). *Abnormal psychology.* Philadelphia: Harcourt Brace Jovanovich.

Hall, C., & Lindzey, G. (1970). *Theories of personality.* New York: Wiley.

Hampton, B. R., & Hulgus, Y. F. (1993). The efficacy of paradoxical strategies: A quantative review of the research. *Psychotherapy in Private Practice, 12,* 53–72.

Hare-Mustin, R. (1987). The problem of gender in family therapy theory. *Family Process, 26,* 15–27.

Harman, R. (1995). Gestalt therapy as brief therapy. *Gestalt Journal, 18,* 77–85.

Harper, R. A. (1959). *Psychoanalysis and psychotherapy: 36 systems.* Englewood Cliffs, NJ: Prentice-Hall.

Harris, A. B., & Harris, T. A. (1990). *Staying OK.* New York: Harper & Row.

Harris, H., & Bruner, C. (1971). A comparison of self-control and a contract procedure for weight control. *Behavior Research and Therapy, 9,* 347–354.

Harris, T. A. (1967). *I'm OK—you're OK.* New York: Harper & Row.

Hartmann, A., Herzog, T., & Drinkman, A. (1992). Psychotherapy of bulimia nervosa: What is effective? A meta-analysis. *Journal of Psychosomatic Research, 36,* 159–167.

Hartmann, H. (1958). *Ego psychology and the problem of adaptation.* New York: International Universities Press.

Hartmann, H., Kris, E., & Loewenstein, R. M. (1947). Comments on the formation of psychic structure. In A. Freud et al. (Eds.), *The psychoanalytic study of the child.* New York: International Universities Press.

Hartshorne, T. S. (1991). The evolution of psychotherapy: Where are the Adlerians? *Individual Psychology, 47,* 321–325.

Hatcher, C., & Himelstein, P. (Eds.). (1976). *The handbook of Gestalt therapy.* New York: Jason Aronson.

Hawton, K., & Kirk, J. (1989). Problem-solving. In K. Hawton, P. M. Salkovskis, J. Kirk, & D. M. Clark (Eds.), *Cognitive behaviour therapy for psychiatric problems.* New York: Oxford University Press.

Hawton, K., Salkovskis, P. M., Kirk, J., & Clark, D. M. (Eds.). (1989). *Cognitive behaviour therapy for psychiatric problems: A practical guide.* New York: Oxford University Press.

Hays, P. A. (1996). Culturally responsive assessment with diverse older clients. *Professional Psychology: Research and Practice, 27*, 188–193.

Hazelrigg, M. D., Cooper, H. M., & Borduin, C. M. (1987). Evaluating the effectiveness of family therapies: An integrative review and analysis. *Psychological Bulletin, 101*, 428–442.

Heath, A. E., Neimeyer, G. J., & Pedersen, P. B. (1988). The future of cross-cultural counseling: A Delphi poll. *Journal of Counseling and Development, 67*, 27–30.

Hebb, D. O., Held, R., Riesent, A., & Teuber, H. (1961). Sensory deprivation: Facts in search of a theory. *Journal of Nervous and Mental Disorders, 132*, 17–43.

Heidegger, M. (1962). *Being and time.* New York: Harper & Row.

Held, B. S. (1991). The process/content distinction in psychotherapy revisited. *Psychotherapy, 28*, 207–217.

Held, B. S. (1995). *Back to reality: A critique of postmodern theory in psychotherapy.* New York: Norton.

Hendricks, I. (1943). The discussion of the "instinct to master." *Psychoanalytic Quarterly, 12*, 561–565.

Henry, W. A. (1990, April 9). Beyond the melting pot. *Time,* pp. 28–31.

Henry, W. P., & Strupp, H. H. (1991). Vanderbilt University: The Vanderbilt Center for Psychotherapy Research. In L. E. Beutler & M. Crago (Eds.), *Psychotherapy research: An international review of programmatic studies.* Washington, DC: American Psychological Association.

Hersen, M., & Barlow, D. (1976). *Single-case experimental designs.* Elmsford, NY: Pergamon.

Hester, R. K., & Delaney, H. D. (1997). Behavioral self-control program for Windows: Results of a controlled clinical trial. *Journal of Consulting and Clinical Psychology, 65*, 686–693.

Highlen, P. S. (1994). Racial/ethnic diversity in doctoral programs of psychology: Challenges for the twenty-first century. *Applied & Preventative Psychology, 3*, 91–108.

Hill, K. A. (1987). Meta-analysis of paradoxical interventions. *Psychotherapy, 24*, 266–270.

Ho, M. K. (1992). *Minority children and adolescents in therapy.* Newbury Park, CA: Sage.

Hoffman, E. (1994). *The drive for self: Alfred Adler and the founding of individual psychology.* Reading, MA: Addison-Wesley.

Hoffman, L. (1981). *Foundations of family therapy: A conceptual framework for systems change.* New York: Basic.

Holland, G. (1973). Transactional analysis. In R. Corsini (Ed.), *Current psychotherapies.* Itasca, IL: Peacock.

Hollin, C. R., & Trower, P. (Eds.). (1986). *Handbook of social skills training.* New York: Pergamon.

Hollon, S. D., & Beck, A. T. (1994). Cognitive and cognitive-behavioral therapies. In A. E. Bergin & S. L. Garfield (Eds.), *Handbook of psychotherapy and behavior change* (4th ed., pp. 428–466). New York: Wiley.

Holroyd, K. A., & Penzien, D. B. (1990). Pharmacological versus non-pharmacological prophylaxis of recurrent migraine headache: A meta-analytic review of clinical trials. *Pain, 42*, 1–13.

Holt, R. R. (1989). *Freud reappraised: A fresh look at psychoanalytic theory.* New York: Guilford.

Hora, T. (1959). Epistemological aspects of existence and psychotherapy. *Journal of Individual Psychology, 15*, 166–173.

Hora, T. (1960). The process of existential psychotherapy. *Psychiatric Quarterly, 34*, 495–504.

Horner, A. (1979). *Object relations and the developing ego in therapy.* New York: Jason Aronson.

Horvath, A. O., & Luborsky, L. (1993). The role of the therapeutic alliance in psychotherapy. *Journal of Consulting and Clinical Psychology, 61*, 561–573.

Houts, A. C., Berman, J. S., & Abramson, H. (1994). Effectiveness of psychological and pharmacological treatments for nocturnal enuresis. *Journal of Consulting and Clinical Psychology, 62,* 737–745.

Howard, K. I., Kopta, M. S., & Orlinsky, D. E. (1986). The dose-effect relationship in psychotherapy. *American Psychologist, 41,* 159–165.

Hoyt, M. F. (1995). *Brief therapy and managed care.* San Francisco: Jossey-Bass.

Hoyt, M. F. (Ed.). (1998). *The handbook of constructive therapies.* San Francisco: Jossey-Bass.

Hull, C. (1943). *Principles of behavior.* New York: Appleton-Century-Crofts.

Hunt, W. A., Barnett, L. W., & Branch, L. G. (1971). Relapse rates in addiction programs. *Journal of Clinical Psychology, 27,* 455–456.

Hyde, J. S. (1991). *Half the human experience* (4th ed.). Lexington, MA: Heath.

Hyman, R. B., Feldman, H. R., Harris, R. B., Levin, R. F., & Mallory, G. B. (1989). The effects of relaxation training on clinical symptoms: A meta-analysis. *Nursing Research, 8,* 216–220.

Integrative Psychotherapy {special issue}. (1996). *Transactional Analysis Journal, 26* (4).

Jackson, D. (1967). The eternal triangle. In J. Haley & L. Hoffman (Eds.), *Techniques of family therapy.* New York: Basic.

Jacobson, E. (1938). *Progressive relaxation.* Chicago: University of Chicago Press.

Jacobson, N. S. (Ed.). (1987). *Psychotherapists in clinical practice: Cognitive and behavioral perspectives.* New York: Guilford.

Jacobson, N. S. (1993, April). *Integrative developments within behavior therapy.* Address to the ninth annual conference of the Society for the Exploration of Psychotherapy Integration, New York.

Jacobson, N. S., & Gurman, A. S. (Eds.). (1986). *Clinical handbook of marital therapy.* New York: Guilford.

Jacobson, N. S., & Margolin, G. (1979). *Marital therapy: Strategies based on social learning and behavior exchange principles.* New York: Brunner/Mazel.

James, M., & Jongeward, D. (1971). *Born to win.* Reading, MA: Addison-Wesley.

Jensen, J. P., Bergin, A. E., & Greaves, D. W. (1990). The meaning of eclecticism: New survey and analysis of components. *Professional Psychology: Research and Practice, 21,* 124–130.

Johnson, W. G., Tsoh, J. Y., & Varnado, P. J. (1996). Eating disorders: Efficacy of pharmacological and psychological interventions. *Clinical Psychology Review, 16,* 457–478.

Jones, E. (1955). *The life and works of Sigmund Freud* (Vol. 2). New York: Basic.

Jones, E. (1957). *The life and works of Sigmund Freud* (Vol. 3). New York: Basic.

Jones, N. S. (1990). Black/white issues in psychotherapy: A framework for clinical practice. *Journal of Social Behavior and Personality, 5,* 305–322.

Jordan, J. V., Kaplan, A. G., Miller, J. B., Stiver, I. P., & Surrey, J. L. (1991). *Women's growth in connection: Writings from the Stone Center.* New York: Guilford.

Kahn, E. (1985). Heinz Kohut and Carl Rogers: A timely comparison. *American Psychologist, 40,* 893–904.

Kanfer, F. H., & Goldstein, A. P. (Eds.). (1991). *Helping people change: A textbook of methods* (4th ed.). Boston: Allyn & Bacon.

Kantrowitz, R. E., & Ballou, M. (1992). A feminist critique of cognitive-behavioral therapy. In L. S. Brown & M. Ballou (Eds.), *Personality and psychopathology: Feminist reappraisals.* New York: Guilford.

Kaplan, A. G., Fibel, B., Greif, A. C., McComb, A., Sedney, M. A., & Shapiro, E. (1983). The process of sex-role integration in psychotherapy: Contributions from a training experience. *Psychotherapy: Theory, Research and Practice, 20,* 476–485.

Kaplan, E. H. (1997). Telepsychotherapy. *Journal of Psychotherapy Practice and Science, 6,* 227–237.

Kaplan, H. S. (1974). *The new sex therapy.* New York: Brunner/Mazel.

Kaplan, H. S. (1987). *The illustrated manual of sex therapy* (2nd ed.). New York: Brunner/Mazel.

Karasu, T. B. (1986). The specificity versus nonspecificity dilemma: Toward identifying therapeutic change agents. *American Journal of Psychiatry, 143,* 687–695.

Karasu, T. B. (1992). The worst of times, the best of times. *Journal of Psychotherapy Practice and Research, 1,* 2–15.

Karpman, S. (1968). Script drama analysis. *Transactional Analysis Bulletin, 7,* 39–43.

Kaslow, F. (Ed.). (1996). *Handbook of relational diagnosis and dysfunctional family patterns.* New York: Wiley.

Kazdin, A. E. (1979). Nonspecific treatment factors in psychotherapy outcome research. *Journal of Consulting and Clinical Psychology, 47,* 846–851.

Kazdin, A. E. (1984). Integration of psychodynamic and behavioral psychotherapies: Conceptual versus empirical synthesis. In H. Arkowitz & S. B. Messer (Eds.), *Psychoanalytic therapy and behavior therapy: Is integration possible?* New York: Plenum.

Kazdin, A. E. (1991). Effectiveness of psychotherapy with children and adolescents. *Journal of Consulting and Clinical Psychology, 39,* 785–798.

Kazdin, A. E. (1994). *Behavior modification in applied settings* (5th ed.). Pacific Grove, CA: Brooks/Cole.

Keane, T. M., Fairbank, J. A., Caddell, J. M., & Zimering, R. T. (1989). Implosive (flooding) therapy reduces symptoms of PTSD in Vietnam combat veterans. *Behavior Therapy, 20,* 245–260.

Keane, T. M., & Kaloupek, D. G. (1982). Imaginal flooding in the treatment of a post-traumatic stress disorder. *Journal of Consulting and Clinical Psychology, 50,* 138–140.

Keen, E. (1970). *Three faces of being: Toward an existential clinical psychology.* New York: Irvington.

Keleman, S. (1971). *Sexuality, self, and survival.* San Francisco: Lodestar.

Keleman, S. (1973, July). We do have bodies and we are our bodies. *Psychology Today,* pp. 64–70.

Kempler, W. (1973). Gestalt therapy. In R. Corsini (Ed.), *Current psychotherapies.* Itasca, IL: Peacock.

Kendall, P. C. (Ed.). (1991). *Child and adolescent therapy: Cognitive-behavioral perspectives.* New York: Guilford.

Kendall, P. C., & Braswell, L. (1992). *Cognitive-behavioral therapy for impulsive children* (2nd ed.). New York: Guilford.

Kernberg, O. F. (1973). Summary and conclusions of "Psychotherapy and psychoanalysis: Final report of the Menninger Foundation's Psychotherapy Research Project." *International Journal of Psychiatry, 11,* 62–77.

Kernberg, O. F. (1975). *Borderline conditions and pathological narcissism.* New York: Jason Aronson.

Kernberg, O. F. (1976). *Object-relations theory and clinical psychoanalysis.* New York: Jason Aronson.

Kernberg, O. F. (1979). Some implications of object-relations theory for psychoanalytic technique. *Journal of the American Psychoanalytic Association, 70,* 207–239.

Kernberg, O. F. (1984). *Severe personality disorders: Psychotherapeutic strategies.* New Haven: Yale University Press.

Kernberg, O. F., Ellis, A., Person, E., Burns, D. D., & Norcross, J. C. (1993, April). *A meeting of the minds: Is integration possible?* Two-day conference sponsored by the Institute for Rational-Emotive Therapy, New York.

Kernberg, O. F., Selzer, M. A., Koenigsberg, H. W., Carr, A. C., & Applebaum, A. H. (1989). *Psychodynamic psychotherapy of borderline patients.* New York: Basic.

Kerr, M., & Bowen, M. (1988). *Family evaluation.* New York: Norton.

Kierkegaard, S. (1954a). *Fear and trembling.* New York: Doubleday.

Kierkegaard, S. (1954b). *The sickness unto death.* New York: Doubleday.

Kieser, D. J. (1966). Some myths of psychotherapy research and the search for a paradigm. *Psychological Bulletin, 65,* 110–136.

Kiesler, D. J. (1996). *Contemporary interpersonal theory and research.* New York: Wiley.

Klass, E. T., & Barlow, D. H. (1991). State University of New York at Albany, Center for Stress and Anxiety Disorders: Psychotherapy research at the phobia and anxiety disorders clinic. In L. E. Beutler & M. Crago (Eds.), *Psychotherapy research: An international review of programmatic studies.* Washington, DC: American Psychological Association.

Klein, D. F., Zitrin, C. M., Woerner, M. G., & Ross, D. C. (1983). Treatment of phobia II. Behavior therapy and supportive psychotherapy. *Archives of General Psychiatry, 40,* 139–145.

Klein, M., Dittman, A. T., Parloff, M. B., & Gill, M. M. (1969). Behavior therapy: Observations and reflections. *Journal of Consulting and Clinical Psychology, 33,* 259–266.

Klerman, G. L., Budman, S., Berwich, D., Weissman, M. M., Damico-White, J., Demby, A., & Feldstein, M. (1987). Efficacy of brief psychosocial interventions on symptoms of stress and distress among patients in primary care. *Medical Care, 25,* 1078–1088.

Klerman, G. L., & Weissman, M. M. (1991). Interpersonal psychotherapy: Research program and future prospects. In L. E. Beutler & M. Crago (Eds.), *Psychotherapy research: An international review of programmatic studies.* Washington, DC: American Psychological Association.

Klerman, G. L., & Weissman, M. M. (Eds.). (1993). *New applications of interpersonal psychotherapy.* Washington, DC: American Psychiatric Press.

Klerman, G. L., Weissman, M. M., Rounsaville, B. J., & Chevron, E. S. (1984). *Interpersonal psychotherapy of depression.* New York: Basic.

Knight, R. P. (1941). Evaluation of the results of psychoanalytic therapy. *American Journal of Psychiatry, 98,* 434–436.

Knobloch, F. (1996). Toward integration through group-based psychotherapy: Back to the future. *Journal of Psychotherapy Integration, 6,* 1–25.

Knobloch, F., & Knobloch, J. (1979). *Integrated psychotherapy.* New York: Jason Arasonson.

Kohut, H. (1971). *The analysis of the self.* New York: International Universities Press.

Kohut, H. (1977). *The restoration of the self.* New York: International Universities Press.

Koss, M. P., & Shiang, J. (1994). Research on brief psychotherapy. In A. E. Bergin & S. L. Garfield (Eds.), *Handbook of psychotherapy and behavior change* (4th ed., pp. 664–700). New York: Wiley.

Kovacs, A. L. (1989). Evoked reflections on psychotherapy's future prospects—Adlerian and otherwise. *Individual Psychology, 45,* 248–260.

Krasner, L. (1988). Paradigm lost: On a historical/sociological/economic perspective. In D. B. Fishman, F. Rodgers, & C. M. Franks (Eds.), *Paradigms in behavior therapy: Present and promise.* New York: Springer.

Kuehlwein, K. T., & Rosen, H. (Eds.). (1993). *Cognitive therapies in action: Evolving innovative practice.* San Francisco: Jossey-Bass.

Kuhn, T. S. (1970). *The structure of scientific revolutions* (2nd ed.). Chicago: University of Chicago Press.

Lam, C. S., McMahon, B. T., Priddy, D. A., & Gehred-Schultz, A. (1988). Deficit awareness and treatment performance among traumatic head injury adults. *Brain Injury, 2,* 235–242.

Lambert, M. J. (1976). Spontaneous remission in adult neurotic disorders: A revision and summary. *Psychological Bulletin, 83,* 107–119.

Lambert, M. J. (1986). Future directions for research in client-centered psychotherapy. *Person-Centered Review, 1,* 185–200.

Lambert, M. J. (1992). Psychotherapy outcome research: Implications for integrative and eclectic therapists. In J. C. Norcross & M. R. Goldfried (Eds.), *Handbook of psychotherapy integration*. New York: Basic.

Lambert, M. J., & Bergin, A. E. (1992). Achievements and limitations of psychotherapy research. In D. K. Freedheim (Ed.), *History of psychotherapy: A century of change*. Washington, DC: American Psychological Association.

Lamson, R. J. (1997). *Virtual therapy*. Paris: Polytechnic International Press.

Lantz, J. (1992). Using Frankl's concepts with PTSD clients. *Journal of Traumatic Stress, 5*, 485–490.

Larson, D. (1980). Therapeutic schools, styles, and schoolism: A national survey. *Journal of Humanistic Psychology, 20*, 3–20.

Layden, M. A., Newman, C. F., Freeman, A., & Morse, S. B. (1993). *Cognitive therapy of borderline personality disorder*. Boston: Allyn & Bacon.

Lazarus, A. A. (1956). A psychological approach to alcoholism. *South African Medical Journal, 30*, 707–710.

Lazarus, A. A. (1958). New methods in psychotherapy: A case study. *South African Medical Journal, 32*, 660–664.

Lazarus, A. A. (1966a). Behavior rehearsal versus non-directed therapy versus advice in affecting behavior change. *Behavior Research and Therapy, 4*, 209–212.

Lazarus, A. A. (1966b). Broad spectrum behavior therapy and the treatment of agoraphobia. *Behavior Research and Therapy, 4*, 95–97.

Lazarus, A. A. (1967). In support of technical eclecticism. *Psychological Reports, 21*, 415–416.

Lazarus, A. A. (1971a). *Behavior therapy and beyond*. New York: McGraw-Hill.

Lazarus, A. A. (1971b). Has behavior therapy outlived its usefulness? *American Psychologist, 32*, 550–555.

Lazarus, A. A. (1971c). Where do behavior therapists take their troubles? *Psychological Reports, 28*, 349–350.

Lazarus, A. A. (1973). Multimodal behavior therapy: Treating the BASIC I.D. *Journal of Nervous and Mental Disease, 156*, 404–411.

Lazarus, A. A. (1976). *Multimodal behavior therapy*. New York: Springer.

Lazarus, A. A. (1981/1989a). *The practice of multimodal therapy*. Baltimore: Johns Hopkins University Press.

Lazarus, A. A. (1989b). Brief psychotherapy: The multimodal model. *Psychology, 26*, 6–10.

Lazarus, A. A. (1991). A plague on Little Hans and Little Albert. *Psychotherapy, 28*, 444–447.

Lazarus, A. A. (1992). Multimodal therapy: Technical eclecticism with minimal integration. In J. C. Norcross & M. R. Goldfried (Eds.), *Handbook of psychotherapy integration*. New York: Basic.

Lazarus, A. A. (1993). Tailoring the therapeutic relationship, or being an authentic chameleon. *Psychotherapy, 30*, 404–407.

Lazarus, A. A. (1997). *Brief but comprehensive psychotherapy: The multimodal way*. New York: Springer.

Lazarus, A. A., Beutler, L. E., & Norcross, J. C. (1992). The future of technical eclecticism. *Psychotherapy, 29*, 11–20.

Lazarus, A. A., & Fay, A. (1984). Behavior therapy. In T. B. Karasu (Ed.), *The psychiatric therapies*. Washington, DC: American Psychiatric Association.

Lazarus, A. A., & Fay, A. (1990). Brief psychotherapy: Tautology or oxymoron? In J. K. Zeig & S. Gilligan (Eds.), *Brief therapy: Myths, methods, and metaphors*. New York: Brunner/Mazel.

Lazarus, A. A., & Lazarus, C. N. (1991). *Multimodal Life History Inventory*. Champaign, IL: Research Press.

Lazarus, A. A., Lazarus, C. N., & Fay, A. (1993). *Don't believe it for a minute! 40 toxic ideas that are driving you crazy*. San Luis Obispo: Impact.

Lazarus, A. A., & Messer, S. B. (1991). Does chaos prevail? An exchange on technical eclecticism and integration. *Journal of Psychotherapy Integration, 1*, 143–158.

Leong, F. T. L. (1986). Counseling and psychotherapy with Asian-Americans: Review of the literature. *Journal of Counseling Psychology, 33,* 196–206.

Lerman, H. (1992). The limits of phenomenology: A feminist critique of the humanistic personality theories. In L. S. Brown & M. Ballou (Eds.), *Personality and psychopathology: Feminist reappraisals.* New York: Guilford.

Lerner, H. (1986). *A mote in Freud's eye.* New York: Springer.

Lerner, H. (1988). *Women in therapy.* New York: Jason Aronson.

Levant, R. F. (1990). Psychological services designed for men: A psychoeducational approach. *Psychotherapy, 27,* 309–315.

Levant, R., & Pollack, W. (Eds.). (1995). *The new psychology of men.* New York: Basic.

Levant, R. F., & Shlien, J. M. (Eds.). (1984). *Client-centered therapy and the person-centered approach.* New York: Praeger.

Levenson, H. (1995). *Time-limited dynamic psychotherapy: A guide to clinical practice.* New York: Basic Books.

Levine, J. L., Stolz, J. A., & Lacks, P. (1983). Preparing psychotherapy clients: Rationale and suggestions. *Professional Psychology: Research and Practice, 14,* 317–322.

Levinson, D., Dorrow, C., Klein, E., Levinson, M., & McKee, B. (1978). *The seasons of a man's life.* New York: Knopf.

Levis, D. J. (1966). Effects of serial CS presentation and other characteristics of the CS on the conditioned avoidance response. *Psychological Reports, 18,* 755–766.

Levis, D. J. (1987). Treating anxiety and panic attacks: The conflict model of implosive therapy. *Journal of Integrative and Eclectic Psychotherapy, 6,* 450–461.

Levis, D. J. (1991). The recovery of traumatic memories: The etiological sources of psychopathology. In R. G. Kumzendorf (Ed.), *Mental imagery.* New York: Plenum.

Levis, D. J. (1993). The power of extrapolating from basic laboratory procedures: The behavioral-cognitive approach of implosive therapy. *Behavior Change, 10,* 154–161.

Levis, D. J., Bouska, S., Eron, J., & McIlhon, M. (1970). Serial CS presentation and one-way avoidance conditioning: A noticeable lack of delayed responding. *Psychonomic Science, 20,* 147–149.

Levis, D. J., & Stampfl, T. (1972). Effects of serial CS presentation on shuttlebox avoidance responding. *Learning and Motivation, 3,* 73–90.

Levitsky, A., & Perls, F. (1970). The rules and games of Gestalt therapy. In J. Fagan & I. Shepherd (Eds.), *Gestalt therapy now.* Palo Alto, CA: Science and Behavior Books.

Lewis, J., M., Beavers, W. R., Gossett, J. T., & Philips, V. A. (1976). *No single thread: Psychological health in family systems.* New York: Brunner/Mazel.

Lidz, T. (1963). *The family and human adaption.* New York: International Universities Press.

Liebman, R., Minuchin, S., & Baker, L. (1974). The use of structural family therapy on the treatment of intractable asthma. *American Journal of Psychiatry, 131,* 535–540.

Liebman, R., Minuchin, S., Baker, L., & Rosman, B. (1975). The treatment of anorexia nervosa. *Current Psychiatric Therapies, 15,* 51–57.

Lietaer, G. (1990). The client-centered approach after the Wisconsin Project: A personal view on its evolution. In G. Lietaer, J. Rombauts, & R. VanBalen (Eds.), *Client-centered and experiential psychotherapy in the nineties.* Leuven, Belgium: Leuven University Press.

Lietaer, G., Rombauts, J., & VanBalen, R. (Eds.). (1990). *Client-centered and experiential psychotherapy in the nineties.* Leuven, Belgium: Leuven University Press.

Liff, Z. A. (1992). Psychoanalysis and dynamic techniques. In D. K. Freedhiem (Ed.), *History of psychotherapy: A century of change* (pp. 571–587). Washington, DC: American Psychological Association.

Linden, W., & Chambers, L. (1994). Clinical effectiveness of non-drug treatment for hypertension: A meta-analysis. *Annals of Behavioral Medicine, 16,* 35–45.

Linehan, M. M. (1993). *Cognitive-behavioral treatment of borderline personality disorder.* New York: Guilford.

Linstone, H. A., & Turoff, M. (Eds.). (1975). *The Delphi method: Techniques and applications.* Reading, MA: Addison-Wesley.

Lipsey, M. W., & Wilson, D. B. (1993). The efficacy of psychological, educational, and behavioral treatment: Confirmation from meta-analysis. *American Psychologist, 48,* 1181–1209.

Lloyd, G. (1984). *The man of reason: "Male" and "female" in western philosophy.* London: Methuen.

Loeschen, S. (1997). *Systematic training in the skills of Virginia Satir.* Pacific Grove, CA: Brooks/Cole.

Loevinger, J. (1976). *Ego development.* San Francisco: Jossey-Bass.

Lohr, J. M., Tolin, D. F., & Lilienfeld, S. O. (in press). Efficacy of Eye Movement Desensitization and Reprocessing: Implications for behavior therapy. *Behavior Therapy.*

London, P. (1964). *The modes and morals of psychotherapy.* New York: Holt, Rinehart & Winston.

London, P. (1986). *The modes and morals of psychotherapy* (2nd ed.). New York: Hemisphere.

London, P. (1988). Metamorphosis in psychotherapy: Slouching toward integration. *Journal of Integrative and Eclectic Psychotherapy, 7,* 3–12.

Lorenz, K. (1963). *On aggression.* New York: Harcourt Brace Jovanovich.

Lorenzo, G. (1989). Current issues in the assessment and treatment of ethnic minority populations. *Psychotherapy in Private Practice, 1,* 133–140.

Lorion, R. P. (1978). Research on psychotherapy and behavior change with the disadvantaged: Past, present, and future directions. In S. L. Garfield & A. E. Bergin (Eds.), *Handbook of psychotherapy and behavior change* (2nd ed.). New York: Wiley.

Lowen, A. (1958). *Physical dynamics of character structure.* New York: Grune & Stratton.

Lowen, A. (1965). *Love and orgasm.* New York: Macmillan.

Lowen, A. (1967). *The betrayal of the body.* New York: Collier.

Lowen, A. (1972). Bioenergetic analysis: A development of Reichian therapy. In G. Goldman & D. Milman (Eds.), *Innovations in psychotherapy.* Springfield, IL: Charles C Thomas.

Lowen, A. (1975). *Bioenergetics.* New York: Penguin.

Lowen, A. (1980). *Fear of life.* New York: Macmillan.

Lowen, A. (1984). *Narcissism: Denial of the true self.* New York: Macmillan.

Luborsky, L. (1984). *Principles of psychoanalytic psychotherapy.* New York: Basic.

Luborsky, L. (1992). The Penn Research Project. In D. K. Freeheim (Ed.), *History of psychotherapy: A century of change.* Washington, DC: American Psychological Association.

Luborsky, L., & Crits-Cristoph, P. (1990). *Understanding transference.* New York: Basic.

Luborsky, L., Singer, B., & Luborsky, L. (1975). Comparative studies of psychotherapies. *Archives of General Psychiatry, 32,* 995–1008.

Luepnitz, D. A. (1988). *The family interpreted: Feminist theory in clinical practice.* New York: Basic.

Luria, A. (1961). *The role of speech in the regulation of normal and abnormal behaviors.* New York: Liveright.

Luthman, S. (1972). *Intimacy: The essence of male and female.* Los Angeles: Nash.

Lyons, L. C., & Woods, P. J. (1991). The efficacy of rational-emotive therapy: A quantitative review of the outcome research. *Clinical Psychology Review, 11,* 357–369.

Maddi, S. R. (1972). *Personality theories: A comparative analysis.* Homewood, IL: Dorsey.

Maddi, S. R. (1978). Existential and individual psychologies. *Journal of Individual Psychology, 34,* 182–190.

Maddi, S. R. (1996). *Personality theories: A comparative analysis* (6th ed.). Pacific Grove, CA: Brooks/Cole.

Mahalik, J. R. (1990). Systematic eclectic models. *The Counseling Psychologist, 18,* 655–679.

Mahler, M. S. (1968). *On human symbiosis of the vicissitudes of individuation.* New York: International Universities Press.

Mahoney, M. J. (1984). Psychoanalysis and behaviorism: The Yin and Yang of determinism. In H. Arkowitz & S. B. Messer (Eds.), *Psychoanalytic therapy and behavior therapy. Is integration possible?* (pp. 303–325). New York: Plenum.

Mahoney, M. J. (1991). *Human change processes: The scientific foundations of psychotherapy.* New York: Basic.

Mahoney, M. J. (1996). Constructivism and the study of complex self-organization. *Constructive Change, 1,* 3–8.

Mahrer, A. R. (1983). *Experiential psychotherapy: Basic practices.* New York: Brunner/Mazel.

Mahrer, A. R. (1986). *Therapeutic experiencing.* New York: Norton.

Mahrer, A. R. (1989a). *Dream work in psychotherapy and self-change.* New York: Norton.

Mahrer, A. R. (1989b). *How to do experiential psychotherapy.* Ottawa: University of Ottawa Press.

Mahrer, A. R. (1989c). *The integration of psychotherapies.* New York: Human Sciences Press.

Mahrer, A. R. (1991). Experiential psychotherapy, simple phobias, and a recasting of prescriptive treatment. *Psychotherapy, 28,* 448–451.

Mahrer, A. R. (1993). The experiential relationship: Is it all-purpose or is it tailored to the individual client? *Psychotherapy, 30*(3), 413–416.

Mahrer, A. R. (1996). *The complete guide to experiential psychotherapy.* New York: Wiley.

Mahrer, A. R., & Fairweather, D. R. (1993). What is experiencing? A critical review of meanings and applications in psychotherapy. *The Humanistic Psychologist, 21,* 2–25.

Malan, D. H. (1976a). *The frontier of brief psychotherapy.* New York: Plenum.

Malan, D. H. (1976b). *Toward the validation of dynamic psychotherapy: A replication.* New York: Plenum.

Malcolm, J. (1978, May 15). A reporter at large: The one-way mirror. *The New Yorker,* pp. 39–114.

Malleson, N. (1959). Panic and phobia. *Lancet, 1,* 225–227.

Manaster, G. J. (1987a). Adlerian theory and movement. *Individual Psychology, 43,* 280–287.

Manaster, G. J. (1987b). Editor's comments. *Individual Psychology, 43,* 1–2.

Manaster, G. J., & Corsini, R. J. (1982). *Individual psychology.* Itasca, IL: Peacock.

Mann, J. (1973). *Time-limited psychotherapy.* Cambridge, MA: Harvard University Press.

Mann, J., & Goldman, R. (1982). *A casebook in time-limited psychotherapy.* New York: McGraw-Hill.

Marcus, E. (1976). Gestalt therapy and beyond. In C. Hatcher & P. Himelstein (Eds.), *The handbook of Gestalt therapy.* New York: Jason Aronson.

Markowitz, J. C. (1997). The future of interpersonal psychotherapy. *Journal of Psychotherapy Practice and Research, 6,* 294–299.

Marks, I. M. (1987). *Fears, phobias, and rituals.* New York: Oxford University Press.

Marlatt, G. A., & Gordon, J. R. (Eds.). (1985). *Relapse prevention: Maintenance strategies in addictive behavior change.* New York: Guilford.

Martin, J., Paivio, S., & Labadie, D. (1990). Memory-enhancing characteristics of client-recalled important events in cognitive and experiential therapy: Integrating cognitive experimental and therapeutic psychology. *Counselling Psychology Quarterly, 3,* 239–256.

Marx, M. H., & Goodson, F. E. (Eds.). (1976). *Theories in contemporary psychology* (2nd ed.). New York: Macmillan.

Maslow, A. H. (1960). Existential psychology: What's in it for us? In R. May (Ed.), *Existential psychology.* New York: Random House.

Maslow, A. H. (1962). Some basic propositions of a growth and self-actualizing psychology. In *Perceiving, behaving, becoming: A new focus for education.* Washington, DC: Yearbook of the Association for Supervision and Curriculum Development.

Massey, R. F. (1989a). Integrating systems theory and TA in couples therapy. *Transactional Analysis Journal, 19,* 128–136.

Massey, R. F. (1989b). Techniques for integrating TA and systems theory in couples therapy. *Transactional Analysis Journal, 19,* 148–158.

Massey, S. D., & Massey, R. F. (1989). Systemic contexts for therapy with children. *Transactional Analysis Journal, 19,* 194–200.

Masters, W., & Johnson, V. (1966). *Human sexual response.* Boston: Little, Brown.

Masters, W., & Johnson, V. (1970). *Human sexual inadequacy.* Boston: Little, Brown.

Masterson, J. F. (1976). *Psychotherapy of the borderline adult.* New York: Brunner/Mazel.

Masterson, J. F. (1981). *The narcissistic and borderline disorders: An integrated developmental approach.* New York: Brunner/Mazel.

Maultsby, M. C., Jr., & Ellis, A. (1974). *Techniques for using rational-emotive imagery.* New York: Institute for Rational-Emotive Therapy.

May, R. (1958a). Contribution of existential psychotherapy. In R. May, E. Angel, & H. Ellenberger (Eds.), *Existence: A new dimension for psychology and psychiatry.* New York: Basic.

May, R. (1958b). The origins and significance of the existential movement in psy-chology. In R. May, E. Angel, & H. Ellenberger (Eds.), *Existence.* New York: Basic.

May, R. (1967). *Psychology and the human dilemma.* New York: Van Nostrand Reinhold.

May, R. (1969). *Love and will.* New York: Dell.

May, R. (1977). *The meaning of anxiety* (rev. ed.). New York: Norton.

May, R. (1981). *Freedom and destiny.* New York: Norton.

May, R. (1983). *The discovery of being: Writings in existential psychology.* New York: Norton.

May, R., Angel, E., & Ellenberger, H. (Eds.). (1958). *Existence: A new dimension in psychology and psychiatry.* New York: Basic.

McClendon, R., Kadis, L. B. (1995). Redecision therapy: On the leading edge. *Transactional Analysis Journal, 25,* 339–342.

McConnaughy, E. A., DiClemente, C. C., Prochaska, W. F., & Velicer, W. F. (1989). Stages of change in psychotherapy: A follow-up report. *Psychotherapy, 26,* 494–503.

McConnaughy, E. A., Prochaska, J., & Velicer, W. (1983). Stages of change in psychotherapy: Measurement and sample profiles. *Psychotherapy: Theory, Research and Practice, 20,* 368–375.

McDaniel, S. H., Hepworth, J., & Doherty, W. J. (1992). *Medical family therapy.* New York: Basic.

McGoldrick, M., & Gerson, R. (1985). *Genograms in family assessment.* New York: Norton.

McGoldrick, M., Giordano, J., & Pearce, J. K. (Eds.). (1996). *Ethnicity and family therapy* (2nd ed.). New York: Guilford.

McGrath, E., Keita, G. P., Strickland, B. R., & Russo, N. F. (Eds.). (1990). *Women and depression: Risk factors and treatment issues.* Washington, DC: American Psychological Association.

McNamee, S., & Gergen, K. J. (1992). *Therapy as social construction.* London: Sage.

Meador, B., & Rogers, C. (1973). Client-centered therapy. In R. Corsini (Ed.),

Current psychotherapies. Itasca, IL: Peacock.

Medieros, M., & Prochaska, J. O. (1993). *Predicting premature termination from psychotherapy*. Manuscript submitted for publication.

Meichenbaum, D. (1977). *Cognitive-behavior modification*. New York: Plenum.

Meichenbaum, D. (1985). *Stress inoculation training*. New York: Pergamon.

Meichenbaum, D. (1986). Cognitive-behavior modification. In F. H. Kanfer & A. P. Goldstein (Eds.), *Helping people change* (3rd ed.). New York: Pergamon.

Meichenbaum, D. (1996). Stress inoculation training for coping with stressors. *The Clinical Psychologist, 49*, 4–10.

Meichenbaum, D., & Goodman, J. (1969). Reflection-impulsivity and verbal control of motor behavior. *Child Development, 40*, 785–797.

Meichenbaum, D., & Goodman, J. (1971). Training impulsive children to talk to themselves: A means of developing self-control. *Journal of Abnormal Psychology, 77*, 115–126.

Meltzoff, J., & Kornreich, M. (1970). *Research in psychotherapy*. New York: Atherton.

Messer, S. B. (1992). A critical examination of belief structures in integrative and eclectic psychotherapy. In J. C. Norcross & M. R. Goldfried (Eds.), *Handbook of psychotherapy integration*. New York: Basic.

Messer, S. B., & Warren, C. S. (1995). *Models of brief psychodynamic therapy: A comparative approach*. New York: Guilford.

Messer, S. B., & Winokur, M. (1980). Some limits to the integration of psychoanalytic and behavior therapy. *American Psychologist, 35*, 818–827.

Meth, R. L., & Pasick, R. S. (1992). *Men in therapy: The challenge of change*. New York: Guilford.

Meyer, A. (1957). *Psychobiology: A science of man*. Springfield, IL: Charles C. Thomas.

Mikesell, R. H., Lusterman, D., & McDaniel, S. H. (Eds.). (1995). *Integrating family therapy: Handbook of family psychology and systems theory*. Washington, DC: American Psychological Association.

Miller, G., Galanter, E., & Pribram, K. (1960). *Plans and the structure of behavior*. New York: Holt, Rinehart & Winston.

Miller, L. (1994). Biofeedback and behavioral medicine: Treating the symptom, the syndrome, or the person? *Psychotherapy, 31*, 161–169.

Miller, R. C., & Berman, J. S. (1983). The efficacy of cognitive behavior therapies: A quantitative review of the research evidence. *Psychological Bulletin, 94*, 39–53.

Miller, S. D., Hubble, M. A., & Duncan, B. L. (Eds.). (1996). *Handbook of solution-focused brief therapy*. San Francisco: Jossey-Bass.

Miller, W. R. (1978). Behavioral treatment of problem drinkers: A comparative outcome study of three controlled drinking therapies. *Journal of Consulting and Clinical Psychology, 46*, 74–86.

Miller, W. R. (1983). Motivational interviewing with problem drinkers. *Behavioral Psychotherapy, 11*, 147–172.

Miller, W. R., & Munoz, R. F. (1982). *How to control your drinking* (2nd ed.). Albuquerque: University of New Mexico Press.

Miller, W. R., & Rollnick, S. (1991). *Motivational interviewing: Preparing people for change*. New York: Guilford.

Miller, W. R., & Sanches, V. C. (1994). Motivating young adults for treatment and lifestyle change. In G. Howard (Ed.), *Issues in alcohol use and misuse by young adults* (pp. 55–82). Notre Dame, IN: University of Notre Dame Press.

Miller, W. R., & Taylor, C. A. (1980). Relative effectiveness of bibliotherapy, individual and group self-control training in the treatment of problem drinkers. *Addictive Behaviors, 5*, 13–24.

Miller, W. R., Zweben, A., DiClemente, C. C., & Rychtarik, R. G. (1992). *Motivational Enhancement Therapy manual: A clinical research guide for therapists treating individuals with alcohol abuse and dependence*. Rockville, MD: National Institute on Alcohol Abuse and Alcoholism.

Minuchin, S. (1970). The use of an ecological framework in child psychiatry. In J. Anthony & C. Kaupernik (Eds.), *The child in his family*. New York: Wiley.

Minuchin, S. (1972). Structural family therapy. In G. Caplan (Ed.), *American handbook of psychiatry* (Vol. 2). New York: Basic.

Minuchin, S. (1974). *Families and family therapy*. Cambridge, MA: Harvard University Press.

Minuchin, S. (1997). *Mastering family therapy: Journeys of growth and tranformation*. New York: Wiley.

Minuchin, S., Baker, L., Rosman, B., Liebman, R., Milman, L., & Todd, T. (1975). A conceptual model of psychosomatic illness in children. *Archives of General Psychiatry, 32*, 1031–1038.

Minuchin, S., Montalvo, B., Guerney, B., Rosman, B., & Schumer, F. (1967). *Families of the slums*. New York: Basic.

Mischel, W. (1968). *Personality and assessment*. New York: Wiley.

Mitchell, S. (1988). *Relational concepts in psychoanalysis: An integration*. Cambridge: Harvard University Press.

Mitchell, S. (1993). *Hope and dread in psychoanalysis*. New York: Basic Books.

Mitchell, K. M., Bozarth, J. D., & Krauft, C. C. (1977). A reappraisal of the therapeutic effectiveness of accurate empathy, nonpossessive warmth, and genuineness. In A. S. Guvman & A. M. Razin (Eds.), *Effective psychotherapy*. New York: Pergamon.

Mitchell-Meadows, M. (1992). Consider culture when counseling. *The APA Monitor, 23*(9), 37.

Mohr, D. V. (1995). Negative outcome in psychotherapy: A critical review. *Clinical Psychology: Science and Practice, 2*, 1–27.

Monti, P. M, Rohsenow, D. J., Rubonis, A. V., Niaura, R. S., Sirota, A. D., Colby, S. M., Goddard, P., & Abrams, D. B. (1993). Cue exposure with coping skills treatment for male alcoholics: A preliminary investigation. *Journal of Consulting and Clinical Psychology, 61*, 1011–1019.

Moore, C. M. (1987). *Group techniques for idea building*. Newbury Park, CA: Sage.

Morganstern, K. (1973). Implosive therapy and flooding procedures: A critical review. *Psychological Bulletin, 79*, 318–334.

Mosak, H., & Dreikurs, R. (1973). Adlerian psychotherapy. In R. Corsini (Ed.), *Current psychotherapies*. Itasca, IL.: Peacock.

Mosak, H., & Shulman, B. (1988). *Life style inventory*. Muncie, IN: Accelerated Development.

Mowrer, O. H. (1947). On the dual nature of learning: A reinterpretation of "conditioning" and "problem-solving." *Harvard Education Review, 17*, 102–148.

Mowrer, O. H. (1961). *The crisis in psychiatry and religion*. New York: Van Nostrand Reinhold.

Mowrer, O. H., & Mowrer, W. M. (1938). Enuresis: A method for its study and treatment. *American Journal of Orthopsychiatry, 8*, 436–459.

Munoz, R. F., Hollon, S. D., McGrath, E., Rehm, L. P., & VandenBos, G. R. (1994). On the *AHCPR Depression in Primary Care* guidelines: Further considerations for practitioners. *American Psychologist, 49*, 42–61.

Murtagh, D. R. R., & Greenwood, K. M. (1995). Identifying effective psychological treatments for insomnia: A meta-analysis. *Journal of Consulting and Clinical Psychology, 63*, 79–89.

Napoli, D. F., & Wolk, C. A. (1989). Circular learning: Teaching and learning Gestalt therapy in groups. *Journal of Independent Social Work, 3*(4), 57–70.

Navarro, A. M. (1993). Effectividad de las psicoterapias con Latinos en los estados unidos: Una revision meta-analitica. *Interamerican Journal of Psychology, 27,* 131–146.

Neill, A. S. (1958). The man Reich. In P. Ritter (Ed.), *Wilhelm Reich memorial volume.* Nottingham, England: Ritter.

Neimeyer, R. A. (1993). An appraisal of constructivist psychotherapies. *Journal of Consulting and Clinical Psychology, 61,* 221–234.

Neimeyer, R. A., & Mahoney, M. J. (Eds.). (1995). *Constructivism in psychotherapy.* Washington, DC: American Psychological Association.

Neressian, E., & Kopff, R. G. (Eds.). (1996). *Textbook of psychoanalysis.* Washington, DC: American Psychiatric Press.

Nichols, M., & Zax, M. (1977). *Catharsis in psychotherapy.* New York: Gardner.

Nikelly, A. G. (1996). Alternatives to androcentric bias of personality disorders. *Clinical Psychology and Psychotherapy, 3,* 15–22.

Norcross, J. C. (1985a). For discriminating clinicians only. *Contemporary Psychology, 30,* 757–758.

Norcross, J. C. (1985b). In defense of theoretical orientations for clinicians. *The Clinical Psychologist, 38* (1), 13–17.

Norcross, J. C. (1987a). A rational and empirical analysis of existential psychotherapy. *Journal of Humanistic Psychology, 27,* 41–68.

Norcross, J. C. (Ed.). (1987b). Special section: Toward a common language for psychotherapy. *Journal of Integrative and Eclectic Psychotherapy, 6,* 165–204.

Norcross, J. C. (1990). An eclectic definition of psychotherapy. In J. K. Zeig & W. M. Munion (Eds.), *What is psychotherapy?* San Francisco: Jossey-Bass.

Norcross, J. C. (Ed.). (1991). Prescriptive matching in psychotherapy: Psychoanalysis for simple phobias? *Psychotherapy, 28,* 439–472.

Norcross, J. C. (Ed.). (1992). The future of psychotherapy [Special issue]. *Psychotherapy, 29*(1), 1–158.

Norcross, J. C. (Ed.). (1993). The relationship of choice: Matching the therapist's stance to individual clients [Special section]. *Psychotherapy, 30*(4).

Norcross, J. C., Alford, B. A., & DeMichele, J. T. (1992). The future of psychotherapy: Delphi data and concluding observations. *Psychotherapy, 29,* 150–158.

Norcross, J. C., & Arkowitz, H. (1992). The evolution and current status of psychotherapy integration. In W. Dryden (Ed.), *Integrative and eclectic psychotherapy: A handbook.* London: Open University Press.

Norcross, J. C., & Beutler, L.E. (1997). Determining the therapeutic relationship of choice in brief therapy. In J. N. Butcher (Ed.), *Personality assessment in managed care: A practitioner's guide.* New York: Oxford University Press.

Norcross, J. C., & Beutler, L. E. (1998). Prescriptive eclectic psychotherapy. In R. A. Dorfman (Ed.), *Paradigms of clinical social work* (vol. 2). New York: Brunner/Mazel.

Norcross, J. C., & Freedheim, D. K. (1992). Into the future: Retrospect and prospect in psychotherapy. In D. K. Freedheim (Ed.), *History of psychotherapy: A century of change.* Washington, DC: American Psychological Association.

Norcross, J. C., & Goldfried, M. R. (Eds.). (1992). *Handbook of psychotherapy integration.* New York: Basic.

Norcross, J. C., & Grencavage, L. M. (1989). Eclecticism and integration in psychotherapy: Major themes and obstacles. *British Journal of Guidance and Counseling, 17,* 227–247.

Norcross, J. C., Karg, R. S., & Prochaska, J. O. (1997a). Clinical psychologists in the 1990s. *The Clinical Psychologist, 50*(2), 4–9.

Norcross, J. C., Karg, R. S., & Prochaska, J. O. (1997b). Clinical psychologists and managed care: Some data from the Division 12 membership. *The Clinical Psychologist, 50*(1), 4–8.

Norcross, J. C., & Napolitano, G. (1986). Defining our journal and ourselves. *International Journal of Eclectic Psychotherapy, 5,* 249–255.

Norcross, J. C., & Newman, C. F. (1992). Psychotherapy integration: Setting the context. In J. C. Norcross & M. R. Goldfried (Eds.), *Handbook of psychotherapy integration.* New York: Basic.

Norcross, J. C., & Prochaska, J. O. (1984). Where do behavior (and other) therapists take their troubles?: II. *The Behavior Therapist, 7,* 26–27.

Norcross, J. C., & Prochaska, J. O. (1986a). Psychotherapist heal thyself: I. The psychological distress and self-change of psychologists, counselors, and laypersons. *Psychotherapy, 23,* 102–114.

Norcross, J. C., & Prochaska, J. O. (1986b). Psychotherapist heal thyself: II. The self-initiated and therapy facilitated change of psychological distress. *Psychotherapy, 23,* 345–356.

Norcross, J. C. & Prochaska, J. O. (1988). A study of eclectic (and integrative) views revisited. *Professional Psychology: Research and Practice, 19,* 170–174.

Norcross, J. C., Prochaska, J. O., & DiClemente, C. C. (1995). The stages and processes of weight control: Two replications. In T. B. VanItallie & A. P. Simopoulos (Eds.), *Obesity: New directions in assessment and management.* Philadelphia: Charles Press.

Norcross, J. C., Prochaska, J. O., & Farber, J. A. (1993). Psychologists conducting psychotherapy: New findings and historical comparisons on the Psychotherapy Division membership. *Psychotherapy, 30,* 692–697.

Norcross, J. C., Prochaska, J. O., & Hambrecht, M. (1985). The Levels of Attribution and Change (LAC) Scale: Development and measurement. *Cognitive Therapy and Research, 9,* 631–649.

Norcross, J. C., Ratzin, A. C., & Payne, D. (1989). Ringing in the New Year: The change processes and reported outcomes of resolutions. *Addictive Behaviors, 14,* 205–212.

Norcross, J. C., Saltzman, N., & Guinta, L. C. (1990). Contention and convergence in clinical practice. In N. Saltzman & J. C. Norcross (Eds.), *Therapy wars* (pp. 242–260). San Francisco: Jossey-Bass.

Norcross, J. C., Strausser, D. J., & Faltus, F. J. (1988). The therapist's therapist. *American Journal of Psychotherapy, 42,* 53–66.

Norcross, J. C., Strausser, D. J., & Missar, C. D. (1988). The process and outcomes of psychotherapists' personal treatment experiences. *Psychotherapy, 25,* 36–43.

Norcross, J. C., & Vangarelli, D. J. (1989). The resolution solution: Longitudinal examination of New Year's change attempts. *Journal of Substance Abuse, 1,* 127–134.

Norcross, J. C., & Wogan, M. (1983). American psychotherapists of diverse persuasions: Characteristics, theories, practices, and clients. *Professional Psychology, 14,* 529–539.

Noyes, R. (1991). Treatment of choice for anxiety disorders. In W. Coryell & G. Winokur (Eds.), *The clinical management of anxiety disorders.* New York: Oxford University Press.

O'Banion, D. R., & Whaley, D. L. (1981). *Behavior contracting.* New York: Springer.

Ockene, J., Kristeller, J. L., Goldberg, R., Ockene, I., Merriam, P., Barrett, S., Pekow, P., Hosmer, D., & Gianelly, R. (1992). Smoking cessation and severity of disease: The Coronary Artery Smoking Intervention Study. *Health Psychology, 11,* 119–126.

Ockene, J., Ockene, I., & Kristellar, J. (1988). *The coronary artery smoking intervention study.* Worcester, MA: National Heart Lung Blood Institute.

Okun, B. F. (1992). Object relations and self psychology: Overview and feminist perspectives. In L. A. Brown & M. Ballou (Eds.), *Personality and psychopathology:*

Feminist reappraisals. New York: Guilford.

O'Leary, K. D., & Wilson, G. T. (1987). *Behavior therapy: Application and outcome* (2nd ed.). Englewood Cliffs, NJ: Prentice-Hall.

Olsen, P. (Ed.). (1976). *Emotional flooding.* New York: Human Sciences.

Omer, H. (1993). The integrative focus: Coordinating symptom—and person—oriented perspectives in therapy. *American Journal of Psychotherapy, 47,* 283–295.

Omer, H. (1997). Narrative empathy. *Psychotherapy, 34,* 19–27.

Oquendo, M., Horwath, E., & Martinez, A. (1992). Ataques de nervios: Proposed diagnostic specific syndrome. *Culture, Medicine and Psychiatry, 16,* 367–376.

Orlinsky, D. E., & Howard, K. I. (1980). Gender and psychotherapeutic outcome. In A. M. Brodsky & R. T. Hare-Mustin (Eds.), *Women and psychotherapy.* New York: Guilford.

Orlinsky, D. E., & Howard, K. I. (1986). Process and outcome in psychotherapy. In S. L. Garfield & A. E. Bergin (Eds.), *Handbook of psychotherapy and behavior change* (3rd ed.). New York: Wiley.

Orlinsky, D. E., & Howard, K. I. (1987). A generic model of psychotherapy. *Journal of Integrative and Eclectic Psychotherapy, 6,* 6–27.

Osborn, A. (1963). *Applied imagination.* New York: Scribner.

Otto, H., & Otto, R. (1972). *Total sex.* New York: New American Library.

Paivio, S. C., & Greenberg, L. S. (1995). Resolving "unfinished business": Efficacy of experiential therapy using empy-chair dialogue. *Journal of Consulting and Clinical Psychology, 63,* 419–425.

Palmer, J. E. (1980). *A primer of eclectic psychotherapy.* Pacific Grove, CA: Brooks/Cole.

Paludi, M. A. (1992). *The psychology of women.* Dubuque, IA: Brown & Benchmore.

Parloff, M. (1976, February 21). Shopping for the right therapy. *Saturday Review,* pp. 14–16.

Parloff, M. B., Waskow, I. E., & Wolfe, B. E. (1978). Research on therapist variables in relation to process and outcome. In S. L. Garfeld & A. E. Bergin (Eds.), *Handbook of psychotherapy and behavior change: An empirical analysis* (2nd ed.). New York: Wiley.

Patterson, C. H. (1984). Empathy, warmth, and genuineness in psychotherapy: A review of reviews. *Psychotherapy, 21,* 431–438.

Patterson, C. H. (1989). Foundations for a systematic eclecticism in psychotherapy. *Psychotherapy, 26,* 427–435.

Patterson, C. H. (1990). On misrepresentation and misunderstanding. *Psychotherapy, 27,* 301.

Paul, G. (1966). *Insight versus desensitization in psychotherapy: An experiment in anxiety reduction.* Stanford, CA: Stanford University Press.

Paul, G. (1967). Insight versus desensitization in psychotherapy two years after termination. *Journal of Consulting and Clinical Psychology, 31,* 333–348.

Pederson, P. (Ed.). (1985). *Handbook of cross-cultural counseling and therapy.* Westport, CT: Greenwood.

Perls, F. (1947). *Ego, hunger and aggression: A revision of Freud's theory and method.* Winchester, MA: Allen & Unwin.

Perls, F. (1969a). *Gestalt therapy verbatim.* Lafayette, CA: Real People Press.

Perls, F. (1969b). *In and out the garbage pail.* Lafayette, CA: Real People Press.

Perls, F. (1970). Four lectures. In J. Fagan & I. Shepherd (Eds.), *Gestalt therapy now.* Palo Alto, CA: Science and Behavior Books.

Perls, F. (1973). *The Gestalt approach and eye witness to therapy.* Palo Alto, CA: Science and Behavior Books.

Perls, F., Hefferline, R., & Goodman, P. (1951). *Gestalt therapy: Excitement and growth in the human personality.* New York: Dell.

Perry, M. A., & Furukawa, M. J. (1986). Modeling methods. In F. H. Kanfer & A. P. Goldstein (Eds.), *Helping people change* (3rd ed.). New York: Pergamon.

Perry, W. (1970). *Forms of intellectual and ethical development in the college years: A schema*. New York: Holt, Rinehart & Winston.

Persi, J. (1992). Top gun games: When therapists compete. *Transactional Analysis Journal, 22*, 144–152.

Persons, J. B., & Miranda, J. (1995). The search for mode-specific effects of cognitive and other therapies: A methodological suggestion. *Psychotherapy Research, 5*, 102–112.

Pervin, L. A. (1993). *Personality: Theory and research*. New York: Wiley.

Peterson, C., Semmel, A., vonBaeyer, C., Abramson, L. Y., Metalsky, G. I., & Seligman, M. E. P. (1982). The Attributional Style Questionnaire. *Cognitive Therapy and Research, 6*, 281–299.

Peterson, C., & Villanova, P. (1988). An expanded Attributional Style Questionnaire. *Journal of Abnormal Psychology, 97*, 87–89.

Piaget, J. (1952). *The origins of intelligence in children*. New York: International Universities Press.

Pinsof, W. M. (1995). *Integrative problem-centered therapy*. New York: Basic.

Pinsof, W. M., Wynne, L. C., & Hambright, A. B. (1996). The outcome of couple and family therapy: Findings, conclusions, and recommendations. *Psychotherapy, 33*, 321–331.

Pipher, M. B. (1994). *Reviving Ophelia*. New York: Putnam.

Polster, E., & Polster, M. (1973). *Gestalt therapy integrated*. New York: Brunner/Mazel.

Polster, M. (1974). Women in therapy: A Gestalt therapist's view. In S. V. Frankl & V. Burtle (Eds.), *Women in therapy*. New York: Brunner/Mazel.

Power, R. N. (1981). On the process and practice of psychotherapy: Some reflections. *British Journal of Medical Psychology, 54*, 15–23.

President's Commission on Mental Health. (1978). *Report to the President*. Washington, DC: U.S. Government Printing Office.

Prochaska, J. O. (1968, May). *Implosive therapy with a severe obsessive compulsive patient*. Paper presented at the University of Michigan Clinical Colloquium, Ann Arbor.

Prochaska, J. O. (1971). Symptom and dynamic cues in the implosive treatment of test anxiety. *Journal of Abnormal Psychology, 77*, 133–142.

Prochaska, J. O. (1979). *Systems of psychotherapy: A transtheoretical analysis*. Chicago: Dorsey.

Prochaska, J. O. (1996). A revolution in health promotion: Smoking cessation as a case study. In R. J. Resnick & R. H. Rozensky (Eds.), *Health psychology through the lifespan: Practice and research opportunities*. Washington, DC: APA Books.

Prochaska, J. O. (in press). Strong and weak principles of progress from precontemplation to action for twelve problem behaviors. *Health Psychology*.

Prochaska, J. O., & DiClemente, C. C. (1982). Transtheoretical therapy: Toward a more integrative model of change. *Psychotherapy: Theory, Research and Practice, 19*, 276–288.

Prochaska, J. O., & DiClemente, C. C. (1983). Stages and processes of self-change of smoking: Toward an integrative model of change. *Journal of Consulting and Clinical Psychology, 51*, 390–395.

Prochaska, J. O., & DiClemente, C. C. (1984). *The transtheoretical approach: Crossing the traditional boundaries of therapy*. Homewood, IL: Dow Jones-Irwin.

Prochaska, J. O., & DiClemente, C. C. (1992a). Stages of change in the modification of problem behaviors. In M. Hersen, R. M. Eisler, & P. M. Miller (Eds.), *Progress in behavior modification*. Sycamore, IL: Sycamore.

Prochaska, J. O., & DiClemente, C. C. (1992b). The transtheoretical approach. In J. C. Norcross & M. R. Goldfried (Eds.), *Handbook of psychotherapy integration*. New York: Basic.

Prochaska, J. O., DiClemente, C. C., & Norcross, J. C. (1992). In search of how people change: Applications to addictive behaviors. *American Psychologist, 47,* 1102–1114.

Prochaska, J. O., DiClemente, C. C., Velicer, W. F., Ginpil, S. E., & Norcross, J. C. (1985). Predicting change in smoking status for self-changers. *Addictive Behaviors, 10,* 395–406.

Prochaska, J. O., DiClemente, C. C., Velicer, W. F., & Rossi, J. S. (1993). Standardized, individualized, interactive, and personalized self-help programs for smoking cessation. *Health Psychology, 12,* 399–405.

Prochaska, J. O., Norcross, J. C., & DiClemente, C. C. (1995). *Changing for good.* New York: Avon.

Prochaska, J. O., Norcross, J. C., Fowler, J., Follick, M., & Abrams, D. B. (1992). Attendance and outcome in a work-site weight control program: Processes and stages of change as process and predictor variables. *Addictive Behavior, 17,* 35–45.

Prochaska, J. O., Rossi, J. S., & Wilcox, N. S. (1991). Change processes and psychotherapy outcome in integrative case research. *Journal of Psychotherapy Integration, 1,* 103–120.

Prochaska, J. O., Smith, N., Marzilli, R., Donovan, W., & Colby, J. (1974). Demonstration of the advantages of remote-control aversive stimulation in the control of headbanging in a retarded child. *Journal of Behavior Therapy and Experimental Psychiatry, 5,* 285–289.

Project MATCH Research Group. (1993). Project MATCH: Rationale and methods for a multisite clinical trial matching patients to alcholism treatment. *Alcoholism: Clinical and Experiemental Research, 17,* 1130–1145.

Project MATCH Research Group. (1997). Matching alcholism treatments to client heterogeneity: Project MATCH post-treatment drinking outcomes. *Journal of Studies on Alcohol, 58,* 7–29.

Prout, H. T., & DeMartino, R. A. (1986). A meta-analysis of school-based studies of psychotherapy. *Journal of School Psychology, 24,* 285–292.

Psychology Today. (1972, May). Letter to the editor.

Rachman, S. J. (1991). The medium-term future. *Behavioural Psychotherapy, 19,* 3–5.

Rait, D. (1988). Survey results. *Family Therapy Networker, 12,* 52–56.

Rank, O. (1936). *Will therapy.* New York: Knopf.

Rapaport, D. (1958). The theory of ego autonomy: A generalization. *Bulletin of the Menninger Clinic, 22,* 13–35.

Raskin, N. J. (1986a). Client-centered group psychotherapy: 1. Development of client-centered groups. *Person-Centered Review, 1,* 272–290.

Raskin, N. J. (1986b). Client-centered group psychotherapy: 2. Research on client-centered groups. *Person-Centered Review, 1,* 389–408.

Raskin, N. J. (1992, August). *Not necessary, perhaps sufficient, definitely facilitative.* Paper presented at the 100th annual convention of the American Psychological Association, Washington, DC.

Rebecca, M., Hefner, R., & Oleshansky, B. (1976). A model of sex role transcendence. *Journal of Social Issues, 32,* 197–206.

Reed, S. D., Katkin, E. S., & Goldand, S. (1986). Biofeedback and behavioral medicine. In F. H. Kanfer & A. P. Goldstein (Eds.), *Helping people change* (3rd ed.). New York: Pergamon.

Reich, W. (1942). *The function of the orgasm.* New York: Orgone Institute.

Reich, W. (1945). *Character analysis.* New York: Orgone Institute.

Reich, W. (1951). *Selected writings.* New York: Farrar, Straus & Giroux.

Reich, W. (1953). *People in trouble.* New York: Orgone Institute.

Reich, W. (1967). *Reich speaks on Freud.* (M. Higgins & C. Higgins, Eds.). New York: Farrar, Straus & Giroux.

Reich, W. (1970). *The mass psychology of fascism*. New York: Farrar, Straus & Giroux.

Reicherts, M. (1998). Gesprachspsychotherapie. In U. Baumann & M. Perrez (Eds.), *Lehrbuch klinische psychologie* (2nd ed.). Bern: Hans Huber.

Reik, T. (1948). *Listening with the third ear*. New York: Farrar, Straus & Giroux.

Reinecke, M. A., Ryan, N. E., & DuBois, D. L. (1998). Cognitive-behavior therapy of depression and depressive symptoms during adolescence: A review and meta-analysis. *Journal of the American Academy of Child and Adolescent Psychiatry, 37*.

Reisman, D. (1961). *The lonely crowd*. New Haven: Yale University Press.

Reiss, D. (1977). The multiple family group as a small society: Family regulation of interaction with nonmembers. *American Journal of Psychiatry, 134*, 21–24.

Rice, L. N. (1988). Integration and the client-centered relationship. *Journal of Integrative and Eclectic Psychotherapy, 7*, 291–302.

Rice, L. N., & Greenberg, L. (Eds.). (1984). *Patterns of change*. New York: Guilford.

Ricks, D. F., Wandersman, A., & Poppen, P. J. (1976). Humanism and behaviorism: Towards new syntheses. In A. Wandersman, P. J. Poppen, & D. F. Ricks (Eds.), *Humanism and behaviorism: Dialogue and growth*. Elmsford, NY: Pergamon.

Rimm, D., & Masters, J. (1974). *Behavior therapy*. New York: Academic.

Riordan, R. J., Mullis, F., & Nuchow, L. (1996). Organizing for bibliotherapy: The science in the art. *Individual Psychology, 52*, 169–180.

Roberts, L. J., & Marlatt, G. A. (1998). Guidelines for relapse prevention. In G. P. Koocher, J. C. Norcross, & S. S. Hill (Eds.), *Psychologists' desk reference*. New York: Oxford University Press.

Roberts, A. H., Kewman, D. G., Mercier, L., & Hovell, M. (1993). The power of nonspecific effects in healing: Implications for psychosocial and biological treatments. *Clinical Psychology Review, 13*, 375–391.

Robertson, M. (1979). Some observations from an eclectic therapist. *Psychotherapy: Theory, Research and Practice, 16*, 18–21.

Robine, J. (1991). Contact, the first experience. *The Gestalt Journal, 14*, 45–60.

Robins, C. N., Helzer, J. D., Weissman, M. M., Orvaschel, H. Gruenberg, E., Burke, J. D., & Regier, D. A. (1984). Lifetime prevalence of specific psychiatric disorders in three sites. *Archives of General Psychiatry, 41*, 949–958.

Robinson, D. (1969). *The Freudian left: Wilhelm Reich, Geza Roheim, Herbert Marcuse*. New York: Harper & Row.

Robinson, L. A., Berman, J. S., & Neimeyer, R. A. (1990). Psychotherapy for the treatment of depression: A comprehensive review of controlled outcome research. *Psychological Bulletin, 108*, 30–49.

Roethilsberger, F., & Dickson, W. (1939). *Management and the worker*. Cambridge, MA: Harvard University Press.

Rogers, C. R. (1939). *The clinical treatment of the problem child*. Boston: Houghton Mifflin.

Rogers, C. R. (1942). *Counseling and psychotherapy*. Boston: Houghton Mifflin.

Rogers, C. R. (1951). *Client-centered therapy*. Boston: Houghton Mifflin.

Rogers, C. R. (1957). The necessary and sufficient conditions of therapeutic personality change. *Journal of Consulting Psychology, 21*, 95–103.

Rogers, C. R. (1959). A theory of therapy, personality, and interpersonal relationships as developed in the client-centered framework. In S. Koch (Ed.), *Psychology: A study of a science*. New York: McGraw-Hill.

Rogers, C. R. (1961). *On becoming a person*. Boston: Houghton Mifflin.

Rogers, C. R. (1970). *Carl Rogers on encounter groups*. New York: Harper & Row.

Rogers, C. R. (1972). *On becoming partners: Marriage and its alternatives*. New York: Delacorte.

Rogers, C. R. (1977). *Carl Rogers on personal power*. New York: Delacorte.

Rogers, C. R. (1980). *A way of being*. Boston: Houghton Mifflin.

Rogers, C. R. (1983). *Freedom to learn for the 80's*. Columbus, OH: Merrill.

Rogers, C. R. (1986). Carl Rogers on the development of the person-centered approach. *Person-Centered Review, 1,* 257–259.

Rogers, C. R. (1987a). Comments on the issue of equality in psychotherapy. *Journal of Humanistic Psychology, 27,* 38–40.

Rogers, C. R. (1987b). Steps toward world peace, 1948–1986: Tension reduction in theory and practice. *Counseling and Values, 32,* 38–45.

Rogers, C. R., & Dymond, R. (1954). *Psychotherapy and personality change*. Chicago: University of Chicago Press.

Rogers, C. R., Gendlin, E., Kiesler, D., & Truax, C. (1967). *The therapeutic relationship and its impact: A study of psychotherapy with schizophrenics*. Madison: University of Wisconsin Press.

Rogers, C. R., & Rablen, R. (1958). *A scale of process in psychotherapy*. Unpublished manuscript, University of Wisconsin, Madison.

Rokeach, M. (1970). Faith, hope and bigotry. *Psychology Today, 3,* pp. 33–38.

Rollnick, S., & Miller, W. R. (1995). What is motivational interviewing? *Behavioural and Cognitive Psychotherapy, 23,* 325–334.

Rosenberg, J. (1973). *Total orgasm*. New York: Random House.

Rosenblatt, A. D. (Ed.). (1991). *Psychotherapy in the future* (GAP Report #133). Washington, DC: American Psychiatric Press.

Rosenthal, R. (1990). How are we doing in soft psychology? *American Psychologist, 45,* 775–777.

Rosenthal, R. (1995). Progress in clinical psychology: Is there any? *Clinical Psychology: Science and Practice, 2,* 133–150.

Rosenzweig, S. (1936). Some implicit common factors in diverse methods of psychotherapy. *American Journal of Orthopsychiatry, 6,* 412–415.

Rosewater, L. B., & Walker, L. E. A. (Eds.). (1985). *Handbook of feminist therapy*. New York: Springer.

Rosman, B., Minuchin, S., Liebman, R., & Baker, L. (1978, November). *Family therapy for psychosomatic children*. Paper presented at the annual meeting of the American Academy of Psychosomatic Medicine, Atlanta.

Ross, A., & Fonagy, P. (1996). *What works for whom? A critical review of psychotherapy research*. New York: Guilford.

Rothenberg, A. (1988). *The creative process of psychotherapy*. New York: Norton.

Rotter, J. B. (1954). *Social learning and clinical psychology*. Englewood Cliffs, NJ: Prentice-Hall.

Rubinstein, G. (1994). Expressions of existential philosophy in different therapeutic schools. *Journal of Contemporary Psychotherapy, 24,* 131–148.

Rush, A., Beck, A., Kovacs, M., & Hollon, S. (1977). Comparative efficacy of cognitive therapy and pharmacotherapy in the treatment of depressed outpatients. *Cognitive Therapy and Research, 1,* 17–37.

Ryle, A. (1990). *Cognitive analytic therapy*. London: Wiley.

Ryle, A. (Ed.). (1995). *Cognitive analytic therapy: Developments in theory and practice*. New York: Wiley.

Sachse, R. (1990). Acting purposefully in client-centered therapy. In P. J. D. Drenth, J. A. Sergeant, & R. J. Tokens (Eds.), *European perspectives in psychology* (Vol I, pp. 65–80). New York: Wiley.

Safran, J. D., & Segal, Z. V. (1990). *Interpersonal processes in cognitive therapy*. New York: Basic.

Salter, A. (1949). *Conditioned reflex therapy*. New York: Farrar, Straus & Giroux.

Saltzman, N., & Norcross, J. C. (Eds.). (1990). *Therapy wars: Contention and* convergence in differing clinical approaches. San Francisco: Jossey-Bass.

Saner, R. (1989). Culture bias of Gestalt therapy: Made-in-USA. *The Gestalt Journal, 12,* 57–71.

Sartre, J. P. (1955). *No exit and three other plays.* New York: Vintage.

Sartre, J. P. (1956). *Being and nothingness.* New York: Philosophical Library.

Sartre, J. P. (1967). *Existential psychoanalysis.* Chicago: Henry Regnery.

Satir, V. (1967). *Conjoint family therapy.* Palo Alto, CA: Science and Behavior Books.

Satir, V. (1972). *Peoplemaking.* Palo Alto, CA: Science and Behavior Books.

Satir, V. (1982). The therapist and family therapy: Process model. In A. Horne & M. Olsen (Eds.), *Family counseling and therapy.* Itasca, IL: Peacock.

Satir, V., & Baldwin, M. (1983). *Satir step by step.* Palo Alto, CA: Science and Behavior Books.

Satir, V., Stachowiak, J., & Taschman, H. (1977). *Helping people change.* New York: Jason Aronson.

Satz, P., & Baraff, A. (1962). Changes in relation between self-concepts and ideal self-concepts of psychotics consequent upon therapy. *Journal of General Psychology, 67,* 191–198.

Saunders, T., Drishell, J. E., Johnston, J. H., & Salas, E. (1996). The effect of stress inoculation training on anxiety and performance. *Journal of Occupational Health Psychology, 1,* 170–186.

Schachter, S. (1971). Some extraordinary facts about obese humans and rats. *American Psychologist, 26,* 129–149.

Schachter, S. (1982). Recidivism and self-cure of smoking and obesity. *American Psychologist, 37,* 436–444.

Schachter, S., & Singer, J. (1962). Cognitive, social and physiological determinants of emotional state. *Psychological Review, 69,* 379–399.

Scher, M., & Good, G. E. (1990). Gender and counseling in the twenty-first century: What does the future hold? *Journal of Counseling and Development, 68,* 388–391.

Scher, M., Stevens, M., Good, G., & Eichenfield, G. A. (Eds.). (1987). *Handbook of counseling and psychotherapy with men.* Newbury Park, CA: Sage.

Schiff, R., Smith, N., & Prochaska, J. (1972). Extinction of avoidance in rats as a function of duration and number of blocked trials. *Journal of Comparative and Physiological Psychology, 81,* 356–369.

Scogin, F., & McElreath, L. (1994). Efficacy of psychosocial treatments for geriatric depression: A quantitative review. *Journal of Consulting and Clinical Psychology, 62,* 69–74.

Segal, L. (1962). Brief family therapy. In A. Horne & M. Ohlsen (Eds.), *Family counseling and therapy.* Itasca, IL: Peacock.

Segal, L. (1991). Brief therapy: The MRI approach. In A. S. Gurman & D. P. Kniskern (Eds.), *Handbook of family therapy* (Vol. 2). New York: Brunner/Mazel.

Seidenberg, R. (1970). *Marriage in life and literature.* New York: Philosophical Library.

Seligman, M. E. P. (1990). *Learned optimism.* New York: Knopf.

Seligman, M. E. P., Abramson, L. Y., Semmel, A., & vonBaeyer, C. (1979). Depressive attributional style. *Journal of Abnormal Psychology, 88,* 242–247.

Selmi, P. M., Klein, M. H., Greist, J. H., Sorrell, S. P., & Erdman, H. P. (1990). Computer-administered cognitive-behavioral therapy for depression. *American Journal of Psychiatry, 147,* 51–56.

Senge, P. M. (1992). *The fifth discipline: The art and practice of the learning organization.* New York: Doubleday.

Serketich, W. J., & Dumas, J. E. (1996). The effectiveness of behavioral parent training to modify antisocial behavior in children: A meta-analysis. *Behavior Therapy, 27,* 171–186.

Shadish, W. R., Montgomery, L. M., Wilson, P., Wilson, M. R., Bright, I., & Okwumakua, T. (1993). The effects of family and marital psychotherapies: A meta-analysis. *Journal of Consulting and Clinical Psychology, 61,* 61.

Shadish, W. R., Ragsdale, K., Glaser, R. R., & Montgomery, L. M. (1995). The efficacy and effectiveness of marital and family therapy: A perspective from meta-analysis. *Journal of Marital and Family Therapy, 21,* 345–360.

Shapiro, D. A., & Shapiro, D. (1982). Meta-analysis of comparative therapy outcome studies: A replication and refinement. *Psychological Bulletin, 92,* 581–604.

Shapiro, F. (1989a). Efficacy of the eye movement desensitization procedure in the treatment of traumatic memories. *Journal of Traumatic Stress, 2,* 199–223.

Shapiro, F. (1989b). Eye movement desensitization: A new treatment of post-traumatic stress disorder. *Journal of Behavior Therapy and Experimental Psychiatry, 20,* 211–217.

Shapiro, F. (1995). *Eye movement desensitization and reprocessing: Basic principles, protocols, and procedures.* New York: Guilford.

Shapiro, F. (1997). *EMDR in the treatment of trauma.* Pacific Grove, CA: EMDR Institute.

Shapiro, F. (in press). EMDR as a treatment for PTSD. *Treatment.*

Shapiro, F., & Forrest, M. S. (1997). *EMDR: The breakthrough therapy for overcoming anxiety, stress, and trauma.* New York: Basic.

Shaw, B. F., & Dobson, K. S. (1988). Competency judgments in the training and evaluation of psychotherapists. *Journal of Consulting and Clinical Psychology, 56,* 666–672.

Shepherd, I. L. (1976). Limitations and cautions in the Gestalt approach. In C. Hatcher & P. Himmelstein (Eds.), *The handbook of Gestalt therapy.* New York: Jason Aronson.

Sherman, A. (1973). *Behavior modification: Theory and practice.* Pacific Grove, CA: Brooks/Cole.

Shirk, S. R., & Russell, R.L. (1992). A re-evaluation of estimates of child therapy effectiveness. *Journal of the American Academy of Child and Adolescent Psychiatry, 31,* 703–708.

Shoham-Salomon, V., & Rosenthal, R. (1987). Paradoxical interventions: A meta-analysis. *Journal of Consulting and Clinical Psychology, 55,* 22–28.

Sifneos, P. E. (1973). *Short-term psychotherapy and emotional crises.* Cambridge, MA: Harvard University Press.

Sifneos, P. E. (1992). *Short-term anxiety-provoking psychotherapy: A treatment manual.* New York: Basic.

Silver, B. V., & Blanchard, E. B. (1978). Biofeedback and relaxation training in the treatment of psychophysiologic disorders: Or are the machines really necessary? *Journal of Behavioral Medicine, 1,* 217–239.

Silverman, L. H. (1976). Psychoanalytic theory: "The reports of my death are greatly exaggerated." *American Psychologist, 31,* 621–637.

Sitharthan, T., Sitharthan, G., Hough, M. J., & Kavanagh, D. J. (1997). Cue exposure in moderation drinking: A comparison with cognitive-behavior therapy. *Journal of Consulting and Clinical Psychology, 65,* 878–882.

Skinner, B. F. (1971). *Beyond freedom and dignity.* New York: Vintage.

Skinner, B. F. (1990). Can psychology be a science of mind? *American Psychologist, 45,* 1206–1210.

Sloane, R. B., Staples, F., Cristol, A., Yorkston, N., & Whipple, K. (1975). *Psychotherapy versus behavior therapy.* Cambridge, MA: Harvard University Press.

Sluzki, C., & Ransom, D. (Eds.). (1976). *Double bind: The foundations of the communicational approach to the family.* New York: Grune & Stratton.

Smith, C., & Lloyd, B. (1978). Maternal behavior and perceived sex of infant: Revisited. *Child Development, 49,* 1263–1265.

Smith, D. S. (1982). Trends in counseling and psychotherapy. *American Psychologist*, 37, 802–809.

Smith, M. (1975). *When I say no, I feel guilty*. New York: Dial.

Smith, M. L., & Glass, G. V. (1977). Meta-analysis of psychotherapy outcome studies. *American Psychologist*, 32, 752–760.

Smith, M. L., Glass, G. V., & Miller, T. I. (1980). *The benefits of psychotherapy*. Baltimore: Johns Hopkins University Press.

Solis, J., & Brink, T. L. (1992). Adlerian approaches in geriatric psychotherapy. *Individual Psychology*, 48, 419–426.

Sollod, B. (1981). Goodwin Watson's 1940 conference. *American Psychologist*, 36, 1546–1547.

Sollod, R. N. (1978). Carl Rogers and the origins of client-centered therapy. *Professional Psychology*, 9, 93–104.

Solomon, L. N. (1990). Carl Rogers's efforts for world peace. *Person-Centered Review*, 5, 39–56.

Solomon, P., Kubzansky, P., Leiderman, P., Menderson, J., Trumbull, R., & Wexler, D. (Eds.). (1961). *Sensory deprivation*. Cambridge, MA: Harvard University Press.

Solomon, R. (1964). Punishment. *American Psychologist*, 19, 239–253.

Solomon, R., Kamin, L., & Wynne, L. (1953). Traumatic avoidance learning. The outcomes of several extinction procedures with dogs. *Journal of Abnormal and Social Psychology*, 48, 291–302.

Solomon, R., & Wynne, L. (1954). Traumatic avoidance learning: The principle of anxiety conservation and partial irreversability. *Psychological Review*, 61, 353–385.

Sperry, L. (1992). Psychotherapy systems: An Adlerian integration with implication for older adults. *Individual Psychology*, 48, 451–461.

Spiegelberg, H. (1972). *Phenomenology in psychology and psychiatry*. Evanston, IL: Northwestern University Press.

Spitz, R. (1945). Hospitalism: Genesis of psychiatric conditions in early childhood. *Psychoanalytic Study of the Child*, 1, 53–74.

Spring, D., Prochaska, J., & Smith, N. (1974). Fear reduction in rats through avoidance blocking. *Behavior Research and Therapy*, 12, 29–34.

Stampfl, T. (1970). Implosive therapy: An emphasis on covert stimulation. In D. Levis (Ed.), *Learning approaches to therapeutic behavior change*. Hawthorne, NY: Aldine.

Stampfl, T. (1976). Implosive therapy. In P. Olsen (Ed.), *Emotional flooding*. New York: Aldine.

Stampfl, T., & Levis, D. (1967). The essentials of implosive therapy: A learning-theory based psychodynamic behavioral therapy. *Journal of Abnormal Psychology*, 66, 496–503.

Stampfl, T., & Levis, D. (1973a). The essentials of implosive therapy: A learning-theory based on psychodynamic behavioral therapy. *Journal of Abnormal Psychology*, 72, 496–503.

Stampfl, T., & Levis, D. (1973b). *Implosive therapy: Theory and technique*. Morristown, NJ: General Learning Press.

Standal, S. (1954). *The need for positive regard: A contribution to client-centered theory*. Unpublished doctoral dissertation, University of Chicago.

Stanton, M., & Todd, T. (1979). Structural family therapy with drug addicts. In E. Kaufman & P. Kaufman (Eds.), *The family therapy of drug and alcohol abuse*. New York: Gardner.

Stanton, M. D., & Shadish, W. R. (1997). Outcome, attrition, and family-couples treatment for drug abuse: A meta-analysis and review of the controlled, comparative studies. *Psychological Bulletin*, 122, 170–191.

Starker, S., & Pankratz, L. (1996). Soundness of treatment: A survey of psychologists' opinions. *Psychological Reports*, 78, 288–290.

Steiner, C. (1967). A script checklist. *Transactional Analysis Bulletin*, 6, 38–39.

Steiner, C. (1971). *Games alcoholics play*. New York: Ballantine.

Steiner, C. (1974). *Scripts people live*. New York: Grove.

Steiner, C. (1990). *Scripts people live* (rev. ed.). New York: Grove/Atlantic.

Stiles, W. B., Shapiro, D. A., & Elliott, R. (1986). "Are all psychotherapies equivalent?" *American Psychologist, 41,* 165–180.

Stricker, G. (1988). Supervision of integrative psychotherapy: Discussion. *Journal of Integrative and Eclectic Psychotherapy, 7,* 176–180.

Strupp, H. H. (1971). *Psychotherapy and the modification of abnormal behavior.* New York: McGraw-Hill.

Strupp, H. H. (1986). The nonspecific hypothesis of therapeutic effectiveness: A current assessment. *American Journal of Orthopsychiatry, 56,* 513–520.

Strupp, H. H. (1992). The future of psychodynamic psychotherapy. *Psychotherapy, 29,* 21–27.

Strupp, H. H., & Binder, J. L. (1984). *Psychotherapy in a new key: A guide to time limited dynamic psychotherapy.* New York: Basic.

Strupp, H. H., & Howard, K. I. (1992). A brief history of psychotherapy research. In D. K. Freedheim (Ed.), *History of psychotherapy: A century of change.* Washington, DC: American Psychological Association.

Stuart, R. (1969). Token reinforcement in marital treatment. In R. Robin & C. Franks (Eds.), *Advances in behavioral therapy.* New York: Academic Press.

Stuart, S., & Bowers, W. A. (1995). Cognitive therapy with inpatients: Review and meta-analysis. *Journal of Cognitive Psychotherapy, 9,* 85–92.

Sue, D. W., & Sue, D. (1990). *Counseling the culturally different: Theory and practice* (2nd ed.). Somerset, NJ: Wiley.

Sue, S. (1988). Psychotherapeutic services for ethnic minorities: Two decades of research findings. *American Psychologist, 43,* 301–308.

Sue, S., Zane, N., & Young, K. (1994). Research on psychotherapy with culturally diverse populations. In A. E. Bergin & S. L. Garfield (Eds.), *Handbook of psychotherapy and behavior change* (4th ed., pp. 783–817). New York: Wiley.

Suinn, R. M., & Richardson, F. (1971). Anxiety management training: A nonspecific behavior therapy program for anxiety control. *Behavior Therapy, 2,* 498–510.

Sullivan, H. S. (1953a). *Conceptions of modern psychiatry.* New York: Norton.

Sullivan, H. S. (1953b). *The interpersonal theory of psychiatry.* New York: Norton.

Sullivan, H. S. (1970). *The psychiatric interview.* New York: Norton.

Sullivan, H. S. (1972). *Personal psychopathology.* New York: Norton.

Svartberg, M., & Stiles, T. C. (1991). Comparative effects of short-term psychodynamic psychotherapy: A meta-analysis. *Journal of Consulting and Clinical Psychology, 5,* 704–714.

Sweeney, T. J. (1998). *Adlerian counseling: A practitioner's approach* (4th ed.). Bristol, PA: Accelerated Development.

Tafrate, R. C., DiGiuseppe, R., & Goshtasbpour-Parsi, F. (1997, August). *A review of treatment efficacy for adult anger disorders.* Paper presented at the annual convention of the American Psychological Association, Chicago, IL.

Talley, P. F., Strupp, H. H., & Morey, L. C. (1990). Matchmaking in psychotherapy: Patient-therapist dimensions and their impact on outcome. *Journal of Consulting and Clinical Psychology, 58,* 182–188.

Task Force on Promotion and Dissemination of Psychological Procedures. (1995). Training in and dissemination of empirically-validated psychological treatments. *The Clinical Psychologist, 48,* 3–23.

Tausch, R. (1990). The supplementation of client-centered communication therapy with other validated therapeutic methods: A client-centered necessity. In G. Lietaer, J. Rombouts, & R. Van-Balen (Eds.), *Client-centered and experiential psychotherapy in the nineties.* Leuven, Belgium: Leuven University Press.

Taylor, S. E. (1990). Health psychology: The science and the field. *American Psychologist*, *45*, 40–50.

Thompson, J. R. (1987). *The process of psychotherapy: An integration of clinical experience and empirical research*. Frederick, MD: University Press of America.

Thoresen, C. E. (1973). Behavioral humanism. In C. E. Thoresen (Ed.), *Behavior modification in education*. Chicago: University of Chicago Press.

Tillich, P. (1952). *The courage to be*. New Haven: Yale University Press.

Tinbergen, N. (1951). *The study of instinct*. Oxford: Clarendon.

Tinsley, H. E., Bowman, S. L., & Ray, S. B. (1988). Manipulation of expectancies about counseling and psychotherapy: Review and analysis of expectancy manipulation strategies and results. *Journal of Counseling Psychology*, *35*, 99–108.

Toffler, A. (1970). *Future shock*. New York: Bantam.

Torgenrud, J. & Storm, C. L. (1989). One-person therapy? An analysis of family therapy schools. *American Journal of Family Therapy*, *17*, 143–154.

Torrey, E. F. (1972). *The mind game*. New York: Bantam.

Tosi, D. J., Rudy, D. R., Lewis, J., & Murphy, M. A. (1992). The psychobiological effects of cognitive experiential therapy, hypnosis, cognitive restructuring, and attention placebo control in the treatment of essential hypertension. *Psychotherapy*, *29*, 274–284.

Truax, C. (1966). Reinforcement and nonreinforcement in Rogerian psychotherapy. *Journal of Abnormal Psychology*, *71*, 1–9.

Truax, C., & Carkhuff, R. (1967). *Toward effective counseling and psychotherapy: Training and practice*. Hawthorne, NY: Aldine.

Turner, S. M. (1997). *Behavior therapy for obsessive-complusive disorder*. Washington, DC: American Psychological Association Videotape Series.

Turner, S. M., Calhoun, K. S., & Adams, H. E. (Eds.). (1993). *Handbook of clinical behavior therapy* (2nd ed.). New York: Wiley.

U.S. Bureau of the Census. (1990). *Current population reports: United States population estimates by age, sex, and Hispanic origin, 1980–1988* (No. 1045). Washington, DC: U.S. Government Printing Office.

U.S. Bureau of Labor Statistics. (1997). *Employment and earnings*. Washington, DC: U.S. Government Printing Office.

U.S. Department of Labor, Women's Bureau. (1988). *20 facts on women workers*. Washington, DC: Author.

Usher, C. H. (1989). Recognizing cultural bias in counseling theory and practice: The case of Rogers. *Journal of Multicultural Counseling and Development*, *17*, 62–71.

van Balkom, A. J. L. M., Nauta, M. C. E., & Bakker, A. (1995). Meta-analysis on the treatment of panic disorder with agoraphobia: Review and re-examination. *Clinical Psychology and Psychotherapy*, *2*, 1–14.

van Balkom, A. J. L. M., van Oppen, P., Vermeulen, A. W. A., van Dyck, R., Nauta, M. C. E., & Vorst, H. C. M. (1994). A meta-analysis on the treatment of obsessive compulsive disorder. *Clinical Psychology Review*, *14*, 359–381.

VandenBos, G. R., Cummings, N. A., & DeLeon, P. H. (1992). A century of psychotherapy: Economic and environmental influences. In D. K. Freedheim (Ed.), *History of psychotherapy: A century of change*. Washington, DC: American Psychological Association.

Veevers, H. M. (1991). Which child—which family? *Transactional Analysis Journal*, *21*, 207–211.

Veroff, J., Douvan, E., & Kulka, R. A. (1981a). *The inner America*. New York: Basic.

Veroff, J., Douvan, E., & Kulka, R. A. (1981b). *Mental health in America*. New York: Basic.

Viswesvaran, C., & Schmidt, F. L. (1992). A meta-analytic comparison of the effectiveness of smoking cessation methods. *Journal of Applied Psychology, 77,* 554–561.

von Bertalanffy, L. (1968). *General systems theory.* New York: George Braziller.

VonGlinow, M. A., & Krzyczkowska-Mercer, A. (1988, Summer). Women in corporate America: A caste of thousands. *New Management, 6,* 36–42.

Vygotsky, L. (1962). *Thought and language.* New York: Wiley.

Wachtel, P. L. (1977). *Psychoanalysis and behavior therapy: Toward an integration.* New York: Basic.

Wachtel, P. L. (1983). *You can't go far in neutral: On the limits of therapeutic neutrality.* Paper presented at the 40th anniversary celebration of the William Alanson White Institute, New York.

Wachtel, P. L. (1987). *Action and insight.* New York: Guilford.

Wachtel, P. L. (1989). *The poverty of affluence: A psychological portrait of the American way of life.* Philadelphia: New Society.

Wachtel, P. L. (1990). Psychotherapy from an integrative psychodynamic perspective. In J. K. Zeig & W. M. Munion (Eds.), *What is psychotherapy?* San Francisco: Jossey-Bass.

Wachtel, P. L. (1991). From eclecticism to synthesis: Toward a more seamless psychotherapeutic integration. *Journal of Psychotherapy Integration, 1,* 43–54.

Wachtel, P. L. (1993). *Therapeutic communication: Principles and effective practice.* New York: Guilford.

Wachtel, P. L. (1997). *Psychoanalysis, behavior therapy, and the relational world.* Washington, DC: American Psychological Association.

Wachtel, P. L., & McKinney, M. K. (1992). Cyclical psychodynamics and integrative psychodynamic therapy. In J. C. Norcross & M. R. Goldfried (Eds.), *Handbook of psychotherapy integration.* New York: Basic.

Wachtel, E. F., & Wachtel, P. L. (1986). *Family dynamics in individual psychotherapy.* New York: Guilford.

Walen, S. R., DiGiuseppe, R., & Dryden, W. (1992). *A practitioner's guide to rational-emotive therapy* (2nd ed.). New York: Oxford University Press.

Walker, M. (1990). *Women in therapy and counselling: Out of the shadows.* London: Open University Press.

Wallerstein, R. S. (1986). *Forty-two lives in treatment.* New York: Guilford.

Wallerstein, R. S., & Weinshel, E. M. (1989). The future of psychoanalysis. *Psychoanalytic Quarterly, 58,* 341–373.

Walter, J. L., & Peller, J. E. (1992). *Becoming solution-focused in brief therapy.* New York: Brunner/Mazel.

Wandersman, A., Poppen, P. J., & Ricks, D. F. (Eds.). (1976). *Humanism and behaviorism: Dialogue and growth.* Elmsford, NY: Pergamon.

Watkins, C. E. (1982). A decade of research in support of Adlerian psychological theory. *Individual Psychology, 38,* 90–99.

Watkins, C. E. (1983). Some characteristics of research on Adlerian theory, 1970–1981. *Individual Psychology, 39,* 99–110.

Watkins, C. E. (1992). Adlerian-oriented early memory research: What does it tell us? *Journal of Personality Assessment, 59,* 248–262.

Watkins, C. E., Lopez, F. G., Campbell, V. L., & Himmell, C. D. (1986). Contemporary counseling psychology: Results of a national survey. *Journal of Counseling Psychology, 33,* 301–309.

Watson, G. (1940). Areas of agreement in psychotherapy. *American Journal of Orthopsychiatry, 10,* 698–709.

Watson, J. B., & Rayner, R. (1920). Conditioned emotional reactions. *Journal of Experimental Psychology, 3,* 1–14.

Watzlawick, P., Beavin, J., & Jackson, D. (1967). *Pragmatics of human communication.* New York: Norton.

Watzlawick, P., Weakland, J. H., & Fisch, R. (1974). *Change: Principles of problem formation and problem resolution.* New York: Norton.

Weakland, J., Fisch, R., Watzlawick, P., & Bodin, A. (1974). Brief therapy: Focused problem solving resolution. *Family Process, 13,* 141–168.

Webster, D. C., Vaughn, K., & Martinez, R. (1994). Introducing solution-focused approaches to staff in inpatient psychiatric settings. *Archives of Psychiatric Nursing, 8,* 254–261.

Weiner, I. B. (1975). *Principles of psychotherapy.* New York: Wiley.

Weiss, B., & Weisz, J. R. (1995a). Effectiveness of psychotherapy {Letter to the editor}. *Journal of the American Academy of Child and Adolescent Psychiatry, 34,* 971–972.

Weiss, B., & Weisz, J. R. (1995b). Relative effectiveness of behavioral versus nonbehavioral child psychotherapy. *Journal of Consulting and Clinical Psychology, 63,* 317–320.

Weisz, J. R., Donenberg, G. R., Han, S. S., & Weiss, B. (1995). Bridging the gap between laboratory and clinic in child and adolescent psychotherapy. *Journal of Consulting and Clinical Psychotherapy, 63,* 688–701.

Weisz, J. R., Weiss, B., Alicke, M. D. & Klotz, M. L. (1987). Effectiveness of psychotherapy with children and adolescents: A meta-analysis for clinicians. *Journal of Consulting and Clinical Psychology, 55,* 542–549.

Weisz, J. R., Weiss, B., Han, S. S., Granger, D. A., & Morton, T. (1995). Effects of psychotherapy with children and adolescents revisited: A meta-analysis of treatment outcome studies. *Psychological Bulletin, 117,* 450–468.

Wells, R. A., & Giannetti, V. J. (Eds.). (1990). *Handbook of the brief psychotherapies.* New York: Plenum.

Werner, H. (1948). *Comparative psychology of mental development.* Chicago: Follett.

Werner, H., & Kaplan, B. (1963). *Symbol formation: An organismic-developmental approach to language and the expression of thought.* New York: Wiley.

Westen, D. (1991). Cognitive-behavioral interventions in psychoanalytic psychotherapy of borderline personality disorders. *Clinical Psychology Review, 11,* 211–230.

Wexler, D. (1974). A cognitive theory of experiencing, self-actualization, and therapeutic process. In D. Wexler & L. Rice (Eds.), *Innovations in client-centered therapy.* New York: Wiley.

Wexler, D., & Rice, L. (Eds.). (1974). *Innovations in client-centered therapy.* New York: Wiley.

Wheeler, G. (1990). *Gestalt reconsidered: A new approach to contact and resistance.* New York: Gardner.

Wheeler, G., & Backman, S. (Eds.). (1994). *On intimate ground: A Gestalt approach to working with couples.* San Francisco: Jossey-Bass.

Whitaker, C. A., & Bumberry, W. M. (1988). *Dancing with the family: A symbolic-experiential approach.* New York: Brunner/Mazel.

Whitaker, C. A., & Keith, D. V. (1981). Symbolic-experiential family therapy. In A. S. Gurman & D. P. Kniskern (Eds.), *Handbook of family therapy.* New York: Brunner/Mazel.

Whitbread, J., & McGowen, A. (1994). The treatment of bulimia nervosa: A meta-analysis. *Indian Journal of Clinical Psychology, 21,* 32–44.

White, R. W. (1959). Motivation reconsidered: The concept of competence. *Psychological Review, 66,* 297–333.

White, R. W. (1960). Competence and the psychosexual stages of development. In M. R. Jones (Ed.), *Nebraska symposium on motivation.* Lincoln: University of Nebraska Press.

White, M., & Epston, D. (1990). *Narrative means to therapeutic ends.* New York: Norton.

White, M., & Epston, D. (1994). *Experience, contradiction, narrative, and imagination.* Adelaide, South Australia: Dulwich Centre Publications.

Wiener, N. (1962). *Cybernetics, or control and communication in the animal and the machine.* Cambridge, MA: MIT Press.

Wilkins, W. (1971). Desensitization: Social and cognitive factors underlying the effectiveness of Wolpe's procedure. *Psychological Bulletin, 76,* 311–317.

Wilkins, W. (1977). Expectancies in applied settings. In A. S. Gurman & A. M. Razin (Eds.), *Effective psychotherapy: A handbook of research*. New York: Pergamon.

Wilkins, W. (1979). Expectancies in therapy research: Discriminating among heterogeneous nonspecifics. *Journal of Consulting and Clinical Psychology*, 47, 837–845.

Wilson, G. T. (1987). Chemical aversion conditioning as a treatment for alcholism: A re-analysis. *Behaviour Research and Therapy*, 25, 503–516.

Wilson, G. T. (1996). Acceptance and change in the treatment of eating disorders and obesity. *Behavior Therapy*, 27, 417–439.

Wilson, G. T., & Agras, W. S. (1992). The future of behavior therapy. *Psychotherapy*, 29, 39–43.

Wilson, G. T., & Fairburn, C. G. (1993). Cognitive treatments for eating disorders. *Journal of Consulting and Clinical Psychology*, 61, 261–269.

Wilson, P. H. (1996). Relapse prevention: Overview of research findings in the treatment of problem drinking, smoking, obesity, and depression. *Clinical Psychology and Psychotherapy*, 3, 231–248.

Wittgenstein, L. (1953). *Philosophical investigations*. New York: Macmillan.

Wittgenstein, L. (1958). *The blue and brown books*. New York: Harper & Row.

Wohl, J. (1989). Integration of cultural awareness into psychotherapy. *American Journal of Psychotherapy*, 43, 343–355.

Wolfe, B. E., & Goldfried, M. R. (1988). Research on psychotherapy integration: Recommendations and conclusions from a NIMH workshop. *Journal of Consulting and Clinical Psychology*, 56, 448–451.

Wolpe, J. (1958). *Psychotherapy by reciprocal inhibition*. Stanford, CA: Stanford University Press.

Wolpe, J. (1973). *The practice of behavior therapy* (2nd ed.). Elmsford, NY: Pergamon.

Wolpe, J. (1989). The derailment of behavior therapy: A tale of conceptual misdirection. *Journal of Behavior Therapy and Experimental Psychiatry*, 20, 3–15.

Wolpe, J. (1990). *The practice of behavior therapy* (4th ed.). Elmsford, NY: Pergamon.

Wolpe, J., & Lazarus, A. (1966). *Behavior therapy techniques*. New York: Pergamon.

Worell, J., & Remer, P. (Eds.). (1992). *Feminist perspectives in therapy: An empowerment model for women*. New York: Wiley.

Wright, J. H., Thase, M. E., Beck, A. T., & Ludgate, G. (Eds.). (1992). *Cognitive therapy with inpatients*. New York: Guilford.

Wright, J. H., & Wright, A. S. (1997). Computer-assisted psychotherapy. *Journal of Psychotherapy Practice and Research*, 6, 315–329.

Yalom, I. D. (1975). *The theory and practice of group psychotherapy* (2nd ed.). New York: Basic.

Yalom, I. D. (1980). *Existential psychotherapy*. New York: Basic.

Yontef, G. (1988). Assimilating diagnostic and psychoanalytic perspectives into Gestalt therapy. *The Gestalt Journal*, 11, 5–32.

Yutrzenka, B. A. (1995). Making a case for training in ethnic and cultural diversity in increasing treatment efficacy. *Journal of Consulting and Clinical Psychology*, 63, 197–206.

Zeig, J. K., & Munion, W. M. (Eds.). (1990). *What is psychotherapy? Contemporary perspectives*. San Francisco: Jossey-Bass.

Zimring, F. (1974). Theory and practice of client-centered therapy: A cognitive view. In D. Wexler & L. Rice (Eds.), *Innovations in client-centered therapy*. New York: Wiley.

Zinker, J. (1991). Creative process in Gestalt therapy: The therapist as artist. *The Gestalt Journal*, 14, 71–88.

Zinker, J. C. (1994). *In search of good form: Gestalt therapy with couples and families*. San Francisco: Jossey-Bass.

Author Index

Subject Index